HUMAN TRAFFICKING AROUND THE WORLD

Human Trafficking Around the World

Hidden in Plain Sight

STEPHANIE HEPBURN
and RITA J. SIMON

 Columbia University Press   *New York*

Columbia University Press
Publishers Since 1893
New York   Chichester, West Sussex
cup.columbia.edu
Copyright © 2013 Columbia University Press
All rights reserved

Library of Congress Cataloging-in-Publication Data

Hepburn, Stephanie, 1977–
  Human trafficking around the world : hidden in plain sight / Stephanie Hepburn
and Rita J. Simon.
      pages cm.
  Includes bibliographical references and index.
  ISBN 978-0-231-16144-2 (cloth : alk. paper) — ISBN 978-0-231-16145-9 (paperback :
alk. paper) — ISBN 978-0-231-53331-7 (e-book)
  1. Human trafficking.   I. Simon, Rita J. (Rita James), 1931–   II. Title.

  K5297.H47 2013
  364.15—dc23

                                                           2013000561

Columbia University Press books are printed on permanent and durable
acid-free paper.
This book is printed on paper with recycled content.
Printed in the United States of America

c 10 9 8 7 6 5 4 3 2 1
p 10 9 8 7 6 5 4 3 2 1

COVER IMAGE: © Getty Images
COVER DESIGN: Julia Kushninsky

References to Internet Web sites (URLs) were accurate at the time of writing.
Neither the author nor Columbia University Press is responsible for URLs that may
have expired or changed since the manuscript was prepared.

To our families and friends
for the steadfast support they
have shown us, and most importantly to the
victims of human trafficking who have
existed in darkness for far too long.

They would not call it slavery, but some other name. Slavery has been fruitful in giving itself names. It has been called "the peculiar institution," "the social system," and the "impediment," as it was called by the General Conference of the Methodist Episcopal Church. It has been called by a great many names, and it will call itself by yet another name; and you and I and all of us had better wait and see what new form this old monster will assume, in what new skin this old snake will come forth.

—FREDERICK DOUGLASS, SPEECH TO THE AMERICAN ANTI-SLAVERY SOCIETY, MAY 1865

Contents

HUMAN TRAFFICKING AROUND THE WORLD

Introduction

We have all seen films that portray the dark and lurid world of human trafficking, depictions that seem sensationalized and exaggerated for cinematic effect. The victims are usually young women forced into an underground sex-trafficking ring, kept on a permanent drug high, and forced to prostitute. Although the plot is horrifying, it is just a story to us—or perhaps it is something that happens in some other part of the world but surely would never occur where we live. Yet the reality is that wherever we may live, regardless of city or nation, some form of human trafficking exists. As of 2005 this global phenomenon reaped an annual worldwide profit of $44.3 billion and affected more than 12.3 million persons. The International Labour Organization (ILO) estimated that 43 percent of victims were trafficked for commercial sexual exploitation, 32 percent were trafficked for forced labor, and the remaining 25 percent were trafficked for a mixture of both or for undetermined reasons (Belser, 2005, p. 4; ILO, 2006). We believed the percentage of forced labor to be higher, and recent ILO global estimates concur. The International Labour Organization now estimates that 20.9 million are victims of forced labor. Within that number it is estimated that 14.2 million people (68 percent) are victims of forced labor exploitation and 4.5 million (22 percent) are victims of forced sexual exploitation. The remainder of victims—2.2 million (10 percent)—are in state-imposed forms of forced labor such as that imposed by rebel armed forces, state militaries, and prisons with conditions that conflict with ILO standards (ILO, 2012, p. 13).

The term *human trafficking* triggers preconceived notions. Sex trafficking has received more coverage in the media than forced labor, so people generally think of it. But it is the element of movement that seems to confuse most, even legislators. The verb *traffic,* according to Merriam-Webster, means to trade or barter. Yet trade in humans does not necessarily involve movement, and international definitions of human trafficking are evolving to include this fact. The crux of human trafficking is its exploitative purpose. Persons of all ages and genders are vulnerable. Women and girls make up 56 percent of persons trafficked for forced labor, while men and boys make up 44 percent. Of those trafficked for forced commercial sexual exploitation, women and girls make up 98 percent; men and boys make up 2 percent. Children constitute 40 to 50 percent of the overall forced labor population (Belser, 2005). While trafficking for forced labor is more prevalent than sex trafficking, many nations are just beginning to include forced labor in their anti-trafficking legislation and statistics. Although we perceive all forms of indentured servitude to be forced labor, a division is often created in legal definitions and anti-trafficking legislation. As a result, throughout the book trafficking for forced labor and for commercial sexual exploitation are presented as two different categories. Other forms of trafficking will also be discussed, such as organ trafficking and Muti murders, which involve killing a person and removing the body parts and organs that are allegedly used for traditional healing purposes. Child sexual tourism, adoption, and marriage for the purpose of sexual exploitation are also examined.

Human trafficking varies not only by type but also by current, that is, by the flow of victims. These currents are categorized in terms of source nation, transit nation, and destination nation. Many nations qualify for all these groupings, but one category is often more prevalent than the others. Another current of trafficking, one that is often ignored, is purely internal or domestic, involving indentured servitude within a nation. Because the anti-trafficking focus has been chiefly on victims of international trafficking, internal trafficking is often absent from the calculus, both in legislation and in practice.

There are common methods used by traffickers, regardless of the type of trafficking, such as false job offers that lure potential victims and exorbitant fees charged for recruitment, visas, travel, housing, food, and the use of tools. These practices keep victims in an endless cycle of debt.

Along these same lines, traffickers often charge victims fines for alleged poor behavior or not meeting certain work quotas. As debts rise exponentially, victims often go unpaid or are underpaid. In order to control and limit the movement of victims, traffickers frequently withhold victims' visas and other identifying documentation, isolate the victims, threaten deportation, threaten to harm the victims or their families, and physically harm the victims. At the beginning of the process, exorbitant recruiting fees, sometimes as high as $40,000, can place victims in a position of debt bondage. In order to pay these fees workers sell their land or that of family members and take out loans with astronomical interest rates. Earning low wages or none and paying high fees for housing, food, and even the use of work tools, the workers can never catch up to their debt, putting them in a position of debt bondage. In cases where the employer paid the costs, the worker is told that before they can receive their wages they have to work off the fees.

There are many definitions of human trafficking, but the Palermo Protocol, otherwise known as the United Nations Protocol to Prevent, Suppress, and Punish Trafficking in Persons, Especially Women and Children, is the worldwide standard for anti-trafficking law and the template on which many nations model their domestic laws. The protocol, which supplements the 2000 United Nations Convention against Transnational Organized Crime, contains three elements that define trafficking of persons. The first element is the act of trafficking, which is the recruitment, transportation, transfer, harboring, or receipt of persons. The second, the means of trafficking, is the threat or use of force or other forms of coercion, abduction, fraud, deception, abuse of power or vulnerability, or giving payments or benefits to a person in control of the victim. The third, the purpose of trafficking, is exploitation. This includes, at a minimum, sexual exploitation, including the exploitation of the prostitution of others, forced labor or services, slavery or practices similar to slavery, servitude, or the removal of organs (UNODC, 2004, p. 42). Of the 24 nations we examined, 21 have ratified the protocol, in whole or in part: Australia, Brazil, Canada, Chile, China, Colombia, France, Germany, India, Iraq, Israel, Italy, Mexico, Niger, Poland, Russia, South Africa, Syria, the United Arab Emirates, the United Kingdom, and the United States. Iran, Japan, and Thailand have not yet ratified the protocol (UNTC, 2011). Ratification of the protocol alone is not a sufficient anti-trafficking measure for a nation. The Palermo Protocol, according to Joy Ngozi Ezeilo, United Nations special rapporteur on trafficking in persons, is not a self-executing provision (OHCHR, 2009); that is, by itself the protocol is not sufficient to bridge the gap between domestic and international law. Those nations that ratify the protocol must also adopt domestic anti-trafficking law, or an additional act of legislation, to harmonize internal legislation to that of the protocol and ensure that the protocol is entirely implemented. Consequently, gauging a nation's anti-trafficking efforts solely on whether they have ratified the protocol is not adequate.

The most prevalent tool used globally to help determine the anti-trafficking status of a nation is the annual U.S. State Department *Trafficking in Persons Report*. The report ranks nations' compliance with the minimum standards of the Victims of Trafficking and Violence Protection Act of 2000 (TVPA). The report gives a breakdown, per country, on the severe forms of human trafficking prevalent in that nation. These forms of human trafficking involve the use of force, fraud, or coercion for the purpose of sex trafficking, involuntary servitude, peonage, debt bondage, or slavery, or, in terms of sex trafficking, the act involves a person less than 18 years of age. The minimum standards for the elimination of trafficking apply to governments of nations of origin, transit, or destination with a significant number of severe-form-of-trafficking victims. Under the TVPA minimum standards, such governments should prohibit severe forms of human trafficking and punish offenders with sentences that are sufficiently stringent and reflect the severity of the crime. Those offenders involved in severe forms of sex trafficking should be prescribed a punishment akin to other grave crimes such as forcible sexual assault. Also, under the standards, the government should make real and continual efforts to eliminate severe forms of human trafficking. Where a nation stands in the report is not without consequence as those nations rated Tier 3, the worst tier, face possible U.S. sanctions. The report has been extremely significant to the global anti-trafficking movement. Not only can nations face U.S. sanctions, but the stigma associated with poor anti-trafficking efforts can create pressure on a nation to improve measures. For instance, according to James Farrer, former director of the Institute of Comparative Culture (ICC) at Sophia University in Tokyo, the U.S. State Department *Trafficking in Persons Report* had a critical impact on the Japanese Ministry of Justice that propelled the nation to adopt the National Action Plan of Measures to Combat Trafficking in Persons in 2004.[1] Despite the importance and significance of the U.S. *Trafficking in Persons Report,* it is impossible to escape that the report is prepared by an agency within the U.S. government. Quite obviously, the data the U.S. government is able to collect can be scarce in nations where it is not on the best of terms with the governments. This indicates that the report alone is not a sufficient guide to determine an accurate picture of the trafficking scenario in nations.

There are other significant sources for human trafficking data, such as the International Organization for Migration and Human Rights Watch, which have both published reports on labor exploitation and immigration issues related to human trafficking, and the United Nations Office on Drugs and Crime, which published its own *Global Report on Trafficking in Persons* in 2009. These reports are helpful, but it is essential to gain an understanding on what is happening on the ground in each nation. In most nations there is a current shift in the perception on what defines human trafficking. This will eventually help shape legislation and, consequently, enforcement of that legislation; but for now, in many nations, there is still a narrow view on what defines human trafficking. For some nations this includes a broad legal definition but narrow enforcement and an even narrower collection of statistics. In other nations there is not even an adequate legal definition. Consequently, government statistics are often innately flawed. We note frequently throughout the book that government statistics are defined by the parameters of what that nation's government determines by law or in practice to be human trafficking. This means that if forced labor or internal trafficking is not included in law or goes unenforced or underenforced then the estimates of how many victims are affected are simply not accurate. Also, in many nations human trafficking is prosecuted under a variety of laws. In fact, traffickers are often charged under lesser offenses instead of the anti-trafficking articles of the nation's Criminal Code. The result is not just that traffickers' face lesser sentencing but also that the offense is miscategorized and is not included in the nation's trafficking statistics. This does not mean that these statistics should be disregarded but that this flaw needs to be stated throughout. We do so and furthermore we include numbers gathered by nongovernmental organizations (NGOs) and newspapers to supplement and illustrate gaps in government statistical collection. For the U.S. chapter we spoke with attorneys working on Gulf Coast trafficking cases and thoroughly compiled post–Hurricanes Katrina and Rita trafficking data, which, to our knowledge, has not been done by any other source to date.

We turn to these sources—case documents, trafficking reports, newspaper articles, and interviews with experts, federal employees, and documentarians—not only for statistical purposes but also to gain a more rounded view of specific cases. For example, in the U.S. chapter we talk about the Cass 23 case, where U.S. Immigration and Customs Enforcement (ICE) knowingly targeted alleged trafficking victims. In order to give a holistic view on the case we used multiple sources: the related case of which the Cass 23 are alleged victims, David et al. v. Signal International LLC et al.; our interview with Barry Nelson, executive director of the Metro Youth Partnership, who aided the workers; the New Orleans Workers' Center for Racial Justice (NOWCRJ) as the Signal case had contact with the New Orleans/Gulf Coast area; and stories by journalist Patrick Springer at *The Forum* newspaper. Springer wrote about the support the workers received and the trial date that was set for the workers. Springer also spoke with Drew Wrigley, U.S. Attorney for the District of North Dakota (this is where the Cass 23 workers were held), and later corresponded with us regarding their conversation. Collectively these sources provided a complete look at the case and the issues that arose. Of course, not every subject has as many layers of sources, but in nations where access to case files is at a minimum or where the government is less than open or simply does not adequately collect data, newspaper articles are essential. For instance, in the Iran chapter, a person who paid to be smuggled from Afghanistan to Iran tells a reporter for *Dawn* about his experience. This gives the victim dimensionality and allows the reader a window into the victim's experience.

There is a dearth when it comes to comprehensive literature on human trafficking, particularly when it comes to forced labor and internal trafficking. In order to gain further clarity on the trafficking status of a nation, we have interviewed experts such as anti-trafficking program coordinators, NGO directors, university researchers and directors, counsel attorneys of landmark trafficking cases, government employees, and even documentarians who have been able to shed light on the victim experience in a respectful and moving way. These experts give us a window into the inner workings of not only the trafficking experience, but what happens afterward. For instance, Helen Duffy, co-counsel for Hadijatou Mani Koraou, the victim in a landmark traditional slavery case in Niger, reveals that even once Mani was released from slavery, a court still ruled, improperly, that a freed slave girl is the de facto wife of her master. This illustrates the strength of customary practices, which often prevails over law, as is seen in this instance. Culture and custom also play a significant role in what is permitted, or ignored, in the sex industry. For instance in Japan, a ¥ 2.3 trillion a-year sex industry is accepted as part of the urban landscape, but talking about sex is not deemed appropriate, creating what Michiko Yokoyama, Public Outreach of the Polaris Project, Japan Office, calls a societal ignorance on the issue of sex trafficking.

Economic factors are also significant in the trafficking status of a nation. For instance, South Africa has four times the GDP of its neighbors. This makes it attractive to both migrants and traffickers. When combined with poor border control, it is easy to see how it became a popular destination for human trafficking in the region. Other nations, such as Russia and the United Arab Emirates, have experienced quick economic growth that resulted in an urgent demand for affordable labor, making them destinations for human trafficking. Political climates and civil unrest further exacerbate the issue. In Colombia, the decades of civil unrest have resulted in a high number of internally displaced persons. Displacement creates vulnerability to a variety of exploitations, including human trafficking. Guerrilla and rebel forces also force and lure children to join their groups. Child soldiers can be found in Colombia and Iraq.

Geographic location is also essential to the trafficking scenario. Yet, it isn't just location, per se, but also grouping that is a factor, at least when it comes to the European Union (EU). For instance, Poland joined the European Union and became part of the Schengen area, where signatory nations are, in essence, a single country for the purpose of travel. As a result, Poland went from primarily a source nation to also a destination and transit country. Porous borders in countries that are surrounded by many other nations, such as Iran, which is bordered by seven other nations, are ideal for cross-border and transnational trafficking. Immigration and border control have become hot button issues worldwide, resulting in a slew of new legislation that often conflicts with these nations' own anti-trafficking laws. For instance, in the United States, when it comes to trafficking victim visa applicants, there is often a race against the clock as to what will happen first—deportation or protection. In France, the government began a controversial deportation of the Roma, a marginalized ethnic group, until the European Parliament put a stop to it. The issue isn't just what nations have done to prevent entry of and deportation of potential trafficking victims, but also national work visa programs that allow an easy means for trafficking to occur. Under-enforced and unenforced work visa programs create loopholes for governments to bring in affordable labor and create an ideal opportunity for unscrupulous employers to exploit and traffic workers. These programs exist in nations such as the United States, Japan, and the United Arab Emirates.

Gender bias is also a factor in the trafficking calculus. In nations where women are not on equal footing with men, they are particularly vulnerable to exploitation, including human trafficking. Not surprisingly, in the post-trafficking experience women often continue to face unequal treatment. This occurs in Iran where, under the government's interpretation of Islamic law, a woman's testimony is worth half of that of a man. Of course this is in direct conflict with Article 3 of the constitution of Iran, but in cases of conflict between the constitution and Islamic law, the principles of Islamic law prevail. Yet, it is not just bias against women that is an issue. Men too face discrimination, particularly in the post-trafficking experience, and in many nations they are simply not acknowledged as victims. The governments of other nations, such as Poland and Japan, recognize that men can be victims, but the lack of shelters specifically designated for men illustrates that they are not yet a priority. (This was also the case in Israel, where male victims were rarely given shelter, but the situation has changed with the inclusion of the Atlas shelter, which is specifically designated for victims of male trafficking.) Part of this distinction is not just based on gender but on the form of trafficking that is deemed more offensive. In many nations sex trafficking is perceived as worse. This is reflected in their anti-trafficking laws, both at national and local levels. For example, the New York State Anti-Trafficking Law treats sex traffickers and labor traffickers differently: sex trafficking is a class B felony with a maximum sentence of twenty-five years' imprisonment, while labor trafficking is a class D felony with a maximum sentence of seven years.

Disparate perceptions of labor trafficking and sex trafficking are a global phenomenon. In many nations, neither the government nor the general population acknowledges forced labor as human trafficking. Sex trafficking has been discussed in the media as human trafficking for far longer, making it more familiar. Even large-budget films have done their part to bring attention to the issue. Labor trafficking is not as "sexy" of a topic, which makes it less attractive to the media. Also, there is an innate response that humans understandably have to the subject of forced sex. Yet forced labor, and the abuse that goes along with it, is no less of an offense. For instance, in Brazil traffickers take forced laborers to desolate locations surrounded by armed guards. One such victim was forced to burn the documentation of fellow workers that had supposedly left the camp of their own free will. The victim soon found heaps of bones nearby in the jungle. In China, a 16-year-old victim was forced to work at an illegal brick factory where he faced beatings and threats of death. Just like the victim in Brazil, the worker was forced to work long hours, often from 4 a.m. to midnight. He was forced to sleep in a dark kiln, and his food consisted of mashed vegetable soup and moldy bread. In order to scare the victim, the kiln boss took him to another kiln to witness the murder of a worker who was deemed to be inefficient. The worker was knocked unconscious and then tossed into a mixing machine where, according to the victim, the worker's body was chopped into tiny pieces within seconds.

We have selected 24 nations that span the Americas (North and South), Europe (East and West), the Middle East, Africa, Asia (East and South), and Australia. Within those regions we chose nations that help the reader understand a broad spectrum of issues that contribute to a nation's trafficking scenario such as economics, geopolitics, and culture. We did not select nations based on which is "worse" or "better" in terms of human trafficking, but instead we wanted a diverse representation of first, second, and third world nations. This helped illustrate the point that all countries experience human trafficking. Of course, the degree varies and some chapters are less compelling than others. It was essential to maintain all chapters in the book—even those that are less gripping—so as to give the reader a realistic look into human trafficking and not to contribute to the sensationalism that is often attached to the topic. The organization of the book was originally based on geography, but upon further examination we decided to group countries under a common characteristic or unique feature. Our rationale is that while there is no denying regional similarity in human trafficking, there are more commonalities between nations than those that are distinguished by region alone. By highlighting a unique feature of a nation's trafficking scenario we were able to group nations together based on an underlying issue that significantly contributes to the problem. For example, nations that have work visa programs that create loopholes and opportunity for human trafficking are placed together. Those countries that do not easily fit under a category stand-alone under a title that explains a characteristic unique to that nation; this is intentional as we did not want the organization of the book to pigeonhole or force a nation under a category that is not an appropriate fit. Along that same thought process, just because a country is grouped under a certain category does not preclude it from fitting elsewhere. Also, while countries may be grouped by a common characteristic, the chapters discuss all aspects of trafficking within each nation and by no means solely, or even primarily, focus on the common characteristic.

In examining human trafficking throughout the world, we looked at the forms of trafficking relevant to a particular nation and the factors that contributed to its trafficking status—such as anti-trafficking legislation, enforcement, the existence and treatment of marginalized groups, and cultural and economic factors (e.g., hardships or even a sudden economic boost). What makes identifying each nation's unique anti-trafficking issues and obstacles critical is not only to recognize potential victims, but also to point to common practices or even national objectives that may be in direct conflict with the specific nation's own anti-trafficking efforts. This book describes the precise picture of human trafficking in 24 nations and illustrates that no nation is exempt.

PART I
Work Visa Loopholes for Traffickers

Theoretically, no government actually encourages traffickers to traffic; yet those in need of inexpensive labor often create work visas that do just that. Among them are the United States, Japan, and the United Arab Emirates (UAE).

The U.S. State Department publishes the globally acknowledged annual Trafficking in Persons Report, and as a result some experts regard the United States as a front-runner in the crusade against human trafficking. Yet the country's failure to monitor and enforce its H-2 guestworker visa program has created ample opportunities for traffickers to exploit and enslave legal migrants. Thus in the aftermath of the 2005 natural disasters Hurricanes Katrina and Rita, high demand for cheap labor to rebuild New Orleans resulted in rampant labor exploitation and human trafficking. Legal migrant workers in the Gulf Coast region were forced to live and work in labor camps surrounded by armed guards, and some had to cook with contaminated water and kill and cook pigeons to survive.

Unlike the United States, Japan has not enacted a comprehensive anti-trafficking law. Although the government took a strong step forward in its 2009 Action Plan to Combat Trafficking in Persons by acknowledging that sex trafficking is not the only form of human trafficking, forced-labor victims continue to be marginalized. As a result of ethnocentric policies, the government prohibits foreign unskilled laborers from working in Japan. But the disparity between the nation's immigration posture and its labor needs has created a quandary. With a demand for inexpensive labor but without an adequate low-wage labor force, Japan uses the government-run Industrial Training Program and Technical Internship Program to create a temporary and low-cost migrant workforce for employers. The stated purpose of the program is to transfer skill, technology, and knowledge to persons of other nations and thereby play a central role in the economic growth of developing nations, specifically those in East Asia. Instead, it has created opportunities for exploitation and human trafficking.

In the UAE, the astonishingly rapid rate of urban development has come at a cost. Migrant workers make up more than 90 percent of the UAE's private-sector workforce. Although workers are promised high-paying jobs, upon arrival in the UAE many earn less than half of what they were promised or are not paid at all. Furthermore, the recruitment of foreign workers involves a system of brokers and agents who charge workers a continual flow of exorbitant fees that they simply cannot pay back, placing them in positions of debt servitude. Although it is illegal for employers in the UAE to withhold worker passports, the common method used by an employer to trigger the deportation of a worker is to turn in the worker's passport to the Ministry of Interior. Thus the law and common practice regarding legal migrant workers contradict each other.

In the United States, Japan, and the UAE, foreign workers' dependence on legal employment is tied to one employer, creating the opportunity for unfair treatment, abuse, and human trafficking. Unscrupulous employers take advantage of the system by withholding worker passports, charging outrageous fees that place workers in positions of debt bondage, forcing laborers to work excessive hours, restricting their movements, and paying them little or not at all. Victims often face the threat of deportation, the threat of bodily harm to themselves or family members, and psychological, physical, and/or sexual abuse at the hands of their employers or the employers' agents.

CHAPTER 1

United States

No one is raiding a factory looking for trafficking victims;
they are looking for illegal immigrants.
—SUZANNE B. SELTZER, PARTNER AT KLASKO RULON STOCK & SELTZER, LLP

The United States, through the Victims of Trafficking and Violence Protection Act of 2000 (TVPA) and other statutes, prohibits all forms of human trafficking as well as many of the activities that surround it, such as confiscating or withholding a person's documents or committing fraud in forced-labor contracting. Those convicted of labor trafficking face imprisonment ranging from 5 to 20 years for involuntary servitude, forced labor, peonage, and domestic servitude. In aggravated circumstances offenders face up to life imprisonment. Sex-trafficking offenders face up to life imprisonment with a mandatory minimum sentence of 10 years for the sex trafficking of minors and a minimum sentence of 15 years for trafficking a minor under the age of fourteen through force, fraud, or coercion (U.S. Department of State, 2000, 2011). Although U.S. anti-trafficking laws are adequately stringent, the nation's visa programs reflect conflicts between its anti-trafficking and immigration agendas (discussed later). The H-1B temporary visa program is designed to attract foreign workers in specialized fields such as technology, engineering, and medicine; the H-2A visa program allows for the temporary hire of nonimmigrant foreign workers to perform agricultural labor; and the H-2B visa program allows for the hire of temporary nonimmigrant workers to perform nonagricultural labor on a onetime, seasonal, peak-load, or intermittent basis (U.S. Department of Labor, 2012a, 2012b, 2012c). The government, however, does not adequately monitor its visa programs, particularly the H-2B visa. Just like the H-1B and H-2A visa programs, the H-2B visa is employer-specific (visa holders suddenly become illegal if they no longer work for the employer identified on their visa applications), but for years it was the lack of regulations and enforcement of the H-2B visa program that left these visa holders the most vulnerable.

THE UNITED STATES AS A DESTINATION

The United States is one of the top ten destinations for human trafficking, with tens of thousands of people brought into the country each year. Until recently experts believed that sex trafficking accounted for most of the victims; today, however, more foreigners are found in labor trafficking. For instance, of the trafficking victims certified by the Department of Health and Human Services (HHS) in 2009, 82 percent of foreign adults and 56 percent of foreign children were labor trafficking victims.[1] Of the foreign trafficking victims identified in 2010, 55 percent of the adults (70 percent men and 30 percent women) and 62 percent of the children (50 percent boys and 50 percent girls) were forced-labor victims (U.S. Department of State, 2010, 2011).

The increase in identified forced-labor victims has resulted in an increase in identified male trafficking victims. In 2008, men made up 45 percent of the 286 adults certified by HHS. This was a 15 percent increase over those certified during 2007 and a 39 percent increase since 2006 (U.S. Department of State, 2009c). In 2009, 58 percent of the 271 labor trafficking victims were men (U.S. Department of State, 2010). On the other hand, sex trafficking continues to primarily target female victims. For instance, 15 percent of foreign adult victims certified in 2009 were sex-trafficking victims; all of them were women. Of the 38 percent child sex-trafficking victims who received eligibility letters, 84 percent were girls and 16 percent were boys. Of foreign child forced-labor victims, half were boys and half were girls. Three percent of adults and 6 percent of children were victims of both sex and labor trafficking (U.S. Department of State, 2010).

The covert nature of human trafficking makes it difficult to ascertain which countries are primary sources for trafficking into the United

States. That said, the certification by HHS gives us a glimpse of some possibilities. For instance, the 286 foreign adults certified by HHS in 2008 were primarily from Mexico (23 percent), Thailand (19.5 percent), the Philippines (16 percent), Korea (4 percent), and China (2.7 percent) (U.S. Department of State, 2009c). The United States is also the most frequent destination for victims trafficked from Latin America and the Caribbean, and one of the top three destinations for persons trafficked from Asia (other than other Asian nations). The primary countries of origin for identified foreign victims in 2010 were the Dominican Republic, El Salvador, Haiti, Honduras, India, Mexico, the Philippines, and Thailand (U.S. Department of State, 2011).

Labor trafficking occurs primarily in domestic and food and care services, garment, and agricultural sectors (Bales et al., 2004, pp. 1, 14). One such case is that of an Egyptian girl, Bennu, who was forced into domestic labor in Irvine, California. In 1999 Bennu's sister Eshe was working for Abdel Nasser Eid Youssef Ibrahim and Amal Ahmed Ewis-abd Motelib when the couple accused Eshe of theft. In exchange for not going to the authorities, the couple demanded the labor of Bennu, and required her parents to pay them roughly 30 dollars a month for 10 years. Bennu and Eshe's parents agreed to the ultimatum, forcing Bennu into domestic servitude. When 10-year-old Bennu arrived in the United States in 2000, the couple confiscated her passport. For two years Bennu worked as a housekeeper for the family and as a nanny to the couple's five children. During that time she did not receive pay or education and faced physical and verbal abuse as well as threats of deportation. The couple told her that her family would reject her if she was deported and tried to return home (Srisavasdi, 2006).[2]

Another alleged forced-labor case, which made headlines throughout the United States, involved roughly 600 Thai nationals brought to Hawaii and the U.S. mainland between 2001 and 2007 by Global Horizons Manpower, Inc. The federal charges, now dismissed, stated that the defendants confiscated the workers' passports and required them to perform farm labor without pay or for nominal wages.[3] The original complaint alleged that the workers were forced to live in overcrowded and substandard conditions (U.S. Department of Justice, 2011a, 2011b). "It's a classic bait-and-switch," said FBI Special Agent Tom Simon. "They were telling the Thai workers one thing to lure them here. Then, when they got here, their passports were taken away, and they were held in forced servitude working on these farms." The complaint also alleged that the defendants used false promises of high-paying jobs to induce the workers to incur excessive debt. In order to secure jobs in the United States, the workers paid recruitment fees of up to $21,000. Many were encouraged to mortgage their homes or farms to make the payment. "In the old days," Simon said, "they used to keep slaves in place using chains and whips. These days, it's done through economic intimidation" (Kerr, 2010). The government suddenly dismissed the criminal charges against the defendants in July 2012, but the U.S. Equal Employment Opportunity Commission is pursuing civil litigation against Global Horizons Manpower as well as six farms where the workers allegedly faced discrimination and deplorable working conditions (Lin, 2012).

The Central Intelligence Agency (CIA) estimates that 50,000 women and children are trafficked each year throughout the United States for commercial sexual exploitation. This category covers a variety of forms, including forced prostitution, sex shows, stripping, and pornography (Kaiser, 2005, p. 1A). Lack of regulation within the U.S. sex industry exacerbates the problem. Although prostitution is illegal except in the state of Nevada, the sale of pornography (aside from child pornography) and the operation of strip clubs are legal but largely unregulated. Strip clubs, which are usually zoned in certain areas, are often used as a front for prostitution. Pornography, which is constitutionally protected under the First Amendment, is pervasive in the United States, with Americans spending roughly $10 billion a year on adult entertainment. Pornography is linked to some of the biggest U.S. corporations; Time Warner, Hilton, Westin, AT&T, and Marriott earn tens of millions of dollars a year in distribution (CBS News, 2004; University of Nevada, 2004). The considerable profits earned by large U.S. corporations come at a cost, as the lack of regulation results in the illegal use of underage and trafficked persons.

A common feature of all forms of human trafficking is the use of exorbitant fees, such as those for transportation and housing, which places victims in a position of debt bondage and makes them vulnerable to a multitude of additional abuses. This phenomenon is clearly illustrated in a case of women and girls trafficked from Mexico to Florida with the promise of housekeeper and waitress jobs. Upon arrival in the

United States, the traffickers raped the women and girls, confiscated their travel documents, and forced them to prostitute. Guards prevented them from leaving the brothels, and if the victims tried to escape they faced severe physical punishment as well as threats of deportation. The women allegedly earned $3 per trick but never received the money. Instead, the traffickers told the women the earnings would go toward the $2,000-per-person transportation fee. To put some perspective on the situation, in order to pay off her debt, each woman would need to have sex with around 667 men. The traffickers also charged the women for room and board and other miscellaneous fees (OAS/PAHO, 2001). The use of fees to create debt bondage is also apparent in an Atlanta case in which Asian women and girls between the ages of 13 and 25 were trafficked to the United States and forced to prostitute until they paid off debts of between $30,000 and $40,000 per person. Conditions in the bordellos resembled those in a prison, with guards, barbed-wire fences, and dogs (Richard, 2000, p. 21).

The lawlessness and high demand for cheap labor that tends to accompany the aftermath of natural disasters can create an atmosphere ripe for human trafficking. Trafficking in New Orleans and other areas devastated by Hurricanes Katrina and Rita began shortly after the storms. To date, at least nine large cases of exploitation in the Gulf Coast region have been documented that may be classifiable as forced labor. The cases involve more than 3,728 alleged victims from Bolivia, Brazil, the Dominican Republic, Honduras, India, Mexico, Panama, Peru, the Philippines, and Thailand.

One such example is that of Thai nationals trafficked to New Orleans after Hurricane Katrina. The victims were forced to work and live in hurricane-damaged buildings riddled with mold and debris without electricity or running water. Some of the victims were eventually discovered inside the Capri Hotel in November 2005 (Andert, 2007, p. 27). Conditions in their living quarters were so squalid that they were forced to cook with contaminated water (Asanok et al., 2007). "They did not have enough food," said attorney Lori J. Johnson of Legal Aid of North Carolina, Farmworker Unit. "At the end, they had to build traps to capture pigeons to eat."[4] The victims' civil complaint states that North Carolina human resource company Million Express Manpower, Inc., used a locally based Thai agent to recruit victims in Bangkok. The victims were promised legal visas and three years of employment at $8.24 per hour. Each paid over $11,000 in fees simply to secure employment (Asanok et al., 2007). In order to pay the employment fee, says Johnson, victims were steered toward lenders who were in league with the traffickers. "To secure the loan, victims had to put up their land and that of family members. Keep in mind that rice farmers in northeast Thailand typically make less than $500 a year. Essentially, there is no way that the workers could pay back the loans on their typical salary in Thailand." Once the victims were sufficiently in debt, Million Express Manpower was safely in the power position—one that it eagerly highlighted to potential employers. "Via word of mouth, [Million Express] Manpower, Inc., began to pitch its labor force as more inclined to work hard because they were so far in debt," Johnson said.

In August 2005 the traffickers brought the victims to the United States with temporary H-2A visas. Upon arrival, armed guards confiscated the victims' return tickets, visas, and passports. The victims spent the first month primarily working on Howell Farms, Inc. in North Carolina before they were taken to perform demolition on Katrina-ravaged buildings in New Orleans (Asanok et al., 2007). "One indicia of trafficking is that the victims are moved from place to place, so that they are kept in disorientation," Johnson said. "They were moved around within New Orleans; each place was worse than the previous. They were housed in the buildings that they were demolishing. The Capri Hotel was the final, and the worst, stop." While in New Orleans, the victims were not paid and were closely supervised by an armed guard to ensure that they did not try to escape. The same guard charged the victims for purchasing their food, but without pay the workers began to go hungry (Asanok et al., 2007). As a result of pressure brought by the Thai embassy, the traffickers had to return the victims to North Carolina in order to meet with embassy representatives—who were beginning to question the victims' whereabouts. "Unable to fit all of the victims into their vehicles, the traffickers left seven in New Orleans with a guard," Johnson said. There were other victims related to this case, some of whom had arrived on a different and previous order. Their whereabouts remain unknown. Others were simply too fearful to participate in the legal proceedings again Million Express Manpower and disappeared before social service providers were able to gain their trust.

Johnson believes that the post-Katrina setting, in which normal community networks had been compromised and the population was in flux, created ideal trafficking conditions. Devastation from a natural disaster, Johnson says, creates a sudden high demand for low-wage and largely unskilled labor. Disruption of the traditional labor supply leaves room for illicit contractors to move in, and new workers can be brought in unnoticed. Additionally, law enforcement personnel are overextended and do not have the resources to monitor a trafficking scenario.

On September 5, 2005, the Occupational Safety and Health Administration of the U.S. Department of Labor temporarily suspended the enforcement of job safety and health standards in hurricane-impacted counties and parishes in Florida, Alabama, Mississippi, and Louisiana. Affirmative-action requirements were also suspended. Within the next several days, the Department of Homeland Security (DHS) suspended for 45 days the requirement that employers confirm employee eligibility and identity, and then-president Bush temporarily suspended the Davis-Bacon Act, lifting wage restrictions for nearly 2 months. Under the act, construction workers are guaranteed the prevailing local wage when paid with federal money (Donato & Hakimzadeh, 2009). These changes, intended to speed recovery in the disaster-ravaged region, also opened the floodgates for worker exploitation and human trafficking. For instance, the number of Department of Labor investigations in New Orleans dropped from 70 in the year prior to Katrina to 44 in the year after—a 37 percent decrease. "The Department of Labor is the federal cop on the workplace safety, wages, and hours beat," Congressman Dennis Kucinich said. "Where was 'Sheriff Labor' during the early months of the reconstruction?" (U.S. House of Representatives, 2007, p. 2).

One of the groups most affected by the lack of regulation was guest-workers. There seems to be a general misperception that all migrant workers are in the United States illegally, but nearly all—98.3 percent—of persons identified as potential forced-labor victims in the Gulf Coast region were visa holders. (See Table 1.1.) Of those 3,663 persons, 72 were H-2A visa holders, 361 were H-1B visa holders, and 3,230 were H-2B visa holders (these are the lowest estimates of the potential victims in the alleged Gulf Coast cases).[5] U.S. companies or their agents recruited most of these workers. This is not uncommon practice. U.S. companies often use guestworker visas to recruit low-skilled foreign workers. In

2005 alone, employers brought in 121,000 guestworkers under the H-2 program (Bauer, 2007, p. 1; U.S. House of Representatives, 2008). What stands out in the data we collected are the high number of alleged trafficked persons in the Gulf Coast who were H-2B visa holders, who, as we have seen, are particularly vulnerable to employer exploitation and abuse.

In 2005, the year the Gulf Coast region was devastated by Hurricanes Katrina and Rita, no government agency claimed ownership of the H-2B program. The Department of Labor stated they had little to no authority to act on behalf of H-2B visa holders. Although statutes existed to protect H-2A visa holders, there was no similar protection for nonagricultural guestworkers. The H-2A program grants workers free housing, access to legal services, employment for at least three-fourths of the total hours promised in his or her contract (this is called the "three-quarters guarantee"), compensation for medical costs and permanent injury, as well as various other benefits (U.S. House of Representatives, 2007). In contrast, wage protection provided to H-2B visa holders was skeletal at best. Employers utilizing the H-2B program were obligated to offer full-time employment that at minimum paid the prevailing wage rate, but because the H-2B visa was established via a 1994 Department of Labor administrative directive instead of through statutory regulation, the Department of Labor claimed to lack the legal authority to enforce its requirements (U.S. Department of Labor, 1994; U.S. House of Representatives, 2007).

Congress exacerbated the problem when in 2005 it vested the Department of Homeland Security with enforcement authority over the H-2B visa program. As a result, the Department of Labor had no authority to enforce the provisions and regulations of the program. According to Kucinich, the Department of Labor had the authority to grant or deny certification for a foreign labor contract through its Office of Foreign Labor Certification, but it could not deny certification for an employer who had been prosecuted for labor law violations. Instead, the Department of Homeland Security was granted complete authority over the enforcement of H-2B contract terms. Irrespective of the statutory limitations impeding the Department of Labor's advocacy on behalf of H-2B workers, the Department of Labor's Wage and Hour Division still had the authority and the responsibility to prosecute employers for

TABLE 1.1
Alleged Gulf Coast Forced-Labor Trafficking Cases

Case	Estimate of potential victims	Country of origin	Visa	Alleged conditions faced by workers	Defendants charged under	Status
David et al. v. Signal International, LLC et al.	500–550	India	H-2B	False promises; exorbitant fees and payroll deductions for room, board, and work-related tools; withheld documents; surveilled labor camps; threat of deportation; threat of harm; detainment; armed guards; unpaid wages	TVPA[a]; RICO[b]; FLSA[c]	Ongoing
Asanok et al. v. Million Express Manpower, Inc. et al.	30	Thailand	H-2A	False promises; exorbitant fees; unpaid wages; withheld documents; threat of deportation; monitored workers' movements; condemned housing; contaminated water; no food; armed guard(s)	TVPA; RICO; FLSA	Won a default judgment but have been unable to collect on the judgment
Daniel Castellanos-Contreras et al. v. Decatur Hotels, LLC et al.	300	Peru, Bolivia, Dominican Republic	H-2B	False promises; exorbitant fees; unpaid wages; retaliatory firing; eviction; position of debt peonage due to high fees and low wages	FLSA	Won in district court but lost on appeal

TABLE 1.1 (continued)

Case	Estimate of potential victims	Country of origin	Visa	Alleged conditions faced by workers	Defendants charged under	Status
Saucedo et al. v. Five Star Contractors, LLC et al.	2,300	Brazil	H-2B	False promises; exorbitant fees; threat of deportation; surveilled labor camp; required to purchase work tools; unpaid wages	FLSA; RICO; breach of contract	Ongoing
Fredi Garcia et al. v. Audubon Communities Management, LLC et al.	13	Honduras	Undocumented	False promises; unpaid wages; threat of eviction and deportation; eviction	TVPA; FLSA	Settled
Israel Antonio-Morales et al. v. Bimbo's Best Produce	42–118[d]	Mexico	H-2A	Threats of arrest, eviction, and deportation; verbal abuse; at least one instance of physical abuse; use of weapon to intimidate workers; harmful and offensive contact with pesticides; withheld documents; unpaid wages	TVPA; FLSA; breach of contract	On administrative hold until the Department of Justice completes its own investigation

Case	Number	Country	Visa type	Abuses	Legal basis/status	Status
Louisiana Labor, LLC (Matt Redd)	130	Mexico	H-2B	False promises; withheld passports; deplorable living conditions; exorbitant housing costs taken out of wages	No suit as of yet	n/a
Mairi Nunag-Tañedo et al. v. East Baton Rouge Parish School Board et al.	361	Philippines	H-1B	Exorbitant fees with accruing interest rates; controlled and withheld visa and social security documents; threat of deportation if they tried to move out of arranged high-rent housing	TVPA. The case is also under investigation by the Department of Labor	Ongoing
Investigation by the Panamanian government[e]	52	Panama	Unknown	Unknown	Unknown	Unknown

[a] Victims of Trafficking and Violence Protection Act of 2000.
[b] Racketeer Influenced and Corrupt Organizations Act (1970).
[c] Fair Labor Standards Act of 1938.
[d] Thirty-seven persons were brought from Mexico to work at Bimbo's in 2005/2006, approximately 39 in 2006/2007, and approximately 42 in 2007/2008. It is unknown how many of the workers came back annually.
[e] U.S. Department of State, 2009c.

Sources: Interviews and correspondence with Mary Bauer, Lori Johnson, Jacob Horwitz, Dan Werner, Stacie Jonas, Robert Anthony Alvarez, and Dan McNeil.

violations of the Federal Labor Standards Act and the Davis-Bacon Act (U.S. House of Representatives, 2007).

Fortunately, in late 2008, discussions between the Department of Homeland Security and the Department of Labor resulted in an agreement that the Department of Labor should be delegated H-2B enforcement authority. Numerous amendments to the Department of Labor regulations updated the procedures for issuing labor certification to employers sponsoring H-2B guestworkers (U.S. Department of Labor, 2008, 2009b). The amendments, unlike the 1994 administrative directive, expressly prohibit employers from passing onto foreign workers the cost of attorney or agent fees, the H-2B application, or recruitment associated with obtaining labor certification. The Federal Register Rules and Regulations state that these are business expenses associated with aiding the employer to complete the labor certification application and labor market test: "The employer's responsibility to pay these costs exists separate and apart from any benefit that may accrue to the foreign worker" (U.S. Department of Labor, 2008, p. 78,039).

TRAFFICKING WITHIN THE UNITED STATES

Sex trafficking is the most common form of human trafficking identified among U.S. citizens. Although HHS identified more than 1,000 internal trafficking victims in 2009, it is extremely difficult to know how many persons this form of trafficking actually affects (U.S. Department of State, 2010). This uncertainty reflects both the hidden nature of the crime and the emphasis studies have placed on international as opposed to internal trafficking. There are estimates on the sexual exploitation of minors within the United States, but there is little information on children and adults trafficked within the United States for forced labor or commercial sexual exploitation (Estes & Weiner, 2002, p. 5; Clawson et al., 2009, p. 4).

Richard J. Estes and Neil Alan Weiner in the report *The Commercial Sexual Exploitation of Children in the U.S., Canada and Mexico* estimate that as of 2001 there were between 244,000 and 325,000 U.S. youths at risk (Estes & Weiner, 2002, p. 150). These numbers may have drastically changed since the release of this report.

The Child Labor Coalition estimates that 5.5 million U.S. youths between ages 12 and 17 are employed. This number does not include illegal employment such as the use of U.S. children in sweatshops (Clawson et al., 2009, p. 6). In 2008 the Department of Labor found 4,734 minors illegally employed. Forty-one percent of cited child labor violations included children working under hazardous conditions, in hazardous environments, and/or using prohibited equipment. Other child labor violations involved children under the age of 16 working too late, too early, or for too many hours (U.S. Department of Labor, 2009a). Grocery stores, shopping malls, restaurants, and theaters, where children are often employed, have historically shown a high level of noncompliance with child labor laws. Children in agricultural employment are also a particularly vulnerable population. In 2009 the Wage and Hour Division cited five agricultural employers for employing children under the legal age of employment to perform labor in North Carolina blueberry fields (U.S. Department of Labor, 2009a). The Association of Farmworker Opportunity Programs estimates that hundreds of thousands of U.S. children, some as young as nine years old, are migrant and seasonal farmworkers (Hess, 2007, pp. 2, 6, 11).

There is a common misconception among Americans that human trafficking within the United States is an underground industry whose victims and abusers are exclusively immigrants. The story of one 15-year-old illustrates that U.S. citizens and legal residents can also become victims of human trafficking. In September 2005 "Sarah" ran away from home and met her traffickers, Matthew Gray (30 years old) and Jannelle Butler (21 years old), through a friend. They took Sarah to an apartment in the Washington Park area of Phoenix, where they bound and gang-raped her.[6] The traffickers then forced Sarah into a dog kennel and with a gun threatened to harm her and her family. When fearful of police, the traffickers hid Sarah in a hollowed-out box spring. The traffickers forced Sarah to prostitute for 42 days. One of her captors, Gray, raped Sarah throughout her time in captivity (Villa & Collom, 2005a; Park, 2008).

In early November Sarah managed to call her mother from Gray's cell phone. Sarah was too scared to give her mother details regarding her captors or on her exact location for fear that they would harm her family. This fear was not unfounded, as Gray knew where her mother and family members lived. Arizona policeman Greg Scheffer says victims often don't call the police, even when given an opportunity to do so, for fear of reprisals (Villa & Collom, 2005b).

After receiving her daughter's phone call, Sarah's mother called the police. The officers made repeat visits to the apartment where Sarah was held and were, at times, just inches away. After Butler was arrested on the last visit and placed in the patrol car, she informed police that Sarah was hidden in the box spring. Butler expressed concern that Sarah might run out of oxygen as she almost fainted the last time she was forced to hide in the compartment. Interestingly, Butler was a victim of similar crimes at age 17. It seems that she subjected Sarah to the same strategy of beatings, threats, and imprisonment that she experienced. Phoenix police sergeant Chris Bray told the *Arizona Republic* that Butler's actions are not uncommon in victims of abuse, specifically child abuse. "It's kind of a battered-child syndrome," Bray said. "It happened to them. They hated it. And then they do it to someone else" (Villa & Collom, 2005b).

CHILD SEX TOURISM

Child sex tourism is a form of exploitation that often takes place off U.S. soil but at the hands of U.S. citizens and legal residents. Many Western men travel to Southeast Asia, particularly Thailand, and pay for sex with children. The humanitarian organization World Vision, which collaborates with the U.S. State Department, HHS, and U.S. Immigration and Customs Enforcement (ICE), estimates that there are 2 million children enslaved worldwide in the commercial sex trade. It also estimates that U.S. citizens make up 25 percent of child-sex tourists globally and up to 80 percent of child-sex tourists in Latin America (World Vision, 2009). In response to the exploitation of children via sex tourism by U.S. citizens and residents, the U.S. government enacted the Prosecutorial Remedies and Other Tools to End the Exploitation of Children Today (PROTECT) Act of 2003, which grants the United States jurisdiction to prosecute its citizens and legal permanent residents who go abroad and pay to have sex with a minor. It does not matter whether the client had knowledge that the child was a minor. Convicted sex tourists face up to

30 years' imprisonment (U.S. Department of Justice, 2006b). Another program, called Operation Twisted Traveler, was launched in February 2009. The program is a collaborative effort by ICE, the Department of Justice, and law-enforcement officials in Cambodia to identify, arrest, and prosecute U.S. citizens and legal residents who travel to Cambodia for child-sex tourism (U.S. Department of Justice, 2009).

As a result of information provided to ICE by the International Justice Mission and Action pour les Enfants, three U.S. citizens were indicted for alleged acts of sex tourism in September 2009. Jack Louis Sporich (75 years old) and Erik Leonardus Peeters (41 years old) were each charged with three counts of having sexual contact with three Cambodian boys, while Ronald Gerard Boyajian (49 years old) was indicted on one count of sexual contact with a 10-year-old Vietnamese girl. If they are found guilty the men face up to 30 years' imprisonment for each count of sex tourism. Reports say that Sporich would drive his motorbike in the city of Siem Reap, tossing Cambodian currency as a means of catching the attention of children (U.S. Department of Justice, 2009).

WHAT HAPPENS TO VICTIMS AFTER TRAFFICKING

Even after rescue or escape, the victim experience is far from over. One concern among social service providers is the large number of persons who are found in agent raids, arrested, and deported without a proper evaluation as to whether they are trafficking victims. Also, internal victims are not typically the focus of anti-trafficking efforts and are marginalized as a result. In 2009, HHS-funded outreach programs identified over 700 potential foreign trafficking victims plus more than 1,000 internal trafficking victims. It is unknown how many of the latter were referred to law enforcement or received services (U.S. Department of State, 2010). Additionally, children continue to be arrested for crimes associated with their trafficking experience. In 2008 at least 643 females and 206 males under the age of 18 were reportedly arrested for prostitution and commercialized vice (U.S. Department of State, 2010). Moreover, although the TVPA provides a federal framework for victim protection, safeguards for trafficking victims are not consistent at state and local levels. Forty-two states have enacted, and are slowly beginning to use, specific anti-trafficking statutes. Only 9 states offer state public benefits to trafficking victims; 18 states permit victims to bring civil lawsuits in state court; 18 states have instituted mandatory restitution; and 9 states require that victims' names and/or locations be kept confidential (U.S. Department of State, 2010).

The United States falls short in several areas when it comes to addressing the post-trafficking experience of victims. These areas include the underutilization of U and T visas (discussed below), the pressure for adult victims to cooperate with law enforcement in order to obtain social services, and the less-than-adequate relationship between social service providers and law enforcement. The Department of Health and Human Services is the only federal agency authorized to grant eligibility letters to minors and certification to adults who are foreign trafficking victims. The agency issued eligibility letters to 50 foreign minors and certified 330 foreign adult victims in 2009, which is an increase from the 31 foreign minors and 286 foreign adult victims granted eligibility or certification in 2008 (HHS, 2009; U.S. Department of State, 2009c, 2010). In 2010 the agency issued 92 eligibility letters to foreign minors and certified 449 foreign adult victims (U.S. Department of State, 2011). Certification and eligibility letters allow victims access to federal services and benefits similar to those received by refugees. With the objective of skill development and self-sufficiency, minors are provided care through the Unaccompanied Refugee Minors program. United States citizens and lawful permanent residents do not need to be certified or to receive a letter of eligibility to obtain services (HHS, 2009; U.S. Department of State, 2009c).

The United States offers immigration relief through continued-presence status to potential trafficking witnesses during the investigation and prosecution of their trafficker(s). In 2008, 225 requests and 101 extensions for continued-presence status were granted (HHS, 2009; U.S. Department of State, 2009c). In 2009, continued-presence status was issued to 299 potential victim-witnesses. In 2010 continued-presence status was issued to 186 potential victim-witnesses (U.S. Department of State, 2010, 2011). Victims can also obtain relief through the U visa (U nonimmigrant status) and T visa (T nonimmigrant status). The U visa is created for immigrants who are victims of crimes. It allows visa holders to apply to become lawful permanent residents and eventually U.S.

citizens. The success of a U visa application turns on whether the victim suffered substantial physical or mental abuse as a result of one or more of a specific list of crimes. Trafficking, rape, torture, sexual assault, sexual exploitation, prostitution, kidnapping, and false imprisonment are among the offenses included. Applicants must also obtain certification by a federal, state, or local government official that the petitioner is likely to be helpful to him or her in the investigation or prosecution of the criminal act of which the applicant is a victim (U.S. Department of Homeland Security, 2009a, 2009c). This visa program seems ineffective in multiple respects. First, it is underutilized. Although Congress created the U visa in 2000, the first visa was not issued until eight years later. At the end of 2008, 13,300 people had filed U visa applications, but only 65 visas were issued, and 20 applications were denied. The number of visas issued is particularly small considering that the Department of Homeland Security can issue up to 10,000 U visas annually, though interim benefits were granted to 10,800 applicants while final decisions on their applications were pending. Second, it is not uncommon for applicants to be placed in detention while awaiting decisions. This practice is in direct conflict with the intent of the TVPA, as it treats the applicant as a criminal instead of a potential victim. It also creates a "race against the clock" situation as to what will happen first—deportation or protection. As of July 2009 roughly 50 U visa applicants were being held in immigration detention centers throughout the nation (Gorman, 2009a, 2009b). Third, the burden on victims to assist law enforcement results in potential obstacles (discussed below).

The T visa provides immigration protection to victims of severe forms of trafficking and allows visa holders to apply to become lawful permanent residents and eventually U.S. citizens.[7] The Department of Homeland Security is authorized to issue up to 5,000 T visas annually. As of October 2008 the department received only 2,300 T visa applications—1,308 of which were approved, 709 were denied or withdrawn, and 212 remained pending. In 2008, 247 T visas were granted to foreign victims of trafficking identified in the United States, and 171 T visas were granted to immediate family members of those persons (Crary, 2005; U.S. Department of Homeland Security, 2009b; U.S. Department of State, 2009c). In 2009, 313 T visas were granted to foreign victims, and 273 T visas were issued to immediate family members of victims. In 2010, T visas were granted to 447 victims and 349 immediate family members of victims. Roughly 500 and 518 T visa holders, including victims and their family members, became lawful permanent residents in 2009 and 2010, respectively (U.S. Department of State, 2010, 2011).

Strict criteria used for issuance of the T visa may be partly responsible for its underutilization. One concern among social service providers is the pressure exerted on victims to assist law enforcement. Since the T visa is more likely to be approved for an adult victim if he or she cooperates with law enforcement, trafficking victims over the age of 18 are encouraged to do so. The language on the I-914, Application for T Nonimmigrant Status, reads: "I have complied with requests from Federal, State, or local law enforcement authorities for assistance in the investigation or prosecution of acts of trafficking. (If 'No,' explain the circumstances.)" (U.S. Department of Homeland Security, 2009b). A victim who has just escaped or was recently rescued from a trafficking experience may simply not be in the right state of mind to help investigators. If interviewed before he or she is ready, the victim may not reveal critical details the police need to pursue the case. Factors in play may include mistrust of police, language barriers, loyalty to the victim's traffickers, psychological reasons such as post-traumatic stress disorder, fear of appearing culpable, and fear of reprisals by traffickers or those in the traffickers' network. Alia El-Sawi, a former Anti-Human Trafficking Program coordinator at Tapestri: The Refugee and Immigrant Coalition against Domestic Violence in Atlanta, Georgia, says victims are more apt to cooperate with law enforcement when the pressure to do so is temporarily lifted:

> Most of the time we give the victim a certain amount of time when we don't visit the topic of prosecuting his or her trafficker(s). After a while, we bring it up in a gentle manner and explain to the victim why it is helpful to talk to law enforcement, so that the traffickers are not getting away with continuing to victimize others. Usually at this point the victim is interested in helping law enforcement investigate and prosecute his or her trafficker(s).[8]

Many social service providers would like to see cooperation with law enforcement eliminated as one of the prerequisites for victim services and visa eligibility. Kavitha Sreeharsha, executive director at Global

Freedom Center in San Francisco, argues that the mandate to aid law enforcement actually hinders the prosecutorial process. She also holds that victims should first be provided with immigration protection. "Providing them with immigration protection without such a requirement will enable crime victims to first rebuild their lives. If they receive such services immediately, we expect that they would eventually cooperate on their own but in a way that would be far more effective."[9]

WHAT HAPPENS TO TRAFFICKERS

Human trafficking provides large profits for traffickers and those associated with trafficking networks. If a trafficking victim forced into the commercial sex industry in the United States must meet a quota of $500 a night, the person exploiting this individual can obtain roughly $182,000 a year, tax-free (Frundt, 2005). The more persons trafficked and exploited, the more profit gained by traffickers and their associates. From a cost-benefit analysis, trafficking is low risk and has high profit margins. Profits commonly range from $1 million to $8 million, and detection of abuse is difficult (Richard, 2000; iAbolish, American Anti-Slavery Group, 2006). Even once authorities suspect criminal activity, demonstrating the use of coercion or force is challenging.

While stringent sentencing does occur (see *United States v. Carreto et al.*, 2006), many traffickers face minimal punishment. In the Bennu case, the defendants, Ibrahim and Motelib, pleaded guilty to holding a person in involuntary servitude, obtaining labor through unlawful force or coercion, harboring an illegal alien, and conspiracy. They received prison sentences of 3 years and 1.8 years, respectively. Additionally, the defendants were ordered to pay Bennu $76,137.60 in restitution. The defendants, foreign nationals, were to face deportation proceedings once they completed their sentences (Srisavasdi, 2006).[10] Gray, the primary trafficker of 15-year-old Sarah, pleaded guilty to two counts of child prostitution, two counts of sexual assault, one count of kidnapping, and one count of aggravated assault. He was sentenced to 35 years in prison (Park, 2008). None of the defendants in this Arizona case were charged with trafficking offenses. Perhaps prosecutors felt that they would be more successful, or that the defendants would receive harsher sentencing, if they pursued tried and true charges such as sexual assault, child prostitution, aggravated assault, and kidnapping. At the time of the July 2006 arrests, Arizona's anti-trafficking law had been in effect for nearly a year.

There continue to be more criminal convictions of sex traffickers than of forced-labor traffickers. For instance, in 2008 the Department of Justice's (DOJ) Civil Rights Division and U.S. Attorneys' Offices secured 77 convictions in 27 sex-trafficking and 13 forced-labor cases (U.S. Department of State, 2009c). The good news is that the number of convicted forced-labor traffickers may be increasing. In 2009 there were 47 convictions in 22 sex-trafficking and 21 labor-trafficking cases, and in 2010 there were 141 convictions in 71 sex-trafficking and 32 labor-trafficking cases (U.S. Department of State, 2010, 2011). The average sentence for convicted traffickers may also be on the rise. In 2008 the average sentence faced by those found guilty of trafficking offenses in the United States was 9.3 years' imprisonment compared to 13 years in 2009. However, the average sentence decreased to 11.8 years in 2011 (U.S. Department of State, 2009c, 2010, 2012).

The Innocence Lost National Initiative, run by the DOJ and the Federal Bureau of Investigation (FBI), is a collaboration of federal and state law-enforcement authorities and victim assistance providers that targets child sexual exploitation. In 2008 the initiative led to the rescue of 245 children and the conviction of 148 offenders (U.S. Department of State, 2009c). In 2009 the initiative led to the identification of 306 children and the conviction of 151 traffickers in state and federal courts (U.S. Department of State, 2010). Under amendments to the TVPA in 2008, the FBI is tasked with incorporating human trafficking offenses in the annual statistics collected from police forces nationwide. This requirement should help to provide a more accurate picture of trafficking in the United States. Collection is expected to begin in early 2013 (U.S. Department of State, 2012).

While attorneys can turn to both the Fair Labor Standards Act (FLSA) and the TVPA to bring civil suit against traffickers, attorneys often utilize only the FLSA. Perhaps this is because the FLSA has been around far longer. Yet there is minimal disincentive to using both. If attorneys utilize both but are unable to satisfy the TVPA claim, the suit can still be won regarding the FLSA claim. It may be that attorneys believe that proceedings will drag on if they involve the TVPA. The difference, of course, between losses for defendants under the FLSA versus the TVPA is that of mere slaps on the wrist versus the stigma associated with human trafficking. Conviction solely under the FLSA seriously undermines the severity of the crime and does not adequately deter a company (and others) from repeating the crime.

Restitution is automatically part of the proceedings in criminal trafficking cases. In 2008 traffickers were ordered to pay more than $4.2 million to their victims (U.S. Department of State, 2009c). Also, in 2009, under 18 U.S.C. § 1593A, sentencing guidelines established equivalent sentencing in peonage, slavery, and trafficking-in-persons cases for whoever knowingly benefits, financially or by receiving anything of value, from participation in a trafficking venture. Under the guidelines the offender cannot simply plead ignorance. The individual is culpable if he or she knew or was "in reckless disregard" of the fact that the venture involved human trafficking (U.S. Department of State, 2010; U.S. House of Representatives, 2010b).

It is important to recognize the various factors that may alter and influence the language and meaning of new legislation, and consequently the sentencing that traffickers face. For instance, the New York State Anti-Trafficking Law contains an obvious discrepancy in its definitions of and penalties for sex versus labor traffickers. Enacted in 2007 under Eliot Spitzer's administration, the New York anti-trafficking law makes it significantly tougher to prosecute labor traffickers than sex traffickers. Attorney Christa M. Stewart, the coordinator of the New York State Anti-Trafficking Program, says the agenda in creating the anti-trafficking law was to hinder prostitution but not necessarily human trafficking. "The anti-trafficking law is more aligned with New York State penal law against promoting prostitution," Stewart said. "If someone is promoting prostitution by using a specific means—i.e., if he is benefiting from someone else's commercial sex act and he also does X, Y, and Z (such as gives a material false statement) then he can be considered a trafficker in New York State."[11]

The final language of New York's anti-trafficking law was strongly influenced by a rift within the anti-trafficking movement and by the interests of agricultural lobbying groups and political figures. According to one social service provider, who wished to remain anonymous, the law reflects a clear connection that lawmakers wanted to make between prostitution and trafficking:

> During the creation of this law there was a strong lobby to merge the two issues. While some advocacy groups pushed for tough laws against both sex and labor traffickers, there was an organized lobbying effort that wanted to curtail strict legislation against labor traffickers, both in definition and in penalties. Agricultural industries were particularly invested in making sure that prosecuting labor traffickers was difficult.[12]

Suzanne B. Seltzer, a partner at Klasko Rulon Stock & Seltzer, LLP, asserts that the original definition of human trafficking, when Spitzer was attorney general, was indentured servitude. Then, when Spitzer became governor, the legislation suddenly had an anti-prostitution emphasis. "We felt that he [Spitzer] turned his back on us," Seltzer said. "The reality is that trafficking is indentured servitude and forced labor—regardless of the type of work. Labor trafficking is as horrible as sex trafficking."[13] The ultimate success of pressure from the various interest groups is reflected in the vastly disparate penalties for sex trafficking versus forced-labor trafficking. "Under the New York State law, sex trafficking is a class B felony with a maximum sentence of 25 years' imprisonment," Stewart said. "Additionally, the patronizing a prostitute offense was increased from a class D misdemeanor to a class B misdemeanor. On the other hand, labor trafficking is a class D felony with a maximum sentence of seven years."[14]

Division within the anti-trafficking movement, says Seltzer, also obstructed a consensus on the language used in the New York anti-trafficking law. "Within the anti-trafficking community, there are those of us who believe labor trafficking is as significant as sex trafficking, and there are others whose primary interest is [eliminating] sex trafficking," Seltzer said. "We sat down together to try to get on the same page as to what should be included in the legislation, but it was a nightmare. We were not able to communicate—it was very tense." Seltzer believes that one reason for the disunity within the anti-trafficking movement is a lack of understanding of the realities of labor trafficking: some people just don't believe, or don't want to believe, that labor trafficking is a real problem:

> Since the general activities—domestic work, farming, factory work, or restaurant work—are all legal activities, there is a perception that "it's not as bad as sex trafficking," because in sex trafficking people are being forced into an illegal activity. I think the opposite is true—that because these activities themselves are legal, those forced into these situations fall under the radar. No one is raiding a factory looking for trafficking victims; they are looking for illegal immigrants.

Seltzer believes sex trafficking is the hot issue because it represents "the sexy topic" targeted by the media:

> The general perception that human trafficking is solely for the purposes of sexual exploitation has an unfavorable effect on the overall anti-trafficking movement. People don't think about how the definition of sex trafficking is narrow and that there may be types of work that you would consider sex trafficking but don't fall under the definition, such as strippers, exotic massage, and cocktail waitresses in topless bars. Additionally, you see sexual abuse in labor trafficking scenarios.

Seltzer points out that use of the anti-trafficking movement to eradicate prostitution and violence against women is disadvantageous. "Violence against women is a terrible thing, but it is not always trafficking, and when conflated with trafficking you hurt both issues," Seltzer said. "This type of agenda hurts the anti-trafficking movement because it ignores many of the people being trafficked—such as victims of labor trafficking and male victims of trafficking—and it harms female victims of violence because it does not address the actual causes of violence against women." Seltzer stresses that society and lawmakers seem to have difficulty understanding the subtleties of labor trafficking. Even people smuggled into the United States of their own volition can face a trafficking experience. "Someone may pay to sneak into the country, but it becomes trafficking when the person helping starts to exploit them," Seltzer said. "It seems that in these instances victims are often seen as culpable."[15]

INTERNAL EFFORTS TO DECREASE TRAFFICKING

In response to the increasing number of trafficking cases, the federal government began an anti-trafficking campaign in 2005. Laws that prohibit trafficking are important, but it is critical that they be implemented and enforced. The U.S. government spent $25 million in 2005 toward enforcement of anti-trafficking laws, raising awareness, and identifying and protecting victims of trafficking (U.S. Department of State, 2009c). The first federal law focused on eliminating human trafficking was the TVPA in 2000. The act requires the U.S. State Department to create an annual *Trafficking in Persons Report*. The report rates each country by way of tiers indicating its efforts and success rates in combatting human trafficking. Countries rated lowest, in Tier 3, face possible U.S. sanctions, such as the withholding of non-trade-related, nonhumanitarian assistance (U.S. Department of State, 2005a, 2009c). The United States did not rank itself in the report until 2010, when it gave itself Tier 1 status, defined as countries whose governments meet all the TVPA's minimum standards (U.S. Department of State, 2010).

In compliance with the TVPA mandate, then-president Bush created the President's Interagency Task Force (PITF) in 2002, whose members include the secretary of state (chair), the director of the CIA, and the attorney general. The objective of the task force is to monitor and combat trafficking in persons and to coordinate the anti-trafficking activities of critical U.S. governmental agencies (U.S. Department of State, 2009b). The Senior Policy Operating Group (SPOG) was created in 2003 to follow up on PITF initiatives and to implement anti-trafficking guidelines and policies. The SPOG also reviews proposed anti-trafficking grants in order to facilitate coherence among the agencies' anti-trafficking programs (U.S. Department of State, 2005a, 2009b).

Despite the nation's historical emphasis on sex trafficking, the U.S. government has taken measures to address labor trafficking. In 2008, 18 U.S.C. § 1351 criminalized fraud in foreign labor contracting. The statute prohibits persons from knowingly (and with intent to defraud) recruiting, soliciting, or hiring a person outside the United States—or attempting to do so—to work on a government contract performed on government facilities outside the United States by means of materially false or fraudulent pretenses, representations, or promises regarding that employment. Offenders face a fine, imprisonment for not more than five years, or both (U.S. House of Representatives, 2010a). In February 2010 the PITF pledged to uphold a system that provides for all trafficking victims, regardless of whether they have lost their freedom through sex trafficking or labor trafficking and regardless of age, gender, or immigration status (U.S. Department of State, 2010).

The Rescue and Restore Victims of Human Trafficking public awareness campaign, established by the HHS Office of Refugee Resettlement, has created anti-trafficking coalitions in 24 cities, regions, and states throughout the United States. The coalitions, which raise awareness and develop local anti-trafficking networks, are made up of law enforcement, social service providers, students, and academics. The Department of Health and Human Services also funds the National Human Trafficking Resource Center, a free calling center (888-373-7888) where social service providers, law-enforcement personnel, community members, and victims can report trafficking incidents and receive referrals and technical assistance (Clawson et al., 2009, p. 28). Of course, accessibility remains an obvious problem. Victims are typically isolated, with no access to a phone, let alone anti-trafficking materials that would alert them to their options. Language barriers can also be a hindrance, though interpreters are available in 170 languages. In 2009 the center received a total of 7,257 phone calls. The calls included 1,019 tips, which resulted in 300 referrals to law enforcement and 697 requests for victim care referrals (U.S. Department of State, 2010). In order to address international trafficking, U.S. agencies between fiscal years 2001 and 2009 obligated an estimated $686 million to international anti-trafficking in persons assistance. Among the giving agencies are the Department of Labor, the Department of State, the United States Agency for International Development, the Department of Justice, and the Department of Health and Human Services (Siskin & Wyler, 2010, p. 7). In support of efforts by nongovernmental organizations and foreign governments to combat human trafficking, in 2005 the U.S. government distributed

$95 million to fund 266 programs in 101 countries. In 2009 the State Department's Office to Monitor and Combat Trafficking in Persons awarded more than $26 million to 93 anti-trafficking programs world-wide (U.S. Department of State, 2005b, 2009a; U.S. Department of Justice, 2006a). The U.S. government appropriated at least $231.3 million to domestic anti-trafficking in persons programs between fiscal years 2005 and 2009. The amount the U.S. government obligated to domestic anti-trafficking in persons decreased from fiscal year 2008 to fiscal year 2009; it dropped from $23.2 million to $19.7 million, respectively. This amount increased to $24.2 million in 2010. This amount does not include the cost of related law enforcement investigations or the cost of administering trafficking-in-persons operations (Siskin & Wyler, 2010, p. 7; Siskin & Wyler, 2012, p. 5).

One hurdle for the United States in its anti-trafficking efforts is the conflict between its anti-trafficking and immigration agendas. This is illustrated in a case in which ICE knowingly targeted alleged trafficking victims. The agency began surveillance on 23 alleged victims in North Dakota after being informed by the workers' employer, Wanzek Construction, that there were anomalies in the workers' employment paperwork. Suspecting the workers of obtaining and using false documents, ICE staged a sham staff meeting in order to arrest them even though ICE knew that the persons detained in the raid were cooperating in a federal investigation against their alleged trafficker, Signal International, LLC.[16] The raid and arrest took place on October 28, 2008, seven months after the trafficking victims had filed suit against Signal in federal court (NOWCRJ, 2008; Springer, 2008a, 2008b). Barry Nelson, executive director of the Metro Youth Partnership in Moorhead, Fargo, and West Fargo, says the Cass 23 (so called because they were held at Minnesota's Cass County Jail) were in dire financial straits while they waited out the lawsuit against Signal:

> As time went on, their finances [deteriorated], and they needed employment. Initially, the workers were encouraged by a warm response from members of Congress and assurances that the case against Signal would take place in an efficient manner. The workers later told me, "Washington, D.C., is very expensive. We had to figure out a way to support ourselves while this [the suit against

Signal] is going on." It was at this point that the victims began dispersing. Some of the men knew of friends who had obtained employment working on the [Tharaldson] power plant in North Dakota. They learned that they were actively recruiting welders and pipefitters.[17]

Nelson says the workers had a good experience working on the power plant. They were treated well and were paid overtime. The workers felt that the employer valued them, and, according to Nelson, Wanzek has stated that the men were excellent workers. Then, on the last day on the job the men received notice that they should come to headquarters. This is when the men were arrested. "It seems coincidental that the employer [Wanzek Construction] felt compelled to perform its civic duty of reporting the men to ICE after the job was complete, after they no longer needed the skilled services of the men," Nelson said. The Cass 23 workers had entered the United States legally with H-2B visas, which they obtained through their alleged traffickers. Because the visas are employer specific, when the men escaped the labor camp and trafficking experience, they lost their visas. If their T visa applications are accepted, the men will be able to legally live and work in the United States for three years and can subsequently apply for permanent resident status (a green card). While waiting for the lawsuit to proceed, the men faced a long time when they could not legally work but needed income to survive. "Their biggest crime was trying to support themselves while the justice system slowly ground on," Nelson said. "I have never seen a situation where people were so victimized and continuously trapped by a system that is ours."[18]

What is most surprising about this case is that the workers were prosecuted regardless of the trafficking assertion. Drew Wrigley, then-U.S. attorney for the District of North Dakota, was aware of the trafficking allegations before he decided to prosecute the workers, but he was more concerned with the workers' visa statuses than with their alleged-victim statuses. "Nothing in those allegations would allow them to disappear in the American mosaic and reappear in North Dakota and obtain employment," Wrigley told *Forum* reporter Patrick Springer (Springer, 2008c). Aside from the fact that Wrigley's actions are in direct conflict with the objective of the TVPA, deporting victim-witnesses can obviously significantly weaken a case against the victims' traffickers.

Like many law-enforcement units, ICE has historically used arrest quotas. Until recently, fugitive tracking teams (consisting of four to seven agents) in the Fugitive Operations Program had to arrest at least 1,000 fugitives per year (Taxin, 2009). The controversial Fugitive Operations Program has received much negative publicity surrounding the large number of noncriminal arrests resulting from agent raids. The Migration Policy Institute reported that 73 percent of nearly 97,000 persons arrested by the Fugitive Operations Program between 2003 and 2008 did not have criminal records.[19] Some experts blamed the large number of noncriminal arrests on the arrest quotas of the Fugitive Operations Program. Additionally, arrest quotas can obstruct efforts to arrest criminal offenders, whose cases can take more time. Then, in August 2009, ICE director John Morton announced the elimination of arrest quotas in the Fugitive Operations Program and stated that the program would focus on criminals who have ignored deportation orders. "The Fugitive Operations Program needs to focus first and foremost on people who have knowingly flouted an immigration removal order, and within that category, obviously we will focus first on criminals," Morton stated. "I just don't think that a law-enforcement program should be based on a hard number that must be met," Morton said. "I just don't think that's a good way to go about it. So we don't have quotas anymore" (Gorman, 2009c, p. 11).

Whereas immigration violations such as illegal border crossing and overstaying a visa have historically been treated as administrative or civil offenses, persons who have ignored deportation orders are now considered fugitives (Mendelson, Strom, & Wishnie, 2009; Rood, 2009). Morton told reporters that he would continue enforcing the law against immigrants who refuse to follow deportation orders. "It is important that the system have integrity," Morton said. "I am not signaling in any way that we are not going to enforce the law against non-criminal fugitives" (Gorman, 2009c, p. 11). According to Tim Counts, a spokesperson for ICE, "80 percent of the fugitive population is non-criminal. While we focus on the worst offenders, we are charged with enforcing the nation's immigration laws." Counts goes on to state that nonfugitives are not in the clear; if discovered, they, too, will be arrested. "If we get leads, we're not going to ignore administrative offenders" (Rood, 2009, p. 1).

Many legal and social service providers were hopeful that the relationship between ICE and legal and social service providers would improve under the Obama administration. And according to Caitlin Ryland of Legal Aid of the North Carolina Farmworker Unit, this seems to be happening. "What we have seen lately is a forging between local law enforcement, ICE, and direct service providers. ICE has indicated to us that they have been given specific instructions [by the Obama administration] to concentrate on employer-focused enforcement actions. We understand this to mean that they are targeting enforcement actions on employers as opposed to workers."[20]

Ryland states that it is in the best interests of trafficking victims for local police, ICE, legal service providers and direct service providers to have a working relationship: "There are many different types of first responders—it may be a migrant housing inspector, a Department of Labor inspector, an NGO, a health clinic, or local law enforcement. A lack of cooperation between groups can be detrimental to trafficking victims. One example is that of a trafficker of one of our clients who was actually able to use an unknowing police officer to further his trafficking scheme."

The trafficker had called local law enforcement in order to stop a victim from leaving the trafficking labor camp. The officer who arrived at the location did not speak Spanish and allowed the trafficker to act as an interpreter between the officer and the trafficking victim. As a result of this interaction, the victim understood—through his trafficker's fraudulent translation of the conversation—that the police officer was demanding that the victim sign a paper indicating that he could not leave the camp without repaying his alleged debt to the trafficker. "If the law enforcement official had been sufficiently trained to see those red flags, then perhaps this person could have had an opportunity to leave the trafficking situation at an earlier date," Ryland said. "Additionally, it might have prevented the trafficker from trafficking others. Instead, the trafficker was actually able to use law enforcement to further his trafficking scheme."

In September 2009 the local ICE office agreed to inform the appropriate legal service providers when they start an enforcement action. In the past, says Ryland, ICE has placed those found at raids in the local jail—in black-and-white-striped suits—and in the same jail as their traffickers and johns:

> ICE has now agreed to let us know when they begin a raid. If they have identified a potential victim they will try to place the victim somewhere other than the jail for the interviewing process, in an effort to minimize re-victimization. Trust between an advocate and a victim is just that [much] more difficult to foster when a person has been unknowingly re-victimized by people who are there to help them. However, ICE informed us that the extent to which they are able to make these alternative interview arrangements depends on the extent of their working relationship with the specific local law-enforcement agency involved in the raid.

One of the challenges in forging relationships between law enforcement and legal and direct services is that they have different professional guidelines. According to Ryland, the victim may not immediately give service providers permission to share information with law enforcement:

> We are bound by a duty of confidentiality, and we understand that there are certain barriers that you have to get over to build trust with your client before they will (a) tell us the whole story and (b) grant us permission to share that story with someone else. However, law enforcement does not always realize that building trust takes time. They don't always understand why a victim wouldn't readily identify himself or herself as a victim of human trafficking.

Another obstacle to building a relationship with police, Ryland said, is the pressure put on local law enforcement: "It seems that local law enforcement has to meet a certain number of convictions for prostitution. For instance, they [law enforcement] may charge a person with prostitution and not drop the charges even when the person is found to be a victim of human trafficking."[21]

Although the United States has taken significant measures to counter human trafficking worldwide as well as nationally, there exists a conflict between the objective of the TVPA to protect and assist victims of trafficking and that of ICE to combat illegal immigration. Those found in raids are often arrested and deported without a thorough evaluation as to whether they are trafficking victims. Such practices not only fail to protect and assist potential victims of trafficking, but also result in the deportation of critical witnesses, which significantly weakens the case against their traffickers. Hopefully, the removal of arrest quotas from the Fugitive Operations Program will help shift the focus so that traffickers and corporations that benefit from the exploitation of trafficked persons become the target of ICE instead of those who have been exploited.

CHAPTER 2

Japan

I apologize to those Brazilians or Peruvians who came to Japan with high hope[s]. Our policy was very wrong. We just wanted the cheap labor, but we don't want to open our market to . . . foreign countries.
—TARO KONO, MEMBER OF THE JAPANESE HOUSE OF REPRESENTATIVES, 2009

Japan has a hyperthriving sex industry amounting to $3 billion a year (Hughes, Sporcic, Mendelsohn, & Chirgwin, 1999; McNeill, 2004). Sex is openly advertised, yet conservative attitudes persist toward the open discussion of sex. According to James Farrer, former director of the Institute of Comparative Culture at Sophia University in Tokyo, this is not a contradiction but rather a reflection of a cultural difference between the West and the East:

> In Japan it is acceptable to be a different person during the day versus the night. It is context appropriate. Japanese society doesn't have the Protestant moral restrictions on sex like [that of] the United States. There has always been a commercial sex industry. For many people the world of the commercial sex industry is a vague and gray area, and they don't get too bothered by it. Particularly in the cities, it is part of the urban landscape—you see it everywhere. It is seen as something that has its place but not in serious daily life. If kept in its place it is not morally significant. At the same time, the culture is modest, and talking about sex is considered immodest.[1]

Michiko Yokoyama, a public outreach program officer at the Japan office of the anti-trafficking group Polaris Project, holds that this cultural dualism fosters ignorance on the issue of trafficking, particularly that of trafficking for commercial sexual exploitation:

There is a lack of social awareness on trafficking issues due to a lack of human rights and sex education at schools, poor media coverage, and the absence of a government campaign on human trafficking. I attended an NGO and government meeting on Japan's new action plan on human trafficking on December 2, 2009. During the meeting a government official from the Ministry of Health mentioned that "many teachers are not willing to talk about issues too shocking for children" and refused to give clear answers as to whether the government is willing to include trafficking issues in human rights education.[2]

According to Japan's Ministry of Foreign Affairs (MOFA), efforts have been made to improve sex education through the subjects of physical education, health, and science (MOFA, 1999). But schools and health organizations do not always cooperate (Matsumoto, 1995). According to Chieko Ishiwata, "The issues of who should be providing sexual education, the extent of it, and how it is taught are extremely complicated." For instance, curriculum guidelines imposed by the Ministry of Culture, Sports, Science and Technology limit the language teachers can use in teaching about sex and what topics they can discuss (Ishiwata, 2011). Masako Ono-Kihara, director at the UNAIDS Collaborating Centre on Socio-Epidemiological HIV Research and associate professor at the Kyoto University School of Public Health, said that teachers of sex education have to walk the line between cultural values and modern lifestyles. "This gap must be eradicated. But at the same time, we must be careful to consider family values where some protected young children might not be ready for explicit information" (Kakuchi, 2004).

Despite what appears to be societal and governmental naïveté on the topic of trafficking, Japan did adopt a national action plan of measures to combat trafficking in persons in 2004. Many skeptics hold that this was simply a political move to appease foreign nations as opposed to an acknowledgment that trafficking is indeed a problem within Japan. According to Farrer, the U.S. State Department *Trafficking in Persons Report* had a big effect on the Japanese Ministry of Justice. "There were open discussions on the topic of trafficking around that time, but they soon subsided. The societal perception is that trafficking probably exists on a small scale but that it is not a big part of the sex industry or that of labor."[3]

JAPAN AS A DESTINATION

Human trafficking accelerated in Japan in the 1980s as a result of rapid economic growth and increased labor demands in bars and restaurants. Persons from Thailand and the Philippines entered the country, often through channels associated with crime syndicates (ILO, 2005). Between 2001 and 2007, MOFA reported 498 identified sex-trafficking victims. The primary countries of origin were Thailand (35.3 percent), the Philippines (23.9 percent), Indonesia (15.3 percent), Colombia (11.6 percent), and Taiwan (8.2 percent) (MOFA, 2008b). Victims are also trafficked to Japan for commercial sexual exploitation from Russia and other nations in eastern Europe, as well as from East Asia and Southeast Asia. Persons are trafficked to Japan from China, Indonesia, and Vietnam for forced labor (U.S. Department of State, 2009). Most foreign persons in the Japanese sex industry are Asian nationals, but a surprising number of victims are from Latin America and the Caribbean. Latin Americans are the largest non-Asian ethnic group in Japan. Roughly 1,700 women are trafficked each year from Latin America and the Caribbean to Japan, primarily for commercial sexual exploitation. The primary countries of origin are Bolivia, Brazil, Colombia, Mexico, and Peru. Other nations of origin are Argentina, Chile, the Dominican Republic, Ecuador, and Paraguay (OAS, 2005).

In the past, foreign nationals were often brought into Japan under the entertainer visa. The law was made more stringent in 2005 and 2006, creating stricter obligations for employers—such as a salary of no less than $2,226.59 per month and increasing disqualification standards for operators, managers, and other regular employees of the inviting organization (MOFA, 2008b). Masatoshi Shimbo, deputy director-general of MOFA's Foreign Policy Bureau, said the measures drastically reduced the number of persons entering the country with the entertainer visa (MOFA, 2008a). And indeed the number of these visas decreased from 134,879 in 2004, to 99,342 in 2005, to 40,000 in 2006 (Hongo, 2006; SMC, 2009). But the visa is still utilized by traffickers. In 2009 it was discovered that a former government official had accepted a $54,000 bribe to facilitate entertainer visas for 280 women from the Philippines. The visas were granted by MOFA. The women were to perform in charity concerts but upon arrival in Japan worked as bar hostesses. No investigation occurred to determine whether trafficking took place in relation to this case. The government cited lack of evidence (U.S. Department of State, 2009). The entertainer visa is certainly not the only visa to have been used in the trafficking of persons. People are also trafficked into Japan under the spouse or child of Japanese national visa category (OAS, 2005). Visas are not always necessary. Many countries such as Argentina, Chile, the Dominican Republic, Korea, and Taiwan have visa exemption arrangements with Japan that allow nationals to stay in Japan for a limited period ranging from 14 days or less to 6 months or less (MOFA, 2012). The largest officially identified group of trafficking victims is female foreign nationals who willingly migrate to Japan but face debt bondage upon arrival. With debts of up to $50,000, the women are forced into labor or commercial sexual exploitation in order to pay back their debts (U.S. Department of State, 2009).

Many experts state that the *yakuza* (organized crime) networks play a significant role in the smuggling and subsequent debt bondage of women—particularly women from China, Thailand, and Colombia— for forced prostitution in Japan (PBS, 2009). Determining the exact extent of yakuza involvement is difficult because of the covert nature of the sex industry. Consequently, the yakuza are able to minimize people's direct knowledge of their involvement. Michiko Yokoyama stated that she had heard many stories involving the yakuza but that it is difficult to know which stories are accurate. "Polaris Project Japan is working with particular focus on victim assistance," Yokoyama said. "We hear many random stories including yakuza, but since our focus is not on researching yakuza networks but on direct assistance to the potential victims of human trafficking, we do not ask further questions. So we do not have much information and are also sensitive about releasing any information that might be without any ground."[4]

Jake Adelstein, a former journalist for the *Yomiuri Shimbun* and author of *Tokyo Vice*, was exposed firsthand to the yakuza networks. In an interview for Reuters, Adelstein, who is a Polaris Project Japan board member, revealed that a friend—who was a prostitute—disappeared when she attempted to help him discover more about what he suspected to be a yakuza human trafficking ring:

> There are times when the street justice the yakuza deal out seems like poetic justice, and there are a few yakuza whom I consider honorable men, in their own way. At the same time, certain factions of the yakuza engage in human trafficking, the production of child pornography, extortion, stock manipulation, pushing drugs, assault, loan sharking and occasionally murder. They can and often do create a lot of human misery, and these days I think they're out of control. (Reynolds, 2009)

The yakuza networks are extremely well organized and stay informed about all crime-related legislation. *The Guardian* reports that members of the Yamaguchi-gumi yakuza—numbering roughly 40,000—are required to study any new anticrime laws in order to identify legal loopholes and avert crackdowns on their activities (McCurry, 2009; Adelstein, 2009). One briefing distributed within a yakuza group reads: "It is now illegal to give financial rewards or promote someone who was involved in a hit against a member of a rival gang. But it is not illegal to give them a salary with a front company and promote them within that organization" (McCurry, 2009, p. 26). Yakuza networks work with organized crime groups from other nations, such as China, Russia, and Colombia. One example involves a Colombian woman living in Tokyo who acted as a broker between Japanese and foreign organized crime networks and a theater for nude dancing in Okinawa. The woman enticed Colombian women and girls with false promises of work as waitresses. Upon arrival in Japan the women were forced to work as nude dancers (Vital Voices, 2004; PBS, 2009).

Prior to adoption of the national action plan, immigration law was typically used to arrest traffickers. In June 2004 Okinawa police arrested the Colombian broker for offenses against the Immigration Control and Refugee Recognition Law on the grounds that the trafficked women were working without work visas (Vital Voices, 2004; PBS, 2009). Immigration law was also utilized to secure the 2002 arrest and prosecution of trafficker Koichi "Sony" Hagiwara. The former head of Japan's largest known human trafficking ring was arrested for brokering two Colombian women into the sex industry. He was sentenced to 22 months' imprisonment and a fine of $3,321.71 (Vital Voices, 2004; PBS, 2009).

Commercial sexual exploitation is the only acknowledged form of trafficking under Japanese law. Forced labor is largely ignored and over-looked. After an official visit to Japan in 2009, Joy Ngozi Ezeilo, the United Nations special rapporteur on trafficking in persons, noted in her preliminary report: "Although trafficking for prostitution and other forms of sexual exploitation constitute the vast majority of the recorded cases in Japan, trafficking for labor exploitation is also of great concern" (OHCHR, 2009b). Forced labor is prohibited but essentially unenforced. Under Article 5 of the Labor Standards Act, "An employer shall not force workers to work against their will by means of physical violence, intimidation, confinement, or any other unfair restraint on the mental or physical freedom of the workers." Offenders face 1 to 10 years' im-prisonment or a fine of between $2,615.32 and $39,233.95 (Labor Stan-dards Act, 2005).

Forced-labor victims seem to be made up primarily of foreign mi-grants, but it would not be a surprise if some of the marginalized Nikkei population—Japanese emigrants and their descendants—were also af-fected. Most of the Nikkei who have returned to Japan are from Brazil, Peru, and Bolivia. In 1990 the Immigration Control and Refugee Recog-nition Act was revised to allow Nikkei back into Japan under the visa status of long-term resident for up to three years, which can be renewed. The work available to them is typically short-term and low-wage labor (MOFA, 2000; Sour strawberries, 2008). Taro Kono, a member of the Japa-nese House of Representatives and at the time a senior vice-minister for justice, said the policy was changed in order to obtain cheap labor. "I was in charge of this immigration," Kono told National Public Radio in a 2009 interview "I apologize to those Brazilians or Peruvians who came to Japan with high hope[s]. Our policy was very wrong. We just wanted the cheap labor, but we don't want to open our market to . . . foreign coun-tries" (Kuhn, 2009).

In the current global economic crisis, Japan's unemployment has been on the rise. In order to reduce these numbers, the government of Japan has encouraged unemployed Nikkei to leave. They are given at least $3,000 plus $2,000 per dependent if they repatriate to the nation whence they originally emigrated (McCabe, Yi-Ying Lin, & Tanaka, 2009; Arudou, 2009). James Farrer said the general population disapproves of this move by the government.

> Japan has a complex view of migrant workers. Currently, there is public support for a more progressive policy that is welcoming to foreigners. The Nikkei were presumably allowed into Japan because they were persons of Japanese origin whose ancestors had been sent away as part of a sponsored emigrant program. Japan needed immigrants, so the Nikkei were, in a sense, invited back to Japan. Now that it has been seen that many Nikkei Latin Americans have not assimilated and are not making much of an effort to be Japanese, the government [has] created a program to send unemployed migrants back. It seems that in general many Japanese see this as an insult and not a good move politically.[5]

Under Japanese law, foreign unskilled laborers are prohibited from employment. Yet there is a demand for such workers. Although the Nikkei were allowed back into Japan to help satisfy this need, certain government programs also created loopholes for employers to obtain low-cost migrant workers. Employers are able to hire foreign unskilled laborers through the government-run Industrial Training Program and Technical Internship Program, revised in 2010 as the Technical Intern Training Program. The programs have resulted in a number of abuses. A 2007 survey by the Justice Ministry cited 449 companies and organizations that were abusing foreign employees hired through job training programs by failing to pay adequate wages (Nambu Foreign Workers Caucus, 2008). In what is designed as an overall three-year program, enrollees are supposed to spend the first year as trainees and the remaining two years as technical interns. Much like the H-2B program in the United States, the worker's dependence on legal employment is tied to one employer, creating the opportunity for unfair treatment and abuse. "Tying workers to one employer for the duration of the three years makes them vulnerable to exploitation, since they might be discharged and forced to leave Japan if they complain about working conditions, and they cannot seek an employer with better conditions," Michiko Yokoyama said. In July 2009 Polaris Project Japan visited four dormitories in the Fukui Prefecture, where Chinese workers in the trainee and technical intern programs were housed. The workers faced inordinate fees as well as inhumane conditions. Yokoyama said that according to government statistics, more than half of the people who come to Japan through the trainee program are from China:

> The two women we met [were part of] the trainee program and paid expensive fees to brokers in China to get to Japan. They paid deposits that would only be returned if they finished the three-year contract. Once in Japan, both faced harsh work conditions that included extremely long hours, low pay, and excessive overtime. In one case the compensation for overtime was only 300 yen [approximately $3] per hour. One of the women had suffered from a beating at the hands of the president of the company. They [the women] fled their companies and were living in a shelter.[6]

According to Ippei Torii, leader of the Zentoitsu Workers Union, the program is not really a training program but simply a means to bring in cheap labor. "Japan doesn't want to damage the façade of being an ethnically homogeneous nation," said Torii in the documentary *Sour Strawberries*. "They [Japan] said they don't accept unskilled workers. So training is used as a pretense to get migrant workers into the country" (Sour strawberries, 2008). One man stated that after applying to participate in the job training system in 2005, when he arrived in Japan from China there was no actual job training. Instead, he was forced to perform agricultural duties:

> I was forced to do a farming job from 5 in the morning through 10 at night every day, without any paid days off. My pay was a little more than 100,000 yen [roughly $1,111.27] a month and my employer banned me from using a cell phone and confiscated my passport. I can't afford to return home, as doing so before I finish the three-year period under the training system would mean that I'd forfeit the deposit, or guarantee money that I managed to raise from my relatives. (Nambu Foreign Workers Caucus, 2008)

Three men from China faced similar circumstances. Their documents and signing stamps were confiscated when they came to Japan as part of the training program but instead were forced to work 365 days a year on a strawberry field in Tochigi Prefecture. Additionally, the men were not paid their wages. Four months before the end of their contracts, they were taken to the airport by force by a private security agency (Sour strawberries, 2008). Torii said the conditions foreign workers face have been worsening with each passing year. Various forms of exploitation such as sexual harassment and skimmed wages are commonplace. "These folks are sometimes called $3-an-hour workers," Torii told National Public Radio. "They are not treated like human beings. They are trafficked like slaves" (Kuhn, 2009). Thus, although the Japanese government acknowledges only trafficking for commercial sexual exploitation, it is the trainee and intern programs that have sparked debate in the Japanese media. According to Farrer:

> Migration is a broad issue, and there are concerns in Japan as to whether the trainee programs are good or bad. Are they [migrant workers] undercutting the Japanese labor market or are they helping small companies? They are overworked, and while they are not well paid, they are paid. The Japanese government doesn't want to open the floodgates to unskilled migrants because they feel they will bring social problems with them. At the same time, the government has pressures to not stop the program and pressures to improve the conditions that trainees face.[7]

The trafficking of children, persons under the age of 18, is a concern in relation to both prostitution and pornography. Under the Law for Punishing Acts Related to Child Prostitution and Child Pornography, and for Protecting Children, production and distribution of child pornography is illegal, but possession is not (Johnston, 2009). According to the National Police Agency (NPA), 1,361 persons were arrested in violation of the law in 2007. Of those, 984 were arrested for child prostitution offenses, which include online dating services and telephone clubs; and 377 were arrested for child pornography offenses—including cases that involved the use of the Internet. The official number of children victimized in 2007 was 1,419—of whom 1,144 were exploited for child prostitution and 275 for child pornography. These numbers reflect an 8.7 percent increase in identified cases of child pornography and a 13.7 percent decrease in identified cases of child prostitution from 2006 (NPA, 2009). Children are trafficked not only for commercial sexual exploitation but also for forced labor. For instance, in 2008 it was discovered that a number of children were trafficked from Paraguay to Japan for forced labor (U.S. Department of State, 2009).[8]

TRAFFICKING WITHIN JAPAN, CHILD SEX TOURISM, AND JAPAN AS A TRANSIT NATION

While trafficking of its own citizens does occur within Japan, only one domestic victim was officially identified between 2001 and 2007 (MOFA, 2008b). In 2008 police raided a sex industry establishment and identified 12 Thai trafficking victims. Three other women were also discovered, but because they were not illegal immigrants they were not taken into custody (U.S. Department of State, 2009). Consequently, it is unknown whether they too were victims of trafficking. The issue here is not that the three women were not taken into custody but rather that the police failed to identify potential trafficking victims at the time of the raid. According to Michiko Yokoyama, 44 percent of phone calls and emails received by Polaris Project Japan are in Japanese. Not all of these calls involve Japanese victims, but many do:

> Debt bondage was typical in the past, but we think the ways victims are controlled by brokers or "boyfriends (pimps)" are getting more sophisticated. In recent years, there have been an increased number of calls and emails from Japanese teenagers in trouble in domestic violence, prostitution, sexually transmitted diseases, or sexual exploitation. In fact 1 in 10 calls/emails are from Japanese teenagers, so we created a new website that focuses on Japanese teenagers, http://www.pol214.com/. It is available on both PCs and mobile phones.[9]

Japan is also a transit nation for persons trafficked to North America from East Asia for commercial sexual exploitation and forced labor

(U.S. Department of State, 2009). Additionally, a significant number of Japanese are sex tourists, traveling to other nations in Southeast Asia—such as the Philippines, Cambodia, and Thailand—to have sex with underage persons. Under the Act on Punishment of Activities Relating to Child Prostitution and Child Pornography, the law allows for extra-territorial jurisdiction over Japanese nationals who have exploited children in another country. There has been one prosecution by the government of a Japanese national for child sex tourism since 2005 (U.S. Department of State, 2008, 2009, 2012). In order to address child pornography, a government team, which had its first meeting on February 4, 2010, works to promote comprehensive anti–child pornography measures (Convention on the Rights of the Child, 2010).

WHAT HAPPENS TO VICTIMS AFTER TRAFFICKING

Although there was a sudden increase in identified victims immediately following the adoption of the 2004 action plan, since 2005 there has been a steady drop in the number (see Table 2.1). There are several possible explanations for this continual decrease. One is that the detection and enforcement that took place immediately after the adoption of the action plan created an intimidating atmosphere for traffickers and thereby a reduction in actual trafficking. Another possibility—one that is more realistic—is that there was a boost of awareness and focus on the topic of trafficking after the adoption of the action plan but that it soon dissipated.

In 2007, 16 of the 43 identified trafficking victims were repatriated to their countries of origin without being referred to the International Organization for Migration (IOM) for risk assessment and formal repatriation processing. Since 2005 this intergovernmental organization has had an established arrangement with the Japanese government to assist victims in repatriation and social integration in their country of origin (U.S. Department of State, 2008, 2009). From 2005 through 2007 the Japanese government gave $844,000 in funding to the IOM for this purpose (MOFA, 2008b). As of March 1, 2010, 176 victims had received repatriation assistance through this program, including 17 children under the age of 18 (Convention on the Rights of the Child, 2010). In

TABLE 2.1
Number of Identified Trafficking Victims in Japan, 2001–2010

Year	Number of identified victims
2001	65
2002	55
2003	83
2004	77
2005	117
2006	58
2007	43
2008	36
2009	17
2010	43
2011	45

Sources: MOFA (2008b); U.S. Department of State (2010, 2011, 2012).

2009 the government decreased its funding to the IOM from $300,000 to less than $190,000. As a result some victims have been unable to return home or to obtain reintegration assistance (U.S. Department of State, 2010).

The government provides temporary shelter for victims of trafficking and domestic violence through the Women's Consulting Office. The office has 47 locations nationwide and enough space for up to 773 temporary residents. Victims at the shelter have access to food, clothing, temporary lodging, as well as medical and psychological treatment. From 2001 through 2006, the office aided 186 trafficking victims (MOFA, 2008b; DAW/DESA, 2009). A number of private shelters and facilities, subsidized by the Ministry of Health, Labour, and Welfare, also grant lodging to female victims. For instance, 54 female trafficking victims were provided shelter in fiscal year 2005. The ministry also budgets medical costs, travel expenses to Tokyo, and interpreter expenses (MOFA, 2008b). Both the Women's Consulting Office and those shelters subsidized by the Ministry of Health, Labour, and Welfare are available solely to female victims; thus not all forms of trafficking and their victims are adequately acknowledged. Japan's 2009 Action Plan to Combat Trafficking in Persons states the government's intention to raise awareness among the general public on the topic of human trafficking. It emphasizes that victims of trafficking in persons include but are not limited to non-Japanese women and children, and that the crime should be tackled by society as a whole (Inter-Ministerial Liaison Committee, 2009). The plan also integrates concerns and suggestions expressed by Joy Ngozi Ezeilo, the UN special rapporteur on trafficking in persons. These include:

> 5. Appropriate shelters for victims of trafficking, and lack of the resources and specialized know-how, including but not limited to language skills, required to provide adequate assistance to victims and avoid their being re-trafficked at a later stage
>
> 9. Human trafficking responses by the State and assistance to victims are gendered and [focus] solely on women and on sexual exploitation; while this is important, other forms of trafficking that affect both men and women, boys and girls must not [be] neglected (Inter-Ministerial Liaison Committee, 2009, p. 3; OHCHR, 2009a).

Nothing in the 2009 Action Plan specifies how men will be helped in terms of shelter or services. The "Protection of Victims of Trafficking in Persons" section of the 2009 Action Plan states that it will provide shelter and support (Inter-Ministerial Liaison Committee, 2009), but the section focuses on services to be provided by the Women's Consulting Offices (presumably for women) and the Child Guidance Centers (for children). There is no mention of men. In 2010, one male victim of sex trafficking received services at an NGO shelter and no males were identified as victims of forced labor or forced prostitution by the government of Japan in 2011 (U.S. Department of State, 2011, 2012).

Under the Immigration Control and Refugee Recognition Act, a special permission for temporary residence can be granted to trafficking victims. This is determined on a case-by-case basis. With special permission from the Ministry of Justice, victims are exempt from forced deportation (MOFA, 2008b). According to Michiko Yokoyama, the special permission from the Ministry of Justice allows victims of human trafficking to stay in Japan only temporarily: "The true purpose of the special permission for residence is to prevent the expulsion of those who overstayed their visas as a result of trafficking. This allows the victim to stay in Japan without arrest while the investigation or some other procedure continues. If the victim wishes to stay in Japan for a longer period, she or he has to obtain another visa."[10] The Immigration Bureau granted special permission for residence to a total of 74 victims in 2005 and 2006; the number decreased from 47 to 27, respectively (MOFA, 2008b). Despite the existence of the special permission for residence, there is only one case of a victim's staying in Japan for more than several months (U.S. Department of State, 2012).

There are no formal procedures in place to aid with victim identification among law enforcement. With a lack of government focus on the topic as well as insufficient training, law enforcement is not adequately proactive in identifying human trafficking cases. Not only may trafficking victims be overlooked, but also they may be punished for acts they committed as a direct result of their trafficking experience. One example involves a Thai victim trafficked to Japan under a promise of working in the restaurant industry. Upon arrival in Tokyo she was sold to a Tokyo brothel and told that she had to pay a debt of $39,215.68. After police raided the brothel in 2009, the victim was forced to serve four months in jail and receive three months of counseling before she was sent back to Thailand (Bangkok Post, 2009).

WHAT HAPPENS TO TRAFFICKERS

In 2005 two articles were added to the Penal Code that criminalize the buying or selling of human beings (Article 226-2) and the transportation of kidnapped persons out of a country (Article 226-3) (DAW/DESA, 2005). Offenders under Article 226-2 face three months' to five years' imprisonment. A person who buys or sells another person for the purpose of transporting him or her from one nation to another faces a sentence of no less than two years' imprisonment with work. The sentence is increased to a maximum of seven years' imprisonment when the offense involves a minor. It is further increased if the person buys or sells another for the purpose of profit, indecency, marriage, or threat to the life or body, with a minimum sentence of one year and a maximum of ten years' imprisonment (DAW/DESA, 2005; Government of Japan, 2006). Offenders under Article 226-3, those who transport a person via kidnapping by force or enticement or a person who has been bought or sold, from one country to another face a sentence of imprisonment and work for no less than two years (DAW/DESA, 2005; Government of Japan, 2006).

According to MOFA, 369 persons were arrested for trafficking offenses from 2001 through 2007. A closer look reveals a yo-yo of arrest numbers—40 in 2001, 28 in 2002, 41 in 2003, 58 in 2004, 83 in 2005, 78 in 2006, and 41 in 2007 (MOFA, 2008b). In 2008 there were 29 prosecutions and 13 convictions reported. In 2009 the government reported prosecuting and convicting 5 persons under Penal Code Article 226-2. The government did not report sentencing data for the offenders. Corruption among authorities continues to be an issue. In December 2009 a senior immigration official was convicted of accepting bribes in exchange for helping to obtain residence permits for female bar workers. The official was sentenced to two years' imprisonment with labor. Despite the stringent prescribed sentences for traffickers, to date the severest punishment has been 5.5 years' imprisonment. Even this sentence is a rarity; traffickers often go unprosecuted, and those found guilty are often given suspended sentences. Eleven of the 13 persons convicted in 2008 received suspended sentences and did not face imprisonment. Six of 14 persons convicted in 2010 received suspended sentences and did not face imprisonment, while another 6 received sentences ranging from 2.5 to 4.5 years' imprisonment, and one trafficker was simply ordered to pay a fine. Eighteen out of 20 persons convicted of human trafficking in 2011 faced imprisonment; sentences ranged from 1.5 to 4 years' imprisonment. There were no forced-labor convictions in 2011 (MOFA, 2008b; U.S. Department of State, 2009, 2011, 2012).

INTERNAL EFFORTS TO DECREASE TRAFFICKING

The issue of trafficking for forced labor has not been sufficiently addressed by the government. Experts hoped that would change with the 2009 Action Plan to Combat Trafficking in Persons. Yokoyama believes the main reason forced labor has been inadequately addressed is a lack of awareness among both the public and government. The 2009 visit from U.N. special rapporteur Ezeilo put international pressure on the government of Japan to address the issue of forced labor. In response, the government included portions of Ezeilo's recommendations and concerns in its 2009 Action Plan. Among them are Ezeilo's commentary on the trainee and technical intern programs: "While this is a well-intended program to be encouraged for its objective of transferring skills and technology to some Asian countries, in a number of cases it is fuelling demand for exploitative cheap labor under conditions that may well amount to trafficking" (Inter-Ministerial Liaison Committee, 2009, p. 3; OHCHR, 2009a). Despite including Ezeilo's recommendations and concerns, the action plan also has some worrisome elements, such as increased regulation of illegal employment and illegal stay. Yokoyama stated that NGOs have raised a concern that the government is more focused on regulating victims as criminals and not placing enough regulation on brokers. "This reflects the fact that both the government and public tend to think [of] the victims as foreigners or Japanese who have committed crimes rather than victims who need protection."[11]

In her preliminary report, Ezeilo stated that Japan needs to increase internal efforts to combat human trafficking at both the local and national levels. Specifically, Ezeilo recommended that Japan increase training and coordination of law enforcement, lessen cases of victim misidentification by creating a more comprehensible identification procedure, sign on to bilateral agreements with nations of origin for those victims trafficked to Japan, and ratify applicable international treaties (UN News Center, 2009). Ezeilo also suggested that Japan improve labor inspections, create a national rapporteur office on human trafficking, increase services provided to victims to ensure that they receive adequate shelter and resources, and make certain that victims have access to judicial remedies and compensation. Lastly, she recommended that Japan improve the relationship between governmental agencies and NGOs (OHCHR, 2009b). In response to Ezeilo's suggestions, the Japanese government established a temporary working group, including NGOs, to develop the 2009 Action Plan to combat trafficking. Unfortunately, that is where the government-NGO collaboration ended. The 2009 Action Plan does not include NGO partnerships.

A significant step taken by the Japanese government is the revision of the Immigration Control and Refugee Recognition Act (Immigration Control Act) to prohibit organizations from collecting deposits from trainees and/or their families or managing the money and/or assets of trainees. The July 2010 revisions also establish a new status of residence for the Technical Intern Training Program. Trainees are now able to receive protection under labor-related laws and regulations, such as the Labor Standards Law and the Minimum Wages Law (JITCO, 2010). The government (through the National Police Agency) has expanded its international anti-trafficking relationships and cooperates with Thailand, Indonesia, the Philippines, Taiwan, and Colombia in the investigation and prosecution of trafficking cases. It also exchanges information with other nations through Interpol in order to identify those suspected of trafficking as well as Japanese nationals staying abroad who have arrest warrants against them for trafficking offenses (MOFA, 2008b; NPA, 2009).

The government of Japan has taken some positive measures on paper to combat human trafficking, but there are numerous gaps and issues with implementation that must be addressed. Law enforcement takes a passive approach in the identification of trafficking victims. After a raid, victims of commercial sexual exploitation are often identified after they have been arrested for immigration violations. Consequently, internal victims of commercial sexual exploitation are less apt to be identified. It would behoove the Japanese government to create formal victim identification procedures that focus on signs of exploitation not just immigration status, increase the anti-trafficking training of law-enforcement personnel, and continue to increase protections of marginalized and vulnerable groups. The government of Japan must also address the lack of prosecutions against traffickers and the prevalence of suspended sentences. In calculating the previously discussed conviction numbers, in 2008 and 2010, roughly 85 percent and 43 percent, respectively, of convicted traffickers received a suspended sentence.

The 2009 Action Plan states that "the definition of trafficking in persons includes not only the buying and selling of persons but also a wide range of activities such as the recruitment or transportation of persons for the purpose of, for example, sexual exploitation, forced labor or services, or the removal of organs" (Inter-Ministerial Liaison Committee, 2009, p. 2). The plan also touches on concerns mentioned by Ezeilo, such as abuses under the Industrial Training Program and Technical Internship Program, and the government's tendency to focus its anti-trafficking efforts on women and sexual exploitation while largely ignoring other forms of trafficking that affect men, women, boys, and girls. Although mention of the latter in the plan is a positive step, there is no specific discussion of how it will deal with these issues. The plan states only that male victims may be identified in the cases of trafficking in persons for the purpose of labor exploitation of non-Japanese workers and that the government will consider establishing protection policies for male victims (Inter-Ministerial Liaison Committee, 2009). Thus far this has not occurred. Revisions such as those to the Immigration Control Act are certainly an excellent first step, though whether these changes will be properly enforced remains to be seen.

CHAPTER 3

United Arab Emirates

The company has all our passports. We can't afford to leave.
I went to a manager here and complained, and she said
if you don't like it here, you can go home.

—DEBT BONDAGE VICTIM IN DUBAI

With a booming economy, the United Arab Emirates (UAE)—made up of seven emirates: Abu Dhabi, Dubai, Sharjah, Ajman, Umm Al-Quwain, Ras al-Khaimah, and Fujairah—has become an attractive destination for foreigners, who constitute over 80 percent of the UAE population. UAE nationals make up 18 percent of the population, Asians 65 percent, Arab expatriates 13 percent, and Europeans 4 percent (Caplin, 2009). Migrants account for more than 90 percent of the UAE's private-sector workforce (U.S. Department of State, 2010). According to Dr. Anwar Mohammed Al Gargash, the minister of state for foreign affairs and chair of the National Committee to Combat Human Trafficking, the UAE has shown its commitment to combat human trafficking not only by endorsing international human rights agreements that focus on the rights of women and children but also by taking "a number of political and legislative measures" (UAE Interact, 2008). Regardless, the prevalent issue of labor trafficking remains mostly overlooked and unenforced. While all forms of trafficking are prohibited under Federal Law No. 51, the labor laws do not adequately safeguard domestic-service workers from forced labor. Additionally, without formal procedures for identifying potential victims among vulnerable populations, sex-trafficking and forced-labor victims continue to be arrested and punished for crimes associated with their trafficking experience such as prostitution or immigration violations (UAE Interact, 2008; U.S. Department of State, 2008, 2010).

THE UAE AS A DESTINATION

As many as 1.2 million persons from India live in the UAE. At least half of this population is made up of migrant workers. Along with Indian nationals, thousands of persons are recruited from Afghanistan, Bangladesh, China, Eritrea, Ethiopia, Indonesia, Iran, Korea, Nepal, Pakistan, the Philippines, Sri Lanka, and Thailand for domestic labor or to participate in the construction industry in the UAE (U.S. Department of State, 2008, 2010). Common abuses that these workers face are unpaid wages, debt bondage from recruitment fees, confiscation of passports, hazardous working conditions, and physical abuse (HRW, 2009). In the laborers' home countries, recruiters offer good wages and low-cost living in the UAE. In order to pay the large fees of up to $4,100 the workers often borrow money from family members, sell personal property, and take out loans from moneylenders, who often charge high interest rates. One labor camp supervisor in Abu Dhabi reveals a crooked system of brokers and agents that swindle large sums of money from Thai workers: "The Thais here mostly paid agents 50,000 baht [roughly $1,450] to get to the UAE, but before that they often had to pay a broker to get to the agent. The main agencies are in Bangkok, but the secondary ones are in the provinces. You might have to pay much more. You might have to pay up to 15 percent interest a month if you've got no collateral to get a loan to pay the fee" (HRW, 2009).

Upon arrival, the workers are commonly in debt and quickly realize that wages are often 50 percent less than what they were promised. A Bangladeshi surveyor's assistant working on Saadiyat Island said he paid an agency $2,900 in exchange for what he thought would be a good job in the UAE: "I sold land to pay for part of the agent's fee, and had to take out a loan for the rest. The agency said I'd get a basic salary of 700 dirhams [roughly $190] per month, but when I got here my salary was only 350 dirhams [roughly $95]. When I first came here I was going to save money for a house, get married, have a child, but now, this isn't really possible" (HRW, 2009).

One worker from Kerala, India, earns $260 a month on Saadiyat Island as a security guard—only 63.4 percent of what he was promised—and is fined if his wardrobe is not up to par: "The agency told me I'd get 1,500 dirhams [roughly $410] a month and Fridays off, but I don't get any days off. And I get fined if my necktie isn't tied right, or my socks are the wrong color—that's 100 dirhams. I've been here for a year. When I got here, a bag of rice cost three dirhams, now it's six. I could have earned more money if I'd stayed back home as a Maruti car salesman" (HRW, 2009).

Other workers simply do not receive pay. One worker from Bangladesh was assigned to build temporary housing on Saadiyat Island but has yet to receive payment: "I paid 250,000 taka [roughly $4,100] to the agency; I sold my land for 60,000 taka [roughly $1,000] and borrowed the rest. When we got to UAE, we signed four papers but they didn't give any to us. First we waited for 14 days, but there was no work. We went for training for steel fixing for 10 days. We've been on the island for two months since then, and we still haven't been paid" (HRW, 2009).

As with temporary work visa programs in the United States, foreign construction workers in the UAE depend on the sponsorship of a single company. Those workers who attempt to seek a better job elsewhere are subject to deportation and are banned from returning to the UAE for one year, except in cases in which the sponsor-employer failed to pay them for more than two months. The employer can trigger the deportation of a worker by simply requesting that the UAE ministries of labor and interior cancel the employee's work permit and residence visa, rendering the employee illegal. Thus unscrupulous recruiters and employers can exploit workers with minimal consequences. Workers have few avenues of protection. While the UAE law prohibits employers from working with agencies that charge worker recruitment fees, UAE officials state that they will not intervene in cases of contract fraud committed by labor agencies outside the country (HRW, 2009).

It is common practice for employers in the UAE to confiscate worker passports. Although UAE law prohibits the confiscation of passports, it also provides an incentive for doing so: companies face heavy fines if they fail to request the government to cancel absconding workers' visas. The accepted practice has been for employers to request the cancellation by turning in the workers' passports to the Ministry of Interior. To prevent workers from leaving, companies inform them that they must pay a fine before their passports will be returned to them. This is what happened to a Nepali worker on Saadiyat Island:

We'd like to leave now, but the company said it would cost us a 2,000 dirham fine [roughly $540]. If we had left the UAE within two months, the company says we could've avoided the fine, because we were still on a temporary permit, but now we have to pay the fine because they say they've done all the work to get the real work permit. The company has all our passports. We can't afford to leave. I went to a manager here and complained, and she said if you don't like it here, you can go home. (HRW, 2009)

On November 7, 2006, Mohammed bin Rashid Al Maktoum, the UAE prime minister, issued a decree ordering the labor minister to implement immediate reforms that addressed housing, transportation, a recruitment process for new labor inspectors, fast-track dispute resolution in federal labor courts, and immediate release from their employer sponsorships for workers who have been cheated on wages or not been paid for more than two months, if they so choose. The prime minister decreed that employers should be required to provide health insurance for low-skill workers. The reforms mandated that workers scheduled for return to their countries of origin be satisfactorily housed and fed while awaiting their departure. In 2007, following the 2006 decree that housing for workers be brought in line with international standards and conventions, the UAE minister of labor stated that the government had closed 100 Dubai compounds and labor camps where workers resided. The compounds housed hundreds to thousands of workers in shared rooms (HRW, 2009). Although these are positive steps, the 2006 decree appears to be mostly unenforced. Public health authorities in Dubai stated that 40 percent of the UAE's 1,033 labor camps violated minimum health and fire safety standards. In 2008 a chickenpox outbreak in a labor camp was linked to unhygienic conditions, and 11 construction workers died in August 2008 when a 30-room residence housing 500 workers caught fire. Some of the workers had to jump out of windows because exits were blocked. In March 2009 the Ministry of Labor's chief inspector said that in order to cut costs companies had cut workers' meals from three to one a day and added as much as 40 percent to their labor camp population without adding space for accommodations (HRW, 2009).

Domestic workers (housekeepers, caretakers) are particularly marginalized because they are not recognized as members of the labor force and are thereby excluded from protection under UAE labor laws. Like many other forced-labor victims, they voluntarily accept jobs in the UAE and face the withholding of their passports, nonpayment of wages, and excessive work hours. In addition, domestic workers commonly face isolation, with minimal to no access to the outside world, which makes it difficult for them to escape and also makes them more vulnerable to physical and sexual abuse. Like foreign construction workers in the UAE, domestic workers are dependent upon their sponsoring employer, but it is their exclusion from protection that augments the sponsor-employer's power and control (Caplin, 2009; HRW, 2010b). In addition to the abuses, domestic victims face poor nutrition. Eleven of 26 Filipina domestic workers interviewed by Human Rights Watch in the July 2006 report *Swept Under the Rug: Abuses Against Domestic Workers Around the World* stated that they were deprived of adequate nutrition. "I don't want to die from starvation and too much work," Rosa Alvarez told HRW. "Breakfast was water and bread, there was no lunch. They would say I can only eat bread. I lost five kilograms [11 pounds] in three months" (Sunderland, 2006).

Trafficking for commercial sexual exploitation is also an issue in the UAE. Women and children from Afghanistan, Armenia, Azerbaijan, Belarus, China, Eritrea, Ethiopia, India, Iran, Iraq, Kazakhstan, Kyrgyzstan, Moldova, Morocco, Pakistan, the Philippines, Russia, Somalia, Tanzania, Uganda, Ukraine, and Uzbekistan are trafficked to the UAE for this purpose. Some women accept positions as hotel employees or secretaries but then are forced into domestic servitude or prostitution (U.S. Department of State, 2008, 2010; UNODC, 2009). It is challenging to determine the exact country breakdown and respective percentages of persons trafficked to the UAE for sexual exploitation, but in 2005 and 2006 the majority (57.1 percent) of identified sex-trafficking victims were from Uzbekistan. Other significant areas of origin were Moldova (17.9 percent) and South Asia (10.7 percent) (UNODC, 2009).[1] It is estimated that roughly 30 percent of the estimated 200 Tajik women in prostitution in the UAE are victims of trafficking. There are also media reports of Iraqi families who knowingly sold their teenage daughters to other Iraqi residents in the UAE for forced prostitution (U.S. Department of State, 2010). In the case of one Iraqi 15-year-old, her father sold her into domestic servitude but instead she was forced into the Dubai sex trade. Her father was given a $6,000 advance payment by a trafficking ring member and promised that his daughter would be returned after completing a one-year contract. "I was a virgin and didn't understand what sex was," the girl told Integrated Regional Information Networks (IRIN), the humanitarian news and analysis service of the UN Office for the Coordination of Humanitarian Affairs. "I was told that they [the traffickers] were going to get good money for my first night with an old local man who paid for my virginity. He was aggressive and hit me all the time" (IRIN, 2006). In order to deter her from running away, her traffickers threatened the young Iraqi girl daily. She managed to escape and return to Baghdad, where she was placed in the care of the Organization for Women's Freedom in Iraq, an NGO.

WHAT HAPPENS TO VICTIMS AFTER TRAFFICKING

The UAE government identified roughly 80 sex-trafficking victims in 2009. Government funds were used to repatriate 30 of the victims; the remaining 50 victims were offered comprehensive services in government-run shelters in Abu Dhabi and Dubai. In 2010 the Abu Dhabi shelter assisted 71 victims of sex trafficking, and the Dubai shelter assisted 49 victims of sex trafficking. The next year, 2011, the number of victims assisted by the two shelters decreased to 29 and 19, respectively. The government opened shelters for female and child victims of trafficking and abuse in Sharjah and Ras al-Khaimah in January 2011. The facilities provided comprehensive services—medical and psychological care, case management, immigration and legal support, educational and vocational training—to female and child victims of trafficking. No victims of forced labor were provided shelter, counseling, or immigration relief by the government (U.S. Department of State, 2010, 2011, 2012; NCCHT, 2010).

In 2011 the Ministry of Interior implemented new victim identification procedures whereby designated personnel at police stations implement operating procedures to identify victims of sex and labor trafficking. The government still has no formal procedures for proactively identifying potential victims among vulnerable populations. Consequently, unidentified victims are often arrested, punished, and deported for crimes associated with their trafficking experience such as prostitution and immigration violations. For instance, persons over the age of 18 are commonly not recognized as victims of forced labor, particularly if they entered the country voluntarily. As a result, if they run away from their sponsor they can face arrest and deportation for immigration violations. Also, women who knowingly found employment in prostitution but faced debt bondage after arrival are often treated as criminals not victims (Noueihed, 2008; U.S. Department of State, 2008, 2010; 2012).

WHAT HAPPENS TO TRAFFICKERS

Under Federal Law No. 51, those who are found guilty of trafficking face imprisonment ranging from one year to life. In 2007, 15 persons were prosecuted and convicted of sex trafficking. Sentences ranged from 9 months to 10 years' imprisonment. In 2009, prosecutions of 36 trafficking cases were initiated. Sentences ranged from one year to life imprisonment (U.S. Department of State, 2008, 2010). Dr. Gargash says the rising number of registered human trafficking cases in the UAE—37 cases in 2011, 58 in 2010, and 43 in 2009, compared to 20 cases in 2008—reflects the country's progress since Federal Law No. 51 was introduced (Sambidge, 2010; U.S. Department of State, 2011, 2012). Yet despite the prevalence of forced labor, investigations and prosecutions are focused primarily on sex trafficking. Only one recruitment agent was referred for prosecution in 2007, and there were no reports of convictions or punishments associated with forced labor (U.S. Department of State, 2008). In 2009 and 2010 there were no investigations, prosecutions, or convictions for forced-labor offenses. In its 2011–2012 report the UAE government reported the ongoing prosecution of one forced-labor case, and in January 2011 two women were charged with forced-labor offenses— they allegedly forced a woman to work in a massage parlor.

As in many other nations, some persons manage to behave with impunity. For instance, the royal family appears to have carte blanche when it comes to illicit conduct. In addition to an alleged instance of torture, it is suspected that 8 family members of the royal family of Abu Dhabi placed

17 people in forced servitude while in Brussels. Belgian authorities are investigating the case, but the UAE does not appear to have an investigation (HRW, 2010a; U.S. Department of State, 2010, 2011, 2012).[2]

The majority (53.8 percent) of convicted traffickers in the UAE in 2005 and 2006 were from South Asia. Other significant regions of origin were eastern Europe and Central Asia (23.1 percent). A significantly lower percentage (11.5 percent) were citizens of the UAE (UNODC, 2009).

INTERNAL EFFORTS TO DECREASE TRAFFICKING

In 2008 General Sheikh Mohammed bin Zayed Al Nahyan, deputy supreme commander of the UAE armed forces and crown prince of Abu Dhabi, donated $15 million to fund the United Nations Global Initiative to Fight Human Trafficking (UNODC, 2011). According to Gargash, the donation is in line with the UAE's commitment to set up a forum "which includes countries, UN agencies, governmental agencies, and [the] non-governmental sector to work together under one umbrella to create unprecedented cooperation in the international community" (UAE Interact, 2008). The UAE government has taken measures to improve anti-trafficking cooperation with source nations. For instance, on December 5, 2009, the governments of the UAE and Armenia signed a bilateral memorandum of understanding on combatting trafficking in persons (UNODC, 2009). This should help improve cooperation between the two nations' law-enforcement agencies on joint cases of trafficking. Within the UAE, the government has increased its training of police on how to identify human trafficking when investigating prostitution cases. Ideally, this step will help to decrease the number of sex-trafficking victims arrested and punished for crimes that occur as a result of their trafficking experience. In addition, in June 2010 the government announced its decision to establish two new shelters in Sharjah and Ras al-Khaimah (Gulf News, 2010), which opened in January 2011. The shelters, however, are solely for women and child victims of human trafficking and sexual exploitation (U.S. Department of State, 2010). Along these same lines, in October 2010 Judge Ahmed Ibrahim Saif announced that Dubai would establish a special court solely designed to hear sex-trafficking cases. The court would give priority to the victims by hearing their testimonies in the first session of the trial and would assist them in returning to their homeland. "The main reason for setting up the court is to protect the interests of the victims and to mitigate the damage inflicted upon them due to such crimes," Saif said. "All the cases referred to the court will concern sexual exploitation and not other forms of trafficking such as forced labor, which means the exploitation of others without pay, or slavery or practices similar to slavery, servitude or the removal of organs." The court was established in November 2010 (Emarat Al Youm, 2010; U.S. Department of State, 2011).

In order to help eliminate debt bondage, the Ministry of Labor announced in October 2007 that foreign workers must be paid via an electronic wage deposit system that can be kept under surveillance. The system has been sustained and continues to expand. It allows the migrant sponsorship program to be monitored by creating an electronic record of direct salary payments. All companies were required to use this system by May 2010. Those companies not in compliance face a prohibition on new hiring. In March 2010, roughly 800 companies that had not complied with the November 30, 2009, deadline were barred from hiring new workers. In order to further tackle labor violations and human trafficking, on November 7, 2006, Prime Minister Mohammed bin Rashid Al Maktoum issued a decree ordering that 2,000 more government labor inspectors be hired. The government hired more than 200 labor inspectors in 2007, bringing the total number of inspectors to around 425 (nowhere near the 2,000 ordered by decree). And in March 2010 the Ministry of Labor announced the formation of a new unit to identify and investigate potential labor-trafficking cases (U.S. Department of State, 2008, 2010; HRW, 2009). In January 2012 the UAE Cabinet of Ministers approved a draft law to protect the rights of domestic workers. The proposed law, according to *Gulf News*, will provide domestic workers with a paid day off per week, two weeks of paid annual leave, holidays, and 15 paid sick days. There are concerns over some aspects of the proposed law, such as that domestic workers who reveal the secrets of their employers are liable to prosecution and penalties (including imprisonment), and that harsh criminal sentences will be imposed on those who encourage a domestic worker to quit her job or offer her shelter. The Federal National Council must approve the legislation before President Shaikh Khalifa Bin Zayed Al Nahyan can sign it into law (HRW, 2012).

For many years children were trafficked into the UAE from Sudan, Bangladesh, Mauritania, and Pakistan to be camel jockeys. These young jockeys often sustained significant injuries from falling off the camels, which can run as fast as 18.64 miles per hour. In June 2005 the UAE imposed a minimum legal age of 18 for camel jockeys. Those found guilty of violating this law face imprisonment of up to three years and/or a fine of $13,670. In April 2007 the government of the UAE along with the governments of Bangladesh, Sudan, Pakistan, Mauritania, and the United Nations Children's Fund (UNICEF) signed a memorandum of understanding in order to compensate and assist those children formerly involved in camel racing in the UAE (IRIN, 2007). The initiative between UNICEF and the UAE resulted in the return of more than 1,000 child jockeys to their home countries, primarily Pakistan. The UAE also allocated an initial $9 million toward integrating and rehabilitating child camel jockeys in their countries of origin (IRIN, 2007). "The integration includes providing the basic services for these children: health services, education services, and protection services," Dr. Ayman Abu Laban, the UNICEF representative for the Gulf countries, told IRIN. "The idea is to give back to these children some of what they've missed from their childhood. At the same time, to give their families a better means of livelihood so they don't have to send children for further exploitation by child traffickers" (IRIN, 2007).

Today the UAE government continues to fund the UNICEF program to provide rehabilitation assistance to repatriated child jockeys (U.S. Department of State, 2010). Of course, the question remains whether the use of children as camel jockeys has actually stopped. *The Independent* reported in 2010 that the practice continues. Photos show the use of underage camel jockeys (some as young as 10 years old) at a February 2010 race in Abu Dhabi. "We are concerned that the fact the race was attended by the police and UAE dignitaries means that child protection is not being taken seriously," Catherine Turner, a child labor expert at Anti-Slavery International, told *The Independent* (Peachey, 2010).

Despite the prevalence of labor trafficking, the UAE's anti-trafficking efforts continue to focus primarily on commercial sexual exploitation. Although forced-labor victims are technically considered trafficking victims under Federal Law No. 51, in practice, identified victims are not provided with shelter, counseling, or immigration relief, nor are they encouraged to participate as witnesses against their employers. Furthermore, victims of forced labor who run away from their sponsors can face arrest and deportation for immigration violations.

PART II
Stateless Persons

"Statelessness" describes people who are not nationals of any country. Forced to exist outside the framework of society, those without citizenship or legal status are unable to access government benefits such as health care and education. If travel and movement within the nation are restricted, stateless persons are hindered from applying for jobs outside of where they live.

This is a significant issue in Thailand, where an estimated 50 percent of the one million hill tribe people lack citizenship, despite the fact that they were born in the nation. Without national identity, members of the hill tribes are marginalized; do not have equal opportunity to health care, property rights, or education; and often face discrimination. Without access to the formal labor market for employment, they are vulnerable to a litany of human rights abuses that include human trafficking, unsafe migration, exploitative labor, sexual exploitation, and an increased risk of HIV infection. The lack of protections not only increases their vulnerability to trafficking but also fails to adequately aid hill tribe victims afterward. For instance, if trafficked outside Thailand, hill tribe people without proof of citizenship may be denied reentry into Thailand.

Palestinians are similarly stateless and face poverty, inequity, discrimination, and violence—all factors that increase a person's vulnerability to human trafficking. In addition to other restrictions, the government of Israel restricts Palestinians' movement in, within, and out of the Occupied Palestinian Territories by means of checkpoints, barriers, gates, roadblocks, and a 436-mile-long wall. There are at least 561 physical obstacles that restrict the movement of approximately 2.4 million Palestinians to gain access to their basic services, places of worship, and families. The checkpoints, and the number of authorities encountered, even determine whether an act of trafficking is internal or international. If the victim encounters both the Israeli authorities and the Palestinian National Authority (PNA) at a checkpoint, the act is considered international trafficking. If the victim just comes across the PNA, it is considered internal trafficking. Palestinian courts have jurisdiction in only some areas, and the Israeli government, the occupying power, does not collaborate with the territories on anti-trafficking efforts or share investigative information.

As stateless people, members of the hill tribes in Thailand and Palestinians in Israel and the Palestinian Territories are at the mercy of the whims of their reluctant (at best) or hostile (at worst) host governments—governments that don't regard them as equal and have the ultimate power to limit the scope of their rights. The result is the utmost in marginalization: trafficking victims have nowhere to turn for justice other than the government that created the inequality that increased their vulnerability to trafficking in the first place. These calls for justice go unanswered.

CHAPTER 4

Thailand

> If the single greatest risk factor to being trafficked is lack of
> citizenship, what they need is citizenship.

—DAVID A. FEINGOLD, DIRECTOR OF THE OPHIDIAN RESEARCH INSTITUTE AND
UNESCO INTERNATIONAL COORDINATOR FOR HIV/AIDS AND TRAFFICKING

The hill tribe people are one of the most marginalized groups in Thailand, despite the fact that they were born there. Many live in poverty and without legal status and the protection of citizenship, and so are vulnerable to various forms of exploitation, including human trafficking. A highland grandmother from the Sripingmuang Akha slum community in the city of Chiang Mai paints a tragic picture of the hill tribe experience. "Without I.D. Cards, the only choices for our children are to beg, sell drugs, or sell their bodies—they are without hope" (UNESCO Bangkok, 2008). Since August 2001, hill tribe children whose parents are registered with "alien status" (which grants permanent residence) are to be granted Thai citizenship, though the registration process for permanent residence and citizenship requires a variety of supporting documents. For instance, a DNA test is required for those who do not have a birth certificate or a witness who can testify on their behalf (Lertcharoenchok, 2001). As a result of the challenges in obtaining citizenship, an estimated 50 percent of the one million hill tribe people in Thailand lack citizenship (UNESCO Bangkok, 2008; Freedom House, 2009).

Legislation in Thailand has set out to improve the protection of trafficking victims and migrant workers. The 2008 anti-trafficking law prohibits trafficking for both commercial sexual exploitation and forced labor. This is a large step, as adult male victims prior to the law were not considered victims and were—if foreign—typically deported (Hongthong, 2007). Prior to the anti-trafficking law, prosecutors used the

Prevention and Suppression of Trafficking in Women and Children Act of 1997 to bring suit against traffickers. The act solely prohibits sex trafficking (Hongthong, 2007). In labor trafficking cases, prosecutors often pressed charges of labor code violations against traffickers. The punishment for labor code violations is minimal, and many traffickers simply faced fines, particularly first-time offenders (U.S. Department of Labor, 2008). The anti-trafficking law is a positive step, but a continuing hurdle for the nation is corruption within its law enforcement. Additionally, despite protections under the law, thousands of foreigners are deported for immigration violations each month without adequate screening to determine whether they are trafficking victims.

THAILAND AS A DESTINATION

The majority of trafficking victims identified in Thailand are migrants who voluntarily travel to Thailand but who are forced, coerced, or defrauded into forced labor or commercial sexual exploitation. Undocumented migrants in particular are especially vulnerable to trafficking. Victims are found working in a variety of industries ranging from maritime fishing, seafood processing, garment production, to domestic labor (U.S. Department of State, 2010). It is difficult to know how many persons are trafficked into Thailand. David A. Feingold, director of the Ophidian Research Institute and UNESCO International Coordinator for HIV/AIDS and Trafficking, says obtaining exact numbers is a challenge because human trafficking is a process, not an event. "A person may leave home and migrate to the nearest town for employment," Feingold said. "If they don't find work, they may venture further. They may end up in Thailand as an illegal migrant worker and then subsequently locked in a shrimp factory where they become a trafficking victim. When it comes to data collection, the data can change depending on when you speak with the person."[1] Still, the breakdown of identified trafficking victims may give a glimpse into the primary countries of origin for human trafficking in Thailand. For instance, foreign victims identified by Thai authorities from 2005 through 2007 were from Laos (713 persons), Cambodia (359), Myanmar (334), Vietnam (13), and China (7).[2] The most prominent forms of exploitation of foreigners identified by Thai authorities between October 2006 and December 2007 were sex work (169), forced labor and factory work (158), house work (44), and begging (18). The majority (76 percent) of these victims were minors (UNODC, 2009).

As the shrimp industry in Thailand continues to boom, the demand for affordable labor has resulted in an industrywide crisis of labor abuse and the trafficking of persons from Laos, Cambodia, and Myanmar (Eckert, 2008). There are roughly 200,000 migrant workers from Myanmar in Samut Sakhon, 130,000 of whom are not legally registered (U.S. Department of Labor, 2008). Those exploited, even those enrolled in Thailand's temporary work program, often do not report labor abuses for fear of deportation (U.S. Department of State, 2009). When the American Center for International Labor Solidarity (Solidarity Center), with field offices in Thailand, looked into the Thai shrimp industry, it found human trafficking, child labor, debt bondage, and a failure to pay promised wages (Eckert, 2008). Additionally, workers in shrimp processing factories face long hours six days a week for modest wages (roughly $4.60 per day, if paid) in hazardous and unhealthy conditions. According to the Solidarity Center, it is "the norm" for the workforce in these factories to be made up of forced and child labor (Eckert, 2008).[3] Thailand is the world's largest exporter of shrimp and tuna. Thirty-seven percent of shrimp and 59 percent of tuna exported to the United States are from Thailand (Solidarity Center, 2008; NOAA Fisheries Service, 2011; United Nations Radio, 2011). In 2006 alone, the United States purchased 193,764,063 kilograms of shrimp from Thailand at a cost of roughly $1.3 billion. "It's essential that people know with absolute certainty that the flow of shrimp into the U.S. market is tainted by shrimp that's processed by the hands of those in slavery," said Mark Lagon, former director of the U.S. State Department's Office to Monitor and Combat Trafficking in Persons (Eckert, 2008).

The 2006 raid of the Ranya Paew shrimp factory in Samut Sakhon brought global media attention to the labor abuses and human trafficking taking place within Thailand's shrimp processing industry. Roughly 800 workers (men, women, and children) from Myanmar were imprisoned in a labor camp monitored by armed guards. The walls surrounding the camp were covered with barbed wire to prevent escape (Cropley, 2007). Workers at the factory were often forced to work unpaid because of supposed accrued debts. Deducted from their wages were housing, food, medicine, safety equipment, and labor agent fees. They worked between 16 and 20 hours a day and were paid $12.97 a month. Those who asked to leave, complained, or made an error on the factory line suffered horrible retribution. Workers faced public humiliation—they were stripped naked, publicly beaten, had their hair shaved or cut, and were paraded in front of their coworkers. Workers who asked for a break had metal rods thrust up their nostrils. Other workers claimed to have been sexually molested as punishment (Solidarity Center, 2008). Exploitation and trafficking of workers in the fishing industry is also a significant issue. In November 2009 authorities and NGOs partnered to rescue 51 Burmese workers from a locked room near a fishing port. It is likely that their captors planned to force the workers onto fishing vessels (U.S. Department of State, 2010).

Many Burmese workers are lured to Thailand by false promises of jobs. For instance, traffickers promised a Burmese worker named Zaw Zaw a job in a local market or factory. With his consent, the traffickers smuggled Zaw Zaw from his home in Myanmar through the jungle into Thailand. During the journey, he and other Burmese workers were beaten, and Thai brokers raped two of the women. They were then passed from broker to broker until they were eventually sold to work on a fishing boat. The conditions on the boat, Zaw Zaw recalled, were unbearable. The workers were beaten, threatened with violence and death, and given only a few hours of sleep at a time. They were also drugged. "I saw the captain put 15–20 amphetamine tablets into a plastic bag and crush them into a powder and then put that into the drinking water," Zaw Zaw told the BBC. "We worked faster and faster but then had terrible headaches afterwards." Three of the men tried to escape. Of the three, two drowned; the other was beaten, tortured with electric shocks, and shot before he was thrown overboard. The captain called Zaw Zaw and the other workers to the deck to witness the murder and then told the workers that this would happen to anyone who attempted escape. In order to avoid a similar fate, Zaw Zaw jumped overboard when the boat was close to shore and hid when the captain's henchmen searched the nearby dunes. He then walked for four days until he arrived at Pattaya City and found a church group that helped him (Leithead, 2011).

Though there is hope that U Thein Sein, the new president of Myanmar, will break from the governmental practices that preceded his presidency, it is the nation's not-so-distant past that pushed many Burmese into mass exodus. In addition to the economic and political instability that has plagued the nation, the systematic rape of women and girls was part of the military's campaign against minority ethnic groups. The 2002 report *Licence to Rape* documents 173 incidents of rape and other forms of sexual violence that involved 625 girls and women, committed by Burmese State Peace and Development Council (SPDC) army troops in Shan State (Shan Women's Action Network, 2002). The 2004 report *Shattering Silences* documents 125 cases of sexual violence committed by the SPDC's military troops in Karen State from 1988 until 2004. According to the latter report, high-ranking military officers committed half of the rapes. Forty percent of the documented rapes were gang rapes, and in 20 percent of the cases the women were killed after the rapes (Karen Women's Organization, 2004; WLB, 2004). The military regime was officially disbanded on March 30, 2011, but there is concern that the new civilian administration is not so different from its predecessor. In fact many in the current administration were a part of the military regime, including President U Thein Sein, who served as the last prime minister of the old military government (BBC News, 2011). Thus far, positive signs are that the president has taken measures to move the nation's government toward democracy and to hinder ethnic conflict. He reshuffled his cabinet in August 2012, which consolidated his power. The latter, some experts say, is a positive step to help the president implement positive change and reform, while other experts worry that this is indicative of weakness within the administration. Skeptics point to the 2012 violence between Buddhists and Muslims in Arakan State and violence between the armed forces and Kachin rebels (Naing, 2012; Myint-U, 2012).

Unfortunately, abuse and discrimination do not simply end with emigration. There are at least one million Burmese in Thailand. Marginalized and without adequate rights and protection, they face trafficking for the purposes of forced labor and sexual exploitation. Along with the hill tribe women and girls, Burmese immigrant women and girls (even those born in Thailand) are often without legal status in Thailand and face gender-based discrimination. They are vulnerable to a litany of human rights abuses that include human trafficking, unsafe migration, exploitative labor, sexual exploitation, and consequently an increased risk of HIV infection (Leiter et al., 2004).

The floods from the 2011 monsoon season affected more than 7 million households and made undocumented migrants even more vulnerable to exploitation and exorbitant transport fees by illicit brokers. In November 2011 the Federation of Thai Industries estimated that losses from the seven hardest-hit industrial estates, involving 891 factories and 460,000 workers, could reach $13 billion (IRIN, 2011). In an October 2011 report, the International Organization for Migration (IOM) estimated there were 1.4 million unregistered workers and family members in Thailand. According to Claudia Natali, the labor migration program coordinator at the IOM office in Bangkok, Thai law, which generally prohibits migrant workers from traveling outside their registered provinces, increases the vulnerability of migrants. "Irregular [undocumented] migrants who have no passport or work permit risk being arrested, but also those with a work permit or ID risk arrest and deportation when they leave the provinces where they are registered" (IRIN, 2011). Aye Than, a Burmese migrant worker who was employed at a furniture factory in Thailand until it flooded, said he had been arrested several times since his work permit expired. In order to be released, Than, who earns $4 per day doing odd jobs, had to pay up to $80 to both Thai and Burmese border immigration officers. "It is impossible for me to pay the fees," Than told IRIN, the humanitarian news and analysis service of the UN Office for the Coordination of Humanitarian Affairs (IRIN, 2011).

TRAFFICKING WITHIN THAILAND AND CHILD SEX TOURISM

Victims trafficked within Thailand are often underage and exploited in the garment, shrimp, and sex industries. Those who are exploited— particularly in the informal economy—tend to be children of ethnic minorities, stateless persons, or migrants, although many children who are Thai nationals are affected as well. For instance, Thailand's Office of the National Commission of Women's Affairs estimates that there are

22,500 to 40,000 Thai nationals under the age of 18 working in prostitution (U.S. Department of Labor, 2009). Experts also estimate that thousands of Thai citizens are trafficked into Thailand's fishing industry (Hongthong, 2007). The nature of this type of trafficking makes it difficult to know the actual numbers. The Mirror Foundation in Thailand has identified and aided in the rescue of a total of 19 men trafficked to work on fishing boats between 2003 and 2007, 27 in 2008, and 138 victims in 2009 (Hongthong, 2007; Bangkok Post, 2010). Eaklak Loomchomkhae, trafficking expert and head of the Mirror Foundation's anti–human trafficking center, states that forced labor is so prevalent in Thailand that male teenagers and adult men have been drugged at bus terminals and brought onto fishing boats while unconscious. When they awaken they are nowhere near shore. "They have no way to escape and must work in a boat until the time it goes ashore," Loomchomkhae told *The Nation*. Some fishing boats go ashore only every five years. Loomchomkhae says corrupt state officials play a prominent role in labor trafficking within the fishing industry (Hongthong, 2007).

The persons particularly susceptible to trafficking within Thailand and abroad are marginalized ethnic minorities such as the northern hill tribe people and children born in Thailand to Burmese parents. The exact number of children born to Burmese migrant workers is unknown, but a study by IOM estimates the number of migrant Lao, Cambodian, and Burmese children under the age of 17 to be roughly 200,000. Nearly 80 percent of all labor migrants in the country are Burmese, with the rest from Cambodia and Laos, which means that the majority of the 200,000 children are likely Burmese (IRIN, 2009). While more than 2,000 children of Burmese migrants are born in Thai hospitals each year, most children born to unregistered Burmese parents are born at their worksites with the assistance of local midwives. Unregistered migrant workers are rightly fearful of facing arrest and deportation if their lack of legal status is discovered, and thus are hesitant to give birth at a state hospital. Despite the clarity of the Civil Registration Act and the fact that state hospitals have been specifically instructed to issue birth certificates to all babies regardless of the legal status of the child's parents, many hospitals still do not issue birth certificates for the children of migrants (Civil Registration Act No. 2, 2008; IRIN, 2009;

Thawdar, The Irrawaddy, 2009a, 2009b). Additionally, changes to the Nationality Act have led to some confusion. Section 7 of the act appears to indicate that nonregistered persons who are born in Thailand may be considered illegal aliens:

> The person who is born within the Thai Kingdom and has not acquired Thai nationality under paragraph one shall reside in the Thai Kingdom under conditions stating [stated] in the Ministerial Regulation, but principles of national security and human rights have to be considered as well. Nevertheless, the person shall be deemed to have entered and resided in the Thai Kingdom without permission under the law on immigration when there is no such Ministerial Regulation still. (Nationality Act No. 4, 2008)

Without a legal identity, marginalized persons are at grave risk of being trafficked. The disadvantages that they face begin as early as primary school. According to David Feingold, although every child in Thailand is entitled to primary education, children without citizenship often go without. "What we found in our sample is that 57 percent of persons without citizenship don't make it to lower primary school [kindergarten to third grade]. From those persons who did make it to primary school, more than half did not make it to upper primary school [roughly third to sixth grade]. This is an example of a situation where the policy is good, but the implementation isn't." Feingold is referring to the Education for All policy launched in August 2005, which intended to grant equal access to education for all children in Thailand. The policy is often not enforced. Aside from cultural biases against migrants, there is also a lack of understanding of the policy on the local level. In addition, language differences, financial hurdles, and physical distances from schools present challenges (IRIN, 2009). Like migrants, unregistered hill tribe people are not only susceptible to arrest and deportation, but are also denied the basic rights granted to citizens. Persons without status cannot vote, own land, register a marriage, or obtain health care. Those without alien resident status or citizenship cannot travel outside their district or go on to higher education because they are unable to receive a certificate upon finishing school, so their employment options are significantly limited.

The restrictions placed upon unregistered highland people make them susceptible to trafficking, both within Thailand and abroad (Lertcharo-enchok, 2001; U.S. Department of State, 2009).

Thailand is a commonly known sex tourism destination, yet the nation has made minimal efforts to reduce the demand for commercial sex acts. Thai authorities do work with NGOs in intermittent police raids to shut down brothels, and the government also conducts awareness-raising anti–child sex tourism campaigns geared to tourists. Some of the primary nations of origin for sex tourists are France, Germany, Italy, Japan, and South Korea. The government does prosecute sex tourists, although prosecution seems to be sporadic. For instance, 20 child sex tourists were prosecuted in 2008, but there were no reported prosecutions in 2009 (U.S. Department of State, 2009; 2010). One potential reason for the government's apathy on the topic of sex tourism may be the significant role sex tourism plays in the Thai economy. Tourism revenues contribute to roughly 6 percent of the GDP. In 2009 14,150 tourists spent $19,421 million, and in 2010 revenues from tourism increased to $23,407 million (National Statistical Office Thailand, 2004; UNWTO, 2011). Some believe that sex tourism accounts for 1 percent of the nation's GDP (Prospect Magazine, 2005). The steady growth in the number of international tourists entering Thailand is likely to continue. In fact, international arrivals to Thailand increased 7 percent between April 2011 and April 2012 (PATA, 2012). This inevitably increased demand in Thailand for commercial sex, with an adverse effect on children (both girls and boys), who as a population are vulnerable to a variety of exploitations, including sexual exploitation. This vulnerability is exacerbated by a lack of national identity, which marginalizes children and does not allow them equal opportunity to health care and education; economic hardship, which compels children to discontinue their education in order to aid in the support of their family; and homelessness—specifically, children that run away from home to escape abuse. Once again, children of ethnic minorities are particularly vulnerable. A study conducted by the Research Institute at Mahidol University, Thailand, found that children of ethnic minorities are trafficked from their highland homes to Bangkok and Pattaya for commercial sexual exploitation. In addition to marginalization created by the nation's citizenship laws, there is neither structure nor sufficient mechanisms within the tourism industry itself to protect children from commercial sexual exploitation (Pimonsaeng-suriya, 2008).

To help bridge the gap and decrease the vulnerability of children, groups such as Friends-International, through the ChildSafe Network, work with the Thai Immigration Authority and the Hotels and Taxi Associations to protect children in Thailand. The program helps identify what restaurants and hotels are safe for children. Additionally, Friends-International's Peuan Peuan in Bangkok program works with more than 350 children and youth every month to provide emergency and long-term support services to Thai, Burmese, Cambodian, and Lao children and youth and their families (Friends-International, Inc., 2011). Also of significance are tourism-related groups that are part of anti-trafficking initiatives that focus on protecting children from sexual exploitation in travel and tourism. One such initiative is called The Code and is co-funded by the Swiss Government (SECO) and the tourism private sector and supported by ECPAT International, a nongovernmental organization that works toward the elimination of child prostitution, child pornography, and the trafficking of children for sexual purposes. Advisory partners to the initiative are UNICEF and the United Nations World Tourism Organization (UNWTO). Accor Hotels has been a core partner in implementing The Code in Thailand (Pimonsaeng-suriya, 2008; The Code, 2011).

It is not just sex tourists who affect the demand for commercial sex acts in Thailand, but also Thai men. Kevin Bales, human trafficking abolitionist and author of *Disposable People: New Slavery in the Global Economy*, states in his book: "For Thai men, buying a woman is much like buying a round of drinks" (Bales, 1999, p. 44). This attitude stems from Thai tradition, whereby a man's worth, according to Bales, could easily be measured in wives, mistresses, and concubines. Those without as many resources could rent instead of own their mistresses through prostitution. Today, thanks to economic growth—7.8 percent in 2010—and an emerging economy (IMF, 2011), Thai men can more regularly afford to pay for sex, and they do. Studies indicate that of those interviewed, up to 90 percent state that their first sexual encounter was with a prostitute. According to Bales, there is general acceptance of this behavior among single Thai men. More surprising is that one-third of women interviewed felt that commercial sex is also appropriate for married Thai men. Bales states that married Thai women are less threatened by the idea of a prostitute than a minor wife or mistress because, while polygamy is technically illegal, children that arise from those relationships are entitled to legal support. Acceptance of the sex industry also exists within the government and is compounded by government corruption. In 2011 a new political party called "Love Thailand" won four seats in the House of Representatives. The party was formed by politician and former brothel owner Chuwit Kamolvisit, known as a godfather of prostitution, who was arrested in 2003 and subsequently exposed the bribes he paid to police to maintain his brothels. His campaign platform in 2011 focused on leading the country's fight against corruption (Duthel, 2011; Branigan, 2011).

While some literature notes that the majority of child sex tourists are situational abusers who do not initially have a particular sexual preference for children, but instead take the opportunity to sexually abuse children as it arises, other literature points to an increased demand for young children among sex tourists and Thai men who pay for sex. This is believed to be, at least in part, a consequence of the fear of HIV infection and the belief that young children are less likely to carry sexually transmitted diseases. Those women and girls who test HIV positive and work in brothels are typically thrown out onto the streets (Bales, 1999; Pimonsaengsuriya, 2008; Batstone, 2010). What is troubling is that while HIV continues to be a significant issue in Thailand, the government has decreased the budget for prevention programs. In 2001 domestic funding for HIV prevention was half of that in 1997. The budget toward prevention decreased from $47.7 million in 2008 to $31.4 million in 2009. At the end of 2009 the estimated number of people living with HIV was 530,000, with 1.3 percent of persons between 15 and 49 infected (National AIDS Prevention and Alleviation Committee, 2010; AVERT, 2011).

TRAFFICKING ABROAD

Thailand is a major source nation for human trafficking. Victims are trafficked to Bahrain, Canada, Denmark, Fiji, Finland, Israel, Malaysia, the Maldives, Qatar, Singapore, South Africa, South Korea, Sweden,

Switzerland, Taiwan, and the United States, among other countries. Of 443 trafficking victims repatriated to Thailand between October 2007 and September 2008, 81.3 percent had been trafficked to Bahrain. A distant second destination country was Malaysia, at 16.5 percent. Most repatriated trafficking victims were trafficked abroad for commercial sexual exploitation and were held in debt bondage by their traffickers. The overall number of human trafficking victims is likely to grow in the years to come, as male trafficking victims are now included in the anti-trafficking law and therefore will (hopefully) be incorporated into trafficking statistics. Some Thai men voluntarily migrate for contract work in the Gulf states, Israel, Malaysia, South Korea, Taiwan, and the United States but may face forced labor and debt bondage upon arrival. During 2009 Thai workers were subjected to forced labor in Poland, Sweden, and the United States for work on farms, at construction sites, and in slaughterhouses (U.S. Department of State, 2010).

For obvious reasons, it is impossible to know the exact number of persons trafficked from Thailand to other nations. The official number of trafficking victims repatriated to Thailand is probably only the tip of the iceberg. In 2010 and 2009, 88 and 309, respectively, were repatriated with help from the governments of the Bahrain, China, Malaysia, Russia, Singapore, South Africa, Sri Lanka, the United Arab Emirates, the United Kingdom, the United States, Vietnam, and Yemen (U.S. Department of State, 2009, 2010, 2011). Thai citizens accounted for 64.5 percent of trafficking victims identified in South Africa in 2005 and 2006. In Australia, Thai victims made up 62.1 percent of persons placed on government victims support between 2004 and November 2008 (UNODC, 2009). In 2009 roughly 20 percent of certified adult trafficking victims in the United States were from Thailand (second only to Mexico). Thailand remained a primary country of origin for victims trafficked to the United States in 2012 (U.S. Department of State, 2012). As discussed in chapter 1, roughly 600 Thai nationals were purportedly victims of the largest alleged human trafficking case in U.S. history. Though the U.S. government dropped the criminal charges against defendants in 2012, the U.S. Equal Employment Opportunity Commission is still pursuing civil litigation (Lin, 2012). The victims entered the United States under the federal agricultural guestworker program between 2001 and 2007. The traffickers allegedly used false promises of high-paying jobs and charged the victims exorbitant recruiting fees of up to $21,000, placing them in a position of debt servitude. The traffickers also allegedly withheld the victims' passports and threatened to deport them (Kerr, 2010; U.S. Department of Justice, 2011a, 2011b). Another U.S. case involves Thai workers hired for agricultural labor but instead forced to perform demolition in hurricane devastated New Orleans. After accepting agricultural employment, 22 Thai workers were brought over to the United States legally on the H-2A visa by a U.S. company, Million Express Manpower, Inc. When they arrived in North Carolina, the traffickers confiscated the victims' transportation and visa documents. One month later the workers were transported from North Carolina to New Orleans to perform building demolition (Asanok et al., 2007). Forced to live in the building that they were demolishing, the victims had no access to clean water and were continuously exposed to mold in the roach-, mosquito-, and fly-infested buildings (Andert, 2007, p. 27). While in New Orleans, the victims were not paid and were closely watched by an armed guard to ensure that they did not try to escape. The same guard charged the victims for purchasing their food, but without pay the workers began to go hungry (Asanok et al., 2007). Eventually, questions from the Thai embassy about the location and situation of the workers forced the traffickers to return the victims to North Carolina. The traffickers could not fit all of the victims into their vehicles and left seven in New Orleans. With the help of service providers in New Orleans and North Carolina, all the victims were able to escape.[4]

WHAT HAPPENS TO VICTIMS AFTER TRAFFICKING

There are at least 138 temporary government-run shelters in Thailand, with at least 1 shelter in every province, along with 9 long-term-stay regional shelters where victims receive food, housing, psychological counseling, medical care, and legal assistance. One of the regional long-term-stay facilities is specifically geared to aid male trafficking victims and their families. In 2009 the Thai government opened 3 additional trafficking shelters for men (U.S. Department of State, 2009, 2010). This is a great step forward for Thailand, as under the former anti-trafficking law males were not acknowledged as trafficking victims (U.S. Department of State, 2009, 2010). While more than 60 women and children were placed in a center for trafficking victims (in Bangkok) after the 2006 raid at Ranya Paew, roughly 200 Burmese men were deported as illegal immigrants (Cropley, 2007; Solidarity Center, 2008; U.S. Department of Labor, 2008).

In 2009 and 2010 the Ministry of Social Development and Human Security reported that 530 and 381 foreign trafficking victims were identified and assisted, respectively. Most of the persons identified in 2009 were victims of forced labor. Seventy-nine Thai citizens repatriated after being trafficked abroad also received assistance. In 2009 Thai immigration authorities reported identifying at least 60 victims of trafficking, and the Ministry of Foreign Affairs reported assisting and repatriating 309 Thai trafficking victims (U.S. Department of State, 2010, 2011). While Thai law protects identified victims from being prosecuted for acts committed as a result of their trafficking experience, thousands of foreigners are deported for immigration violations each month without adequate screening to determine if they are trafficking victims (U.S. Department of State, 2010). For instance, adult trafficking victims are sometimes detained in government shelters for several years. Foreign victims cannot opt to reside outside the shelters. Even though foreign trafficking victims are not offered legal alternatives to deportation, they may not leave before Thai authorities are ready to repatriate them. Additionally, while Thailand's anti-trafficking law grants foreign victims the right to seek employment while awaiting conclusion of legal processes, the government does not appear to actually provide victims with this right (U.S. Department of State, 2010, 2012).

Victims are encouraged to participate in the prosecution of their traffickers, but they are not required to do so and will receive social services and shelter regardless. The government, as an incentive for victims to participate in the investigation and prosecution of their traffickers, aids victims of forced labor in recovering compensatory damages from employers. Victims are not systematically made aware of this option, and some NGOs report that a number of victims are pressured to participate in the criminal cases against their traffickers (U.S. Department of State, 2009, 2010). Trafficking-related court proceedings move slowly. The victims in the 2006 Ranya Paew case who were not deported stayed in Thailand for more than two years during proceedings against the shrimp factory. In 2008 the court awarded 66 victims $950 each in compensation. This allowed two victims—Kyi Kyi Thein and her daughter—to rebuild their lives in Myanmar (IRIN, 2010).

Whatever the outcome of a court case, the trafficking experience can have lasting detrimental psychological and physical effects on victims. Children and adults exploited in the commercial sex industry commonly contract sexually transmitted diseases and face unwanted pregnancies. One such case is that of Ning, who was sold into sex trafficking by her father at the age of 13. Upon her return to Thailand from Australia she discovered that she was infected with HIV. Filmmaker Luigi Acquisto, who interviewed Ning for his 2005 documentary *Trafficked* as well as for his 2011 film *Trafficked—The Reckoning,* says Ning's experience is similar to that of other trafficked children. "The incidence of HIV in children who are trafficked is very high, as is the incidence of suicide, drug dependency, and adult lives as prostitutes. Ning is HIV positive. She has made several serious suicide attempts, as evidenced by the deep transverse scars on her wrist. She was a serious drug user and has an alcohol problem. She fits the profile of a trafficked child." Ning's trafficking experience has had a lasting psychological impact. "The psychiatric tests she underwent a few years ago established that she is suffering from post-traumatic stress and depression. The long-term effects on victims of the crime of sex trafficking are horrific."[5]

Trafficked followed two Thai trafficking victims, "Ning" and "Noi." The film ended with two seemingly very different outcomes. Ning was happily married, had given birth to a baby boy, and the New South Wales Victims Compensation Tribunal in Australia had ordered that she be paid $50,000 from a government fund for crime victims. On the other hand, Noi, who it seems was trafficked at the age of 21 from Malaysia to Sydney (the details are unclear), was a heroin addict and ill when immigration authorities picked her up. When she arrived at Sydney's Villawood Immigration Detention Centre she was suffering from malnutrition and acute pneumonia, and while there her condition continued to worsen. Unfortunately, her health problems somehow went unnoticed by staff. Reports indicate that she vomited into a bucket for more than 60 hours while at the detention center. The coroner's shocking report on her death as well as the treatment she faced in the center made headlines throughout Sydney. As time has passed, says

Acquisto, Ning's trafficking experience also seems to have continued to have an adverse impact on her life: "Ning's life follows closely the trajectory of Noi's life. At the time [during the filming of *Trafficked*] the story ended well for one [victim] and badly for the other: Ning survived and Noi died. This was too simple a resolution. The lives of the two women, both trafficked to Sydney in 1995, were very similar. Noi was a heroin addict, attempted suicide, and, like Ning, found herself trapped by her former life as a sex slave." Chapter 17 provides details about Ning and Noi's trafficking experiences.

WHAT HAPPENS TO TRAFFICKERS

The primary enforcement agency for human trafficking in Thailand is the Anti-Human Trafficking Division (AHTD) of the Royal Thai Police. The AHTD investigated 134 trafficking cases between June 2008 and November 2009 (U.S. Department of Labor, 2010). The Office of the Attorney General reported that prosecutors initiated 17 trafficking-related prosecutions in 2009 and 8 in January and February of 2010 (U.S. Department of State, 2010). The number of persons prosecuted for human trafficking is minimal, and sentencing varies. For instance, in 2008 Thai courts convicted 3 Thai citizens, all women, for sex trafficking. Two of the women had forced children into prostitution; the other woman had trafficked two women to Italy for commercial sexual exploitation. The women were sentenced to 34, 50, and 14 years' imprisonment, respectively. In 2009 there were at least 8 trafficking-related convictions, 5 of which involved labor trafficking. Under the 2008 anti-trafficking law, all forms of trafficking are prohibited, and the law prescribes penalties ranging from 4 to 10 years' imprisonment. The sentences in these 8 cases ranged from 2 years' imprisonment to death. Some convicted offenders were released while awaiting appeal. In November 2009 Thai courts convicted 2 Thai citizens for subjecting Burmese migrants to forced labor in their Samut Sakhon shrimp processing factory. The offenders were sentenced to 5 and 8 years' imprisonment. This was the first human trafficking conviction involving Thailand's fishing and related processing industries. The 2009 case of 51 rescued Burmese workers is still under investigation, although one person has been convicted in this case. He was sentenced to 2 years' imprisonment. Authorities have not arrested any offenders involved in the 2006 case of 39 deaths on a fleet of six fishing vessels. The victims were not provided with food and died from malnutrition. In 2010 and 2011 the Thai government reported 18 and 12 convictions in trafficking-related cases, respectively. Three traffickers in the 2006 Ranya Paew case were convicted in December 2010; each was sentenced to 20 years in prison. In another case, a person who ran a fraudulent employment agency involved in the trafficking of Thai workers abroad was sentenced to 4 years' imprisonment (U.S. Department of State, 2009, 2010, 2011, 2012).

Reports indicate that police, soldiers, immigration officers, and local officials accept bribes and/or turn a blind eye to trafficking or are actually involved in the trafficking itself (Freedom House, 2009). Officials found to be complicit in human trafficking are supposed to face harsher sentencing. Under the 2008 anti-trafficking law, any official who commits offenses under the anti-trafficking act "shall be liable to twice the punishment stipulated for such offense" (Royal Thai Government, 2008). The question is whether this provision will actually be enforced. A police officer suspected of human trafficking in 2007 did not face trafficking charges but instead was fired, convicted, and fined for smuggling illegal aliens into the country. The government holds that there was not enough evidence to substantiate a trafficking charge. In 2009 there were reports of corruption of local police, but there is no information as to whether these cases were investigated or prosecuted. In 2011 there were three ongoing investigations of local law enforcement officials who allegedly took bribes from brothels that harbored child sex-trafficking victims (U.S. Department of State, 2009, 2010, 2012). David Feingold says the critical step to prevent human trafficking is to address the issue of legal identity rather than through the prosecutorial system:

> There is no country in the world where prosecution has been shown to have an impact on the aggregate of trafficking. While I support prosecution for the purpose of justice, it does not deter trafficking. If you think it is a 1 in 1,000 chance that you will be caught, then you may take your chance. Regardless of nation, there is very little prosecution against traffickers. Yes, you need a legal framework and good laws in place, but you need to do something

about the underlying structural issues. If you don't do anything about that you are not going to have much success. Worldwide you have this same problem of various aspects of legal identity that make people vulnerable. To correct this is the most efficient step forward to eliminating trafficking.[6]

INTERNAL EFFORTS TO DECREASE TRAFFICKING

As part of an effort to address the prevalence of workplace exploitation, the Thai government has begun to target inspections at workplaces where the worst forms of child labor are likely to exist. The Department of Labor Protection and Welfare prioritizes inspections of small factories and workplaces where there is a high concentration of migrants, young laborers (15–17 years old), and hazardous labor. It also launched the National Policy and Plan to Eliminate the Worst Forms of Child Labor (2009–2014), which is designed to protect both Thai and non-Thai nationals. The government also established women and child labor protection centers to help target sex and labor trafficking at the local level (U.S. Department of Labor, 2009). The Children and Women Protection Police Division has national jurisdiction over anti-trafficking investigations, while the Transnational Crime Coordination Center and the Office of the Attorney General's Center Against International Human Trafficking conduct strategic planning for anti-trafficking efforts and collect and analyze trafficking information (U.S. Department of State, 2009). Theoretically, these measures should help synchronize and organize anti-trafficking efforts, but inadequate cooperation between police and prosecutors as well as rapid staff turnover within the divisions has created investigative delays.

In 2009 the Thai government implemented the Nationality Verification and Granting an Amnesty to Remain in the Kingdom of Thailand to Alien Workers Program. It extended the period of the nationality verification process and allowed illegal workers from Myanmar, Cambodia, and Laos to stay temporarily in Thailand so long as they had already registered and received work permits during 2009 in accordance with certain cabinet resolutions (Extension, 2010).[7] The objective of the program is to register and protect undocumented migrants by bringing them into the formal labor market and providing them with related benefits. Paradoxically, the provisions of the program—such as the travel requirements and fees associated with the nationality verification process—can actually increase vulnerability to debt bondage and trafficking. According to Joy Ngozi Ezeilo, the United Nations special rapporteur on trafficking in persons, the nation's anti-trafficking efforts are hindered by weak and fragmented implementation and enforcement of the 2008 anti-trafficking law. Perhaps in part to address this chronic issue, in May 2011 the Thai government passed a regulation to implement a provision in the 2008 anti-trafficking law that grants foreign victims the right to seek employment while awaiting conclusion of legal processes. This is a positive step, but equally important is addressing another concern expressed by Ezeilo, which is that implementation and enforcement are often hampered by deep-rooted corruption, especially among low-cadre law enforcement officers at provincial and local levels (OHCHR, 2011; U.S. Department of State, 2011).

In addition to corruption, multiple other issues pose obstacles to the Thai government's anti-trafficking efforts. For instance, although victims are technically protected under the anti-trafficking law, migrants still face deportation before a proper screening determines whether they are victims of trafficking. It is a positive step that the government has begun workplace inspections of locales where they believe the worst forms of child labor exist and that it has launched a national policy plan to eliminate this issue. Still, children age 15 and older have few protections in the industries of agriculture, sea fishing, and domestic work—areas where they continue to face exploitation and perform hazardous labor. Additionally, education is compulsory only until age 16. This creates a scenario where children are more likely to be part of the workforce and not adequately protected. Finally, the issue of citizenship must be properly addressed for the highland people and children born to Burmese migrants in Thailand.

Israel and the Occupied Palestinian Territories

They succeeded in executing their plot by exploiting, for their own profit, the economic and social distress of their victims.
—BASSEM KANDALAFT, ATTORNEY OF THE NORTHERN DISTRICT PROSECUTION IN ISRAEL

Israel's Anti-Trafficking Law of 2006 prohibits all forms of human trafficking. The strength of the legislation is its breadth of application: it does not require the means of trafficking to be identified (UNODC, 2009). The weakness in the law is that it imposes significantly more stringent sentencing on sex traffickers than on labor traffickers. Violators under the law face up to 16 years' imprisonment for the sex trafficking of an adult, up to 20 years' imprisonment for the sex trafficking of a child, up to 16 years' imprisonment for slavery, and up to 7 years' imprisonment for forced labor (U.S. Department of State, 2009). In the Occupied Palestinian Territories (OPT), anti-trafficking law is fragmented. The drafting of a new criminal code is in progress, but for now the Egyptian penal law of 1960 and the Jordanian penal law of 1937 prevail in the West Bank and Gaza Strip, respectively (SAWA/UNIFEM, 2008). Overall, the current legal framework in the OPT is a jumble of Egyptian, Jordanian, Palestinian, Ottoman, and British laws. It also includes Israeli military orders. Even more confusing is that, generally speaking, different laws apply to the West Bank and the Gaza Strip, which results in the lack of a unified legal framework, inconsistencies, and gaps in the current legislation. Furthermore, these laws do not reflect President Mahmoud Abbas's 2009 significant endorsement of CEDAW, the Convention on the Elimination of All Forms of Discrimination Against Women (WCLAC & DCAF, 2012). What is consistent is that the applicable penal laws in the OPT do not provide sufficient protection to women and girls, especially in instances of gender-based violence. The laws in the OPT as they relate to human trafficking result in sentencing that is far less stringent than in Israel. Traffickers who force persons into prostitution by using threats, drugs, or deceit face a prison sentence ranging from 1 to 3 years. In order to deter the use of forced marriage as a means of human trafficking, in 2008 Tayseer Tamimi, a Palestinian judge and chief of the High Council of Sharia Jurisdictions, issued an order to all judicial courts and the Ministry of Women's Affairs. The order stipulates that in order for a marriage to transpire the woman must consent, she must be more than 18 years of age, the couple must have secured a residence to live in after they are married, all medical examinations required for the marriage should be completed and the man should not have AIDS, and there must be no legal or religious conditions hindering a marriage (SAWA/UNIFEM, 2008).

As is the case in many nations, obtaining accurate statistics on human trafficking in Israel and the OPT is challenging. Human trafficking is often investigated under other offenses such as soliciting prostitution, kidnapping, causing a person to engage in prostitution, and pandering. As a result, these crimes are reported separately and not included in trafficking statistics (UNODC, 2009). One concern in obtaining an accurate picture of human trafficking in Israel and the OPT is the Israeli government's attempt to limit the presence of NGOs. In September 2009 the Interior Ministry stopped granting work permits to foreign nationals working in NGOs operating in East Jerusalem and the OPT. Instead, the NGOs were granted tourist visas that prevented them from working. Some of the groups adversely affected were Save the Children, Doctors Without Borders, and Oxfam International (Hass, 2010a). In March 2010 the Interior Ministry stopped issuing the restrictive tourist visas and stated that the previous system would be restored temporarily. Historically, NGO workers in the region registered with the International Relations Department at the Social Affairs Ministry and were issued B1 visas—temporary unrestricted work visas—by the Interior Ministry. The Interior Ministry now aims to make the Ministry of Defense responsible for international NGOs in the territories. NGOs argue that this move would subjugate them to the Israeli military, in direct conflict with the intent and purpose of the NGOs (Hass, 2010b).

ISRAEL AS A PRIMARY DESTINATION

Persons from China, India, Nepal, the Philippines, Romania, Sri Lanka, Thailand, and Turkey voluntarily and legally migrate to Israel for low-skilled contract labor in the areas of construction, agriculture, and health care. The Knesset reported that as of December 31, 2010, 33,439 "infil-trators" had entered Israel from Egypt, 26,164 of whom received a temporary residence 2(a)(5) permit (Knesset, 2011a). This is the most common permit given to anyone residing in Israel who holds no other permit and is not in detention. Most asylum seekers in Israel hold this permit. The visa gives the holder no legal or social rights, but it does allow employers to hire asylum seekers. However, it is not considered a work permit (Dickman, 2011). The majority of these "infiltrator" migrants were from Eritrea (18,262) and Sudan (7,992). The numbers of persons entering Israel from Egypt is on the rise—13,686 in 2010 compared to 4,827 in 2009 (Knesset, 2011a). Upon arrival in Israel, some migrant workers face forced labor, their passports and travel documents are withheld, and their movements restricted. They also encounter non-payment, threats, and physical intimidation and abuse. Others are charged exorbitant fees by recruitment agencies (between $1,000 and $10,000) that place them in a position of debt bondage. The national origins of Israel's forced laborers vary by employment sector. The largest identified groups of labor-trafficking victims are Thai agricultural workers, Chinese construction workers, and Filipino, Indian, Nepalese, and Sri Lankan domestic and nursing care workers. Caregivers are particularly vulnerable to retracted visa status when employers fail to arrange their visas. Persons are also trafficked from Russia, Ukraine, Lithuania, Moldova, Uzbekistan, Belarus, China, and Mongolia for sexual exploitation. Typically, organized crime groups engage in this type of trafficking and traffic the victims from Egypt into Israel (U.S. Department of State, 2009, 2010a).

Historically, more sex-trafficking victims are identified and receive shelter than forced-labor victims. For instance, from 2005 through 2007, of victims who received shelter, 258 were sex-trafficking victims and 6 had been trafficked for forced labor (UNODC, 2009). Although all the forced-labor victims in the statistic received shelter in the year following passage of the 2006 law, none of them were men; it seems clear not only that forced-labor victims remained highly unidentified but also that male victims had little access to services and shelter. This is changing. In 2009–2010, 21 male victims of slavery and forced labor were housed in the 35-bed Atlas shelter for male trafficking victims; in 2010, 63 men were referred to the shelter; and as of December 2010, 13 men were housed there. As of the same date, 20 women were housed in the Maagan shelter, a 35-bed shelter for female trafficking victims. The number of persons referred to the two shelters by law enforcement and judicial officials remained similar in 2011 for female but not male victims. That year 16 women and 10 men were referred to the Maagan and Atlas shelters, respectively (UNODC, 2009; U.S. Department of State, 2010b, 2011, 2012). Victims who received shelter in 2005 and 2006 were from Ukraine (31), Moldova (18), Russia (13), Uzbekistan (7), China (5), South Asia (3), other countries of eastern Europe and Central Asia (2), and South America (1). The 6 victims of forced labor who received shelter in 2007 were from Sri Lanka, China, Nepal, and Ukraine (UNODC, 2009).

The largest account of human trafficking to be discovered in Israel is that of an organized crime syndicate whose members were arrested in Tel Aviv in March 2009. In a two-year period, the ring allegedly trafficked more than 2,000 women from Belarus, Moldova, Russia, Ukraine, and Uzbekistan to Israel for commercial sexual exploitation (IRIN, 2009; Goren, 2009). According to Chief Superintendent Pini Avraham of the Tel Aviv Police's Central Unit, "The suspects essentially went on a shopping spree for women throughout the former Soviet Union" (Goren, 2009). "We are talking about over 2,000 women who, we suspect, were forced to work as prostitutes via threats and violence, in Israel and Cyprus and, later, in Belgium and England as well."

The primary suspect in the case is Rami Saban, a mobster who is allegedly closely related to one of Israel's mafia families, the Abutbul crime organization (IRIN, 2009; Goren, 2009). Saban was previously under investigation for smuggling hired killers from Belarus to assassinate Nissim Alperon, a leading Israeli mobster figure and a member of the rival Alperon clan. He allegedly ran the intricate trafficking network by utilizing agents in nations such as Ukraine, Belarus, and Moldova. Over 20 suspects in several other countries—such as Russia and the Turkish Republic of Northern Cyprus—were also arrested in relation to this case (Goren, 2009). The key players in the trafficking ring each earned between $267,952.85 and $803,858.55. The victims were offered employment as waitresses or caretakers (Jerusalem Post, 2009). After they were flown to Egypt and smuggled into Israel, the women faced harsh and violent conditions (Goren, 2009). Forced into debt bondage, the women had to prostitute without pay until the pimps' payments were met (IRIN, 2009). While the ring initially focused on trafficking women to Israel, they moved the operation to Cyprus when some of their Israeli and Russian partners were arrested in 2008. "There, they opened strip joints that employed dozens of women as prostitutes using threats and violence," Avraham said (Goren, 2009).

Although Israel is primarily a destination nation for international human trafficking, a small number of persons are reportedly trafficked from Israel to Ireland and the United Kingdom for commercial sexual exploitation (U.S. Department of State, 2009).

TRAFFICKING WITHIN ISRAEL AND THE OPT

Criticism by outside nations and NGOs of international sex trafficking in Israel caused the government to take action. The government passed its anti-trafficking law in 2006, and law enforcement has subsequently increased the identification of foreign victims. Victims are often identified when law enforcement finds they are missing visa documents—a red flag that a trafficker or pimp has withheld such documents in order to curtail the victim's movements, or that the person has been smuggled into the country. While the identification of foreign victims has increased, the demand for prostitution remains the same. Consequently, NGOs estimate that hundreds of Israeli women are trafficked within the nation, primarily in the cities of Tel Aviv and Haifa. "The demand for sex did not change, and the [gap] had to be filled. Israeli women filled it," Adi Willinger, the trafficking coordinator at Hotline for Migrant Workers, told *Haaretz*. One victim of internal trafficking was drugged, beaten, and raped by her trafficker. The trafficker also threatened to harm her children and family members if she did not comply with his demands. What makes this story particularly unusual is that the trafficker in this case was the victim's husband. As the victim stated, her husband would say: "You're mine; I control you. You are not yours. You do not belong to yourself." Na'ama Ze'evi Rivlin, manager of the state-run Shalit shelter, says many of the traffickers in internal cases of sex trafficking are the husbands of the victims. One issue is that police do not generally recognize the trafficking of Israeli citizens within Israel as human trafficking. As a result, internal trafficking cases are often ignored. "[The police] deny the existence of this phenomenon," Willinger told *Haaretz*. "They claim there is no such thing as internal trafficking in Israel" (Zebede, 2009).

Palestinian women are also forced into prostitution, particularly in the cities of Jerusalem in Israel and Ramallah in the West Bank (SAWA/ UNIFEM, 2008). For instance, two sisters—ages 13 and 14—were repeatedly sold by their father to Palestinian men inside Israel. Utilizing the temporary Urfi marriage, the father would collect money and then sell the girls again. One of the sisters, now 18 years old, told field researchers that she has married around 12 men under the Urfi marriage:

> I ran away from my last marriage, as the wife of my husband knew of my pregnancy and tried to burn me. My baby was put in a kindergarten in Beit Jalla, and I have never seen him. As I turn 18 years old, I will have to leave this safe house, but I cannot return to my family and have no place to go. A year ago, my relatives took me and made me marry my cousin as a mean to protect me, but the judge forced me to get a divorce, as there is no legal evidence of my divorce from my last husband. And after I got the divorce for my last Urfi marriage, my cousin refused to marry me again. (SAWA/ UNIFEM, 2008)

The girl's sister ran away from their father and returned to search for her last husband. She killed him and is now in a Nablus prison (SAWA/ UNIFEM, 2008).

Factors that increase a person's vulnerability to human trafficking are poverty, inequity, discrimination, and violence. Palestinian girls and women in the OPT face a range of restrictions and discriminations, not only politically but also culturally (SAWA/UNIFEM, 2008). As with anyone living inside the fractured territories, the movements of girls and women are restricted by numerous checkpoints, barriers, gates, roadblocks, and the 436-mile-long wall. At least 561 physical obstacles restrict the movement of approximately 2.4 million Palestinians to their basic services, places of worship, and families (OCHA, 2007). On account of gender, women in the territories also face obstacles presented by an increasingly conservative culture. As a result, many girls and women avoid leaving their homes not only in order to protect themselves from arrest, harassment (verbal and sexual), and detainment by Israeli officials but also to deter potential negative talk that could incite physical and/or verbal retribution by family members (Menkedick, 2010). Girls and women in the territories face a great deal of violence. A study by the Palestinian Women's Information and Media Center found that 77.1 percent of Palestinian women and girls in the Gaza Strip have encountered violence of some sort. Fifty-two percent have experienced physical violence, and 15 percent sexual violence. The study indicates that 67 percent are exposed to verbal violence, 71 percent to psychological violence, and 44.6 percent to multiple forms of violence (Kliger, 2009).

TRAFFICKING OF ORGANS

In April 2010 an organ-trafficking ring was discovered in Israel when a victim from East Jerusalem filed a complaint with the Department for Fraud and Misappropriations in northern Israel. Members of the syndicate included two lawyers and a retired Israeli general as well as traffickers and their agents. All the donor-victims in this case were Israeli citizens, as were most of the transplant candidates. Thus far, the trafficking ring is known to be responsible for at least 10 transactions between victim-donors and organ candidates (Khoury & Ashkenazi, 2010). "The ring is operating throughout Israel and not only in the north, and appeals to the public through local media and internet," a police official told the Israeli daily *Haaretz*. "The organ traffickers somehow receive details about potential transplant candidates and they offer them their services" (Ma'an News Agency, 2010). Having responded to an advertisement that promised $100,000 for the removal and use of a kidney, the first victim to complain to law enforcement underwent a medical examination and was subsequently flown to Azerbaijan, where her kidney was extracted. After surgery the woman was returned to Israel without the money she was promised (Khoury & Ashkenazi, 2010). The department received other similar complaints in which the syndicate demanded at least $120,000 for a kidney transplant from clients but offered to pay organ donors only about $10,000. Many donors received smaller sums or no pay at all. The donors also signed contracts and filled out fraudulent documents claiming a family relationship between the donor and the organ recipient (Ma'an News Agency, 2010).

The donors underwent medical screenings in which they were categorized by medical condition and blood type. If they were a match for a recipient, they were typically flown to eastern Europe, Ecuador, or the Philippines. They were then returned to Israel without medical documentation and often had untreated medical complications from surgery. In order to cover their tracks, the traffickers tried to hide the donors' Israeli medical records, making it immensely difficult for donors to be treated if they became ill following the surgery (Ma'an News Agency, 2010; BBC News, 2010). During the investigation the police found transplant candidates on their way abroad to have surgery. Some were at Israel's Ben-Gurion International Airport awaiting departure. Other fraud victims were already abroad and due to return to Israel after police notified them that some of the traffickers had been arrested (Ma'an News Agency, 2010). "The defendants operated in an organized, systematic and ongoing manner, and traded in human beings like they were objects being passed from hand to hand, for the sake of harvesting their kidneys," attorney Bassem Kandalaft of the Northern District Prosecution wrote in the indictment. "They succeeded in executing their plot by exploiting, for their own profit, the economic and social distress of their victims" (Roffe-Ofir, 2010).

Although organized crime rings perform much of human trafficking, it often could not occur without the collusion of official personnel. For instance, in this particular case, one of the suspects was a retired Israeli army reserve brigadier-general who had been awarded a medal of valor in the 1973 Arab-Israeli War. Other suspects in the case were two lawyers as well as organ traffickers and their agents (Ma'an News Agency, 2010; Khoury & Ashkenazi, 2010).

WHAT HAPPENS TO VICTIMS AFTER TRAFFICKING

Victims of international sex trafficking who manage to escape do have access to shelters and a variety of social services. The government has supervised and funded a local NGO shelter operation for foreign victims of sex trafficking. In 2008 it allocated $1.25 million to the shelter for the purposes of medical care, security, and operations. In the same year the shelter assisted 44 women, 12 of whom were referred by law enforcement. The shelter offers medical treatment, psychiatric and social services, stipends, temporary residency, and work permits to foreign female victims of sex trafficking. It has been reported that the shelter is reluctant to accept victims with children and that victims who attempt to access medical or psychological care outside the shelter cannot do so unless they have first paid for insurance (U.S. Department of State, 2009).

As with all nations, one challenge for prosecutors is convincing victims to testify against their traffickers. Many victims fear retribution if they testify, a concern that is not without merit. In the sex-trafficking case that involved Israeli mobster Rami Saban, the prosecutors and NGOs expressed concern that the suspects would use any means possible to harm the victims who testified or planned to testify against them. Their concerns were realized when a victim who planned to testify against the traffickers was killed in a hit-and-run incident in Uzbekistan. The traffickers allegedly arranged the murder (IRIN, 2009; Goren, 2009; Jerusalem Post, 2009). Fear of harm and retribution at the hands of one's traffickers does not dissipate simply because the victim has been rescued. Intimidation and abuse are commonly used means to maintain control over victims during the trafficking experience—a technique that Saban and his colleagues relished. Police have in their possession recordings of Saban ordering the physical punishment and murder of victims who refused to prostitute (IRIN, 2009). A suspect turned state witness who had exclusive access to the syndicate and its operations provided the recordings (Goren, 2009; Jerusalem Post, 2009). Saban allegedly put a gun to one woman's head and beat her when he suspected that she had tried to escape. He also allegedly assaulted two women for refusing to comply with his demands and locked one of the women in an office for a week as punishment (Jerusalem Post, 2009).

The government's anti-trafficking efforts still focus primarily on foreign victims of sex trafficking. As a result, internal and international victims of forced-labor and internal sex-trafficking victims often go without shelter, medical, and psychological services. Fortunately, this situation is slowly changing. Protective services were made available for the first time to Israeli victims of sex trafficking and international forced-labor victims in early 2009. Additionally, in response to the growing issue of internal sex trafficking, the government has created two state-funded shelters for Israeli women forced into prostitution. The Knesset also passed the Legal Aid Law (Amendment 9), which grants free legal aid to victims of trafficking and slavery (U.S. Department of State, 2009; Zebede, 2009). Another positive step is that in February 2009 the minister of justice signed Penal Regulations 5769-2009, which allows the confiscated property and funds of trafficking offenders to be distributed to victims as well as NGOs and government agencies to support victim rehabilitation programs (U.S. Department of State, 2009).

Historically, male victims of human trafficking have not been acknowledged. For instance, all of the 382 trafficking victims who received shelter between 2004 and 2007 were women (UNODC, 2009). This fact further illustrates the marginalization of male trafficking victims, who are often victims of forced labor. Fortunately, this too is beginning to change: in 2008 the Ministry of Social Affairs solicited bids for the creation of three facilities for labor-trafficking victims and selected an NGO to operate them. The bids included a shelter for women, a shelter for men, and three short-term apartments. As a result, the Atlas shelter for male victims of slavery and forced labor housed 50 men during 2009. The Israeli government reports that all trafficking victims in the shelters received temporary visas and work visas upon request. Also, the Ministry of Interior (MOI) published procedures for granting temporary visas to victims of slavery and forced labor. This step resulted in temporary visa extensions for 27 victims trafficked for commercial sexual exploitation and 17 victims of forced labor in 2008. Unfortunately, in January 2010 the MOI announced its intention to cancel the policy of issuing B1 visas to trafficking victims.[1] It is unclear whether this decision will in fact be implemented. In 2010 and 2011, B1 visa requests continued to be approved by the MOI. NGOs note that some requests, including those by persons who entered Israel through Sinai,

Egypt, have not been granted (U.S. Department of State, 2009, 2010a, 2011, 2012).

One concern is what happens to persons from the OPT who are trafficked to Israel. Typically, persons from the territories who are found to be in Israel illegally are summarily returned to the territories without an investigation as to whether they are trafficking victims. This practice makes victims vulnerable to potential retribution and re-trafficking when they are returned to the same set of circumstances that made them initially vulnerable to human trafficking. The most common patterns of trafficking movement between Israel and the OPT are from Israel to the West Bank; from the West Bank into Israel and East Jerusalem; within the West Bank; and from the Gaza Strip into Israel. Those trafficked into Israel and within the territories are predominantly from Nablus, Jenin, Hebron, Ramallah, Al-Ram, Jerusalem, and the Gaza Strip. However, some of the women trafficked into the West Bank from Israel are from Russia and Ukraine (SAWA/UNIFEM, 2008).

The fragmentation and limited scope of the Palestinian judicial system often leaves Palestinian victims of human trafficking without legal redress. Persons who live in the OPT can be deemed internal or international victims of trafficking depending on how many authorities they encounter. For instance, if the victim encounters the Israeli authorities and the Palestinian National Authority (PNA) at a checkpoint, then the act is considered international trafficking. If the victim just comes across the PNA then it is considered internal trafficking. Another critical concern is that the authorities in Israel and the OPT do not collaborate on anti-trafficking efforts or share investigative information (SAWA/UNIFEM, 2008).

WHAT HAPPENS TO TRAFFICKERS

Saban, the primary suspect in the sex-trafficking case, was charged in March 2009 with 23 felony offenses that included operating a brothel, managing a brothel, solicitation, conspiracy to commit a crime, assault, forgery, money laundering, forcing a person to leave her country of residence to work as a prostitute, and harassing witnesses. This was not the first time Saban had been accused of human trafficking. He was convicted and sentenced to 31 months in prison for human trafficking in 2001. He was also found guilty of operating a brothel a year later (Jerusalem Post, 2009).

In 2008 there were 9 cases investigated for alleged sex trafficking, 6 indictments filed, and 6 convictions obtained against traffickers in Israel. This is 32 fewer convictions than in 2007. Sentences ranged from 4 months to 7 years in prison as well as fines. During the same recording period, 12 prosecutions remained ongoing, and 8 cases were awaiting appeal (U.S. Department of State, 2009). From 2003 through 2006 there were 154 cases of human trafficking and 1,577 trafficking-related cases investigated; and 117 traffickers were convicted. Of persons who received sanctions during that time, 2 received less than one year, 56 received between 1 and 5 years, 50 received between 5 and 10 years, and 24 received more than 10 years (UNODC, 2009).

All trafficking offenders convicted in 2005 and 2006 were involved in trafficking for commercial sexual exploitation. In 2007 two persons were convicted of trafficking for the purposes of organ removal (UNODC, 2009). The latter statistic may reflect the broadened reach of the 2006 anti-trafficking law and an increased awareness among law enforcement that other forms of trafficking besides sex trafficking do occur. Still, enforcement seems to lag behind realities. For instance, in 2010, although the government convicted seven persons under trafficking statutes, it did not secure any convictions for labor trafficking. The government also convicted six sex traffickers under nontrafficking statutes; although the cases were prosecuted under trafficking statutes, the charges were reduced during plea negotiations. The sentences for sex traffickers convicted under trafficking statutes ranged from 6 months' community service to 8.5 years' imprisonment, while prison sentences for those convicted under nontrafficking statutes were between 24 months and 7.5 years. Of precedential significance is that in 2011 the government convicted two labor traffickers under the trafficking statute for the forced labor of a Filipina domestic worker. The government also convicted an alleged labor trafficker under a non-trafficking statute. He was sentenced to 8 years' imprisonment. Fifteen sex-trafficking offenders were also convicted in 2011, some of whom were charged under the trafficking statute but convicted under reduced charges based on limitations of available evidence. Sentences for the sex traffickers ranged from 8 months' to 5 years' imprisonment. While labor trafficking convictions still lag behind those of sex traffickers, authorities are taking some measures to address the issue. Authorities revoked the recruitment licenses and special permits to recruit foreign workers of 18 recruitment agencies in 2009–2010, and investigations and prosecutions of labor traffickers are increasing. For example, during 2008 the government opened 24 investigations in alleged cases of forced labor and opened 48 investigations into the unlawful withholding of the passports of migrant workers (U.S. Department of State, 2009, 2010, 2012). During 2009 police opened 61 investigations of cases involving forced labor and 28 investigations of cases involving the withholding of passports. The government initiated the prosecution of 32 suspected offenders on charges of forced labor, exploitation of vulnerable populations, and withholding a passport. In 2010 the Israeli government obtained 3 convictions against those who extracted recruitment fees from foreign workers; sentences ranged from 15 to 50 months' imprisonment. The government also revoked the license of one recruitment agency for charging migrant workers illegal fees (U.S. Department of State, 2010a, 2011).

INTERNAL EFFORTS TO DECREASE TRAFFICKING

The national coordinator for anti-trafficking efforts provides anti-trafficking lectures to army units, municipal workers, social workers, and students. The Authority for the Advancement of Women, the Ministry of Education, the State Attorney's Office, and the Ministry of Justice's Legal Aid Branch sponsor anti-trafficking lectures, seminars, and conferences throughout the country (U.S. Department of State, 2009). In an effort to decrease the demand for commercial sex in Israel, the Knesset drafted a private bill in 2008, the Prohibition of the Use of Paid Sexual Services Law, which would criminalize clients who pay for sexual services in the commercial sex industry. The bill prescribes six months' imprisonment or enrollment in an education program for first-time offenders (Ministry of Justice, 2010). Another bill, Increased Penalties for Prostitution Advertising, passed on March 28, 2011, aims to reduce commercial sexual exploitation. Under the law, offenders who advertise or facilitate information for prostitution services face sentencing or a fine. The offense is punishable by 5 years' imprisonment if the service advertised would be performed by a minor and 3 years' imprisonment if the provider is an adult. Courts are authorized to double the fine on corporate offenders (Ministry of Justice and the Ministry of Foreign Affairs, 2009; Knesset, 2011b).

In order to aid women in prostitution—including sex-trafficking victims—in December 2008 the Ministry of Health and Social Affairs put $2.5 million toward emergency apartments in Tel Aviv and Haifa, a mobile clinic, and a hotline. Seventy women benefited from the project, but none were identified as trafficking victims. In 2008 the Committee of Directors General approved and circulated procedures to identify labor-trafficking victims to relevant government entities and NGOs. It has been reported by NGOs that the guidelines were not implemented and that the Detention Tribunal that reviews immigration violation cases still misclassifies labor-trafficking cases on a regular basis, with the result that these victims are detained and deported. One potential safeguard against the forced labor of caregivers is a system launched by the interministerial committee for licensing nursing recruitment agencies and employing foreign caregivers. The system allows workers who legally enter the country to obtain other employment if they lose or choose to leave their job (U.S. Department of State, 2009). There remains a somewhat strained relationship between the government's intent to protect foreign workers and the belief that foreign workers are taking jobs away from Israeli citizens. For instance, the Socio-Economic Agenda for 2008–2010, recommendations made to the government of Israel by the National Economic Council, was adopted by the government on April 22, 2007, which reveals its resolve to further reduce the number of foreign workers. The National Economic Council reports that the majority of legal foreign workers are employed in construction, agriculture, and care for the elderly and are competing for jobs with Israelis at the lower wage levels. Consequently, the government states that there is no choice but to continue severely reducing their number (National Economic Council, 2007). In line with this, on May 16, 2011, the Knesset passed the Entry into Israel (Amendment No. 21), which grants the MOI the authority to establish a cap on the number of times a foreign worker who works in home health care for the elderly may transfer to a new employer. The stated objective of the law is to prevent misuse of visa and residence permits (Knesset, 2011c). NGOs have expressed concern about the new law because it binds labor migrants in home health care to their employers, increasing their vulnerability to exploitation and human trafficking (Cohen & Mozgovaya, 2011).

As with other nations, it appears that Israel's recent immigration and anti-trafficking agendas are in direct conflict. The new Entry into Israel amendment binds foreign workers to sectors and geographic regions, and migrants who are found in violation for more than 90 days will be deported (Knesset, 2011c). The result could be similar to the treatment of temporary worker visas in the United States, which has created employer dependence and the opportunity for employee exploitation and deportation without thorough investigation of whether the worker is a trafficking victim. One recent concern expressed by experts and confirmed by the Knesset's Research and Information Center is that anti-trafficking efforts have diminished since the newly created immigration and border control authority (the Oz unit) replaced the Immigration Police. NGOs assert that Oz inspectors do not convey information to police when they encounter a suspected crime against migrant workers. NGOs also report that all labor trafficking prosecutions since the initiation of the Oz unit were a result of NGO efforts, not of investigations by the government (U.S. Department of State, 2010a).

Israel has taken numerous positive anti-trafficking steps on paper. It remains to be seen whether implementation will be successful and what continuing impact the new immigration policies will have on the nation's anti-trafficking efforts. While the anti-trafficking law encompasses victims of forced labor, the government has largely failed to identify these victims and to prosecute the employers who exploit them. In 2009, 61 forced-labor cases were opened, but these cases face long delays. For instance, the first forced-labor indictment under the anti-trafficking law was filed in 2008 and was still pending in 2010. The same is true for internal trafficking for commercial sexual exploitation. The government has taken measures on paper to provide internal victims with shelter and services, but law enforcement often fails to identify these victims.

It would aid victims greatly if the Israeli government and authorities in the OPT would collaborate in sharing information on trafficking cases and investigations. Otherwise this gap in communication will continue to provide traffickers with a loophole where they can exploit Palestinian women in Israel and the OPT without consequences. These women are extremely marginalized and have little access to assistance whether in Israel or the OPT.

PART III
Unrest, Displacement, and Who Is in Charge

The displaced person's experience is often littered with the death and murder of loved ones, rape, physical abuse, and the pillage of land and property. Uprooted, displaced persons have lost their support system, and with the ghosts of their experiences in tow, they are forced to migrate to a different town or nation. Continued uncertainty, financial strain, and lack of legal and/or societal inclusion go hand-in-hand with displacement, which results in acute vulnerability to human trafficking.

In Colombia, civil unrest has resulted in between 3.6 and 5.2 million internally displaced persons. The Constitutional Court in Colombia has ruled that the disparity between the rights guaranteed to internally displaced persons by domestic law and the inadequate resources and institutional capacity of the government to protect these rights has resulted in an "unconstitutional state of affairs." Forced to work and live outside the periphery of society, displaced persons have minimal access to education, health care, and housing. Countless paramilitary groups exist in Colombia and are notorious for the violence and havoc they wreak on communities, particularly those of Afro-Colombians and indigenous people. They seize land and cause displacement throughout the countryside, and they use children to further their objectives. Children are forced to be soldiers, sexual partners, and workers in the illegal drug trade.

As a result of the U.S. invasion of Iraq, an estimated 4.8 million Iraqis were displaced between 2003 and 2009. Children, who make up 38–40 percent of those internally displaced in Iraq, face abduction and violence, and are used by Iraqi insurgent groups as spies or scouts, to plant improvised explosive devices, and as suicide bombers. Externally displaced Iraqis don't have it any easier. In Syria, host to the largest number of externally displaced Iraqis, the economic and social situation of Iraqi refugees has made them immensely vulnerable to human trafficking. Fifty Iraqi females are imprisoned on prostitution charges each week in Syria; many are trafficking victims.

Syria, since March 2011, is experiencing its own civil unrest. Despite the government's agreement with the Arab League, Syrian security forces have continued violence against civilians. As a result of army defections, the Syrian government claims that the opposition has become more militarized. The human rights violations by President Bashar al-Assad and his regime were the impetus for the uprising, yet a November 2011 opinion poll revealed that 55 percent of polled Syrians do not want him to resign. For many, the desire for Assad to stay in power is based on a fear for the future of the country. As the death toll and potential for civil war increase, there is the real threat of a deterioration of society, lawlessness, continued violence, displacement, economic hardship, and the absence of a just law-enforcement and judicial system (which is already in question). This situation sets the stage for a continuing increase in numerous human rights violations, including exploitation and human trafficking.

In Colombia and Iraq there remains the question of who is in charge. On the surface, the rebel groups in Colombia are disconnected from the government; but former paramilitary commanders and experts say the guerrillas are merely the armed wing of a multiheaded monster. Those in charge of the economic and political arms of the paramilitary groups, they say, are high-level officials, politicians, members of the public security forces, business leaders, contractors, and foreign investors. The degree of collusion between members of the government and the paramilitaries is not yet known, but it is suspected that the real leaders of the paramilitaries are those who currently exercise political power.

Just over a year after the United States invaded Iraq, the U.S. was an occupying power that claimed to have no responsibility as the occupying authority. By that point, the U.S. government had handed sovereignty back to Iraq multiple times, yet it still remained the occupying power and in ultimate control of the nation. As an occupying power, the United States handled appointments and dismissals and even granted itself, its contractors, and the Iraqi military immunity from the Iraqi legal system. Under a U.S. order (CPA Order 17), the Coalition Provisional Authority (CPA) and the Multi-National Force, along with foreign liaison missions, their personnel, property, funds, and

assets, and all international consultants, including contractors and subcon-
tractors, were immune from the Iraqi legal process. In June 2004 the U.S.
government also imposed a formal policy to ignore human rights abuses com-
mitted by the Iraqi military. Under the policy, coalition troops were barred
from investigating any violations committed by Iraqi troops against other
Iraqis. Thus those assigned to protect civilians were also, as enforcement per-
sonnel, in a unique position to exploit them with immunity.

For internally displaced persons in Colombia, without significant changes
and protections of indigenous and Afro-Colombian communities, it doesn't
much matter who legally rules the country when paramilitaries continue to rule
their lives. In Iraq, the Iraqi government passed legislation to rescind CPA Order
17 in 2008, but the legislation does not specifically address how past incidents
will be addressed. In the United States there is at least one large lawsuit against
a U.S. contractor under the Trafficking Victims Protection Reauthorization Act.
A suit was brought against Kellogg Brown & Root and its Jordanian subcontrac-
tor Daoud & Partners for allegedly trafficking Nepali workers in Iraq; twelve of
whom were kidnapped and executed by insurgents. The case is ongoing, and a
trial date has been set for April 29, 2013.

CHAPTER 6

Colombia

> Whether it was the police, the army, or the paramilitaries: when
> they said "go to the front," you had to go, and it was hard
> because we had to walk for days without sleep and hardly
> eating anything. I was saddest when I saw friends die.
>
> —ESTELLE, A CHILD SOLDIER

Understanding Colombia's trafficking scenario depends upon understanding the displacement that has resulted from decades of civil unrest. As recently as December 2009 there were between 3.6 and 5.2 million internally displaced persons (IDPs) in Colombia. This number places the nation on par with Sudan, the country with the largest displacement situation in the world (4.9 million) (IDMC, 2009; IOM, 2011). The Observatory on Human Rights and Displacement reported that 89,000 people were displaced in the first half of 2011. The government reported lower numbers and stated that 44,000 people were registered during that time (IDMC, 2011). The nonprofit and nonpartisan U.S. Office on Colombia reported in 2004 that women in particular have been disproportionately displaced by the armed conflict. The report stated that over 50 percent of Colombian IDPs were women, and over 70 percent were either women or children (USOC, 2004). Displaced Colombians have little access to education, health care services, and housing (UNCRC, 2000). Consequently, they are more vulnerable to exploitation, including human trafficking and domestic violence. The report stated that 52 percent of Colombian displaced women faced domestic abuse compared to 20 percent of nondisplaced women (USOC, 2004).

Despite the assurance of equal rights and protections for all Colombian citizens under the constitution, Colombia has had a longstanding division between the wealthy and poor, with little to no social or economic mobility for those not born into the upper class. The inflexible social hierarchy created opportunity for guerrilla and paramilitary groups to insert themselves into the fabric of Colombia under the guise of helping the disadvantaged. Groups such as the Revolutionary Armed Forces of Colombia (FARC) and the National Liberation Army (ELN) are Marxist revolutionary guerrilla groups that claim to represent the interests of the rural, and more recently the urban, poor (Hanson, 2009); yet both groups have forcibly taken land from the poor. Afro-Colombians in particular have been unable to protect their land rights from paramilitary and guerrilla forces. While land titles are inalienable, paramilitary and guerrilla forces are not known to abide by the letter of the law (UNHCR, 2004).[1] Guerrilla and paramilitary groups also recruit disadvantaged children within Colombia to further their objectives. They use children as combatants, informants, messengers, sexual partners, transporters, placers of bombs, guarders of hostages, kidnappers, spies, and workers in the illegal drug trade (U.S. Department of Labor, 2004; U.S. Department of State, 2010a, 2010b).

To address the situation, the Colombian government has tried to weaken guerrilla and paramilitary groups. In a series of attacks and counterattacks, it has been a roller coaster of a struggle. In 2008 the attacks against the guerrilla and paramilitary groups appeared to be effective—particularly when it seemed that the FARC was weakened. But the conflict regained strength in 2009 and 2010. The paramilitary armed groups were remobilized and continued to commit significant human rights violations, threatening security in Colombia's cities (IDMC, 2009). The government struck back, and in September 2010 Colombian security forces killed Víctor Julio Suárez Rojas (a.k.a. Mono Jojoy), the second in command of the FARC, and roughly 20 other FARC members in a massive air strike in the region of La Macarena in the department of Meta in central Colombia (Alsema, 2010).

At certain times, the attacks by the Colombian government on the guerrilla and paramilitary groups have reaped short-term positive results, but experts emphasize that unless the political and economic powers behind the organizations are identified, they will never truly diminish. Imprisoned former leaders of the dissolved paramilitary group the United Self-Defense Forces of Colombia (AUC) say paramilitary organizations include high-level officials, politicians, members of the public security forces, business leaders, contractors, and foreign investors (Vieira, 2010).

TRAFFICKING WITHIN COLOMBIA

Internal trafficking and child labor are major issues in Colombia. Forced labor of boys and sex trafficking of young girls has historically been in large part a result of the strength of the paramilitary and guerrilla groups who use children to further their objectives. Forced marriage; involuntary domestic servitude; forced labor in sweatshops, grocery stores, and farms; forced begging; and forced street vending have also been reported (U.S. Department of Labor, 2004; UNODC, 2009a; U.S. Department of State, 2010a, 2010b).

Displaced persons are particularly susceptible to trafficking everywhere. There are discrepancies between the Colombian government's estimate of IDPs and that of other monitors. For instance, in 2009 the government reported that slightly more than 120,000 persons were internally displaced, while a national monitor estimated the figure to be closer to 290,000 (IDMC, 2009). Regardless, the number of displaced persons continues to be strikingly high. While most of the displacement in 2009 resulted from small-scale events, 80 large-scale events resulted in the displacement of 19,000 people. Most of the displaced persons from the large-scale events were Afro-Colombian and indigenous persons in the departments of Antioquia, Chocó, Cauca, Nariño, and Valle del Cauca. About half of the larger displacements took place in Nariño, a department in the west that borders Ecuador and where numerous assassinations of indigenous people were reported in 2009 (IDMC, 2009).

Internally displaced persons are entitled to emergency state assistance, but they must register and be certified by the government. Women in rural areas are less likely to possess identification than men. Also, there is a negative stigma associated with registration. In 2004 it was estimated that 60 percent of IDPs were not registered and as a result did not receive aid (USOC, 2004). Under-registration of IDPs continues to exist not only because of lack of information, stigma, or fear, but also because of a high rate of application rejections. The latter issue is one that the government has begun to address (IDMC, 2009). Displacement also means that IDPs have a particularly difficult time obtaining economic and social benefits and are excluded from the formal labor market. In 2009, 89 percent of IDPs failed to earn the minimum salary of $260 per month and relied primarily on informal work (IDMC, 2009). The informal economy is not regulated, and workers are vulnerable to exploitation, including internal and international trafficking. The larger cities in Colombia, such as Bogotá, Cali, and Medellin, receive the most IDPs. The cities have tried to improve their response to receiving IDPs but face coordination and budget constraints. Displaced persons also flee to the nearby countries of Ecuador, Venezuela, and Panama (IDMC, 2009).

The Colombian government and other monitors report a range of estimates regarding the number of child soldiers used by guerrilla and military groups. The organization War Child International estimated that there were at least 14,000 child soldiers in Colombia in 2007, half of whom it believed were used by the FARC and the ELN. The children were commonly recruited in their neighborhood and at school. Other children were kidnapped from their school as they left at the end of the day. In 2009 the Colombian government estimated that guerrilla and paramilitary groups forcibly recruited thousands of children (U.S. Department of State, 2010a, 2010b). The previous year, the Ministry of Defense gave more specific estimates, stating that more than 4,600 FARC members and more than 1,300 ELN members were minors and that most guerrilla fighters had joined the guerrilla ranks as children. In 2009 the United Nations Children's Fund (UNICEF) and the Colombian Family Welfare Institute estimated that the number of children participating in illegal armed groups was between 10,000 and 13,000. These are the most recent estimates on the total of child soldiers in Colombia. Colombian authorities did report that they identified 483 cases of children recruited by armed groups in 2011. In the same year 835 children participated in the reintegration program for child soldiers found in the ranks of armed groups. In its effort to recruit children, the FARC issued letters to indigenous communities delineating a policy to conduct child recruitment. Recipients were warned not to challenge the policy (U.S. Department of State, 2010b, 2012). Carlos, 10 years old, recalled what it was like when these groups came to his town:

I was very young, around 6 years old, when the army, the guerrillas, and the paramilitaries came to our neighborhood. They were
fighting in the mountains, and the boys who lived there came
down to our neighborhood. One day my mother was ill and she
said, "I am going to buy pills." The guerrillas were outside the shop
and said, "Come here, we will give you a pill." It was not a pill, but
a bullet. I was very frightened. These people were walking around
and guarded the villages day and night. (War Child International,
2007)

Not all child soldiers are directly forced to work for the guerrilla and
paramilitary groups. Other factors cited for joining are ideology, lack
of socioeconomic options, a love of weapons, and desire for protection
or revenge (War Child International, 2007). For some children it is an
exchange of one harsh life for another. One child soldier, Estelle, was
repeatedly raped by her stepfather from the age of 5 to 11 and beaten
throughout her early childhood by her mother. At 11 years of age, Estelle
was recruited by the FARC and became a child soldier in constant fear
of being killed:

Whether it was the police, the army, or the paramilitaries: when
they said "go to the front," you had to go, and it was hard because
we had to walk for days without sleep and hardly eating anything.
I was saddest when I saw friends die. When I was thirteen I wanted
to run away. In the group I experienced war, hunger, and cold and
saw people die. One day I did run away. I was sent ahead as a scout
and suddenly my courage left me. I sat down and all I could do was
cry. When I heard music I looked out across the valley. Then, I
stopped thinking and ran down a little road and kept running.
(War Child International, 2007)

In addition to children used by guerrilla and paramilitary groups,
child labor is used in the production of at least eight products in Colombia: clay bricks, coal, coca, coffee, emeralds, gold, pornography, and
sugarcane. Coca production also involves forced labor of adults (U.S.
Department of Labor, 2009). The exploitation of children through sex
tourism is also a problem, particularly in the coastal cities of Cartagena

and Barranquilla. Many of the child victims have been displaced from their rural homes because of the unrest. In 2004 it was estimated that 1,500 boys and girls were victims of sexual tourism in Cartagena, some as young as 9 years old (Arrington, 2004; U.S. Department of State, 2010a). The U.S. State Department's 2010 *Trafficking in Persons Report* states that although some men experience forced labor, forced prostitution of women and children remains a larger problem (U.S. Department of State, 2010a). This claim is questionable, particularly when the number of children who are forced child soldiers for the guerrilla and paramilitary groups is included in the calculation. It is more likely that the number of forced-labor and sex-trafficking victims is equal, or close to it. Regardless, investigations focus primarily on sex trafficking. For instance, out of 159 investigations in 2008 and 215 investigations in 2009, there were only 2 and 80 investigations of forced labor, respectively (U.S. Department of State, 2010a). Still, the increase from 2 to 80 is positive and noteworthy.

A particular challenge for the Colombian government in its struggle against its guerrilla and paramilitary groups is the lack of cooperation by neighboring Venezuelan and Ecuadoran authorities. Leaders of the FARC and the ELN have sought refuge in both nations. One such case is that of Luciano Marín Arango (a.k.a. Iván Márquez), a member of the FARC whom the Colombian government believes to be in Venezuela (El Universal, 2009). Colombia's intelligence agency, the Departamento Administrativo de Seguridad (DAS), believes that Luciano Marín Arango and other high-level rebels move back and forth between Colombia and Venezuela, specifically hiding in bordering municipalities of Machiques, Venezuela, which borders Cesar in Colombia, and in Nula, Venezuela, which borders Arauca in Colombia. The DAS states that 28 FARC camps exist in Machiques and Nula and have enough space to house up to 1,500 persons (Palmer, 2010; Pachico, 2010). Other FARC leaders are likely hiding in Venezuela's Perijá National Park. The DAS believes that Venezuelan military officials and civilians help the FARC guerrillas by providing them with arms and food (Palmer, 2010; Pachico, 2010).

Relations between the Colombian and Venezuelan governments are not optimal. In July 2010 Luis Alfonso Hoyos, Colombia's ambassador to the Organization of American States (OAS), gave a presentation to the

OAS that included a series of photographs, maps, coordinates, and videos that, according to the Colombian government, are proof of the presence of illegal armed groups in Venezuelan territory. In response, Venezuela's OAS ambassador, Roy Chaderton, stated that Colombia's evidence was not valid and disapproved of the use of the OAS as a platform for presenting it (OAS, 2010). In the case of Luciano Marín Arango, the Colombian government emphasizes its frustration with Venezuelan authorities. "One would like that, in accordance with international obligations related to judicial cooperation, Venezuela's authorities would capture, take to court, and extradite or deport him [Luciano Marín Arango] to Colombia," said Gabriel Silva, Colombia's Defense Minister (El Universal, 2009).

The government of Colombia has also had tension with its neighbor Ecuador, specifically surrounding an event in 2008 when the Colombian army carried out a raid on a FARC camp in Ecuador. The army killed FARC leader Luis Edgar Devia Silva (a.k.a. Raúl Reyes) and retrieved his computers (Begg, 2010). The Ecuadoran government believed this act undermined its sovereignty and wanted the Colombian government to hand over Reyes' files, which the Colombian government claimed contained evidence of collusion between the Ecuadoran government and the FARC. More recently the governments of Colombia and Ecuador have been trying to restore their relationship, but the files were a serious point of contention. Former Colombian president Álvaro Uribe refused to provide the files, but President Juan Manuel Santos handed them over on the day of his inauguration in August 2010 (Begg, 2010). Recently Ecuadoran and Colombian authorities have jointly investigated several trafficking cases (U.S. Department of State, 2010a). This development may indicate that relations between the two nations are on the mend.

Colombia is also a destination nation for human trafficking for forced labor (domestic servants, vendors, and beggars) and commercial sexual exploitation. The majority of victims identified by state authorities in Colombia between 2005 and August 2007 were from Honduras (19 persons) and Ecuador (4 persons) (UNODC, 2009a; U.S. Department of State, 2010a, 2010b). Another country of origin is Peru. An anonymous Interpol investigations officer revealed that in 2008 a trafficking ring holding 30 Peruvian nationals captive was dismantled. The laborers had been forced to work in the city of Bucaramanga (Martínez, 2009).

TRAFFICKING ABROAD

Colombia's civil unrest has significantly contributed to its existence as a primary source nation of human trafficking for the Western Hemisphere. In 2005 it was estimated that many of the 45,000 to 50,000 Colombian nationals working abroad as prostitutes were trafficking victims (U.S. Department of State, 2006; HRI, 2006). Fortunately, this number appears to be on the decline. For instance, Colombians made up more than 35 percent of trafficking victims in Spain in 2000 and 2001. This number decreased to 10 percent by 2006. Between 2001 and 2007, nearly 12 percent of identified trafficking victims in Japan were from Colombia. While the number spiked to 43 victims in 2003, it dropped to zero in 2006 and 2007 (MOFA, 2008; UNODC, 2009b). Regardless, international trafficking of Colombians remains an issue. Persons from Colombia are trafficked to the Caribbean, Europe, Asia, North America, and other Latin American countries for forced labor and commercial sexual exploitation (UNODC, 2009a; U.S. Department of State, 2010a). One such case involves 30 Colombian women lured by false jobs and taken to a brothel in Ibarra, Ecuador. Fortunately, the women were discovered within several days (Martínez, 2009). In September 2009, 54 Colombian women were reportedly detained in a Trinidad and Tobago prison. According to Ilba Miriam Hoyos Castañeda, assistant attorney general for the rights of child, adolescent, and family, the women were victims of a Colombian-Venezuelan network that trafficked women to Venezuela and Trinidad and Tobago. What is of particular concern is that in December 2009, 26 of the Colombian victims were reportedly still being held in a penitentiary in Trinidad and Tobago (Vanovac, 2009; El Colombiano, 2009). The articles regarding this case do not state explicitly that the women were trafficked for commercial sexual exploitation, nor is it clear whether the initial number was incorrect or whether 28 of the women had been previously released.

Colombians also face forced labor abroad. For instance, in 2009, 56 Colombian forced-labor victims were discovered on a Venezuelan shrimp farm (U.S. Department of State, 2010a). The Venezuelan government is investigating the case. In another case, a Colombian woman, María, accepted employment as a domestic worker in a U.S. city (for protection, the victim does not disclose the exact location). Upon arrival in the

United States, María's captors confiscated her passport, forced her to perform domestic duties daily from 5 a.m. to midnight, and gave her only vegetables to eat. As a result of the limited diet and the long hours of labor, María's weight plummeted from 128 pounds to 90 pounds during the 39 days of forced labor. She was not allowed to contact her family, and in fact her captors blocked the phone to ensure that she had no means to contact anyone outside the home. With the help of a neighbor, María contacted the police. Unfortunately, the police did little more than force her captors to return Maria's passport to her and reprimand them for mistreating her. Frightened by the police visit, María's captors told her that if she did not sign a paper exonerating them from all responsibility, they would report her to the police and make false charges against her so that she would face years in jail. María managed to escape when her captors were sleeping. The neighbor drove her to a shelter for human trafficking victims (Martínez, 2009).

WHAT HAPPENS TO VICTIMS AFTER TRAFFICKING

The government does not operate shelters for trafficking victims but does refer victims to local NGOs. Authorities do provide psychological and medical care, access to financial and employment assistance, and legal support. Although, the government does not have formal procedures for the identification of trafficking victims among vulnerable populations such as displaced persons or prostitutes, authorities do have an interagency anti-trafficking operations center to refer those victims who have been identified to service providers. The operations center also allows authorities to track criminal investigations and prosecutions as well as to collect nationwide information and statistics regarding trafficking crimes. During 2009 the government identified 155 victims of transnational trafficking, half of them forced-labor victims and half sex-trafficking victims. The majority were adults. Seventy-eight percent of the victims were provided with services. In 2010 the government identified 338 child soldiers; 76 transnational trafficking victims, made up equally of forced-labor and sex-trafficking victims; and 15 internal trafficking victims. It is unclear how many of the victims received services, though the child soldiers were referred to the government's Family

Welfare Institute for services. Victims who assist in the investigation and prosecution of their trafficker(s) are provided housing through the nation's witness protection program, though most victims do not come forward because of fear of retaliation (U.S. Department of State, 2010a, 2010b, 2011). Their concerns are not without merit. Those who participate in the witness protection program often do not blend into their new environment, and want to contact family and friends from home. Also, harm can come to family members remaining in the trafficked person's hometown (Pearson, 2002; U.S. Department of State, 2006). Out of 80 trafficked women assisted between 1997 and 2000, only 4 filed a formal report with authorities. Instead, it is officials or family members of victims who bring most cases of trafficking forward. In 2009 only 4 victims participated in prosecutions against their traffickers (Anti-Slavery International, 2002; U.S. Department of State, 2010a). There is no specialized legal mechanism that grants temporary residence status to foreign victims, but authorities can provide victims with temporary permission to stay in the nation on a case-by-case basis. Victims are also eligible for humanitarian assistance through the government (U.S. Department of State, 2010a). It is unclear how often, if ever, temporary status is granted to victims.

The Colombian government does provide some support to Colombian victims trafficked abroad, though the reported numbers are erratic at best. Consular officials reported aiding 22 victims in 2008, 110 in 2009, 106 in 2010, and 9 in 2011. One hurdle is that victim services overseas are limited to consular districts with at least 10,000 Colombian residents. Consequently, their services are not typically available to victims in isolated areas. The International Organization for Migration has helped Colombian victims obtain protection and services in the country where they were trafficked and has safely brought them back to Colombia. Officials have also set up interviewing facilities at the international airport in Bogotá, in order to greet returning victims and debrief them on their rights and the procedures on bringing charges against their traffickers (U.S. Department of State, 2006, 2010a). Interpol officers state that while Colombian anti-trafficking law is sufficiently stringent, a significant increase in anti-trafficking training must take place so that victims are not treated as culpable parties to their own trafficking experience. "During legal proceedings we often see victims being 'hammered' with questions like 'why did you go?' or 'how could you not realize it was a bogus offer?'" Interpol officers told the news agency Inter Press Service (Martínez, 2009).

WHAT HAPPENS TO TRAFFICKERS

While the number of convictions of those who have committed trafficking offenses is not high, it does appear, generally, to be on the rise. The United Nations Office on Drugs and Crime (UNODC) states that from 2003 to September 2009, only 3 prosecutions and 3 convictions for trafficking in persons were recorded (UNODC, 2009a). The U.S. State Department reports a higher number of convictions: 2 in 2005, 10 in 2006, 6 in 2007, 16 in 2008, 14 in 2009, 17 in 2010, and 16 in 2011. Sentencing of traffickers also appears to be increasing. In 2005 persons convicted of trafficking offenses received 9 years' imprisonment compared to 48 months to 6.5 years in 2006, 4 to 12 years in 2007, 4.5 to 14 years in 2008, 7 to 27 years in 2009, 7 to 23 years in 2010, and 2 to 26 years in 2011. Moreover, the number of trafficking investigations were increasing over all, until 2011: 49 in 2006, 182 in 2007, 159 in 2008, 215 in 2009, 144 in 2010, and 72 in 2011. The number of investigations of labor trafficking increased from 2 in 2008 to 80 in 2009 (U.S. Department of State, 2006, 2007, 2008, 2009, 2010a, 2011, 2012). Particularly noteworthy is that the government attained its first labor trafficking conviction in 2010. What is concerning and potentially regressive is that the majority of investigations in 2011 focused on transnational sex trafficking; there was only one reported investigation of forced child labor. Furthermore, all 16 convictions in 2011 were obtained in transnational sex-trafficking cases. Despite the window of increasing investigations between 2006 and 2009, it seems that sex tourism has continued to slip under the radar. For instance, there were no reported prosecutions or convictions of child sex tourists in 2009, 2010, or 2011 (U.S. Department of State, 2010a, 2011, 2012).

INTERNAL EFFORTS TO DECREASE TRAFFICKING

In 2002 Colombia made human trafficking a specific offense. The law prohibited promoting, inducing, constraining, enabling, financing, co-operating, or participating in a person's transfer within the national territory or abroad by resorting to any form of violence, ruse, or decep-tion, for exploitation purposes, to lead such person to work in prostitu-tion, pornography, debt bondage, begging, forced labor, servile marriage, slavery for purposes of obtaining financial profit, or any other benefit either for himself or for another person (Pearson, 2002). In August 2005 new anti-trafficking legislation (Law 985) was adopted. Under the law, a victim's consent is irrelevant when defining situations of human trafficking, which means defendants cannot raise consent as a means of defense. Offenders face a minimum sentence of 13 to 23 years' impris-onment. The law also assigned the Interinstitutional Committee to Combat Trafficking in Persons the task of developing a comprehensive national action plan to eliminate human trafficking and to coordinate anti-trafficking policies (U.S. Department of State, 2006; UNODC, 2009a). Reforms to the penal code in 2011 increased fines for trafficking minors. The government also reformed penalties for using minors in the commission of crimes and established sentences of 10 to 20 years' imprisonment (U.S. Department of State, 2012). While the government has made moderate progress in increasing awareness of human traffick-ing, it relies a great deal on the work of international groups and NGOs to do the bulk of public awareness anti-trafficking campaigns.

There exist various official units that focus on human trafficking and related offenses. In 2007 the Public Prosecutor's Office established a National Unit of Human Rights that focuses on human trafficking. The DAS also has a unit that concentrates specifically on trafficking investigations and operates under the direction of Interpol (UNODC, 2009a; IOM, 2009). As part of the 2008 Comprehensive National Strat-egy Against Trafficking in Persons (Act 4786), the Ministries of Justice and Interior and the United Nations Office on Drugs and Crime field office implemented an Anti-Trafficking in Persons Operational Center (Centro Operativo Anti-Trata de Persona). The center's objective is to coordinate authorities' efforts to investigate and prosecute traffickers and provide assistance to victims (Act 4786, 2008; UNODC, 2009a; IOM,

2009). The Register Information System on Trafficking in Persons (Registro de Informacíon de Trata de Personas, RITRA) was created to assist in the coordination of trafficking case information. Launched in 2007, RITRA collects information from various institutions that deal with trafficking cases, such as direct assistance organizations and criminal justice agencies (UNODC, 2009a).

Colombia has strengthened and continued international anti-trafficking cooperation efforts with Argentina, Bolivia, Ecuador, El Salvador, Guatemala, Mexico, Nicaragua, Panama, Trinidad and Tobago, and the United States. The anti-trafficking partnerships focus on the repatriation of trafficking victims and trafficking investigations (U.S. Department of State, 2010a, 2011). Since January 2005 Japan and Colombia have worked jointly to eliminate human trafficking of Colombians to Japan, an effort that has involved significant obligation on both sides. Japan has agreed that Colombian victims are allowed to stay in Japanese shelters for extended periods as opposed to immediate deportation back to Colombia. Colombia has agreed that once victims return to Colombia, they will be offered immediate care. Colombian and Japanese officials have agreed to make efforts to exchange information on both victims and traffickers (Asahi Shimbun, 2005; U.S. Department of State, 2006). The Colombian government has also agreed to expand efforts to ensure that passports are not forgeries, and Japan has agreed to increase its enforcement of traffickers, who are often involved in organized crime mafias (Asahi Shimbun, 2005).

All 32 departments in Colombia have anti-trafficking committees, though they vary in degree of activity. Of concern is that civil society actors state that some of the committees exist only in name. In 2009 the government put together a national workshop for departments to discuss the challenges they face and the best practices. In addition, the Ministry of Education has introduced an anti-trafficking component into the education curriculum, specifically in sex education. And in contrast to many other nations, in an unusual but potentially beneficial anti-trafficking measure, Colombian authorities have trained 171 journalists to improve awareness and increase accurate media coverage of the trafficking situation in Colombia (U.S. Department of State, 2010a, 2012).

While all of these measures are certainly positive, one key step to reducing human trafficking in Colombia is to halt the civil unrest.

Significant efforts and successes have occurred. Eight former leaders of the now demobilized AUC paramilitary group have been imprisoned and charged with crimes against humanity (Vieira, 2010). These paramilitary leaders have committed more than 42,000 crimes and have sought a reduced prison sentence of eight years under the controversial Justice and Peace Law in exchange for demobilizing their troops and confessing their crimes (Gill, 2009; Vieira, 2010). The Constitutional Court ruled that the demobilized paramilitaries could obtain the legal benefit of the Justice and Peace Law only if they confessed the complete truth. In response, the eight former commanders pointed out that there are other culpable persons who also need to be brought to justice for their involvement in paramilitary activities: high-level officials, politicians, members of the public security forces, business leaders, contractors, and foreign investors (Vieira, 2010).

The eight paramilitary leaders wrote a letter to Iván Cepeda, congressman-elect and spokesperson for the Movement of Victims of State Crimes, and Gustavo Petro, former presidential candidate for the Alternative Democratic Pole. In the letter, the imprisoned former commanders stated that their disarmament and demobilization and the "half truth and half justice" were "worth nothing" if those persons in higher positions who "personify" the paramilitary evaded responsibility and remained protected by political and economic power. The commanders emphasized that "land speculation, seizure and concentration of agricultural property, violence and displacement in the countryside, and the consequent social injustice against the rural people, entail and involve situations still unknown" (Vieira, 2010). Camilo González, director of the Institute of Studies for Development and Peace, agreed that there are multiple layers of culpability. "What they say is true. They were merely the armed wing of paramilitarism. Here we have a many-headed monster, with the armed, political, and economic heads. They are interrelated, and each one has a small piece of the other."

Those displaced by the unrest continue to be marginalized. In an effort to push the government to adequately protect IDPs, in 2009 the Constitutional Court declared the right of IDPs to be included in the registry and directed the government to address under-registration through various means. These include registering persons whose applications were rejected in previous years, sharing information between government databases and the IDP registry, and registering children born to IDPs after the family's registration date (IDMC, 2009). In the same year the Constitutional Court upheld its 2004 ruling that the lack of response by the government represents an unconstitutional state of affairs. Throughout 2009 the court made 12 decisions obligating the government to take action. In response, various government agencies drafted a comprehensive reform of land policy (IDMC, 2009). In October 2011 the court echoed its previous sentiments that the government's response to internal displacement amounted to an unconstitutional state of affairs, and ordered the government to adopt a wide range of measures and report on the implementation and outcomes of the measures. Months before, on June 10, 2011, President Santos signed into law a new Victim and Land Restitution Law (Ley de Victimas y de Restitución de Tierra, Law. 1448) aimed to restore land to Colombians who have been forced from their homes by violence. Under the law, victims of conflict, including IDPs, will be provided redress. An approved finance plan of $500 million will support its implementation. Some remaining problems have been identified in the Victims' Law, including in the property restitution section—such as how to ensure the safety of returning individuals and communities as unrest and conflict continue; and although the Constitutional Court confirmed the right of Afro-Colombian communities to be consulted in the process of adopting and implementing the law, the communities report that this has not been sufficiently done. The implementation of the law began on January 1, 2012 (IDMC, 2011; ABColombia, 2012).

The primary and underlying issue of Colombia's trafficking status is the nation's civil unrest. As Cepeda and González emphasized, it is not only the armed wings of paramilitary groups that need to be stopped but also the economic and political powers behind them. As the eight imprisoned AUC leaders noted, a number of high-level and powerful people continue to collude in trafficking. If the underlying powers of these organizations are not dismantled, paramilitary and guerrilla groups will continue to create instability in the nation and displace citizens. In addition to Colombia's internal efforts, it is essential that Colombia obtains support from neighboring Venezuelan and Ecuadoran authorities to aid in the capture of FARC and ELN leaders who cross the border into their domain. Without their help, there is little possibility that Colombia's trafficking situation will improve. For those persons already displaced, Colombia needs to properly address the registration of IDPs and restitution in the form of social and economic benefits. If these steps are not taken, IDPs will continue to be a population vulnerable to human trafficking and child labor.

CHAPTER 7

Iraq

We wanted to make sure our military, civilians, and
contractors were protected from Iraqi law.
—FORMER AIDE OF PAUL BREMER

Since the U.S. invasion of Iraq in 2003, an ongoing question has been
"Who's in charge?" Investigative journalist Nir Rosen says that although
the United States remained the occupying power, it claimed to no longer
be responsible as the occupying authority after Iraq gained sovereignty
in June 2004. "It's kind of an absurd claim, because they've [the United
States], since 2004, handed sovereignty back to Iraq several times, most
recently just in September of this year [2010]," Rosen told *Democracy
Now.* "But they remain the occupying power. They were the ones training and funding and appointing and firing. They were the ones who
controlled the country and ruled the country" (Democracy Now, 2010).
Despite its claim to not be in charge, the U.S. government instituted
policies creating immunity from Iraqi law and the Iraqi legal process
for U.S. contractors and Iraqi military personnel. This step has left marginalized persons, including those groups most vulnerable to human
trafficking, with little to no recourse against offenders that fit this criterion. In 2004, two days before he left Iraq, Coalition Provisional Authority (CPA) administrator Paul Bremer signed into effect CPA Order
No. 17. The order made the Multi-National Force–Iraq (MNF–I), the
CPA, foreign liaison missions, their personnel, property, funds and assets, and all international consultants immune from the Iraqi legal process. In June 2004 the U.S. government also imposed a formal policy to
ignore human rights abuses committed by the Iraqi military. Revealed

by WikiLeaks, an order known as "Frago 242" barred coalition troops from investigating any violations committed by Iraqi troops against other Iraqis (Democracy Now, 2010).

Aside from the obvious waiver of culpability for the U.S. military, the CPA order made contractors (under Section 4) not subject to Iraqi law or the Iraqi legal process in matters relating to the terms and conditions of their contract or subcontract (CPA, 2004). When explaining why the order was issued, one of Bremer's former aides told *Newsweek,* "We wanted to make sure our military, civilians, and contractors were protected from Iraqi law" (Hirsh, 2007). The transitional administration maintained CPA rules and regulations when in March 2004 it adopted Article 26 of the Transitional Administrative Law of Iraq, which states: "[T]he laws, regulations, orders, and directives issued by the Coalition Provisional Authority pursuant to its authority under international law shall remain in force until rescinded or amended by legislation duly enacted and having the force of law" (Mason, 2009). In December 2008 the Iraqi government did pass legislation to rescind CPA Order 17, but the legislation does not specifically address how past incidents will be addressed (HRW, 2008; Risen, 2008).

Before the U.S. invasion of Iraq, in 2002, President George W. Bush instituted a policy that called for the prosecution of government contractors and employees who engaged in human trafficking, and for the suspension or disqualification of companies that participated in such practices. Still in force, the policy has proved to be nearly impossible to put into effect in Iraq. Experts say that this state of affairs exists not only because of limited investigative resources and judicial hurdles but also because authorities are ignoring the evidence. "Zero prosecutions [suggest] zero effort to enforce the law," Martina Vandenberg, a lawyer and former Human Rights Watch investigator, told the *Washington Post* (Schwellenbach & Leonnig, 2010).

Those persons not under the protection of immunity who committed crimes in Iraq were and are subject to the Iraqi constitution, penal code, and labor code. The Iraqi constitution prohibits slavery, forced labor, trafficking of women and children, and the sex trade. In February 2012 the Iraqi parliament passed a comprehensive anti-trafficking law, which establishes trafficking as a separate offense and prescribes punishments for sex trafficking and labor trafficking (Lavender, 2012). Before the new law was passed, there was no specific law to address human trafficking, so attorneys primarily turned to trafficking-related articles under the penal code such as rape, forcible sexual assault, kidnapping, detention, and unlawful seizure. Maximum sentences range from 7 to 15 years' imprisonment, which can be increased to life imprisonment if the offense results in the victim's death (IILHR, 2010; Republic of Iraq, 2010). The labor code prohibits slavery and similar practices, including forced labor, child trafficking, and compulsory recruitment of minors for use in armed conflict; child prostitution; illicit activities such as drug trafficking; and work likely to harm the health, safety, or morals of children. Those who violate the labor code provisions pertaining to work performed by children may be penalized by imprisonment for 10 days to 3 months or fines (U.S. Department of Labor, 2009). Despite this assortment of somewhat applicable laws, trafficking offenders rarely faced prosecution, and victims of trafficking continued to be arrested and punished for crimes associated with their trafficking experience such as prostitution and document/passport fraud. The new law establishes sentences of up to 15 years' imprisonment, which can be increased to life imprisonment if the offense results in the victim's death (Lavender, 2012). The exact language of Article 1 of the law uses terms similar to those used in the Palermo Protocol in defining human trafficking:

> First: For purposes of this law, the term "Human Trafficking" shall indicate recruiting, transporting, housing, or receiving individuals by force, threat to use force, or other means, including by coercion, kidnapping, fraud, deception, misuse of power, exchange of money, or privileges to an influential person in order to sell and exploit the trafficked individuals by means of prostitution, sexual abuse, unpaid labor, forced labor, enslavement, beggary, trading of human organs, medical experimentation, or by other means. (Presidency Council, 2012)

The government then defines trafficking victims to be "the person who suffered from material or moral damage caused by one of the crimes stipulated in this law." This means that attorneys will have to prove "material" or "moral" damage in order to succeed under the law. The law would be much more enforceable had this second portion been left out.

Of positive significance is that consent is irrelevant, meaning that consent cannot be used as a defense (Presidency Council, 2012).

INTERNAL TRAFFICKING

As in many other nations, child labor is a serious issue in Iraq. In fact, 12.4 percent of children between the ages of 5 and 14 work. Boys account for a larger share than girls—15.1 percent compared to 9.6 percent, respectively. Most working children in Iraq are employed in a family business, and rural children are employed at a higher rate than children living in urban areas. Children also work on the streets selling items or begging, and in hazardous conditions in automobile shops and on construction sites. They are also used by Iraqi insurgent groups to plant improvised explosive devices, as suicide bombers, and as spies or scouts (U.S. Department of Labor, 2009). "We have evidence that the phenomenon of criminal gangs and terrorist groups recruiting juveniles—either by threatening them or luring them with money—has increased recently," Hamza Kamil, a spokesman for the Iraqi Human Rights Ministry, told IRIN, the humanitarian news and analysis service of the UN Office for the Coordination of Humanitarian Affairs. "We urge the government, NGOs, and international organizations working in Iraq to run comprehensive programs for these children to distance them from any militant influence" (IRIN, 2008).

Under Iraq's labor law, the minimum age for employment is 15. The law prohibits the employment of anyone under the age of 18 in areas that are detrimental to the worker's health, safety, or morals. Specifically, young workers are not supposed to work underground, underwater, or with dangerous or hazardous substances or equipment. The legal requirements surrounding employment of young workers are a pre-employment medical examination and a maximum workday of seven hours. Workers must obtain a break after four hours and a daily break of one hour. One caveat is that youths (ages 15 and older) who work for their family are excluded from the daily maximum of work hours and the medical examination (U.S. Department of Labor, 2009).

Children in Iraq have suffered tremendously from the ongoing violence. Students and teachers were the targets of violent crimes and sectarian killings, particularly in Baghdad and Mosul. The killings, closures of schools, and fear of child abduction resulted in a dramatic decrease in student attendance. "Most of the available information is extracted from a wide range of different sources but can rarely be sufficiently verified," stated the UN secretary-general in a report to the UN Security Council. "It remains clear, however, that Iraqi children suffer most in the ongoing violence. Statistics from United Nations partners and Iraqi authorities suggest that approximately half of all Iraqi refugees are children, as are as many as 38 to 40 percent of internally displaced persons" (United Nations Security Council, 2007).

Militants also use children to advance their agendas. For instance, in March 2007, militants used two children to facilitate passing a car through an MNF–I checkpoint in Baghdad. The car was blown up, killing five persons, including the two children (United Nations Security Council, 2007). In July 2008 more than 1,000 juveniles were in the custody of Iraqi and U.S. forces. "Most of these juveniles [currently held in prisons] were being used [by the militants] either for transporting bombs to areas the militants can't enter due to security cordons, or to daub walls with anti-government graffiti," Hamza Kamil told IRIN (IRIN, 2008). It has been reported that such youths have faced abuse in both MNF–I and Iraqi-run facilities (Coalition to Stop the Use of Child Soldiers, 2008; United Nations Security Council, 2007). Of additional concern is that the United States identified a significant number of Iraqi children—even those as young as 13—as "enemy combatants." The United States captured and detained roughly 2,400 persons under the age of 18 in Iraq between 2003 and 2008 (Pincus, 2008). The use of children as spies or informants by insurgent groups is a direct violation of basic human rights. The status of children as enemy combatants is troubling because as a result child victims are not only exploited by insurgent groups but then face punishment for being exploited (Coalition to Stop the Use of Child Soldiers, 2008). "Juveniles and former child soldiers should be treated first and foremost as candidates for rehabilitation and reintegration into society, not subjected to further victimization," Jamil Dakwar, director of the American Civil Liberties Union's (ACLU) human rights program, said in a statement (Pincus, 2008).

Since the U.S. invasion of Iraq, there has also been an increase in prostitution rings, human trafficking, and the number of exploited women, girls, and boys in the commercial sex industry and the drug trade. With social upheaval and rising unemployment, the number of persons vulnerable to trafficking, such as orphans and separated children, has increased. Children placed in orphanages are not always safe. Some staff members of orphanages and charitable organizations have trafficked young children for the purposes of prostitution (U.S. Department of State, 2003; Global Policy Forum, 2005; Bennett, 2006; U.S. Department of Labor, 2009). Traffickers often prey on families that are financially destitute. They encourage parents to prostitute their children. One mother stated that the prostitution of her young sons, ages 13 and 14, provided an income for the family: "We are a poor family and my husband cannot work because he has serious epilepsy. Three months ago, Abu Weled [the leader of a commercial sex ring] came to our house offering us money if we let our two teenage boys work with them. Thanks to him, today we have a good income. People may find it surprising, but at least we can eat now and I'm proud of them" (Global Policy Forum, 2005). Weled's gang also exploited girls under the age of 16. While boys received roughly $10 per trick, the ring reportedly charged roughly $50 per sexual encounter (Global Policy Forum, 2005).

When the Organization of Women's Freedom in Iraq (OWFI) interviewed Iraqi females detained for prostitution in Baghdad's Kadhimiya prison, it was discovered that most were runaways (often trying to escape sexual abuse) or sold into prostitution by their families, and/or destitute. Sixty-five percent of the 72 persons interviewed were under the age of 18. Some of the victims had been recruited and prostituted by Iraqi brothel owners; others had been trafficked to brothels by taxi drivers and even police. A number of the victims had been forced into fake and temporary marriages so as to be trafficked within Iraq or to other countries. When determining the overall picture of prostitution and sex trafficking in Iraq, OWFI's 2010 report stated that it "looked like an octopus with its head in Baghdad while the limbs reached out to Damascus, Dubai, Jordan, and the Emirates" (OWFI, 2010).

In addition to continuing reports of the internal trafficking of Iraqi women, girls, and boys for the purposes of forced prostitution, there have been reports that some Iraqi boys are trafficked internally for organ trafficking. In such instances, Baghdad hospitals did not question the organ donation because the father of the donor-child was often present (U.S. Department of State, 2010).

IRAQ AS A DESTINATION

Men and women from Bangladesh, Ethiopia, Georgia, India, Indonesia, Jordan, Nepal, Pakistan, the Philippines, Sri Lanka, Thailand, and Uganda face forced labor in the areas of domestic work, construction, and security in Iraq. They often experience the withholding of their passports and official documents, employer refusal to honor employment contracts, and threats of deportation. Some persons from these nations willingly accept jobs in Jordan or Kuwait but are instead forced or tricked into involuntary servitude in Iraq. Others knowingly migrate to Iraq but are subjected to forced labor upon arrival (Simpson, 2006; U.S. Department of State, 2010). One case of forced labor involved 14 women from Uganda promised jobs on U.S. military bases in Iraq. Instead, they were forced to work for private Iraqi families and received lower wages than promised. Some of the women were also locked in rooms, had their passports withheld, and were physically and/or sexually abused by either the employer or the recruitment agent. Forced labor has also been a significant problem on U.S. military bases in Iraq. Thousands of foreign laborers have been trafficked into Iraq via human brokers and subcontractors, had their passports confiscated, and been forced or coerced to work in menial positions on U.S. bases (Simpson, 2006; U.S. Department of State, 2010).

One of the largest U.S. contractors in post-invasion Iraq was Kellogg Brown & Root (KBR), which at the time was a Halliburton subsidiary.[1] The company stated that roughly 35,000 of 48,000 people hired under a 2005 privatization contract were imported from nations other than Iraq and the United States (Simpson, 2006; KBR, n.d.). In 2004, thirteen men, ages 18 to 27, were recruited by KBR subcontractor Daoud & Partners in Nepal to work in a five-star hotel in Amman, Jordan. Instead, they had their passports seized when they arrived in Jordan and were informed that they would be working in a military facility in Iraq. While in transit they were stopped, kidnapped, and later militant insurgents executed 12 of the men. The one survivor was forced to work in a warehouse in Iraq for 15 months, supervised by KBR, before KBR and Daoud & Partners allowed him to return home to Nepal (Simpson, 2006; Hedgpeth, 2008; Handley & McOwen, 2009). In August 2006, the law firm Cohen Milstein Hausfeld & Toll, PLLC filed suit against Daoud & Partners. In April 2008 the presiding judge in the U.S. Department of Labor's Office of Administrative Law ruled that the men's families were entitled to death benefits and ordered Daoud & Partners to pay $1 million to the families of 11 of the victims (Switzky, 2008). In April 2009 the same firm filed suit against KBR and Daoud & Partners, claiming that KBR and its Jordanian subcontractor had trafficked Nepali workers. In response to a series of attempts by KBR and Daoud & Partners to get out of the suit, courts denied KBR's motion to dismiss and the subsequent appeal, and jurisdiction was upheld over Daoud & Partners. A trial date has been set for April 29, 2013 (Ramchandra Adhikari et al. v. Daoud & Partners et al., 2009; Business Wire, 2012).

Mike Thibault, co-chair of the Commission on Wartime Contracting in Iraq and Afghanistan, states that subcontractors continue to use human trafficking to fill open job positions in both Iraq and Afghanistan. Once in Iraq, the workers have their passports taken away and are placed in debt bondage. "We're talking about individuals that were hired from foreign countries in order to come into Iraq but were told they were going to be working in places like Dubai and Kuwait. And when they showed up, they were flown into Iraq," Thibault told Federal News Radio (Kubota, 2010). In February 2010 the U.S. State Department alerted the U.S. army of a potential case of human trafficking in Iraq. The case allegedly involved subcontractor supervisors working for the Army and Air Force Exchange Service who had recruited women in their nations of origin and promised the women jobs as beauticians in Dubai. Instead, the women were "forced to surrender their passports, transported against their will to Iraq, and told they could only leave by paying a termination fee of $1,100." An Army Criminal Investigation Command spokesman said the allegations were investigated and not substantiated (Schwellenbach & Leonnig, 2010).

Reports suggest that at least one-third of the approximately 200,000 contracted employees in Iraq and Afghanistan work for subcontractors. One concern is the immunity that was granted to contractors under CPA Order No. 17. Under the order, contractors and subcontractors were not subject to Iraqi laws or regulations in matters relating to the terms and conditions of their contracts, including licensing and registering employees, businesses, and corporations. Contractors were defined as "non-Iraqi legal entities or individuals not normally resident in Iraq, including their non-Iraqi employees and subcontractors not normally resident in Iraq, supplying goods or services in Iraq under a contract" (CPA, 2004). A broad array of contracts was covered under Order 17. It included contract or grant agreements with the CPA or any successor agreement. The order also protected contract or grant agreements with a sending state to supply goods or services in Iraq, where that supply was to or on behalf of the MNF–I; for humanitarian aid, reconstruction or development projects approved and organized by the CPA or a sending state; for the construction, reconstruction, or operation of diplomatic and consular missions; or until July 1, 2004, to or on behalf of foreign liaison missions. Also included were contracts for security services provided by private security companies to foreign liaison missions and their personnel, diplomatic and consular missions and their personnel, and the MNF–I and its personnel, international consultants, or contractors (CPA, 2004).

In terms of forced labor and debt bondage, of particular interest is the immunity granted to contractors and subcontractors in Iraq for the purposes of construction, reconstruction, or development projects. Today the U.S. government claims to have no direct oversight over contractors because it has no direct contractual relationship with them. Prime contractors are legally responsible for managing subcontractors, but their supervision has often been ineffective and inadequate. "Subcontracting is a normal business practice," said Christopher Shays, co-chair of the Federal Commission on Wartime Contracting in Iraq and Afghanistan. "But what makes sense for an office-renovation project in Maryland can create some unique risks when the contractor is hiring subcontractors in a combat zone half a world away" (Commission on Wartime Contracting, 2010).

TRAFFICKING ABROAD

Iraqi women and girls as young as 11 years old are trafficked for sexual exploitation to Iran, Jordan, Kuwait, Lebanon, Qatar, Syria, Turkey, and the UAE. Iraqi citizens are also trafficked to Europe; in fact they account for 1 percent of the identified trafficking victims in the Netherlands. Iraqi females are often lured by traffickers with false promises of work or are convinced by family members to prostitute as a means of economic opportunity, to pay off debts, or to resolve disputes between families. Traffickers use temporary marriages (*muta'a*) to transport women and girls within Iraq as well as to neighboring nations, particularly Syria, for sexual exploitation (U.S. Department of State, 2010).

Ousting the Iraqi government and all previous existing systems of security resulted in border vulnerabilities and security weaknesses in the cities of Iraq. This situation has made women particularly vulnerable to a variety of crimes such as kidnapping, sexual assault, and human trafficking. One trafficking ring sold 128 Iraqi women to Saudi Arabia in 2008 and 2009. The ring was made up of Iraqi police officers, members of the Governorate's Council (a political party), and security officials. Shyaa Hmoud Salman, an Iraqi police officer involved in the ring, testified that they set up a branch of an NGO and offered legitimate employment as a lure:

> I was only one of many other men who were summoned to the city of Mosul by the Saudi-Arabian Abou Mansour on March 18, 2007. The agreement was that he [would] pay us $3,000 for every young woman brought from Diyala. After a few days, we went to the city of Diyala where we started a branch of the Arab Humane Organization NGO after we paid its owner an amount of money. We announced that we [would] pay a $200 salary to young women, which we did with a big number until we gained their trust. With many we tried seduction and alluring. The first group we sent were 20 women. (OWFI, 2010)

Salman went on to state that Mansour raised the inducement price to $5,000 per woman:

> We told the women that they [would] be working in Saudi Arabia, and we convinced them to get rid of a life of poverty and stress under their strict families' control. We were able to convince and send a total of 128 [women] from Diyala City to Saudi Arabia,

through the city of Mosul. We had learned beforehand that they [would] be sold to tourist houses where they [would] be sexual servants and [would] prostitute for a living, but [would] not be allowed to say anything to anyone. (OWFI, 2010)

There are reports that Iraqi children are also trafficked internally and abroad. Some are trafficked for adoption and others for sexual abuse. Officials and aid agencies point to corruption, inadequate law enforcement, and porous borders as contributing factors. The child traffickers use threats, force, coercion, abduction, fraud, deception, abuse of power or vulnerability, or give payment or benefits to a person in control of the victim. One police officer told *The Guardian* that at least 15 Iraqi children were sold each month for these purposes. Officials believe that the 12 or more criminal gangs that operate in Iraq offer $312 to $6,239 per child (Sarhan, 2009). Trafficking syndicates use intermediaries who pretend to work for NGOs to negotiate with the families. The syndicate prepares the change of names, furnishes new birth certificates, and adds the child to the passport of the intermediary who will take the child outside the country. "Before we try to negotiate with any family, we study their living conditions, their debts, the goods they own, and when we feel that the relatives are suffering with unemployment and cannot feed their children, we make our approach that in most of the time is welcomed as we are seen as aid workers," an anonymous source involved in human trafficking told *The Guardian* (Sarhan, 2009). The source stated that the readiness of underpaid government employees to help with the falsification of documents makes child trafficking from Iraq cheaper and easier than elsewhere. Colonel Firaz Abdallah, part of the investigation department of the Iraqi police, says corruption in many departments of the government makes it difficult for traffickers to be caught and children to be retrieved:

When those children come to the airport or the border, everything looks correct and it is hard for us to keep them inside the country without significant evidence that the child is being trafficked. A couple of weeks ago we caught a couple with a six-month-old baby leaving by car from the Iraqi border to Jordan. One of our police officers found the age difference between the couple strange and asked our office to check. After arresting them we found out that the girl was sold by her parents and was going to be taken to Amman, then after that, to Ireland where a family had already paid for the baby. (Sarhan, 2009)

One mother cited life in a displacement camp, unemployment, and lack of support to explain why she sold two of her children. "I did anything possible to keep them with me, but I lost my husband while I was pregnant with my fifth child and life became too hard. I love all my children. I know that the families who adopted them will give a good life, food, and education that I would never give" (Sarhan, 2009). Aid agencies warn parents that these children are often sexually exploited. "We tried to approach many of these families to alert them about what can happen with their kids but we have been threatened and two aid workers were killed after they tried to prevent a child negotiation," said Ahmed Sami, an aid worker. The source involved in human trafficking stated that traffickers prefer babies, but occasionally families request children between the ages of one and four. It is unknown what happens to the children who are trafficked. The source was told by a colleague that one of the babies sold in 2008 was used for organ transplants (Sarhan, 2009).

WHAT HAPPENS TO VICTIMS AFTER TRAFFICKING

Just after the U.S. invasion, an armed gang took a young woman from an orphanage. The 18-year-old was sent to several brothels before being brought back to Baghdad, drugged with pills, dressed in a suicide belt, and sent to bomb a cleric's office. Instead, the teen went to the police and was subsequently sentenced to seven years in prison. The prison director says the sentence was imposed to protect her from the gang (Bennett, 2006).

In addition to facing a harsh cultural stigma, it is not uncommon for victims to be punished for crimes associated with their trafficking experience. Coercion is not recognized in Iraqi courts as a legal defense for engaging in unlawful acts. Child victims forced to act on behalf of insurgent groups face prosecution for terrorism offenses. The same is the case for sex-trafficking victims who are prosecuted for prostitution and can spend several months in detention awaiting trial (U.S. Department of State, 2010). One such case involved two sisters, ages 14 and 15, who escaped their traffickers in Dubai (UAE) and reported them to police. After being returned to Iraq, they were imprisoned for carrying false passports. Their traffickers were rumored to be back on the streets after paying their way out of prison. "I don't know what to do if the prison administration decides to release me," said Asmah, age 14. "We have no one to protect us" (Bennett, 2006). Prostitution is illegal in Iraq, and those arrested face detainment for three to four months. Almost half the women in the central women's prison Kadhimiya (Baghdad) have been convicted of prostitution. Others face death. Between 2006 and 2008 there were mass killings of women in the cities of Basra and Umara. Some of the women were accused of prostitution while others were convicted of being unveiled and wearing makeup (OWFI, 2010).

Some child-trafficking victims are placed in protective facilities, orphanages, and foster care, but others are placed in juvenile detention centers. Foreign victims are not granted legal protection against removal, nor are they provided temporary or permanent residency status or other relief from deportation. In the case of the 14 women from Uganda, the Iraqi government did assist in their repatriation. There are no formal procedures available to officials to systematically refer victims for services, although two government ministries do refer juvenile and adult detainees to medical screenings if they report abuse. Also, no formal procedures exist to help identify trafficking victims among vulnerable groups such as prostitutes and foreign workers. Lastly, the government does not fund shelters for trafficking victims; all care of trafficking victims is administered by NGOs (U.S. Department of State, 2010).

WHAT HAPPENS TO TRAFFICKERS

There is no official mechanism in place to collect data on trafficking offenses or enforcement in Iraq. Thus far, there is no evidence that the Iraqi government has successfully prosecuted traffickers. In 2010 the Iraqi government did initiate a human rights and criminal investigation into an alleged occurrence of labor trafficking. This resulted in the issuance of two arrest warrants. It is unknown whether the alleged traffickers faced prosecution or sentencing. What is known is that the few existing trafficking investigations are slow going. For instance, a 2008 investigation into an alleged incident of human trafficking by the director of a women's shelter in the Kurdistan Regional Government (KRG) area was not complete as of June 2010 (U.S. Department of State, 2009; 2010). Additionally, cases are often misclassified, dismissed, or ignored. For instance, traffickers that were part of the syndicate that trafficked 128 women from Iraq to Saudi Arabia were released, and the police officers who were part of the ring were transferred. The case— while obviously human trafficking —was categorized as terrorism and closed (OWFI, 2010).

INTERNAL EFFORTS TO DECREASE TRAFFICKING

The passage of the anti-trafficking law is an enormously positive step, but overall, human trafficking has been a low priority for those groups in charge of anti-trafficking efforts—the Ministries of Interior of both Iraq and the KRG. As a result, cases often go uninvestigated. Also, there is no mechanism to collect data on enforcement or offenses of human trafficking. Child labor is supposed to be regulated and enforced by the Ministry of Labor and Social Affairs, but again enforcement is minimal, as the ministry lacks resources and inspectors (U.S. Department of Labor, 2009).

Unstable national security, corrupt officials, dire financial circumstances, and the insecure position of Iraqi women, children, and migrant workers have created an atmosphere ripe for human trafficking. Of particular concern is the CPA Order 17 immunity that the United States granted to contractors and subcontractors. Order 17 was rescinded, but the ramifications of the order continue to have an effect. Forced-labor abuses by contractors and subcontractors are still taking place, yet the onus appears to fall on no one. Victims of trafficking face severe social stigma and continue to be punished for crimes associated with their trafficking experience. The government's anti-trafficking law has created a comprehensive definition of human trafficking and criminalizes all forms of trafficking. If properly implemented, it could significantly improve the treatment of victims, emphasize victim protections, and grant adequate tools to law enforcement in the investigation and prosecution of trafficking offenses.

CHAPTER 8

Syria

Refugees are especially vulnerable to human trafficking. Prolonged displacement and uncertainty, coupled with increased financial pressure, can adversely affect the scope and severity of sexual and gender-based violence among refugees in Syria, including the trafficking of women and children.

—RENATA DUBINI, UNHCR SYRIA REPRESENTATIVE

In January 2010 the Syrian government adopted counter-trafficking Legislative Decree No. 3. The new law includes a definition of trafficking, protection measures for victims, punishment for perpetrators and those who benefit from the offense, the establishment of shelters for victims, and the creation of a counter-trafficking unit (Moschella, 2010). Under the new law, which became effective April 2010, trafficking is the inducing, transportation, kidnapping of persons in order to use them for financial or other gain. Sexual abuse of children is also regarded as human trafficking. Offenders face a minimum of 7 years' imprisonment and a fine of $21,459.23 to $64,377.68 (Sawah, 2010). The law provides a legal framework, albeit skeletal, for prosecuting traffickers and those who commit trafficking-related offenses. It also creates a legal foundation for protecting victims. What the law does not provide is a clear definition of human trafficking, nor does it specifically criminalize the sale of children and child pornography (UNCRC, 2012). Despite the law, the Syrian government often punishes victims for crimes that occur during the trafficking experience, such as prostitution and immigration violations. On the other hand, traffickers are rarely prosecuted. Though the adoption of the anti-trafficking law is highly significant, there have been delays in its execution. For instance, the executive order required to implement the new law was not issued until more than a year later. In addition to the absence of a clear definition of trafficking, there is a lack of clear procedures for the identification, interview, and referral of victims (UNCRC, 2012; U.S. Department of State, 2012). Without procedures, prosecutions and adequate protection for victims have been hindered. Also, the status of Syria's national plan of action against human trafficking, which the government began drafting in early 2010, is unknown (U.S. Department of State, 2010, 2011, 2012).

Of course, the new law and subsequent changes took place before and during the pronounced unrest that began in Syria in mid-March 2011. It began in Dara'a, where demonstrators set fire to the headquarters of the ruling political party, the Ba'ath Party. They chanted demands, which included the release of all political prisoners, trials for those who shot and killed protesters, and a halt to Syria's longstanding emergency law, which was imposed in 1963 and allows security agencies to detain people without arrest warrants and hold them for lengthy periods without communication (New York Times, 2011; HRW, 2011). In response, police opened fire on the demonstrators, killing one person and injuring numerous others. President Bashar al-Assad seemed initially to waver between offers of political reform and violence, ultimately choosing the latter (New York Times, 2011; Associated Press, 2011). The estimated number of dead killed by Assad loyalists, which the United Nations believes to be over 5,000, continues to rise (UN News Centre, 2011). The Syrian regime claims that 2,000 government soldiers have died during conflicts with the opposition, which has been increasingly militarized as a result of army defections (Peel, 2012). In September 2012 the UN News Centre stated that more than 18,000 people, mostly civilians, had died since the uprising against Assad began (UN News Centre, 2012). Though anger over human rights violations by Assad and his regime is the driving force behind the uprising, a November 2011 opinion poll revealed that 55 percent of polled Syrians did not want him to resign. For many the desire for Assad to stay in power was based on fear for the future of the country (Doha Debates, 2012). As divisions deepen and fighting continues as the nation sinks further into civil war, the factors that contribute to an optimal environment for human trafficking also increase. Unrest and forced migration, as can be seen in Colombia and Iraq, creates immense vulnerability to abuse and exploitation, including human trafficking. As the conflict continues it is difficult to see what the exact consequences will be, but so far an increasing number of Syrian refugees have fled to Iraq, Jordan, Lebanon, and Turkey, while other nearby nations are bracing for a potential influx of Syrians.

SYRIA AS A DESTINATION

Primarily a destination nation, persons are trafficked to Syria for commercial sexual exploitation, domestic servitude, and forced labor. Women and girls are trafficked from eastern Europe, Iraq, Kyrgyzstan, Morocco, and Somalia for commercial sexual exploitation. Other women willingly come to Syria seeking employment only to find themselves in situations of involuntary servitude. This is the situation of cabaret dancers, often from Belarus, Morocco, Russia, Somalia, and Ukraine. Some of these women are forced into prostitution, their passports are withheld, and they are prohibited from leaving their work premises. Also, women from Ethiopia, Indonesia, the Philippines, Sierra Leone, Somalia, and Sri Lanka, among other nations, accept positions in Syria as domestic servants but face involuntary servitude. Contracts that the women sign prior to departure are often changed once in Syria, passports are withheld by the employer or recruitment agency, and the women are often confined to the private residences where they work. The government of Ethiopia has prohibited its citizens from accepting employment in Syria, but this move has not stopped the flow of Ethiopian workers into the nation. Men and women are also trafficked from Indonesia for forced labor and debt bondage in the areas of construction, agriculture, and manufacturing (U.S. Department of State, 2008, 2010, 2012). Determining exact numbers is a challenge, but according to the Blas F. Ople Policy Center, the majority of the 6,000 Filipino women working illegally in Syria are trafficking victims. Susan Ople, head of the Ople Center, says most victims are first trafficked to other nations such as Oman, Jordan, Kuwait, and the United Arab Emirates. "The first human trafficking case that the Ople Center ever handled was that of a Filipino domestic worker whose passport and contracts were sold from Dubai to Oman to Damascus, Syria, way back in 2006," Ople said. "Even during that time we were surprised to find out that we had 6,000 Filipino women illegally employed in Syria" (ABS-CBN, 2011). In 2011 the International Organization for Migration (IOM) identified at least 95 Filipino domestic workers believed to be trafficking victims in Hama and Homs (U.S. Department of State, 2012).

Syria is host to the largest externally displaced Iraqi population in the region, many of whom remain in need of urgent assistance as the economic and social situation of this vulnerable population has worsened (IOM, 2010b). Some Iraqi women and girls are forced to prostitute by their families or criminal gangs, with temporary marriages used as a means to do so (U.S. Department of State, 2010). The exact number of Iraqi refugees in Syria is disputed. The UN, on the basis of Syrian government figures, initially estimated that roughly 4.8 million Iraqis were displaced from their homes between 2003 and 2009, and that an estimated 2 million persons fled to neighboring countries, primarily Syria and Jordan (GAO, 2009). In September 2008 the government of Syria reported that 1.2 million Iraqis held residence permits. The Office of the United Nations High Commissioner for Refugees (UNHCR) believed these numbers to be an overestimate and, by deactivating 58,000 files, revised downward the number of Iraqi refugees registered in Syria to a total of 165,493 registered at the end of April 2010 (IRIN, 2010). In 2012 there were 102,000 registered Iraqi refugees, though the government of Syria estimated the total number of Iraqi refugees to be 1 million (IRIN, 2012). The reality is that many Iraqi refugees do not want to register, and the UNHCR has had difficulty reaching out to them. "If we look at the numbers officially registered, such a small minority has been reached," Elizabeth Campbell, a senior advocate at Refugees International, a U.S. advocacy group, told IRIN, the humanitarian news and analysis service of the UN Office for the Coordination of Humanitarian Affairs. "Not many refugees are returning." In 2010 those refugees who did not pick up food vouchers for two months and who did not make contact with the office for more than four months had their files deactivated (IRIN, 2010).

The current unrest in Syria makes the situation for Iraqi refugees all the more tenuous. Food prices have risen, and ways out of Syria have diminished. Furthermore, the warfare that Iraqis escaped is once again present in their everyday lives. For many Iraqis, the choices are limited to staying in Syria and returning to Iraq, where the situation is not much better. As noted above, an estimated 1 million Iraqis still live in Syria and have chosen to stay, so far. Others, in small numbers, have fled Syria into Turkey, Lebanon, and Jordan. Refugees are forbidden from formal employment in Syria, so many Iraqis are employed in the informal sector, which is less regulated and makes workers more susceptible to abuse and human rights violations, including human trafficking. In the informal sector, many refugees work in hotels or tourism, industries that have been hit hard by the unrest (IRIN, 2012).

Without means of finding employment to take care of their children, Iraqi female-headed families in Syria remain particularly vulnerable to human trafficking. Consequently, international organizations such as the IOM have made significant efforts to aid this population. In October 2010, through the Syrian Arab Red Crescent Association, the IOM distributed 800 hygiene kits—which included mops, shampoo, soap, toothbrushes, toothpaste, tissues, and other materials—to Iraqi female-headed families in Syria and victims of trafficking who were assisted in two shelters in Damascus and Aleppo (IOM, 2010a). The initiative is part of a wider $2.05 million program funded by the European Union that aims to provide comprehensive assistance and protection to vulnerable Iraqi female-headed families and victims of trafficking in Syria. The program includes medical aid, psychosocial assistance, and vocational training as well as long-term assistance to help vulnerable families and victims of trafficking engage in income-generating activities (IOM, 2010a). "Refugees are especially vulnerable to human trafficking," said Renata Dubini, the UNHCR Syria representative. "Prolonged displacement and uncertainty, coupled with increased financial pressure, can adversely affect the scope and severity of sexual and gender-based violence among refugees in Syria, including the trafficking of women and children" (Moschella, 2010).

In addition to the vulnerabilities of Iraqi refugees within Syria, the social upheaval and deteriorating conditions in Iraq have put Iraqi women who remain in Iraq at risk for human trafficking (IRIN, 2008). As its neighbor, Syria is a common destination. Hana Ibrahim, founder of the Iraqi women's group Women's Will, estimated in 2007 that 50,000 Iraqi women and girls were in prostitution in Syria (Hassan, 2007). "It is not possible to say how big the trafficking problem from Iraq to Syria is, but we know it does exist," Ann Maymann, protection officer for UNHCR Syria, told IRIN. "It is something that has been kept quiet because people are afraid to talk about it" (IRIN, 2006). In 2003 an 11-year-old Iraqi girl was forced to marry her cousin and was then sold to traffickers; she was forced to dance in private homes and nightclubs in Syria. Four years later she was pregnant, imprisoned on charges of prostitution, and was to be deported back to Iraq before the UNHCR intervened (IRIN, 2008).

TRAFFICKING ABROAD, CHILD SEX TOURISM, SYRIA AS A TRANSIT NATION, AND TRAFFICKING WITHIN SYRIA

Syrian citizens are trafficked abroad for sex and forced labor. For instance, Syrian women are trafficked for commercial sexual exploitation to Lebanon. Other Syrian women voluntarily go to Lebanon using "artiste" visas to work in cabarets and nightclubs but end up having their passports withheld and their movements restricted. Some are forced into prostitution and face threats and physical abuse. Also, men and women from Syria voluntarily find employment in Qatar as domestic servants and laborers, but some face involuntary servitude and debt bondage: pay is withheld; movements are restricted; travel documents, passports, and exit permits are withheld; and they are forced to perform a different job than originally agreed. Additionally, some face threats of legal action, threats of arbitrary detention and deportation, false charges, and sexual and/or physical abuse (U.S. Department of State, 2008).

Syria is a source nation for organ trafficking to other nations. It is difficult to ascertain exact numbers for this form of human trafficking, but in 2010, 11 traffickers were arrested for trafficking organs from Syria to Egypt. Part of a larger syndicate, the traffickers bought and sold kidneys harvested from more than 150 persons from Aleppo's slums in 2009. The Syrian donor-victims were sent to Cairo, where their kidneys were sold to patients from Saudi Arabia and the United Arab Emirates (AFP, 2010; Rashwan, 2010; Al-Masry Al-Youm, 2010). The newspaper *Al-Masry Al-Youm* reports that while kidneys on the Cairo black market can cost as much as $15,000, donors do not typically receive more than $2,500. The majority of the payment goes to participating hospitals, laboratories, and middlemen (Al-Masry Al-Youm, 2010).

Syria is a growing child sex-tourism destination. Tourists are mostly from the Middle East, primarily from Saudi Arabia and Kuwait. Syria is also a transit country for human trafficking. East Africans, Iraqi women and girls, and Southeast Asians are trafficked through Syria to Europe, Kuwait, Lebanon, Saudi Arabia, and the United Arab Emirates for forced prostitution. An unknown number of Syrian citizens are also trafficked within Syria. There is anecdotal evidence of the trafficking of children within Syria for forced labor, and there are uncorroborated allegations that children have been used as soldiers by the opposition (U.S. Department of State, 2010, 2012).

WHAT HAPPENS TO VICTIMS AFTER TRAFFICKING

The Syrian government lacks procedures for identifying potential trafficking victims among vulnerable populations. Consequently, victims of trafficking face detainment, punishment, and deportation on charges of prostitution and/or violating immigration laws, such as carrying expired entry papers (IRIN, 2008; U.S. Department of State, 2008, 2010). Under Article 509 of the Criminal Penal Code, prostitution is illegal and is punishable with up to three years' imprisonment or a fine of up to $115 (IRIN, 2008). Sybella Wilkes of UNHCR Damascus says up to 50 Iraqi women are imprisoned on prostitution charges each week. "Some are professionals but many are forced into it by gangs or family members," Wilkes said (IRIN, 2008).

Some victims initially arrested for crimes committed in association with their trafficking experience have been identified as trafficking victims and subsequently referred to shelters. In 2008 and 2009 the Syrian government donated building space for two shelters, one in Damascus and one in Aleppo, specifically designed for trafficking victims. The two shelters are operated by local NGOs and offer legal, medical, and psychological counseling services. Approximately 30 female trafficking victims received aid from the Damascus shelter in 2009. The Aleppo shelter opened in January 2010. In 2009 the Ministry of Social Affairs and Labor referred 21 Asian trafficking victims to the Damascus shelter. In 2010 the two shelters offered medical, legal, and psychological counseling services to 160 women and 3 girls. At least 12 cases involved human trafficking, specifically the forced labor or prostitution of Iraqis. Such referrals are performed on an ad hoc basis and are inconsistent. At times NGOs or international organizations have to secure the release of these victims from detention centers (U.S. Department of State, 2010, 2011). Also, Syrian authorities have been known to release imprisoned Iraqi women and minors to their traffickers, and child-trafficking victims of commercial sexual exploitation are not referred to protective services provided by NGOs but instead are sent to juvenile detention facilities (U.S. Department of State, 2008). During 2011 the government did not refer any trafficking victims to the shelters (U.S. Department of State, 2012). Victims are not encouraged to assist in the investigation or prosecution of their traffickers, nor are they provided with a legal alternative to removal to their country of origin. As a result victims are left in a position where they can face retribution from their traffickers (U.S. Department of State, 2010).

WHAT HAPPENS TO TRAFFICKERS

Before the passage of Legislative Decree No. 3, there were laws that could be used to prosecute trafficking-related offenses, but were not. For instance, those who sexually exploit underage children can be prosecuted under Article 3 of Law 10 (1961). The law prohibits prostitution of a minor under the age of 16 with penalties ranging from one to seven years' imprisonment. Also, the General Penal Code imposes a three-year prison term and a fine for exploitation of prostitution by force, fraud, or coercion. The use of false documentation can be prosecuted under Decree 29 of 1970. The decree stipulates that "any foreigner who tries to enter the country with false documents and anyone who aided that person is subject to imprisonment of three months to one year." Additionally, Prime Ministerial Decision No. 81 of 2006 outlines working-condition guidelines for domestic employees, but penalties for violating the decree are vague and light. The fine for violating the law is $2 or imprisonment for an unstipulated duration (UN International Convention on the Protection of the Rights of All Migrant Workers and Members of Their Families, 2008; U.S. Department of State, 2008). Lastly, Legislative Decree No. 59 (2004) prohibits illicit trading in human organs and in bacteriological and toxic material. It also prohibits organized prostitution (Syrian Arab Republic, 2004).

Despite the existence of these laws, they have not been enforced against traffickers. Although the 2010 passage and implementation of the comprehensive anti-trafficking law (Legislative Decree No. 3) represents a vast improvement, experts express concern that the anti-trafficking law does not give a clear definition of human trafficking. Thus far there is little information on the success of the decree, and other existing statutes continue to be highly underenforced against traffickers (U.S. Department of State, 2010, 2011). There are no reports of prosecutions against traffickers from 2007 through 2011 (U.S. Department of State, 2008, 2009, 2010, 2011, 2012). Syrian officials did arrest the 11 alleged organ traffickers in October 2010 and asked Interpol to issue an international arrest warrant for the Syrian members of the network living in Cairo (AFP, 2010).

INTERNAL EFFORTS TO DECREASE TRAFFICKING

Legislative Decree No. 3 is a significant step in Syria's anti-trafficking measures. In 2010 the government began drafting a national plan of action against trafficking, but the current status of the plan is unknown. The government does monitor public- and private-sector industries with surprise inspections to ensure that children under the age of 15 are not employed. The nation has not released statistics on the results of the inspections (U.S. Department of State, 2010, 2012).

Domestic servants are not protected under Syria's labor laws, but Decree No. 27 of March 2009 and Decree No. 108 of December 2009 provide stricter regulations regarding the recruitment and employment of domestic workers. These decrees allow the Prime Minister's Office to revoke an agency's license if it imports domestic workers under the age of 18 or under false pretenses; physically abuses, tortures, or exploits a domestic worker; or fails to repatriate domestic workers at its own expense. The decrees also require that employment contracts be issued by the Ministry of Interior and contain regulations regarding the stipulation of monthly paychecks and other necessities such as food, clothing, medicine, and housing (U.S. Department of State, 2010). While these are positive steps, experts say that enforcement mechanisms are still lacking (HRW, 2011). Enforcement is a universal concern with all new decrees related to this topic. The Ministry of Interior launched a specialized anti-trafficking directorate in June 2010. The agency is charged with investigating cases, training law enforcement, raising public awareness, and cooperating with foreign entities. It is also designated to track and report annually on the government's anti-trafficking efforts. The agency, which has established a working relationship with the IOM and Interpol, opened an office in Damascus and has hired over 200 personnel. Since the unrest, it is unclear whether the anti-trafficking directorate is fully operational. The number of prosecutions against traffickers appeared to be on the rise (prior to the unrest), though the accuracy of these numbers is debated. The Ministry of Foreign Affairs reports that 45 alleged trafficking cases were prosecuted under the anti-trafficking law in 2010 (11 in Damascus, 20 in the Damascus countryside, 5 in Aleppo, 4 in Hassakeh, 3 in Hama, 1 in Deir al-Zour, and 1 in Edlib). Local observers in Aleppo say that they knew of only 3 investigated cases, instead of the 5 reported by the ministry. The observers state that none of the cases can be effectively prosecuted until a law is adopted that clearly defines victims of human trafficking and provides procedures to implement Legislative Decree No. 3. There were no known prosecutions of or convictions for human trafficking in 2012 (U.S. Department of State, 2010, 2011, 2012).

Syria has recently taken numerous legislative anti-trafficking steps, but it is unknown whether enforcement will actually occur. Both before and since passage of the new decrees, there has been little information on the incidence of arrests, investigations, prosecutions, and sentencing of traffickers and persons who have committed trafficking-related offenses. Existing laws that could have been used in lieu of a comprehensive trafficking law were not. Both socially and within the government, victims are still often perceived as criminals themselves, as is illustrated by the continuing arrest, punishment, and deportation of victims. A positive sign of potential change is that after their arrest some persons have been referred to shelters for human trafficking victims.

Syria might show more progress if it created formal procedures for identifying potential victims among vulnerable populations such as migrants, refugees, and children.

In the meantime, the civil unrest is bound to have a continuing adverse impact on the people of Syria. Unrest creates vulnerabilities, such as displacement and economic hardship, that can make people susceptible to a variety of exploitations, including human trafficking. On account of the unrest, forced migration is a large issue affecting Syria. In fact, more than 228,000 Syrians have fled to neighboring countries. As a result Lebanon and Iraq are host to thousands upon thousands of Syrian refugees, more than 40,000 and 15,000, respectively. At 80,000 and 72,000 Syrian refugees, Turkey and Jordan are hosting even more (UN News Centre, 2012; Bulos, 2012). Syrians who remain in Syria face ongoing conflict, particularly those in Aleppo, Damascus, Dara'a, Hama, and Homs. Conflict has a powerful adverse impact on health, as it disrupts access to health care services. Without proper access to health care, children are particularly vulnerable to malnutrition and disease. This is true both for children who remain in Syria and for those living in refugee camps elsewhere (UN News Centre, 2012). Of course, health care is only one hostile effect of civil war—poverty, violence, and social upheaval make Syrians vulnerable to numerous human rights violations, including human trafficking. The scenario for Syrians is not dissimilar to that for the people of Iraq. The current trafficking situation for Iraqis—both those inside the nation and refugees—offers insight into what likely will come next if the situation for Syrians does not improve soon.

PART IV
Conflation

Human smuggling is often conflated with human trafficking, but they are not the same. In Canada, this confusion permeates society and the media, and even politicians use the terms interchangeably. The significance of the error cannot be underscored enough. The act of smuggling involves the procurement, for financial or other material benefit, of the illegal entry of persons into a nation where they are not nationals or residents. This is characterized by a consensual agreement between the customer (the person to be smuggled) and the smuggler that terminates upon arrival at the destination. In contrast, human trafficking involves an act of recruiting, transporting, transferring, harboring, or receiving a person through the use of force, coercion, or other means for the purpose of exploiting them. Of course, the exchange between customer and smuggler is rarely clear-cut. Smugglers often charge exorbitant fees, and the act of smuggling is a dangerous endeavor that can result in death. For example, in some cases the containers used to transport people lack sufficient oxygen, resulting in suffocation. Additionally, smuggled persons are extremely vulnerable to abuse, exploitation, and human trafficking. While smuggling can turn into human trafficking, the distinction is important: not all persons who are smuggled experience human trafficking. Confusing these terms can result in an inadequate response that is not tailored to the specifics of each issue. In the Canadian media, the two terms are often used interchangeably, and smugglers are frequently labeled as human traffickers, furthering the general population's misunderstanding on the subject. The government also conflates the two, and as a result it has been difficult to determine the extent of human trafficking because statistics often combine both trafficking and smuggling.

Without knowing the scope of human trafficking in Canada, it is difficult to know how best to address it. Likewise, using the two terms interchangeably places the focus on movement, specifically movement into Canada. The emphasis on movement can be seen in the nation's Immigration and Refugee Protection Act, the only anti-trafficking law in existence in Canada until 2005, when Canada amended the Criminal Code to include the offense of trafficking in persons. Under the act, both the offenses of smuggling and human trafficking include "coming into Canada" as an element. It makes sense that movement is discussed in the immigration act, but its inclusion also illustrates why the act was not sufficient in addressing human trafficking. Movement is not a necessary element of human trafficking, and making it such diminishes the focus on other forms of trafficking, such as internal trafficking. Though movement is not a necessary element of the offense of human trafficking in the Criminal Code, the government of Canada continues to focus on movement into the nation. This can be seen in the 2012 adoption of the Protecting Canada's Immigration System Act, which included the controversial Bill C-4 (formerly Bill C-49), initially purported by the government to be an anti-trafficking bill when in fact it primarily focused on limiting the rights of refugees smuggled into the nation, illustrating once again that the conflation of the terms smuggling and human trafficking continues.

CHAPTER 9

Canada

Some cases are like charging someone with assault when they
murder someone. We should be charging someone with the
most serious charge that their conduct warrants.

—BENJAMIN PERRIN, FOUNDER OF THE NGO FUTURE GROUP

All forms of human trafficking and associated offenses, such as receiving material or financial gain as a result of trafficking, are prohibited in Canada. Child sex tourism is illegal, as is transnational trafficking. Destroying or withholding a person's travel documents or identification to assist human trafficking is also prohibited. The government prosecutes all forms of trafficking, including offenses such as forcible confinement, sexual assault, extortion, kidnapping, threats, and prostitution-related crimes (U.S. Department of State, 2007a, 2007b). Some advocates state that while the anti-trafficking laws are sufficient, the resources allotted to services—such as long-term assisted housing—and the monitoring of labor conditions are not. Experts also point to a need for stronger anti-trafficking training of local law-enforcement personnel, who are often the first to come into contact with trafficking victims (U.S. Department of State, 2007a, 2007b, 2012; Akin, 2010).

The Canadian government has recently amplified its efforts to keep out illegal immigrants. An anti–illegal immigrant agenda can often counteract a nation's ability to properly protect and provide services to victims of human trafficking because it tends to overpower the need to protect trafficking victims who are commonly violators of immigration law by the nature of their trafficking experience. Until recently, because of international treaty obligations, Canada accepted anyone who arrived on its shores and claimed refugee status (Akin, 2010). The issue of refugee status was raised most recently in response to the arrival of 492

Sri Lankan Tamil refugee claimants in August 2010. The refugees were aboard the MV *Sun Sea* when they landed in British Columbia. In reaction, the government did not amplify its anti-trafficking efforts under existing law but instead created Bill C-49 (now Bill C-4), the Preventing Human Smugglers from Abusing Canada's Immigration System Act (Akin, 2010; Dhillon, 2011; CCR, 2012). In support of the bill, government sources have been quoted in the media arguing that the bill is designed to put a stop to human trafficking rings (Akin, 2010). What is clear is that the bill places the emphasis on border control and immigration as opposed to human rights. In terms of the government's discussion of the bill, it is difficult to determine whether the conflation of human trafficking and smuggling was intentional and if by purporting that the bill furthered the nation's anti-trafficking objectives it was able to garner more support. In June 2012, the Protecting Canada's Immigration System Act, which included Bill C-4, was approved (CIC, 2012). Years later it has not yet been determined whether the refugees aboard the MV *Sun Sea* were victims of a trafficking scheme, though the government stated it suspected so because of the exorbitant fees the refugees were charged, 75 percent of which was to be paid once in Canada, creating a potential scenario of debt bondage (Canadian Immigration Information Centre, 2011). Recent details show that the passengers paid $5,000 to $10,000 in advance and pledged to pay 10 to 20 times that amount if the ship made it to Canada (Bell, 2012b). Those who orchestrated the operation are believed to have netted a profit of $1.6 million (Perrin, 2011). Of concern is that attorneys for MV *Sun Sea* passengers said that the migrants were held in custody by the Canada Border Services Agency and would not be released until they paid off the smuggler. "It's become this weird perversion of the law where we're forcing people to pay these debts," said attorney Gabriel Chand, who represented some of the migrants who were aboard the vessel. "They're selling their land, their jewelry, so that they can pay these debts so they can be released from custody." Attorney Eric Purtzki, who represented some of the passengers, told the *Globe and Mail* that paying off the debt undoubtedly played a role in their release. Jason Kenney, minister of citizenship, immigration and multiculturalism, said the attorneys were incorrect. "The government of Canada wouldn't countenance facilitating someone paying [such a debt]," Kenney said (Dhillon, 2011).

While members of the Conservative Party of Canada want to stop allowing passengers of unannounced boats to claim asylum, others like New Democratic Party MP Olivia Chows believe this step would result in a regression in immigration law (Whittington, 2010). "Sometimes we are generous, sometimes we are not, with tragic consequences," Chows told the *Toronto Star*, referring to Ottawa's well-known decision to turn away Jewish refugees from Nazi Germany in the 1930s. "That's why we have a refugee law and we should follow the law and treat these individuals equally under Canadian law," she said (Whittington, 2010). As of August 2012, 15 of 492 MV *Sun Sea* passengers had been granted refugee status (Bell, 2012a).

CHILD SEX TOURISM AND CANADA AS A TRANSIT NATION AND DESTINATION

Experts have believed for many years that Canada is primarily a transit nation for human trafficking. In 2004 the Royal Canadian Mounted Police (RCMP) estimated that 1,500 to 2,000 persons from other nations were trafficked annually through Canada into the United States and that only 600 to 800 were trafficked annually to Canada as a destination. The RCMP also estimated that some Canadians were trafficked within Canada (U.S. Department of State, 2007a). Certain forms of trafficking such as internal trafficking and forced labor are just now coming to light. It is likely that while Canada remains a transit nation, it may also be more of a destination country and a nation of internal trafficking than was previously believed.

Persons trafficked through Canada are primarily women from Asia (chiefly from South Korea) and eastern Europe. Many of these women are trafficked into the United States (U.S. Department of State, 2007a, 2007b, 2010). NGOs believe that the number of persons trafficked through Canada is much higher than the RCMP estimates—closer to 15,000 (Fitzpatrick, 2006). Women are believed to constitute the primary group of victims brought to Canada for commercial sexual exploitation there. As in other nations, this is the form of trafficking that has been most sensationalized in the media. Persons are also trafficked to Canada for forced labor in sweatshops, farming and fishing, agriculture, processing plants, and domestic work (CityNews, 2006; Fitzpatrick, 2006; U.S. Department of State, 2010). Victims are from China, Hong Kong, Moldova, the Philippines, Romania, South Korea, Taiwan, and Ukraine. Eastern European women and Latin American women are more often trafficked to eastern Canada, Montreal, and Toronto, while Asian women are more regularly trafficked to Vancouver and western Canada (U.S. Department of State, 2007b, 2010).

The government's primary focus on sex trafficking makes it difficult to determine the actual extent of forced labor. Most labor victims enter the nation legally and are subjected to forced labor after arrival. NGOs report a higher incidence of forced labor in Alberta, British Columbia, and Ontario than elsewhere in the nation (U.S. Department of State, 2010). One alleged instance of forced labor involves Khaira Enterprises Ltd., a subcontractor paid $286,979.83 by the government to clear brush in British Columbia. The contract was suspended in 2010 when it was found that 25 workers—mostly African immigrants—were found living in squalor without drinking water or bathing facilities (Bolan, 2010). The typical day for workers included traveling 2 to 3 hours into the bush, working 10 to 12 hours, and traveling another 2 to 3 hours back to the makeshift camp. The workers also allegedly faced threats, racist comments, insufficient food, and bounced paychecks (Bolan, 2010). Jim Sinclair, president of the British Columbia Federation of Labour, said that the federation asked the Ministry of Labour to undertake an independent investigation of what happened. Sinclair said that all the workers are still owed tens of thousands of dollars for their months at the bush camp. "It is clear that these people weren't protected," Sinclair told the *Vancouver Sun*. "It's clear that enforcement failed. We had Third World conditions in British Columbia" (Bolan, 2010).

The territories and provinces, rather than the federal government, have been primarily responsible for enforcing labor standards and combatting forced labor. Ontario enacted the Employment Protection for Foreign Nationals Act (Live-in Caregivers and Others) in December 2009. The act amends the Employment Standards Act (2000) to include employment protections for temporary foreign workers in the domestic-service sector. It prohibits taking or retaining property from a foreign worker, or intimidating, penalizing, or attempting or threatening to intimidate or penalize a foreign national because he or she requests compliance with the law, makes inquiries about his or her rights, files a complaint with the Ministry of Labour, exercises or attempts to exercise a right under the act, gives information to an employment standards officer, or is required or is going to testify or participate in a proceeding under the act. Violators are subject to a fine and/or possibly imprisonment of no more than 12 months if the offender is an individual. Corporations are subject solely to fines of up to $512,432 depending on whether the company has had previous convictions, and if so, how many (Legislative Assembly of Ontario, 2009). In April 2011 amendments to the Immigration and Refugee Protection Act (IRPA) came into effect and established an improved compliance structure for the federal temporary foreign worker program. Among the reforms are guidelines for compensation to temporary foreign workers in instances of employer liability, additional criteria for the live-in caregiver program, and increased consequences for employers that are noncompliant (U.S. Department of State, 2012).

Canada has yet to ratify the more general International Labour Organization (ILO) Convention No. 29 on Forced Labor. The convention, adopted in 1930, prohibits all forms of forced or compulsory labor, defined by the ILO as "all work or service exacted from any person under the menace of any penalty and for which the said person has not offered voluntarily" (NUPGE, 2009). Canada has also not ratified ILO Convention No. 98, Right to Organize and Collective Bargaining (1949) or ILO Convention No. 138, Minimum Age (1973) (NUPGE, 2010). Still, Canada has adopted some of the ILO conventions related to human trafficking. For instance, in 1959 it ratified Convention No. 105, Abolition of Forced Labor, prohibiting forced or compulsory labor as a means of political coercion. It also ratified the Convention on Maritime Labor in July 2010, which requires that seafarers have rights to decent work conditions and allows Canada to inspect foreign ships in its ports to determine compliance with modern labor standards (NUPGE, 2009, 2010). Cleopatra Doumbia-Henry, director of the ILO's International Labor Standards Department, believes that the ratification of the ILO Convention on Maritime Labor "demonstrates a re-engagement by Canada with international labor standards, being that it's the first convention ratified by Canada in ten years" (NUPGE, 2010).

Canada is not only a transit and destination nation for human trafficking but also a significant source country for child-sex tourists, citizens who travel abroad to engage in sex with children. Since 1997, roughly 136 formal charges have been filed against Canadian citizens who allegedly sexually exploited children in other countries. In 2008 the government obtained two convictions against Canadian sex tourists compared to none in 2009, one in 2010, and none in 2011 (U.S. Department of State, 2010, 2011, 2012).

TRAFFICKING WITHIN CANADA

The conflation of smuggling and human trafficking has created significant hurdles in Canada, where, historically, statistics have combined cases of smuggling and human trafficking, so that it is impossible to properly examine the extent of human trafficking. From 2002 until 2005, the only anti-trafficking law in existence was the IRPA, which includes the offense of human smuggling (section 117) and the offense of human trafficking (section 118) (Department of Justice, Canada, 2001; RCMP, 2010). The issue is that the emphasis of the act is on violations of immigration, not human rights. For instance, the human trafficking section is only applicable when persons are trafficked across a border into Canada (RCMP, 2010). In the first case of human trafficking on which the IRPA was used, the accused offender was acquitted on the charge of human trafficking but convicted of human smuggling and prostitution-related offenses, which illustrates its ineffectiveness as a tool to prosecute traffickers. In 2005 the government of Canada amended the Criminal Code to include the offense of trafficking in persons. This change permits prosecutors to focus on the human rights violation aspect of human trafficking, which does not always involve borders, rather than those aspects potentially related to immigration. Even with the change, conflation of the two issues continues. One adverse result is that the nation's anti-trafficking efforts have focused primarily on persons entering Canada, which has marginalized victims of internal trafficking. The reality is that persons, some of whom are as young as 12 years old, are trafficked internally within Canada for commercial sexual purposes. The offenders are often part of organized crime syndicates. Unsurprisingly, exact numbers are unknown. One reason is that the issue of internal trafficking is just now beginning to be acknowledged in Canada, but recent data indicate that the numbers are significant. In fact, in February 2012 all but 4 of 57 ongoing human trafficking prosecutions involved internal sex trafficking (U.S. Department of State, 2012). Girls of the aboriginal communities—a particularly marginalized population—are targeted by sex traffickers. Other groups that are also vulnerable are children in protective care, the homeless, and sexually exploited youths (CISC, 2008; Perrin, 2009a).

As in other nations, the age of sex-trafficking victims in Canada appears to be decreasing. Without solid numbers it is difficult to know whether this trend is perception or reality, but there has been enough of a change to attract the attention of the Criminal Intelligence Service Canada (CISC). "Across the country, organized crime networks are actively trafficking Canadian-born women and underage girls inter- and intra-provincially, and in some instances to the United States, destined for the sex trade," the CISC stated in an August 2008 strategic intelligence brief (CISC, 2008).

In order to determine the scope and nature of the internal trafficking of children, the RCMP conducted 175 interviews with police and service agencies in Vancouver, Prince George, Kamloops/Kelowna, Calgary, Edmonton, Prince Albert, Fort McMurray, Regina, Winnipeg, the Greater Toronto Area, Ottawa, Montreal, Fredericton/Marysville, St. John's, Moncton, St. John, Halifax, and Gander. The report indicates that some populations of children are at particular risk of sexual exploitation, including vulnerability to sex trafficking. Among them are runaways, unwanted children, youths living independently (when they reach 16 years of age), and children who use the Internet to solicit sex-trade clients. In some cities, black and aboriginal children within these groups are particularly vulnerable (Dalley, 2010). One case of internal trafficking is that of a 17-year-old Canadian girl trafficked for commercial sexual exploitation. The girl's trafficker, Michael Lennox Mark, pleaded guilty but then received two years' credit for one year in pretrial custody. He spent only a week in custody after his conviction. The victim declined to give her victim impact statement in court when she was informed how soon her trafficker would be released (Parliament of Canada, 2010c). Canadian-born persons can also become victims of forced labor. Christine Barker is one such victim. A Canadian citizen allegedly enslaved by Khaira Enterprises Ltd., Barker was mistreated and unpaid. At times she and other workers were refused food. Some of the workers also faced death threats. Barker saw a supervisor threaten to kill a Congolese co-worker and then throw a knife at him. "When we started the work refusal, that's when the camp conditions got even worse; showers were denied," Barker told the *Vancouver Sun*. "We were refused food because we weren't working for him at that time" (Bolan, 2010). Barker has since been unable to collect employment insurance because the company, Khaira, claimed on her documents that she quit (Bolan, 2010).

WHAT HAPPENS TO VICTIMS AFTER TRAFFICKING

As recently as 2006, potential victims were treated as illegal migrants and often deported without any sort of screening to determine if they were trafficking victims. Benjamin Perrin, founder of the Future Group (an NGO), says victims were deported without any psychological counseling or emergency support. "There was no system in place to protect victims," Perrin said (Chan, 2007). In June 2007 immigration guidelines were amended to enable immigration officials to better assist and protect foreign trafficking victims. The guidelines extended the temporary residence permits (TRPs) from 120 to 180 days, which can be renewed at the termination of the 180-day period (this varies with each individual case). Yet between May 2006 and February 2009, only 26 permits were issued, and only 18 of those went to trafficking victims. In 2011, 53 TRPs were issued to 48 foreign trafficking victims. Five of the TRPs were first-term permits, and 48 were renewals (CIC, 2007; UNODC, 2009; U.S. Department of State, 2012). Victims are now allowed to apply for work permits, and there are no fees for either the work visa or TRP. Victims are eligible for psychological and trauma counseling, dental care, and essential and emergency medical care. Also, while victims are encouraged to testify in cases against their trafficker(s), their ability to obtain temporary or permanent status does not depend on it (CIC, 2007; U.S. Department of State, 2010). Other victims opt to seek residency via humanitarian or refugee immigration applications instead of utilizing the TRP. They do so in part because benefits are perceived to be more secure and the immigration status associated with humanitarian or refugee applications may be more familiar to immigration officials (U.S. Department of State, 2010). Canada receives more than 30,000 refugee claims a year, and each refugee determination process averages 16 months (Whittington, 2010).

Support services for trafficking victims are generally provided at the provincial level, so the type and quality of the services vary. Most jurisdictions do provide victims with shelter, short-term counseling, and rape counseling, and also feature initiatives targeted at aiding aboriginal women. Additionally, NGOs provide victim services such as resettlement, shelter, and employment assistance (U.S. Department of State, 2010).

WHAT HAPPENS TO TRAFFICKERS

Under the IRPA, the only anti-trafficking law in existence between 2002 and 2005, cross-border traffickers can face a maximum of life in prison and fines of up to $1.025 million. Thus far, few prosecutors have used the IRPA for cross-border trafficking. The first person charged under the human trafficking law was massage parlor owner Michael Wai Chi Ng (U.S. Department of State, 2007a; RCMP, 2010). Ng was accused of bringing two women from China into Canada after promising them waitress jobs and then forcing them to work as prostitutes. In 2008 Ng was sentenced to a 15-month jail term for falsifying immigration documents, human smuggling, procuring sexual intercourse, and running a common bawdy house (brothel). He was acquitted on the charge of human trafficking. The British Columbia Court of Appeal increased Ng's sentence by 12 months on the grounds of inadequate sentencing for the prostitution-related convictions. Ng faced a total of 27 months' imprisonment (Perrin, 2009b; RCMP, 2010).

In 2005, Bill C-49: An Act to Amend the Criminal Code (Trafficking in Persons) was passed, adding sections 279.01 to 279.04 to the Criminal Code. These sections make trafficking in persons a criminal offense, allow charges of human trafficking to fall under multiple jurisdictions,

and go beyond the focus on immigration. The act prohibits the recruitment, transport, transfer, receipt, concealment, or harboring of a person,
or the exercise of control, direction, or influence over the movements of
a person, for the purpose of exploitation. It also prohibits a person from
benefiting economically from trafficking and prohibits the withholding
or destruction of identity, immigration, or travel documents to facilitate
trafficking in persons. Penalties are up to 14 years' imprisonment for
human trafficking, with a 5-year minimum for minors. The first charge
under section 279.01 occurred in 2007. As of November 15, 2009, of 33
persons charged under section 279.01, 5 had been convicted. Charges
were dropped against 2 of the accused because of a victim's absence in
court, while 3 others were acquitted of the human trafficking charges
but found guilty under trafficking-related charges such as assault with
a weapon, kidnapping, aggravated sexual assault, and forcible confinement. Human trafficking convictions have resulted from guilty pleas,
not from judicial pronouncements (Barnett, 2006; RCMP, 2010).

Of concern is the use of 2-for-1 credit granted to traffickers. For
example, in the sentencing of Michael Lennox Mark, one year in pretrial custody was counted as two (Rabson, 2009). Likewise, in the case
of Laura Emerson, her sentence was reduced by 16 months for the 8
months and 10 days that she spent in pretrial custody (Payton, 2009).
In October 2009 federal legislation placed a cap on credit for time
served at 1-to-1. The law will permit judges to give credit at a maximum
ratio of 1.5-to-1 only when the circumstances can justify it. Judges are
required to explain the circumstances (CBC News, 2009; Parliament
of Canada, 2010a).

Until recently, Canada did not have a minimum sentence for those
who commit trafficking offenses. In order to change this, MP Joy Smith
introduced Bill C-268. Passed in June 2010, the law amends the Criminal
Code to create a minimum prison sentence of five years for offenses involving the trafficking of persons under the age of 18 (Parliament of
Canada, 2010b; Cherry, 2010). Perrin, who helped draft Bill C-268, says
the new law (section 279.011) is only one part of the solution. He believes
part of the problem is that trafficking cases are often filed under different
offenses, even though anti-trafficking law has existed in the Criminal
Code since 2005. "Some cases are like charging someone with assault
when they murder someone," Perrin told the *Toronto Sun*. "We should be

charging someone with the most serious charge that their conduct warrants" (Cherry, 2010).

While the number of persons trafficked through, to, and within Canada are estimated to be in the thousands, the number of reported investigations and prosecutions is low. Convictions are even less common (UNODC, 2009). In late February 2010 there were 32 trafficking cases before the courts. The cases involved 40 alleged traffickers and 46 victims. Ninety-seven percent of the cases involved sex trafficking. In 2009 there were 1 conviction under trafficking-specific laws and 3 under other Criminal Code offenses, such as sexual assault and living off the proceeds of prostitution. The sentences ranged from six to nine years' imprisonment. As of late February 2011 there were 46 human trafficking cases before the courts, involving 80 victims and 68 accused offenders. There were 2 convictions under trafficking-specific laws. The offenders received sentences of 6 years' imprisonment and 30 months of credit for pretrial custody. There were also at least 7 convictions under non-trafficking specific offenses; 2 of these offenders were sentenced to 34 months' imprisonment. The other sentences were not reported. In 2011 there were 3 convictions of sex traffickers under trafficking-specific laws. One of the offenders received a sentence of 30 months' imprisonment, including credit for pretrial custody. Another offender was sentenced to time served after spending just over a year in jail. Six other sex-trafficking offenders were convicted under other sections of the Criminal Code; sentences ranged from two years' suspended to nine years' imprisonment. Of significance is that the government of Canada attained its first forced labor conviction in 2012 (U.S. Department of State, 2010; 2011; 2012).

INTERNAL EFFORTS TO DECREASE TRAFFICKING

Officials and border agents often screen vulnerable persons detained for immigration violations for signs of human trafficking. Additionally, Canadian consular officials and domestic law and social service officials receive training in identifying trafficking victims and the assistance and protections available to them. NGOs are given funding by the government through the Victims Fund, which has an annual budget of

$11.6 million to fill in potential gaps in services for trafficking victims. In addition, the government is making $5.38 million available over five years to create new child advocacy centers or to enhance existing ones in Canada (U.S. Department of State, 2007b; Department of Justice, Canada, 2012).

The government has increased its anti-trafficking prevention measures through awareness campaigns, which distribute anti-trafficking materials and support an anti-trafficking website. The most recent awareness campaign is called Blue Blindfold and includes radio, print, and television spots (Mayes, 2010). While these materials and the website may help those in the community better identify victims, they are less accessible to actual victims, who tend not to be allowed out on their own and are threatened with bodily harm or death to ensure that they will not attempt escape.

According to MP Joy Smith many Canadians are simply oblivious to human trafficking. "The average Canadian is not aware of the victims in their cities and communities who are held in bondage, threatened and brutalized as they try to seek help, if they try to seek help. Predators are making vast amounts of money off their suffering" (Fitzpatrick, 2006). Smith said that the passage of Bill C-268 is a victory, but much more needs to be done, particularly concerning victim protection and services:

> It's been brought up to the forefront and now, there has to be an awareness both at the provincial and federal level that this is happening right under the public eye. This coordination has to happen to ensure that, number one, the laws are put in place to arrest and make sure that these perpetrators stay away from their victims, and number two, there has to be, in my opinion, the rehabilitation piece, where victims are counseled, where they're helped to get a new education, get jobs and helped to get out of this horrific crime. (Cherry, 2010)

Although prostitution is legal in Canada, many of the surrounding activities, such as owning a bawdy house, are not. In response to a 2010 constitutional challenge by three sex industry workers, the Ontario Superior Court held to be unconstitutional three anti-prostitution laws that are often used to prosecute traffickers (such as prohibiting living on the avails of prostitution and operating a bawdy house). The federal government appealed and lost in March 2012 when the Ontario Court of Appeals upheld the decision of the Superior Court (CBC News, 2010; U.S. Department of State, 2012). Some anti-trafficking experts support the global decriminalization of prostitution and associated activities, with the hope that increased transparency would minimize opportunity for human trafficking. Others hold that nations simply do not have infrastructures in place to sufficiently monitor and regulate the sex industry. Valerie Scott, a sex worker and one of the applicants in the 2010 case, said that the decision reduces the risk of violence for sex workers. "We don't have to worry about being raped and robbed and murdered. This decision means that sex workers can now pick up the phone, and call the police and report a bad client. This means that we no longer have to be afraid, that we can work with the appropriate authorities" (CBC News, 2010).

Canada is consistently moving forward in terms of anti-trafficking legislation, but the government's persistent conflation of human trafficking and smuggling as well as its determination to limit the rights of refugees based on their form of entrance into the nation, is a step backward. Furthermore, the number of convictions is nominal. Sentences are insufficiently stringent, and many convicted offenders still receive inflated credit for pretrial custody.

PART V
Conflicting Agendas

A global economic crisis has caused many governments to tighten restrictions on immigration; among them are France and Italy. In doing so, these governments have created immigration policies that are in direct conflict with their anti-trafficking agendas and pose the most significant challenge to granting victims proper treatment and services as well as investigating and prosecuting traffickers.

In Italy the conflict has resulted in a focus on the illegal status of a person, not on whether he or she is a victim of human trafficking. Illegal migrants commonly face fines and expedited deportation without proper screening to determine whether they are in fact trafficking victims. This state of affairs not only allows traffickers to evade culpability; it also creates a setting in which victims are denied proper treatment and services and are returned to nations where they may face retribution or re-trafficking. The Italian government, often commended on its victim-centric focus, has approved a security package that includes the option to deport prostitutes. Prostitution and human trafficking are not synonymous, but the uniform deportation of street prostitutes means that potential victims are not screened before deportation. The policy also treats potential victims as criminals and, by deporting them, places these persons in a position where they are at risk of re-trafficking and potential retribution by traffickers. To decrease the number of illegal immigrants in Italy, the government made an agreement with Libya that permits Italy to return and reroute boat migrants to Libya. These persons are not screened for signs of human trafficking prior to return.

The French government has also taken measures that focus on immigration to the detriment of its anti-trafficking agenda. One population that is particularly vulnerable to human trafficking in France, and elsewhere in Europe, is the Roma ethnic group. In August 2010 the government of France began to deport Roma persons, and though, after some controversy, this was eventually stopped, it is reported that Roma continue to face discrimination. Another problematic policy issue is the transit zones (zone d'attente) *that allow the government to treat persons physically in France as though they are outside the nation. The result is that those detained in the zones have restricted rights and face rapid deportation. Among those adversely affected by the policy are unaccompanied child trafficking victims. Border police lack screening procedures to adequately identify victims and have a history of immediately deporting these children. There are even instances where the border police have allowed traffickers to visit their child victims in detention. The zones facilitate instances of human trafficking by allowing the transport of victims to their destination or transit nation to continue without question.*

The European Court of Human Rights, which ensures compliance with EU law and rules on the interpretation and application of the treaties that establish the EU, held in the 2010 case of Rantsev v. Cyprus and Russia *that member nations of the European Convention on Human Rights, such as France and Italy, must provide safeguards to aid and protect potential victims of human trafficking. The court held that such safeguards include a state's immigration rules, which must address relevant concerns relating to tolerance, facilitation, or encouragement of trafficking. The anti-immigration measures by Italy and France hinder each step of the anti-trafficking process. By deporting potential victims and marginalized persons, these nations prevent not only the proper identification of victims, but also their access to proper treatment and services, and their right to be a part, if they wish, of the prosecutorial process against their traffickers.*

CHAPTER 10

Italy

Here I found true hell. A world of daily violence perpetrated by men,
and by other women, and also by our own families who
pretend they're not aware, and take their part of money.
—ISOKE AIKPITANYI, SEX-TRAFFICKING VICTIM

It is estimated that roughly 40,000 people are trafficked for commercial sexual exploitation in Italy. Trafficking cases are categorized under a variety of laws, most commonly Articles 600, 601, and 602 of the Penal Code, but determining the scope of labor versus sex trafficking is difficult as the current collection and distribution of comprehensive law enforcement data does not separate forced labor from forced prostitution convictions (UNODC, 2009a, 2009b; U.S. Department of State, 2012a).

There is a conflict between Italy's agenda to keep out immigrants and its effort to properly aid trafficking victims. Until this conflict is resolved, foreign victims will continue to lack access to the services to which they are entitled; face arrest and deportation without a thorough investigation of whether they are trafficking victims; and be returned to their country of origin, where they may be vulnerable to retribution from their trafficker(s).

ITALY AS A PRIMARY DESTINATION AND AS A TRANSIT NATION

Italy is both a destination and a transit nation for human trafficking. Women and children are trafficked into Italy from Albania, Bulgaria, China, the Middle East, Moldova, Morocco, Nigeria, North and East Africa, Romania, Russia, South America, Ukraine, and Uzbekistan for forced prostitution. Persons from Albania, China, Cote d'Ivoire, Morocco,

Pakistan, Poland, and Romania face forced labor, mostly in the agricultural sector in the south but also in sweatshops throughout the nation. Victims identified by law enforcement between 2003 and 2007 were primarily foreigners. Nations of origin were Romania (68.5 percent), Nigeria (7.5 percent), Thailand (5.9 percent), Albania (4.4 percent), and Brazil (3.7 percent) (UNODC, 2009a; U.S. Department of State, 2010a).

Children are particularly vulnerable to child labor and other forms of trafficking, especially those who are unaccompanied. Experts estimate that there are about 24,000 unaccompanied minors in Italy. The law prohibits employment of children under the age of 15 (with some exceptions) and places restrictions on employment in unhealthy or hazardous occupations for girls under the age of 21 and boys under the age of 18. The Italian government appears to sufficiently enforce the formal economy, but enforcement of the informal economy presents a challenge. Child laborers from China, the Philippines, and North Africa, ages 15–18, work primarily in the service and manufacturing sectors. Most arrive with their parents, but some are unaccompanied (U.S. Department of State, 2010b). Children are also believed to be a vulnerable population for sexual exploitation and forced begging. The Ministry of Interior estimates that children make up 20 percent of the total trafficking and smuggling victims from Romania. Of that 20 percent, the ministry estimates that 75 percent are engaged in prostitution. One example is a Romanian girl trafficked under the promise of a caretaker job in Sicily. Instead, the traffickers—one Italian and three Romanians—repeatedly raped and abused her, took her passport, isolated her, and forced her to prostitute (U.S. Department of State, 2010b). In June 2010 Italian and Romanian authorities dismantled a large syndicate that trafficked more than 150 women, including minors, from Romania to Monza and Milan as well as other Italian cities for the purposes of commercial sexual exploitation. The 57-person trafficking ring was made up primarily of Romanians but also included several Italians, one Albanian, and one Egyptian. The majority, if not all, of the arrests took place in Romania (AFP, 2010).

Of concern is the recent increase in Nigerian women and girls who are trafficked to Italy for forced prostitution. After the United Kingdom, Italy is host to the largest number of Nigerians in Europe. Experts believe that the majority of 10,000 Nigerian women and girls engaged in prostitution in Italy are trafficking victims (Germano, 2001; IOM, 2006; Aminu, 2010). In the 1980s a demand for low-skill labor in the agricultural and services sectors in Italy caused an influx of Nigerian workers. The Nigerian women who came to work in the sex industry during this time were probably not trafficking victims, but in the 1990s the increased challenges of migrating and settling in Europe created a ripe opportunity for human traffickers. Persons migrating from Nigeria to Italy were promised legitimate employment and charged high fees by alleged recruiters and/or smugglers. Upon arrival they were forced to prostitute in order to repay their debt (Carling, 2005).

Jørgen Carling of the International Peace Research Institute says there is a systematic pattern in human trafficking from Nigeria to Italy. First, family and friends often put the victim in touch with a smuggler. The smuggler then puts the victim in contact with a madam/sponsor who finances the travel. Costs range between $500 and $2,000 for the necessary documents and between $8,000 and $12,000 for travel expenses, though victims are typically charged much higher fees amounting to somewhere between $40,000 and $100,000. It is these charges that place the victims in debt bondage (Carling, 2005). The victim then enters into an emigration pact with the sponsor that obligates the victim to repay the sponsor in exchange for safe passage to Europe. This agreement is affirmed by a traditional ceremony that in effect establishes a contract not only with the sponsor, but also with the local priest and the victim's community. Increasingly, victims and their families enter into a formal agreement with the sponsor and even use family assets as security (Carling, 2005). Some of the women do not know that they will be working in the Italian sex industry. Others are aware that they will be prostituted but are unaware of the conditions they will face upon arrival. The women are transported to Europe via air, land, or through the Sahara by smugglers. Those who are transported by land are often raped and forced to have sex with border officials. Upon arrival in Italy, the women often live and work under the control of a Nigerian madam and a male assistant. The victims are often indentured—working between one and three years to pay off their debt. They frequently are forced to work as low-wage street prostitutes in the suburbs or along intercity highways (Carling, 2005, 2006).

One case of human trafficking from Niger to Italy is that of Isoke Aikpitanyi, a woman from Benin City, Nigeria, who accepted a job in London. Instead she was sold to a criminal group that sent her to Turin, Italy, where she faced debt bondage and was forced to prostitute in order to pay the $42,000 that she "owed" traffickers. Aikpitanyi was beaten and raped and in one instance was nearly stabbed to death (Povoledo, 2007; Zaccaro, 2009). "Here I found true hell," Aikpitanyi told the Inter Press Service. "A world of daily violence perpetrated by men, and by other women, and also by our own families who pretend they're not aware, and take their part of money" (Zaccaro, 2009). Fortunately, Aikpitanyi was able to escape her trafficking scenario. Today she is an advocate for trafficked persons and coauthor of the book *Le ragazze di Benin* (The Girls in Benin City). "I made a promise with myself that I would help them [other victims] as a sort of therapy to heal a wound I know will never heal," Aikpitanyi told the *New York Times*. "Sometimes all they need is someone to listen" (Povoledo, 2007).

Persons are also trafficked to Italy for forced labor. Some of the primary source nations are Albania, Bangladesh, China, Cote d'Ivoire, Ghana, Morocco, Pakistan, Poland, Romania, and Senegal. Of 291 forced-labor victims who received assistance from NGOs between 2005 and 2009, the top countries of origin were Egypt, India, Morocco, and Romania. Seventy-one percent of the victims were male, and more than half went to Italy voluntarily. Sixty-seven percent of female forced-labor victims and 48 percent of male forced-labor victims received deceptive employment offers; 25 percent worked in the construction industry, 17 percent worked as caregivers, and 14 percent worked in the agricultural sector. In March 2008 a Chinese entrepreneur was charged with abetting illegal immigration and exploiting 47 Chinese victims, including 6 minors and 2 pregnant women working and living in a sweatshop near Reggio Emilia. In May 2010 police arrested the Chinese owner of a textile factory near Perugia and charged him with exploiting 15 Chinese illegal laborers. The laborers were working and living in poor conditions at the textile factory. According to one NGO, 90 percent of foreign seasonal workers are unregistered and two-thirds are in the country illegally, and thus vulnerable to human trafficking (U.S. Department of State, 2010a, 2010b, 2011b, 2012b). Italian police reported identifying 410 victims of labor exploitation in 2009 and 640 victims in 2010 (U.S.

Department of State, 2011a). In 2009 labor inspectors discovered 98,400 unregistered workers working in the agricultural sector. In fact 79.5 percent of the 100,600 inspected farms employed unregistered workers. Unregistered workers are extremely vulnerable to human trafficking, typically in the form of forced labor and debt bondage (U.S. Department of State, 2010b).

In January 2010, race riots brought to public view the labor exploitations of African immigrants, particularly in Italy's agricultural sector. Two immigrants were injured when white youths fired air rifles at a group of farm workers in Rosarno. "Those guys were firing at us as if it was a fairground," a worker said. "They were laughing, I was screaming, other cars were passing by, but nobody stopped." In the ensuing riot the laborers smashed cars with bricks. Fifteen farm laborers were arrested and 19 were injured. The next day more than 2,000 Africans went to the town center to demonstrate against the shootings and their living and working conditions. They chanted, "We are not animals." It is difficult to know exactly how many migrant workers are employed in the Calabria region of Rosarno, but as of 2007 the Italian General Confederation of Labor estimated the number at roughly 26,400. Over 19,400 of the workers did not have permits to be in Italy, and thus were susceptible to exploitation. They earned $28 per day for 9-hour days but were forced to hand over a quarter of what they earned to the Ndrangheta, a large crime organization in Italy (Day, 2010).

Flavio Di Giacomo, a spokesperson for the International Organization for Migration (IOM), told the *New York Times* that the riots reveal the conditions faced by migrant workers in Italy. "This event pulled the lid off something that we who work in the sector know well but no one talks about: That many Italian economic realities are based on the exploitation of low-cost foreign labor, living in subhuman conditions, without human rights" (Day, 2010). After the riot, the police began to bulldoze the shanty encampments where many of the workers lived. It is unclear whether the migrant workers left the encampments voluntarily or were forced to leave. The workers were then taken to detention centers. Roberto Maroni, then-minister of the interior, stated in a television interview that those with residence permits or those who requested political asylum were free to leave the immigration centers. All others were to be deported (Donadio, 2010). It is unknown whether the detained workers in this case were properly and systematically screened for human trafficking. What is known is that only eight migrants requested residence permits as trafficking victims. Many of the migrants in detention did possess temporary residence permits, but it is unknown if they were allowed to stay in the country. The Italian government reported granting some of the workers asylum and deported the rest (U.S. Department of State, 2010a).

In addition to Romanians, Nigerians, and most recently, Moroccans (these are the top three countries of origin for assisted victims in Italy), there has also been an increase in the number of Bulgarians trafficked to Italy. One case involves a Bulgarian family that was trafficked by Italian circus owner Enrico Raffaele Ingrassia; his son, William Ingrassia; and his son-in-law, Gaetano Belfiore. The family was forced to work between 15 and 20 hours per day for $133 a week and to live in a vehicle used to transport animals. Any attempts to escape resulted in physical punishment. The mother was forced to cook, the father was forced to perform manual labor, and the two daughters were forced to perform dangerous acts such as entering a tank full of piranhas and draping snakes around their bodies. One of the girls developed wounds from where snakes bit her or constricted too tightly around her abdomen, but she was never taken to the hospital by her captors. The traffickers were charged with holding the Bulgarian family in slavery and breaching international human rights conventions (Owen, 2008; Truscott, 2008).

On February 25, 2009, Carabinieri officers of the Italian armed forces arrested 11 Bulgarian Roma accused of trafficking minors from Bulgaria to countries in western Europe. Victims were forced to marry other Roma and to commit crimes such as shoplifting, burglary, and pickpocketing (U.S. Department of State, 2010b).

TRAFFICKING WITHIN ITALY, SEX TOURISM, AND TRAFFICKING ABROAD

Italian citizens made up 9 percent of the trafficking victims identified by law enforcement authorities in Italy between 2003 and 2007. This is likely to be an underrepresentation, as internal trafficking cases often go unreported or are classified under other offenses (UNODC, 2009a).

Italy is also home to a large number of sex tourists, persons who travel abroad to have sex with minors. The NGO ECPAT (End Child Prostitution Child Pornography and Trafficking of Children for Sexual Purposes) estimates that each year 80,000 Italian men travel to Brazil, the Czech Republic, Kenya, Latin America, and Thailand for sex (U.S. Department of State, 2010a). Italy's anti–child sex tourism program permits domestic courts to try citizens and permanent residents who engage in sex tourism outside the country, even if the offense is not a crime in the country where the incident occurred. Nevertheless, the government has not reported prosecuting any such offenders (U.S. Department of State, 2010a, 2010b, 2011a, 2012a).

Italian nationals are also trafficked abroad. The United Nations Office on Drugs and Crime (UNODC) states that Italian nationals, along with Romanian nationals, account for a large part of the trafficking victim population in France (UNODC, 2009b).

WHAT HAPPENS TO VICTIMS AFTER TRAFFICKING

An operational system for the referral of identified victims has been established by the authorities and accredited NGOs that provides a wide range of assistance and support services within the Ministry for Equal Opportunity Social Assistance and Integration Program for trafficked persons (UNODC, 2009a). That said, because Italy does not have an established national referral process, the referral process for victims varies from region to region (U.S. Department of State, 2012a). In 2009 the Italian government along with local authorities earmarked $12.7 million for victim assistance programs. In collaboration with the IOM, the state helps reintegrate victims to their home in a responsible manner. In 2008 roughly 1,100 trafficking victims—including 100 men and 50 children—entered social protection programs (U.S. Department of State, 2010a).

Italy does not have a formal reflection period during which victims can recuperate and determine whether to assist law enforcement, but authorities do informally grant this period to victims and do not limit it to a fixed number of days. This, importantly, grants victims the critical element of time to best determine their next course of action. Under Article 18 of the immigration law, once a victim has been identified, he or she can pursue social or judicial procedure. Judicial procedure requires cooperation with law enforcement while social procedure only requires a statement submission by social services or an accredited NGO on behalf of the victim (UNODC, 2009a; U.S. Department of State, 2012a). Under both the social and judicial procedures, victims are granted a renewable temporary residence permit and may eventually obtain a residence permit for work or education. From 2003 through 2006 roughly 950 foreign victims obtained residency permits as compared with 664 in 2008 and 810 in 2009. The number decreased to 527 in 2010. In 2011, at 1,078, the number was higher but likely includes permits granted to victims of other types of exploitation (UNODC, 2009a; U.S. Department of State, 2010a, 2011a, 2012a). Adult victims receive a six-month residency permit, which can be renewed if the victim has obtained employment or is enrolled in a training program (U.S. Department of State, 2010a). National and local authorities provide minor trafficking victims automatic residency permits—valid until age 18—and access to education and other assistance programs (U.S. Department of State, 2010b).

The biggest challenge in granting victims proper treatment and services is the nation's competing anti-trafficking and immigration agendas. While Italy has a victim-centered anti-trafficking approach, NGOs believe that there has been a recent decrease in proactive identification of trafficking victims by the government. The result may be an underidentification of victims and forced deportation without a thorough evaluation as to whether they are indeed trafficking victims. Illegal migrants commonly face fines and expedited deportation (U.S. Department of State, 2010a, 2011a). In addition to the issues surrounding the 2010 race riots, other state actions reveal this critical clash of national interests. Italy entered into an agreement with the government of Libya in 2008 that allows Italy to forcibly return and reroute boat migrants back to Libya. These persons are not given any screening to determine whether they are trafficking victims. Italy temporarily suspended the agreement in February 2011 and reentered it in December 2011 (U.S. Department of State, 2010a; *Tripoli Post*, 2011; Watkins, 2011). Further prioritizing its immigration stance over its anti-trafficking agenda, in November 2010 the Italian government approved a security package that includes the option of deporting prostitutes, even those who are European Union citizens, who work on the streets (European Parliament, 2010).

WHAT HAPPENS TO TRAFFICKERS

Human trafficking is prosecuted under Articles 600, 601, and 602 of the Penal Code. Article 600 forbids placing or holding a person in conditions of slavery or servitude; Article 601 prohibits trafficking in human beings; and Article 602 prohibits the sale and purchase of slaves (UNODC, 2009a). Those found guilty under any of the articles face between 8 and 20 years' imprisonment; sentences are increased by 33 percent to 50 percent if the offenses are perpetrated against persons under the age of 18, or for the purposes of sexual exploitation, prostitution, or organ removal (Chamber of Deputies and Senate, 2003).

There has been a recent decrease in arrests and prosecutions for human trafficking. The local and national anti-Mafia bureaus conduct and coordinate trafficking investigations. There were 1,723 prosecutions initiated against traffickers between 2004 and 2007; 861 were prosecuted under Article 601, 594 under Article 600, and 268 under Article 602 (UNODC, 2009a). In 2008 only 365 human trafficking suspects were arrested. Trial courts convicted 138 offenders in 2008, 166 in 2009, and 174 in 2010. While prescribed sentences for human traffickers are sufficiently stringent, the sentences actually received by traffickers in 2008 were lower than the prescribed amount. On average, the traffickers received sentences of four years' imprisonment (U.S. Department of State, 2010a, 2012a). There is a significant difference in the severity of sentencing given to those prosecuted under the trafficking law versus other offenses. For instance, the average sentence for those charged under the trafficking law is 6.5 years' imprisonment, while those convicted under slavery and underage prostitution laws are given average sentences of 1.5 and 3.5 years' imprisonment, respectively (U.S. Department of State, 2012a).

Romanians were the largest population of persons under prosecution in Italy for trafficking offenses between 2003 and 2007 (22.8 percent). The other significant groups of alleged traffickers were Italians (21.4 percent), Albanians (18.5 percent), and Nigerians (15.2 percent) (UNODC, 2009a). Experts report that traffickers in Italy have become more sophisticated, moving the sexual exploitation of their victims from the streets to less visible locales such as hotels, clubs, and discos. Traffickers also move victims from place to place in order to evade police detection.

These practices have made it more challenging for authorities to identify not only potential victims but also their traffickers (U.S. Department of State, 2010a, 2010b).

INTERNAL EFFORTS TO DECREASE TRAFFICKING

Because of Italy's emphasis on restricting immigration, there is a continuing marginalization of migrants. On July 2, 2009, Italy's parliament approved a law that criminalizes illegal immigration, which is punishable by a fine and an immediate order to leave the country. The law also permits the creation of unarmed citizen patrol groups to help police keep order. There are also reports that police occasionally use excessive force against persons, particularly Roma and immigrants detained in connection with common criminal offenses or in the course of identity checks (U.S. Department of State, 2010b).

Italy's expanded efforts to keep illegal immigrants from entry has also resulted in a controversial agreement with Libya in 2008 that allows Italian officers to patrol the Libyan coast. Under the Treaty of Friendship, Partnership and Cooperation between the Republic of Italy and the Grand Arab Libyan Popular Socialist Jamahiriya, all migrants departing the Libyan coast (not just Libyan nationals) may be turned back before reaching Italian soil. Thus far, at least 17,000 migrants bound for Italy from Libya have been prohibited entry. The UN Refugee Agency and the Council of Europe's commissioner for human rights have criticized the policy and expressed concern that returned immigrants may have been eligible for asylum in Europe but instead were returned to a country that has not signed international conventions on protection of refugees. Human Rights Watch and Amnesty International criticized the government for its failure to screen foreigners and to identify refugees, unaccompanied minors, and victims of trafficking (U.S. Department of State, 2010b). Then-Italian prime minister Silvio Berlusconi stated he entered into the agreement "for less illegal immigrants and more oil" (Fruehauf, 2011). The returned and rerouted refugees are housed in several detention camps across Libya, camps that were built by the Italian government. Experts state that the conditions in the camps are vile and that migrants and asylum seekers face a variety of human rights violations, including arbitrary detention, unfair trial (if they have access to a trial at all), disappearance, torture, and death (Fruehauf, 2011). In September 2010 the Libyan coast guard, with the Italian Guardia die Finanza (the police force responsible for dealing with financial crime and smuggling) on board the patrol boat, fired at suspected boat migrants to prevent them from heading toward Italy. There were no casualties, and it turned out that the "migrants" were actually Italian fisherman. The Libyan government apologized for having mistakenly opened fire on the boat, and Roberto Maroni, the Italian interior minister at the time, proposed that the Libyans perhaps mistook the fishing boat for a boat with illegal migrants. According to Bill Frelick, the Refugee Program director at Human Rights Watch, "The Libyans and Italians appear to agree that it was a mistake to shoot at Italian fishermen, but imply that it's OK to shoot at migrants. The bullet-riddled boat shows a reckless use of potentially lethal force that would have been just as bad if it had actually targeted nonthreatening migrants" (HRW, 2010).

Despite Italy's protective laws, reports indicate continuing discrimination against women, Roma, and immigrants in Italy. This further marginalizes these populations and increases their vulnerability to a variety of exploitations, including human trafficking. Italy's immigration and anti-trafficking agendas are in conflict. This has resulted in a focus on the illegal status of a person and not whether the individual is a victim of human trafficking. Consequently, persons are not properly screened and are returned to nations where they may face retribution or re-trafficking. Also, the sentencing of traffickers is not sufficiently stringent. While the laws are adequate in prohibiting human trafficking and enslavement, perpetrators commonly face sentences below the minimum prison requirement of eight years. Lastly, Italy is in dire need of a comprehensive strategy to address human trafficking. There should be an increase in communication among all trafficking-related organizations and agencies, including those focused on immigration. This would improve proper victim identification, case classification, investigations, and prosecutions of traffickers.

CHAPTER 11

France

We need money, we need food. We can live in Romania, but we have
no job and in this village each family has about 10 kids. We are
members of the European Union and we have rights.

—IIORDAN MARIAN, A ROMA FORCIBLY EXPELLED FROM FRANCE

In March 2003 human trafficking was made an offense in France under
the Internal Security Law. The nation prohibits trafficking for the purposes of forced labor or sexual exploitation via Article 225-4-1 of the
Penal Code (CRC, 2009). Those found guilty face up to 7 years' imprisonment and a fine of $209,275 for trafficking an adult and up to 10 years'
imprisonment and a fine of $2.1 million for the trafficking of a minor.
This can be increased to life imprisonment (French Republic, 2005;
UNODC, 2009a). Authorities also utilize other articles of the Criminal
Code to prosecute trafficking offenders, such as soliciting prostitution
and subjection to working and living conditions that are incompatible
with human dignity (UNODC, 2009a).

Nevertheless, immigrant and Roma populations, which are particularly vulnerable to human trafficking, continue to be further marginalized by the French government. Also, unaccompanied children, some
of whom are trafficking victims, enter France and are sometimes sent
to their final destinations without adequate protection (HRW, 2009;
U.S. Department of State, 2009).

FRANCE AS A DESTINATION

Persons are trafficked into France for commercial sexual exploitation and
forced labor primarily from Africa (Cameroon, Ghana, Guinea, Morocco,

Nigeria, and Togo), Asia (Indonesia), Brazil, the Caribbean, and Europe (Albania, Austria, Bulgaria, Hungary, Moldova, Poland, and Romania). Additionally, persons of the Roma ethnic group and unaccompanied minors in France continue to be vulnerable to forced begging (U.S. Department of State, 2008, 2010). The trafficking of women and children for the purpose of domestic servitude is also a problem. The NGO Committee Against Modern Slavery (CCEM) has reported that this abuse often transpires at the hands of diplomats serving in France. Such persons benefit from diplomatic immunity. In 2010 the NGO noted that the Saudi Arabian diplomatic community often violated French labor laws and that roughly 10 percent of cases of modern slavery in 2009 involved diplomats as employers, compared to 8 percent in 2008 (Embassy of the United States in Paris, France, 2010; U.S. Department of State, 2010).

As is the case with all nations, it is difficult to determine how many persons face human trafficking in France. The French government estimates that the majority of the 20,000 women in France's commercial sex trade are victims of trafficking. An estimated 75 percent of them are foreigners (U.S. Department of State, 2012). In 2005 and 2006 the Central Office for the Suppression of Trafficking in Human Beings (OCRTEH) registered 2,407 persons as victims of commercial sexual exploitation; 1,757 of the victims were foreign nationals (UNODC, 2009a). From January to September 2008, 98 persons were identified as forced-labor victims. Twenty-three victims were from China, another 23 were from Brazil, 13 were from Poland, and 7 were from Morocco (UNODC, 2009a).

The most prevalent economic sector of forced labor is construction (35 percent). Forced labor was also found in the garment industries (19 percent); agriculture (18 percent); and hotels, bars, and catering (15 percent). Persons from Brazil, central Europe, and North Africa were often exploited in the construction sector. Persons from China were more commonly exploited in the catering and textile sectors, while persons from Poland and North Africa were detected in the agriculture sector (UNODC, 2009b; U.S. Department of State, 2010). In fact, persons from Africa are highly vulnerable to both sex trafficking and forced labor in France. Between 1994 and 2009, African women made up the majority of the more than 500 trafficking victims assisted by the CCEM in France. Nearly 30 percent of the victims arrived in France as minors (People's Daily, 2008; Embassy of the United States in Paris, France, 2010).

Both males and females are victims of the offense "soliciting prostitution," but the majority of identified victims from 2003 through 2006 were female—4,148 females compared to 158 males. However, the number of identified males is on the rise—18 in 2003 compared with 17 in 2004, 41 in 2005, and 82 in 2006 (UNODC, 2009a). The number of women trafficked from Bulgaria to France has been an ongoing problem. In 2007, 10 Bulgarians were arrested for trafficking at least 105 Bulgarian women and girls to France for commercial sexual exploitation from 2002 through 2005. "We received 13 European arrest warrants from the French authorities, but three of the wanted men are outside Bulgaria," said Darina Ivanova, of the National Investigation Service. "The other ten were arrested in the towns of Pazardzhik and Plovdiv" (IOL, 2007).

This case illustrates both the coordination that must occur for international arrests and the need for and importance of international collaborations. Fortunately, French officials make a significant effort to collaborate with the authorities of common source nations of persons trafficked to France. In April 2010 a specialized operation between French and Bulgarian officials resulted in the arrest of 7 persons in Varna, Bulgaria, and 20 persons in Nice, France, who were allegedly part of a sex-trafficking ring. In October 2010, 9 Bulgarians were arrested in Germany for allegedly trafficking Bulgarian women to Germany and France for commercial sexual exploitation (Novinite, 2010). "The trafficking of women from Bulgaria to France is alarming, especially in the past few years," Bulgarian Interior Minister Tsvetan Tsvetanov told the Focus News Agency. "I hope that with the co-operation between the Bulgarian and French services, those channels will be stopped" (Sofia Echo, 2010).

Internal trafficking of French citizens also occurs, both for commercial sexual exploitation and for forced labor. Twenty-seven percent of the 2,407 identified sex-trafficking victims and 20.4 percent of the 98 identified forced-labor victims were French citizens (UNODC, 2009a).

A population that is particularly vulnerable to human trafficking throughout Europe, including France, is the Roma ethnic group. Most Roma in Europe are EU citizens, which entitles them to certain rights, including the right to move and reside freely in the EU. In August 2010 France began a controversial deportation of Roma persons from France.

The office of then-president Nicolas Sarkozy put out a statement purporting the expulsions to be an anti-trafficking effort. The office called Roma camps "sources of illegal trafficking, of profoundly shocking living standards, of exploitation of children for begging, of prostitution and crime" (BBC News, 2010b). The government did not screen camp inhabitants to determine whether they were victims of human trafficking, but instead systematically destroyed camps and deported Roma (some of whom the president's office itself said were "exploited"). In the first month roughly 1,000 Roma persons were deported and sent to Romania and Bulgaria. France stated that it was acting in line with EU law and that it would urge the Romanian government to integrate the Roma in Romania. "France will call [Romania] for commitments on police and judiciary cooperation, the fight against human trafficking and integration of Roma in Romania," Pierre Lellouche, the French European affairs minister, said (BBC News, 2010a).

France insisted that it was abiding by EU law, but the European Parliament had serious concerns that the country was targeting Roma and Travellers (persons, including Roma and non-Roma, with itinerant lifestyles). As a result, it passed a resolution calling on France to suspend the deportation of Roma and demanding that the European Commission (EC) and EU governments take action to integrate the Roma (COE, 2006; BBC News, 2010a). "[The European Parliament] urges those authorities immediately to suspend all expulsions of Roma, at the same time calling on the [European] Commission, the Council and the Member States to intervene with the same request," states the adopted text of the resolution (European Parliament, 2010).

Claude Moraes, a member of the European Parliament, said the resolution "places the European Commission under renewed pressure to begin legal action against the French authorities for failing to respect the rule of law in the way it has been targeting the Roma as an ethnic group" (BBC News, 2010a). One Roma forcibly expelled from France is Iiordan Marian. He stated that French police forced him onto a plane and smashed his camp. He was given $420 in compensation. "We need money, we need food. We can live in Romania, but we have no job and in this village each family has about 10 kids," Marian told *Sky News*. "We are members of the European Union and we have rights" (Rossi, 2010).

In October 2010 France submitted plans to bring its legislation into line with EU law on freedom of movement. As a result, the EC will not begin infringement procedures against France over the expulsion of Roma (UPI, 2010). While on its face France appears to be toeing the line by halting the forced expulsion of Roma, the EC should keep a close eye on the treatment of Roma in France to ensure that they do not continue to be marginalized and vulnerable to human trafficking and other forms of exploitation. NGOs report that there continues to be discriminatory targeting of the Roma by the French government, and Victoria Vasey, the legal director for the Hungary-based European Roma Rights Center, stated that expulsions "are still primarily occurring in France and Italy" (Phillips & Chrisafis, 2011). In August 2012 France renewed its efforts to shut down camps and remove the Roma who were living there. On August 9, authorities raided 2 camps near Lille, and 240 Romanian Roma (evicted from camps in the Lyon area) were evicted to Romania. The camps near Lille were home to roughly 200 Roma, including 60 children. The government of France said these 240 Roma left for Romania voluntarily and were paid up to $387 each to leave. The issue is that in the past Roma accepted voluntary return only after receiving an order to leave—this is what the government is deeming voluntary. This is significant because voluntary return sidesteps court review of the removals (HRW, 2012).

WHAT HAPPENS TO VICTIMS AFTER TRAFFICKING

Victims are granted shelter for an initial 30-day period in order to determine their legal options. NGOs offer medical and psychosocial support as well as housing and shelter (U.S. Department of State, 2008; UNODC, 2009a). Those victims who assist in the prosecution of their traffickers are granted witness protection and a three-to-six-month stay permit, which can be renewed biannually. The stay permit affords an individual the right to work in the country. The fee for the residence permit is $407. Each renewal costs $103, and the visa validation tax is $177. Fees are not waived for trafficking victims (Coatnet, 2004; U.S. Department of State, 2008). A trafficking victim who assisted in the prosecution of their trafficker may receive a Permanent Resident Permit (10 years), if and only if, the defendant is successfully convicted. Local prefects do have the discretion to grant permanent residency to victims, but often victims are not informed of this option. The permit is renewable and grants the holder the same working conditions and benefits as those of the French, such as social security, family allowance, unemployment benefits, and pension (Coatnet, 2004; U.S. Department of State, 2008, 2012).

The government reports that authorities identified and referred 799 trafficking victims to NGOs for assistance in 2009. In 2010, 688 victims were identified, and in 2011, 654 victims were identified, but the government did not report the number of victims it referred for assistance in either year. There is no official method to track and collect data on the actual number of identified victims who are referred to shelters and assistance (U.S. Department of State, 2010, 2011, 2012). Victims continue to be punished for offenses related to their trafficking experience. One explanation lies in the "passive solicitation" offense listed under the Internal Security Act; another lies in the difficulty law enforcement has in distinguishing between trafficking victims and other workers in the sex industry (French Republic, 2005). The interpretation of passive solicitation is up to the discretion of the police officer (Coatnet, 2004). As a result, trafficking victims continue to be arrested and punished on the grounds of solicitation (Amnesty International Canada, 2006; U.S. Department of State, 2008). These practices not only punish victims for offenses related to their trafficking experience but also deter victims from going to the authorities.

In a 2010 decision the European Court of Human Rights held that member nations of the European Convention of Human Rights, such as France, must provide safeguards to aid and protect potential victims of trafficking. This includes laws surrounding immigration:

The Court considers that the spectrum of safeguards set out in national legislation must be adequate to ensure the practical and effective protection of the rights of victims or potential victims of trafficking. Accordingly, in addition to criminal law measures to punish traffickers, Article 4 requires member States to put in place adequate measures regulating businesses often used as a cover for human trafficking. Furthermore, a State's immigration rules must address relevant concerns relating to encouragement, facilitation or tolerance of trafficking. (ECHR, 2010)

In France there are guidelines for identifying victims, but they need stronger implementation, particularly among first responders. Persons who are trafficked into the sex industry continue to be arrested and fined for solicitation and immigration violations, and often face deportation without proper screening to see if they are victims of human trafficking (Amnesty International Canada, 2006; U.S. Department of State, 2009, 2010, 2012). Failure to identify victims or to provide sufficient protections and treating foreign victims as illegal migrants are not limited to the sex industry. A 2009 Human Rights Watch report, *Lost in Transit*, noted that the failure of French law to distinguish between adults and unaccompanied children results in the return of children to transit nations or their country of origin, or in sending children onward to their final destinations without sufficient safeguards. The report stated that from January 2008 to July 2009, 1,500 children arrived at Roissy Charles de Gaulle Airport in Paris and were denied entry and detained by police in what French officials call transit zones (*zone d'attente*). The transit zones allow France to treat a person who is physically in the country as if he or she is still on the outside. In this case, the transit zone includes Paris hotels and hospitals, and even courtrooms that are more than 12 miles from the airport (HRW, 2009).

Some of the children were trafficking victims, others were fleeing persecution in their home countries, and some were arriving to join family members in France. Instead of receiving protection, the unaccompanied children faced detention with adults, humiliating treatment by police, little to no protection from traffickers, and obstacles to filing for asylum. Of the 1,500 children, roughly 30 percent were deported to their country of origin or to a country through which they had transited on their journey to France, or continued their journey to their final destinations. The remaining children were granted access to France (HRW, 2009). This practice facilitates human trafficking by allowing for the completion of the trafficking route or returning victims to a country where they face re-trafficking, retribution, and/or persecution.

The French government continues to target immigrants, and it is not just the encampments of Roma that are targeted. In September 2009 French police dismantled a migrant camp in Calais and arrested 276 persons from Afghanistan and Pakistan, 135 of whom were teenagers. Their fate was determined on a case-by-case basis. Authorities stated that some of the migrants would apply for asylum in France, others would be returned to their country of origin or Greece—the country where most of the migrants had entered the EU (Audi & Brothers, 2009). French officials touted the demolition as an anti-trafficking measure, but experts criticized the government's response and believe it increased the migrants' vulnerability to trafficking (U.S. Department of State, 2010).

WHAT HAPPENS TO TRAFFICKERS

The 2003 anti-trafficking law was first used in 2007 to convict 2 persons of sex trafficking. There were only 33 trafficking convictions under the anti-trafficking statute in 2007 and 19 in 2008. In 2011 there were 85 known human trafficking convictions. Historically, prosecutors have utilized the offense of labor and living conditions against human dignity in cases of forced labor and the anti-pimping statute when prosecuting sex traffickers (U.S. Department of State, 2008, 2010, 2012; UNODC, 2009a). Even the government's urging prosecutors to charge cases under the trafficking statute, along with other applicable charges, has not made much of a dent. Generally speaking, prosecutors are more comfortable with the established case law of the longstanding anti-pimping laws. Pimping has been illegal since the late 1940s. Fortunately, penalties under the anti-trafficking statute and the anti-pimping laws are equally stringent. In 2006, 505 pimps were arrested and prosecuted under the anti-pimping statute. In 2008 there were 523 prosecutions that utilized the anti-pimping statute. Sixteen percent of those cases involved original arrests for trafficking-specific offenses. In 2011 there were 508 convictions under the statute, with 15 percent of original arrests in these cases involving trafficking-specific offenses (Lichfield, 2005; U.S. Department of State, 2008, 2010, 2012; UNODC, 2009a).

The Office for the Prosecution of Illegal Labor (OCLTI) focuses on forced-labor cases under the offense of labor and living conditions against human dignity. Roughly 100 forced-labor cases were investigated in 2006 and also in 2007. From January to September 2008, 32 forced-labor cases were investigated and involved 55 alleged offenders (UNODC, 2009a). In addition to the 19 persons convicted under the anti-trafficking statute in 2008, 26 trafficking offenders were convicted for the forced prostitution of children. The maximum sentence in all 45 convictions was 7 years' imprisonment (U.S. Department of State, 2010). In March 2009 the government convicted 2 French nationals for aggravated sex-tourism offenses committed in Southeast Asia. Both received 7 years' imprisonment. At least 1 other offender was convicted for aggravated trafficking under Article 225-4-2 in 2009 (U.S. Department of State, 2010, 2011). The government also utilized other offenses to prosecute traffickers. Seventeen trafficking offenders were convicted of the prostitution of children, and roughly 79 were convicted under the anti-pimping statute in 2009. The majority of trafficking offenders received sentences between 2 and 10 years' imprisonment, though this was increased in aggravated cases. In 2010 the French government sentenced 2 traffickers to 30 years' imprisonment, and 10 others received sentences between 2 and 25 years' imprisonment (U.S. Department of State, 2011).

It is often assumed that all traffickers are foreign nationals. But of the 55 suspected forced-labor offenders in France identified between January and September 2008, 42 percent were citizens. There were also a number of foreign traffickers. Eight suspected offenders were citizens of Turkey, seven were from North Africa, six were from central Europe, five were from China, and five were from Portugal (UNODC, 2009a). It is also commonly believed that persons are exclusively exploited by persons of the same nationality. This is not always the case. In 2008 the OCLTI registered 37 cases of forced labor that were prosecuted under different offenses. Of those cases, 50 percent involved French nationals exploiting French nationals or foreigners, 26 percent involved foreigners exploiting their own nationals, and 24 percent involved foreigners exploiting persons of a nationality other than their own (UNODC, 2009b).

INTERNAL EFFORTS TO DECREASE TRAFFICKING

In January 2009 the government broadened its anti-trafficking law to include a specific definition of forced labor, further increasing the protections granted under the statute (U.S. Department of State, 2010). The hope was that the broadening of the statute would result in increased utilization of the anti-trafficking statute in trafficking cases. Thus far there has been an increase, but other statutes are still more regularly used. The issue is that using non-trafficking-specific charges—such as pimping—can adversely affect international collaborations on trafficking cases (U.S. Department of State, 2012).

The government collaborates with other nations to ensure the safe return and medical care of victims sent back to their home of origin. In addition to the government of Bulgaria, the government of France collaborates with the governments of Brazil, Cameroon, Ghana, Nigeria, Romania, and Ukraine to combat the trafficking of women from those nations to France for commercial sexual exploitation (People's Daily, 2008; U.S. Department of State, 2010, 2012). In 2009 the government dismantled 40 trafficking rings in France and cooperated with authorities in other nations to dismantle an additional 14 networks (U.S. Department of State, 2010). "We want to ensure that there are concerted efforts between our European neighbors and the source countries," said Jean-Marc Souvira, the head of the Central Office for the Suppression of Trafficking in Human Beings (OCRTEH) (People's Daily, 2008). OCRTEH is a government-run agency under France's central criminal investigation department. It focuses on sexual-exploitation trafficking cases and as of 2007 had 32 officers working full-time on the issue (People's Daily, 2008; UNODC, 2009a). Between 2005 and 2008 OCRTEH broke up over 25 African prostitution rings within France (People's Daily, 2008; Embassy of the United States in Paris, France, 2010). Patience Ashorkor Quaye, deputy superintendent of police in Accra, Ghana, concurred with Souvira that a collaborative effort among many nations is the best means of eliminating trafficking. "Ghana cannot wage the fight against a global phenomenon on its own," Quaye said (People's Daily, 2008).

Some experts and politicians believe that licensed brothels could be a positive anti-trafficking step. Prostitution is not illegal, but pimping, procuring, or solicitation is. Chantal Brunel, a member of the National

Assembly of France, says legalizing brothels might help protect persons from trafficking. "Prostitutes are finding themselves even more badly treated and damaged than before," Brunel said. "We have to stop their exploitation" (Davies, 2010). Brunel believes that the focus needs to be on making the sex trade safer and transparent as opposed to exerting efforts to stamp out prostitution: "Women selling sex should be allowed to do so legally on special licensed premises. This would free thousands of women from the exploitation they suffer at the hands of pimps and criminal gangs and offer them much more security than they currently have on the streets. It would give them a legal taxable income and they would not be handing over large sums of their earning[s] to a pimp" (Telegraph, 2010).

Opinion polls indicate that a significant number of French citizens may agree. One poll found that 59 percent of respondents supported Brunel's position to reintroduce brothels (Davies, 2010). While transparency of the commercial sex industry is certainly ideal, whether it can actually be regulated and monitored within France is unknown.

The largest hurdle in the French government's anti-trafficking efforts is its own immigration policies. The systematic destruction of camps— both of Roma (in violation of EU law) and of other immigrants—makes these persons homeless and even more vulnerable to exploitation, including human trafficking. The French government has maintained that deportation of Roma to Romania has been voluntary, but voluntary return seems to have occurred after the living quarters of the Roma have been destroyed and they have received orders to leave, putting into question the actual voluntariness of their return. Also of concern are unaccompanied child trafficking victims who enter transit zones and are not offered adequate protection. In fact, some are sent to their final destinations—simply allowing the trafficking cycle to be completed. Others are returned to their country of origin, which makes the victims vulnerable to re-trafficking and retribution.

PART VI
Gender Apartheid

In some nations, strict sex segregation and socio-sexual and economic dis-crimination against women and girls make equality in life and justice impossi-ble. This gender apartheid pervades all aspects of female existence; it saturates the human, political, economic, social, and cultural experience. It not only makes females more vulnerable to human trafficking, but it also hinders them from attaining equal justice under the law in the post-trafficking experience.

In Iran the segregation of men and women is enforced in public spaces. Women are not allowed to socialize openly with men who are not relatives or who are unmarried. They must sit in specific reserved sections on the bus and must enter public buildings, airports, and universities through a separate en-trance from men; they must stay in "women only" areas when swimming, skiing, or at the beach. Health care is also segregated, and there are not enough trained female physicians and health care professionals to meet the needs of all the women and girls in Iran. A woman may initiate divorce for a limited number of reasons, while a man does not need to state a reason to divorce. The age of criminal responsibility begins at age 8 years and 9 months for girls and age 14 years and 7 months for boys. Under the Penal Code, a woman may not go out in public without an appropriate hejab; *those who do face lashings and fines. The fact that there is no clear legal definition of an appropriate* hejab *creates an arbitrariness that places the decision on appropriateness in the hands of morality police and judges. A man may have up to four wives as well as temporary wives; a* sigheh *(temporary marriage) is a loophole that is used for prostitution and human trafficking.*

Article 3 of Iran's constitution states that women and men have the same rights and protections, yet it also states that the principles of Islamic law are the supreme law. This state of affairs poses significant challenges for female trafficking victims. For instance, a significant hurdle to obtaining equal justice for female victims is that under the Iranian government's interpretation and application of Islamic law, a woman's testimony is worth half of that of a man. Furthermore, while human trafficking is criminalized, so too are the moral offenses victims commit during the trafficking experience such as illegal border crossing, prostitution, or extramarital affairs. Punishments are severe; at times victims are sentenced to death. This was the case of a 16-year-old sex-trafficking victim who was publicly hung for crimes against chastity committed during her trafficking experience. Aside from the diminished worth of a female's testimony, the knowledge of potential punishment and execution strongly deters victims from coming forward. This situation further marginalizes the victim and also allows traffickers to continue the abuse and exploitation of females with impunity. The punishment of females for crimes associated with their trafficking experience is likely to continue. At the February 2010 Trafficking in Persons Working Group in Vienna, the Iranian delegate stated that the government of Iran would not accept recommendations that called for absolving trafficking victims for their crimes. The delegate went on to state that while the victim status of a woman may be taken into account by the judge, he opposed the idea that such a woman should not be prosecuted. In January 2012 the government of Iran adopted a new Penal Code, which retains adverse differential treatment in the punishment, age of responsibility, evidentiary standards, and compensation of females as compared to males.

Note: Throughout chapter 12 we refer to the Penal Code, which specifically means the Penal Code of 1991, unless otherwise specified. Any noteworthy changes to the code that arise from the 2012 Penal Code are discussed.

Iran

There are many young runaway girls—I say this confidentially.
More than 4,000 young girls have come to our city. That's a lot.
On any street corner I can pick up ten girls.

—A MULLAH IN IRAN

A 16-year-old sex-trafficking victim was publicly hung in 2006. Her crime was engaging in acts incompatible with chastity. The town governor congratulated the religious leader who sentenced the young girl on his firm approach (U.S. Department of State, 2006). Just two years earlier, Iran had taken significant steps toward eliminating human trafficking within its borders. In 2004 the Iranian Parliament ratified an anti-trafficking law that prohibits the trafficking of persons by means of a threat, use of force, coercion, abuse of power or of position of vulnerability of the victim for prostitution, removal of organs, slavery, or forced marriage (UNODC, 2007; Hosseini-Divkolaye, 2009). In the same year Iran signed separate memorandums of understanding with Afghanistan, the International Labour Organization, the International Organization for Migration (IOM), and Turkey. Iran also conducted a study focusing on the trafficking of women (U.S. Department of State, 2005).

Despite these significant anti-trafficking steps, victims continue to face punishment for moral offenses resulting from their trafficking experience, including imprisonment, beatings, and execution (Hughes, 2006). Other significant problems are the lack of enforceable anti-trafficking mechanisms and that substantial disjunctures persist among policy, the judiciary, and law enforcement (UNODC, 2007; ODVV, 2009).

IRAN AS A DESTINATION AND TRANSIT NATION

Migration to, through, from, and within a nation must always be considered when examining the trafficking scenario of a country. Iran has some of the highest emigration and immigration flows in the world. The country is also acutely susceptible to cross-border and transnational crime because of economic, political, and geographic factors. Both human trafficking and migrant smuggling have become sources of increasing regional concern (IOM, 2009). Bordered by seven nations, Iran is a frequent destination for people fleeing those countries; it has become a refugee haven for Afghanis, Iraqis, and Pakistanis. Iran is also an ideal transit location for persons who voluntarily migrate or are trafficked to Greece, the Gulf states, Europe, and Turkey (IOM, 2009; IRIN, 2010; U.S. Department of State, 2010).

Young Afghan men in particular take serious risks to travel to Iran, where they pay smuggling networks between $400 and $600 and seek informal jobs, often with construction companies. Determining the exact number of persons who immigrate to Iran from Afghanistan is challenging. What is known is that from 2006 through 2009 Iran deported roughly 1 million Afghan illegal migrants (IRIN, 2009). Some Afghan deportees claim that they faced incarceration for weeks and physical abuse at the hands of Iranian security forces prior to deportation. "I was working on a construction site when the police arrested me . . . they beat me up with bats and then put me in a cell for three days, after which they sent me back to Afghanistan without allowing me to collect my salary and settle debts in Iran," one deportee told IRIN, the humanitarian news and analysis service of the UN Office for the Coordination of Humanitarian Affairs (IRIN, 2009). Smuggling is not the same as human trafficking, but smuggled persons are vulnerable to human rights violations, including human trafficking. In 2010 the Iranian government continued to deport Afghanis without any screening to determine whether they were in fact trafficking victims (U.S. Department of State, 2011).

Throughout the world the terms *smuggling* and *human trafficking* are commonly conflated. For instance, in 2010 it was reported that Rahman Malek, Pakistan's interior minister, had ordered an inquiry into reports that human traffickers were using the porous Baluchistan border with

Iran to transport people to Europe. This statement came immediately after Iran had deported 85 persons back to Pakistan. The Pakistani citizens were caught living in Iran without valid immigration documents (IANS, 2010). The Pakistanis were likely smuggled into Iran across the Taftan border. Although smuggling is not the same as human trafficking, it can certainly turn into a situation of human trafficking. Men and women voluntarily migrate to Iran from Bangladesh, Iraq, and Pakistan for construction, agricultural, or domestic work. Once in Iran some of these workers find themselves in scenarios of debt bondage or involuntary servitude where they face threats, abuse (sexual or physical), nonpayment of wages, and/or restriction of movement. Similarly, women from Azerbaijan and Tajikistan migrate to Iran to find employment and subsequently face forced prostitution (U.S. Department of State, 2010).

In March 2008, 23 victims of human trafficking were returned to Pakistan from Iran. The victims (men, women, and children) had been forced to work on a banana orchard in the agricultural Zarabad area of Iran by their trafficker, Iranian national Umer Makrani. "We were taken to Iran by Umer Makrani's agents, who assured us that we would get paid in Iran and would not have to bear travel expenses," Hashim, one of the victims, told *Dawn* (Kahn, 2008). Hashim stated that when they reached Iran, they were provided with food but were not paid any wages for their work. "The landlord used to threaten us against venturing out of his agricultural land, warning that the Iranian police might arrest [us] as illegal immigrants," Hashim said (Kahn, 2008).

The smuggling experience into Iran is treacherous. In 2009 a transport container was discovered at a truck stand in Quetta, Pakistan. The container held roughly 105 Afghanis headed to the Iran border. At least 45 persons in the container died from lack of oxygen. Shams-ur-Rehman, one of the passengers, said the air conditioner in the container was not working: "After an hour-and-a-half into the journey, we began to feel suffocated. We desperately tried to inform the driver by banging on the container, but maybe he couldn't hear us because there was a big gap between the container and the driver's cabin. I saw people falling over each other due to suffocation. One could see death close at hand. It was frightening" (Wahab, 2009).

Despite the dangers, the Baluchistan border will likely continue to be the transit point to Iran for those fleeing Pakistan and Afghanistan.

One Pakistani man hoping to be smuggled to Iran and then to Europe is Muhammad Fayyaz. "I saw a sign saying 2,256 km to Tehran as we left Quetta, and I realized how long my journey would be," Fayyaz told IRIN. "But I am determined to make it out to Iran, and then to Europe" (IRIN, 2010). Akbar Sarki, an Anti–Human Trafficking Cell senior officer, said that talks were under way to fence the Pakistan-Iran border with barbed wire in order to stop human trafficking. "We are coordinating with border patrol officials of neighboring countries to stop this activity," Sarki told the *Daily Times* (Khan, 2010).

Once people are in Iran, the nation's ports are a means to transport them to the Arabian Peninsula and the southern Mediterranean region. Children from Afghanistan and Iran are trafficked to the Persian Gulf region for camel jockeying and sexual exploitation (Vaidya, 2008; Hosseini-Divkolaye, 2009). Women and girls are trafficked from Afghanistan and Azerbaijan to Iran for forced marriage, commercial sexual exploitation, or involuntary servitude as laborers or beggars, while Afghan boys are forced to prostitute in male brothels in southern Iran (U.S. Department of State, 2008a, 2010). Yakin Ertürk, a former United Nations special rapporteur on violence against women, its causes and consequences, stated in a 2006 report that there had been a worrying increase in the trafficking of girls and women. In his report he said: "Most of the trafficking is said to occur in the eastern provinces and mainly in border towns with Pakistan and Afghanistan where women are kidnapped, bought, or entered into temporary marriage in order to be sold into sexual slavery in other countries" (UNODC, 2006).

Although inadequately protected borders create an opportunity for both smugglers and traffickers to transport their victims, reports also cite collusion among Iranian authority and security agencies as a contributing factor. While experts believe the problem to be widespread, the actual extent of corruption is unknown. However, it is clear is that criminal organizations are somehow able to consistently transport human trafficking victims, migrants, drugs, and arms across the Iranian borders with Pakistan and Afghanistan (U.S. Department of State, 2010).

INTERNAL TRAFFICKING WITHIN IRAN AND TRAFFICKING ABROAD

The minimal access to Iran by NGOs and international bodies hinders the collection of full and accurate data on human trafficking and anti-trafficking efforts there (U.S. Department of State, 2005, 2007, 2008b, 2010; Hughes, 2006).[1] Within Iran there is little comprehensive field research on the methods and number of Iranian persons trafficked, though there has been some research conducted on the status and forms of human trafficking that affect its citizens. One such study reveals that Iranian females are most commonly trafficked to Pakistan and the United Arab Emirates (UAE) (Fehresti, 2010). The victims who are taken to Pakistan are typically from poor families. They marry in Iran and are then taken to brothels in Pakistan. The majority of these girls have no idea that they are being trafficked. While they are forced to prostitute, they are not paid; their husbands or family receive the profits. The victims who are trafficked to Dubai (UAE) are generally young—ages 10 to 16—and have greater social standing and education than the girls trafficked to Pakistan. The girls trafficked to Dubai commonly become engaged to prominent Arab individuals, or the girls' families grant the trafficker(s) permission to take the girls across the border in exchange for money. Some of the girls travel to Dubai knowing that they will work in prostitution while others are abducted and taken out of Iran without their families' knowledge (Fehresti, 2010). Experts estimate that every day 45 Iranian girls run away from home for reasons such as poverty and maltreatment. A significant portion of these girls are picked up by human traffickers and end up in brothels abroad (Fehresti, 2010). The Women's Freedom Forum states that thousands of Iranian girls, many of whom are between 13 and 17 years of age, are sold to men in Afghanistan. Trafficked women and children have also been sent to France, Germany, Iraq, Kuwait, Pakistan, Qatar, Turkey, the UAE, and the United Kingdom for commercial sexual exploitation, forced marriage for the purpose of sexual servitude, drug trafficking, and forced labor (Hughes, 2006; Hosseini-Divkolaye, 2009; U.S. Department of State, 2010).

Trafficking within Iran occurs as well. Women and girls are primarily trafficked internally for the purpose of forced prostitution or forced marriage. In circumstances of forced marriage, "husbands" sometimes force the women and girls into prostitution and involuntary servitude as beggars or laborers to provide income, pay debts, or support the drug addiction of family members (U.S. Department of State, 2010). One means of trafficking Iranian women within Iran or to other nations is through a temporary marriage (*sigheh*). Iranian women have also been subjected to forced prostitution through temporary marriages to men from Pakistan and the Gulf states (U.S. Department of State, 2010). Akbar Hashemi Rafsanjani, former president of Iran, explained the intent and purpose of *sigheh* as a way to organize a potential corruption of ethics in a controlled and legal manner. "It has been considered that under certain circumstances when a man and a woman are not able to marry on a permanent basis they need to satisfy their instincts," Rafsanjani told *60 Minutes*. "It is not possible for everybody to have a permanent marriage" (Rafsanjani, 1997). Rafsanjani stated that there are multiple reasons that a traditional marriage may not be possible, such as financial obstacles or geographic ones. He also noted that widows who lose their husbands still need to satisfy their instincts on a temporary basis:

> This could be accomplished through an official agreement or contract between two parties. For whatever the time. This brings an order to the relations. Faith of the children would be clear. It addresses the issue of the woman in respect to her expenses as she will not be able to marry for a while. Psychologically speaking, this is a legal act, not a forbidden act that everyone is fearful of. In the Shiite school of thought, everybody accepts it. We believe this is a solution to sexual problems. (Rafsanjani, 1997)

Mostafa Pour-Mohammadi, Iran's former interior minister, has said that marriage is a human need and that people should use temporary marriage to solve social problems, not just for sex. Overall, temporary marriages are highly taboo in Iranian society; they are perceived as merely a cover for prostitution (Harrison, 2007). Nahid Persson Sarvestani's 2004 film *Prostitution Behind the Veil* highlights the use of temporary marriages within Iran. In the documentary, Habib, a 65-year-old man, decides to obtain a *sigheh*, an extra "wife" whom a man can marry for a fee. His new "wife to be" is Leila, a 17-year-old girl. "She is my third *sigheh*," Habib tells the mullah who is to marry them. "My second one ends in two days. She was my *sigheh* for a year and a half. She was a teacher." The mullah who presides over the marriage discusses the issue of runaway girls in Iran. "There are many young runaway girls—I say this confidentially," the mullah says. "More than 4,000 young girls have come to our city. That's a lot. On any street corner I can pick up ten girls." The mullah then asks Leila how long she wants to be married to Habib. She says, "Two months." The mullah responds by stating that he will not perform a temporary marriage of less than six months. Leila agrees to the fixed period. Habib and Leila discuss the fee he must pay her. For the six-month period Habib will pay Leila $200. In the end, the *sigheh* lasted only two weeks, as Leila left for another city once she obtained the money (*Prostitution behind the veil*, 2004).

For many Iranian girls and women, prostitution is the only way to earn an income. Despite the fact that prostitution is strictly illegal, in 2004 there was a 635 percent increase in the number of teenage girls in prostitution in Iran. In Tehran alone there were an estimated 84,000 women and girls in prostitution. Unemployment of roughly 28 percent among youths 15–29 years of age and 43 percent unemployment of women ages 15–20 created a particularly economically vulnerable population. The rising number of drug addicts, street children, and young female runaways contributed further to create a highly marginalized population (Hughes, 2004, 2006).

Men who work within trafficking networks often target poor families, offering to marry their daughters—some no older than 12 years old. These girls are often forced to prostitute or to beg for money (Hughes, 2006). Attorney Norma Ramos, the executive director of the Coalition Against Trafficking in Women–International, stated that gender apartheid has created a social-political condition not hospitable to equality for women and girls. The enforced segregation of men and women is pervasive in all aspects of public life. In addition to using separate entrances to public buildings, women must sit in reserved sections on the bus, and they must follow a strict dress code or face lashings and fines. Segregation and inequality affect all facets of the female experience in Iran, ranging from the age of criminal responsibility, which is age 8 years, 9 months for girls compared to age 14 years, 7 months for boys, to a woman's limited right to divorce and limited freedom of movement (Hepburn & Simon, 2007; Reporters Uncensored, 2010; Biklou, 2012).

Ramos says that as long as women and girls continue to be a marginalized population, they remain vulnerable to human trafficking (Reporters Uncensored, 2010). The only way to diminish the marginalization of any population is to create and enforce equal rights and treatment of that group. In the case of Iran, the only way to stop the vulnerability of girls and women to human rights violations, including human trafficking, is to create and enforce equal rights and treatment of girls and women. This means discontinuing the segregation of women from men in public life, as equality in a separate-but-equal approach to any population is innately fictional. Unfortunately, bringing about equality for women in Iran is easier said than done. While Article 3 of the Constitution of Iran states that men and women have the same rights and protection under the law, it also makes clear that the principles of Islamic law (*shariah/shari'a*) are the supreme law. Article 20 states: "All citizens of the country, both men and women, equally enjoy the protection of the law and enjoy all human, political, economic, social, and cultural rights, in conformity with Islamic criteria" (Islamic Republic of Iran, 1979). This poses a significant challenge for the anti-trafficking movement, as religious law, not state law, prevails. So even if amendments were made to the constitution or if a Penal Code was adopted that equalized the sexes, these changes would be deemed null and void if they contradict Islamic law. Also, the Guardian Council, which is tasked with ensuring that laws passed by parliament are in accordance with Islamic law, would not approve it.

In 2012 the government adopted a new Penal Code. The text of the code illustrates the government's objective to appease the international community but not make any significant changes. Soon after the code was adopted, a member of government and a government spokesperson announced that stoning and the execution of juveniles no longer existed in the code. It turns out that this is not true. Yes, children who commit crimes deemed to be less serious do not face corporal punishment, but those of maturity (girls who have reached the age of 8 years and 9 months and boys who have reached the age of 14 years and 7 months) who commit *hadd* offenses such as illicit (outside of marriage) sex (*zina*), theft, homosexual acts, or consumption of an intoxicant face the same sentencing as adults.[2] Under Islamic law, *zina* is punishable by 100 lashes or death by stoning. In the Penal Code, under the chapter on *zina*, unmarried persons who commit *zina* face flogging. Yet the chapter is silent on those who are married. This makes it appear as if stoning is no longer the sentence for married persons who commit *zina*, but a closer look at the code, specifically Articles 172 and 198, illustrates that the immutable sentence of stoning for married persons who commit *zina* still exists. Under Article 198, *zina* must be proved by the testimony of two just men and four just women for unmarried persons and by the testimony of at least three just men and two just women for married persons. As it stands now, both human trafficking and the moral crimes a victim may commit during the trafficking experience are criminalized. This means that persons who are trafficked and, for example, commit *zina* as a result of their trafficking experience can face flogging (if unmarried) or death (if married). Victims face detainment, punishment, and, if a foreign national, deportation for their moral crimes (Hosseini-Divkolaye, 2009; ODVV, 2009; Nayyeri, 2012).

WHAT HAPPENS TO VICTIMS AFTER TRAFFICKING

The State Welfare Organization for Social Affairs assists victims and those at risk of trafficking through social emergency centers, which provide health care, counseling, and legal services. In addition, the organization administers temporary housing facilities for women, which are available to, but are not specifically designed for, trafficking victims (Hosseini-Divkolaye, 2009). Iran does not have a process to identify trafficking victims, and law-enforcement officials do not differentiate between victims of trafficking and undocumented migrants. Overall protective measures for victims are still weak. As a result, victims do not typically receive the requisite support and protection that they need. Victims of human trafficking in Iran often face detention, deportation (if a foreign national), and punishment for crimes they committed during their trafficking experience such as illegal border crossing, prostitution, or extramarital affairs. One such case is the 16-year-old victim of human trafficking for commercial sexual purposes who was publicly hung for crimes against chastity that she committed during the trafficking experience (U.S. Department of State, 2006, 2010; Hosseini-Divkolaye, 2009; ODVV, 2009).

Female sex-trafficking victims face immense challenges in obtaining justice against their trafficker(s). The first challenge is the application in Iran of Islamic law, which maintains that a woman's testimony is worth half that of a man.[3] For instance, under Article 198 of the new Penal Code, illicit—out of marriage—sex, punishable by flogging or stoning, may be proved by the testimony of two just men and four just women for unmarried persons and by the testimony of at least three just men and two just women for married persons (Nayyeri, 2012). The second hindrance is that women who have been forced to prostitute are vulnerable to execution for adultery (U.S. Department of State, 2010). The government does not encourage trafficking victims to aid law-enforcement authorities in their investigation and prosecution of trafficking cases. Victims from other nations are typically detained for a short time and then returned to their country of origin, where they may face hardship or retribution. The nation offers no legal alternative to deportation (U.S. Department of State, 2008b, 2010).

WHAT HAPPENS TO TRAFFICKERS

No amalgamated information on the total number of persons convicted of human trafficking offenses is available, but there is sporadic evidence that some traffickers in Iran have been convicted. Of course, it is difficult to know what this means in relation to the scope of human trafficking in Iran, particularly since internal trafficking and forced labor go mostly unacknowledged. In 2003, 53 Afghan refugee tribesmen were sentenced to a total of 281 years' imprisonment, 222 lashes, and fines for ensnaring girls with marriage offers and then trafficking them to Pakistan for commercial sexual exploitation. Additionally, an Iranian court sentenced 27 people to from 14 months to 10 years' imprisonment for trafficking of young girls to the UAE for commercial sexual exploitation. In 2004 a woman and her accomplice husband were arrested and convicted for trafficking young girls and women to work in a brothel in the northern city of Qazvin. In the same year, 20 members of a human trafficking ring in the city of Bileh Savar were arrested and convicted (U.S. Department of State, 2003, 2004). An international smuggling network based in Tehran was disbanded in 2007. The trafficking ring smuggled women and girls from Central Asia through Iran, and then to the Gulf states. Twenty-five people were arrested for their involvement in the group. It is unclear how many of the smuggled persons were trafficking victims. It is also unknown how many of these individuals were prosecuted and sentenced (U.S. Department of State, 2008a).

Officials have also been arrested for their involvement with human trafficking. Some members of the Islamic Revolutionary Guard Corps and the State Security Forces were arrested in 2006 for engaging in commercial sexual exploitation of children (some as young as 13 years old). The victims were also arrested, most likely for engaging in prostitution (U.S. Department of State, 2007).

Traffickers receive inconsistent sentences, ranging from three years' imprisonment to death (U.S. Department of State, 2003, 2004). The variability results in part from whether the Penal Code or the anti-trafficking law is applied. For instance, if the Penal Code applies, those who encourage or facilitate people to enter prostitution or promiscuity face 1 to 10 years in prison, which is not much different than sentences under the Anti–Human Trafficking Law. But if the offense is held to jeopardize the moral health, values, and social security of Iran, then offenders face increased punishment or death. If the Penal Code does not apply, then the extent of punishment is determined by the Anti–Human Trafficking Law, which imposes between 2 and 10 years' imprisonment and a fine. The fine is either twice the amount earned by the offender or the amount promised to the offender by a third party (Fehresti, 2010). Under Article 8 of the Anti–Human Trafficking Law, all assets, whether movable or unmovable, are to be seized by the government. Zahra Fehresti, the author of an analysis of trafficking legislation in Iran, has suggested that victims could be reimbursed with the seized assets (Fehresti, 2010). This step has not yet been taken by the Iranian government, but it would surely be a useful strategy.

INTERNAL EFFORTS TO DECREASE TRAFFICKING

Although some portions of the Penal Code address offenses related to human trafficking—such as abduction and procurement of sex—there was a clear need for a more comprehensive anti-trafficking law. The 2004 Anti–Human Trafficking Law filled in some of the gaps. For instance, the Anti-Trafficking Law does not permit consent by the victim to reduce a trafficker's liability. The result is that any contract that undermines a person's basic rights—such as dignity or moral qualities—is rendered void (Fehresti, 2010). But although the Anti–Human Trafficking Law has been ratified, it is not effectively enforced. Specifically missing from the law is a mechanism to coordinate law-enforcement (UNODC, 2007).

The Anti–Human Trafficking Law comes into play only if the Penal Code does not cover the offense. Furthermore, the Anti–Human Trafficking Law is deemed invalid in instances in which it contradicts Islamic law, which is considered the supreme law (Fehresti, 2010). Additionally, there is a lack of continuity between the Anti–Human Trafficking Law and the Penal Code. Under the Anti–Human Trafficking Law, an offender who traffics a person younger than 15 years of age faces a maximum of 10 years' imprisonment. Under the Penal Code, the same offender faces a maximum penalty of 15 years' imprisonment (Islamic Republic of Iran, 1991). The same is true in instances of attempted human trafficking. The punishment for offenders who initiate "coercion, threat, or force the victims to comply against their wills but fail to do so due to factors out of their control" (Anti–Human Trafficking Law) or who attempt "conspiracy against lives or assets of people even if it fails" (Penal Code) can face different sentencing for the same crime. Sentencing ranges from 6 months to 2 years, 6 months to 3 years, or 3 to 5 years' imprisonment depending on whether the Anti–Human Trafficking Law or the Penal Code is used (Fehresti, 2010).

Another concern is that the Anti–Human Trafficking Law appears to be based on the notion that human trafficking involves transit—either in or out of a country. The premise that trafficking includes actual transport of a person is a common misconception that can be detrimental to the nation's anti-trafficking measures. It can also further marginalize persons trafficked within Iran. One step that could help to create continuity between law and practice is for Iran to ratify the Protocol to

Prevent, Suppress and Punish Trafficking in Persons, Especially Women and Children, supplementing the United Nations Convention against Transnational Organized Crime. This step would push the government of Iran to create a uniform definition of human trafficking within Iran as well as create continuity of law between Iran and nearby nations that are signatories to the protocol such as Armenia, Azerbaijan, Oman, Saudi Arabia, Turkey, and Turkmenistan (UNODC, 2008).

Contradictions exist between the definitions of and penalties for trafficking and trafficking-related offenses, and there is an inconsistent pattern in the arrest, prosecution, and sentencing of traffickers. Victims consistently face arrest and punishment for crimes associated with their trafficking experience. As indicated by the Iranian delegate at the February 2010 Trafficking in Persons Working Group in Vienna, who stated that the government of Iran would not accept recommendations that called for absolving trafficking victims of their crimes, this state of affairs is not likely to change in the near future. The delegate stated that while the victim status of a woman in prostitution might be taken into account by the judge, he opposed the idea that such a woman should not be prosecuted (U.S. Department of State, 2010). This creates a situation in which victims are understandably fearful of seeking justice against their trafficker because, once the incident is reported, the victim is under scrutiny and punishable for crimes committed under duress. The term *gender apartheid,* used by attorney Norma Ramos to describe the situation of women in Iran, may sound extreme, but the unequal standing of women and men has laid the foundation for a highly marginalized population. Women and girls are not only limited in their daily endeavors such as walking in public or riding the bus but also in the eyes of the judiciary, where the testimony of a woman is worth half that of a man. The result is that human trafficking cannot properly be addressed simply through anti-trafficking laws. In order to take steps toward the elimination of human trafficking, Iran must adequately address the contradictions that exist between policy, religious law, and the social practice toward women.

PART VII
Social Hierarchy

In some nations a strict social hierarchy creates a marginalized population that is immensely vulnerable to exploitation, including human trafficking. In other nations the social hierarchy subjects people to hereditary slavery wherein a person faces indentured servitude or slavery upon birth. To be clear, slavery is human trafficking; the exploitation included in the definition of human trafficking is "at a minimum, the exploitation of prostitution of others or other forms of sexual exploitation, forced labor or services, slavery or practices similar to slavery, servitude or the removal of organs" (United Nations Convention Against Transnational Organized Crime, 2004).

In India, where the law prohibits slavery, the Scheduled Castes (formerly the Untouchables) and Scheduled Tribes face the majority of caste prejudice and social and economic marginalization. Religion plays a significant role in this hierarchy: under Hinduism all persons are not created equal. Between slavery and debt bondage, NGOs estimate that tens of millions of Indian citizens are affected by human trafficking in India, the majority of whom are members of the Scheduled Castes. At least 2 million persons of the Scheduled Castes are bonded laborers. Unlike the debt bondage that occurs in most of the world, where a person's debt is a result of exorbitant fees that he himself has been charged, in India a person is born into a position of debt bondage and indentured servitude. Children are forced to work off debts that were incurred even generations ago. In other cases an exchange is made between parents and a trafficker. The trafficker gives the parents a financial advance, sometimes with the false assurance that the child will receive an education and learn a trade. The child is then bonded to the trafficker and must work off the advance. In a study of children in two rehabilitation centers, those most susceptible to trafficking were children of the Scheduled Castes and the Other Backward Classes; the most vulnerable population was female children of the Scheduled Castes. The children were forced to work in a variety of industries such as domestic labor, brick kilns, stone quarries, and agriculture. Children of the slave castes are subjected not just to hereditary slavery and bonded labor but also to sex trafficking. The caste system assures discrimination and marginalization—inferior education, position, and status—of the "low castes" and makes social and economic mobility nearly impossible. As a result even victims who manage to escape a scenario of human trafficking are vulnerable to re-victimization and other forms of exploitation and abuse.

As in India, traditional slavery and practices analogous to slavery are illegal but continue to be real problems in Niger, where an estimated 8,800 to 43,000 persons are subjected to traditional slavery. Although the Nigerien government acknowledges that slavery does exist, it denies the prevalence of the practice and claims that NGO estimates are exaggerated. Within minority ethnic groups a caste system exists in which slavery is ascribed at birth; slaves are forced to work as agricultural workers, shepherds, domestic servants, and sexual servants. Some female slaves are a fifth wife or sadaka *and are forced to work as domestic laborers and sex servants. The few victims of hereditary slavery who have turned to Niger's judicial system have found no redress there; offenders continue to receive suspended sentences and reduced fines.*

In China, the household registration (hukou) system, which establishes permanent legal residence, has created a legal two-tier caste structure in which people are defined by the place they were born and whether they are rural or urban. The upper caste is the urban nonagricultural population, and the lower caste is the rural agricultural population. Before 1998 children inherited the hukou *of the head of household; today children can choose to inherit the* hukou *of either parent. The workers who move to cities but cannot fulfill the requirements to attain permanent residence have a status similar to that of illegal migrant workers in other nations; they face discrimination; are without the free compulsory education, urban employment, public housing, free medical services, and retirement benefits granted to holders of urban hukou registration; and have minimal protection against unsafe working conditions and exploitative employers. There are at least 200 million Chinese migrant workers throughout China. Although these migrant workers can obtain temporary work permits, they often face long work hours and the threat of nonpayment. Their children also face discrimination and inequality; in Beijing alone 400,000 children between the ages of 6 and 18 are without Beijing* hukou *and face restrictions on registering for most public schools. The incentive to maintain the* hukou *system is that it is economically beneficial for local governments; it creates a low-cost labor force that by law does not have to be afforded equal access to public services. Though there is widespread pressure on the government to abolish the system or at least equalize all citizens' ability to change residence and eliminate rules that bond access to public services to urban* hukou *status, those who speak out publicly face job discipline and expulsion.*

CHAPTER 13

India

> When we got hungry we would ask for some food, like biscuits,
> but they would always refuse it. If we would ask for money they would say
> "there is no money." They said if we didn't work they would beat us.
>
> —A FORCED-LABOR VICTIM

Generally speaking, persons from the most disadvantaged socioeconomic strata are most vulnerable to exploitation, including human trafficking. In India these differences are exacerbated by a strict caste system, leaving many persons born into indentured servitude and slavery. According to Dr. Joseph D'souza of the Dalit Freedom Network, trafficking is a huge problem, both in terms of its negative impact on communities and in terms of the massive size of slavery today: "With all the general information coming from the UN, the U.S. State Department, and various non-profit organizations, I know it is easy to miss a particular issue like the nexus of caste and slavery. India may appear to be simply another poor country. But it is a very complex culture with a root issue of caste discrimination behind some of our social ills" (Human Trafficking Project, 2010).

India's constitution explicitly prohibits discrimination on the basis of religion, race, caste, sex, or place of birth; yet prejudice persists. In what is called the silent apartheid, those most marginalized by the caste system are persons of the Dalit/Scheduled Castes (SC), formerly known as the Untouchables; the Scheduled Tribes (ST); and the Other Backward Classes (OBC). "Together these groups are classically known as the Sudras or the slave/vassal castes," D'souza explained in an article on Dalit emancipation:

Scheduled means they are listed in a special index appended to the Constitution. Backward Castes are those whose rank and occupational status are above that of Dalits, but who still remain socially and economically depressed. The Scheduled Castes were until recently also known as the Untouchables because they were deemed literally untouchable by the upper castes. The Scheduled Tribes were defined as Criminal Tribes because they occasionally challenged, with arms, the dominance of the local landlords. (D'souza, 2006)

Statistically, the Other Backward Classes constitute the majority of Hindus in India and are estimated to be 52 percent of the population. But it is the Scheduled Castes and Tribes who face the majority of caste prejudice and subjugation. India's 2001 census data reveal that Scheduled Castes and Scheduled Tribes makeup 24.4 percent of the national population, with 66 percent of these from the Scheduled Castes and 34 percent are the Scheduled Tribes (Heitzman & Worden, 1995; NACDOR, 2001; Shahin, 2001; D'souza, 2006; Negi, 2006). The accuracy of the 2001 census was regarded with a great deal of skepticism. One reason was that the census choices were limited. D'souza and John Dayal, the secretary-general of the All India Christian Council, told the press in 2001 that they believed the government had underhanded political motives in dictating that persons who belong to the Scheduled Castes choose from a category of only three religions:

> We are deeply apprehensive of the government's motives in dictating that those people who declare they belong to a Scheduled Caste must choose religious affiliation from a limited three categories arbitrarily fixed by the government. A Scheduled Caste, or Dalit, Indian citizen is being forced to choose only between the Hindu, Sikh and Buddhist faiths, and is not allowed to claim that he belongs to the Muslim, Christian, animist, indigenous, agnostic, or no-faith categories. To deny the Scheduled Castes the religion of their choice violates the constitutional provision of freedom of faith. Caste, like parentage and place of birth, is the inalienable primary identity of persons and important to them in their continuing struggle to break free of 3,000 years of suppression. (Shahin, 2001)

Many activists see the limited census classifications as a way to try to force the Dalit people to continue to exist in the caste system of Hinduism, in which all persons are not created equal. The Dalit have utilized a rejection of Hinduism at least since the 1930s as a means to break away from a caste system that has oppressed them and offered no socioeconomic mobility. In the 1931 census more than 450,000 persons registered themselves as members of the new Dalit faith called Ad Dharam (Original Religion), and as recently as February 2010 a new faith called Ravidassias was announced by persons of the lower castes in the Punjab region to counter the continued social discrimination that they face in the region (Shahin, 2001; Singh, 2010).

NGOs estimate that tens of millions of citizens are affected by human trafficking in India, most of whom are from the Dalit population. At least 2 million of these victims are Dalit bonded laborers; many born into indentured servitude and forced to work off the "debts" of previous generations (Asian Development Bank, 2002; Anti-Slavery International, 2009; U.S. Department of State, 2009, 2012).

TRAFFICKING WITHIN INDIA

The most prevalent form of trafficking in India occurs within the nation to its own citizens, mainly for forced labor. The victims are men, women, and children forced to work off debts by laboring in brick kilns, rice mills, and embroidery factories or by toiling as agricultural workers or domestic servants. Additionally, Naxalites, a Maoist communist armed group, have forcibly recruited children into their ranks (U.S. Department of State, 2009, 2010).

India has the largest number of child laborers in the world (Asian Development Bank, 2002; U.S. Department of State, 2009). According to India's 2001 census, there were 12.67 million child laborers in 2001. The 2010 Census numbers are more challenging to interpret because while, under the Juvenile Justice Act of 2000, persons are deemed to be children until 18 years of age, the census divides the labor age groups into 5–9 years of age, 10–14 years of age, and 15–19 years of age (the latter being the obvious challenge). If all categories are added together, then it appears that there were 45 million child laborers in 2010. The obvious flaw is that this includes laborers who were 19 years old. The number of child laborers drops to 12.6 million, similar to the number in 2001, when the 15–19 age group is excluded, but this too does not accurately reflect the number of child laborers, as it excludes those that are ages 15–18. Therefore, it can only be accurately said that the number of child laborers in 2011 ranged somewhere between 12.6 million and 45 million (Kumar, 2011). One such case of child labor is that of a boy who accepted a job under the promise of legitimate employment but instead faced forced labor and inhumane treatment:

> They came and told us to go with them, and said they'd give us 3,000 Rupees [roughly $65] a month. That we'd work for two or three hours a day and live on the premises. But they took us there and made us work for 12 or 13 hours. They'd wake us up at six in the morning, and only allow us to come back at nine or ten at night. There they would make us do polishing work for two days then stitching work for two days. Sometimes they would make us drag sacks that would weigh 45 or 60 kilos. When we got hungry we would ask for some food, like biscuits, but they would always refuse it. If we would ask for money they would say "there is no money." They said if we didn't work they would beat us. (Bamforth et al., 2009)

Kailash Satyarthi, founder of the NGO Bachpan Bachao Andolan (BBA), helps rescue trafficking victims and has found that children often become the victims of forced labor through fraudulent placement agencies. Through these agencies traffickers sell and buy children for a minuscule amount of money. "There are many children who have been sold and bought even for less than animals," Satyarthi told *The Guardian* (Bamforth et al., 2009). The BBA not only helps rescue trafficked children but also establishes rehabilitation centers where the children can obtain an education as well as social, leadership, and vocational training. The objective is to help the children overcome the delays and detriments trafficking has caused in their education and health, so that the children will eventually be able to integrate back into mainstream society (BBA, 2010). In 2007 and 2008 Patricia Aliperti, a Rotary World Peace fellow at the International Christian University in Tokyo, interviewed 40 children at the three BBA rehabilitation centers, Mukti Ashram, Balika Ashram, and Bal Ashram. The results give a glimpse into the various types of exploitation that children face as well as the classes or castes most affected by child labor and trafficking. Thirty percent of the children interviewed were identified as bonded laborers because they received few to no wages. These children were either bonded with their families or returned home nightly. Five of these children were from OBC, three were from SC, one was from ST, one was from the Upper Caste, and two were of unknown status.

Debt bondage in India develops in several ways, Aliperti explained: "Many children are born into it, having to work off debts that were incurred generations ago. Others have parents who are deceived by traffickers who offer them money with a false promise that the child will receive an education and can learn a trade, bonding the child to work off the advance. Additionally, some parents pledge their children's labor in return for a financial advance, which also results in the child having to pay off the advance."[1]

Twenty of the children whom Aliperti interviewed had been sent away from their families during their trafficking experience. Of these children, 9 belonged to the SC, 4 were Muslim, 3 were of the OBC, 1 was of the ST, and 3 were of unknown status. Caste plays a large role in shaping who is most vulnerable to human trafficking in India. Unsurprisingly, Aliperti's data reveal that the interviewees most susceptible to trafficking were children of the SC (12 children) and the OBC (8 children), with the most vulnerable population being female children of the SC (7 children). During their trafficking or child-labor experience, the children worked in various industries such as domestic labor (5 boys, 4 girls), brick kilns (3 boys, 4 girls), hotels (5 boys), stone quarries (4 boys), and agriculture (3 boys). Other areas of labor were jari embroidery factories (1 boy), school hostels (1 boy), carpet looms (1 boy), and trucker helper (1 boy) (Aliperti, 2009).

Forced labor is not the only form of human trafficking in India. Adults and children are also trafficked for commercial sexual exploitation. As in labor trafficking, those most vulnerable are persons of the low castes, specifically women and girls. Young boys are also vulnerable, some as young as 10 years old. As HIV/AIDS becomes more of a concern for clients, the age of those forced into prostitution is decreasing. It is estimated that there are more than 20,000 female sex-trafficking victims in Delhi brothels—many as young as 12 or 13 years of age. The majority of these girls and women are forced to work in brothels until their debts are repaid, somewhere between four and eight years (Asian Development Bank, 2002). Another area of high commercial sex trafficking is the red-light district of Kamathipura in Mumbai, an area known for sex tourism and pedophilic activity. It is estimated that Mumbai generates more than $400 million annually in revenue from the estimated 100,000 girls and women who service roughly 600,000 clients per day (Asian Development Bank, 2002). Sex tourism, specifically child-sex tourism, is widespread not only in Mumbai but also in other major cities and towns in India with tourist attractions, even in religious pilgrim centers such as Guruvayoor, Puri, and Tirupati. Indian nationals engage in child-sex tourism within India and, to a lesser extent, in Nepal (U.S. Department of State, 2010).

Each year during the monsoon rains, thousands of people in India die while others face displacement and a complete upheaval of their lives. This instability and movement create circumstances ripe for human trafficking. According to Vijay Kumar, activist and former child laborer, in such settings many children become prey to traffickers:

> After the floods, the people lost all their savings and belongings and only escaped with their lives. Most sought refuge in community halls, government buildings, schools and relief camps. The traffickers also went there. When I went home, I asked the villagers who were living in tents and huts, if any of these traffickers had been seen after the floods. The villagers said that many people approached them asking to take their children to Delhi because they had nothing to eat in their house. And they also gave them some money. So after the floods it's almost natural for the traffickers to come. There were many children who got separated from their families who were washed away and still haven't been found. So whenever these disasters strike, child trafficking increases. (Bamforth et al., 2009)

It is not only the annual floods that create a suitable atmosphere for human trafficking but also the successive droughts that are wreaking havoc on the livelihood of local farmers, apparently as a result of climate change and environmental abuse. Bharat Dogra, a fellow at New Delhi's Institute of Social Sciences, says climate change has adversely impacted the crops in the Bundelkhand region of central India, leaving many farmers insolvent and vulnerable to loan sharks. "Before, a bad year would lead to a good year," Dogra told the *Los Angeles Times*. "Now climate change is giving us seven or eight bad years in a row, putting local people deeper and deeper in debt. I expect the situation will only get worse" (Magnier, 2009). Sanjay Singh, founder of the NGO Parmarth Samaj Sevi Sansthan, points to specific environmental abuses such as the cutting down of hardwood trees in the region and the growth of soybeans, a legume that demands more water than the region's ever-diminishing rainfall provides. "This led to a never-ending cycle of loans," Singh explained. "Droughts and climate change after 2000 [were] the final nail in the coffin." Loan sharks charge farmers exorbitant annual interest rates, some as high as 60 percent. Often human trafficking occurs as a result of these debts, Singh said. "Powerful people give loans backed by clothes, tools, land and sometimes women as collateral, figuring they can sleep with them if they're not repaid. It's a completely feudal thought process" (Magnier, 2009). On account of insurmountable debt and interest rates, many farmers have no choice but to forfeit their land and in some cases have been forced into indentured servitude in order to work off their debts (Magnier, 2009).

The idea that education can aid children at the lowest socioeconomic level is certainly not new, but what is novel is the creation of a model that could help successfully re-integrate child trafficking victims into society. This is exactly what is occurring in India through the BBA rehabilitation center Bal Ashram, where boys are given a nonformal, formal, cultural, and human rights education. They also receive social development, vocational, leadership, and physical training (Aliperti, 2009). Most children at Bal Ashram start with nonformal education that focuses on literacy, creativity, dialogue, and human rights. The objective is to mainstream the children into formal education, but in using nonformal education the center aims to teach children to be active participants in their education. The BBA believes the return of bonded and child laborers to their homes without rehabilitation would be "hollow and meaningless," as it would simply re-immerse them in a system of potential exploitation (BBA, 2010). The Bal Ashram believes that offering boys an opportunity to obtain a well-rounded educational experience may help insulate them from future exploitation and give them the tools to make a better life for themselves.

At the Bal Ashram the boys receive basic and formal education, but what is most intriguing is the center's focus on social and human rights issues. The boys explore the topics of child labor, child marriage, and poverty as well as women's rights, gender equity, and environmental protection. The goal of the center is to build and promote confidence and leadership, but most importantly the center allows the children to simply be children (BBA, 2010). Aliperti reported that Bal Ashram has facilities for up to 80 children. "It is located in a part of Rajasthan that is conducive to real rehabilitation. With open fields in a rural area, the children have plenty of room to run and play." One graduate of the Bal Ashram rehabilitation center, a 13-year-old former child laborer, took a stand that resulted in a statewide change. When his government-run village school began to charge student fees, he responded by protesting to the regional magistrate, who in turn filed a petition. The Jaipur court ordered that all monies be returned to the parents, and the Rajasthan State Human Rights Commission ordered that schools in the state not charge student fees.

Another graduate of the Bal Ashram was a 17-year-old who had been a victim of bonded labor in order to pay off a loan incurred by his father. He was later trafficked for forced labor at a school hostel. After eight years at the Bal Ashram, he had learned Hindi, obtained a formal education, and actively participated in trying to promote education, peace, and international awareness on the issue of marginalized children. Once he realized that he could not apply for a passport without a birth certificate, he helped 550 children from Rajasthan to obtain their birth certificates. In 2006 he received a Children's Peace Prize and spoke at a summit for world peace in Italy attended by the Dalai Lama. The young man continues to be particularly focused on the relationship between education and poverty, in which corruption plays a detrimental role. "Corruption and bribes are a big problem," he told Patricia Aliperti. "The government has the ability to help poor families and give them education, but officials keep about 90 percent in their own pockets and use only 10 percent for people" (Aliperti, 2009).

One more success story is that of a 15-year-old ninth-grader who at the time Aliperti interviewed him had been at the Bal Ashram for seven years. He participated in the 2005 Children's World Congress and the South Asian March Against Child Trafficking. He pushed his local school to expand to cover eighth though twelfth grades, to create a playground, and to install access to tap water for drinking and washing. He managed to increase the number of teachers in the local primary school from four to eight. He also succeeded in enrolling in school at least ten children from a poor Muslim area in a Jaipur slum by promising their parents that the children would receive free school materials until fifth grade. His long-term goal is to become a doctor to help poor families. "The poor become poorer and the rich richer," the boy told Aliperti. "If the poor get sick they die, but the rich are taken to the hospital as soon as possible. My priority is for the poor marginalized people in society whose needs are deprived" (Aliperti, 2009).

After rehabilitation, these children go back to their respective villages where they either enroll in schools or get jobs, if they are 18 or older. But even with the benefits of rehabilitation and education, the children will once again be vulnerable to child labor and trafficking. In 2008, just a year after the initial interviews, Aliperti returned to India to conduct a follow-up round of interviews but was able to reach only 10 of the 40 children. Aliperti suspects that some of the other children returned to child labor or were once again trafficked:

> People do what they need to in order to survive. Poor children don't get the benefits of education because they may have to help provide for their families. But it is education that helps diminish a child's vulnerability to labor and trafficking. When a child is at school they get a midday meal which alleviates food expenses and they don't have to do labor—of course they study and help their families and some may still work a few hours per day, but school keeps them out of long workdays and hard labor while giving them the tools for greater opportunity.[2]

The prospects for rescued girls, who attend the Balika Ashram for rehabilitation, are less certain. In contrast to the Bal Ashram, the Balika Ashram provides girls with no access to formal education. According to Patricia Aliperti, the girls there "receive social class and vocational training such as sewing and cosmetology." The teacher at the school told Aliperti that the girls do not attend the formal village schools because it is unsafe for them to go outside the center alone. "It makes one wonder about the fate of girls," said Aliperti. "I suppose other factors come into play that limits the rescue of girls, such as the exploitation occurring behind closed doors—domestic labor, sexual abuse, and the social bias preferring boys rather than girls."

Seven of the ten children whom Aliperti was able to trace the following year (2008), along with an eleventh child interviewed only in 2008, were boys that had remained at the Bal Ashram rehabilitation center. This outcome illustrates the success of the Bal Ashram program but highlights the problem with follow-up once the children return home as well as the lesser success of the Balika Ashram.

TRAFFICKING ABROAD

Each year thousands of citizens from India who work abroad in Europe, the Middle East, and the United States face forced labor and debt bondage. Some experience fraudulent recruitment and are placed directly in situations of forced labor or commercial sexual exploitation in the destination country while others face debt bondage as a result of substantial fees charged by unscrupulous recruiters and employers (U.S. Department of State, 2009). Fees often include recruitment costs, ongoing housing fees, food costs, and even payment for the tools used on the job. The debts are supposedly taken from the victims' wages, but of course the wages are never enough to discharge the inflated debt that the victims owe. Thus victims find themselves in a position of involuntary servitude facing nonpayment of wages, restrictions on their movements, the withholding of their travel documents, and the threat and actuality of physical and/or sexual abuse.

One case of alleged debt bondage involved 500–550 persons from India trafficked to the United States Gulf Coast region after Hurricane Katrina.

They were allegedly trafficked by the U.S. company Signal International, LLC. As stated in the complaint filed by the victims, recruitment advertisements promised permanent residence in the United States for workers. In fact Signal intended to use the workers only temporarily. Recruitment and other fees totaled roughly $20,000 per victim. Fees included the cost of travel, recruitment, skill tests, and immigration processing. Additionally, recruiters told applicants that permanent residence could also be offered to the workers' spouses and children for a fee of around $1,500. In order to ensure that they received their final payment from the workers, Sachin Dewan, the labor recruiter hired by Signal, required that the workers hand over their passports either just before or after their consular interviews. "The passports were returned to the workers once they had arrived in Bombay and gave Dewan (or his agents) the third installment of approximately $6,000," said Dan Werner, deputy director of the Immigrant Justice Project at the Southern Poverty Law Center and co-counsel for the plaintiffs. "Within an hour the workers were in a taxi to the airport and on their way to the United States."[3]

The sacrifices the workers had to make in order to come up with the money for fee payments often involved taking out substantive loans and borrowing money from family members. Werner reported that the workers obtained money wherever they could get it—including loans from loan sharks who charged astronomical interest rates:

Many of the men speak of having to sell their family jewelry— jewelry that is passed from generation to generation through marriage and has both cultural and symbolic value for these families. The men also sold or took out loans against their property. They did whatever it took to come up with the money. They were investing in what they believed to be a whole new life in the United States. At times this involved workers transporting suitcases and duffel bags full of Indian rupees to their traffickers. Some traveled with as much as 295,538 INR [roughly $6,000] in their possession. Just imagine their desperation to be willing to haul suitcases and duffel bags full of that amount of cash down city streets.

Upon arrival in 2006 and 2007, the workers allegedly were forced to live in dirty, crowded, remote, fenced, and guarded camps in Orange,

Texas, and Pascagoula, Mississippi. The workers were shocked by the conditions. Through other employers, many of them had previously worked outside India, predominantly in the United Arab Emirates and Singapore. "In the UAE," Werner explained, "the workers lived in furnished apartments paid for by their employer. Two workers shared a decent-sized room with a common area." But in these camps they were placed in single rooms that housed 22 to 24 people: "Each housing unit appeared as though multiple trailer-like structures had been pushed together, with the interior walls removed, creating single modular structures. The aisles between many of the bunk beds were barely large enough for a human body, so that a person had to turn his body sideways to walk through them. A worker's only privacy was his bunk, so many workers used drapes to create some semblance of privacy."[4]

There was one gate to each camp, which was surrounded by a chain-link fence and monitored by a guard. Although technically the workers were allowed to come and go, the camps were far from any stores or other services. When workers returned to the camp, the gate guard checked bags and other personal belongings. Everything that the workers did was closely monitored. In addition to isolating the victims, the company compounded the workers' indebtedness by deducting various fees from their wages, such as weekly rent and meal costs and even the cost of job-related toolkits. In this situation it was difficult or impossible for the workers to accrue enough earnings to repay their debts in India (David et al. v. Signal International LLC, complaint, 2008).

If workers complained, the traffickers threatened deportation as well as other serious harm. When some of the workers objected to the conditions they faced, Signal tried to deport them. In response to complaints from Sabulal Vijayan (one of the workers), Sachin Dewan made a threatening call to Vijayan's wife and told her that Sabulal needed to stop "making trouble at Signal." Such threats and actions amplified fear among the workers. Soon after the call, Signal guards illegally detained some of the workers, including Vijayan (David et al. v. Signal International LLC, complaint, 2008). Some of the workers, according to Werner, had begun to gather at a local Catholic church to discuss the conditions at the camp:

> Signal got wind of these meetings, and one morning sent Signal
> management through the housing units with pictures of five men

asking, "Have you seen this person?" Some of the men in question had become worker leaders who organized the offsite meetings. This was a public display by Signal designed to keep the other workers quiet. People were abruptly roused from sleep in order to look at the photos. When the five men were found, they were detained and closed in a common room with guards outside, who at one point were armed. Not only were the five workers illegally detained, but also this act increased fears in all the workers. Signal wanted to ensure that the workers did not continue to organize.[5]

Signal allegedly told the workers that the five men were being deported because they were "complaining." Some of the men saw deportation under so great a burden of debt as a fate worse than death; it would be humiliating for them to return to India and their families with nothing to show for all their sacrifices. When told that he was going to be deported, Vijayan, one of the detained organizers, asked to use the bathroom, and, once inside, he slit his wrists. "When found, Vijayan was released and taken by coworkers to the [hospital] emergency room," Werner said. Concurrently, after learning of the exploitation of the Signal workers, local community activists began to gather outside the camp. The pressure was on for Signal to release the workers, which it eventually did later that morning. Once freed from their traffickers, the workers contacted the U.S. Department of Justice and also filed a class action against Signal in federal court on March 7, 2008 (David et al. v. Signal International LLC, complaint, 2008). The case is still ongoing.

INDIA AS A TRANSIT NATION

Persons from Nepal and Bangladesh are trafficked through India for commercial sexual exploitation and forced labor in the Middle East. In 2008 over 500 girls from Nepal in transit to the Gulf region were jailed in India on charges of using false documents (U.S. Department of State, 2009). Although it is unknown whether they were trafficking victims, the number involved indicates the high volume of migration through India. According to a report by then-solicitor general Gopal Subramaniam, the estimated number of women and girls entering prostitution every day is 200—of whom 20 percent are under the age of 15. The report went on to state that somewhere between 5,000 and 7,000 girls from Nepal are trafficked into India each year. The ages of girls trafficked has dropped from 14–16 years of age to 10–14 years of age (Hindustan Times, 2010; U.S. Department of State, 2010).

WHAT HAPPENS TO VICTIMS AFTER TRAFFICKING

Trafficking victims often face intimidation to persuade them to drop the case against their traffickers. For instance, in 2007 an NGO worker told *The Telegraph* how a rescued victim from Nepal was repeatedly deposed and continually asked embarrassing questions in an attempt to get her to withdraw the charges. As a result of such intimidation, as well as an understandable and legitimate fear of retribution, combined with the fact that cases move very slowly through the overburdened judicial system, many victims simply opt to not testify against their traffickers (Dastidar, 2007; U.S. Department of State, 2009). In addition, victims commonly face charges for crimes associated with their trafficking experience such as soliciting customers for sexual services or using false travel documents. Section 8 of the Immoral Trafficking Prevention Act of 1986 (ITPA) allows for the arrest of trafficked women for soliciting. NGOs have pushed for this to be dropped so that victims are not doubly victimized by the trafficking experience and the judicial system. Since 2006 the Indian government has continued to debate proposed amendments to this law that would eliminate Section 8 and grant victims more protections (Dastidar, 2007; U.S. Department of State, 2009, 2011, 2012).

Pressure for an increased anti-trafficking effort is coming not just from NGOs but also from India's own Supreme Court. In a 2010 decision the Supreme Court stated that there should be an increase in anti-trafficking cooperation between the government and NGOs, specifically when concerning children forced into the commercial sex industry. The court went on to highlight the conditions faced by exploited child prostitutes and the lack of resources available to them. "See the condition of sex workers, whenever the police conduct raid[s], only they are arrested and traffickers get away scot-free and no legal aid is available to them," said Justices Dalveer Bhandari and Ananga Kumar Patnaik (Hindustan Times, 2010). The court mentions that the lack of regulation has contributed to the spread of AIDS, stating that sex workers are forced to continue working even after contracting the retrovirus. "Most of the sex workers are HIV positive and are continuing with their profession. They will only multiply disease. Steps must be taken to curb this," said the justices (Hindustan Times, 2010).

Under national and state law, certified victims of forced and bonded labor are entitled to receive benefits, including compensation. Yet implementation of protection programs and compensation laws remains unsatisfactory (U.S. Department of State, 2009). According to Patricia Aliperti, victims of debt bondage are supposed to receive 20,000 rupees (roughly $434.05). "But they have to first get a certificate from the police. While the compensation is just supposed to be for victims of debt bondage, NGOs such as the BBA do a good job of helping rescued children receive rehabilitation money by classifying them as bonded laborers, since their pay was likely nonexistent or below the minimum wage." However, not all victims get certified. Without the help of NGOs, victims typically have no idea that compensation exists. "When an NGO is involved it helps the victims to exit their trafficking situation, and the victims are given guidance on how to maneuver through the system. For instance, the BBA brings police when they conduct raids. They immediately take the rescued children to the police station to obtain statements and certificates while they are there so that they don't have to go back and follow up with the police, which is difficult in India."[6]

Fortunately, the implementation of protection and compensation for bonded labor victims may be improving slightly. In 2009 police and NGO personnel in Tamil Nadu and New Delhi rescued 161 bonded child laborers; all the children received shelter, and some received part of their statutory rehabilitation packages. Sixty-six other bonded child laborers were also rescued in 2009; they were awarded release certificates, but it is unclear whether they received rehabilitation funds. Another 364 bonded laborers were rescued in Uttar Pradesh and Bihar during the same year; only 185 of them received their rehabilitation packages, totaling roughly $78,000 in government rehabilitation funds. In 2010 the Ministry of Labor and Employment reported that 865 bonded laborers were rescued and that nearly $170,000 was distributed in rehabilitation funds. NGOs reported in 2011 that there are delays in obtaining release certificates, and whether victims obtain the funds is inconsistent (U.S. Department of State, 2010, 2012). Under the Swadhar Scheme, which has an annual budget of $1 million, the government grants support to more than 13,000 women and girls in distress who are without social and economic support. They are provided with shelter, food, clothing, and counseling, as well as legal and clinical support. The program also provides rehabilitation through education, awareness, and behavioral training (U.S. Department of State, 2009; Government of India, Ministry of Human Resource Development, 2010). Among those benefiting from the program are victims of trafficking for commercial sexual exploitation, victims of sex crimes, widows, prisoners, persons who are mentally challenged, persons with HIV/AIDS, survivors of natural disaster, and victims of terrorist/extremist violence (U.S. Department of State, 2009; Government of India, Ministry of Human Resource Development, 2010).

The government, through the Ministry of Women and Child Development's Ujjawala comprehensive program, has taken measures to address prevention, rescue, rehabilitation, reintegration, and repatriation of victims trafficked for commercial sexual exploitation by providing funding for state projects that address these specific issues. One sponsored project under the program is a fund that provides victims with temporary financial relief of $200 in the state of Andhra Pradesh. In 2009 the Andhra Pradesh Department of Women and Child Development disbursed $10,435 in interim relief to 48 sex-trafficking victims for medicine, travel, clothing, and other necessities. The ministry allocated $118 million for the year 2011–2012 to fund 153 projects in 17 states under the Ujjawala program (Government of India, Ministry of Women and Child Development, 2007; U.S. Department of State, 2009, 2010, 2012). Despite these positive steps, the standard of care for victims of commercial sexual exploitation is inconsistent. Many victims simply do not receive comprehensive services (U.S. Department of State, 2009, 2012). Also, there appears to be no shelter that is geared to adult victims of forced or bonded labor, and no shelters that focus on male adult trafficking victims.

WHAT HAPPENS TO TRAFFICKERS

Under the ITPA, traffickers for commercial sexual exploitation face a minimum of 7 years to life in prison. Bonded labor, forced labor, and child labor are prohibited under the Bonded Labor System Abolition Act of 1976, the Child Labor (Prohibition and Regulation) Act of 1986, and the Juvenile Justice Act of 2000. Violators face a light sentence of up to 3 years. Kidnapping and selling minors into prostitution are prohibited under Sections 366(A) and 372 of the Penal Code. Prescribed penalties are a maximum of 10 years in prison and a fine (U.S. Department of State, 2009).

The overall number of anti-trafficking prosecutions and convictions in India is minimal, though some areas have had more success than others. In 2008 officials convicted 30 sex traffickers in Andhra Pradesh, Bihar, Goa, Maharashtra, and West Bengal. Between October 2008 and February 2010 Andhra Pradesh courts convicted 55 traffickers and clients; sentences ranged from 4 to 14 years' imprisonment. Convictions in Andhra Pradesh were less stringent against 118 brothel owners and pimps who were convicted in 2010 under the Immoral Trafficking Prevention Act and the Indian Penal Code; most were sex-trafficking cases. Sentences ranged from 3 to 7 years. In 2008, 89 Mumbai cases resulted in the sentencing of clients and sex traffickers with sentences of up to 5 years' imprisonment, though some of the Mumbai sex-trafficking victims were sentenced for solicitation. The charge carries a $2 fine. However, when the Mumbai court issued 164 ITPA convictions against pimps and brothel owners in 2010, most of which were sex-trafficking cases, the victims were not fined. In 2011 Mumbai courts convicted 125 sex-trafficking offenders; sentences were up to 3 years' imprisonment (U.S. Department of State, 2009, 2010, 2011, 2012).

Even though the government's anti-trafficking efforts have increased, most forced-labor offenders go unpunished or face minimal punishment. In 2009 an NGO reported that it had worked with police to facilitate the conviction of five bonded-labor offenders but that the offenders were only sentenced to one to two days' imprisonment and a fine of $45. In 2010 there were two landmark cases involving convictions of forced-labor traffickers. In the first case, in Tamil Nadu, each of three forced-labor traffickers was sentenced to 5 years' imprisonment and a fine. The second set of convictions took place in Uttar Pradesh, where 5 traffickers were each sentenced to 14 years' imprisonment. In 2011, according to NGOs, there were convictions of 6 offenders for forced and bonded labor; 4 of the offenders were sentenced to 1 year in prison, and 2 offenders were charged with fines (U.S. Department of State, 2010, 2011, 2012).

India's Supreme Court has requested that the government increase the severity of punishment for those who commit trafficking offenses and has recommended an increase in enforcement, specifically a separate police wing to counter child trafficking. "The government needs to understand clearly that child trafficking is the priority area," said the justices. "There are several aspects. There should be a special investigative agency to deal with trafficking and plug the loopholes" (Hindustan Times, 2010). Believing that enforcement and prosecution of traffickers will act as a deterrent, the court stated that without this step India is likely to continue as a hub for human trafficking, specifically for children exploited in the commercial sex industry. "The most serious problem is the use of children for sex trade. While this crime is growing, hardly any case is registered. If a case is registered, it will have a deterrent effect" (Hindustan Times, 2010). The Supreme Court went on to mention the lack of enforcement in areas with a high volume of cross-border trafficking such as Nepal and the northeast border with Bangladesh, stating that the current police presence is ineffective and that a special agency should exist to deal with this type of trafficking.

INTERNAL EFFORTS TO DECREASE TRAFFICKING

In 2009 the government made an initial investment of $19 million for the purpose of expanding its number of anti–human trafficking units. To date it has established at least 47 such task forces within local law-enforcement agencies. The units are responsible for investigating human trafficking cases and have contributed in cases against sex traffickers. It is unclear whether the units have contributed to labor-trafficking prosecutions. The effectiveness of the units seems inconsistent, depending on the location. Additionally, NGOs state that some units lack funding and personnel (U.S. Department of State, 2010).

While anti-trafficking efforts have been predominantly focused on trafficking for commercial sexual exploitation, the government is beginning to take legislative measures against trafficking for forced and child labor. In an effort to combat child labor, the government approved a nationwide model in January 2009 that merges the national educational and poverty alleviation programs (U.S. Department of State, 2009). In 2012 India's cabinet approved changes to the Child Labor (Prohibition and Regulation) Act of 1986 that will establish a minimum age of 14 years for employment and 18 years for hazardous work. The changes must first be approved by Parliament (ILO, 2012). In July 2009 an amendment to the Emigration Act increased penalties for Indian labor recruitment agencies involved in deceptive recruitment practices and/or the trafficking of laborers (Ministry of Overseas Indian Affairs, 2009). Ranbir Singh, the protector general of emigrants, said that every year approximately 1 million workers from India find low-skill jobs in the Middle East/Gulf region and Southeast Asia. "They are the workers who are generally poor, less educated and vulnerable to exploitation and other malpractices. They are the people we have to look after" (Thaindian News, 2009).

Although the government put together a comprehensive plan in 2008 to work with NGOs to prevent and combat human trafficking, the government's post-trafficking programs are geared primarily toward women and child victims of sexual exploitation. While the law appears to be increasingly protective of child and adult victims of forced labor and debt bondage, there is still minimal government focus on rehabilitation services for adult victims. Particularly marginalized are adult male trafficking victims, who have little access to shelters, services, and rehabilitation programs. Also, the issue of caste remains a serious problem in India. It would help improve the trafficking situation if this issue was properly addressed and programs were successfully implemented that would equalize its citizens. Until then, people of the low castes will continue to face inferior education and status that make them vulnerable to human trafficking.

CHAPTER 14

Niger

> My master has four wives. We, the slaves, were doing all the housework like
> cooking, fetching water and firewood, and working on farms.
> I was beaten so many times I would run to my family.
> Then, after a day or two, I would be brought back.
>
> —HADIJATOU MANI KORAOU, BORN INTO SLAVERY

In February 2010 a military junta led by Salou Djibo deposed then-president Mamadou Tandja and suspended the constitution and the cabinet. Approved by referendum in October 2010, the new constitution gave the army until April 6, 2011 to restore civilian rule, which it did, and on April 7, 2011, elected president Mahamadou Issoufou began his term (BBC News, 2010; IFES, 2010; VOANews, 2011a, 2011b). Before handing over leadership, the transitional government enacted the country's first specific law to address human trafficking in December 2010, Order No. 2010-86. The comprehensive anti-trafficking law prohibits all forms of trafficking, including slavery and practices analogous to slavery. Offenders face 5 to 10 years' imprisonment, or 10 to 30 years' imprisonment if the victim is a child. The law also allows victims to file civil suits against their traffickers (U.S. Department of State, 2011). Prior to the anti-trafficking law, prosecutors used Niger's trafficking-related statutes to prosecute traffickers, though there were no laws that addressed the sex trafficking of adults. Forced labor is prohibited through the Nigerien Labor Code. Those found guilty of forced-labor offenses face minimal sentencing that ranges from six days to one month in prison and a fine of between $48 and $598. Profiting from or encouraging child begging is prohibited under Article 181 of the Penal Code, and procurement of a child for prostitution is prohibited under Articles 292 and 293 (ILO, 1996; U.S. Department of State, 2010).

Traditional slavery continues to be a serious problem in Niger. In addition to the anti-trafficking law, Article 270 of the Penal Code prohibits slavery. Under the code those found guilty of slavery offenses are supposed to face a penalty of 10 to 30 years' imprisonment. Yet an estimated 8,800 to 43,000 persons are subjected to traditional hereditary slavery within the nation. The Nigerien government acknowledges that slavery does exist, but considers NGO reports on the number of persons enslaved to be an exaggeration and denies its prevalence and severity (Anti-Slavery International, 2008c; U.S. Department of State, 2009, 2010).

TRAFFICKING ABROAD

There are reports of Nigerien girls entering into sham marriages with citizens of Nigeria, Saudi Arabia, and the United Arab Emirates. Upon arrival in these countries, the girls are often forced into involuntary domestic servitude. Other Nigerien girls enter into fake marriages and are forced into prostitution (U.S. Department of State, 2010, 2012). Nigerien girls are particularly vulnerable to these sham marriages because of cultural pressure on girls to marry at an early age. It is a common practice in Niger for girls to be married off by their parents by the age of 12, a custom that has begun to be exploited by international traffickers (IRIN, 2009a). In fact, according to UNICEF, one-third of girls in Niger are married before the age of 15 (Mebrahtu, 2012). The reasons for the persistence of this tradition include religion and poverty. One mother in Agadez said that marriage is the prescribed way of life for Muslims and that the practice of a girl's marrying early deters potential family dishonor. "I'd rather marry my daughters to whomever rather than have them picking up unwanted pregnancies in the streets of Agadez," the mother said (IRIN, 2009a).

Despite the fact that some parents have faced arrest and imprisonment for marrying off their daughters before the legal age, due to the severe food crisis in Niger the number of early childhood marriages is not likely to dwindle anytime soon. "People are eating leaves to survive," said Achirou Oumarou, the director of a regional hospital in Maradi. In the hospital where Oumarou works, 5 percent of babies are typically born weighing less than five pounds; this increased to 8 percent in 2012. The incentive to marry off a daughter is in part because it fetches a dowry, which includes animals and cash (Raghavan, 2012). Moutari Mamane, regional coordinator for the NGO Association in Favor of the Suppression of Child Labor in Niger, said that parents are often unaware that this custom can result in the sexual exploitation of their daughters. "Parents don't realize what their daughter can go through in the country she is sent to," said Mamane. "All too often, they fall prey to sexual exploitation, violence and all kinds of mistreatment" (IRIN, 2009a). A law has been proposed that would raise the legal age for marriage from 15 to 18. As of September 2012 the proposed law had not yet been adopted. Seyna Saidou, a judge in Agadez, said that even if the law is adopted, implementation and enforcement are unlikely. "The problem with marriage in Niger is that it's governed by customs, which allow parents to marry their girls to whomever they want and at any age," Saidou told IRIN, the humanitarian news and analysis service of the UN Office for the Coordination of Humanitarian Affairs (IRIN, 2009a; Callimachi, 2012).

Nigerien citizens, primarily women and children, are also trafficked abroad through false promises of jobs where they face involuntary domestic servitude, forced labor, and forced commercial sexual exploitation. The most common destinations are Benin, Cameroon, Europe, Mali, the Middle East, and North Africa. In 2005 and 2006, Nigerien citizens made up 1.4 percent of identified trafficking victims in Benin (UNODC, 2009; U.S. Department of Labor, 2009b; U.S. Department of State, 2009, 2010). People from Niger have also been trafficked to the United States. One such case is that of Marie, a woman in her early twenties trafficked to the United States to be a nanny. In exchange for performing nanny duties for a single family, Marie was promised wages and an education. But when she arrived, her traffickers confiscated her passport, birth certificate, and the temporary visa that they had used to bring Marie into the country. Her responsibilities encompassed much more than what she had agreed to do. "She was not only the full-time nanny," said Alia El-Sawi, former Anti-Human Trafficking Program coordinator at Tapestri, Refugee and Immigrant Coalition Against Domestic Violence in Atlanta, Georgia. "She was also assigned to cook, clean, do laundry, and perform yard work."[1] Marie's traffickers locked her inside the home to ensure that she could not leave. When not performing duties, Marie was restricted to her room. "She was forbidden from using the phone," El-Sawi said. "She did not have contact with her family or anyone outside the home for several years. If she asked to leave the house or make any phone calls, she was severely beaten with some type of object on her face and body."

TRAFFICKING WITHIN NIGER

Slavery is prohibited under the anti-trafficking law and Article 270 of the Nigerien Penal Code, but traditional slavery persists and is practiced by minority ethnic groups such as the Toureg, Maure, and Peule. Within these groups, a caste system exists in which slavery is ascribed at birth and passed from one generation to the next. Slaves are forced to work as shepherds, agricultural workers, domestic servants, and sexual servants (Kaye, 2008; Anti-Slavery International, 2008e; U.S. Department of Labor, 2009b). One highly publicized case of traditional slavery in Niger involves the enslavement of a woman named Hadijatou Mani Koraou. Born to a slave, Mani came into the world as the property of her mother's owner. At the age of 12 she was sold to El Hadj Soulemayne Naroua for $543.05 as a fifth wife, or *sadaka*. Under this arrangement Mani was not legally a wife, but a slave acquired to work as both servant and concubine (ECOWAS, 2008).

Mani's experience was probably not unlike that of any other *sadaka*; under this arrangement, forced sexual relations are commonplace. The first sexual attack happened when Mani was 12 years old; Naroua sneaked up on her when she was working in the fields. Thereafter she suffered sexual abuse or beatings whenever Naroua perceived her to be disobedient (ECOWAS, 2008). "My master has four wives," Mani told the BBC. "We, the slaves, were doing all the housework like cooking, fetching water and firewood, and working on farms. I was beaten so many times I would run to my family. Then, after a day or two, I would be brought back" (BBC News, 2008). Under pressure from the human rights organization Timidria, Naroua released Mani from slavery in 2005. The liberation certificate was signed by Mani and Naroua, and countersigned and stamped by the village chief. Mani tried to leave after receiving the certificate, but Naroua prevented her from doing so, stating that she was his wife (INTERIGHTS, 2009a). This claim, of course, was false, as the consent of both parties is required for a marriage to be deemed legal in Niger. Other requirements are a religious ceremony and payment of a dowry, none of which had transpired during Mani's enslavement (Anti-Slavery International, 2008b).

Mani was eventually able to escape under the pretext of visiting her sick mother (ECOWAS, 2008). She then appealed to the local civil and traditional tribunal, which found that no marriage existed between Mani and Naroua. In response, Naroua filed an appeal with the local high court, which ruled that under customary law a slave girl is the de facto wife of her master when freed. This ruling is in direct violation of both Niger's domestic law and international antislavery laws that Niger has ratified. Mani appealed to Niger's Supreme Court, which quashed the high court's decision, composed it differently, and then sent the case back to the high court (Anti-Slavery International, 2008b, ECOWAS, 2008). During that time and with the consent of her brother, Mani married a man of her choosing. In response, Naroua filed suit against Mani for bigamy. The high court judge found Mani guilty and sentenced her, as well as her husband and brother, to six months' imprisonment. Each was also fined $113.14. Mani appealed the verdicts in the Court of Appeals in Niamey, but the court deferred sentencing until the judgment by the divorce judge had been decided. Nonetheless, it did order a provisional release of Mani and her family members. At the time of release they had each served two months of their sentences (Anti-Slavery International, 2008b).

What Mani did next, and the verdict that resulted, are significant. With the help of local attorneys and human rights organizations, Mani brought a case against the Nigerien government before the Economic Community of West African States (ECOWAS) Community Court of Justice on April 7, 2008, for failure to implement laws against slavery (Pflanz, 2008; Anti-Slavery International, 2008b).[2] "I was wrongly jailed, not because of anything I did but because of slavery, and today there is no more slavery, so I wanted the court to vindicate me, to give [me] my rights which I was denied some four years ago, to compensate me," Mani told the BBC (BBC News, 2008).

This was the first time that the ECOWAS Community Court had heard a slavery case and the first time that the court sat in Niger. The case turned on the fact that the Republic of Niger—through its judges—had the opportunity and obligation to protect Mani when she came before them. The court highlighted the fact that one of the Niger judges had not denounced the act of slavery against Mani, but instead said: "The marriage of a free man with a slave woman is lawful, as long as he cannot afford to marry a free woman and if he fears to fall into fornication." The ECOWAS court stated that the judge's recognition of Mani's slave status without denouncing it was a form of "acceptance, or at least tolerance, of this crime or offense." The Nigerien judge, according to the court, had an obligation to bring a criminal prosecution or punish the crime or offense (of slavery) "as need be":

> The Court considers that the slavery situation of the applicant [Mani], although it was due to a particular individual acting in a so-called customary or individual context, gave her the right to be protected by the Nigerien authorities, be they administrative or judicial. Consequently, the defendant [the Republic of Niger] becomes responsible under international as well as national law for any form of human rights violations of the applicant founded on slavery because of its tolerance, passivity, inaction and abstention with regard to this practice. (ECOWAS, 2008)

The ECOWAS court found Niger in breach of both its domestic antislavery laws and those existing under the treaty of ECOWAS, all ratified by Niger. The court also awarded Mani $22,626.94 in restitution, to be paid by the Nigerien government (INTERIGHTS, 2009a). The landmark decision serves as precedent to all members of the ECOWAS (Pflanz, 2008). The Republic of Niger accepted the verdict and paid the fine in March 2009 (U.S. Department of State, 2009). In response to the decision, Mani said:

> It was very difficult to challenge my former master and to speak out when people see you as nothing more than a slave. But I knew that this was the only way to protect my child from suffering the same fate as myself. Nobody deserves to be enslaved. We are all equal and deserve to be treated the same. I hope that everybody in slavery today can find their freedom. No woman should suffer the

way I did. With the compensation I will be able to build a house, raise animals, and farm land to support my family. I will also be able to send my children to school so they can have the education I was never allowed as a slave. (INTERIGHTS, 2009b)

In addition to traditional slavery, Nigerien children are trafficked for forced labor in the agricultural sector, gold mines, stone quarries, as well as for domestic servitude, commercial sexual exploitation (particularly in Zinder and Birni-N'Konni, both cities that border Nigeria), and forced begging. While traffickers often mislead parents with promises of bright futures for their children, some parents are more involved in the process of trafficking their children within Niger. For instance, some parents facilitate in the trafficking of boys for forced cattle herding. Sometimes the boys manage to escape and return to their parents with signs of psychological and physical abuse, but parents frequently return the boys to their employers (U.S. Department of State, 2009).

Some forced-labor cases stem from the traditional practice of sending boys to koranic teachers (marabouts) to receive an education. This may include an apprenticeship or vocational component. The National Nigerien Association of Human Rights states that koranic teachers are often implicated in domestic and cross-border child trafficking from Niger, often for forced begging and manual labor. Amadou Idrissa, coordinator at the nonprofit Niger Association to Deal with Delinquency and Prevent Crime, says it is difficult to estimate the number of koranic students (*almajiris*) in Niger because marabouts move their classes frequently and their attendance lists are unreliable. The most recent data available from the Ministry of Education reveal that in 2004 there were 384,000 students registered with more than 50,000 Koranic schools in Niger. In 2009 the NGO Arewa Youth Mobilization reported that 30 percent of youths from northern Niger are almajiris (Kumolu, 2012). Begging for alms is part of these students' daily routine. "These youths are completely dependent on their teachers, at least for their food," Idrissa told IRIN (IRIN, 2009b). Oumarou Garba, a koranic teacher, says that Islamic principles do sanction child begging to a degree: "Once the child has received his daily quota in his tin can, he should return to his koranic teacher to pursue his religious studies and not stay on the streets. These children should under no condition serve to enrich their teacher. But certain rogue teachers take advantage of this situation to deprive children entrusted to them of an education" (IRIN, 2009b).

Children who work are vulnerable to health risks, physical injury, and exploitation, including human trafficking. The minimum age for employment is 14 (16 for hazardous labor), but roughly 66 percent of Nigerien children between ages 5 and 14 work. In fact more children in that age group work (66.2 percent) than attend school (31.1 percent). Because education is compulsory only until age 12, many children are thrust into the labor market before they are of legal employment age; as a result they are particularly vulnerable to seeking or accepting jobs that are off the grid and unregulated (U.S. Department of Labor, 2009b). Child labor can be found in Niger's production of gold, salt, trona, and gypsum. Children also work in domestic jobs and as street vendors, beggars, dishwashers, and porters. They work in welding, carpentry, metalwork, and at slaughterhouses. Those who work at slaughterhouses face significant health and safety risks, while girls working in domestic servitude and street vending are at particular risk of physical and sexual harassment. Children who work as porters are at risk for physical injury from carrying heavy loads. A 2009 study revealed a high incidence of child worker injuries. Of 400 children who were interviewed, 38 percent reported having been injured at work (U.S. Department of Labor, 2009a, 2009b).

NIGER AS A DESTINATION AND TRANSIT NATION

Women and children are trafficked from Benin, Burkina Faso, Cameroon, Gabon, Ghana, Mali, Nigeria, and Togo to and through Niger for forced labor in agriculture and fishing, spare-parts shops and street vending, mining (gold mines and stone quarries), domestic servitude, and commercial sexual exploitation. Those who transit into Niger typically continue on to North Africa and western Europe. Teenage girls are trafficked from Nigeria through Niger to Libya and then shipped to Europe for sexual commercial exploitation. The girls are offered lucrative legitimate jobs in Europe by trafficking recruiters. When they arrive, their passports are confiscated, and they are forced into prostitution (U.S. Department of State, 2009, 2010). This is exactly what occurred when a Nigerian trafficker, Samuel Osagie, transported at least 21 girls from Nigeria through Niger to Libya. When he was apprehended in Nigeria in 2008, it was discovered that Osagie resided in Libya with 21 trafficking victims, 16 of whom were teenage girls. After their rescue the Nigerian girls informed officials that Osagie had arranged with their parents for the girls to obtain legal employment in Libya as maids. He planned to deduct the transportation fee of $1,272 each from their wages. "The work promise is a ruse," Oemi Bio Ockiya, the head of the Nigerian Immigration Department in Kano, told IRIN. "The truth of the matter is that they were going to pay the fees from the money they would make from prostitution in Europe" (IRIN, 2008).

Although Nigeria has begun using passport-reading machines to deter the use of false passports, according to Ockiya, traffickers are constantly changing their tactics to work around new enforcement strategies. In response to the state-of-the-art passport-reading machines, traffickers simply drive the victims to Niger, then to Libya, and then ship them to Europe; the border between Nigeria and Niger is simply too vast for adequate police enforcement (IRIN, 2008). Because Niger has fewer personnel and resources than Nigeria, the porous border between the two nations is significantly underpoliced. According to an anonymous Niger official, this is an issue that has to be tackled collectively (IRIN, 2008).

WHAT HAPPENS TO VICTIMS AFTER TRAFFICKING

The Nigerien government provides little direct assistance to trafficking victims, but it does refer them to NGOs on an ad hoc basis. The government has no formal system for the identification and referral of trafficking victims, nor does it offer any legal alternative to removal of foreign victims who face potential retribution or hardship upon return to their country of origin. The Ministry of the Interior does provide short-term housing of roughly one week to repatriated Nigeriens, some of whom are trafficking victims. However, while most victim assistance appears to be conducted by NGOs, local authorities have aided NGOs in the rescue, rehabilitation, and return of child-trafficking victims, though the government did not assist any foreign victims with repatriation in 2011 (U.S. Department of State, 2009, 2010, 2012).

Unfortunately, the ECOWAS court decision may not have the widespread impact on current practices and enforcement of anti-slavery legislation that NGOs had hoped for. One case that highlights this concern is that of Assibit Wanagoda, enslaved for 50 years. Wanagoda's duties encompassed anything that her master, Tafane Abouzeidi, requested, such as collecting water and firewood, milking camels, herding goats, moving heavy tents to ensure that the lady of the house was well shaded, and even acting as the outdoor pole for her master's tent amidst horrendous rain and winds (BBC News, 2004; The Independent, 2004; Anti-Slavery International, 2008d). After escaping in 2004, Wanagoda pressed charges against Abouzeidi. Nearly four years later a Niger court ordered that she be awarded the equivalent of $3,321.06 in restitution for her years of enslavement. Abouzeidi received a one-year suspended sentence and a fine of $165.79. In December 2008, just two months after the Mani case was decided, the Niamey Court of Appeals dismissed the case, stating that there were no grounds to prosecute Abouzeidi (Anti-Slavery International, 2008a; U.S. Department of State, 2009). Another enslavement case, *Midi Ajinalher v. Hamad Alamine and three brothers*, was pending from 2006 to at least 2011. There have been no reported developments in the case. Further evidence that the nation's focus on traditional slavery has once again waned is that in 2008 the government provided assistance to 40 victims of traditional slavery; in 2011 it provided assistance to none (U.S. Department of State, 2009, 2010, 2011, 2012).

WHAT HAPPENS TO TRAFFICKERS

Most traffickers do not face arrest, and those who do are often released without charge. For instance, in 2008 11 persons were arrested for offenses related to the trafficking of 81 children. Five of them were charged with the abduction of minors; the remaining 6 were released without charge (U.S. Department of State, 2009). In 2009 police and prosecutors rescued 78 trafficked children, but no arrests were made because the children's families had sent them to look for work. Two alleged traffickers accused of trafficking 8 children (6 girls and 2 boys) for prostitution were arrested but then released after serving two months in jail.

Marabouts arrested for exploiting children for economic purposes are commonly released soon after. For instance, in December 2011 police arrested five marabouts suspected of forcing children to beg but then released them all after two days in police custody (U.S. Department of State, 2010, 2012).

Under the Penal Code, those found guilty of practicing slavery can face up to 30 years' imprisonment, but prosecutions are rare, and stringent sentencing is even less common. For instance, in July 2006 Seidimou Hiya was found guilty of the offense of slavery and sentenced to a year's imprisonment with a suspended sentence of four years. He was also ordered to pay a fine of $836. On appeal, Hiya's sentence was reduced to an 18-month suspended sentence and a fine of $167 (Kaye, 2008). This outcome is not unlike the sentencing of Naroua, the person who enslaved Mani. His original sentence for slavery was a year's imprisonment and a fine of $1,140.47. He was also ordered to pay Mani $2,280.94 in damages. Naroua filed an appeal with the local high court, and in June 2009 the tribunal gave him a suspended sentence of three years and reduced his payment to Mani to $1,140.47.[3] But the trend to issue suspended sentences to traffickers may be on the decline. In 2009 there was at least one known conviction. A man found guilty of having a slave was sentenced by the tribunal of N'Guigmi to five years' imprisonment and a fine of $20,000 in damages to the victim. He was also ordered to pay $2,000 to the government and to an anti-slavery NGO. It is unknown if he appealed the decision and, if so, whether the sentence, fine, and damages were reduced (U.S. Department of State, 2010). In June 2010 a court convicted two traffickers, who had prostituted five girls under the age of 15, under a statute prohibiting the corruption of minors. Each of the traffickers received a sentence of six months' suspended imprisonment and a fine of roughly $100. This case occurred before the adoption of the anti-trafficking law in December 2010. The hope was that, with the new law, the identification of human trafficking cases would increase, as would prosecutions and sentencing. However in 2011 the government investigated only two suspected cases of human trafficking and did not prosecute or convict any offenders (U.S. Department of State, 2011, 2012).

INTERNAL EFFORTS TO DECREASE TRAFFICKING

The adoption of the 2010 anti-trafficking law and the proposed law that would raise the legal age for marriage to 18 (nothing has happened with this proposal since 2009)—if implemented and passed, respectively— could significantly improve the trafficking scenario in Niger. Helen Duffy, co-counsel for Mani, says passing laws that reject practices such as child marriage and slavery is an important element in protecting citizens, but it is not enough. Under the law, Niger's obligation to protect its citizens is tied to its obligation to ensure that its laws are understood and enforced. The Mani case illustrates that the Niger courts were unaware of the nature and effect of their own laws. According to Duffy, it is critical not only that laws are in place, but that they are implemented: "There was a law criminalizing slavery in Niger when Hadijatou [Mani] and seven other *sadaka* were being held in Souleyman Naroua's house, and it made little difference to them. Hopefully, this [the ECOWAS decision] will act as a catalyst to educate and increase awareness among judges and, more broadly, society. This is an essential prerequisite to eradicating slavery and child marriage."[4]

Duffy also states that in Niger there is an inherent link between discrimination and slavery. She believes the Mani case was not just about slavery, but also inequity based on sex and social origin: "Hadijatou was sold as a sexual and domestic slave because she was a woman and because she had inherited her mother's servile status. In turn, a representative of her mother's master sold her to someone who was entitled under custom to own slaves because of his 'noble' status. This case demonstrates how extreme the effects of discrimination based on sex and social origin can be, and how important it is to challenge this fundamental problem." Although discrimination against women and traditional slavery continue, the Mani case opened up a much-needed national dialogue on the practice of slavery. "For the first time, on the evening of the court hearing, people were acknowledging and debating openly in public the fact that slavery exists," says Duffy. "This is an essential prerequisite to its eventual eradication, though there remains a long and challenging road ahead."

The government of Niger has taken some significant anti-trafficking steps. For instance, in 2008 it amended the armed-forces bylaws to prohibit troops from participating in or facilitating of human trafficking.

It has also cooperated with the anti-trafficking efforts of other nations, such as Mali and Togo. In 2008 these efforts resulted in the arrest of one trafficker from Togo and three from Mali. In 2009 Nigerien authorities transferred one suspected trafficker to the custody of Interpol Mali (U.S. Department of State, 2009, 2010).

Slavery in Niger is blatantly downplayed. Not only does the government fail to acknowledge the widespread nature of this practice, but the judicial system issues suspended sentences and reduced fines to those who are found guilty of the practice. When a crime that is stipulated to carry a sentence of 10 to 30 years' imprisonment is reduced to a suspended sentence, the severity of the crime is significantly undermined. Also, Niger's laws have created numerous weaknesses regarding child labor. The minimum age for work is 14 (16 for hazardous work). The law regarding hazardous labor does not discuss safety, supervision, instruction, or training—all areas that need to be addressed to properly protect child workers from harm. Another issue of vulnerability is that education is compulsory only until age 12, but children cannot legally work until age 14. In the interval many children enter the labor force illegally and thus become vulnerable to unregulated markets. Increasing the compulsory age of education to at least 14 would eliminate this gap. The 2010 adoption of an anti-trafficking law is a significant positive step for Niger as it creates a comprehensive definition of trafficking that allows victims to file civil suits against their traffickers. If implemented properly, it could help to ensure that traffickers face more stringent sentencing and decrease the trend of suspended sentences, though much of this depends on the courts. Thus far, no convictions have occurred since the new law was adopted.

CHAPTER 15

China

Forced labor and child labor in China are illegal,
but some local governments don't care too much.
—LIU CHENG, PROFESSOR OF LABOR LAW AT SHANGHAI NORMAL UNIVERSITY

Almost every known form of human trafficking can be found in China. Foreign persons and Chinese nationals are trafficked to and within China for commercial sexual exploitation. Chinese citizens are also trafficked abroad for forced labor and commercial sexual exploitation. But the most prevalent form of trafficking involves the forced labor of Chinese men, women, and children within the nation. Forced labor occurs even in government-run programs that target school-age children and in facilities such as prisons and compulsory rehabilitation centers.

James Farrer, former director of the Institute of Comparative Culture at Sophia University in Tokyo, stated that it is no surprise that various forms of trafficking exist in China:

China is like a whole world in one country. It has the first, second, and third worlds all wrapped into one. The first world exists in the top-tier cities like Beijing, Shanghai, and Guangzhou. People earning the top 1 percent of incomes live in those cities and have lives similar to individuals in the developed world. Persons who live in second-tier cities have upward mobility, while those in the third-world areas perform farming as well as migrant and industrial labor. China also has a fourth world made up of persons of ethnic minority and subsistence farmers who largely live in the western regions and are economically, culturally, and socially marginalized.[1]

A study cited by the United Nations Inter-Agency Project on Human Trafficking examined trafficking cases reported in 800 print media articles in 2006 and 2007. Fifty-eight percent of the articles reported on the sectors in which victims were trafficked. Nineteen percent of victims were trafficked for forced prostitution, 9 percent faced exploitation in the entertainment industry, hairdressing, or massage parlors, while others faced forced labor in brick kilns (9 percent), manufacturing (4 percent), domestic labor (3 percent), and forced begging (3 percent) (UNIAP, 2008). The study also indicates that the two primary trafficking methods used were fraud and deception (37 percent) as well as kidnapping (26 percent) (UNIAP, 2008). The national Ministry of Public Security (MPS) believes 50 percent to 60 percent of reported trafficking victims are trafficked into the entertainment industry, most of them girls 16 to 20 years of age (Xinhua News Agency, 2006; UNIAP, 2008).

Chinese government statistics reveal the limitations of the definition of trafficking. Under Article 240 of China's Criminal Code, trafficking is the abduction, kidnapping, buying, fetching, sending, or transfer of a woman or child for the purpose of selling (Xinhua News Agency, 2006; UNIAP, 2008). Forms of coercion—other than abduction—are not included. Under the legal definition of trafficking, girls over the age of 14 who are in the commercial sex industry are not automatically considered trafficking victims. The law does not cover forced labor, involuntary servitude, debt bondage, or the trafficking of adult males. Sentences range from 5 years' imprisonment to death. Article 358 prohibits forced prostitution; offenders face 5 to 10 years' imprisonment. Article 244 bans forced labor by employers. The prescribed penalty was a fine or up to 3 years' imprisonment until February 2011, when the government raised the prescribed penalty to 3 to 10 years' imprisonment and a fine. Culpability was expanded to include those who recruit, transport, or assist in forcing others to labor (Ministry of Justice, 2010; U.S. Department of State, 2009, 2011).

TRAFFICKING WITHIN CHINA

Although China is a source, transit, and destination nation for human trafficking, the majority of trafficking occurs within the nation itself.

Internal trafficking of Chinese citizens is estimated to exceed 250 million people (Xin, 2012). Not surprisingly, economic disparities play a role in shaping which areas are source provinces and which are destinations for human trafficking. At least partially to blame is China's household registration (*hukou*) system. The registration system creates a caste structure in which people are defined by the place where they were born and whether they are rural/lower caste or urban/upper caste (Wong & Rigg, 2011). Historically, children inherited the *hukou* status of the head of household, but since 1998 children have been able to choose to inherit the *hukou* location and type (urban or rural) of either their mother or father (CECC, 2006). Regulations for urban residence permits have been relaxed for those who can satisfy strict housing and high income requirements. For instance, applicants must fulfill the legal requirements of a stable source of income and a stable place of residence (CECC, 2006). As Farrer noted, "You can change your registration more easily if you have gone to university, particularly if you went to a highly respected university in a large city. This was not the case twenty years ago."

Those who are wealthy and educated experience preferential treatment, while workers who perform low-wage jobs face significant barriers in obtaining urban permanent residence. Under the regulations in one city in Zhejiang Province, unskilled laborers must live in the city for five years in order to qualify for a local *hukou*. On the other hand, business owners may qualify after paying two years of taxes that total more than $732. Skilled and educated persons do not have to reside in the city for a specified amount of time in order to qualify (CECC, 2006). As stated by Farrer, in China the shift in status within the levels of society depends on geographic mobility, but the registration obstacles make such mobility difficult and thereby solidify the inherent inequality between the worlds. The result is that workers who move to cities but cannot fulfill the requirements are left without sufficient public services like health care and education for their children. "If you don't have an urban registration then the best segments of employment are off limits to you. It is the third and fourth worlds in China that are really left behind, placing people in untenable situations. When you have all four worlds in one nation the result is large income gaps and a potential for different forms of migration, trafficking, and forced labor."

In an unusual move, on March 1, 2010, thirteen newspapers—including the *Southern Metropolis Daily*, the *Economic Observer*, the *Metropolis Times* of Kunming, and the *Chongqing Times*—joined in an editorial call for social reform of the *hukou* system. The appeal stated: "China has suffered from the *hukou* system for so long. We believe people are born free and should have the right to migrate freely, but citizens are still troubled by bad policies born in the era of the planned economy and [now] unsuitable" (Branigan, 2010). Immediately after the appeal ran, Zhang Hong, deputy editor of the *Economic Observer*, was fired, and other editors were given warnings. The newspapers had timed their statement to coincide with the government's nine-day annual plenary session. However, Premier Wen Jiabao's administration made no changes to the system (Lam, 2010; Branigan, 2010).

Although it is difficult to change one's household registration, rural *hukou* migrants are able to obtain temporary permits allowing them to find employment in cities. Moving where there are job opportunities, those who cannot meet the requirements to attain permanent urban residence have a status similar to that of illegal migrant workers in other nations: they face discrimination; lack access to the free compulsory education, urban employment, public housing, free medical services, and retirement benefits granted to holders of urban *hukou* registration; and have minimal protection against unsafe working conditions and exploitative employers (Windrow & Guha, 2005; ADB, 2006). Farrer said that there are roughly 200 million Chinese migrant workers in China. "Migrant workers don't have strong connections in the city and have few social resources. This creates a reliance on others to set up their jobs and makes them vulnerable to employer exploitation. As a result of badly enforced labor laws, many migrant workers face long work hours in factories as well as the threat of not receiving pay." Children of migrant workers also face discrimination and inequality; in Beijing alone 400,000 children between the ages of 6 and 18 are without Beijing *hukou* and face restrictions on registering for most public schools (Xiaohuo, 2010).

Economic differences among provinces play a large role in the flow of human trafficking in China. An analysis of media articles on 301 trafficking cases indicated that Fujian, Shangdong, and Guangdong are the main destination provinces, while Yunnan and Guizhou are the primary source provinces for human trafficking. This pattern makes sense, as the latter have some of the lowest per-capita GDPs in China, while Fujian, Shangdong, and Guangdong have some of the highest (UNIAP, 2008). Citizens, many of them children, are victims of forced labor within China. Sometimes intercepted while traveling by deceptive persons who offer food, shelter, and work, people are then forced into situations of servitude. One such case is that of a brother and sister, Su Jinpeng (age 16) and Su Jinduo (age 18), who disappeared after traveling in Qingdao. The siblings, who were cheated out of money when they tried to purchase their return tickets, were taken in by a seemingly kind woman who gave them food and shelter for the night. She also offered the children a means to earn their return fare by selling fruit. When they agreed, the brother and sister were put on a bus and taken to a factory where they were forced to make bricks. Su Jinpeng was able to escape several days after arrival to the factory and return home. His father was able to rescue Su Jinduo a few days later (French, 2007). This story is not an anomaly. In April 2008 a Chinese newspaper uncovered a widespread child forced-labor network in Guangdong Province that reportedly trafficked thousands of children as young as 7 years old. Primarily of the Yi minority, the children were taken from poor and rural areas of Sichuan Province and then sold in labor markets to factory owners in the southeast of China (U.S. Department of State, 2009).

In 2007 at least 568 trafficking victims were discovered in brick factories and mines in the northern Shanxi and central Henan Provinces. Of that number at least 10 persons were mentally handicapped and 51 were children. Among the traffickers was Heng Tinghan, a foreman of a brick kiln in Shanxi Province detained in June 2007 for exploiting 32 persons (Taipei Times, 2007). One of his victims was Chen Chenggong (16 years old). Approached by a man at the Zhengzhou train station, Chenggong was offered a job that paid between $117 and $132 per month. He accepted the position and the next day boarded a van along with nine other workers (Yanzhao Metropolis Daily, 2007). In the van Chenggong noticed long knives and steel pipes placed under the seats—instruments that were later used to threaten and beat workers. Perhaps because they too noticed the weapons or maybe they simply sensed that something was awry, eight of the workers tried to escape when they had an opportunity—including Chenggong. "I was too nervous," Chenggong told the *Yanzhao Metropolis Daily.* "I raced along the direction of the front of the van. Heng Tinghan and the driver chased after me. I tried to scale the iron wire fence by the expressway. Before I got up there, they reached me with their steel pipes and knives. They grabbed my foot and pulled me down" (Yanzhao Metropolis Daily, 2007).

Chenggong was then taken to work at an illegal brick factory, where the traffickers beat and threatened to kill the workers. Chenggong was forced to work from four in the morning until at least until eight at night and often until midnight. He slept in a damp kiln, and his meals consisted of water, mashed vegetable soup, and moldy bread. In order to demonstrate that the threats were not idle and to spread further fear among the workers, the kiln boss took Chenggong to another kiln to witness the murder of a worker who was not working "properly." Chenggong said that the worker was knocked unconscious and then tossed into a mixing machine, where the body was chopped into tiny pieces within seconds. Chenggong was then told by the kiln boss to tell the other workers what he had witnessed (Yanzhao Metropolis Daily, 2007). Another particularly devastating case of child labor is that of 13 primary-school children killed in an explosion in November 2009. The children were working in a Guangxi workshop producing fireworks (U.S. Department of State, 2010).

While child and forced labor are technically illegal, it is difficult to ascertain whether the lack of enforcement is a result of remoteness, the hidden nature of the crime, corruption, or some combination of the three. One mother, Zhang Xiaoying, who visited over 100 brick factories in the Shanxi Province in search of her missing 15-year-old son, said that at one factory police demanded bribes. Once inside the factory Xiaoying was horrified by the inhumane conditions there: "We finally got into that place, and I saw people hauling carts of bricks with great difficulty. Some of them were very small, and the ropes they pulled left tracks of blood on their shoulders and backs. Others were making bricks, standing by the machines. They had to move the bricks from the belt very quickly because they were hot and heavy and they could easily get burned or hurt by the machines" (French, 2007).

Liu Cheng, a professor of labor law at Shanghai Normal University, stated that these forced-labor scenarios may be a result of a government-business alliance. "Forced labor and child labor in China are illegal, but some local governments don't care too much," Cheng told the *New York Times* (French, 2007).

One source of concern is the number of government-sanctioned work-study programs that are simply a veiled means to supply elementary school children to factories and farms for forced labor. The children face dangerous conditions and excessive hours with mandatory overtime. In 2008 the Xinjiang provincial government forced thousands of its students into child labor through the work-study program in order to meet the annual harvest quota (U.S. Department of State, 2009). Government-sponsored labor programs like the Transfer Surplus Workforce Outwards program have also forced children to work without even the pretense of study; many of the child laborers are members of the Uighur (Turkic) ethnic group. For example, a government transfer program exploited more than 300 Uighur children under the age of 18 by forcing them to work thousands of miles from home at a shoe factory in China's southeastern Guangdong Province. Longfa Shoe Factory, where the children were working, is owned by Taiwan-based Dean Shoes Co. Ltd., which supplies footwear to the U.S. company Nike, Inc. Spokespersons for both Nike and Longfa Shoe Factory denied the allegation that underage workers were being used and said hiring underage workers would violate company policies. Allegedly, officials pressured some families to participate in the program and forced the children to use faux or swapped identification cards that made it appear as though they were older. For instance, one 16-year-old girl was instructed by government officials to swap identity cards with her older sister. The father of another teen who was also forced to swap identification with her older sister was told that if he resisted having his 16-year-old daughter work for the program, the government would cancel his government poverty aid. "My older daughter in Karamay City filled the form out for my younger daughter," the father said. "Then my younger daughter set off [for Guangdong] on April 20, 2008. It [will be] one year this April" (Juma, 2009).

Not only have government-sanctioned and -sponsored programs resulted in forced labor; so too has the national government's compulsory drug detention program. As a result of China's 2008 anti-drug law, at any given moment approximately half a million people are in rehabilitation centers. In 2011 alone 216,000 former drug users were detained in 165 centers (U.S. Department of State, 2012). Government officials and security forces are allowed to incarcerate suspected drug users for up to seven years without a trial or any other judicial oversight (Human Rights Watch, 2010). No evidence is required to legitimize arrest. According to one former detainee interviewed by Human Rights Watch, a person does not need to be a drug user to be harassed and arrested by police under the anti-drug law. "Even if you're not using you will be detained if the police know you have used drugs in the past or you look like someone who has" (Human Rights Watch, 2010: p. 24). A Human Rights Watch report stated that China's compulsory detoxification centers not only deny drug users treatment but also use them as forced labor and administer physical abuse (Human Rights Watch, 2010).

Police corruption seems to play a part in determining which civilians are arrested and placed in the detoxification centers. Those who have the money to pay off the police may be able to prevent arrest; those without the means cannot. Chou, a former detainee, said that he was leaving work when several police in plain clothes ambushed him.

> They started beating me and put handcuffs on me. No one on the street tried to help because they just assumed I was a criminal. The police said if I didn't give them 3,000 yuan [$440] they would put me in detox. They brought me to my house and told me if I didn't get the money they would keep beating me. They waited while I was inside and waited while my family found 3,000 RMB from relatives. I was so scared. (Human Rights Watch, 2010: p. 24)

Article 43 of the anti-drug law states that the addict will be given physiological or psychological treatment or physical rehabilitation training: "The compulsory isolation center for drug rehabilitation shall, in light of the kind of narcotic drugs that a drug addict ingests or injects and the degree of his addiction, etc., give him physiological or psychological treatment or physical rehabilitation training, as the case may be" (Human Rights Watch, 2010: p. 16). If appropriately interpreted, it seems that labor without pay may be by definition part of a patient's rehabilitation. This ambiguity seems to create a loophole for rehabilitation centers to force patients to work against their will and to profit financially from their labor. Former detainees of drug rehabilitation centers in Yunnan Province said that they were not only refused basic medical care but also faced beatings and 18-hour workdays without pay making trinkets and shoes. "The point of being put in a drug detention center is not to quit drugs, it is to work," Jian, a former detainee, told Human Rights Watch. "There is no medicine to take when you first get in and there is no methadone or anything else. They don't put us there to get healthy, they put us there to work. . . . We get up at five in the morning to make shoes. We work all day and into the night. That's all it is" (Human Rights Watch, 2010: p. 28).

Other detainees are selected to use physical force against inmates who are considered inefficient. The incentives of becoming an enforcer are immunity from work and access to higher-quality food. Deng, a former detainee, said that the last time he was in drug detention he didn't finish his work on time and was badly beaten: "They beat me all over my back and butt and wouldn't let me sleep. They say it's the police who guard detox, but really they use other detainees because the police don't want to be responsible if someone dies. The people who are chosen have much better situations than normal detainees. They don't have to work, they get food that is more than just rice and spoiled vegetables" (Human Rights Watch, 2010: p. 30).

How many deaths occur in rehabilitation centers is unknown. Former detainees did state in the report that when an unnatural death occurs, family members of the deceased are paid not to look into the matter. Former detainees say those families that push officials to investigate what happened to their loved ones face threats (Human Rights Watch, 2010).

Like those in compulsory detoxification centers, criminal suspects in detention centers face forced labor, abuse, and torture and are denied medications. Unnatural deaths also occur. As stated in the Human Rights Watch report, official Chinese government statistics indicate that in the first four months of 2009 15 detainees died of unnatural deaths in official detention centers. Since then the government has equipped criminal detention centers with closed-circuit television security monitors. It has not yet done so in any of the compulsory detoxification centers (Chou, 2006; Human Rights Watch, 2010).

CHINA AS A DESTINATION AND AS A TRANSIT NATION

Though certainly less prevalent than trafficking within China, trafficking of persons from bordering nations into China is on the rise. Predominantly from Vietnam and Myanmar (Burma), females and boys are victims of trafficking for commercial sexual exploitation through adoption and matchmaking services. Also believed to be on the rise is the number of persons trafficked from Laos to China and from China to Malaysia and Thailand for commercial sexual exploitation (Guihua, 2009). Of similar ancestry, those on the border of Laos and China often speak the same language and have like customs. However, the starker economic situation on the Laos side has created a drive for cross-border migration to China and a ripe opportunity for human trafficking. "We have to brace ourselves for more cases," said Hang Lintao, deputy director at the Criminal Investigation Section at the Yunnan Public Security Bureau (Guihua, 2009).

Zhao Xianming, a narcotics police officer in Mengla County, says cross-border matchmaking services burgeoned at the same time as Chinese agricultural laborers went to Laos to replace poppy production with the growth of cash crops such as rubber, fruit, and rice (China Daily, 2003; Guihua, 2009). "Most victims are teenage girls from mountainous areas in northern Laos, who were lured by job or marriage opportunities at the other side of the border," Xianming told the Xinhua News Agency. One such case involved two girls (ages 14 and 15) from Laos promised legitimate employment at a restaurant in a neighboring county in Laos. Instead their trafficker, a native of Laos who is married to a Chinese citizen, attempted to traffic the girls into China. He was stopped at the border. "Thanks to the timely communication with the Lao side," said Xianming, "the two girls were rescued at the border crossing and handed over to the Lao police the same day"(Guihua, 2009).

Women who flee to China from North Korea are vulnerable to forced labor and sexual servitude. Some are sold into forced marriages with Chinese nationals; others are forced to work in the sex industry (U.S. Department of State, 2009). One such case is that of Kim Chun-ae, who was smuggled to China in pursuit of her eldest daughter who had gone missing; Chun-ae assumed her daughter had fled to China. After Chun-ae and another daughter entered China, they were directed to a safe house. Accepting a job as a cook, Chun-ae soon realized that the camp was actually just a holding space before women were sold to local farmers as brides. When Chun-ae's 16-year-old daughter disappeared from the camp, Chun-ae met a broker who promised to find her daughter in exchange for marriage. The broker was abusive and raped her habitually. "I was locked into a house and raped every night," Chun-ae told The *Telegraph*. "My teenage daughter was sold three times by traffickers. She was recycled" (Spencer, 2005).

Some experts point to the lopsided gender ratio as a contributing factor in the demand for the trafficking of women into China. According to a 2011 estimate, there are 45,543,936 more men than women under the age of 64 (CIA, 2011). China's cultural pressures to produce male offspring and the one-child policy have resulted in the frequent abortion of female fetuses, particularly in rural areas. The Chinese Academy of Social Sciences says that these "extremely common" sex-specific abortions are a critical factor in the gender imbalance (BBC News, 2010). According to James Farrer, "Infanticide of girls and the gender imbalance pre-existed this policy. What the policy has done is put pressure on families to make certain choices that they might not have made on their own. This has resulted in sex-selective abortions."[2]

Obtaining exact numbers is difficult because not all parents register their female infants, but in terms of recorded statistics it seems that only 100 girls are born for every 118 boys. In some provinces the gender gap increases to 130 boys for every 100 girls born (BBC News, 2010; Haixing, 2012). Yu Xuejun, head of the Policy and Legislation Department of the National Population and Family Planning Commission, says this is in part due to a lack of effective social security in rural areas. With only one-tenth of farmers covered by social security, many turn to their sons for support as they age. Additionally, there is simply a favoring of males as laborers. "In the countryside boys are preferred because they are better labor[ers] than girls and labor is always the top priority" (China Daily, 2004).

The Chinese Academy of Social Sciences believes that by 2020 more than 24 million Chinese men of marrying age may find themselves without spouses (BBC News, 2010). The gender imbalance has created a situation in which men at the bottom of the socioeconomic ladder must scramble for a wife. According to Farrer, Chinese law outlawed marriage as a financial exchange in 1950, and marriage patterns changed as a result. "For example, the young couple is more important than the parents in the relationship. At the same time, gifts are still part of the wooing process. Those without financial means are unable to offer such gifts leaving them at a distinct disadvantage for finding a wife."[3]

Experts had the foresight to realize the adverse impact the lopsided gender ratio would have on not only marriage but also on birth and marriage rights and the exploitation of women. "The shortage of women will have enormous implications on China's social, economic and development future," said Khalid Malik, then-UN resident coordinator in China, in 2004. "In the next decade, we could have as many as 60 million missing women. People are exercising their preferences, but the consequences for society are huge. The skewed ratio of men to women will have an impact on the sex industry and human trafficking as well" (China Daily, 2004). Years after Malik's statements it seems that he was correct. The *Global Times* reported that the increasing imbalance has resulted in abductions, human trafficking, forced prostitution, and illegal marriages in areas with an excess number of men (The Telegraph, 2010). Vice-Premier Li Keqiang announced in January 2010 that China would continue to pursue a low birthrate while actively coping with problems such as the sex-ratio imbalance and the aging of the population (Xinhua News Agency, 2010a).

TRAFFICKING ABROAD

Roughly 600,000 Chinese citizens, mostly males, leave China annually to work abroad. This number does not include persons who have left the country without documentation. Another population that is believed to migrate at an increasing rate is young Chinese women between the ages of 17 and 25. Experts believe that the majority of Chinese migrant workers move through unregulated channels (UNIAP, 2008). Doing so makes them vulnerable to trafficking and other forms of exploitation. Men, women, and children of China are trafficked to other parts of Africa, Asia, Europe, and North America. Some are baited by legitimate employment but face forced labor or commercial sexual exploitation upon arrival. Others pay large transportation fees, face debt bondage, and are forced to pay off the debts via forced labor or commercial sexual exploitation (U.S. Department of State, 2009).

In a story that narrowly follows the formulaic pattern of trafficking for commercial sexual exploitation, three Chinese nationals, James Xu Jin, San Shan Ying, and Chou Xiu Ying, were found guilty of trafficking by a Ghanaian court in 2009. Under the guise of legitimate restaurant employment, the traffickers lured 10 Chinese girls to Ghana, 3 of whom were still missing when the traffickers were convicted. Upon arrival the traffickers confiscated the passports and travel documents of the girls and forced them to prostitute. The traffickers charged clients $70 per night or $40 per hour. The girls received none of the proceeds, as they were informed that they had to work off a $6,000 debt that included their travel and airfare costs (GhanaWeb, 2009). Trafficker James Xu Jin convinced his neighbors, the parents of an 18-year-old girl, to allow him to take their daughter to Ghana to work in a restaurant. He assured them that she would be safe. Instead she was sent to casinos and forced to prostitute. When she refused to have sex, Jin severely beat her and charged her a fine of $50 per day. "I had no choice but to do as I was told because I could not raise that amount," the girl told the court (GhanaWeb, 2009). The traffickers also ran a brothel out of a home whose front room was designed to mimic the appearance of a restaurant and two separate rooms in the back were utilized for sex. Despite the traffickers' insistence that the girls went to the restaurant to sing, the court noted that it was during singing that the clients selected the girl they would purchase for sex (GhanaWeb, 2009).

WHAT HAPPENS TO VICTIMS AFTER TRAFFICKING

Whereas trafficking victims were formerly viewed as criminals because of their immigration status, some experts believe that there has been a shift in general perceptions and sympathies concerning trafficking victims because the focus has shifted to child protection. Still, not all child-trafficking victims are acknowledged. For instance, although boys are trafficked for sex, they are not recognized under the anti-trafficking law as victims. Li Ping, director of communications for Save the Children, asserts that all victims of trafficking need to be acknowledged and protected in order to reduce trafficking (Guihua, 2009). Instead victims continue to face arrest and sentencing for acts associated with their trafficking experience. For instance, foreign victims of forced commercial sexual exploitation often face arrest for prostitution and are later penalized for immigration violations. One example concerns 200 women smuggled into China under the false pretense of employment, sold, and then forced to marry Chinese men. In 2008 the women were arrested and put in jail for immigration violations. Some of the women were sent back to Myanmar (Burma); others faced three-month prison sentences in China for violating immigration laws (U.S. Department of State, 2009). Experts hold that victims continue to be punished for crimes associated with their trafficking experience because of police corruption and also a lack of an efficient procedural system to identify victims.

There is an inadequate number of shelters in China, and most that exist are temporary, not specifically geared to trafficking victims, and provide few to no services for repatriated persons. On account of China's legal definition of trafficking, male and adult victims of labor trafficking are not recognized and thereby have no access to services (U.S. Department of State, 2009, 2010). Rehabilitation centers exist in both Guangxi and Yunnan Provinces. Victims are supposed to be given counseling before being sent back to their nation of origin (Guihua, 2009). Yet repatriation often occurs without any rehabilitation services. This is particularly true of North Korean trafficking victims, who commonly face punishment upon return for unlawful acts that occurred as a result of their trafficking experience. In China there is no legal alternative to deportation for victims who face hardship or retribution if returned to their nation of origin (U.S. Department of State, 2009, 2010). Thus when Chun-ae and her daughter were eventually caught by police in China and sent back to North Korea, they were imprisoned in a gulag. Chun-ae and her daughter managed to escape, and they now live in Seoul, South Korea, with Chun-ae's eldest daughter and son (Spencer, 2005). Women who have children as a result of their "marriages" to Chinese nationals are often targeted and face additional abuse in the gulags. Those who are pregnant as a result of their buyer marriage sometimes undergo forced abortions or their infants are killed at birth. Other infants face abuse at the hands of North Korean gulag guards.

For example, Chun-ae witnessed North Korean gulag guards beat one baby on the head. The guards said: "Why should we feed Chinese seed when we have nothing to eat?" (Spencer, 2005).

One positive effort is the collaboration between China's Ministry of Civil Affairs and the International Organization for Migration (IOM) on an IOM-funded training module to help in the identification, protection, and reintegration of foreign trafficking victims. Another group that aids victims and provides them with rehabilitation and legal counseling through their provincial offices is the All-China Women's Federation (U.S. Department of State, 2009). However, internal trafficking victims have minimal to no access to social services. Of 167 children rescued from factories near Dongguan, none received protection or rehabilitation. Furthermore, not one of the victims discovered in Ghana has received any assistance from the Chinese government (U.S. Department of State, 2009). In the case of forced laborer Chenggong, the Hongdong government gave him a letter of apology and compensation of $732. He stated that the condolence money and letter simply did not make up for his experience. "The torture that we suffered and the amount of labor that we performed [are] worth more than 5,000 yuan," Chenggong said (Yanzhao Metropolis Daily, 2007).

WHAT HAPPENS TO TRAFFICKERS

The Ministry of Public Security reported that it investigated 2,566 potential trafficking cases in 2008. In 2009 the ministry obtained 2,413 convictions against traffickers. In evaluating this number it is important to recognize that the government conflates human trafficking and smuggling, making it difficult to discern which cases involve trafficking versus smuggling or both (U.S. Department of State, 2009, 2010). Smuggled persons can become trafficking victims, but the act of smuggling itself does not automatically make them victims of human trafficking. What is true is that smuggled persons are often in a position of vulnerability that can put them at risk for a range of exploitation, including human trafficking. The most recent trafficking data not only conflates human trafficking and smuggling but also conflates human trafficking and abduction and illegal adoption offenses, making it even

more challenging to determine the nation's exact anti-trafficking efforts (U.S. Department of State, 2012).

Investigation, enforcement, and prosecution of traffickers are sporadic and inconsistent at best. Once traffickers are found guilty, penalties
vary depending on involvement and the number of trafficking offenses,
among other factors. Some traffickers face four or five years' imprisonment while others face death. In one case, five men were found guilty in
January 2010 of abducting and selling three children. The man deemed
to be the principal criminal, Xiao Yuande, faces life in prison. The four
remaining traffickers face prison sentences of 6 to 13 years and also
must collectively pay a fine of $11,765 (Xinhua News Agency, 2010b).
Another case involved the trafficking of 88 women and one 11-year-old.
The traffickers promised the victims factory jobs where they were to
package tea and sunflower seeds. Instead, traffickers took the workers to
a sham factory where they pretended to be managers and workers of the
factory in order to keep the illusion of legitimacy. Soon after arrival at
the fake factory, the traffickers sent the victims to other provinces supposedly to purchase raw materials, but instead the women were sold as
wives. The ringleader, He Kaixun, was sentenced to death while two
other members, Luo Qin and Wang Yongqing, were sentenced to death
with a two-year reprieve, a period during which, if they show genuine
regret for their crimes, the sentence can be commuted to life imprisonment. Other members of the trafficking ring face two years' to life imprisonment (People's Daily, 2008).

INTERNAL EFFORTS TO DECREASE TRAFFICKING

A national action plan in China has been implemented and aims to help
rescue and resettle women and children who have been abducted and
trafficked.[4] The plan emphasizes that killing or abandoning baby girls
will be severely punished (Beijing Review, 2009). It is unknown whether
this aspect of the plan has been enforced. The 2012 national plan of
action for anti-trafficking efforts was to be released in December 2012
(U.S. Department of State, 2012). Also, to help identify victims who may
have been too young at the point of trafficking to identify their true
names and origins, the MPS launched a DNA database for missing chil-

dren in May 2009. This tool will allow 43 cross-national laboratories to compare and share DNA data and could be invaluable in the nation's anti-trafficking efforts (Guihua, 2009). Public Security Vice-Minister Zhang Xinfeng has called on all police to try to obtain more information from the public in missing persons cases. To aid in investigations, blood samples are supposed to be routinely collected from parents of confirmed missing children, rescued children, homeless children, and children of unknown origins who may have been trafficked (RFA, 2010).

Aside from the humanitarian motivation, the government has a strong incentive to stop organized crime, including that related to human trafficking. Farrer said, "Organized crime has been linked with groups that are a threat to the state. The government sees all of those who organize separately from the state as a similar type of threat. This includes so-called cults or unofficial religious movements, underground political movements, and organized crime." Yet one of the government's obstacles may involve their own officials and police. Prostitution is illegal, and the government is reluctant to make it permissible. Of course the contradiction is that China has a substantial sex industry of saunas, massage parlors, barber shops, and karaoke bars that would not be able to exist without strong connections with police and, in some areas, a robust relationship with organized crime groups. According to Farrer, women in the commercial sex industry are sometimes abused or harassed by police and organized crime groups, depending on the locality. "The police know what these places are and what they are doing. Of course, as one police officer told me, 'We know what they are doing, but with the way that they are organized you can't easily catch them in the act.'"

When crimes do occur, citizens may be wary of seeking help from the police because of the general perception that the police are not trustworthy. According to Farrer, "Whether police are in collusion with the crime, turn a blind eye, or are simply not concerned with these issues—the citizens and police are not at all on the same page. Also, there are not enough police. China is an underpoliced society, so there are not enough people to solve crimes."[5]

In December 2009 the government ratified the 2000 UN Trafficking in Persons Protocol in order to harmonize China's anti-trafficking standards and definitions with those of the international community (Jia, 2010). The protocol obligates China to prohibit all forms of trafficking and to bring its domestic laws into conformity with international standards within 24 months (U.S. Department of State, 2010). "We've been faced with more organized and more professional cross-border human trafficking crimes in recent years," Vice–Foreign Minister Li Jinzhang told *China Daily*. "So it is necessary to strengthen international cooperation to fight the crime" (Jia, 2010). If realized, the protocol would be implemented on the Chinese mainland and the Macao Special Administrative Region, but not in Hong Kong (Jia, 2010). As of 2012 no comprehensive anti-trafficking legislation had been enacted in line with the protocol (U.S. Department of State, 2012). International collaborative efforts have already helped the MPS identify over 44,507 cases of trafficking involving women and children between 2000 and 2007. Approximately 133,000 victims were rescued during that time, and more than 6,000 victims (women and children) were identified from April through October 2009 (Jia, 2010). In order to increase the efficiency and coordination of anti-trafficking efforts, in 2004 Cambodia, China, Laos, Myanmar (Burma), Thailand, and Vietnam signed a Memorandum of Understanding on Cooperation Against Trafficking in Persons in the Greater Mekong Subregion (Guihua, 2009).

As the most populous nation in the world, it is not surprising that China is presented with an immense human-trafficking challenge. The lack of a comprehensive anti-trafficking law, minimal enforcement, corruption among officials, and abuse of its own programs compound an already significant problem. The nation's anti-trafficking efforts are seriously inadequate in the areas of victim identification, shelters, counseling, medical aid, reintegration, protection, and other forms of rehabilitative assistance. This situation is exacerbated by the fact that not all acts and means of trafficking are criminalized, so that many victims are left without recourse and their traffickers go unpunished. Still, the nation took a significant and positive step in ratifying the 2000 UN Trafficking in Persons Protocol. This step compels China to adopt a clear and comprehensive definition of human trafficking in its criminal law. It will put pressure on China to create a law that protects male and female victims equally and prohibits all acts of trafficking, such as the recruitment, transportation, transfer, harboring, or receipt of persons, whether for forced sex or forced labor. If properly implemented, it will result in the much-needed inclusion of all means of trafficking, such as physical or psychological coercion, including debt bondage, though thus far no legislation has been enacted to bring the nation's laws in line with the protocol. The amendment of Article 244 of the Criminal Code to increase the prescribed penalty and to broaden culpability to include those who recruit, transport, or assist in forcing others to labor is a significant first step, but many more need to be taken.

PART VIII
Muti Murder

One of the most horrifying forms of human trafficking occurs in the name of traditional medicine. Muti murder (muti is the word commonly used for traditional medicine in South Africa) involves abducting people, killing them, and harvesting their body parts for use in ritual or cult practices. Believers in these rituals hold that the use of human body parts is more potent than other muti and can bring about wealth, luck, and fertility. Identified victims in South Africa include babies and toddlers, young boys and girls, and adults; the victims are found missing body parts such as heads, hearts, kidneys, tongues, ears, breasts, and genitalia. Many female victims are raped beforehand.

Studies indicate that the human body parts used in traditional medicine in South Africa tend to come from persons killed in South Africa or in Mozambique. Experts estimate that somewhere between 12 to 300 muti murders occur per year in South Africa. Determining exact numbers is nearly impossible, as murders are not categorized by type. Moreover, by the time some potential muti murder victims are discovered, decomposition has occurred or predators have eaten at the body, so that determining the cause of death is difficult.

One challenge in addressing the problem is the strong community belief in traditional medicine. Someone who believes in a traditional healer will often consult with a healer before implementing recommendations from a physician. The government continues to meet with traditional healers to discuss the measures necessary to stop muti killings and the demand for rituals that in-

volve harvested human body parts. The immense trust in healers allows them to promote awareness far more effectively than anti-trafficking advocates could do alone. Experts believe that healers' involvement is crucial to raising awareness on the danger muti killings pose to those who practice traditional medicine.

CHAPTER 16

South Africa

Sometimes we rape them. We call it "washing the hands."

—A SOUTH AFRICAN HUMAN TRAFFICKER

As is the case with all nations, human trafficking in South Africa cannot be properly evaluated in isolation from its specific culture, economy, and laws. Because South Africa has four times the GDP of its neighbors, it is an attractive destination for both migrants and traffickers. Insufficient control over the nation's vast borders, lack of a comprehensive anti-trafficking law, and the demand for body parts used in traditional healing also contribute to South Africa's unique trafficking scenario. Although South Africa is primarily a destination for human trafficking, it also serves as a transit nation, and its citizens are also trafficked both internally and abroad (NPA/ HSRC, 2010).

As HIV/AIDS becomes more of a concern among clients, the demand for underage children for commercial sexual exploitation is increasing in all of South Africa's trafficking streams (NPA/HSRC, 2010). Social workers and officers of the Child Protection Unit (CPU) estimated in 2000 that there were 28,000 child prostitutes in South Africa (Molo Songololo, 2000). This statistic continues to be recounted in the media and expert reports even though the data is more than a decade old. According to Patric Solomons, director of the child advocacy group Molo Songololo, this is in part because South Africa does not have a central data collection in place. "As for the numbers . . . we have no idea how big the problem is," Solomons said. Since 2000, according to Solomons, there has been an increase in the detection, investigation, and prosecution of child prostitution–related cases. Yet it is still a prevalent problem.

"Our experience tells us that child sexual exploitation is more widely practiced than we would like to believe; that it is complex in nature and often parents, adults, police, social workers, community, etc., turn a blind eye . . . street prostitution and prostitution of children in brothels and drug-dens are often exposed by media and police raids; however, sexual exploitation of children by "respected adults" in local communities by ordinary men, employed, unemployed, married, unmarried [is] more common." Solomons says that it is not just men who are involved in the sexual exploitation of children. "There is a role played by older prostitutes and women who facilitate the prostitution of children or procure children for sexual use by clients on demand."[1] Carol Bews, assistant director of the NGO Jo'burg Child Welfare in Marshalltown, says the nation's history has led to poverty and a distorted view regarding the sexualization of children:

> People have been subjected to oppression and poor living conditions. As a result, there is a lack of boundaries because people live on top of each other. We have a high use of children in sexual exploitation, which has led to our current culture—it is entrenched in our current way of being. Children are seen as sexual objects because they are perceived to be sexually mature at a much younger age than that of persons in other countries. For example, an 11-year-old can be perceived to be sexually mature. As a result, it is believed that it is okay for a person to have sex at a far younger age.[2]

Slavery, servitude, and forced labor are prohibited under provisions in the South African Bill of Rights, dating from 1996. Trafficking for commercial sexual exploitation is punishable under the 2007 Sexual Offenses and Related Matters Amendment Act (SOA) and the 2005 Children's Act 38. Still, these forms of trafficking persist. Comprehensive anti-trafficking legislation, called the Prevention and Combating of Trafficking in Persons Bill was introduced in South Africa's Parliament in March 2010. In November 2011 the Department of Justice and Constitutional Development revised the bill, and in August 2011 the department began to draft implementation regulations. As of September 2012 the bill had not yet passed.

SOUTH AFRICA AS A DESTINATION

Persons from Bulgaria, China, India, Pakistan, the Philippines, Romania, Russia, Taiwan, Thailand, and Ukraine are trafficked to South Africa for forced labor and commercial sexual exploitation. South Africa is also a destination for persons trafficked from other African nations—Angola, Burundi, Cameroon, the Democratic Republic of Congo, Ethiopia, Kenya, Lesotho, Malawi, Mozambique, Nigeria, Rwanda, Senegal, Somalia, Swaziland, Tanzania, Uganda, and Zimbabwe —for commercial sexual exploitation and forced labor (U.S. Department of State, 2009, 2010; NPA/ HSRC, 2010). Shelter information offers a glimpse into the country breakdown of trafficking victims in South Africa. Of 93 trafficking victims sheltered by the International Organization for Migration (IOM) in South Africa in 2005 and 2006, the majority (64.5 percent; 60 persons) were from Thailand.[3] Other significant countries of origin were India (9 persons), the Congo (7 persons), Mozambique (5 persons), and Zimbabwe (4 persons) (UNODC, 2009).

The economic wealth of South Africa is a key factor in making it a trafficking destination. Its GDP in 2003 was $159.9 billion—four times greater than that of its neighbors and roughly 24 percent of Africa's entire GDP. By 2012 South Africa's GDP had risen to $408.2 billion (UNESCO, 2007; World Bank, 2012). According to Nde Ndifonka, the media and communication liaison for the IOM, South Africa is perceived as the land of opportunity in the region. "It is therefore easy for traffickers to lure victims with promises of a better life. Millions of migrants come each year and their particular vulnerabilities during and after the journey to the country can lead them into a trafficking situation."[4]

The lack of sufficient patrolling along the vast borders between South Africa and its neighbors has enabled the smuggling of migrants and the transport of trafficking victims into the country. "This movement is undocumented; when these people are offended they do not even report to the police because they are here illegally," said Sibongile Manana, a member of the Executive Council in Mpumalanga. "They are even used by criminals to commit crime because we do not have their fingerprints" (Ndawonde, 2009). An additional concern is that officials accept bribes in the international trafficking of persons. Amanda Ledwaba, head of law enforcement at the Department of Home Affairs, addressed this issue at a February 2008 IOM workshop on human trafficking. Ledwaba told workshop participants that 90 percent of the illegal border crossings into the country took place with the involvement of officials and police (Cole, 2008).

One case that illustrates such collusion is that between South African police and Giang Brooderyk, a 34-year-old trafficker from Thailand. Brooderyk, with the help of her connections in the Department of Home Affairs, the police, and the aviation industry, was able to transport victims between Thailand and South Africa with fraudulent travel documents. She allegedly recruited Thai girls, under the guise of employment at a massage parlor, to force them to work as prostitutes at her brothel in South Africa. When arrested in November 2009, she was charged with immigration violations—specifically, for assisting the girls to enter the country illegally (SAPA, 2009). In the absence of a comprehensive anti-trafficking law, prosecutors have utilized immigration and other trafficking-related offenses to arrest and prosecute traffickers. Another case of police collusion is that of a trafficking syndicate that allegedly trafficked 30 to 40 women per month from Mozambique to South Africa between 2004 and 2010. The women were lured by the promise of waitress jobs in the restaurant and hotel industry but were forced to prostitute upon arrival in South Africa. Those who resisted were raped and beaten. The syndicate was made up of 15 citizens from Mozambique and several Chinese citizens. The main transporter was Nando Matsingi, who lived in Johannesburg. Each week he drove from South Africa to Maputo, Mozambique, to pick up the "sold" women and take them to South Africa. Policemen helped him transport the women illegally across the border. "I do this very often," Matsingi told undercover Media24 journalists who pretended to be interested buyers and secretly taped conversations with the traffickers.[5] "I took three girls last week. . . . One was Chinese and the other two were Mozambicans." The quoted cost to purchase one girl or woman was $687 (AllAfrica, 2010).

The IOM estimates that each year nearly 1,000 women and children are trafficked across the Mozambique border into South Africa. Not all victims are lured by false promises of legitimate employment; child victims are often ensnared by relatives or family acquaintances. This is exactly what happened to Jabu, a 10-year-old girl from a small Mozambique village near the Lebombo border. One day Jabu was walking to buy bread for her mother when she was intercepted by a friend of her mother. The woman told Jabu that she must accompany her to the bread shop but instead took the girl to Rosettenville, Johannesburg, where she was forced to prostitute and was raped at gunpoint (Carte Blanche, 2007). In addition to false recruitment and confiscation of travel documents, rape is a common characteristic of trafficking. It is often used as a fear tactic to deter victims from attempting escape. "Sometimes we rape them," said a trafficker to an undercover investigative team. "We call it 'washing the hands'" (Attwood, 2009).

Although insufficiently manned border posts and corrupt border officials have created easy opportunities for traffickers to transport victims, an internal push within law enforcement may help change this pattern. "IOM has trained over 1,500 officials in South Africa, including those at several border posts and within airports to detect cases of trafficking," said Nde Ndifonka. "There is growing momentum within law enforcement to increase their understanding and role in combating the crime. This is hopefully a step forward to decreasing the possibilities and potential for corruption."[6] Corruption is also a problem in other branches of South African law enforcement. Carol Bews noted that one of the focus topics at an anticorruption workshop in the Southern African Development Community (SADC) region was the collusion of police at brothels where there is forced prostitution. Experts at the workshop asserted that brothels in prostitute-dense areas of Johannesburg do house trafficking victims but "will never be raided by police because the police are in collusion with these brothels. They themselves go in and receive sexual services."[7]

Although anti-trafficking efforts in South Africa tend to focus primarily on commercial sexual exploitation, persons are also trafficked for forced labor, often in the form of sweatshop work, farm labor, or domestic servitude. Men from China and Taiwan are trafficked for forced labor in mobile sweatshop factories located in Chinese urban enclaves. The factories are able to evade South African labor inspectors by moving the sweatshops to neighboring nations such as Lesotho and Swaziland (U.S. Department of State, 2009). Another example of forced labor is the case of 11-year-old Nellie, who was abducted from her home in Swaziland. Taken while her family was out, Nellie was trafficked to the town of Barberton in the Mpumalanga province of South Africa. Forced to do domestic work and hard labor, Nellie was beaten if she did not complete all the work assigned by her trafficker. "She would come back and find that I hadn't done all the work she had given me," Nellie told *Carte Blanche*. "She would beat me up for that. The work was too much for me and so I couldn't finish it in time" (Carte Blanche, 2007).

In some cases persons voluntarily migrate to South Africa but face forced labor upon arrival. For instance, young men and boys from Malawi, Mozambique, and Zimbabwe voluntarily migrate to South Africa to work on farms but are then exploited by unscrupulous employers, sometimes working for months with little to no pay while facing conditions of involuntary servitude. These same employers have the workers arrested and deported after reporting them as illegal immigrants (U.S. Department of State, 2009; 2012).

TRAFFICKING WITHIN SOUTH AFRICA

South African citizens are trafficked from rural to urban areas for prostitution; domestic servitude; agricultural work; forced marriage, known as *ukuthwala*; begging; food service; *muti*, the removal of body parts and organs for use in traditional healing; street vending; drug trafficking; and other forms of criminal activity (U.S. Department of State, 2009; NPA/HSRC, 2010).

South African children are mostly trafficked within the nation from poor rural areas to urban areas such as Bloemfontein, Cape Town, Durban, and Johannesburg. They face forced labor in street vending, food service, begging, criminal activities, and agriculture or are subjected to sex trafficking and involuntary domestic servitude. The tradition of *ukuthwala*—the forced marriage of girls as young as 12 to adult men—is still practiced in remote villages in the Eastern Cape. This leaves the girls vulnerable to forced labor and commercial sexual exploitation. NGOs estimate that 60 percent of the trafficking victims in South Africa are children (U.S. Department of State, 2010). One example of child trafficking within South Africa involved children—some as young as 13—trafficked from Mossel Bay and Upington to Cape Town by a man named Boere and forced to work at fruit and flower stands without pay (Donne, 2007). Since the case against Boere took place after the Children's Act was signed into law but before it came into effect on April 1, 2010, police had to charge him with other related offenses. The initial charge of abduction was soon dropped because some of the parents had given Boere consent to transport their children to Cape Town. "He is now free to keep bringing in children who then end up on the street," Sandra Morreira, director of the nonprofit group the Homestead Projects for Street Children and chair of the Western Cape Street Children's Forum, told the *Cape Argus* (Donne, 2007). According to Solomons, without a comprehensive anti-trafficking law prosecutors charge offenders with trafficking-related offenses, which is limiting and also makes it a challenge to prosecute those whose who did not commit the actual trafficking but were part of the scheme. "There is very little protection against child trafficking besides charging [perpetrators] for offenses such as kidnapping, sexual assault and child labor," Solomons told the *Cape Argus* (Donne, 2007).

Local gangs compete with international organized crime syndicates for control of both the local drug trade and the trafficking of children in South Africa. The gangs give out local loans, and when debtors are unable to repay, their children are forced to work off the debt through commercial sexual exploitation or drug trafficking (NPA/HSRC, 2010). Ndifonka said that a critical step in the anti-trafficking process is to raise awareness among parents and children. "The purpose of such campaigns is to ensure that children and their parents are equipped to ask the right questions and recognize the warning signs of opportunities that might lead them into a trafficking situation, regardless of its nature."[8]

According to Carol Bews, the large population of children who are on their own because their parents are ill with HIV or have died of AIDS are particularly vulnerable to exploitation and abuse:

HIV and AIDS are quite a concern in South Africa. Children of those infected and ill are in an incredibly vulnerable position. There are at least 25,000 children who have received services from community-based organizations in our area of operation. In terms of all of South Africa, it is estimated that there are 4 million orphaned and vulnerable children. These children often have to nurse their parents through the late stages of AIDS or have been orphaned. There are children as young as four and five wandering around the community on their own. We don't have protocol to deal with missing children or safeguards to protect them. So children are often kidnapped for a variety of reasons, including human trafficking. Traditionally in more rural areas there is more of a sense of community where people take care of each other, but in the urban areas it is really just survival for these children.[9]

In some rural areas of South Africa muti (or muthi) killings are performed to obtain human body parts for use in ritual practices. The rituals are believed to bring wealth and fertility. One victim of a muti killing was a 10-year-old girl named Kgomo Masego whose mutilated body was found hidden in the bushes near the train station. A *sangoma* (shaman) and six other persons were charged with her abduction, rape, and murder. There was conflicting testimony about whether her womb and breasts were removed before she was strangled. Her body parts were sold for $604.70 (SAPA, 2011). The suspects are allegedly tied to similar murders of three other young girls. Officials believe that all the girls were killed for the use of their body parts in muti (SANews, 2010a; Hosken, 2010). Another case involved the murder of nine women in the province of KwaZulu-Natal. Each woman was missing body parts such as ears, tongues, breasts, and genitalia. Some of the women had been raped before they were murdered. One of the alleged murderers was a *sangoma* (SANews, 2010a).

In response to muti murders, the Department of Women, Children, Youth, and People with Disabilities met with the National Traditional Healers Organization in 2010 to determine how to halt this form of trafficking and the demand for human body parts. "There have been some localized initiatives to either understand or respond to the problem," said department spokesperson Sibani Mngadi. "We need to understand this problem from a national perspective as it has affected many areas in the country and find appropriate solutions" (SANews, 2010a). Nceba Gqaleni, chair of the Indigenous Health Care Systems Research Department at the University of KwaZulu-Natal, says that muti murders form part of the human trafficking in South Africa. He also states that healers are horrified that this crime is committed in the name of traditional medicine. "Traditional healers that I work with have expressed disgust," Gqaleni said. "They do not have the mechanisms to deal with this. To use a body part as medicine is criminal, it is not traditional healing. Good intelligence gathering to understand what drives and motivates it and who is behind it is needed" (SANews, 2010a).

Members of the Traditional Healers' Association of Mozambique (AMETRAMO) believe that persons who use human body parts in their rituals are not traditional healers but instead scam artists who exploit desperate persons. "There are crooks, who are not traditional healers, [who] commit several atrocities like the extraction of human organs; sometimes even after extracting the human organs they take the body of the victim to the railroad to simulate a running over by the train," a group of AMETRAMO traditional healers told Human Rights League interviewers (Fellows, 2008: p. 19).

One reality that anti-trafficking advocates face is the strong community belief in traditional medicine. Raising community awareness on the issue of muti murders and how to distinguish between an authentic healer and extortionists can be achieved only with the help of traditional healers. "People don't talk about it openly," Carol Bews said. "But what is true is that if someone believes in a traditional healer they will consult with a healer before they will implement any recommendation from a social worker, service provider, or even doctor. People turn to healers for guidance, and there is a high level of trust and belief in what they promulgate. Healers can access the community far better than we can." The collaboration between healers and child advocates has been successful in other arenas. Jo'burg Child Welfare has partnered with local traditional healers to raise community awareness on the topic of AIDS. "There used to be a belief that a person could be cleansed of HIV through sex," Bews said. "By building a relationship with traditional healers we have been able to spread the word in Johannesburg on how to protect oneself and stop the spread of HIV. The healers that we work with are a positive group of people. Those persons who do muti murders are a different group."[10] Nde Ndifonka agrees with Bews' sentiment that in order to bring awareness to a community, NGOs must work with those who are trusted within the community: "Culture is a way of life. Hence awareness-raising activities in communities where there are practices that perpetuate human trafficking would have to be well designed to demonstrate the harm to those within the community. This can be difficult, as the message must come from those [who] are trusted within the community, and is not always well-received by outsiders."[11]

Gérard Labuschagne of the South African Police Services (SAPS) Investigative Psychology Unit says that some South African provinces, such as Limpopo, have responded to muti trafficking by creating task teams specifically designed to focus on this type of murder (SANews, 2010a). Experts believe that most muti murders go unreported and estimate that somewhere between 12 and 300 muti killings occur per year. Determining accurate data on the number of muti murders that occur in South Africa per year is hindered not only by the lack of reporting but also by the fact that crime statistics in the nation do not differentiate among types of murder (Dynes, 2003; Labuschagne, 2004). Additionally, depending on when the body is found, it can be difficult to determine whether a murder was committed to obtain body parts because of decomposition before the body is found. Labuschagne said, "Predators may eat a body, destroying wound sites and mutilation that might be a result of . . . mutilation for non–muti related purposes" (SANews, 2010a).

The human body parts used in traditional medicine in South Africa often come from persons killed there or in Mozambique. As an interviewee stated in the 2008 report *Trafficking Body Parts in Mozambique and South Africa*, ritual killings are common in South Africa. "It's like a daily bread. We do not even get shocked when a person is missing and found dead with body parts removed. . . . body parts sale is common here" (Fellows, 2008: p. 29). One case in which a muti murder occurred in Mozambique for trafficking body parts to South Africa is that of a 10-year-old boy who was followed home and murdered. His organs were extracted and his body discarded in a river. The boy's body lacked his head, heart, kidneys, and genitalia. The body parts were never found. Community members believe that the body parts were bound for a Zion Christian Church in South Africa (Fellows, 2008: p. 19).

One interviewee for the report on trafficking body parts said that she witnessed at least three to four cases per month along the Mozambique–South African border, where the body parts were being transported into South Africa: "And it does get a lot worse at the end of November and in December. People want more money in these months. . . . In December there are a lot more people crossing and the control is much worse. . . . The people that cross these things have their schemes—they know who is going to be working, and at what time they will be working, to let them cross" (Fellows, 2008: p. 24). The interviewee went on to describe three specific cases of attempted body-parts trafficking that she witnessed in October 2008. All three were caught by the South African border patrol:

> The first case happened at the beginning of October. The police border [patrol] caught male and female sexual organs from adults hidden in the middle of Matapa leaves. A 40-something lady was carrying the bag with those inside. The second case was in middle October. A lady . . . was caught carrying a head and the sexual organ of a male child . . . around 10 years old. She was carrying several bags with several things inside and she [hid] the material inside plastic bags with ice on the middle of the food. The third case, it was [at] the end of October, around 2 weeks ago. A man . . . was carrying meat inside a freezer bag. At the bottom [hidden] were 5 male genital organs from adult men. The police border [patrol] opened the freezer bag and asked him where he was taking all that meat and started searching until he found that. (Fellows, 2008: p. 24)

The motivation for customers who participate in rituals or "treatments" that utilize human body parts is the belief that traditional medicine is more powerful when it contains human body parts. Customers often turn to healers to help them obtain wealth or to cure a problem such as infertility. One client in South Africa stated that she was instructed by a *sangoma* to use a belt of children's fingers and penises in order to cure her infertility. She was also given a concoction to drink—which she believes contained blood from a human—and a piece of flesh that seemed to be from a human organ. As instructed she sliced, cooked, and ate pieces of the flesh daily. She paid the healer $542 for these items: "I went to that sangoma and he gave me muti to drink, a mixture of herbs—and another muti that I had to burn at night. You could see that it was like a heart from a person. That muti to drink, it was three bottles. Those bottles when I was drinking that muti, it looked like blood. I don't know what to say, because when I was drinking I wanted to vomit. I wanted to vomit that muti. I was starting to be scared. I thought I cannot drink this" (Fellows, 2008: p. 26). When asked where the fingers and genitalia came from, the client answered, "They kill babies." The researchers asked the woman whether she questioned the healer regarding the contents of the muti. She responded, "No, I was so desperate. I was so sick, so sick . . . that if someone told me to go to the toilet and eat I would do it" (Fellows, 2008: p. 27).

Researchers conducted 139 interviews for the 2008 report on trafficking body parts. The interviews revealed 43 cases of alleged body-parts trafficking in South Africa. Fourteen cases occurred in Mpumalanga—7 of which were firsthand accounts and 7 of which were hearsay; 17 cases occurred in Limpopo—4 firsthand accounts and 13 hearsay; 9 cases occurred in the Free State—4 firsthand reports and 5 hearsay; and 3 hearsay accounts occurred in KwaZulu-Natal (Fellows, 2008: 32). As in India and China, in South Africa there is little to no follow-up from police in cases of missing persons. In the case of a colleague who suddenly went missing, one social service provider quickly found the police of minimal help in investigating the case. "When she went missing, it was left to her family and us to do the follow-up, not the police," the anonymous source said.[12]

CHILD SEX TOURISM, SOUTH AFRICA AS A TRANSIT NATION, AND TRAFFICKING ABROAD

The primary destinations for child sex tourism in South Africa are Port Elizabeth, Johannesburg, Durban, and Cape Town, where the persons prostituted are predominantly children between 10 and 14 years of age (NPA/HSRC, 2010). Many of the victims are children recruited from rural towns in South Africa. Child prostitution in the cities is believed to be run by local criminal rings and street gangs (U.S. Department of State, 2009, 2010). South Africa is also a transit nation for human trafficking. Persons from China, Lesotho, Malawi, and Swaziland are trafficked through South Africa (Independent Online, 2007). To a lesser extent, citizens of South Africa are trafficked to Ireland, Israel, Macao, the Netherlands, Switzerland, the United Arab Emirates (UAE), the United States, and Zimbabwe for sexual exploitation and forced labor. The IOM identified eight recorded cases of South African citizens trafficked abroad between 2004 and 2008 (U.S. Department of State, 2010; NPA/HSRC, 2010). In a 2010 case, South African men were recruited by local employment agencies to drive taxis in the UAE. When they arrived in November 2009 they were placed in a labor camp. The workers had responded to a newspaper ad and were told by the recruitment agent that they would be paid $2,423.63 per month. Copies of one driver's pay slips showed that he barely earned $54 per shift and worked multiple back-to-back shifts. Deducted from the wages was the cost of living in the labor camp, roughly $200 per month. The *National* reported that the 20 cab drivers, now back in South Africa, and the cab company settled. It is unclear what this means and if the exploitation rose to the level of human trafficking (Kwong, 2010; U.S. Department of State, 2010).

WHAT HAPPENS TO VICTIMS AFTER TRAFFICKING

Foreign trafficking victims often go undetected or face arrest for crimes associated with their trafficking experience such as prostitution and immigration violations. Women in prostitution are at times too hastily screened without a thorough investigation into whether they are trafficking victims. Also, say NGOs, potential foreign trafficking victims are overlooked as a result of law enforcement's continuing focus on deporting undocumented migrants (U.S. Department of State, 2012). This pattern reflects a lack of sufficient anti-trafficking training among law enforcement. Twenty-seven Chinese trafficking victims who were arrested in a brothel raid in March 2008 were subsequently deported to China for immigration and employment violations. The traffickers in this case were also arrested in the brothel raid and deported (U.S. Department of State, 2009). Deporting both victim and trafficker both hinders prosecution and enhances the potential for retribution or re-trafficking. Nde Ndifonka says victims of trafficking live in constant fear as a result of the trauma they have experienced: "This may at times cause the victims to be afraid of testifying against their traffickers. The safety and privacy of a victim has to be upheld at all times during the rehabilitation process. There is a 14-day stay on deportation, which has, in practice, been extended to allow for comprehensive assistance to be provided to victims of trafficking. Under the new [anti-trafficking] law, [if passed], these protections would be greatly increased."[13]

Victims are often undetected or arrested for offenses they commit related to their trafficking experience because essential personnel—such as first responders—are not sufficiently trained to identify trafficking victims. "Persons not getting sufficient training are the police, emergency service providers, and the division of community safety," Bews said. The National Prosecuting Authority of South Africa (NPA), the IOM, and NGOs run anti-trafficking trainings, though attendance seems to be sporadic. The other issue is that NGOs, who simply do not have an adequate number of personnel, are carrying out much of the anti-trafficking training efforts. "While NGOs do anti-trafficking training, it is on an ad hoc basis. There is just not the same coordination [as with the IOM and NPA]. It is hit or miss." Fortunately, the IOM has been able to train over 10,000 government officials from the SADC, whose member nations are Angola, Botswana, the Democratic Republic of the Congo, Lesotho, Madagascar, Malawi, Mauritius, Mozambique, Namibia, Seychelles, South Africa, Swaziland, Tanzania, Zambia, and Zimbabwe. The immigration officials, police, social workers, and NGOs of all these nations are likely to come across victims of trafficking, Ndifonka said. "The efforts have yielded benefits; the IOM has seen more identification of victims and questioning of victims because more victims are receiving assistance as opposed to being summarily deported."[14]

Collaborative anti-trafficking efforts among African nations are essential. Since organized crime entities around the world cooperate with one another in human trafficking, it is impossible to combat trafficking in South Africa without international cooperation. Malusi Gigaba, former deputy minister of Home Affairs, says: "SADC and [other] African countries must all be urged to provide their nationals with identity and travel documents to make it easier and safer for them both to be identifiable at home as well as to travel abroad. We need further to harmonize both our immigration and trafficking legislation in the region and continent so that we can all have common instruments to combat human trafficking" (SANews, 2010b).

Police have begun to implement victim protection provisions in the SOA and the Children's Act. Persons identified or suspected of being victims of trafficking are to receive services and shelter at NGO facilities designated for victims of gender-based violence, rape, domestic abuse, and sexual assault (U.S. Department of State, 2009). There are no shelters available for male victims of human trafficking. The Department of Social Development (DSD) is the only agency authorized to refer human trafficking victims to registered private shelters. Through a collaborative effort with SAPS and NGOs, the DSD helps victims to prepare for court and aids them through the trial and/or repatriation process (U.S. Department of State, 2010). Foreign victims who agree to remain in witness protection programs while awaiting the trial of their traffickers can also receive long-term assistance. The DSD and SAPS give each other formal notice of cases to ensure that victims receive services in a timely manner and that evidence and testimony are efficiently gathered (U.S. Department of State, 2010).

While the recent implementation of the Children's Act and the potential passage of the Prevention and Combating of Trafficking in Persons Bill are positive steps in South Africa's anti-trafficking efforts, the ability of service providers to actually enforce these laws remains unknown. Bews said that whereas child-protection services are a government responsibility in most other countries of the world,

> to a large extent the Children's Act is to be implemented by NGOs, with no additional funding from the government. The reality is that we don't have enough registered social workers. As an NGO we get a subsidy from the government, but while the responsibilities may increase, the funding does not. The subsidy has not increased over the past two years. We don't have the staff and resources to do anything but superficial work. As a result, we deal with cases of circumstantial neglect as opposed to other, more challenging cases.[15]

Another concern is that forced-labor victims, particularly men, do not have the same access to services and shelters as victims of sexual exploitation. This form of trafficking often goes undiscovered, as it is not a focal point of internal anti-trafficking efforts. According to Bews, "Labor inspectors from the Department of Labor simply aren't checking for this [trafficking for forced labor]. The reality is that without proper training they won't detect it. It is a worrying situation." And it is difficult to know how many victims have received assistance, because there are no official statistics, and law-enforcement records continue to classify victims of trafficking for commercial sexual exploitation as victims of domestic abuse, rape, and gender-based violence (U.S. Department of State, 2009). IOM shelter information reveals that in 2005 and 2006, 66 sex-trafficking victims (25 in 2005 and 41 in 2006) were sheltered by IOM compared to 27 victims of forced labor. However, awareness of forced labor among officials and service providers may be on the rise. For example, from 2005 to 2006 the number of forced-labor victims sheltered by IOM more than doubled, from 7 to 20 (UNODC, 2009). In 2011, 13 multipurpose shelters with staff trained to assist trafficking victims aided 59 trafficking victims (U.S. Department of State, 2012).

The victim breakdown in 13 criminal cases analyzed in the 2010 NPA report provides a glimpse into the identified forms of trafficking, the countries of origin, and the ages of those trafficked to and within South Africa (NPA/HSRC, 2010). The cases primarily involve trafficking for commercial sexual exploitation. One case involved trafficking for forced labor, and two toddlers (3 years old) were suspected to have been abducted and murdered for the removal of body parts. All the victims in the cases were female. Twenty of the girls and women were from eastern Europe, 15 from Thailand, 10 from South Africa, and 3 unknown. The victims trafficked from eastern Europe to South Africa were between the ages of 20 and 30. Those trafficked from Thailand to South Africa were age 18 and up; those trafficked within South Africa were from age 13 to the early twenties. Most of the victims trafficked within South Africa were under the age of 18. Four of the 13 cases were withdrawn because witnesses (the trafficking victims) disappeared before the cases went to trial (NPA/HSRC, 2010).

André Neethling, the SAPS provincial coordinator for child protection in Gauteng, says many trafficked girls are introduced to drugs soon after being abducted, and as a result are problematic witnesses. "These children are very erratic," Neethling told *Carte Blanche*. "They would support you now. When they get the urge for drugs again, they would run away from the place of safety. So we have a very low success rate in terms of prosecution of these people [traffickers]" (Carte Blanche, 2007). One concern is not only the lack of prosecutions against traffickers but also the long delays in cases that do go forward. In 2010 Carol Bews noted that one case involving three girls trafficked from Mozambique to South Africa for commercial sexual exploitation had been ongoing for 18 months:

> It has been a long time, and those young girls have been kept in South Africa during that long period of time. The justice system is letting them down by leaving them hanging for so long. The young girls are sitting in shelters. The hope that they would get retribution is just not likely. It was covered by the SOA when the case started, but the attorneys could not utilize the Children's Act because it was not yet implemented. It is common for cases to take a long time to work through the justice system. By the time the case is in court the witnesses can't remember a lot of the details and thereby become unreliable witnesses. When I have taken a case through court I had to be like a dog with a bone. Dockets quickly get lost and delays frequently occur.[16]

WHAT HAPPENS TO TRAFFICKERS

Historically, in the absence of a comprehensive anti-trafficking law, prosecutors have utilized immigration violations and other trafficking-related offenses to bring traffickers to trial. For instance, in March 2010 the government used racketeering laws to convict two traffickers, Basheer Sayed, a South African national, and Somcharee Chuchumporn, a Thai national, who trafficked women from Thailand to South Africa for prostitution. While the women did know that they would be working as prostitutes, they did not know the conditions they would face upon arrival (South Africa—The Good News, 2010). NPA spokesman Mthunzi Mhaga said the defendants were responsible for managing operations and activities at the brothel. "The premises were therefore identified as the central operational point for the unauthorized and unlawful activities. There was therefore an existence of an organized human trafficking structure where females were being sexually exploited for a profit" (South Africa—The Good News, 2010). Sayed and Chuchumporn were convicted in the Durban Regional Court for racketeering, contravention of the SOA and Immigration Act, and money laundering.

They face a maximum sentence of life imprisonment or a fine of $13.55 million. The victims have since returned to Thailand (South Africa—The Good News, 2010). In November 2010 sentencing of Sayed and Chuchumporn was postponed to allow the defendants to apply to have their convictions set aside. The couple wanted the conviction to be reviewed by the Pietermaritzburg High Court on the grounds that the court interpreter in the original trial had not taken the prescribed oath and had not translated fluently. In June 2012 the couple asked the Pietermaritzburg High Court for a retrial. The court has not yet made a judgment (Independent Online, 2010; Regchand, 2012).

It is a positive sign that, lacking a comprehensive anti-trafficking law, the NPA uses existing legislation. The SOA, the Children's Act 38, and the Prevention of Organized Crime Act have all been utilized to investigate and charge persons suspected of trafficking for commercial sexual exploitation (U.S. Department of State, 2009). Sex traffickers have also faced prosecution for trafficking-related offenses such as kidnapping, rape, and indecent assault. The problem is that convictions under these associated crimes typically result in less stringent penalties than those that would be covered under an all-inclusive anti-trafficking law. In cases of cross-border trafficking, the government has no jurisdiction to charge perpetrators with kidnapping if the act occurred in a different country (Stuurman, 2008).

In the 13 human trafficking criminal cases highlighted in the 2010 NPA report, there were 4 withdrawals because of missing witnesses, 2 convictions, 2 acquittals, and 3 cases were still pending at the time of the report. The majority of the traffickers involved in these cases were from South Africa or Thailand. In addition, one trafficker was from Mozambique, one was from Nigeria, and one was from Malawi. Forty-five of the alleged traffickers in the 13 cases were women, and 21 were men (NPA/HSRC, 2010). One sex trafficker was convicted in 2011 for trafficking three Mozambican girls into commercial sex and sentenced to life imprisonment. In February 2012, a sex trafficker was sentenced to 23 years' imprisonment for the sex trafficking of a Swazi woman after fraudulently offering her a job. Labor traffickers are rarely prosecuted, but in May 2008 Aldina "Diana" Hdonegildo dos Santos from Mozambique was charged under the SOA and South Africa labor laws. The woman allegedly forced three children into domestic servitude and prostitution. After several delays and interruptions, the trial resumed before the Pretoria Magistrate's Court in February 2009. The case was still ongoing as of June 2012. In 2011, five suspected traffickers were apprehended, including two labor traffickers and two allegedly complicit police officers (Club of Mozambique, 2008; U.S. Department of State, 2009, 2010, 2012).

Suspended sentences and/or simple fines for traffickers are a serious problem in South Africa. Of 18 traffickers convicted in 2010, nearly all were given fines and/or suspended sentences. Even the 2 convicted traffickers who had to serve prison time had their sentences significantly reduced as a result of suspended time: a 16-year sentence was reduced to 2 years and a 14-year suspended sentence, and a 5-year term was reduced to 2 years with a 3-year suspended sentence (U.S. Department of State, 2011). Lengthy prosecutions are typical. Most prosecutions opened in South Africa between 2006 and 2009 had not been concluded as of 2010 (U.S. Department of State, 2010). The reality is that most traffickers are not caught and that they quickly adapt their trafficking style depending on a nation's specific strengths and weaknesses. For instance, traffickers often do not use Durban International Airport, particularly when trafficking women from Thailand, because they know that they will be traced. Instead they traffic victims through Johannesburg's O. R. Tambo Airport or bring the victims into South Africa by road (Cole, 2008). "The sad reality is [that] traffickers are way ahead of us," said Bongiwe Mlatsha, coordinator of the KwaZulu-Natal office of IOM, at the February 2009 IOM workshop on human trafficking. "They are smart and they are already making their plans. They will check on the gaps, and then close them. We lag far behind" (Attwood, 2009).

INTERNAL EFFORTS TO DECREASE TRAFFICKING

South Africa ratified the United Nations Palermo Protocol in February 2004, but the protocol does not encompass all forms of trafficking specific to South Africa. The language in the pending anti-trafficking bill expands upon the UN protocol in order to address the forms of trafficking that are specific to South Africa. For instance, the bill covers forced marriages, child labor, the trafficking of body parts, and trafficking within national borders, as well as the impregnation of a female against her will for the purpose of selling her child when born. Other forms of trafficking covered under the bill are debt bondage, forced labor, removal of body parts, servitude, and sexual exploitation (NPA/HSRC, 2010).

Knowing the extent of human trafficking in a nation is essential to determining the optimal means to combat it. The 2010 NPA report emphasized that there is a dearth of empirical research on human trafficking in South Africa (NPA/HSRC, 2010). According to Carol Bews, obtaining accurate statistics on *any* crime in South Africa is a challenge: "Rape, child abuse, and child sexual abuse are all reportable conditions, but the government statistics on them are either nonexistent or absolutely unbelievable. It is estimated that in South Africa one in three children are sexually abused. We have a specialized unit, and we see the numbers that come in of persons requiring services. But when you put that together with the low numbers from the police, it just doesn't add up."[17] Nde Ndifonka said that obtaining statistics related to human trafficking is a daunting task because of the hidden nature of the crime—it is not visible to local populations, police, or others who may be in a position to report it:

> Victims who end up in sexual exploitation are often controlled by their traffickers and have limited freedom of movement. Those who are exploited for the purpose of domestic servitude may also find themselves enslaved behind closed doors, away from public view. As a result of the limited awareness of human trafficking, many who are in these situations do not identify themselves as victims of the crime; likewise, many law-enforcement personal are also unaware and unable to identify cases. Without such awareness required for external or self-reporting, many human trafficking cases go undocumented or are documented as other crimes.[18]

Ndifonka also states that the lack of comprehensive anti-trafficking legislation is a hurdle to obtaining accurate statistics. It is also an obstacle to every aspect of the nation's anti-trafficking efforts. The passage of the Prevention and Combating of Trafficking in Persons Bill would allow prosecutors to go after not only perpetrators directly linked to trafficking but also those who are responsible behind the scenes. Also, traffickers would face more stringent sentencing. The legislation would allow for prosecution of all forms of human trafficking, not just trafficking for commercial sexual exploitation. It excludes consent as a defense, regardless of whether the victims are adults or children. It also carries a variety of penalties for crimes associated with trafficking, such as tampering with travel documents in furtherance of trafficking or intentionally benefiting from the services of someone who has been trafficked. Under the clauses of the last seen revision of the bill, tampering and intentionally benefiting from the services of a person who has been trafficked carry a prescribed fine (the amount not yet known) or imprisonment for a period not exceeding 10 and 15 years, respectively (NPA/HSRC, 2010).

In addition to the media and advocates who have focused on the passing of the anti-trafficking bill, in the years before the nation hosted the 2010 FIFA World Cup there was strong pressure on the government to decriminalize prostitution. Jackie Selebi, then national commissioner of the South African Police Service Police, who was later jailed in 2010 after he was found guilty of taking bribes from a drug dealer, stated that legalizing prostitution would allow police efforts that are typically used in policing such activity to be better spent elsewhere (Mbanjwa, 2007; NPR, 2007; BBC News, 2012). Some anti-trafficking advocates supported the proposal and argued that decriminalizing prostitution would help regulate the sex industry and thereby limit potential trafficking. Professor Vasu Reddy, acting director of the Gender and Development Unit at the Human Sciences Research Council of South Africa, asserted that the soccer event would have a ripple effect on human trafficking if the sex industry was not decriminalized. "[South Africa is] fertile ground for human trafficking . . . we need to ensure that by 2010 we have laws governing prostitution in order to regulate it, and laws to govern human trafficking" (Mbanjwa, 2007). Other experts believe that regulating the sex industry is simply not feasible. "The IOM is against it [legalizing prostitution], because the police and home affairs won't be able to control it," said Bongiwe Mlatsha at the February 2009 IOM workshop on human trafficking. "We simply don't have the capacity" (Attwood, 2009). Bews believes in theory that legalizing prostitution would be an excellent step, but that it simply is not realistic: "Holland has legalized the sex industry, and they have the infrastructure to do so.

But we don't have the same structure. I don't think it is practical in South Africa, at least not now. One of the issues in South Africa is that we administratively put laws into place that we don't have the resources to actually implement. If passed, this would be one more instance of a strong law on paper, but not in practice."[19]

According to former Chief Justice Pius Langa, trafficking is attributed to a demand for sex, organized crime syndicates, extreme poverty, war, unemployment, lack of food, and traditional practices that commodify women: "As long as these realities exist it will be extremely difficult to abolish trafficking completely, but it is equally dangerous to use these realities as an excuse for not going the whole hog in fighting trafficking. [It] will require a combination of extended research, legislative measures, improved policing and prosecution practices and judicial awareness" (Mail & Guardian, 2007).

In an effort to improve the situation of vulnerable children, the government has implemented monthly payments called child support grants since 1998. Those who qualify to apply for the grant are impoverished primary caregivers earning less than $98 or less than $134 a month (depending on where the caregiver and child live); the grant itself is for the child, not the caregiver. The grants have been associated with reduced poverty, improved health, and significantly increased school attendance and performance for the child. Still, there are significant constraints on the nation's capacity to offer social protection for children. Birth certificates are required to qualify for services, but more than 20 percent of babies are not registered by their first birthday. Other documents that are necessary for application for the grant are proof of income and—if the applicant is unemployed—an Unemployment Insurance Fund card. Moreover, the child protection system lacks the staff and financial resources to aid the majority of children who need assistance (Williams, 2007; U.S. Department of Labor, 2009; South Africa Department of Social Development, n.d.).

Although South Africa is taking regulatory steps to improve the identification of victims, improve the services provided to victims, and ensure that victims are not punished for crimes associated with their trafficking experience, there is a shortage of social service providers available to implement the laws. Also, while local NGOs, the NPA, and the IOM do their best to provide anti-trafficking training, the instruction and attendance are not consistent enough to ensure that the majority of immigration personnel, border patrol, police, and other enforcement personnel have adequate knowledge about the issue. An increase in training could not only help in the identification of victims but also bring attention to corrupt enforcement officials.

The large number of children with ill or deceased parents in South Africa creates a highly vulnerable population that is susceptible to a variety of abuses, including human trafficking. There needs to be a greater government focus on protecting these children and ensuring that they are sheltered from exploitation and harm. Another group that could benefit from more attention from the South African anti-trafficking movement is men. Law enforcement focuses little attention on debt bondage and indentured servitude; as a result there is little consideration for human trafficking victims who are men. These victims—men and women—need to have access to shelters and social services provided to other victims of human trafficking.

Muti murders are probably the most shocking form of human trafficking in South Africa. Collaborations between traditional healers and social service providers, such as those suggested by Bews and Ndifonka, may be the optimal way to address this form of human trafficking within local communities. Without cooperation from trusted traditional healers, muti murders and the demand for body parts are likely to continue.

PART IX
Hard-to-Prove Criterion
and a Slap on the Wrist

Throughout the world the severity of the crime of human trafficking is often undermined by a lack of government responsiveness to the issue—a lack of enforcement and minimal investigations. This pattern is exacerbated by the hard-to-prove trafficking criterion, which results in prosecutors' charging defendants with less directly related and less severe offenses that result in minimal or suspended sentences.

In Australia the number of criminal prosecutions and convictions remains low, and the average sentence is 7 years and 10 months. One hurdle that prosecutors face is a result of the anti-trafficking law itself, which exists in two discrete divisions, 270 and 271. Anti-trafficking experts maintain that the essential element in defining human trafficking is not the movement of persons but rather the exploitative purpose. The exploitative purpose of trafficking is addressed under Division 270, which prohibits slavery, sexual servitude, and deceptive recruiting. Division 271 focuses on the movement of victims. The problem is that, thus far, prosecutors in forced-labor cases have not used both divisions; they depend solely on Division 271, improperly placing the emphasis, and burden of proof, primarily on movement.

In the United Kingdom, prosecutors must prove intent both to transport and to exploit the victims. This double-intent criterion ignores the realities of internal trafficking of citizens and migrant workers. The Sexual Offences Act 2003 prohibits trafficking into, within, or out of the United Kingdom for sexual exploitation; the Asylum and Immigration (Treatment of Claimants, etc.) Act 2004 prohibits trafficking to, within, or out of the country for the purposes of labor and other exploitation, including organ removal or benefit fraud (fraud-ulently attaining state benefits). The problem is that these acts place as much judicial focus on the movement of victims as on the exploitative purposes of the trafficking. The requirement that prosecutors demonstrate a trafficker's intent to arrange or facilitate travel, arrival, or departure to, from, or within the United Kingdom for the purpose of exploitation significantly weakens their ability to succeed. As a result, prosecutors often opt to use lesser of-fenses to prosecute traffickers. This strategy reduces both the severity of the sentence and the level of protection and support afforded to victims.

In some nations only sex trafficking is recognized under the law. Until March 2011 Chile criminalized only child prostitution and transnational trafficking for the purpose of sexual exploitation. The former law, Article 367 of the Penal Code, did not criminalize forced labor of children or adults or in-ternal sex trafficking of adults. Because government statistics thus far reflect only offenses covered under the earlier law, it is impossible to determine to what extent other forms of human trafficking exist. For example, child labor is practiced widely in Chile. Experts estimate that 200,000 children between the ages of 5 and 17 work under unacceptable conditions, and the average age of child laborers is 12. But how many of these children are victims of forced la-bor is undetermined. Victims not covered by the earlier law were without legal remedy and comprehensive services and thus were vulnerable to repeat exploi-tation. The new law is comprehensive: it prohibits trafficking for the purpose of sexual exploitation, including pornography; forced labor or services; slavery or practices similar to slavery; or the removal of organs. This is a significant step, but effective implementation will require comprehensive training of po-lice, social service providers, immigration officials, and judges on the new law and how to properly and proactively identify and investigate all forms of hu-man trafficking. It will also require changing the practice, common among judges in Chile, of suspending sentences of less than five years.

In Germany the law adequately protects victims of all forms of human trafficking. It is in the implementation of the law that victims are not treated equally. The government focuses its anti-trafficking efforts primarily on sex trafficking and is just beginning to identify the issues of forced labor and se-vere labor exploitation. Male victims of human trafficking are particularly marginalized; most counseling centers that provide specialized services for traf-ficking victims support only women. And both labor traffickers and sex traffickers are still apt to receive light or suspended sentences. For example, of the 135 sex traffickers convicted in 2009, 75.6 percent received nominal to no jail time. There were only 10 convictions of labor traffickers in 2009, and none of the offenders was sentenced to imprisonment. The result of these sentencing patterns is that the vast majority of traffickers go unpunished.

CHAPTER 17

Australia

She vomited into a bucket for 60-plus hours while at the detention center.
The coroner's shocking report on her death as well as the treatment
she faced in the center made headlines throughout Sydney.

—LUIGI ACQUISTO, FILMMAKER

Australia's Pacific Solution of 2001–2007 is no longer in existence, but it is important to mention the measures the nation has taken to fulfill its immigration agenda. John Pace, Amnesty International delegate, said Australia's means of dealing with illegal immigrants during this time aided in the smuggling of human persons. "The policy has clearly failed to stop desperate asylum-seekers trying to reach Australia, and the people smuggling rings have not been broken," said Pace in an Amnesty International press release. "While the government has been creating a 'fortress Australia,' hundreds of men, women and children fleeing persecution and attempting to reach safety are being arbitrarily detained in camps and on boats, often in very poor conditions" (Amnesty International, 2001).

Under the Pacific Solution, asylum seekers were sent to detention camps located on two Pacific island nations—Papua New Guinea and Nauru. The intent was not only to create a solution for dealing with illegal immigrants but also to deter illegal immigrants from attempting to seek asylum in Australia. The incident that triggered the Pacific Solution was the August 2001 rescue of 400 migrants from a sinking boat by a Norwegian cargo ship named the *Tampa*. The migrants were predominantly Afghanis fleeing the Taliban and religious persecution, hoping to seek asylum in Australia. The asylum seekers had paid thousands of dollars to smugglers who ensured them of a new existence in Australia. Instead, the *Tampa* was refused entry to the mainland of Australia, and the refugees were sent to detention camps in Nauru and Papua New Guinea (BBC News, 2002, 2007).

In return for housing asylum seekers in detention camps, the two islands received significant financial compensation from the Australian government. According to the BBC, there are reports that the former president of Nauru, René Harris, received $20 million to house more than 1,000 asylum seekers (BBC News, 2002, 2007). Pace stated that diverting boats to other countries in exchange for aid and money amounts to a trade in human misery. "The Australian government should instead increase efforts towards an international solution that tackles root causes of refugee movements and people smuggling. It should treat asylum-seekers fairly and humanely, and not push boats away from Australian waters." The Pacific Solution came to an end in 2007 (Amnesty International, 2007).

Although the two activities are often conflated, human trafficking and human smuggling are not the same. However, persons who are smuggled are often vulnerable to a variety of exploitations, including human trafficking. Furthermore, smuggled persons who are also trafficking victims are often deported without an adequate screening to determine whether they are trafficking victims. Human trafficking is prohibited under Divisions 270 and 271 of the Australian Commonwealth Criminal Code. Division 270 criminalizes slavery, deceptive recruitment, and sexual servitude. Penalties are up to 7 years' imprisonment for deceptive recruitment, 15 years for sexual servitude, and 25 years for slavery. In June 2005 Division 271 was added to the Criminal Code to include the offenses of child trafficking, internal trafficking, and debt bondage. These offenses also come with a penalty of up to 25 years in prison (University of Queensland, 2009c, 2009d). Children are particularly vulnerable to forced labor and commercial sexual exploitation. With this in mind, the expanded legislation prohibits compulsory and forced labor of both adults and children. Furthermore, under the 1994 Australian Crimes (Child Sex Tourism) Amendment Act, it is an offense for residents or citizens to travel abroad for sexual commercial purposes with minors under the age of 16 (U.S. Department of State, 2007a). Initially those found guilty of child sex tourism faced a maximum sentence of 17 years in prison, but under the Crimes Legislation Amendment (Sexual Offenses Against Children) Act, enacted in April 2010, prescribed penalties for child sex tourism increased to 20 years' imprisonment and up to 25 years' imprisonment for aggravated offenses (Parliament of Australia, 2010a; U.S. Department of State, 2010). In August 2007 the Migration (Employer Sanctions Amendment) Act went into effect. Under the act, employers face 2 to 5 years' imprisonment for exploiting others for sexual servitude, slavery, or forced labor (U.S. Department of State, 2008). The law—through the Crimes Legislation Amendment (Slavery, Slavery-Like Conditions and People Trafficking) Bill 2012—may soon expand again to create new offenses of forced labor, forced marriage, organ trafficking, and harboring a victim (Parliament of Australia, 2012).

While the anti-trafficking law is sufficiently stringent, enforcement is not. There are only a small number of prosecutions per year, and convictions are an even greater rarity. The prosecutions that do exist tend to be focused on trafficking for commercial sexual exploitation. In 2010 the government convicted five sex-trafficking offenders and no labor traffickers. In 2011 the government obtained its first conviction against a labor trafficker.

AUSTRALIA AS A DESTINATION

Australia is primarily a destination country for human trafficking. Persons, mostly women and girls, are trafficked into the country for commercial sexual exploitation. Men and women are trafficked into the nation for forced labor (U.S. Department of State, 2009). A primary group of victims is foreign workers who migrate temporarily to Australia for work but upon arrival have their travel documents taken from them, face debt bondage, fraudulent recruitment, threats, and confinement. These victims are primarily from China, India, Ireland, the Pacific Islands, the Philippines, and South Korea. These abuses against migrant workers are just beginning to get recognized as human trafficking. In many cases the workers face conditions synonymous with forced labor and debt bondage. Some employers use the 457 Temporary Worker Visa Program as a means to subject workers to debt bondage and forced labor. In response the Department of Immigration and Citizenship moved to improve monitoring of the program. As a result, in 2007, 123 employers were temporarily prohibited from hiring migrant workers, and 273 employers received warnings for not paying laborers the minimum wage (U.S. Department of State, 2008).

In 2008 the commonwealth workplace ombudsman investigated a case of forced labor involving hundreds of Indian migrant workers in the country on tourist visas. Allegedly the Rorato Nominees tomato farm and factory in Jerilderie were using their workers as forced labor (ABC News, 2008). The Indian nationals were allegedly subjected to confinement, foul living conditions, and human rights abuses and were forced to pay thousands of dollars in job enrollment and housing fees. At least two migrant workers claimed that their supervisor, Sam Prassad, sexually assaulted them. Prassad was an agent sourced to Rorato by Primary Contracting Services (PCS). These were not the first alleged incidents of sexual misconduct filed against Prassad; three Australian nationals brought individual suits in 2002. The cases were settled out of court, and without admitting liability Rorato and Prassad paid each woman $8,102.07 in general damages (Duff, 2008a, 2008b, 2009).

One worker, Mahesh Prajapati, was maimed and injured for life by a forklift in the Rorato warehouse. Although Rorato claimed that the incident was Prajapati's own fault, the company and PCS were prosecuted and found negligent for breaching the Occupational Health and Safety Act (Duff, 2008b). Rorato and its director were fined $75,961.73 and $7,596.42, respectively. PCS and its director were fined $70,899.96 and $7,090.02 (Gillis Delaney Lawyers, 2008). Prajapati described the inhumane living conditions that he and the other workers faced. "My wife and I lived with 15 others. No furniture, no beds. We all paid $60 each per week but it has since become $75" (Duff, 2008a).

The Australian Centre for the Study of Sexual Assault reported in 2005 that debt-bonded prostitution was the primary form of trafficking in Australia (Fergus, 2005: p. 3). The exact number of these persons trafficked for sex to Australia annually is disputed. Research by Project Respect indicates that the figure is at least 300, while the Scarlet Alliance, Australian Sex Workers Association, believes the number to be 10 (Parliamentary Joint Committee on the Australian Crime Commission, 2004: p. 21; Craig, 2007). Recognized as a form of slavery under the Australian Criminal Code, victims of debt bondage often face "debts" ranging between $40,523.62 and $50,651.26. In order to pay off debts, women are forced to have sex with roughly 18 to 20 men per day, often without condoms. The women are also frequently beaten, raped, and threatened with further harm if they attempt to run away. Those who attempt to run away are often starved and beaten (Fergus, 2005: p. 3). Women trafficked in the Australian sex trade are from China, eastern Europe, Southeast Asia, South Korea, and Taiwan (U.S. Department of State, 2009). According to Project Respect, most women trafficked for commercial sexual purposes in Australia enter the country on Thai passports. Experts believe that many of these women may have already been trafficked to Thailand from Myanmar (Burma) (Fergus, 2005: p. 16). In 2011, of identified foreign victims who received services, most were from Indonesia, Malaysia, the Philippines, and Thailand (U.S. Department of State, 2012).

Some women who are trafficked for sexual commercial purposes travel to Australia with the knowledge that they will be working in legal or illegal brothels. What they do not know is that upon arrival they will face debt bondage or involuntary servitude. Others travel to Australia under the promise of legitimate employment and are forced into commercial sexual exploitation upon arrival (U.S. Department of State, 2007a). One problem, as reported by the Australian Crime Commission (ACC), is the use of deceptive practices masking debt bondage in contract terms and conditions (U.S. Department of State, 2007a). Clearly, one cannot consent to indentured servitude or debt bondage, but the use of a signed contract can help employers to manipulate their victims into believing that they have done just that.

The government of Australia signed and ratified the 2000 UN Trafficking in Persons Protocol, in 2002 and 2005, respectively. The United Nations General Assembly passed Article 3(b) to the Protocol in 2000, which states that the consent of a victim who has been trafficked is irrelevant when the trafficker threatens the victim or uses force or other forms of coercion, abduction, fraud, or deception. In addition, consent is immaterial when the trafficker utilizes abuse of power "or of a position of vulnerability [of the victim] or of giving or receiving of payments or benefits to achieve the consent of a person having control over another person, for the purpose of exploitation" (Fergus, 2005: p. 4; UNODC, 2012). The Parliamentary Joint Committee on the Australian Crime Commission did not appear to understand this distinction when it stated "Many of the trafficked women who are detected by DIMIA [Department of Immigration, Multicultural and Indigenous Affairs] or police have voluntarily come to Australia with the intention of working in the sex industry, and cannot be considered victims of sexual servitude" (Parliamentary Joint Committee on the Australian Crime Commission, 2004: p. 44).[1]

A landmark case that brought great media attention and pressure for legislative change in Australia was the one against human trafficker Gary Glazner in 2000. With the help of agents in Thailand, Glazner purchased women from Thailand for $15,195.97 to $18,237.68. Known as contract girls, the women agreed to Glazner's three-option contract. Of course it was Glazner, not the women, who determined which option would be utilized. In each case, the women were indebted to Glazner until they paid off their contract through prostitution. According to their contract the women were to work off their debt by performing 500 half-hour sexual services without payment. Glazner earned roughly $31,843.43 from each contract girl (after deducting the purchase cost). There are 40 known victims, but officials suspect that there were four to five times more contract girls. If this number is accurate, then Glazner earned more than $5 million from human trafficking. Although the contract girls had willingly gone to Australia to work as prostitutes, Glazner restricted their movements, kept them in debt bondage, and withheld their passports. In order to prevent escape, Glazner confined the women. When one victim escaped by crawling down a tree from the second story of their living quarters, Glazner promptly cut down the tree and barred the windows. He also kept a loaded gun in sight to deter escape attempts (Ford, 2001).

Australian authorities say that sex-trafficking networks are composed primarily of individual operators or small organized crime groups. These organizations and individuals often rely on larger organized crime groups to secure fraudulent documentation for trafficked women (U.S. Department of State, 2007a). Glazner enlisted the help of two migration officers to obtain first temporary visas and then work permits for the women while their refugee status was being reviewed by DIMIA. Most of the visitor visas had expired prior to review of their status and work permit applications. As a result, many, if not all, of the women were in breach of their visa conditions (Ford, 2001).

While prostitution is licensed and legal or decriminalized in many areas, numerous other brothels are operated illegally. As a result there is not adequate regulation of the industry, and many trafficking victims slip under the radar (U.S. Department of State, 2007a). The lack of enforcement and regulation in the Australian sex industry is of greatest concern with regard to the forced sexual exploitation of minors. One such victim is Ning, who was barely a teenager when she was trafficked into Australia for commercial sexual exploitation. In 1995, when she was 13, traffickers took Ning from Thailand to Australia with the permission of her father; her expectation was that she would be employed as a nanny (Craig, 2007; Mercer, 2007). According to filmmaker Luigi Acquisto, it was later revealed that Ning's father knowingly sold his daughter into sex slavery.[2]

When Ning arrived in Australia, she was forced to pay off a "debt" of $35,182.07 through prostitution. Ten days after her arrival immigration officials raided the brothel, but by then she had been coerced into working as a prostitute. Ning states that she was forced to have sex with as many as 100 men during the period before the raid. During those days she was not allowed to leave the house where she and the other women slept. If the women did not cooperate, the traffickers took them to a beating room (Craig, 2007; Mercer, 2007). Although this story is like that of many trafficking victims, what makes it unique is that Ning is the first former child sex slave to be compensated as a victim of human trafficking for commercial sexual exploitation in Australia. In acknowledging the post-traumatic stress and depression that Ning faced on account of being trafficked into the Australian sex trade, the New South Wales (NSW) Victims Compensation Tribunal ordered that she be paid $50,244.05 from a government fund for crime victims (Craig, 2007; Mercer, 2007).

Acquisto, who interviewed Ning for his documentary *Trafficked*, said Ning initially felt as though she had done something wrong. "She felt ashamed, and she carried that with her for a long time, even though she was only 13 at the time when she was trafficked. She realizes . . . that she was in fact a victim, that she didn't do anything wrong, and that justice, to some extent, has been done" (Mercer, 2007). Acquisto views the tribunal's decision as a positive, but not final, step in working toward the elimination of trafficking:

The culmination of our work with Ning was the awarding of 50,000 Australian dollars [roughly 50,244.05 U.S. dollars] to her as compensation for the crimes that happened to her when she was trafficked to Australia. This was a historic decision, the first of its kind in Australia and possibly the world. I felt great satisfaction at being part of the process that led to this decision. My wife and co-producer, Stella Zammataro, worked with Ning for two years putting together the application, gathering the materials required, and lodging the application. This was a labor-intensive task and one that required excellent knowledge of English and a high level of organizational and negotiating skills. Hopefully, Ning's case has set a precedent, but it will not be one that future victims will be able to benefit from without considerable support from a solicitor or NGO.

Fiona McLeod, a human rights attorney and former president of the Australian Women Lawyers, helped Ning file her claim and expressed her belief that the outcome could pave the path for other victims to pursue claims against their traffickers. "I am hopeful that the success of the compensation claim will at least educate other trafficking victims about the possibility of making claims," McLeod told the *Age* (Craig, 2007).

Some internal trafficking does occur in Australia, though to what degree is unknown. For instance, indigenous teenage girls face forced prostitution at rural truck stops (U.S. Department of State, 2009). Indigenous females are a marginalized population that faces discrimination in the Australian criminal justice system, particularly in sexual-assault cases (McGlade, 2006). The marginalization of this group makes it difficult to know how many are affected by trafficking and whether the trafficking is limited to commercial sexual exploitation or extends to forced labor. Thus far the government has not identified or prosecuted any internal trafficking case (U.S. Department of State, 2012).

WHAT HAPPENS TO VICTIMS AFTER TRAFFICKING

Since July 2009, when changes to the Support for Victims of People Trafficking Program and the People Trafficking Visa Framework went into effect, temporary services for suspected victims increased from 30 to 45 days. The objective of the extension is to allow for an extended recovery period in which victims have more time to consider their options (FaHCSIA, 2009). Victims of trafficking have access to support services regardless of whether they assist police in the investigation and prosecution against their trafficker(s) (U.S. State Department, 2010). Those victims who are willing but unable to assist may be eligible for 90 days of support. Eligibility is determined on a case-by-case basis. Formerly, those who made a "significant" contribution to an investigation were eligible to obtain a Witness Protection Trafficking Certificate. Today any contribution to an investigation warrants eligibility. The new amendments collapsed the Temporary and Permanent Witness Protection Visas for trafficking victims into one permanent visa. The visa includes not only victims but also immediate family members inside and outside Australia (FaHCSIA, 2009). Between 2004 and 2006, 58 visas allowing persons to remain lawfully in Australia were granted to victims or witnesses assisting in an investigation. In 2010 Permanent Witness Protection (Trafficking) Visas (Class DH) were granted to 20 victims and 9 family members. In 2011 the government granted 48 Permanent Witness Protection Visas to victims and their family members (U.S. Department of State, 2007b, 2011, 2012).

Victims can also apply for a protection visa as refugees. Permanent visas are granted to those who have obtained a temporary visa for two years. The visas for trafficked persons also come with a variety of benefits—administered by the government's Support for Victims of People Trafficking Program—ranging from food, living allowances, and counseling, to shelter. As of January 2007, 35 persons had been assisted in this program. In 2010 the government identified and assisted 31 potential victims of trafficking, all foreign; 20 were potential sex-trafficking victims, and 11 were believed to be forced-labor victims. Eight of the victims were men. In 2011 the government identified 11 victims; 6 were forced-labor victims (FaHCSIA, 2009; U.S. Department of State, 2007b, 2009, 2011, 2012).

There is a history of arrest, detention, and deportation of trafficking victims in Australia. For instance, many of Glazner's victims fell through the cracks and were sent to detention centers for visa violations. And once it became known that the female victims had not themselves filled out the visa applications in their names, the applications became invalid. The women were kept in detention until the hearing, and afterward the trafficked women were deported to Thailand—regardless of the fact that many of them feared retaliation against themselves and their families upon their return. The police and the Office of Public Prosecutions faced difficulties with DIMIA in allowing the witnesses to stay in the country even for the hearing. Throughout that time, Glazner was out on bail (Ford, 2001).

Another example of a trafficking victim marginalized by DIMIA is that of Noi, a Thai citizen trafficked to Australia for commercial sexual exploitation. Picked up for an immigration violation in 2000, Noi was arrested and placed in the Villawood Immigration Detention Center, where she died from malnutrition and acute pneumonia. Luigi Acquisto said Noi's obvious deteriorating condition went unnoticed by staff. "She vomited into a bucket for 60-plus hours while at the detention center. The coroner's shocking report on her death as well as the treatment she faced in the center made headlines throughout Sydney." The trafficking experiences of Ning and Noi are described in chapter 4.

WHAT HAPPENS TO TRAFFICKERS

The 2000 case against Glazner, as well as lobbying by NGOs, resulted in federal policy and legislative initiatives. Glazner himself received a fine of only $31,386.53 and a suspended sentence of 18 months' imprisonment, despite being found guilty on five counts of providing unlicensed prostitution and two counts of living on the earnings of prostitution. On appeal before Victorian Supreme Court of Appeal, Glazner was given a suspended sentence of 30 months' imprisonment, and the fine was reduced to $30,388.81 (Ford, 2001). Also a matter of concern is the joke that the County Court presiding judge, William White, made before the jury. Seized from Glazner's home were "free passes" granting men a service with the lady of their choice. The judge remarked: "There are eight gentlemen of the jury—do we have eight freebies for them?" (Ford, 2001). White's statement blatantly undermined the severity of the crime.

From February 2007 to 2008, the Transnational Sexual Exploitation and Trafficking Teams and the Australian Federal Police conducted 27 investigations, 80 percent of which were related to sex trafficking. In the same reporting period there were 7 trafficking-related cases before the courts involving 15 defendants, 3 of which were in the appeals phase. Of the four convictions for trafficking, one trafficker was sentenced to 8 years' imprisonment; presumably this was the longest of the four sentences (U.S. Department of State, 2008). In December 2008, in a highly publicized case that involved the sex trafficking of two Thai nationals, Keith William Dobie was sentenced to 5 years' imprisonment for the forced prostitution of the two women (University of Queensland, 2011c). Neither of these sentences is adequately stringent. The number of successful prosecutions continues to remain low. In 2009 and 2010 the government convicted four and five sex traffickers, respectively. Sentencing for offenders in 2010 ranged between 2 and 12 years' imprisonment (U.S. State Department, 2010, 2011). Available data indicate that sentences for sex trafficking range between 2 years and 3 months to 14 years' imprisonment. The average sentence is 7 years and 10 months. The average time an offender must serve before being considered for parole is 5 years and 2 months (University of Queensland, 2010, 2011c). There has been only one conviction for labor trafficking; the trafficker was sentenced to community service and a fine (U.S. Department of State, 2012).

One hurdle for prosecutors is that movement is a required element of the offense of trafficking in persons, Division 271. The result is that without being able to prove movement, the prosecutor will not succeed in the case. This improperly places the focus on the movement of victims, not on the exploitative purpose.[3] Transnational trafficking and domestic trafficking are prohibited under Division 271, but movement is a required element of both. The distinction is that the common element required in transnational trafficking is entry/exit into/from Australia (271.2), while the common element required in domestic trafficking is the transportation of another person from one place in Australia to another place in Australia (271.5). A separate offense of debt bondage is also inserted into Division 271 and does not include movement as a requirement. Unfortunately, the penalty—12 months for debt bondage or 2 years in cases of aggravated debt bondage—is insufficiently stringent. Furthermore, the guidelines give room for a significant amount of subjectivity, as courts are instructed that they may have regard to any of the matters listed, which include the economic relationship between the two persons, the terms of agreements (written or oral, between the victim and another person, not necessarily the persons being accused), and the personal circumstances of the victim (Australian Government, 2005). Contrarily, Division 270 focuses solely on the exploitation itself, and includes and defines the offenses of slavery and sexual servitude. It also includes the offense of deceptive recruiting for sexual servitude (Australian Government, 2012). The issue for prosecutors in cases of forced labor is determining what offenses are likely to be the most successful, as the specific offense of forced labor is not yet included in the Criminal Code. When used in conjunction, the two divisions seemingly cover multiple ways to prosecute a trafficker for forced labor offenses. That way, if one fails it does not preclude success under one of the other offenses. Thus far there have been only two prosecuted cases of labor trafficking, and in both cases only Division 271.2 (transnational human trafficking) was used. This placed the emphasis of the cases on the movement, not the exploitation of the victims. This occurred in the 2011 case of *R. v. Trivedi*, Australia's first conviction for labor trafficking. The offender was charged under Division 271.2 (1B). He was convicted, but the conviction resulted from a guilty plea. This is significant as it means that the judgment against Trivedi was a result of his own declaration of guilt, not a result of a jury determining that he was guilty. In a similar case in 2007 an alleged offender also charged under 271.2 (1B) pleaded not guilty and was acquitted by a jury, illustrating that Division 271.2 alone may not be sufficient to prosecute labor traffickers. In sex-trafficking cases, the charges nearly always include offenses listed in Division 270 and sometimes include offenses listed in Division 271. The exception is *R. v. Dobie*, in which the sex trafficker was charged under 271.2 (2B) and pleaded guilty (University of Queensland, 2011a, 2011b).

The dearth of criminal prosecutions for labor trafficking makes it difficult to conclude whether Division 271 is not strong enough to stand alone. In the two labor-trafficking cases in which there have been criminal prosecutions, *R. v. Trivedi* and *R. v. Yogalingham Rasalingham*, the alleged offenders were charged under 271.2(1B): facilitating the entry of another person to Australia, being reckless as to the exploitation of that other person. The definition of slavery in Division 270 could have also been applied: "the condition of a person over whom any or all of the powers attaching to the right of ownership are exercised, including where such a condition results from a debt or contract made by the person." Yet prosecutors did not use this division, despite the victims' slave-like conditions. Perhaps the prosecution teams believed that proving slavery would be unsuccessful. In the case of *R. v. Trivedi* the trafficker facilitated the victim's travel to Australia and helped the victim obtain the necessary travel documents. The victim was forced to live in a storeroom at the back of the restaurant, bathe in the kitchen, and work for 12 hours a day, seven days a week. His pay was nominal and irregular, and he had limited access to his passport and was physically and mentally abused (University of Queensland, 2011a, 2011b). In *R. v. Yogalingham Rasalingham*, the alleged trafficker denied arranging for the victim's travel. Instead, he directed the victim to a travel agent in India who made all the arrangements, including obtaining a visa to enter Australia. Upon arrival in Australia the alleged trafficker forced the victim to work seven days a week, sometimes for more than 15 hours a day; did not pay the victim or transfer any money to the victim's family in India (per their agreement); and withheld the victim's documents, including his passport (University of Queensland, 2009b).

According to Janice G. Raymond of the Coalition Against Trafficking in Women, the essential element in human trafficking is not the movement of persons but rather the exploitative purpose (Raymond, 2001: p. 5). Amendments to the Australian anti-trafficking law that focus on the exploitation of forced labor itself as opposed to the movement of persons would be more accurate and far more useful to prosecutors, and in turn to victims. Draft legislation proposed in November 2011 would create new offenses of forced labor, forced marriage, organ trafficking, and harboring a victim. These changes were proposed in August 2012 with the Crimes Legislation Amendment (Slavery, Slavery-Like Conditions and People Trafficking) Bill 2012 (Parliament of Australia, 2012).

INTERNAL EFFORTS TO DECREASE TRAFFICKING

Since July 2007 the Australian government has allocated $600,000 per year to the Australian Institute of Criminology (AIC) to conduct research into the trafficking of persons in Australia and the Asia-Pacific region. The hope is to gain greater understanding of the trafficking scenario through evidence-based data and to tailor the nation's anti-trafficking response accordingly. One hurdle to gathering accurate forced-labor statistics, according to the AIC, is that forced-labor cases can be prosecuted under various criminal provisions. Furthermore, there is no separate offense of labor trafficking in the Criminal Code (David, 2010).

Following criticism of the treatment of migrant workers in Australia, Barbara Deegan—an industrial relations expert and member of the Australian Industrial Relations Commission—was appointed by the deputy prime minister and the minister for immigration and citizenship to review the integrity of the 457 temporary worker visa program. Deegan consulted with unions, overseas workers, industry representatives, and agencies. Her 2008 report proposed 66 changes that would help protect migrant workers from employer exploitation (Deegan, 2008). The fiscal 2008–2009 budget included $19.8 million to improve arrangements for temporary worker visas. The Migration Legislation Amendment (Worker Protection) Act 2008 went into effect on September 14, 2009. The amendment aims to enhance the framework for the sponsorship of foreign workers seeking entry to Australia for work. The objective is to better define employer obligations, facilitate improved communication among governmental agencies, and increase the screening, monitoring, and sanctioning of participating employers (Deegan, 2008; Department of Immigration and Citizenship, 2009). The Worker Protection Act was amended by the Fair Work (State Referral and Consequential and Other Amendments) Act 2009. The provisions address the powers that may be exercised by an inspector when investigating and monitoring noncompliance by sponsors (Department of Immigration and Citizenship, 2009).

Still, persons who enter under the program continue to face exploitation. Pearse Doherty, an Irish Sinn Féin politician who is concerned for Irish workers in Australia, says that Australian trade unions have dubbed "457 visa" workers as "bonded labor." "Any workers beholden to their employer for their residency rights are naturally going to be vulnerable to exploitation and reluctant to speak up if their rights are being abused" (An Phoblacht, 2012). Fortunately, the government announced in March 2012 that it will establish a fast-track pathway from the temporary skilled subclass 457 visa to permanent residence under the employer-sponsored visa program. Chris Bowen, minister for immigration and citizenship, says this will enable skilled migrants to settle and work in regional and metropolitan Australia. "We know these workers can do the job and are ready to make a commitment to Australia, so it makes sense to streamline their pathway to permanent residence," Bowen said (Department of Immigration and Citizenship, 2012a).

In August 2007 Australia launched a five-year initiative to give a total of $21 million in support of Indonesia's anti-trafficking efforts. The project provided training of judges, prosecutors, and police on identifying trafficking victims and how to effectively prosecute traffickers. "Without committed police, prosecutors and judiciary it will never be possible to combat the traffickers or to seek justice for the victims of this terrible crime," Bill Farmer, the Australian ambassador to Indonesia, told reporters (Khalik, 2007). The hope is that teamwork between nations will help decrease human trafficking throughout the world. "Trafficking is a multinational problem that would need multilateral cooperation to prevent it," Bambang Hendarso Danuri, chief of the Indonesian National Police, told reporters (Khalik, 2007).

The government has also funded reintegration and return programs in Asia. One focused solely on Thai trafficking victims; another targeted trafficked children and women in Asia. The Australian government was also the co-founder and co-chair of the Bali Process on People Smuggling, Trafficking in Persons, and Related Transnational Crime. Additionally, the government funded the Asia Regional Cooperation to Prevent People Trafficking project (2003–2006) and then the Asia Regional Trafficking in Persons Project (2006–2011), which operated in Burma, Cambodia, Laos, and Thailand, and the objective of which was to combat trafficking by strengthening the criminal judicial process (U.S. Department of State, 2007a; ARTIP, 2011).

The anti-trafficking laws in Australia are becoming increasingly comprehensive. Yet there is a dearth of prosecutions generally, and particularly in cases of employers involved in debt bondage and the involuntary servitude of migrant workers, as is illustrated in the abuse of the 457 worker visa program. Thus far there has just been one conviction for labor trafficking. In order to properly address forced labor, a specific offense of forced labor needs to be added to the Criminal Code, which will occur if the new bill is passed and properly implemented. Otherwise, prosecutors in forced-labor cases will continue to use a legal instrument that improperly places the emphasis on the movement rather than the exploitation of victims. Finally, those found guilty of human trafficking and related offenses face inadequate sentencing that diminishes the severity of the crime.

CHAPTER 18

United Kingdom

The Home Office still want[s] to send me back.
No one has pursued the man [her trafficker].
—EVA, A SEX-TRAFFICKING VICTIM

The United Kingdom prohibits all forms of trafficking under the 2003 Sexual Offences Act, the 2004 Asylum and Immigration Act, and the 2009 Coroners and Justice Act. Authorities have taken significant measures to identify and provide care to women who are trafficked for sexual exploitation and have launched aggressive law-enforcement efforts against trafficking. Despite these efforts, ill treatment and deportation of trafficking victims is still a problem.

THE UNITED KINGDOM AS A DESTINATION

Persons from Africa, Asia, and eastern Europe are subjected to forced labor and commercial sexual exploitation in the United Kingdom. Women and children are trafficked to the United Kingdom for sexual exploitation through organized international gangs. Migrant workers (some of whom are children) are trafficked to the country for forced labor in construction, food processing and food services, restaurants, domestic labor, and agriculture (U.S. Department of State, 2007a, 2007b, 2010). For instance, children, mainly from Vietnam and China, face debt bondage by Vietnamese organized crime gangs for forced work on cannabis farms. Persons from China also make up a large percentage of women forced into prostitution in England and Wales. Nigerian nationals make up one of the highest percentages of identified victims, and there has been a significant increase in the number of identified victims from Uganda. There are also reports of diplomats who exploit domestic workers. These diplomats take advantage of the facts that the workers' immigration status is dependent on them and that they are often immune from prosecution (U.S. Department of State, 2010, 2011, 2012).

While prostitution among consenting adults is legal, running a brothel, loitering for the purpose of prostitution, or trafficking for sexual exploitation is not (ACPO, 2011). The Home Office in 2003 estimated that there were 4,000 victims of human trafficking for sexual purposes at any given time. In 2009 the Home Affairs Committee increased this estimate to 5,000 victims, and in 2010 the ACPO estimated that 2,600 women involved in off-street prostitution in England and Wales were trafficking victims; most (2,200) were from Asia, primarily China (Lipscombe, 2012). The number of persons rescued helps give a glimpse of the number of persons trafficked, though—as experts say—this is likely only the tip of the iceberg. Between April 2009 and September 2010 the U.K. government, through the Border Agency and police, reported identifying 379 potential trafficking victims, 89 of whom were children. In 2010 authorities also rescued 15 trafficking victims in Northern Ireland (U.S. Department of State, 2011). In 2011 the government identified and referred 294 potential trafficking victims; at least 117 were later determined to have been trafficked. Not counting internal trafficking in the U.K., the most common countries of origin for the victims were Lithuania, Romania, and Slovakia. Victims typically have a similar story: they are brought into the country under false pretenses of legitimate employment; subjected to debt bondage by being charged an inordinate amount of money for "travel expenses"; and deprived of their documentation. Traffickers often threaten victims with violence and even death. Some traffickers live up to these threats by utilizing physical and sexual abuse (U.S. Department of State, 2007a, 2007b).

One example of a victim lured to the United Kingdom through false promises of employment is Eva. A family friend promised her a legitimate job abroad when she was 15 years old. Instead, she was forced to prostitute in London. "He never beat me, but I was scared of him," Eva said. "[I was] worried he would kill me." Eva had no money or travel documents, but when given the opportunity she escaped. When she applied for asylum in the United Kingdom she was mistreated. "When

I applied for asylum the security guard started shouting questions at me," Eva said. "[He asked] where was I staying, why did I not have any documentation. I just broke down. They didn't believe I was 17, so I was taken to Brozefield prison." With the help of her church and local NGOs, she obtained legal representation and was released from the prison. "The Home Office still want[s] to send me back," Eva said. "No one has pursued the man [her trafficker]" (Lewis, 2006).

According to Klara Skrivankova, trafficking program coordinator at Anti-Slavery International in London, "At the moment, there are many more people identified for sex trafficking than labor trafficking. However, the reality is that the majority of forced-labor cases are not identified and thus are not included in those numbers." Skrivankova has seen forced labor in enterprises such as food processing, the garment industry, catering, and hospitality. "You see trafficking often when there are temporary jobs and where there is a chain of subcontractors," Skrivankova said. "People become agents to supply labor, and thus the responsibility is removed."[1]

As in many other nations, the persons most vulnerable to forced labor in the United Kingdom are migrant workers. Skrivankova believes this situation reflects the interrelationship between victims' lack of access to labor rights and the impunity granted to employers (Skrivankova, 2010). One such case is that of Yi-Song, a Chinese citizen who paid smugglers $20,802. Once he was in the United Kingdom his employer did not allow him and the other 10 workers to leave the premises and did not pay them for their first two weeks of employment. For food, the workers were given instant soup and tea three times a day. They earned nominal wages of $81.60 per week and were forced to work 20 or more hours a day, sleeping in 3-to-4-hour shifts so that they could continue to work. When they complained, the employer threatened to call the police and have them deported (Skrivankova, 2010).

Another case of forced labor is that of Pushpa, a domestic worker. Her employer withheld her passport and forced her to sleep on the floor in the living room. She was not allowed to leave the home, and her employer told her that if she attempted to do so, she would be reported to the police and deported. Pushpa went unpaid for two months—an alleged probation period. After that she was given a check for $326.49. Since she was never allowed to leave the home, Pushpa could not cash the check, so in reality she was never paid. In addition to her duties at the employer's home from six in the morning to eight at night, Pushpa was forced to clean various office buildings that the employer's cleaning firm was hired to clean. She worked each night until midnight. Upon return to the home, she was not allowed to sleep until her employer went to bed. She also faced an attempted rape by her employer's son and friends. While the cases of both Yi-Song and Pushpa fit under the criteria of forced labor and labor law violations, the irregular status of the victims prohibits them from access to labor law remedies. The latter simply helps to perpetuate the immunity granted to unscrupulous employers (Skrivankova, 2010). The dependency of migrant domestic workers on their employer, and in turn their vulnerability, were further increased in 2012 when the government reestablished a restrictive visa regime to prohibit domestic workers in the United Kingdom from changing employers (Mantouvalou, 2012).

Human trafficking also occurs within the United Kingdom. British nationals are vulnerable to exploitation and forced labor in the workplace, and children are trafficked internally for prostitution. In fact, in 2011 the United Kingdom was one of the primary nations of origin for victims identified by the U.K. government (Skrivankova, 2010; U.S. Department of State, 2010, 2012). To a lesser extent British nationals are trafficked abroad. One such case involves persons of the Traveller community (persons, including Roma and non-Roma, with itinerant lifestyles) trafficked for forced labor in the United Kingdom and later in Norway and Sweden. The victims worked 12-hour days for six days a week laying asphalt and tiles for private individuals; their weekly wages were $15.39. In addition, the workers faced abuse and physical violence. For instance, the traffickers shaved the workers' heads to demonstrate that the victims were their prisoners (Skrivankova, 2010).

WHAT HAPPENS TO VICTIMS AFTER TRAFFICKING

As in many nations, in the United Kingdom a conflict exists between the government's agendas to control immigration and to properly aid trafficking victims. This conflict is salient in the fact that the U.K. Border Agency, whose primary focus is immigration issues, is also the lead

anti-trafficking agency; and this may hinder its ability to properly identify, protect, and support victims of trafficking. For example, 49 officially recognized trafficking victims identified from April through December 2009 by the Border Agency and police through the National
Referral Mechanism (NRM) were not effectively referred. Instead, 27
victims were housed in an immigration detention center and 22 were
housed in a young offenders' institution. NGOs maintained that the
NRM also failed to ensure that identified victims were properly referred
to special care providers. In 2011 NGOs reported that trafficking victims continued to be inadvertently deported or that they faced other
penalization as offenders (U.S. Department of State, 2010, 2011, 2012).

Government funding is a significant issue in the nation's anti-
trafficking efforts. Various groups, including law enforcement and NGOs,
have been adversely affected. For instance, the only law-enforcement
team exclusively dedicated to the investigation of human trafficking
closed after just two years in operation. The government cited lack of
funds as the reason. This is a loss for victims, as the unit was known for
its victim-centered approach. Some of the officers from the unit have
been added to a new team that addresses trafficking abuses (U.S. Department of State, 2010).

Anti-trafficking organizations have also been negatively affected by
funding. One such group is the Poppy Project, a group widely recognized as the United Kingdom's leading organization for female trafficking victims. The organization, run by the charity Eaves, provides ac-
commodation and support services for adult women trafficked into the
United Kingdom for sexual exploitation or domestic servitude. From
2009 through 2011 the project provided accommodations and support
services for 161 victims for an average of 8 months each. It provided
additional support to 326 other victims (Channel 4 News, 2011). In 2011
the government decided not to renew the project's contract, which
could have an adverse effect on the accessibility of specialized services
available to trafficked women (Hill, 2011). Initially Eaves thought the
project would face a reduction in funding from the government of 40
percent or more and that in turn would reduce the number of days victims could receive services. "At the moment the minimum services that
can be provided for a victim of trafficking are for 45 days," said Abigail
Stepnitz, the Poppy Project's national coordinator. "Ideally we would

be looking at a minimum of 90 days. Not only is that what is considered best practice by the Council of Europe, but that is what many other European governments have implemented" (Channel 4 News, 2011). The contract instead went to the Salvation Army, where the funds are still designated to help trafficking victims (Hill, 2011). Fortunately, the Poppy Project survived the funding loss and continues to serve female trafficking victims. It is now the largest independently funded counter-trafficking support and advocacy organization in the United Kingdom (Asylum Aid, 2012).

To address the fact that victims continue to be charged and prosecuted for offenses related to their trafficking experience, in 2009 the government published updated legal guidance to emphasize the role of prosecutors in identifying potential trafficking victims who may have committed crimes while under duress or coercion by their trafficker, and in 2011 the government issued amended legal guidance to prosecutors instructing them not to prosecute trafficking victims for any crimes committed as a direct result of their trafficking. Even so, a boy from Vietnam was convicted of cannabis cultivation despite evidence of coercion, threats to his life, and the fact that he was locked in the factory. In 2011 an appeals court affirmed the decision and said that the exploitation was not tantamount to forced labor (U.S. Department of State, 2010, 2012). Through asylum, deportation of victims can be avoided for those who face retribution or hardship if forced to return to their home country. Asylum is granted on a case-by-case basis. The government can also grant victims who do not qualify as refugees the immigration status of humanitarian protection (HP) or discretionary leave (DL). Both HP and DL status give victims the opportunity to work, obtain housing, education, travel documents, family reunion, overseas travel, and health care. HP status grants victims a stay of five years, at the end of which they can apply for indefinite leave to remain and thereby begin the process of naturalization. DL status grants a stay of 6 months to 3 years or until victims reach the age of 17 and a half, depending on the type of case (ECRE, 2009). The majority of asylum requests are denied. Of the 20,930 initial asylum application decisions made in 2006, 79 percent of requests were refused, 10 percent of requests were granted asylum, and 11 percent were granted HP or DL (Office for National Statistics, 2007). At the end of 2010 roughly 22.6 percent of initial applications for asylum were granted; of those persons who were not granted asylum at the initial decision, 24.6 percent were successful on appeal (Asylum Aid, 2012).

The asylum process is not always fair. Thousands of people are detained annually and can be held in detention for long periods solely because they have applied for asylum (there are 11 immigration removal centers in the United Kingdom). Also, there is an accelerated procedure for assessing asylum—called the Detained Fast Track (DFT)—that is intended for claims by men or women that, according to the U.K. Border Agency, can be decided quickly. These detainees are automatically entitled to legal representation for their initial asylum claim, though often DFT detainees have no legal representation at their asylum appeal (Cutler, 2007; Politics.co.uk, 2010). Many women who enter the DFT asylum process lack access to adequate health care and legal representation. Detainees interviewed at Yarl's Wood Immigration Removal Centre remarked that they were regarded as criminals as opposed to asylum applicants and that supporting evidence was treated like fabrication as opposed to fact (Cutler, 2007).

Few women at Yarl's Wood win their asylum cases, but the percentage of successful applications may be slowly on the rise. In 2005 only 1 percent of applicants were granted approval at initial decision compared to 4 percent in 2008 (Cutler, 2007; Skrivankova, 2010). The government maintains that the low percentages reflect unfounded claims, but experts point to lack of preparation time and of legal representation at appeal (Cutler, 2007). In 2008, roughly 25 percent of women initially assigned to the DFT procedure were eventually moved into the standard asylum procedure. This does not mean that the fast track is not still highly utilized, and the odds of success at Yarl's Wood Immigration Removal Centre continue to be dismal. Ninety-one percent of appeals were refused in 2008 and the first half of 2009 (HRW, 2010b).

Human Rights Watch believes that the fast track system cannot handle complex trafficking cases. The DFT asylum process does not allow enough time for lawyers or other representatives to obtain a client's trust. Experts believe trust to be essential in allowing the lawyer/representative to obtain information regarding the victim's claim or to obtain medical or other evidence needed to verify the claim. Those on the fast track have little time to prepare a legal case, and only a few days to appeal if refused. "The 'Detained Fast Track' system doesn't meet even the basic standards of fairness," said Gauri van Gulik, a women's rights researcher at Human Rights Watch. "It is simply not equipped to handle rape, slavery, the threat of 'honor killings,' or other complex claims, and yet such cases are handed to it regularly" (HRW, 2010b).

Under a guidance note by the Home Office in 2008, the fast track is listed as unsuitable for certain categories of people. The list includes those whose cases should not be determined quickly, such as unaccompanied children seeking asylum, women who are more than 24 weeks pregnant, persons requiring 24-hour nursing care, and persons for whom there is independent evidence of trafficking or torture. The caveat on the latter is that victims of trafficking or torture who do not have evidence with them when they apply for asylum—such as expert reports and medical reports—can end up being placed in the fast track program (HRW, 2010a). One such case is that of Laura from Sierra Leone, who after experiencing multiple rapes and a forced abortion as well as watching the beheading of her father was trafficked to the United Kingdom. None of these issues was identified during the screening interview, and Laura was placed in the fast track program. During the interview the screening officer called Laura a liar and asked: "Why do you come to this country that doesn't want you?" After significant intervention by an NGO, Laura was transferred out of the fast track and eventually granted refugee status (HRW, 2010a).

The DFT asylum process has raised consternation even within the government, particularly in regard to trafficking victims. In May 2009 the House of Commons Home Affairs stated its uneasiness with the system:

> We are concerned that the Government's laudable aims of deterring fraudulent applications for asylum and speeding up the decision processes for genuine asylum seekers may disadvantage the often severely traumatized victims of trafficking. . . . Removing people from the fast track does not mean that their cases would be examined less rigorously; it just means that there would be more time in which evidence of trafficking might be adduced. (HRW, 2010a)

Foreign victims of trafficking who decide to cooperate with law enforcement are granted a 45-day reflection period and a renewable one-year residence permit. The government's specialized shelter houses adult female trafficking victims, including victims of involuntary domestic servitude. In 2009 the shelter assisted 260 trafficking victims; 96 women were provided aid within the shelter, and 164 were supported on an outreach basis. Many victims are excluded from the shelter because of the government's strict criteria for admission—victims must be over the age of 18; be a victim of trafficking that involves prostitution or domestic slavery within three months of referral; be willing to cooperate in the prosecution of their trafficker; and must have been trafficked into the United Kingdom from another nation (U.S. Department of State, 2010).

There is a dearth of victim services in the United Kingdom. Historically the government's anti-trafficking focus has been on foreign sex-trafficking victims. This is slowly changing, but children, British nationals, and men tend to be the most marginalized of the trafficked groups in terms of access to shelter and services. The U.K. government has simply not established comprehensive services for men, and child victims are inadequately placed in foster care or other general social service programs. What is worse is that some rescued children placed in the care of local authorities may be vulnerable to their traffickers, as acknowledged by the U.K. government in 2009. In 2011 experts reported that a number of rescued children placed in the care of local authorities continued to go missing (U.S. Department of State, 2010, 2011, 2012).

Klara Skrivankova said that over the past decade awareness about the issue of human trafficking has increased, but progress is still needed in the post-trafficking experience. On December 17, 2008, the United Kingdom ratified the Council of Europe Convention on Action against Trafficking in Human Beings, which went into force on April 1, 2009. According to Skrivankova, before ratification of the convention there was an ad hoc approach to providing assistance to victims: "the laws that we have are theoretically beneficial. . . . However, it is about how the law is implemented and whether the victim is actually benefited. We have yet to see whether the government will implement the laws in a robust way that actually benefits the victims of trafficking."[2]

WHAT HAPPENS TO TRAFFICKERS

The United Kingdom prohibits all forms of trafficking through its 2003 Sexual Offences Act and its 2004 Asylum and Immigration Act. Offenders face prescribed maximum penalties of 14 and 10 years' imprisonment, respectively (U.S. Department of State, 2010). In order to utilize the 2003 and 2004 trafficking laws, prosecutors must prove intent to both transport and exploit the victim (Government of the United Kingdom, 2003, 2004; U.S. Department of State, 2010). The double-intent criterion seems particularly unsuited to instances of trafficking within the United Kingdom, both in regard to British citizens trafficked internally and in regard to migrant workers who travel voluntarily to the United Kingdom but then experience involuntary servitude. Under the 2003 Sexual Offences Act and the 2004 Asylum and Immigration Act, the trafficker must have intent to move the victim—even if just from one part of the country to another. This requirement wrongly places equal judicial focus on the movement of the victim and the exploitative purpose. Demonstrating the trafficker's intent to move the victim for the exploitative purpose is a challenge, as migration routes often involve independent and facilitated movement. The latter usually involves a number of middlepersons, not all of whom are the same people who exploited the victim. That is not to say that interagents do not have culpability, but rather to illustrate that proving the trafficker's intention to move the victim for the exploitative purpose is difficult, and in many cases impossible (David, 2010). Requiring that the prosecution prove a trafficker's intent to arrange or facilitate travel, arrival, or departure to, from, or within the United Kingdom for the purposes of exploitation severely weakens the ability of prosecutors to succeed in utilizing the anti-trafficking laws. Consequently, prosecutors often use lesser offenses to prosecute traffickers. Prosecuting a trafficker under a lesser offense not only typically reduces the severity of the sentence for traffickers but also deprives the victim of an appropriate level of protection and support (Puffett, 2010).

In December 2009 the government passed the Coroners and Justice Act to explicitly criminalize slavery. Importantly, movement is not a precondition to the applicability of this act. Provisions went into force in April 2010. In Scotland this offense was introduced in Section 47 of the Criminal Justice and Licensing (Scotland) Act 2010 (Government of the United Kingdom, 2009; Skrivankova, 2010; U.S. Department of State, 2012). The 2009 Coroners and Justice Act, which prescribes up to 14 years' imprisonment, not only creates provisions relating to the new offense of slavery, servitude, and forced or compulsory labor; it also includes criminal law provisions relating to a new offense of possession of prohibited images of children (Government of the United Kingdom, 2009). It typically takes a while for a new law to get off the ground, as prosecutors universally prefer to use tried and true offenses. In 2010 there were no prosecutions under the 2009 Coroners and Justice Act, but in 2011 that changed, and 11 offenders of slavery and servitude were prosecuted under the act. Not surprisingly, the other two acts were used more often in the same year; 87 offenders were prosecuted under the 2003 Sexual Offences Act and 29 under the 2004 Asylum and Immigration Act (U.S. Department of State, 2012). Time will tell how successful the new act is in terms of convictions.

The average sentences for traffickers—even when prosecuted under the anti-trafficking laws—are quite low and have been so for the past several years. The average prison sentence for traffickers was four years in 2007, five years in 2008, and four years and five months in 2009 (U.S. Department of State, 2010). Of the 35 human traffickers convicted between April and December 2010, 24 were sex traffickers convicted under the Sexual Offences Act or other trafficking-related offenses, and 8 were labor traffickers, 2 of whom were convicted under the Asylum and Immigration Act. Data on sentencing for the labor traffickers were not available, but it is surely significant that those prosecuted under the Sexual Offences Act were given harsher sentences than those convicted for sexual offenses under other laws. The average sentence for persons convicted under the Sexual Offences Act was 3 years and 8 months' imprisonment compared to 2 years and 6 months' imprisonment given to those convicted under other laws. In 2011 the average penalty for convicted trafficking offenders was 2 years and 3 months' imprisonment; the average sentence for non–sex trafficking sentences was 4 years and 7 months (U.S. Department of State, 2012). This is significant because it illustrates that the government is beginning to take measures against non–sex trafficking offenses. Heftier sentences were handed out in January 2011 to Bogdan Nejloveanu and Marius Nejloveanu, a father-and-son trafficking team that forced five Romanian women to prostitute. They were sentenced to 6 and 21 years' imprisonment, respectively. The women were beaten, starved, and sexually assaulted. Marinela Badea, one of the victims, said that when she tried to escape she was punished: "I got punched, a knife in my head, my hair was pulled until it came out." Other 2011 cases involved 2 British citizens sentenced to a total of 19 years' imprisonment for forcing 100 children into prostitution and a forced-labor case that involved a retired doctor who received a 2-year suspended sentence for subjecting her domestic worker from Tanzania to conditions of slavery (Daily Mail, 2011; Townsend, 2011). Suspended sentences, whereby traffickers serve no jail time, undermine the severity of the crime. Forced labor continues to be insufficiently addressed. An NGO that specializes in the care of migrant domestic workers in the United Kingdom stated that it knew of 22 forced-labor trafficking victims who reported their trafficking experience to police. Only four of the cases were investigated as trafficking crimes. That said, in 2012 two offenders of forced labor were given substantial sentences. A Romanian couple found guilty of subjecting a seven-year-old Romanian girl to domestic servitude was sentenced to nine and a half years in prison (for the man) and nine years (for the woman) (U.S. Department of State, 2010, 2012).

In the United Kingdom, most prosecutions and convictions of traffickers and trafficking-related offenders take place in England, though in 2011 Scotland and Northern Ireland attained their first human trafficking convictions. Of the two offenders in Scotland, one was sentenced to 3 years and 4 months' imprisonment, while the other was sentenced to 18 months (U.S. Department of State, 2012). The trafficking offender in Northern Ireland was given a 3-year sentence for the trafficking charge, 18 months of which were given "on-license," which means that the person will not be imprisoned during that time but will have to adhere to certain conditions (similar to probation) (Queen v. Matyas Pis, 2012).

Human trafficking offenses in England, Northern Ireland, and Wales are governed by the 2003 Sexual Offenses Act, the 2004 Asylum and Immigration Act, and the 2009 Coroners and Justice Act. Scotland's human trafficking offenses are prosecuted under the Criminal Justice (Scotland) Act 2003, which is the equivalent of the U.K. Sexual Offenses

Act. The provisions of the U.K. Asylum and Immigration Act 2004 extend to Scotland. The trafficking provisions in both acts were amended and extended by section 46 of the Criminal Justice and Licensing (Scotland) Act 2010 (the same as the 2009 Coroners and Justice Act). Under either act, offenders face up to 14 years' imprisonment (Scottish Government, 2012).

INTERNAL EFFORTS TO DECREASE TRAFFICKING

In 2006 the government established the Serious and Organized Crime Agency (SOCA) and the United Kingdom Human Trafficking Centre (UKHTC). The UKHTC, led by SOCA, is a multi-agency center that provides a central point for operational coordination and expertise, including that of police and law enforcement, on human trafficking. The UKHTC also promotes the development of a human rights approach toward trafficking victims and works with other groups including NGOs to improve the standard of care and protection given to victims as well as to increase awareness and understanding in the area of criminal justice on the complexities involved with human trafficking. It also develops training modules to help attorneys prosecute traffickers more effectively (U.S. Department of State, 2007a, 2007b; UKHTC, 2008; SOCA, 2012).

In February 2006 the government launched the multi-agency Operation Pentameter 1, a policing operation designed to combat trafficking. This led to raids on more than 375 massage parlors and brothels, the discovery of 88 victims of trafficking for commercial sexual exploitation, the arrests of more than 150 people for trafficking-related offenses, and the seizure of $348,500 (Lewis, 2006). Operation Pentameter 2 (UKP2), was launched in March 2007 and completed in July 2008 (Cambridgeshire Constabulary, 2009). Tim Brain, Association of Chief Police Officers (ACPO) lead on Pentameter 2 and chief constable of Gloucestershire Constabulary, said that the mission of UKP2 was to discover the extent of human trafficking in the United Kingdom as well as to "put in place all means available to prevent anyone else falling victim to this evil trade, and rescue those who are being held in such situations" (Police Oracle, 2007). Some opponents of the task force alleged that police also used the operation as a means of finding and deporting illegal immigrants (Lewis, 2006).

With the support of Europol and Interpol, the United Kingdom is part of the European G6 Initiative Against Human Trafficking, which involves six countries: the United Kingdom, Poland, Italy, the Netherlands, Spain, and Ireland (Department of Justice, Equality and Law Reform [Ireland], 2007). In 2010 the U.K. government opted out of the new EU directive on preventing and combating trafficking in human beings and protecting its victims. In March 2011 the nation reconsidered and announced its intention to opt in. Under the directive, the U.K. government would be mandated to consolidate and broaden its definition of human trafficking, strengthen efforts to fight child trafficking and enhance child protection, and develop a victim-centered approach in protection, provision of services, and prosecution (Equality and Human Rights Commission, 2011; EU, 2011).

The ready availability of U.K. government data on trafficking makes it easier for the government, NGOs, and experts to properly gauge the trafficking scenario and the governmental response as well as to identify what gaps exist and how the nation can improve. This transparency is obviously intentional and reinforces confidence in the nation's resolve to properly address human trafficking. But although the United Kingdom has taken positive steps to protect both victims of sex trafficking and forced labor, its efforts are hindered by the nation's immigration agenda. This problem is illustrated by the misuse of the Detained Fast Track system and the use of the U.K. Border Agency as the lead anti-trafficking agency.

It is an enormously positive step that the 2009 Coroners and Justice Act does not include movement as an element. In fact, movement is not mentioned at all. As previously discussed, the double-intent criterion currently imposed on prosecutions of trafficking through the 2003 Sexual Offences Act and the 2004 Asylum and Immigration Act places undue weight on one specific act of movement instead of its exploitative purpose. It also puts pressure on prosecutors to opt for lesser offenses against traffickers. The resulting lesser sentences seriously undermine the severity of the crime and allow traffickers to face minimal punishment while victims are left without adequate support and protection.

Prosecutors who do not feel that they can succeed in a case against a potential trafficker by utilizing the anti-trafficking laws are left with few alternatives. This is particularly true in forced-labor cases, where remedies under the nation's labor laws are not available to workers with illegal status. In such cases, victims are treated as criminals while unscrupulous employers continue to exploit workers with impunity. Some experts say that there has been a gradual shift in the interpretation of the two acts by prosecutors and judges that veers away from cross-border movement and toward the exploitation itself. That said, it would make the acts clearer to amend them and eliminate movement altogether.

CHAPTER 19

Chile

I saw that other kids were doing it. All of them did it out of need.
— FRANCISCO, A 15-YEAR-OLD SEX WORKER

Even though slavery was abolished in 1823, making Chile one of the first nations in South America to take this step, the nation had no specific criminal offense of trafficking in persons until March 2011. Prior to the 2011 anti-trafficking legislation, Chile criminalized only international trafficking for sexual exploitation and sex crimes against children (UNESCO, 2004; UNODC, 2009). The Penal Code did not criminalize forced labor of children or adults, nor did it criminalize internal sex trafficking of adults. The new comprehensive anti-trafficking legislation was originally proposed in 2002 and defines and distinguishes the criminal offenses of human trafficking and smuggling (UNODC, 2009; U.S. Department of State, 2011). The 2011 Migrant Smuggling and Trafficking law passed unanimously in March 2011 and lays out specific rules for the protection of victims and a special method of investigation, all in accordance with the 2000 UN Trafficking in Person Protocol. Under the 2011 Migrant Smuggling and Trafficking Law, a trafficker is now defined as "whoever by violence, intimidation, coercion, deception, abuse of power, exploitation of a position of vulnerability or dependency of the victim, or the giving or receiving of payments or other benefits to achieve the consent of a person having control over another, captures, transfers, harbors or receives individuals to undergo some form of sexual exploitation, including pornography, forced labor or services, slavery or practices similar to slavery, or the removal of organs." Offenders face up to 15 years' imprisonment. The new law includes measures that focus on preserving the physical and psychological integrity of victims; it also increases enforcement options for police, including the use of undercover agents and wire-tapping in trafficking investigations (El Colombiano, 2011; Republic of Chile, 2011).

CHILE AS A DESTINATION AND TRAFFICKING ABROAD

Until the 2011 Migrant Smuggling and Trafficking law came into effect, all those identified by state authorities as trafficking victims had been adult foreign victims of commercial sexual exploitation. The majority of victims of adult sex-trafficking to Chile are from other South American countries such as Argentina, Bolivia, Colombia, Ecuador, Paraguay, and Peru who are forced to work in nightclubs and illegal brothels. It is difficult to ascertain which of these nations are primary source countries, but of 38 persons identified as trafficking victims by the public prosecutor's office in 2006 and 2007, 24 were from Peru, 11 were from Argentina, and 3 were from other South American nations (IOM, 2009; UNODC, 2009). It is also estimated that a small number of Chilean girls and women are trafficked to Argentina, Bolivia, Peru, and Spain for prostitution. Traffickers use a multitude of tactics ranging from newspaper advertisements for domestic help to convincing economically disadvantaged families that their child is being given the chance for a better life (U.S. Department of State, 2007a, 2010).

Despite the government's long-standing anti-trafficking efforts focused solely on sex trafficking, persons are trafficked in Chile for both forced labor and commercial sexual exploitation. A July 2009 International Organization for Migration (IOM) study gives a glimpse into the breakdown of the types of trafficking that occur in Chile; some of its findings, such as those on internal trafficking, will be discussed in further detail later in the chapter. The study examined 36 cases of trafficking that involved 147 foreign and local victims. The majority of the identified victims (87.7 percent) were foreign nationals, and the greatest number of identified victims were trafficked to Valparaiso. With 1.7 million inhabitants, the city is the third largest in Chile. The victims were primarily Chinese nationals and victims of forced labor. Santiago, the nation's capital, ranked second in the number of identified trafficking victims. Victims were primarily adults trafficked for commercial sexual exploitation (IOM, 2009). Thirty percent of interviewees in this study said that they were conned by false job advertisements in newspapers; other victims said that a recruiter had lured them. The Chinese forced-labor victims—almost exclusively male—stated that they had answered newspaper advertisements printed in a local newspaper in Sichuan Province, an area devastated by the May 12, 2008, earthquake, where approximately 70,000 persons were killed (IOM, 2009; New York Times, 2009). The men entered Chile legally and were forced to work in mines and restaurants. Chinese women also entered the nation legally and were forced to work as prostitutes in massage parlors in Santiago (IOM, 2009).

An alleged case of forced labor in Chile that has received much media attention is that involving Francisco Javier Errázuriz, a former presidential candidate and senator. He was indicted for allegedly trafficking 150 Paraguayan workers, at least 2 of whom are reportedly minors, to work in his vineyard in Pichilemu. The workers, who were brought into Chile on tourist visas, stated that they were deceived about their prospective working conditions. Reports in the media state that the victims faced poor working conditions and were fed one meal per day and saltwater. These reports state that the workers did not receive payment on account of inflated fees for food and shelter that were deducted from their wages (Tauran, 2011; Rivera, 2011). Two lawsuits, representing 54 workers, were filed in June 2011 against the former senator. The workers seek to obtain remuneration and compensation for damages (Quillier, 2011). Additionally, Francisco Javier Errázuriz and his two companies, Errázuriz Ovalle Vineyards and Fruit SA and Livestock and Crop Coast SA, were fined $215,914.13, $19,333.82, and $27,094.28, respectively, by the municipality of O'Higgins for employing the workers without the required authorization. In November 2011 the Rancagua Appeals Court upheld the decision (El Mercurio, 2011; La Tercera, 2011).

TRAFFICKING WITHIN CHILE

Trafficking within Chile is a significant problem, although exact numbers on internal trafficking are difficult to determine, as it was not criminalized until March 2011. Adult victims of internal trafficking continue to be marginalized. The government has increased its anti-trafficking efforts regarding the commercial sexual exploitation of children, yet the exploitation of children for both child labor and commercial sexual exploitation remains a serious concern. In fact, a 2009 UNICEF study in Argentina, Chile, and South Africa concluded that there were 11 times as many inter-province child migrants as international ones (van de Glind, 2010). Those persons identified as underage victims in the afore-mentioned July 2009 IOM study were Chileans who had traveled within Chile and were forced to work in nightclubs and brothels. Traffickers closely monitored the internal trafficked victims, and when working in brothels the victims were usually watched by an adult sex worker (IOM, 2009). One such victim is an orphan named Francisco. He ran away from a Chilean orphanage and turned to life on the street at the age of 7. At 15 he had already been exploited for sexual commercial purposes for half of his life. "I saw that other kids were doing it," Francisco said. "All of them did it out of need." Francisco said he worked in the sex trade in order to eat (Ross, 2003).

Sexual exploitation of children is a critical problem that the Chilean government denied for many years. This changed when a high-profile case in 2003 involved child prostitution and 65,000 online pedophile networks were discovered. In response, Chile took a stronger legal stance on the abuses of children (Ross, 2003, 2004; U.S. Department of State, 2007a, 2007b). The case was brought against a well-known businessman, Claudio Spiniak. Spiniak was accused of conducting a pedophile prosti-tution ring that included a clientele of high-powered businesspersons and politicians. Spiniak and six associates were charged with a variety of offenses ranging from rape to inciting child prostitution. Two legislators were questioned but not charged in the case (D'Alessandro & Tobar, 2004). Adult prostitution is legal, but brothels are not. Prior to the Spiniak case, police often arrested prostitutes under the charge "offense against morality." Prostitutes faced fines of $96 or five days' imprisonment. Since the case of Spiniak, the law has quickly tightened, making it illegal to induce a person under the age of 18 to have sex in exchange for financial gain or drugs (D'Alessandro & Tobar, 2004; U.S. Department of State, 2006).

Child labor in the formal economy is allowed for children between the ages of 15 and 18 with the express consent of a parent/guardian.

Under the law, children must also continue to attend school. They may not be employed in particular types of labor such as working in an underground mine, a nightclub, or any place that serves alcohol. Children may not work more than an 8-hour day or between the hours of 10 p.m. and 7 a.m. (unless they work for a family business) (U.S. Department of Labor, 2004, 2007; ADOC, 2009b). Yet child labor, predominantly in the informal economy, has remained a problem. Approximately 200,000 children between the ages of 5 and 17 work under unacceptable conditions, working a weekly average of 18.5 hours (children ages 5 to 14) and 39.5 hours (adolescents) (U.S. Department of State, 2007a). In 2005 the National Service for Minors (SENAME) released a report of 1,123 cases of children and adolescents in "the worst" adverse child labor scenarios. Fifty-eight percent were involved in hazardous jobs such as mining or worked with toxins/chemicals. Twenty-four percent were exploited in commercial sex labor, while 14 percent were involved in other illegal activities. Sixty-eight percent of the children/adolescents were boys (U.S. Department of State, 2007a). At that time SENAME estimated that 4,000 children were involved in the commercial sex industry in Chile. Other reports estimated the number to be as high as 15,000. Some of the child victims were as young as 5 years old (Ross, 2004). UNICEF stated in a June 2009 report that child labor in Chile was on the rise. The Labor Ministry of Chile denied the claim, citing legislation, programs, and campaigns to combat child labor since 2003 (ADOC, 2009a).

The UNICEF report—which was prepared in collaboration with the Chilean workers' organization Vicarías de Pastoral Social y de los Trabajadores—stated that the average age of child laborers in Chile was 12 and that they worked on average four hours per day and earned $8.86 per week. The majority (97.1 percent) of children who worked still attended school (ADOC, 2009a). The International Work Organization and Chile's Ministry of Work found that there were 240,000 children and adolescents between 5 and 17 years old working in Chile. They also stated that 64 percent of minors who worked in Chile were part of the poorest 40 percent of the population and that 40 percent of adolescents who worked and studied fell behind in their school work (ADOC, 2009b). In collaboration with the Solidarity and Social Investment Fund, UNICEF published a manual designed to help parents to detect potential child labor situations as well as tools and resources to find economic alternatives. The manual received support from government and public agencies (ADOC, 2009b).

WHAT HAPPENS TO VICTIMS AFTER TRAFFICKING

The government provides child victims of commercial sexual exploitation with comprehensive services. SENAME works with international organizations, NGOs, and local offices to ensure that child victims are not returned to high-risk or abusive situations. It provides services specifically geared to children subjected to commercial sexual exploitation through a national network of 16 walk-in centers. In 2011 it assisted 1,168 child victims. While it is unknown how many of the children assisted at the centers were trafficking victims, it is safe to assume that some were. In 2011 the service funded a residential shelter specific to child sex-trafficking victims and provided the children with legal services. Adult victims of sex trafficking are not provided with comprehensive services, but they have access to some social services, such as eligibility for housing and public health services at government-run women's shelters. Adult sex-trafficking victims are generally referred to NGOs and international organizations, some of which receive government funding. There are no specialized shelters for adult trafficking victims yet, but the government plans to fund a shelter specifically designated for female adult trafficking victims that will be run by an NGO. Forced-labor victims and adult internal victims of sex trafficking continue to be marginalized, even since the implementation of the new law. There are no specialized services for forced-labor victims (child or adult), though the government sometimes does offer limited services. For instance, authorities in 2011 provided Paraguayan forced-labor victims with temporary lodging at a hotel and gave the victims food and medical attention (U.S. Department of State, 2010, 2012).

The government encourages adult foreign victims of sex trafficking to assist in the investigation and prosecution of their traffickers. Those who participate are provided with medical care, psychological counseling, and witness protection. They may remain in the country during the proceedings against their trafficker(s) and can later apply for residency status (U.S. Department of State, 2010). Victims other than nationals or permanent residents in the country are entitled to submit an application for temporary residence status for a minimum period of six months, during which they may decide to exercise criminal and civil actions against their trafficker and initiate proceedings to regularize their legal residence status. To further protect foreign victims, under no circumstances can a victim who has applied for a residence permit be repatriated. According to the 2011 Migrant Smuggling and Trafficking Law, repatriation would be harmful to the victim's mental and physical integrity because of the crimes that have been committed against him in his country of origin (Republic of Chile, 2011). An agreement between the Public Ministry and the Ministry of Interior allows for humanitarian visas for trafficking victims who want to stay in Chile during the trial against their trafficker. Experts state that some foreign victims received these visas during 2009, and the Chilean authorities issued humanitarian visas in 2010 to foreign sex-trafficking victims who wished to participate in the investigation of their traffickers (U.S. Department of State, 2009, 2010). Since the passage of the 2011 Migrant Smuggling and Trafficking Law, Chilean officials do investigate possible cases of forced labor, but the government does not have formal procedures to proactively identify trafficking victims among vulnerable populations or to refer them to services, although some agencies do have guidelines for victim identification (U.S. Department of State, 2012).

WHAT HAPPENS TO TRAFFICKERS

In lieu of a comprehensive anti-trafficking law, before March 2011 prosecutors utilized Article 367 of the Penal Code (now repealed) to bring suit against those who committed transnational sex trafficking. Those found guilty faced up to 3 years in prison and a fine of $827. The punishment was increased up to 20 years' imprisonment when the victim was a minor, if violence or intimidation was used, if there was abuse of authority, if deception was used, or if the trafficker took advantage of the victim's circumstances. Sex crimes against children are prohibited under Article 361 of the Penal Code; prosecutors often use this law to prosecute cases of internal trafficking of children for prostitution. Prescribed penalties range from 10 to 20 years' imprisonment (U.S. Department of State, 2007a, 2007b, 2010). Under the 2011 Migrant Smuggling and Trafficking Law, penalties range from 5 years and a day to 15 years' imprisonment and increase to a minimum of 10 years and a day if the victim is a child. Offenders also face a fine of 50 to 100 monthly tax units (UTM). The UTM is a unit of account used in Chile for tax purposes and fines that is updated for inflation. The value of the UTM in September 2012 was approximately 84 U.S. dollars (Mazars, 2011; Republic of Chile, 2011; U.S. Department of State, 2011; Banco Central de Chile, 2012).

One concern is the common practice of judges to suspend sentences of less than 5 years. As a result, trafficking offenders often do not receive jail time (U.S. Department of State, 2010). This practice seriously undermines the severity of the crime. Historically, there have been few convictions of human traffickers. Only two persons were convicted of trafficking in 2006 and one person in 2007. The persons convicted in 2006 received sentences of between 1 and 5 years and 5 and 10 years, respectively (UNODC, 2009). From April through December 2008, the government obtained 10 convictions ranging from fines to 30 months' imprisonment (U.S. Department of State, 2009). Convictions and sentencing may be on the rise. In the case of Spiniak, in August 2008 the Supreme Court increased his sentence from 7 to 12 years' imprisonment for the sexual abuse of 4 underage persons. Additionally, the Supreme Court convicted him of facilitating prostitution and producing pornography (Bernasoni, 2008). In 2010 sentences ranged from roughly 1 and a half to 6 years' imprisonment (U.S. Department of State, 2010, 2011).

Prior to passage of the new law, investigative efforts focused exclusively on child prostitution and cross-border sex trafficking. In 2009 the government opened 128 trafficking-related investigations; 108 involved promoting or facilitating child prostitution, and 22 cases involved cross-border sex trafficking. Additionally, six active police officers were charged with facilitating child prostitution. In 2010 the courts obtained 34 convictions; 26 were for cross-border sex trafficking, and 8 were for promoting or facilitating the prostitution of children (U.S. Department of State, 2010, 2011, 2012). The lack of criminalization of internal trafficking and forced labor hindered victims' access to legal remedies and services and placed victims in a position that made them vulnerable to repeat exploitation. Offenders of internal trafficking and forced labor were able to escape penalization and imprisonment for their crimes. Even since the 2011 Migrant Smuggling and Trafficking Law was passed, investigations primarily focus on child prostitution and transnational sex trafficking. The number of human trafficking investigations gives a glimpse into the government's anti-trafficking focus. In 2011 authorities investigated 46 cases of transnational sex trafficking and 104 cases of promoting or facilitating child prostitution. These cases were all investigated using earlier statutes, not the 2011 Migrant Smuggling and Trafficking Law. In 2011 authorities did use the new law to investigate a small number of labor trafficking and sex-trafficking cases, at least three of which resulted in prosecutions. This is not surprising, as it usually takes a while for a new law to get used as law enforcement personnel and prosecutors adjust to the changes. Convictions in 2011 exclusively use previous statutes. This is most likely because many of the offenders were charged before the 2011 Migrant Smuggling and Trafficking Law was passed. In 2011 the government convicted 30 offenders for the facilitation or promotion of prostitution of minors, and 4 offenders were convicted under the transnational sex-trafficking statute (U.S. Department of State, 2012). In September 2012 the government obtained its first conviction under the 2011 Migrant Smuggling and Trafficking Law. The case involved the trafficking of persons from the Dominican Republic for commercial sexual exploitation. As of this writing the traffickers were not yet sentenced (Radio Universidad de Chile, 2012).

INTERNAL EFFORTS TO DECREASE TRAFFICKING

The government, before and after passage of the new law, has made significant strides in training officials and provides funding for anti-trafficking programs and projects geared to help prevent trafficking and to aid victims. In partnership with the IOM, in 2009 the government conducted eight anti-trafficking training sessions throughout the nation and focused on the identification and treatment of victims. More than 600 police, prosecutors, and immigration officials participated. Since the 2011 Migrant Smuggling and Trafficking Law went to effect, the government has continued to focus on funding and training. For instance, in 2011 SENAME had a budget of roughly $2.6 million for the 16 NGO-run centers that aid children subjected to commercial sexual exploitation. In the same year authorities provided specialized training on trafficking for prosecutors and social workers, and the government continued to give mandatory anti-trafficking and human rights training to military troops prior to deployment in international peacekeeping missions (U.S. Department of State, 2012). Since the 2003 Spiniak case and before the new law went into effect, the government has made consistent and considerable efforts to hinder the commercial sexual exploitation of children. As part of this agenda, in July 2009 the government investigated high-risk areas for child prostitution. Prosecutors and police collaborated in mapping the primary areas of commercial sexual exploitation with specific focus on detecting child prostitution. Since the new law went into effect, the government has continued these efforts and in order to raise the public's attentiveness to the issue of child prostitution, SENAME continues awareness campaigns (U.S. Department of State, 2010, 2012).

The government's anti-trafficking focus remains primarily on child victims of commercial sexual exploitation and transnational sex trafficking. Protection of forced labor and adult internal sex-trafficking victims has ranged from insufficient to nonexistent. Because neither form of trafficking was criminalized until March 2011, traffickers knew that the penalties would be light. With Chile's passage of the comprehensive 2011 Migrant Smuggling and Trafficking Law, if and when properly implemented, the potential exists for the identification of all victims and the investigation, prosecution, and conviction of their traffickers. The remaining challenge is ensuring that in practice all forms of human trafficking are identified; that traffickers are adequately investigated, prosecuted, and convicted; and that all identified victims have equal access to services. For now there continue to be positive changes, but they are slow and still leave many victims marginalized and traffickers with a mere slap on the wrist.

CHAPTER 20

Germany

> When recognized by the authorities, those without legal status
> run a high risk of being deported to their country of origin
> without being able to claim their rights.
> —HEIKE RABE, GERMAN INSTITUTE FOR HUMAN RIGHTS

The number of human trafficking investigations in Germany has significantly risen since 2005, the year the anti-trafficking laws were added to the Penal Code. Jorg Ziercke, the chief commissioner of the Federal Criminal Police Office (Bundeskriminalamt; BKA), says the number of investigations rose from 317 in 2005 to 534 in 2009. "This means an increase of 70 percent over five years and 11 percent last year alone," Ziercke said. "We attach great importance to this form of criminal activity because the human dignity of the victims is violated" (Press TV, 2010). While the rise in human trafficking investigations could reflect an increase in human trafficking, it more likely indicates an increase in anti-trafficking awareness among law enforcement. What is worrying is that roughly 20 percent of the 534 preliminary investigations in 2009 involved alleged trafficking victims under the age of 21, with 8 percent of the overall cases involving children younger than 14 (Press TV, 2010).

Heike Rabe of the German Institute for Human Rights (DIMR) said the increase in underage victims may be in part a result of the 2005 Offenses Against Personal Freedom Amendment to the criminal law. Under the amendment, said Rabe, persons under the age of 21 are considered trafficking victims if they are persuaded into prostitution: "No force or physical/mental abuse or even taking advantage of a helplessness arising from being in a foreign country is required. In comparison all these actions are required when a victim is older than 21. This makes it easier to prosecute and convict perpetrators [of trafficking persons under 21]. Therefore, cases that involve victims younger than 21 are more often reflected in statistics."[1]

Before 1995 only trafficking for the purposes of sexual exploitation was defined as human trafficking in Germany. Today the law also prohibits forced labor, deprivation of liberty, severe forms of coercion, and transplantation (Zündorf-Hinte, 2010).

GERMANY AS A DESTINATION AND CHILD SEX TOURISM

The most identified form of human trafficking in Germany is that for commercial sexual exploitation. In 2008, 676 sex-trafficking victims were identified, with women and girls making up 89 percent of the victims. Identified foreign victims of sex trafficking were primarily from Romania (20 percent), Bulgaria (18 percent), Poland (5 percent), and Hungary (5 percent). There was a particularly large increase in the number of Romanian, Bulgarian, and Nigerian victims between 2007 and 2008—a 108 percent, 55 percent, and 32 percent increase, respectively. Experts believe the increase in Romanian and Bulgarian trafficking victims into Germany is in part a result of the accession of the two nations into the European Union (EU) in 2007. This has made it easier for citizens of Romania and Bulgaria to enter, stay, and work in Germany (Bundeskriminalamt, 2009: pp. 8, 9).

There are four primary ways in which persons are trafficked into the German sex industry. Some victims are violently forced to migrate and perform sex work. Others voluntarily migrate on the basis of false promises of legitimate employment as a domestic worker, caretaker, restaurant employee, or dancer. Upon arrival they are charged exorbitant fees and are forced to prostitute by their traffickers in order to pay off the alleged debts. Some other victims voluntarily migrate to Germany with the knowledge that they will be working in the sex industry but are unaware of the conditions they will face—abuse, limited movement and choice, and threats of physical harm to their family. Lastly, some women travel to Germany under a fictitious marriage with a German national and are forced to prostitute upon arrival. The BKA stated that in 2010, 36 percent of sex-trafficked persons knowingly signed on to perform sex work. This statistic dropped to 27 percent in 2011. These persons were all deceived about the actual circumstances they would face (Bundeskriminalamt, 2011: p. 10; Bundeskriminalamt, 2012: p. 11).

Forced labor, which is prohibited under Section 233 of the Penal Code, is also a significant problem in Germany. Persons face forced labor in various sectors such as the food industry (catering), cleaning, agriculture, food processing, construction, fairground entertainment, transportation, and labor in private households (au pairs/nannies, caretakers, and domestic help) (Follmar-Otto & Rabe, 2009: p. 62). Over the past decade at least 1,000 persons from China have been brought to Germany for forced labor in restaurants (U.S. Department of State, 2010). The BKA identified 27 cases of forced labor in 2008. This is a significant drop from the 92 cases identified in 2007. The 2008 cases involved 96 victims—55 males and 41 females. Most of the victims were trafficked into domestic work or into the catering industry (Bundeskriminalamt, 2009: p. 11). In 2010 most of the 41 victims were male (76 percent) and most were from China (30), Romania (6), and Vietnam (2) (Bundeskriminalamt, 2011: p. 12). In 2011 most of the 32 victims identified were female (75 percent) and most were from Poland (14) and Romania (10). The victims were primarily exploited in the agricultural (18), domestic (4), and catering (3) sectors (Bundeskriminalamt, 2012: p. 13). Heike Rabe stated that these statistics probably do not accurately reflect the amount of labor trafficking that actually occurs: "The relevant actors— counseling centers, police, prosecutors, judges, and labor inspectors— are still not that familiar with how to apply the section [Section 233 of the 2005 Offenses Against Personal Freedom Amendment]. Second, the BKA report began to count and analyze the offense only in 2007. The statistics are young and therefore are probably still poorly developed."[2]

The largest population of sex-trafficking victims in Germany consisted of German citizens until 2011, when there were more identified Romanian victims than German victims. In 2008, 28 percent of identified sex-trafficking victims were German; in 2009 the share was 24.8 percent. In 2010, 19.8 percent of identified sex-trafficking victims were German, which was just slightly higher than the 19.5 percent of such victims who were Romanian (Bundeskriminalamt, 2009: p. 8, 2010: p. 12, 2011: p. 8). In 2011, the first year German citizens did not make up the largest group of identified victims, Romanians made up 26 percent of identified sex-trafficking victims, while Germans made up 22 percent

(Bundeskriminalamt, 2012: p. 9). Among sex-trafficking victims who were minors, German citizens made up 56 percent of identified victims (Bundeskriminalamt, 2012: p. 11; Zündorf-Hinte, 2010). As stated by Rabe and affirmed by the BKA, the large number of identified minors may reflect the fact that provisions of the Penal Code, specifically Section 232, allow for easier identification of underage persons than of any other group (Bundeskriminalamt, 2009: p. 9). The prosecution need only to demonstrate that the trafficker induced the underage person to participate or continue to participate in a sexually exploitative activity. The burden of proof is much heavier to demonstrate that a foreign adult has been trafficked for commercial sexual exploitation.

Child-sex tourism involving Germans who go abroad to pay for sex with young girls and boys is also a problem. One such case involved an HIV-infected 66-year-old German sex tourist who went to Thailand to sexually abuse young girls at least 400 times; one of the victims was just 11 years old, and several others were 14 (BNO News, 2011). Another case involved an HIV-positive German sex tourist who sexually abused children in Cambodia. Since 1994 he has served multiple sentences for child sex tourism; the most recent sentence began in 2008 in Germany. In 2007, before his last arrest, he allegedly had sex with several boys aged 11 to 13 and tried to rape one of them (ECPAT, 2009). In December 2011 German authorities charged a 51-year-old German citizen with nine counts of sexually abusing children in Thailand. Although some sex tourists are prosecuted in Germany, most German sex traffickers face prosecution in the countries where the offenses took place (U.S. Department of State, 2012).

WHAT HAPPENS TO VICTIMS AFTER TRAFFICKING

Experts believe that labor trafficking is a significant problem in Germany. But of the 772 victims identified in 2008, 676 were identified as sex-trafficking victims and only 96 were identified as forced-labor victims. In 2009 the number of identified sex-trafficking victims increased to 710 and the number of identified forced-labor victims decreased to 23. In 2010 the number of identified sex-trafficking victims decreased to 610 and the number of identified forced-labor victims increased to 41. In

2011 the number of identified sex-trafficking victims increased to 640 and the number of identified forced-labor victims decreased to 32 (Bundeskriminalamt, 2009: pp. 10, 11, 2010: p. 12, 2011: pp. 8, 12, 2012: pp. 9, 13; Zündorf-Hinte, 2010). One potential reason for the low number of identified forced-labor victims is that there is no system in place to identify and assist trafficked persons other than those of commercial sexual exploitation. As a remnant of earlier anti-trafficking criminal law, human trafficking police units still focus mainly on "red-light crime" and forced prostitution (Follmar-Otto & Rabe, 2009: p. 27). It is customs officials, not police, who typically encounter trafficking victims outside the sex industry such as those in catering, cleaning, and construction. As a result, these victims are often perceived as undeclared workers and illegal migrants—not trafficking victims (Follmar-Otto & Rabe, 2009: p. 27).

Despite Germany's overall anti-trafficking efforts, there has not been enough emphasis on victim rights. This is an issue for nearly all nations. "[National anti-trafficking policies] usually build on the model of three P's—Protection, Prevention and Prosecution (with great emphasis on prosecution)—without adequate consideration for the three R's—Rehabilitation, Reintegration and Redress for victims," Special Rapporteur Joy Ngozi Ezeilo said at the May 13, 2009, General Assembly Interactive Thematic Dialogue Debate "Taking Collective Action to End Human Trafficking" (OHCHR, 2009).

One significant issue is the overall under-identification of trafficking victims without legal status. According to Heike Rabe, unidentified victims without legal status who are arrested by German police commonly face potential detainment and deportation:

> Those without legal status who do not want to cooperate or are fearful of cooperating with the authorities are very likely to be deported to their country of origin without being able to claim their rights—for example, their right to compensation and remuneration. They are legally entitled to claim their rights in courts, but there are legal and factual barriers, so that this rarely ever happens. For example, one crucial barrier is that judges have to report the plaintiff to the immigration authorities when they discover that a plaintiff does not have a residence permit.[3]

Victims are granted a reflection period to decide whether they want to cooperate in the investigations against their traffickers. The duration of the reflection was increased from one month to three months in 2011 (U.S. Department of State, 2012). Police and NGOs report that victims are commonly fearful of retribution and thus reluctant to aid law enforcement. Those victims who agree to be witnesses are granted renewable temporary residence permits for the duration of the trial proceedings against their trafficker(s). They also are eligible to receive shelter, legal assistance, vocational support, medical services, and psychological care through 39 NGOs that are fully funded by the Federal Family Ministry. Victims who face retribution—such as severe threats in their country of origin—may obtain long-term residence permits (Follmar-Otto & Rabe, 2009: pp. 60, 64; U.S. Department of State, 2012).

NGOs focus primarily on adult females (U.S. Department of State, 2012), so men are often left without equal access to services and shelters. Rabe said that she did not know of any shelter in Germany that is accessible to men:

> The overwhelming majority of counseling centers that provide specialized services for trafficked person exclusively support women. Migrant and refugees organizations as well as trade unions provide services to both men and women, but they are not specialized in trafficking. Trade unions do not run shelters. Their services focus on labor law and the representation of their members in out-of-court settlements and in labor court proceedings.

The government does pay the basic cost of victim repatriation under the Reintegration and Emigration Program for Asylum-Seekers in Germany and the Government Assisted Repatriation Program. The program is administered by the International Organization for Migration and offers payment for transportation, gas, and travel costs to victims. It also provides start-up cash assistance for victims of 35 select nations—among them Nigeria, Russia, and China. However, some of the excluded nations are primary source nations for trafficking into Germany—such as Romania, Bulgaria, Poland, Slovakia, Czechoslovakia, and Thailand (IOM, 2012). The right to compensation is specified under the Council of European Convention on Action Against Trafficking in Human Beings.

While Germany signed the convention in 2005, the government has not yet ratified it (Council of Europe, 2012). According to Rabe, this will soon change, as the government is about to ratify the convention.[4] Regardless, German law allows victims to participate in criminal court proceedings and to claim wages, compensation, and damages. But, says Heiner Bielefeldt, United Nations special rapporteur on freedom of religion or belief and former director of the DIMR, advisory services and assistance to aid those victims in their claims are inadequate.

> Exercising legal rights goes beyond the hoped-for—and often desperately necessary—material compensation and also holds a great deal of symbolic importance for trafficked persons. This is a way for them to regain their sense of being independent subjects, often after having long experienced a total loss of self-determination over their own lives. Active advocacy for one's own rights offers an opportunity to restore and increase awareness of one's own self-worth. But the chances of success are minimal without advice and assistance along this arduous path. (Follmar-Otto & Rabe, 2009: p. 7)

The reality is that many victims who participate in criminal proceedings still do not receive compensation. One attorney interviewed by the DIMR stated that only 30 percent of the women she represented in court received compensation during criminal proceedings. Several counseling centers revealed that only a small minority of women who testified at criminal trials received compensation: 2 out of 34 at one counseling center, 2 out of 124 clients at another center, and 2 out of 22 at a third center (Follmar-Otto & Rabe, 2009: p. 68). The small number of victims who do receive compensation in criminal proceedings are primarily women who have been trafficked for sexual exploitation. The amount received is typically between $1,298.81 and $5,195.26, although a few victims have received higher amounts between $15,584.63 and $38,961.59. "What frequently occurs during criminal proceedings is that perpetrators, through their legal counsel, offer a full admission of guilt and payment of compensation that is generally between 1,000 and 4,000 euros [$1,299 and $5,196], far less than what the trafficked persons would have been entitled to," Heike Rabe said. "Most compensation is paid as damages for pain and suffering."[5] Some women also received state compensation payments under the German Crime Victims' Compensation Act (Opfer-entschädigungsgesetz), which does not include either damages for pain and suffering or compensation for damage to property or financial losses. Instead, the compensation is payment of a pension based on persistent effects of the injury and income-based payments to replace lost wages. The court's findings establish the offense, the consequences, and the causality for approval of state compensation. The compensation typically involves a small pension of $168.88 to $389.63 per month (Follmar-Otto & Rabe, 2009: p. 76).

In response to the few claims made by victims for financial compensation, the DIMR on June 2, 2009, in cooperation with the Remembrance, Responsibility and the Future Foundation, launched "Forced Labour Today—Empowering Trafficked Persons." Under the project, DIMR undertook to run a legal aid fund, offer advanced training and symposiums, and develop guidelines for an initial 3-year-period. The fund cooperates with NGOs, attorneys, and trade unions on a case-by-case basis. The fund represents victims of human trafficking or labor exploitation and helps them to apply for funding from the legal aid fund. One strong benefit of the program is that lack of legal status is not a hindrance. Additionally, the victim does not need to report the incident to the police, and the act of trafficking does not have to be proved by law enforcement. "The professional assessment of NGOs, lawyers, or trade unions is sufficient, as we want to separate victims' rights from the willingness of trafficked persons to testify as witnesses in criminal proceedings," Rabe said. In return for attorney costs and court expenses, victims must make their cases available to the fund so that they can be analyzed and published. Anonymity is guaranteed.

Labor victims are seldom identified and thus less commonly pursue claims against their trafficker(s). Figures and facts are limited, but NGO reports indicate that labor victims simply do not know about their rights. When victims do file claims against their traffickers, said Rabe, they do not commonly make compensation claims, despite their entitlement to do so:

Victims of labor trafficking who were physically or mentally abused and suffered damages are legally entitled to claim compensation. The German legal system does not understand the idea of punitive damages [damages meant to punish the wrongdoer in a civil suit], which means that victims can claim compensation "only" for damages for pain and suffering as well as for material damages. Therefore, damage claims cannot be compared to claims asserted in the United States, for example.[6]

Since victims rarely pursue any sort of claim, the German judicial system has little to no experience with labor-trafficking cases, so there is a lack of precedent for prosecutors to utilize. This commonly deters victims from filing suit against their trafficker(s). Unlike proceedings in criminal courts, in civil and labor proceedings the plaintiff has to initiate the claim. Then the courts must rule on a decision based on the legal issues raised in the claim. "As long as courts do not receive complaints, the judicial system will not develop the necessary experience," Rabe said. Some men and women have successfully filed wage claims. For instance, one victim through out-of-court negotiations was paid $29,241.29 for two years of back wages. But very few have received adequate compensation for work actually done or for illness attributed to the working conditions that they faced. Instead, the victims commonly received payment only for working hours that are typically performed in that specific sector where they faced forced labor (Follmar-Otto & Rabe, 2009: p. 73).

WHAT HAPPENS TO TRAFFICKERS

The government primarily investigates, arrests, and convicts sex traffickers. In 2008, 785 persons were suspected of sex trafficking. German nationals made up 40 percent of these suspected traffickers, Bulgarians made up 11 percent, and Romanians and Turkish nationals each made up 8 percent. In 2009 German nationals made up 36 percent of the 777 trafficking suspects. Bulgarians made up 16 percent compared to Romanians (10.5 percent) and Turks (10.4 percent). In 2010 German suspects again made up the largest share, but less so at nearly 26 percent, followed by Bulgarian suspects at 20 percent and Romanian suspects at 13 percent. In 2011 Germans made up 28 percent of trafficking suspects compared to Romanian suspects (17) and Bulgarian suspects (14) (Bundeskriminalamt, 2009: p. 7, 2010: p. 10, 2011: p. 7, 2012: p. 8). Typically traffickers receive minimal sentencing. Seventy-one percent of the 579 traffickers convicted in West Germany and East Berlin between 2003 and 2006 received 1 to 5 years' imprisonment. Twenty percent of the traffickers received less than one year's detention (UNODC, 2009). In fact it is common practice for judges in Germany to suspend sentences of two years or less. Of 131 adults convicted of sex trafficking in 2008, 70 percent received suspended sentences or fines. Of the 9 adults found guilty of labor-trafficking offenses, 89 percent received a fine or a suspended sentence (U.S. Department of State, 2010). Of 135 sex traffickers convicted in 2009, 75.6 percent received nominal to no jail time. There were only 10 convictions of labor traffickers in 2009, and none of the offenders was sentenced to imprisonment (U.S. Department of State, 2011). In 2010 the vast majority (80 percent) of the 115 convicted traffickers did not have to face jail time. The remaining 23 convicted sex traffickers faced sentences ranging from 2 to 10 years in prison. Thirteen labor traffickers were convicted in 2010, but none was sentenced to imprisonment (U.S. Department of State, 2012). The suspended and negligible sentencing undermines the severity of the crime.

The German government works with law-enforcement officials in Southeast Asia to investigate German sex tourists, where they face trial either in the destination country or in Germany (U.S. Department of State, 2011). The previously mentioned 66-year-old HIV-infected sex tourist was prosecuted in Germany for sex tourism committed in Thailand. In March 2011 he was sentenced to nine years' imprisonment (BNO News, 2011). The HIV-infected man who went to Cambodia to sexually abuse children was sentenced to six and a half years in 2008. When his sentence is complete he will serve a lifelong preventative detention, where prisoners are placed in distinct institutions or separate areas within prisons or jails (ECPAT, 2009; Saas, 2012).

While Germany is beginning to identify the significant issues of forced labor and severe labor exploitation, it still focuses primarily on sex trafficking. Male victims of human trafficking are particularly marginalized and do not have adequate access to services or shelter. It is also of concern that a high number of human traffickers received suspended or minimal sentences. And while traffickers face minimal consequences, unidentified victims without legal status commonly face detainment and deportation without a thorough investigation as to whether they are in fact trafficking victims.

PART X
Transparent Borders

Unmonitored or undermonitored borders are a chronic challenge to the deterrence of human trafficking. They provide ideal opportunities to smugglers and traffickers. In most cases this lack of coverage is a result of a nation's inability to manage its borders effectively; but in some cases nations create transparent borders that result in similar problems.

This is the case in Poland, which was once primarily a source nation but is now also a transit and destination country for trafficking. Poland joined the European Union (EU) in May 2004 and became a signatory to the Schengen Agreement in 2007. Experts believe that the scale of trafficking in Poland has increased as a result. The 25 member nations of the Schengen Area enjoy enhanced police and judicial cooperation, which increases the efficiency of extraditions and transfers of jurisdiction in criminal judgments. Members also benefit from the Schengen Information System, a database that allows national border-control and judicial authorities to obtain information on persons or objects. Member nations function as a single country for purposes of travel: all internal borders are eliminated, and one single external border creates a vast visa-free area allowing the free movement of people, goods, and capital. It is the lack of border checks that contributes to the increase of human trafficking within the Schengen Area, including Poland, which sits on this region's easternmost border. Poland's location on the border not only makes it vulnerable to trafficking within the region, but also makes it vulnerable to trafficking into the Schengen Area because it is an entry point into the region.

Some experts argue that anti-trafficking cooperation among nations in the Schengen Area is not as strong as that among other EU nations. The EU provides a framework of cooperation between member nations and legal obligations on preventing and combatting trafficking in human beings. In 2010 Poland took steps to bring its domestic laws into conformance with EU and other international law by adopting its own comprehensive definition of trafficking. But despite the amendment of its Penal Code, in practice some forms of trafficking remain mostly ignored.

CHAPTER 21

Poland

There is a stereotype that trafficked persons are victims [of] their own wish.
—STANA BUCHOWSKA, LA STRADA INTERNATIONAL

The magnitude of human trafficking in Poland has grown since the nation joined the European Union in May 2004 and became a signatory member of the Schengen Agreement in 2007 (OHCHR, 2009a, 2009b). Poland is part of the easternmost border of the Schengen Area and, consequently, is an entry point into the area for illicit activities, including human trafficking. The 25 member nations of the Schengen Area enjoy enhanced police and judicial cooperation, which promotes more efficient extradition and transfer of jurisdiction in criminal prosecutions. Signatories also benefit from the Schengen Information System, a governmental database—intended to improve law enforcement and national security—that allows national border-control and judicial authorities to obtain information on persons or objects (European Union, 2009).

Another feature of the Schengen Agreement has brought both benefits and disadvantages, at least in relation to human trafficking. The member nations of the Schengen Area function as a single country for purposes of travel. In essence, all internal borders are eliminated, and instead the nations use one single external border (European Union, 2009). Citizens of member nations are not checked at the borders of other signatories. The predictable result is an increase in human trafficking among member nations. According to Joy Ngozi Ezeilo, the United Nations special rapporteur on trafficking in persons, the lack of border checks has contributed to Poland's becoming a transit and destination nation for human trafficking in addition to its preexisting status as a source nation: "The scale of trafficking in persons is not only serious in Poland but has been somewhat aggravated . . . by virtue of Poland joining the European Union and also acceding to the Schengen zone. These developments unarguably helped to transform Poland from being mainly a source country to clearly becoming a transit and a destination country combined" (OHCHR, 2009a, 2009b). The Polish government does sometimes implement border checks. For instance, during the monthlong Euro 2012 soccer tournament, Poland reestablished random border checks with Germany and other EU countries (Seattle Times, 2012). In order to further protect Poland's border from human trafficking during the tournament, 130 European border officers from 23 European countries were deployed to back up Polish border guards at the eastern border and at major airports (Human Trafficking Foundation, 2012).

Poland has ratified multiple international human rights treaties, including the Council of Europe Convention on Action Against Trafficking in Human Beings (2005) and the 2000 Protocol to Prevent, Suppress and Punish Trafficking in Persons, Especially Women and Children (the Palermo Protocol), supplementing the UN Convention Against Transnational Organized Crime. Yet Poland did not have a comprehensive domestic anti-trafficking definition or law until May 2010. Before that, sex traffickers were prosecuted under Articles 203 and 204 of Poland's Penal Code, and forced labor was prosecuted under Article 253 and organized-crime statutes. Since there were no specific provisions in domestic law that defined or addressed labor trafficking, prosecutors relied heavily on trafficking definitions in the Palermo Protocol when pursuing cases against traffickers (U.S. Department of State, 2009; UNODC, 2009a). In her preliminary findings and recommendations at the end of her official visit to Poland in 2009, Ezeilo stated: "Domestic application of international law appears to require some form of transformation despite the constitutional provision that encourage[s] direct application of international law. . . . the Palermo Protocol . . . is not self-executing and would therefore require an additional act of the legislature to be fully implemented in Poland" (OHCHR, 2009b).

Upon ratifying the UN Convention Against Transnational Organized Crime in November 2001, Poland was obligated to take appropriate measures to conform its domestic legislation to that of the convention.

In 2010 Poland amended Article 115 of its Penal Code to provide a clear and comprehensive definition of human trafficking, and Article 189a replaced a previous prohibition on trafficking in persons and introduced criminal liability for preparations to engage in human trafficking (CRIN, 2011). The new law prohibits all form of human trafficking through Articles 115.22, 115.23, and 189a, which replace Articles 253, 204 Sections 3 and 4, and 203, respectively. Penalties prescribed under Article 253 range from 3 to 15 years' imprisonment, and penalties prescribed under Articles 203 and 204 range from 1 to 10 years' imprisonment (U.S. Department of State, 2011; European Union, 2012). The trafficking of human organs and tissue is prohibited under the Trafficking in Human Organs and Tissue Act (OHCHR, 2009b).

POLAND AS A DESTINATION AND TRANSIT NATION

With the fall of communism—and with law-enforcement and other agencies busy with the transformation and reorganization of Poland's political system—came less regulation and porous borders that made the nation vulnerable to a variety of organized crimes, including human trafficking. Freedom of movement replaced stringent policies, and at the same time prostitution changed form in Poland, shifting from a primary existence in hotels and restaurants to massage parlors and revival clubs. The demand for prostitution expanded at an estimated rate of 3,200 or 3,300 per year (Wiśniewski, 2010). These factors, along with accession to the European Union in May 2004 and the Schengen Agreement in 2007, transformed Poland from primarily a source nation to also a destination and transit nation for human trafficking.

Determining the exact number of people affected by human trafficking as it relates to Poland—as a nation of origin, transit, and destination—is a challenge. The European Institute for Crime Control and Prevention estimates the number of trafficking victims to exceed 15,000 persons annually, whereas the National Public Prosecutor's Office states that there were 3,170 victims between 1995 and 2008 (Wiśniewski, 2010). This discrepancy probably arises, at least in part, from the fact that before 2010 a variety of laws were used to prosecute traffickers in Poland, but only two—Articles 253 and 203—were frequently included in released trafficking data on convicted traffickers (U.S. Department of State, 2010). Another reason is that forced labor is just beginning to be identified, and although there have been some highly publicized cases of the trafficking of Poles in other nations, forced labor is generally unidentified (Wiśniewski, 2010). According to Stana Buchowska, co-founder of La Strada and national coordinator of La Strada Foundation Against Trafficking in Persons and Slavery, based in Poland, the identi-fication of trafficked persons for the purpose of forced labor remains a significant challenge. "There were cases reported when the border guards [in Poland] wrongfully identified a group of exploited migrant workers as irregular migrants rather than trafficked persons," Buchowska wrote. "An efficient system of monitoring and evaluation . . . to measure the impact of anti-trafficking activities implemented is also lacking in Po-land" (Buchowska, 2011).

Persons are trafficked to and through Poland from other nations in Europe, Africa, and Asia for commercial sexual exploitation and forced labor. During the 15-year period of 1995–2010 the majority of foreign vic-tims were from Ukraine (350), Belarus (311), Bulgaria (87), Romania (24), Moldova (21), and Russia (15). Other nations of origin were Latvia (8), Vietnam (8), Bangladesh (7), Lithuania (6), Sri Lanka (4), Mongolia (3), Costa Rica (2), Kenya (1), Senegal (1), Niger (1), Uganda (1), Djibouti (1), Germany (1), the Dominican Republic (1), and the Philippines (1) (Min-istry of Interior and Administration, 2010). In 2008 alone, 315 persons were identified as victims of human trafficking by the National Public Prosecutor's Office; 65 were of Ukrainian origin (IOM, 2010). Foreign victims made up 20.3 percent of identified trafficking victims between 1995 and 2008. The majority—80.6 percent—were from Ukraine and Belarus (Ministry of Interior and Administration, 2010, 2011). Since 2010 the National Consulting and Intervention Centre for Victims of Traffick-ing has collected data on victims. Of those interviewed, most forced-labor victims were from Ukraine (49 percent), Thailand (16 percent), and Nepal (7 percent). Others were from Azerbaijan, Bangladesh, Uzbekistan, and Vietnam. Victims were discovered in the agricultural, fishing, trans-port, and domestic sectors as well as in cigarette production. Some victims were also forced to perform physical work in marketplaces (Eu-ropean Union, 2012).

Select human trafficking cases give a glimpse into the types of human trafficking that are identified in Poland. One case, discovered in 2009 by the Metropolitan Headquarters of Police, involved a syndicate that allegedly trafficked women from Bulgaria and forced them to prostitute in Poland and other European nations. Over 40 persons were detained, and more than 30 were charged with forcing persons to prostitute, extortion, participation in an organized-crime group, and robbery with violence. Twenty persons were held in pretrial custody (General Headquarters of Police, 2010). Another case, led by the Rzeszów Central Investigation Bureau in 2007, involved an organized-crime group that forced women and children from Ukraine and Moldova to beg for money in Polish cities. Four persons were charged with participation in an organized-crime group engaged in human trafficking—recruiting, transportation, violence against women and children, and forced begging (General Headquarters of Police, 2010). At the end of 2009, 12 trafficking victims from Bangladesh were transported to Poland to work in the fish-processing industry. Traffickers forced the victims to work in a shipyard, did not pay them, threatened them, and subjected them to poor living conditions. In relation to this case, one person was detained and charged with participation in an organized-crime group dealing with human trafficking and infringement of the labor law. An international warrant was also issued in this case (General Headquarters of Police, 2010).

While most of the identified cases of human trafficking in Poland involve commercial sex, Ezeilo says trafficking for forced labor is on the rise and that labor inspectors appear to lack the necessary training for effective oversight (OHCHR, 2009a). Migrant workers are often deported without a proper evaluation as to whether they are trafficking victims. One such case involved at least 58 Thai migrant workers who faced forced labor in Poland's agricultural sector in 2010. The workers paid money to Kitti Brothers Recruitment and Thai Syntax Travel Service, two primary recruitment companies who send Thai workers to Poland. Once in Poland, the victims were sent to work under the supervision of two local recruitment agencies, NOBA and East West. The workers were each charged between $3,695.15 and $12,317 in brokerage fees in order to reserve supposed jobs that paid between $1,848 and $2,771 per month—wages that the workers never received (Bunnag, 2010; Charoen-suthipan & Tansubhapol, 2010). Once in Poland, the victims were forced to work without a permanent employer—in direct violation of Polish law. Some of the workers claimed that they were misled about the type of work they would be doing. One worker was promised that he would work in a noodle factory but instead was forced to work on a farm. The majority of workers were forced to work on swine, chicken, strawberry, and flower farms (Bunnag, 2010; Charoensuthipan & Tansubhapol, 2010). "Several workers were forced to work on the farms for 24 hours a day, but did not get overtime for months in a row," said Janya Yimprasert, chair-woman of the Union of the Thai Overseas Workers. "Their living conditions are also bad" (Bunnag, 2010).

The recruitment firms took various measures to deter the workers from filing suit against them. The wife of one of the workers stated that the recruitment firm told her that if her husband did not take any legal action against their organization, the firm would help him get home to Thailand (Charoensuthipan & Tansubhapol, 2010). Thirty-three of the workers were arrested and detained by Polish police, and at least 20 were charged with not having work permits and were ordered to leave the country. Not only did Polish officials not identify the workers as victims of human trafficking, but also the workers were charged with illegal entry even though they had allegedly entered Poland legally with appropriate work permits and documents (Bunnag, 2010; Charoensuthipan & Tansubhapol, 2010).

Yimprasert filed a petition on March 19, 2010, with the Polish Embassy in Bangkok, asking it to solve the problem of Thai worker exploitation in Poland by recruitment firms and employers. Yimprasert discussed with labor officials the possibility of obligating the Thai and Polish recruitment companies to compensate the 58 forced-labor victims. She asked that labor officials compel Polish employers who hire Thai laborers to follow the employment law and recommended—as a possible means to hinder exploitation—that the Polish Embassy temporarily stop granting visas to Thai workers in order to pressure employers to improve the working conditions that they offer their migrant workers. She also urged cooperation between the Thai and Polish governments in aiding victims of forced labor (Bunnag, 2010).

Common techniques used by traffickers are false job promises, high fees or alleged debts, rape, and withholding of the victim's documentation. One case demonstrating the use of many of these techniques involves a 23-year-old woman trafficked from Uganda to Poland in 2009. The young woman met a Polish trafficker who offered her well-paid employment in Europe. He informed her that she did not need money or documentation and that he would arrange the entire journey. During the trip from Uganda to Poland the woman was raped multiple times (Polish Radio External Service, 2009a). These techniques—such as the false offer of employment and withholding documentation—allow traffickers to lure in victims and exert control over them. The use of rape also allows traffickers control over their victims and creates fear that they will suffer physical harm if they disobey or attempt to escape. Upon arrival in Warsaw, the woman was able to escape when her trafficker left her alone in a vehicle. Police believe that she then spent the night underground near the city's central train station before contacting the Department for Foreigners at the local border-guard office. The woman received medical treatment from a clinic and also received services from the Ministry of the Interior and Administration's Program for the Support and Protection for Victims of Human Trafficking (Polish Radio External Service, 2009a).

It is not just migrant forced-labor victims who are deported without a thorough investigation as to whether they are victims of human trafficking, but also foreign sex-trafficking victims. According to Poland's Ministry of Interior and Administration, it is difficult to impossible to determine the number of sex-trafficking victims who arrive in or pass through Poland. The ministry states that the deportation policy may well contribute to the problem, as foreign women staying in Poland illegally are immediately deported. As a result the victims are unable to incriminate and testify against the perpetrators. Of women who were identified as victims of sex trafficking, those from Bulgaria were most commonly forced to perform roadside prostitution; Ukrainian women were typically sold to escort agencies. In nearly all identified cases, a citizen in the country of origin cooperated with the traffickers. Most commonly the victims accepted false offers of employment in sales or agricultural work, but sometimes they migrated to Poland on their own and then faced exploitation upon arrival. Those who are trafficked into Poland are often resold, so that discovering their whereabouts is difficult to impossible. The primary destinations for sex trafficking are Warsaw, Płock, Żyrardów, Radom, Rzeszów, and Białystok (Ministry of Interior and Administration, 2008).

TRAFFICKING WITHIN POLAND AND TRAFFICKING ABROAD

Citizens of Poland are trafficked to Austria, Belgium, Finland, Germany, Italy, the Netherlands, the Scandinavian countries, Ukraine, and the United Kingdom for forced labor and commercial sexual exploitation (U.S. Department of State, 2012). In 2008, 179 Polish victims of human trafficking were returned to Poland from Kiev, Ukraine (IOM, 2010). In 2006 Poles made up 5 percent of detected victims in the Netherlands, 10 percent of detected victims in Germany, and 13 percent of forced-labor victims in France, primarily in the agricultural sector (UNODC, 2009b). Forced labor of Poles abroad, or at least the identification of the practice, appears to be on the rise. In 2006, under the Polish and Italian operation Terra Promessa, police uncovered a case of more than 100 Polish workers who had been recruited by newspaper and Internet advertisements for attractive and well-paid agricultural jobs in Foggia, southern Italy. Upon arrival the workers faced appalling conditions and were forced to work for nominal pay under supervision by armed guards. They were charged excessive fees that placed them in a position of servitude and faced physical and psychological abuse; they were sometimes beaten until they passed out, threatened or attacked by dogs, and deprived of food and water as punishment. At night they were locked in the premises, where they slept with no running water, electricity, or furnishings. The rescued workers were given assistance by Italian and Polish NGOs, while Italian and Polish police—with the assistance of Europol—made arrests (Plant, 2009; Ministry of Interior and Administration, 2008).

Like people in many other nations, most Poles associate human trafficking with prostitution. As a result, victims tend to be reluctant to come forward. "Trafficking in persons is not only trafficking into forced prostitution and the sex business, but also forced labor, slavery-like practices, trafficking into begging, petty crimes, transplantation of organs, and many other purposes," Stana Buchowska told the Polish Radio External Service (Bielawska, 2008). In 2008 La Strada International, which provides trafficking victims with therapy, legal services, and job training, launched an awareness campaign called "On the Right Track" to highlight the realities of human trafficking in the hopes of chipping away at the marginalization and stigmatization of human trafficking victims (Bielawska, 2008). Buchowska said that societal assumptions perpetuate these misconceptions: "There is a stereotype that trafficked persons are victims [of] their own wish. It is necessary to increase the knowledge about the problem and . . . to educate society [on] how to prevent this situation, what are the safe steps of job migration. Around 2 million Poles migrated in search [of] job[s], and job migration is one of the factors conducive to trafficking. People are not aware enough and they do not double-check the job offers" (Bielawska, 2008).

La Strada estimates that roughly 7,000 Poles fall victim to human trafficking each year, and the Polish research agency TNS OBOP (Center for Public Opinion Research) states that 20 percent of Poles have worked abroad. Twenty percent of those polled by TNS OBOP said they would respond to a suspicious job offer of good wages with no qualifications required (Bielawska, 2008; Polish Radio External Service, 2010a). In order to inform Poles about the potential dangers of working abroad, the International Organization for Migration (IOM) collaborated with the advertising agency Saatchi and Saatchi, MTV Networks Poland, and the Ministry of Interior and Administration on an awareness TV spot. "We hope that the campaign will contribute to better understanding that human trafficking is a fact, and will encourage persons considering working abroad to carry out thorough background checks of their prospective employers and workplaces abroad," said Anna Rostocka, the head of the IOM office in Poland. "We want them to become suspicious of particularly attractive offers and talk about their plans with friends and family, to leave their contact details behind and keep their travel documents safe. Our aim is for the labor migration to become safe and bring positive changes in people's lives" (IOM, 2010).

One case of deceptive job recruitment and practices is that of a dozen women from Poland who applied for housecleaning jobs but instead were sold to an escort agency by a trafficking ring located in northern

Poland. The four traffickers—two women and two men—recruited women in dismal financial situations and promised them legitimate employment in Germany. Once the victims crossed over the Polish border, the traffickers took away their identification and sold the women to escort agencies that forced the women to work as prostitutes. "The women were intimidated and kept in a closely guarded house," said Jan Kosciuk, a spokesperson for police in northern Poland. "What made matters worse, they did not speak German" (Polish Radio External Service, 2009a). Another instance of Poles trafficked abroad is that of babysitters and housekeepers who faced forced labor and abuse in Sweden by a 46-year-old mother of four. The workers received $1.00 per day or nothing at all. They were forced to live in a small room in the trafficker's apartment, were constantly monitored, and were even forced to steal clothing for their trafficker. If they were deemed disobedient the trafficker would shave their heads (Polish Radio External Service, 2010b; Simpson, 2010).

Polish citizens are also trafficked internally. While exact numbers are difficult to obtain, shelter numbers may shed some light on the situation, though these numbers probably include both internal victims and Polish citizens who were trafficked abroad and returned home. Of trafficking victims provided with shelter by La Strada International in 2005 and 2006, 35 were from Poland, 6 from Bulgaria, and 5 from Ukraine (UNODC, 2009b). Poland's Ministry of Interior reports that of the 934 victims identified in 2009 and 2010, 77.3 percent were Poles (Ministry of Interior and Administration, 2011).

WHAT HAPPENS TO VICTIMS AFTER TRAFFICKING

The government of Poland grants legal protection and temporary stay permits to trafficking victims, while housing, medical, and psychological assistance for victims are typically provided by NGOs (UNODC, 2009a). In 2008 the government increased direct assistance to its sole trafficking shelter by 40 percent (to $70,000) and in April 2009 awarded an additional $215,000 in emergency funding to keep the shelter open through December 2009. The government also expanded its network of specialized crisis intervention centers from 30 to 37. The centers serve victims of domestic violence and human trafficking (U.S. Department of State, 2009). According to Poland's Ministry of Interior, 611 victims were identified in 2009 and 323 in 2010 (Ministry of Interior and Administration, 2011). The U.S. Department of State provided different estimates, reporting that in 2009 at least 206 victims of human trafficking were identified by the government—123 of whom were children in prostitution—and in 2010 a total of 338 victims were identified, 85 by the government and 253 by NGOs. Half of those identified by NGOs were forced-labor victims, and half were sex-trafficking victims. The government-funded and NGO-run National Intervention-Consultation Center for Victims of Trafficking provides assistance to foreign and Polish victims. The center provided assistance to 253 victims in 2010 and to 133 victims in 2011. The U.S. trafficking reports stated that many of the identified victims received government-funded assistance— most of the 315 victims in 2008 and 193 of the 206 victims identified in 2009. The 2012 U.S. trafficking report stated that Polish police identified 304 victims of trafficking in 2011 (U.S. Department of State, 2009, 2010, 2011, 2012; IOM, 2010).

Foreign victims of trafficking, whether third-country nationals or EU citizens, are entitled to receive the same social welfare benefits provided to Polish citizens, including crisis intervention assistance, shelter, food, clothing, and a living allowance. Foreign victims are granted a 90-day reflection period during which they are allowed to stay in Poland and obtain assistance while they decide whether to cooperate with law enforcement. The reflection period is underutilized: only two foreign-trafficking victims used it in 2008, none used it in 2009 or 2010, and two used it in 2011 (U.S. Department of State, 2009, 2010, 2011, 2012). Foreign and Polish victims are no longer required to be identified by or to cooperate with local law enforcement in order to receive government-funded emergency assistance, though reports indicate that police encouraged victims to cooperate immediately with law enforcement and forgo the reflection period. International organizations state that foreign victims who declined to participate in law enforcement investigations were not classified as trafficking victims or offered the reflection period and related services. Those foreign victims who choose to cooperate are allowed to stay in the country during the investigation and prosecution of their trafficker (U.S. Department of State, 2009, 2010). The victim/

witness support is initiated by the Ministry of Internal Affairs and implemented by La Strada Foundation but is available only to those who agree to cooperate with law enforcement. Again, some experts are concerned that victims who choose not to cooperate with law enforcement may not be granted victim status and thus may not receive emergency victim assistance. Twenty-one victims assisted law enforcement with trafficking investigations in 2008, and 22 in 2009. Two foreign victims were granted temporary residency permits to stay in Poland while awaiting completion of the prosecution against their traffickers in 2009 (U.S. Department of State, 2009, 2010). Aside from the victim/witness support program, La Strada provides social assistance to all migrant trafficked persons, regardless of whether they aid law enforcement (Buchowska, 2007). Of course, without temporary residency permits granted by the government, foreign victims who do not cooperate with law enforcement remain in a vulnerable position. To address this issue, in October 2011 the Polish government signed an agreement with the IOM to ensure that assistance is provided to foreign trafficking victims regardless of whether they cooperate with law enforcement. Additionally, the agreement requires a risk assessment for each victim to ensure that the person will be safe upon return to his or her nation of origin (U.S. Department of State, 2012).

Another critical obstacle to the prevention of re-trafficking and the rehabilitation of victims is that victims—regardless of whether they are returning to Poland as their country of origin, were trafficking within the nation, or whether Poland was the destination for trafficking—face isolation, stigmatization, marginalization, and social exclusion. These factors can make victims hesitant to step forward; furthermore, the victims themselves often do not recognize that they are victims of a serious crime. The onus on proper identification rests with the government, as does creating apparatuses of social and labor inclusion so that victims can more easily reintegrate into society, which helps to diminish the risk of further vulnerability and exploitation of identified victims. To develop and implement a model of social and labor inclusion, the pilot project IRIS (Identification—Reintegration—Independence—Sustainability) was launched in 2006. The pilot was designed to offer Polish nationals a full range of support such as identification and crisis intervention; motivation, empowerment, coaching, and vocational training;

and internships and employment. The model was developed and implemented by a formal partenership among NGOs, La Strada Foundation, the Center for Empowerment of Women, the Labor Office of the city of Warsaw, the Warsaw Social Welfare Center, and the Ministry of Social Policy and Labor (Buchowska, 2007). While this is exactly what Poland and all other nations need, the pilot focuses only on the social and vocational occupation integration of women victims of trafficking (Wroblewski, 2009; Ministry of Interior and Administration, 2011).

In 2009 the government allocated $298,000 to assistance for victims of human trafficking, including $59,000 for a shelter designed for adult female victims. In 2011 the government allocated $250,000 for victim assistance. As of now, there are no specialized shelters for male trafficking victims. Although the government has made significant strides in providing male victims with assistance and shelter, many of them are housed in shelters for the homeless as well as halfway homes for recently released prison inmates. In January 2010 the government housed seven male trafficking victims in a government-run crisis center and enrolled them in the Victim/Witness Protection Program to ensure that they had access to care. In 2011 male victims were housed in coed crisis centers (U.S. Department of State, 2009, 2010, 2012). There is no specific law concerning protective measures for child victims of human trafficking in Poland, though children who are identified by law enforcement as victims of trafficking are granted the same aid as adults—including medical, psychological, and social support, legal assistance, safe shelter, and an interpreter if needed. Unaccompanied minors are directed to care centers for minors, and the custodial court appoints them legal representatives. Foreign unaccompanied minors may apply for a residence permit (European Union, 2012).

Compensation is a significant factor in making victims whole, or as close to it as possible, after surviving human trafficking. According to Joy Ngozi Ezeilo, an award of compensation by the court is "an important aspect of redressing loss of earnings, violation of human rights and harm suffered in general" (OHCHR, 2009b). In Poland, victims can claim compensation within a civil action and/or within criminal proceedings. Despite the existence of this framework, Stana Buchowska noted that in only a small number of cases do victims receive compensation. "It is due to the lack of experience and knowledge [of] how to proceed"

(Buchowska, 2007). Ezeilo pointed out that judicial proceedings in trafficking cases are also inordinately long: on average they last about two years. In her preliminary report she suggested that "efforts should be made by the Ministry of Justice and the judiciary to shorten the period and provide early case closure that will bring succor to victims and reduce trauma suffered, while redirecting focus to victims' full reintegration and rehabilitation" (OHCHR, 2009b).

Victims do sometimes face arrest, prosecution, and punishment for crimes they committed while under duress or in relation to their trafficking scenario. This occurred in the previously mentioned case of the Thai trafficking victims arrested for immigration violations. Also, in 2011 the Organization for Security and Cooperation in Europe reported that a Polish court prosecuted three identified victims of human trafficking as members of an organized crime syndicate despite evidence that the victims' families were threatened and that the victims' salaries were withheld (U.S. Department of State, 2012).

WHAT HAPPENS TO TRAFFICKERS

One hurdle that prosecutors faced until May 2010 was the lack of a clear legal definition of human trafficking in Poland's Penal Code (U.S. Department of State, 2009, 2011). In lieu of a clear definition and comprehensive law, prosecutors turned to trafficking-related laws. Under Article 203, whoever subjected another person to practice prostitution—through force, illegal threat or deceit, or by abusing a relationship of dependence or by taking advantage of a critical situation—faced between 1 and 10 years' imprisonment (Interpol, 2009). Article 204 of the code prohibited benefiting financially from the prostitution of other persons, luring or abducting other persons abroad to prostitute, or inducing or facilitating other persons to prostitute in order to benefit financially. Penalties ranged from up to 3 years' imprisonment for the exploitation of adult victims to up to 10 years' imprisonment when the victim was underage (Sykiotou, 2007; Interpol, 2009). Article 253 was used to prosecute forced labor and illegal adoption. The act of trafficking persons, even with the victim's consent, was subject to imprisonment for no less than three years. In addition to prohibiting the buying and selling of human beings, the article banned the organization of illegal adoption of children, carrying a prison sentence of three months to five years (Sykiotou, 2007; Garnier, 2009).

Nowhere in these articles was human trafficking actually defined. Additionally, Articles 203 and 204 focused solely on forced prostitution. One possible solution would have been to amend Article 253 to include a thorough definition of human trafficking and to broaden the number of prosecutable offenses to criminalize all forms of human trafficking—including but not limited to debt bondage, involuntary servitude, peonage, slavery, organ trafficking, forced marriage, and forced prostitution.

Each year roughly 80 percent of traffickers brought to trial in Poland's courts are citizens of Poland; the remainder are primarily Bulgarians and Ukrainians. A significant number of cases—up to 36 percent—are dismissed on the basis of nonoccurrence of a crime or lack of evidence (Ministry of Interior and Administration, 2011). The statistics provided by the National Public Prosecutor's Office reveal no clear pattern in the number of persons charged with human trafficking. To date, 2003 saw the largest number of persons (134) charged with human trafficking. The number decreased to 39 in 2004, 42 in 2005, and 36 in 2006. In 2007, 62 persons were charged (UNODC, 2009a). There were 57 persons convicted of human trafficking in 2008, 52 in 2009, 28 in 2010, and 28 in 2011 (U.S. Department of State, 2010, 2012).

Historically, one challenge to collecting trafficking data in Poland has been the numerous laws under which a trafficker could be prosecuted. The 2009 and 2010 data on convicted traffickers include only the number of persons convicted under Articles 253 and 203. The majority of traffickers receive suspended sentences. For instance, in 2007, 2008, and 2009, 57 percent, 53 percent, and 52 percent of traffickers received suspended sentences, respectively. The remaining 43 percent (2007) and 47 percent (2008) received sentences of 1 to 5 years' imprisonment. The remaining 48 percent of convicted traffickers in 2009 received sentences ranging from 3 months to 10–15 years' imprisonment. In 2010 offenders received sentences ranging from 2 months' to 5-8 years' imprisonment; roughly 50 percent received suspended sentences, and about 1 in 5 convicted offenders received sentences of at least

2 years (U.S. Department of State, 2009, 2010, 2011, 2012). Suspended sentences undermine the severity of the crime and put traffickers back in a position where they can traffic again.

INTERNAL EFFORTS TO DECREASE TRAFFICKING

The government is taking significant steps to combat human trafficking. It provides anti-trafficking training to judges, prosecutors, law enforcement, and military personnel. The Central Team for Combating Trafficking in Human Beings, Human Organs, Child Pornography and Pedophilia (the Central Anti-Trafficking Police Unit) was established in 2006; roughly 500 police officers were assigned to the unit full-time in 2008. To facilitate coordination and supervision of trafficking cases in all 17 regional police anti-trafficking units, the government transferred the Central Anti-Trafficking Unit of the Polish National Police to the Central Bureau of Investigation in January 2011 (U.S. Department of State, 2011). In March 2009 the Central Anti-Trafficking Police Unit issued a set of guidelines to regional police units on identifying persons trafficked for forced begging (U.S. Department of State, 2009; UNODC, 2009a).

In 2007 Suzanna Hof, international coordinator of La Strada International, told Radio Netherlands Worldwide: "We opened the borders for a lot of new European [Union] member states, and for the first time in the last two years we [have seen] more trafficking cases from Poland and the Czech Republic even in the Netherlands" (Campbell & Thorne, 2007). To deter the trafficking of Polish citizens working abroad, the Ministry of Foreign Affairs published a guidebook in 2008 describing the dangers of labor exploitation. The government also conducted a public campaign to raise awareness among Polish labor migrants about how to identify fraudulent recruitment and human trafficking as well as what to do if they are trafficked (U.S. Department of State, 2009). Of course the problem with such public-awareness campaigns is that they are unlikely to be accessible to their target audience.

In response to these and other widespread concerns, the government revised its anti-trafficking statutes. But practical implementation of the law is also essential. One abiding problem is that not all forms of trafficking are being recognized and dealt with. According to Stana Buchowska, the nation must improve its identification procedures to target cases of trafficking for all purposes, including forced labor, slavery-like practices, domestic servitude, forced begging, and petty crimes (Buchowska, 2011).

To improve the identification of forced-labor victims, the national police and border guard updated their referral procedures, which include identification tools for all forms of human trafficking and place particular emphasis on forced labor. The new procedures were adopted when the revised law on foreigners was passed (U.S. Department of State, 2012). In August 2011 President Bronislaw Komorowski signed the revised law on granting protection to foreign nationals (called the Law on Legalization of Stay of Some Foreigners on the Territory of the Re-public of Poland and on the Amendment to the Act on Granting Protection to Foreigners within the Territory of the Republic of Poland and Act on Foreigners). The law introduces regularization of stay of undocumented migrants and rejected asylum-seekers in Poland. It also introduces the concepts of relocation and resettlement. Under the law, asylum seekers whose asylum applications were rejected before January 1, 2010, but who have stayed in Poland without interruption are eligible to apply for legalization of their stay. The law also allows for the transfer of refugees from another country of asylum to Poland (UNHCR, 2011).

In order to improve support for child victims of trafficking, a comprehensive model for the support and protection of minor victims is currently in development. Since late 2009, the Program for Support and Protection of Minor Victims has been tested as a regional pilot project. One objective of the program is to harmonize existing procedures concerning the protection of children. Additionally, the Polish government plans to develop a system of support for child victims by increasing training of law enforcement and other critical personnel and establishing a chain of safe shelters able to adequately support child victims of trafficking (European Union, 2012).

Poland took crucial action in amending its laws to define human trafficking and related offenses in its Penal Code. But in order to adequately protect the rights of all trafficked persons the nation must also improve its identification procedures and its methods of collecting and analyzing data to address all forms of human trafficking. The updated referral procedures and identification tools are certainly a significant step. Poland must also ensure that victims who choose not to cooperate with law enforcement receive emergency victim assistance. The nation also needs to create shelters specifically for male victims and for child victims of trafficking in order to ensure that they obtain proper assistance and rehabilitative care. Finally, the government needs to end the widespread practice of awarding suspended sentences to human traffickers.

PART XI
Fear Factor

It is not uncommon for victims to fear testifying against their trafficker. In nations where it is more likely than not that the trafficker will not be imprisoned, victims are rightly fearful of retribution. Yet it is not just victims who are scared.

In Mexico, local law enforcement, prosecutors, and judges are fearful of pursuing trafficking cases in areas where human trafficking is prevalent and organized crime is strong. This fear is justified as crime groups have continued to target law enforcement and anti–human-trafficking advocates. In January 2012 a local drug cartel in Ciudad Juárez, Chihuahua, killed five police officers and pledged that it would kill one officer a day until Julian Leyzaola, the police chief, resigned. Attacks on police by organized-crime syndicates are not likely to stop anytime soon. Between October 2011 and January 2012 some 60 police officers in Ciudad Juárez were killed (Juan Carlos Llorca, 2012; Stratfor Global Intelligence, 2012).

Federal judges are also fearful of organized-crime syndicates and have been reluctant to try trafficking cases, not only because the anti-trafficking law is new and the judges are not familiar with it, but also because they are fearful of retribution. Pervasive corruption among public officials at all levels and in all branches of government makes the power of organized-crime groups appear limitless. The result is that traffickers perceive everything as negotiable: even after facing charges, they can simply pay off witnesses, judges, and prosecutors. Until 2007, criminal cases were closed to the public, a practice that created a secretive and ideal environment where corruption could flourish. This should change as Mexico slowly implements multiple judicial reforms legislated in 2007.

CHAPTER 22

Mexico

They don't care about destroying people's lives, because what they want
is money. What they want is to dominate the world by having a lot of women
to themselves. They feel like gods before a woman who has no defenses
because she's been beaten, and they totally mistreat them horribly.

—A VICTIM OF THE CARRETO FAMILY TRAFFICKING RING

In November 2007 Mexico passed a federal anti-trafficking law called
the Law to Prevent and Sanction Trafficking in Persons. Additionally,
Mexico City (the Federal District) and all 31 states have criminal codes
that include trafficking in persons as a crime. The Federal District and
the state of Chiapas have separate legislation that criminalizes trafficking and mandates social assistance for victims (ABA, 2009; U.S.
Department of State, 2012).[1] Under federal law, acts of human trafficking include promotion, solicitation, offering, delivery, transfer, receipt,
obtaining, and facilitation. The means included under the law are physical violence, moral violence, deception, and abuse of power. The forms
of exploitation that are covered include sexual exploitation; forced labor
or services; slavery; practices similar to slavery; servitude; and removal
of organs, tissue, or its components (ABA, 2009). In June 2012, then-
president Felipe Calderón signed the General Law to Prevent, Punish
and Eradicate Trafficking in Persons Crimes and for the Protection and
Assistance of Victims of These Crimes, which increases sentencing of
traffickers and trafficking-related offenders to up to 40 years' imprisonment, which can be increased to 60 years for violent crimes. The president also amended the Penal Code to criminalize the killing of a female
because of gender (femicide); offenders face 40 to 60 years' imprisonment
(EFE, 2012).

Mexico is an origin, transit, and destination nation in trafficking for
both forced labor and commercial sexual exploitation. As in all nations,

determining the actual number of persons trafficked in Mexico is difficult. Experts estimate that each year more than 20,000 Mexican children
are victims of sex trafficking. In 2008 Mexican law-enforcement
officials identified 55 trafficking victims of forced labor and commercial sexual exploitation in Mexico—27 males and 28 females. At least
259 victims were identified in 2010, but the number of identified victims decreased in 2011 to 160 (ABA, 2009; U.S. Department of State,
2009, 2012). Mexico City's human rights commission estimated in 2011
that 10,000 women were victims of human trafficking in the capital
city, but there were only 40 investigations and 3 convictions of human
trafficking in the city in 2010 (CNN, 2011b). A 2012 Attorney General's
Office report on sex trafficking states that at least 47 sex-trafficking rings
operate in Mexico and that an estimated 800,000 adults and 20,000
children are trafficked each year. The human trafficking crime syndicates operate in Veracruz, Chiapas, Puebla, Oaxaca, Tlaxcala, Baja California, Chihuahua, Guerrero, and Quintana Roo, as well as in Central
America. According to NGOs, human trafficking is estimated to generate
$26.6 billion annually in Mexico (EFE, 2012; Mexico Institute, 2012).

The government has taken steps to improve victim protections, but
Mexico's society is generally unaware of the seriousness of human trafficking. When he was president, Calderón stated that this must change.
"We have to create a unified front to end human trafficking in Mexico,"
he said. "This front is not limited to police or officials, this front starts
in the streets, in the neighborhoods and in the communities" (CNN,
2011b).

TRAFFICKING ABROAD

Men, women, and children are trafficked from Mexico to the United
States for forced labor. Additionally, organized-crime trafficking syndicates traffic women and girls to the United States for commercial sexual
exploitation (U.S. Department of State, 2009). In 2007, 42 of the 303
certification and eligibility letters given to trafficking victims in the
United States were granted to Mexican citizens. The U.S. Department of
Health and Human Services certified 289 foreign adult victims of trafficking in 2008. Sixty-six of those persons certified were from Mexico,

making it the primary country of origin for persons trafficked to the United States (U.S. Department of State, 2009).

As is discussed in detail in chapter 1, the U.S. H-2B program has resulted in the exploitation of numerous workers, many of them Mexican nationals. In 2005 employers brought in 121,000 nonagricultural guestworkers. Seventy-five percent of these workers were from Mexico. The highly utilized H-2B program not only offered U.S. employers an easy means for cheap labor, but also because the program was not regulated it created opportunity for unscrupulous employers to place workers in debt bondage, indentured servitude, and slavery (Bauer, 2007; U.S. House of Representatives, 2008). In December 2008 the Employment and Training Administration of the U.S. Department of Labor (DOL) amended its regulations for issuing labor certifications to employers sponsoring H-2B guestworkers (U.S. Department of Labor, 2008, 2009a). These steps may help the DOL to adequately monitor the program.

Visa holders also face exploitation under the H-2A program. One such case is that of 42 to 118 guestworkers from San Luis Potosí, Mexico, who were forced to perform agricultural labor in the United States from 2006 through 2008. Charles Relan, the owner of Bimbo's Best Produce in Amite, Louisiana, allegedly confiscated the workers' passports and H-2A visas. In addition to threats and the physical abuse of at least one worker, Relan also fired a shotgun over the workers' heads to deter them from attempting escape (Antonio-Morales et al. v. Bimbo's Best Produce, Inc. et al., 2009).

Mexican nationals are also trafficked to nations other than the United States. Mexicans made up 5.1 percent of trafficking victims identified in El Salvador from 2005 through 2007, and 9 percent of identified trafficking victims in Nicaragua in 2006 and 2007 (UNODC, 2009).

While organized criminal networks are highly involved in human trafficking, additional trafficking of persons occurs by individuals and family groups (ABA, 2009). One such family trafficking ring is that of the Carreto family. In what would seem like an unlikely circumstance, a 61-year-old grandmother managed a sex-trafficking ring out of Mexico. Based in Tenancingo, Tlaxcala, Consuelo Carreto Valencia and other members of the Carreto family forced Mexican women into the commercial sex industry in Mexico and the New York City metropolitan area. The ring was made up of Consuelo Carreto Valencia and her sons

Gerardo Flores Carreto and Josué Flores Carreto, as well as other family members such as nephews Eloy Carreto Reyes and Eliú Carreto Fernández and daughter-in-law María de los Ángeles Velásquez Reyes (DeWeese, 2004; U.S. Department of Justice, 2007a, 2007b; ICE, 2008; Semple, 2008). The trafficking ring was discovered when a victim's mother contacted the U.S. embassy in Mexico City in December 2003 to say that her daughter had been kidnapped and was being held against her will in New York. The communication sparked an investigation of the Carreto trafficking organization, launched by U.S. Immigration and Customs Enforcement (ICE) in 2003, which revealed that the male members of the group lured women into a romantic relationship and forced them to prostitute in Mexico and the United States. The women were systematically controlled through the use of physical abuse and the threat of not allowing them to have contact with their children. These were not empty threats, as the children of the trafficking victims were in the physical custody of Carreto Valencia in Tenancingo or with other Carreto family members (ICE, 2007; U.S. Department of Justice, 2007b).

ICE agents, in collaboration with the local New York City Police Department, raided two apartments in Queens, where they found five trafficking victims along with Gerardo Flores Carreto, Josué Flores Carreto, Eliú Carreto Fernández, and Daniel Pérez Alonso (U.S. Department of Justice, 2005). In the raid, officials were able to locate and rescue the daughter of the woman who had contacted the U.S. embassy and four other trafficking victims (U.S. Department of Justice, 2005; ICE, 2007). Additionally, all but one of the children of the victims have been rescued by the Mexican government and reunited with their mothers in the United States (U.S. Department of Justice, 2007b).

Carreto Valencia was extradited from Mexico to the United States in January 2007. Although she initially denied wrongdoing, she later pleaded guilty (in 2008) and admitted that while in Mexico she received wire transfers from New York and that she was acutely aware that the funds were a byproduct of the commercial sexual exploitation of the women her sons trafficked from Mexico to the United States. Carreto Valencia pleaded guilty to one count of sex trafficking, in violation of 18 U.S.C. § 1591, Sex trafficking of children or by force, fraud, or coercion (DeWeese, 2004; U.S. Department of Justice, 2007a, 2007b; ICE, 2008; Semple, 2008).

Not only did Carreto Valencia manage the syndicate; she was also the recipient of the majority of the network's earnings (United States v. Carreto et al., 2009). The ring made hundreds of thousands of dollars in profits from forced commercial sexual exploitation of at least 50 women. The women were forced to have sex with up to 20 men per day and earned between $25 and $35 per act, which they were forced to give to the brothel owners and the Carretos. The Carretos and the brothel owners split the wages 50/50. With their cut, the Carretos wired money to family bank accounts in Mexico. The majority of money from their operations in both Mexico and New York went to Carreto Valencia (De-Weese, 2004; U.S. Department of Justice, 2007a, 2007b; ICE, 2008; Semple, 2008; United States v. Carreto et al., 2009).

At least three of the victims were forced to have abortions so that they could continue to be exploited for commercial sex (United States v. Carreto et al., 2009). One of the victims was raped and exposed to savage beatings by Pérez Alonso and also forced to watch the beatings of another victim by Josué Flores Carreto. Pérez Alonso controlled every aspect of the victim's life—she was not permitted to leave the apartment without a chaperone except to go to and from the brothels. The victim's purse was searched daily, and Pérez Alonso seized all monies found. Additionally, the victim faced physical brutality when she came home with less money than expected or when Pérez Alonso felt that she had disobeyed his orders. She became pregnant twice by Pérez Alonso and was forced to have abortions as a result (United States v. Carreto et al., 2009).

Another victim had a similar experience, and during the sentencing of the Flores Carreto brothers and Pérez Alonso, she responded when the issue of severity of sentencing was raised: "I just heard that it is not appropriate that they be sentenced to the number of years that they were sentenced because they did not kill anyone. But as far as I am concerned, it is a death. . . . I was five months pregnant when Josué arrived in New York. He caused me to abort and as far as I'm concerned . . . a human being [should not] be killed in that way (United States v. Carreto et al., 2009).

A source related to the case says the Carreto men would initially romance their young female victims. Some were just 17 years old, and at least one was only 14 years old at the time of trafficking. "Often the women were sitting in the plaza or attending weekend dances when they were approached by one of the men," said the source, who wished to remain anonymous. "Initially, it was a normal courtship. However, once the men managed to get the women alone they would rape them."[2] Once a victim was raped, physical isolation typically came next. Many of the women, said the source, were sent to the home of Carreto Valencia, where their movements were restricted:

> The Carreto Valencia home was a compound of buildings, further aiding in isolation. Carreto Valencia waged a psychological campaign of demeaning the women—treating them as worthless. Restraint does not have to be physical but rather a collection of coercive forces brought to bear on the victims such as psychological degradation, humiliation, shame, isolation, poverty, naïveté, and conflicting feelings about the traffickers.

Understandably, the women felt they were in a hopeless situation. Furthering the manipulation of the women, a number of the victims' children were kept in the physical custody of the Carreto family. "The consistent threat was that the children were going to be kept from their mothers if they did not cooperate," the source said. When the women were brought to the United States, the children remained in the physical custody of Carreto Valencia and other Carreto family members. The victims feared that they would never see their children if they did not follow their traffickers' orders. During the sentencing phase of the trial, one victim forced by Gerardo Flores Carreto to prostitute at the age of 14 asked the court to be reunited with her daughter: "The only thing I would like to ask you is that my daughter be returned to me because he took her away. She is eight years old and I don't even know her and they still have her. . . . I have an idea that she is with her [Carreto Valencia's] family but only because of the process that I am undergoing in Mexico for the custody" (United States v. Carreto et al., 2009).

TRAFFICKING WITHIN MEXICO

Men and boys from southern Mexico are subjected to forced labor in northern Mexico. Mexican forced-labor victims are also found in other parts the country. For example, on December 3, 2009, Mexico City police discovered 107 forced laborers making clothespins and shopping bags in a factory disguised as a drug rehabilitation center. Many of the workers had been kidnapped. Officials reported that the victims showed signs of physical and sexual abuse as well as malnourishment—they were given only rotten vegetables and chicken feet to eat. One of the workers escaped and informed the authorities. Twenty-three persons were arrested and charged with human trafficking in relation to this case (McAdams, 2010; U.S. Department of State, 2010). Child labor is used in Mexico in the production of green beans, chili peppers, coffee, cucumbers, eggplants, melons, onions, sugarcane, tobacco, tomatoes, and pornography (U.S. Department of Labor, 2009b).

Child-sex tourism is also growing in Mexico. Many child-sex tourists are from the United States, Canada, and western Europe. Unsurprisingly, the areas where child-sex tourism seems to be most prevalent are in tourist areas or northern border cities such as Acapulco, Cancún, Tijuana, and Ciudad Juárez. The Mexican government does not appear to prosecute sex tourists, but in 2007 it did assist with a U.S. child-sex tourism investigation involving a U.S. citizen in Ciudad Juárez. The defendant was convicted and sentenced in the United States (U.S. Department of State, 2008, 2010).

MEXICO AS A DESTINATION AND TRANSIT NATION

Persons from Central America, primarily from El Salvador, Guatemala, and Honduras are trafficked via Mexico into forced labor and the commercial sex trade in the United States and, to a lesser extent, Canada and western Europe. Persons from Africa, Asia, the Caribbean, eastern Europe, and South America are trafficked to Mexico for commercial sexual exploitation and forced labor, and some of these are trafficked on to the United States (U.S. Department of State, 2009, 2010). Central Americans, particularly Guatemalans, are trafficked to Mexico for forced labor, often in the agricultural industry. Unaccompanied minors from Central America who travel through Mexico to meet family members in the United States are vulnerable to human trafficking, particularly near the Guatemalan border (U.S. Department of State, 2010). Those identified as trafficking victims in Mexico from 2005 through 2007 were from Argentina (8 people), Honduras (4 people), other Central American nations (4 people), other South American nations (2 people), East Asia (2 people), and Central Europe (1 person) (UNODC, 2009).

WHAT HAPPENS TO VICTIMS AFTER TRAFFICKING

One concern with the 2007 federal anti-trafficking law is that the regulations required victims to press charges against their traffickers in order to obtain assistance. Gretchen Kuhner, founder and co-director of the Institute for Women in Migration in Mexico and author of the American Bar Association's *Human Trafficking Assessment Tool Report for Mexico*, said that a more humane and realistic prosecuting strategy would allow victims to receive assistance without having to first press charges against their traffickers. "Victims are often initially wary of law enforcement—they frequently feel like criminals themselves, are scared of deportation, and are fearful of pressing charges against their traffickers."[3] Prosecutors need strong witnesses, and victims need time away from the trafficking experience to trust law enforcement and to feel strong enough to participate in a criminal proceeding. "The reality is that prosecutors can't tell victims in good conscience that the trafficker[s] will likely be imprisoned if they agree to press charges, because chances are that the trafficker will not be imprisoned," so victims are understandably fearful of retribution.[4] In 2010 the National Institute of Migration (INM) issued a directive requiring immigration officials to offer foreign victims an unlimited period of reflection to determine whether they want to participate in the prosecution of their trafficker. Victims can also request to stay in the country without providing evidence against their traffickers. Currently this directive applies only to INM employees (U.S. Department of State, 2011).

Another problem with the 2007 law is that it did not contain a clause rendering victim consent irrelevant. Consequently, the burden of proof could shift to the victim if he or she was over the age of 18. It is unknown whether the issue of victim consent presented problems for prosecutors, as it was not raised in a federal prosecution. Kuhner believes the absence of a consent-is-irrelevant clause was due in part to a societal misperception that trafficking for commercial sexual exploitation is the same as prostitution, which is culturally tolerated in Mexico. Although prostitution is legal, pimping or running a brothel is not. Offenses related to prostitution are not typically prosecuted. When a case is pursued against a pimp, Kuhner explained, the prostitute has to identify that person:

> In the proceedings, the women have to identify their pimp. But that relationship is often complex—sometimes the pimp is her boyfriend or husband, and the women often end up dropping the charges. So, there is a frame of mind that a woman has to say that she was *not* consenting. This may be why the clause has not been included—there is a cultural assumption that a trafficking victim, at least in terms of commercial sexual exploitation, can consent.[5]

Today at least seven Mexican states have statutes that make victim consent irrelevant if any of the means of trafficking are established (ABA, 2009; U.S. Department of State, 2010). In 2010 there was a draft law under consideration by the Mexican Congress that would address the issue of consent, increase victim protections, and add clarification in the area of government responsibilities. In 2011 the government did enact reforms that raised trafficking to the level of a serious crime, established enhanced victim identity protections, and allowed for preventative detention of suspected traffickers, but the reforms did not address the issue of consent (U.S. Department of State, 2011, 2012). The issue of consent was not properly addressed until the passage of the new anti-trafficking law in 2012, Article 40 of which states that consent by the victim, regardless of age, will not constitute grounds for excluding criminal responsibility (Government of Mexico, 2012a).

The government has increased its focus on shelter availability for trafficking victims. Historically, although the social welfare agency operates shelters for children who are victims of violence (including trafficking victims), there has been a lack of government-funded shelters specifically oriented to trafficking victims. In 2007 the Attorney General's Office donated a residence, confiscated from a convicted drug trafficker, for use as a shelter geared to adolescent victims of human trafficking, specifically sexual exploitation. Camina A Casa was renovated, is fully operational, and is able to accommodate up to 25 victims. As of 2012, more than 100 girls have received long- or short-term care through the recovery program (USAID, 2009; U.S. Department of State, 2009; iEmpathize, 2012). In 2009 the Specialized Prosecutorial Unit for Violent Crimes against Women and Human Trafficking (FEVIMTRA) opened a high-security shelter in Mexico City specifically for female victims of sex trafficking and other violence including kidnapping, as well as to women whose family members have disappeared or been murdered. Victims are not allowed to leave the shelter unaccompanied, which the government states is because of safety concerns. The shelter is designed to provide legal, medical, and psychological services to victims. The nation's social welfare agency runs general shelters for children under the age of 13 who are victims of violence; it is unknown how many children housed in these shelters are trafficking victims. The government also supports a national network of shelters and emergency attention centers for female victims of violence, though few of these shelters offer specialized care for trafficking victims. The government continues to fail to provide adequate shelter services for male victims (ABA, 2009; U.S. Department of State, 2010, 2012).

Some NGOs also run shelters, which provide not only safe lodging but also social assistance and in some cases legal representation to trafficking victims (ABA, 2009; U.S. Department of State, 2009). Although the government frequently refers trafficking victims to NGOs, there has been little inclusion of NGO representatives in the interagency anti-trafficking committee. Such involvement would aid in gathering trafficking statistics (ABA, 2009; U.S. Department of State, 2009). Along with NGOs, some international and religious groups also provide shelter and services to trafficking victims. However, services in some regions remain inadequate, and some shelter organizers are fearful of retribution and are therefore reluctant to aid trafficking victims (U.S. Department of State, 2012).

The INM directive requires immigration officials to offer foreign victims the option to stay in the country, independent of any decision to testify against their traffickers. There is no official policy, Kuhner said, but the directive offers nonimmigrant status to victims of crimes or those eligible for humanitarian status. "Over 100 trafficking victims thus far have been able to regularize their immigration status. The theory is that they should be able to continue to renew their status every year for 10 years, and then become a permanent resident if they decide to remain in Mexico." Despite the directive, nongovernmental agencies and international organizations state that, in practice, legal alternatives to deportation are not often provided. Instead, officials sometimes hand over identified trafficking victims to INM for deportation because of their lack of legal status. Also, unidentified victims are often housed in detention centers and subsequently deported (U.S. Department of State, 2012).

WHAT HAPPENS TO TRAFFICKERS

The 2007 federal anti-trafficking law stipulated 6 to 12 years' imprisonment or 9 to 18 years' imprisonment if the victim was a child or lacked mental capacity. The penalty increased by half if the trafficker was a public official. In addition to imprisonment, the minimum sanctions against those found guilty of trafficking offenses included a fine of 500 to 1,500 days of the federal minimum wage, or between $2,462 and $7,386. Legal entities faced additional penalties such as dissolution and suspension. The 2012 anti-trafficking law increases penalties to up to 40 years' imprisonment, which can be increased to 60 years for violent crimes (EFE, 2012). Traffickers can face further charges under the Federal Criminal Code and state criminal codes that address trafficking-related crimes such as rape, murder, false imprisonment, and assault (ABA, 2009; U.S. Department of State, 2009, 2010).

The 2007 federal anti-trafficking law was sufficiently stringent, but implementation was not adequate, making evident the possible hurdles in the implementation of the 2012 anti-trafficking law. In some states, despite the fact that federal jurisdiction is invoked in organized-crime cases, traffickers are prosecuted as pimps under the individual state's criminal code. This is a less grave offense than trafficking, which under the federal law is a felony (ABA, 2009). Classifying trafficking cases as pimping can also significantly hinder the collection of accurate trafficking statistics. "Because trafficking cases typically utilize other offenses (such as pimping or smuggling) instead of anti-trafficking law, we have no way to know which of these cases are associated with trafficking," Kuhner said.

Like the U.S. anti-trafficking law, Mexico's federal anti-trafficking law covers only cases in which it is possible to prove federal jurisdiction. "This has caused problems for federal prosecutors," Kuhner said. "What prosecutors would like is for human trafficking to be a federal crime much like smuggling or organized crime." This hope was realized in 2011 when the government amended the constitution and established human trafficking as a serious crime (Government of Mexico, 2012b). Eighteen states have passed their own trafficking laws, helping to strengthen criminal codes and establishing state regulations for trafficking prevention, and all 31 states and the Federal District have added some sort of anti-trafficking penal code reforms, but not all the reforms outlaw every form of human trafficking. As a result, inconsistencies among state penal codes and laws on human trafficking cause confusion among law enforcement and problems in inter-state prosecutions (U.S. Department of State, 2011, 2012).

One hurdle in the nation's anti-trafficking efforts, according to Kuhner, is that local law enforcement, prosecutors, and judges are fearful of trying trafficking cases in areas where human trafficking is prevalent and organized crime is strong. Kuhner explained:

> They are fearful of prosecuting people that they know—friends, family, and neighbors. In some areas, such as Tenancingo, Tlaxcala, forcing women into prostitution has occurred for generations. It took place before the modern concept of trafficking. When it began, families initially forced women into prostitution within Tlaxcala. As the network expanded, women were sent to other areas in Mexico such as Tijuana. Over time this merged into an international trafficking network that occurs within migration networks.[6]

Law-enforcement officials are also wary of investigating and prosecuting trafficking cases for fear of retribution (ABA, 2009). This fear is not unwarranted; activists and political figures involved in trying to bring an end to organized crime in Mexico at times have been met with retribution. One such case is the brutal murder of José Nemesio

Lugo Félix, general coordinator of information at the National Center for Planning and Analysis to Combat Organized Crime. Lugo Félix was murdered in 2007 in Mexico City (U.S. Embassy in Mexico, 2007). "Nemesio Lugo Félix was heading up the anti-trafficking initiative," Kuhner said. "No one knows who murdered him—there was never any conclusion to the investigation. He had told a reporter here in Mexico that there was corruption within the government agencies. He had too much information and was pushing in the wrong places."

Even at the federal level, judges prefer to hear lesser criminal charges against traffickers—such as the charge of pimping—and have been reluctant to hear trafficking cases that use the federal anti-trafficking law (ABA, 2009). "Prosecutors report that judges often reject trafficking charges," Kuhner said. "They are told to use a different criminal charge, like pimping. This is likely in part because the concept of anti-trafficking law is new and judges are not familiar with it, but it is also likely in part because the judges are fearful around the topic of trafficking because of its association with organized-crime groups."

Despite these challenges, investigations, prosecutions, and some convictions do occur. In 2008 FEVIMTRA opened 24 trafficking investigations; 13 cases involved commercial sexual exploitation while 11 involved labor exploitation. In the same year FEVIMTRA filed a prosecution in a forced-labor case in the state of Chiapas. The Office of the Attorney General has prosecuted three cases involving the trafficking of women for commercial sexual exploitation. At least 10 state-level cases, 1 in Michoacán and 9 in Chihuahua, have utilized the charge of trafficking in persons (ABA, 2009; U.S. Department of State, 2009). The first conviction under the 2007 anti-trafficking law took place in December 2009, when a federal judge convicted five people. The offenders were convicted for trafficking Mexican women and girls to the United States for commercial sexual exploitation. Also in 2009 Mexico City's special prosecutor for trafficking sentenced a trafficker to 10 years' imprisonment (U.S. Department of State, 2010). In 2010 Mexico City's Attorney General's Office convicted four trafficking offenders. Sentences ranged from 4 to 17 years' imprisonment. In the same year the federal government, through FEVIMTRA, also attained its first conviction and sentence for forced labor. The trafficker, who was sentenced to 9 years' imprisonment, has appealed his sentence. In 2011 Mexican authorities at the federal and state levels convicted 14 traffickers. All of the convicted offenders were sex traffickers; there were no known convictions of forced-labor traffickers. Sentences ranged from 6 to 16½ years' imprisonment (U.S. Department of State, 2012). In March 2011 Jean Succar Kuri, a prominent Cancún businessman who forced children into prostitution, was convicted of child pornography and corruption of minors. He was sentenced to 13 years' imprisonment and ordered to pay $6,585.93 in fines and $26,854.08 to each of the victims. A federal court increased his sentence to 112.5 years in August 2011, though under the Federal Criminal Code Succar Kuri faces a maximum of 60 years' imprisonment (Alcocer, 2011; Mosso, 2011).

INTERNAL EFFORTS TO DECREASE TRAFFICKING

Although the former federal anti-trafficking law was passed in 2007, the regulations to the law were not issued until February 27, 2009 (ABA, 2009). The long-term impact of the 2011 and 2012 regulations remains to be seen. The lack of formal procedures among most states for identifying trafficking victims in vulnerable populations—such as migrant workers and people in prostitution—remains an issue. Still, there is some progress. The government does periodically raid brothels in order to identify victims of commercial sexual exploitation. For instance, in 2011 authorities in Ciudad Juarez raided two dozen bars, hotels, and boarding houses. In the raids they arrested 1,030 persons (500 men and 530 women) suspected of human trafficking and sexual exploitation (U.S. Department of State, 2010; CNN, 2011a). Also, Mexican immigration agents have implemented a system for identifying potential trafficking victims—particularly children—entering or exiting Mexico, and referring these victims to care providers. In 2009, 1,333 migration officers received anti-trafficking training that focused on identifying and interviewing trafficking victims. Government-sponsored training on identifying human trafficking does take place, but NGOs report that many state and local public officials do not differentiate between human trafficking offenses and smuggling (U.S. Department of State, 2010, 2012). Additionally, training of judges on federal anti-trafficking law has been inadequate (ABA, 2009). "There has not been systematic and ongoing training of judges," Kuhner said. "Additionally, it is difficult to convince the judges to change and accept prosecutors classifying the crimes as trafficking."

NGOs also report that a number of public officials, local law enforcement, and immigration personnel are corrupt. These officials help traffickers to falsify documents, discourage victims from reporting crimes, ignore trafficking activity, and accept bribes and sexual services in exchange for their collusion (U.S. Department of State, 2009, 2010, 2012). Kuhner said that bribery is extremely prevalent:

> People pay off witnesses, judges, and prosecutors. To a trafficker everything is negotiable. There are obviously exceptions, but Mexico is still extremely weak in terms of corruption within the criminal justice system. Public opinion of the system is that politicians and persons in power [operate with] impunity. Currently, criminal cases are closed to the public. The secretive nature of the process makes it easy to see how corruption would occur.[7]

Still, on rare occasions some corrupt officials do face investigations, prosecution, and conviction. For instance, in 2007 two immigration officials were arrested for their leadership in a crime syndicate that included human trafficking. In December 2010 the officials were convicted and received sentences of 12 and 8 years' imprisonment, respectively. In 2009 a high-level immigration official was investigated for suspected involvement in human trafficking, but was officially cleared by a federal judge in 2010. In 2011 there were no reported prosecutions or convictions of public officials for trafficking offenses (U.S. Department of State, 2011, 2012).

In 2008 the constitution was reformed to transform the criminal judicial system from an inquisitorial to an adversarial one. Kuhner believes this should change the way investigations are handled. "The basic presumption of innocent until proven guilty should be implemented," Kuhner said. "There will be more open trials where lawyers are able to present their cases orally instead of through filing documents with the judge. This will change how evidence is produced and presented. Additionally, the trials will be more open—the public will be allowed to observe."[8]

The criminal justice system of Mexico does not include juries; thus the judge alone considers witness testimony and how much weight, if any, should be given to it. Part of the reform is the inclusion of a *juez de control,* a judge in charge of ensuring due process for the person under investigation and the effective application of criminal law (Hernández, 2008; Justice in Mexico Project, 2009). The introduction of the due process judge creates separation of powers in the judiciary, as the judge who determines whether a suspect is indictable is not the same person who will make a final determination of guilt. The due process judge will ensure that a criminal case is properly handled during the investigation, preliminary hearing, and indictment, and is responsible for determining whether a suspect's rights should be limited during the trial phase (such as by a restraining order, detention, or house arrest) and whether he should be released on bail or on his own recognizance until a verdict is delivered. The due process judge will issue the final sentence in cases in which the defendant accepts a plea bargain, and will oversee alternate dispute resolution processes, such as the use of mediation (Shirk, 2010). Theoretically, the due process judge will be a safeguard against corruption and ensure the proper use of the investigative process. Thus far, implementation of comprehensive reform of the criminal justice system has been slow. Only a handful of states have made substantive changes (HRW, 2012). Because of lack of efficiency and transparency in the criminal justice system, less than 25 percent of crimes are reported, and only 1 percent to 2 percent of crimes result in sentencing (Shirk, 2010).

In 2011 then-president Felipe Calderón approved several changes to Mexico's constitution aimed at cracking down on human trafficking. The decree amends Articles 19, 20, and 73 of the Federal Constitution. Article 19 was amended to add human trafficking to the list of crimes for which a judge will order the preventative detention of an alleged offender, meaning that those accused of human trafficking will be imprisoned during trials. Article 73 was amended to empower the Federal Congress to issue federal laws on human trafficking. Article 20 was amended to include a guarantee to protect victim identity and personal data in compliance with the minimum safety measures required in criminal proceedings (CNN, 2011a; Gutierrez, 2011). "It is important that they [victims] can give their testimony to the authorities and to society without being at risk," then-president Calderón said (CNN, 2011b).

The former president gave Mexico's Congress 180 days from the date of the decree, July 14, 2011, to approve a new nationwide human-trafficking law that would reform and streamline how authorities handle such cases across the country. "There are thousands and thousands of cases, in a society that is still unaware of the seriousness of this crime," he said. "We have to break through this curtain . . . that is hiding from the Mexicans a criminal reality that is in front of us" (CNN, 2011a). In August 2012 Mexico's lower house of Congress passed an anti–human-trafficking bill that establishes preventative and punitive measures and provides aid to victims. Signed into law by then-president Calderón in June 2012, the new law includes sentences of up to 40 years for offenders convicted of sexual exploitation and abuse, which can be increased to 60 years. It also creates a fund to provide care to victims. The law targets not just the traffickers themselves but also the entire chain of exploitation, ranging from persons who entrap victims, to those who exploit them, to those who hold them against their will, to the clients who pay for sexual services with the victims (EFE, 2012; Government of Mexico, 2012a; Mexico Institute, 2012). The new law sets out to improve coordination for the prevention, prosecution, and punishment of human trafficking among the federal, state, and municipal levels of government. It also grants additional tools to investigators, such as tracking people and cooperating with informants. Repatriation of victims is examined more holistically, and victims in danger of retribution in their country of origin are not to be deported. Also, the law mandates reparations to victims in a comprehensive manner and the creation of a Fund for Protection and Assistance to Victims of Trafficking in Persons Crimes, which will include the confiscated property of offenders. In addition to the above reforms, Calderón also amended the Penal Code to criminalize femicide—the killing of a woman because of gender—punishable by 40 to 60 years' imprisonment. In September 2012 a coordination center for the investigation and prosecution of crimes on trafficking in persons was created to improve the coordination of trafficking cases. Part of the Attorney General's Office, the agency is tasked with investigating and prosecuting trafficking offenses when committed by organized crime, and with establishing emergency mechanisms to assist victims of crime. The agency can receive complaints and has the power to order arrests of alleged perpetrators (CNN, 2012a, 2012b; EFE, 2012; Government of Mexico, 2012a, 2012b).

While the above changes are essential and significant steps, not all recent measures taken by the government have been positive. For instance, the government reduced the budget for the National Program to Prevent and Combat Trafficking to $313,000 from $4.2 million in 2011 because of budgetary issues. Additionally, in September 2011, then-president Calderón established Provictima, a new agency designed to assist victims of all crimes. In order to support the new agency, funding was shifted from other agencies, including FEVIMTRA. The division of responsibilities between Provictima and FEVIMTRA is unclear. Some experts have indicated that Provictima has an inadequate budget and facilities and unqualified personnel (Brundage, 2012; U.S. Department of State, 2012).

The Mexican government, specifically FEVIMTRA, distributes anti-trafficking materials as part of its anti-trafficking campaign (U.S. Department of State, 2009). Such approaches are of doubtful effectiveness in reaching potential victims. "Prevention campaigns need to be targeted to certain sectors," Kuhner said. "It can be beneficial to inform persons in harvesting camps or prostitutes on their rights and how to identify trafficking, but the information and type of campaign should be specific to each audience."

Mexico participates in bilateral cooperative anti-trafficking agreements with Guatemala, El Salvador, and the United States. Under these agreements, the nations pledge to exchange information for the purposes of investigating, prosecuting, and extraditing those who have committed trafficking offenses. Mexico is part of the Regional Committee against Trafficking in Persons in Mexico, Central America, and the Caribbean; the Regional Conference on Migration; and High Level Groups on Border Security with Guatemala and Belize. Mexico cooperates with the United States through the Security and Prosperity Partnership for North America; the Operation against Smugglers (and Traffickers) Initiative on Safety and Security; and the Plenary Group for Law Enforcement and its Subcommittee on Trafficking in Persons (ABA, 2009).

Still, cooperation between Mexico and other nations does not always occur without a hitch. This can be seen in the case of the Carreto family. Propelled by the U.S.-Mexico anti-trafficking partnership, the traffickers Carreto Valencia and Velásquez Reyes were found and arrested by Mexican authorities. Yet the Mexican government released Velásquez Reyes and did not extradite her to the United States. She remains a fugitive, and U.S. officials believe that she remains in Mexico (U.S. Department of Justice, 2006, 2009). An anonymous source states that Velásquez Reyes and Carreto Valencia were arrested in Mexico after the case broke in the media. "However, after a year and a half, the Mexican cases were dismissed or Velásquez Reyes and Carreto Valencia were acquitted," the source said. "While both women were named in the U.S. indictment, only Consuelo was produced and sent to the U.S., while María was let go."

There have been some convictions under Mexico's 2007 federal anti-trafficking law, but judges remain hesitant to allow cases to move forward under federal anti-trafficking law. They prefer that prosecutors press charges utilizing other laws, such as pimping. The result is that traffickers receive lighter sentences. Trying trafficking cases under different crimes also poses a challenge to obtaining accurate trafficking statistics. Judges and prosecutors need to obtain thorough training on the 2012 federal anti-trafficking law so that its use in courts can increase and offenders can be properly prosecuted and sentenced.

The Mexican government and NGOs appear to have established a strong relationship. However, including more NGO representatives in the government's interagency anti-trafficking committee would help create a more comprehensive perspective on trafficking within the nation and would aid in gathering trafficking statistics. Finally, although the comprehensive reform of the criminal justice system is significant and positive, slow implementation has allowed for continued corruption and inequality.

PART XII
Poverty and Economic Boom

When rapid economic growth moves nations such as Russia and Brazil out of decades of comparative poverty, the inevitable dislocations change the patterns of human trafficking there. As a nation experiences economic development it becomes attractive to migrant workers from other nations and also draws nationals from poorer sections to wealthier ones. By 2020 Russia and Brazil, along with China and India, are expected to be among the world's six largest economies.

As rapid growth in the Russian economy brings constant increases in the cost of living, the average Russian struggles ever harder to make ends meet. The poverty rate continues to decline, but progress has been slow. Those who are economically marginalized still have incentives to migrate to wealthier areas in Russia or to other nations, and they remain vulnerable to exploitation and human rights abuses, including human trafficking. The large cities are also epicenters of trafficking homeless and orphaned children for prostitution, pornography, begging, and selling drugs or stolen goods. During such times of great economic change, the supply of potential victims seems unlimited. As a result, traffickers have no financial incentive to ensure victims' well-being or health.

In 2011 Brazil became the world's sixth-largest economy. The nation has vast natural resources and a growing middle class. Some experts believe that the growing middle class is helping improve the trafficking situation within Brazil, particularly by decreasing the number of child laborers. But income inequality remains high, and the pairing of poverty with a booming economy and a need for inexpensive labor in the burgeoning agricultural sector creates a scenario for potential exploitation and human trafficking. Today Brazil leads the biofuel movement with sugarcane ethanol, and at least half of forced laborers in the country have been found on sugarcane plantations. The average life expectancy of sugarcane cutters—from the time they begin work—is 10 years. Anti-trafficking experts would be among the first to challenge the claim that sugarcane ethanol is a "clean" fuel.

CHAPTER 23

Russia

> A woman came up to me at the train station. She offered me part-time work in Germany as a nanny. I said "yes." When I got there, though, she took away my passport. Then she drove me to a bar on the edge of town.
>
> —NATASHA, SEX-TRAFFICKING VICTIM

The depiction of young Russian women as sex slaves is sensationalized in movies and the media. A decade ago this image was not necessarily false, but recently the number of Russian citizens trafficked abroad appears to have significantly declined. One reason is probably the nation's economic resilience. Like other nations, Russia was adversely affected by the 1998 and 2008 global economic crises. Yet it maintained consistent economic growth after each crisis, averaging 7 percent economic growth since 1998, 4.1 percent growth in 2010, and 4.8 percent GDP expansion in the third quarter of 2011 over the same quarter in 2010. While growth is projected to continue, Kaspar Richter, the World Bank's country sector coordinator for economic policy in Russia, projects that the rate of growth will decline from 4.3 percent in 2011 to 3.5 percent in 2012, and stay at 3.6 percent in 2013 (Economy Watch, 2010; Trading Economics, 2011; International Business Times, 2011; World Bank in Russia, 2012). According to Jim O'Neill, chairman of asset management at Goldman Sachs, along with Brazil, India, and China, Russia will soon enter the top five world economies. O'Neill, who coined the acronym BRICs (Brazil, Russia, India, and China) to designate the four emerging economies, believes that by 2020 the four economies will be responsible for nearly 50 percent of the increase in global GDP (Inman, 2011; Goldman Sachs, 2011; Reuters, 2011; Polina, 2011). These boosts in economic growth have resulted in a need for affordable labor, making this source and transit nation also a destination for human trafficking (U.S. Department of State, 2010). The Migration Research Center estimates that 1 million people are exposed to exploitative labor conditions characteristic of human trafficking in Russia, such as withholding of documents and pay, physical abuse, and poor living conditions (U.S. Department of State, 2012).

Exact statistics on the amount of trafficking that occurs in Russia are impossible to come by. According to Tatyana Azhakina, chief deputy head of the Criminal Investigation Department of Russia's Interior Ministry, the number of identified trafficking cases declined by 50 percent from 2010 to 2011. "If we talk figures, 58 cases [of] human trafficking were opened in 2008, 94 in 2009, 103 in 2010, and 48 in the first 11 months of this year," Azhakina said at a December 2011 international conference on combatting human trafficking (ITAR-TASS, 2011c). Of course, the number of identified cases does not typically reflect the actual number of trafficking cases, and although these data could illustrate a decrease in human trafficking, it may instead reflect a decrease in the proper identification of victims and a lack of data collection of all trafficking-related offenses. Despite specific anti-trafficking laws, traffickers are often charged under lesser offenses. Offenders charged under anti-trafficking Articles 127.1 (used against sex traffickers) and 127.2 (used against forced-labor traffickers) of the Criminal Code face up to 6 years' imprisonment and up to 5 years' imprisonment, respectively (U.S. Department of State, 2008, 2010; UNODC, 2009a; McCarthy, 2010). The country lags behind in identifying victims and the post-trafficking experience. Few municipalities in Russia have systems in place to identify trafficking victims. When victims are identified there are minimal resources to aid and address their needs, as the government does not supply adequate funding to local anti-trafficking NGOs.

RUSSIA AS A DESTINATION AND TRANSIT NATION

Russia is a destination and transit country for both forced labor and commercial sexual exploitation (Chance, 2008). There is debate over which form of trafficking, overall, is more prevalent in Russia. For instance, Chief Deputy Azhakina stated in December 2011 that roughly 70 percent of victims in Russia were trafficked for the purpose of sexual slavery, while 24 percent were victims of forced labor (ITAR-TASS, 2011a). On the contrary, the International Labour Organization reported in May 2009 that while the global spotlight has predominantly focused on sex trafficking, forced labor of undocumented and documented workers is the most predominant form of trafficking in Russia (ILO, 2009). Second only to the United States, Russia has one of the largest migration populations in the world (HRW, 2009; Narizhnaya, 2011). "The huge movements of people mean there will always be space for traffickers to exploit the situation," said Enrico Ponziani, then-Moscow chief of mission for the International Organization for Migration (IOM) (Narizhnaya, 2011). The Ministry of Internal Affairs and border-authority statistics reveal that more than 12 million migrants enter Russia each year. Determining the exact number of migrants who work in Russia is tricky. Official statistics—based on work permits—showed that there were 460,000 labor migrants with work permits in 2004, but of course many migrant workers are illegal and do not have work permits. Experts estimate that labor migrants probably account for between 5 and 7 percent of the workforce in Russia, inhabiting a shadow economy that is estimated to make up between 22.4 and 40 percent of the nation's GDP. The lack of safe migration channels and legislative protections often leads migrants to take risks that place them in precarious positions (Tiurukanova, 2006).

It is estimated that two-thirds of illegal migrants in Russia are from other member nations of the Commonwealth of Independent States (CIS); this is likely so because of the transparent borders between member states (Tiurukanova, 2006).[1] The high prevalence of human trafficking-related exploitation against CIS migrants working in the shadow economy can be seen in Moscow and Stavropol. Of interviewed CIS workers in Moscow and Stavropol, 25 percent and 47 percent, respectively, had been coerced to work with no payment or vague payment terms; the movements of 31 percent and 26 percent of the workers were restricted; 30 percent and 15 percent of the women interviewed were forced to prostitute; 13 percent and 6 percent experienced physical abuse; 27 percent and 35 percent experienced psychological abuse; passports were confiscated in 23 percent and 24 percent of cases; and debt dependency resulted in 18 percent and 16 percent of cases (Tiurukanova, 2006). Men, women, and children from Belarus, Kyrgyzstan,

Moldova, Tajikistan, Ukraine, and Uzbekistan are subjected to forced labor in Russia—often in the construction industry, in textile shops, and in agriculture (U.S. Department of State, 2010). A 2011 case involved citizens of Uzbekistan who recruited workers there and helped them with the necessary documents. When the workers arrived in Vladivostok, Russia, the traffickers took away their passports and forced the victims to work without pay at construction sites and in the agricultural sector (ITAR-TASS, 2011b). It is not just citizens of CIS countries who experience trafficking; traffickers also subject about 40,000 North Koreans to forced labor conditions in Russia's Far East logging industry. The Democratic People's Republic of North Korea (DPRK) regime continues to recruit workers for bilateral contracts with Russia and other foreign governments, providing contract labor for logging camps operated by North Korean companies in the Russian Far East. There are reports that the DPRK government withholds up to 85 percent of the workers' wages and controls their movements (U.S. Department of State, 2010, 2012). According to a report by E. V. Tiurukanova and the Institute for Urban Economics for the UN/IOM Working Group on Trafficking in Human Beings, trafficking for labor exploitation is the most common type of human trafficking in Russia:

> Based on the figure that 10–30 percent of all illegal migrants in Russia, i.e., 3–5 million people, face some form of human trafficking-related or slavery-related exploitation, it is possible to estimate that the number of victims of such exploitation among migrants coming to Russia approaches 1 million. While this assumption does not mean that all these people are permanent victims of trafficking, it does suggest that these individuals do form an at-risk group, whose position may near slavery. (Tiurukanova, 2006: p. 35)

Yelena Burtina of the Moscow-based human rights group Civic Assistance says that foreign workers are often enticed by the assurance of good working conditions. When they arrive in Russia their travel documents are withheld, and they often face nonpayment and police harassment. "There is no need to force them to stay in their workplace because they have nowhere to go with no money and no documents,"

Burtina told *Radio Free Europe/Radio Liberty*. "As soon as they step out of the door, they are going to be detained by police. So there is no need to chain them and force them to stay" (Saidazimova, 2008). In June 2008 police raided a worksite and found 50 Uzbek migrant laborers forced to work 14-hour workdays without pay. The women on the site also reportedly faced sexual abuse (Saidazimova, 2008). Other examples of forced labor or exploitative conditions are employers who sell their laborers for a nominal fee (a little more than $100 each) or persons who obtain what seems to be legitimate employment but are simply not paid for their labor. One such example is a migrant laborer from Uzbekistan who was never paid for a job that he performed in Moscow. "Last winter, we built three cottages, but haven't been paid yet," the laborer told *Radio Free Europe/Radio Liberty* (Saidazimova, 2008). Migrant workers from Tajikistan were recruited in 2008 through television advertisements that featured a Ministry of Interior of Tajikistan representative complimenting the employment agency Vostok-Farm. The workers signed agreements with Vostok-Farm to work in construction, but upon arrival their passports were withheld and they were forced to dig stones in quarries with mere hand tools. When some of the workers refused to comply, they were told: "Whether you want to work or not, you will work. We will deport you." The victims worked in the quarries for 85 days without pay and were forced to live in an abandoned refrigerator truck and two cargo containers with dirty mats and cots. For the entire period they were given only two large containers of water; in desperation they frequently drank rainwater from puddles or water that they boiled from a nearby swamp. Workers who refused to work were not given food for two days. The IOM commissioned Yakub Marufov, a lawyer, to investigate the case, where he found slavery-like conditions. "I saw that indeed the conditions were horrible," Marufov told Human Rights Watch. "The cargo trailers were not equipped for people to live in, and there was no potable water." The next day a representative of the Migration Service of the Ministry of Interior of Tajikistan and Russian Federal Migration Service (FMS) officials arrived on the worksite. The FMS fined the employer for illegal employment of foreigners and forced him to return the workers' passports. However, when the General Prosecutor's Office of Tajikistan opened an investigation into possible trafficking in persons, the case was closed for lack of evidence of a crime (HRW, 2009).

People are also trafficked to Russia for commercial sexual exploitation. Victims from Africa and Central Asia are lured with false promises of legitimate employment or educational opportunities; others are kidnapped (Chance, 2008; U.S. Department of State, 2010). Children from Ukraine and Moldova are subjected to forced prostitution and forced begging in Moscow and St. Petersburg. Russia is also a transit nation for those trafficked to the United Arab Emirates from Armenia and Uzbekistan for commercial sexual exploitation. In 2004 Russia's Ministry of Internal Affair's Department to Fight Organized Crime and Terrorism and police authorities in Armenia collaborated in the prosecution of an organized criminal group that trafficked women from Armenia to Dubai through Moscow for commercial sexual exploitation (Tiurukanova, 2006). Russia is a source nation for sex tourists and remains a destination for child sexual tourism. The sexual tourists who travel to Russia are primarily from the United States and western Europe (U.S. Department of State, 2008, 2010). In 2004 two British citizens and Moscow pimps made an agreement over the Internet regarding the sexual services of boys under the age of 14. The pimps were found guilty of enticing vulnerable male minors into prostitution whom they sold for a fee to men for sexual exploitation. In relation to this case Moscow's Central District Prosecutor's Office opened a criminal case for the offense of trafficking in minors as well other charges (Tiurukanova, 2006). Alexander Krasnov of the Ministry of Interior Police blames poorly controlled migration and lack of legislation on the trafficking scenario in Russia. "First of all, we have virtually open borders, and badly controlled migration flows from nearby countries," Krasnov said. "Secondly, we still don't have a basic law that defines victims' rights. At the moment, it's mostly aid agencies that deal with it" (Chance, 2008).

TRAFFICKING WITHIN RUSSIA AND TRAFFICKING ABROAD

The Russian economy continues to grow, but with an average monthly salary of $737.50 (September 2011 estimate) the average Russian still struggles to make ends meet. The cost of living in Russia is high, and even the cost of essential food fluctuates. Fifty-three percent of the population earns only enough for food, clothing, and utilities (Alexandrova, 2011). Average monthly wages vary widely by location; for instance, the average monthly salary in Moscow is $1,219.26 compared to $406.20 in Orel. The minimum monthly wage in most regions is $145 (WageIndicator Foundation, 2011). Although the poverty rate has steadily declined, the progress has been slow. The poverty rate was 12.8 percent in 2011—affecting roughly 18.1 million people—compared to 12.6 percent in 2010, 13 percent in 2009, 13.4 percent in 2008, 13.3 percent in 2007, and 15.2 percent in 2006. The projected poverty rates for 2012 and 2013 are 12.2 and 12.3 percent, respectively (World Bank in Russia, 2012).

The weighty burden of poverty makes Russians vulnerable to trafficking within Russia and abroad. While there is often a focus on the instability that results from international migration, the adverse effects of migration also affect those who migrate from one part of a nation to another. Data suggest that the majority of women in the commercial sex industry in Russia's large cities are migrants from other nations or from neighboring small towns and villages. It is estimated that more than half of Moscow's commercial sex workers have lived in Moscow for less than one year, while the remainder have lived in Moscow for no more than two to five years. The lack of a network and support makes them more vulnerable to exploitation and human rights abuses, including human trafficking. Young girls are particularly vulnerable. One trafficking case revealed more than 20 girls from the ages of 15 to 17 recruited by criminal gang members in Borisoglebsk City, Russia, for waitress jobs in Moscow. Instead the girls were forced to work as prostitutes in brothels or along highways. Those who did not earn the requisite $2,800 per month faced physical and psychological abuse (Tiurukanova, 2006).

Russian men, women, and children are also subjected to debt bondage and forced labor in Russia's agricultural and fishing sectors, the construction industry, and in textile shops. Russian children are trafficked to St. Petersburg and Moscow for forced begging and commercial sexual exploitation (U.S. Department of State, 2008, 2010). An estimated 560,000 Russian children are homeless, and thus at risk of abuses, including labor exploitation. Homeless and orphaned children are particularly vulnerable to involvement in the informal economy, such as prostitution, pornography, begging, and selling drugs or stolen goods. While involving a minor in prostitution and creating or circulating pornography depicting a known minor are punishable under the Criminal Code, the Criminal Code does not include a definition of child pornography, nor does it criminalize the possession of child pornography. The primary hubs for child trafficking and the commercial sexual exploitation of children are Moscow and St. Petersburg (U.S. Department of State, 2008, 2010; U.S. Department of Labor, 2010).

Under the Labor Code, the minimum age of employment is 16. Children who have completed their general education and are 15 years of age may work; also, children 14 and older may work in the performing arts, so long as the work will not harm their health or moral development. Children under 18 are prohibited from engaging in night work, dangerous work, underground work, or labor that may be harmful to their health or moral development. This includes carrying heavy loads and the production, transportation, and sale of toxic substances, including tobacco, alcohol, and drugs (U.S. Department of Labor, 2010). Regardless of the law, children work on the street performing dangerous activities such as repairing cars, collecting trash, and carrying heavy loads. In rural areas children primarily work in the agricultural sector. As a result, many children are exposed to potentially dangerous machinery, tools, and harmful pesticides, and are made to carry heavy loads. The Federal Labor and Employment Service, which is responsible for enforcing child-labor laws, reported 10,000 violations in 2008 (U.S. Department of Labor, 2009, 2010).

Russian men and women are trafficked to Armenia, China, Japan, the Middle East, and South Korea, for forced labor. Women from Russia are trafficked for commercial sexual exploitation in Australia, China, Germany, Greece, Israel, Italy, Japan, the Middle East, New Zealand, Poland, Spain, South Africa, South Korea, Thailand, Turkey, and Vietnam. Also, Russian women and children are trafficked to Kazakhstan and forced into prostitution (U.S. Department of State, 2008, 2010; U.S. Department of Labor, 2010).

It was during the fading existence of the Soviet Union that, according to Louise I. Shelley, professor at George Mason University and founder and director of the Terrorism, Transnational Crime and Corruption Center, there was a startling increase in prostitution at hotels and restaurants. "But this was not the familiar sight of poorly educated prostitutes soliciting men on the streets. Often the women were multilingual and educated. Never alone, they were always accompanied by highly visible thugs, the most typical gangster element of organized crime" (Shelley, 2010: p. 18). There is a close relationship between organized crime and the commercial sex industry in Russia, and experts believe that many of the women involved are victims of trafficking. In 2001 Russian and French authorities discovered an organized criminal group in Russia that recruited Russian women to work in France as dancers and waitresses at variety shows and strip clubs. The traffickers use forged documents to get the women into France and then, through threats and physical abuse, forced them to prostitute on the street without pay. The traffickers were from Armenia, France, Georgia, Russia, and the former Yugoslavia. After the fall of communism there was a flow of women and girls from Russia and other eastern European nations dispersed globally into the sex trade. Common points of transport out of Russia, among others, were the Baltic route through Lithuania, the central European route through Warsaw and Prague, the Caucasus (or Georgian) transit route, routes through Egypt, and the China-Siberia and the China–Primorsky Region routes (Tiurukanova, 2006). The women were dubbed "the Natashas"; in fact any woman from eastern Europe— regardless of whether she was from the Czech Republic, Moldova, Romania, Russia, or Ukraine—was given the name (Malarek, 2004). A 2006 report estimated that between one-fifth and one-third of the 175,000 women who left Russia each year—between 35,000 and 58,333—were victims of trafficking (Tiurukanova, 2006). Shelley stated that unlike in China, where the trafficking style lends itself more to long-term business activity, the human trafficking business in Russia is more oriented toward immediate profit. "The Russians, who historically have been sellers of natural resources rather than traders, treat their trafficking business as a commodity market," wrote Shelley in a 2005 book. "The human resource of women is plundered like the precious metals, oil, and gas of the former Soviet Union with no thought to the investment of the profit of this trade in the domestic economy" (Stoecker & Shelley, 2005).

More recently the number of Russian citizens identified as international trafficking victims has decreased, at least in Europe and Turkey. In Germany, Russian citizens accounted for a large share of the trafficking victims identified from 2002 through 2005, ranging from around 11 percent to 25 percent. This decreased in 2006 and 2007 to a little over 5 percent. A similar pattern is seen in Turkey, where from 2004 through 2008 the number of identified Russian trafficking victims decreased from more than 25 percent to 5 percent. In Spain, identified Russian trafficking victims decreased from 9 percent in 2001 to 3.5 percent in 2006 (UNODC, 2009b). Despite the decrease, the trafficking of Russian citizens abroad is still a significant problem. Some victims are lured by supposed well-paid jobs such as nanny or waitress positions that are advertised in local Russian newspapers. Other victims are approached and offered employment. One such victim was offered a nanny position while she stood at a train station. "A woman came up to me at the train station," the victim ("Natasha") told *BBC News*. "She offered me part-time work in Germany as a nanny. I said 'yes.' When I got there, though, she took away my passport. Then she drove me to a bar on the edge of town" where she was forced to prostitute (Rosenberg, 2003).

Mariana Solomatova of the Angel Coalition said that legitimate employment is a common tactic. "Natasha's no exception," Solomatova told *BBC News*. "Most women don't expect to be enslaved—they think they're going for legitimate work, like nannies or waitresses. In most cases their passports are taken away. They're threatened. They're told they'll go to prison. They're too afraid to complain" (Rosenberg, 2003). In order to uncover the workings of the Russian trafficking mafia, reporter Yaroslava Tankova went undercover and attached herself to a group of women who had been offered waitress positions overseas. The women were trafficked through Egypt and smuggled across the desert into Israel. Upon arrival the women had their passports confiscated and were sold into the Israeli sex trade. "One of the girls nearly died from sunstroke," Tankova told *Russia Today*. "Another was raped by an Arab guard. He used a plastic bag instead of a condom. We were treated like meat. One man hit me, but the other guards intervened. They didn't want the commodity spoilt before it was sold" (Russia Today, 2008).

Victims not only face rape, beatings, and other abuses, but sometimes they are killed. This may be what happened to Oxana Rantseva, a Russian languages student trafficked to Cyprus. After accepting a job as a translator, the 20-year-old was instead forced to sign a dancing contract. "Oxana didn't expect that she would have to work as a dancer, and she especially did not expect that she would have to perform [sexual services]," attorney Lyudmila Churkina told the *Moscow News* (Arutunyan, 2010). Nine days after Oxana escaped, Marios Athanasiou—the manager of the nightclub Zigos Cabaret, where Oxana was forced to work—found her in a disco and took her to the police. Officials believe that Athanasiou had hoped police would deport Oxana so that he could get another dancer to replace her, but police found Oxana's status legal and asked Athanasiou to take her to an immigration office at 7 a.m. (Arutunyan, 2010). At 6 a.m. Athanasiou took Oxana to the apartment of another Zigos Cabaret employee. Just half an hour later Oxana was found dead in the street. The balcony of the apartment was open, and a bedspread was tied to a railing (Arutunyan, 2010). A Cyprus court ruled in 2001 that Oxana's death was an accident, but a separate autopsy conducted in Russia found that she may have been killed. Russian forensic officials found "that Ms. Rantseva had died in strange and [unclear] circumstances requiring additional investigation, [which] were forwarded to the Cypriot authorities." Russian officials' request for a new investigation was denied (Arutunyan, 2010).

Oxana's father, Nikolai Rantsev, filed suit in the European Court for Human Rights in Strasbourg. The court found that Cyprus and Russia had failed to protect Oxana from human trafficking and fined Cyprus $53,544 and Russia $2,677.20 (Arutunyan, 2010). After the ruling, Cyprus acknowledged that it had violated articles of the Convention for the Protection of Human Rights and Fundamental Freedoms, and agreed to pay damages to Rantsev. It also appointed three independent criminal investigators to probe into Oxana's death. Russia, which has not ratified the Council of Europe Convention on Action Against Trafficking in Human Beings, has yet to respond to the ruling (Burkov, 2010; Arutunyan, 2010; ECHR, 2010). The Parliamentary Assembly of the Council of Europe (PACE) has asked Russia to sign and ratify the convention. "Russia will have to change its legislation," Jannick Devaux, PACE representative of the assembly's Equal Opportunities Committee, told the *Moscow News*. Because the Duma has to ratify it, "it will take some time, but the faster they do it the better" (Arutunyan, 2010).

WHAT HAPPENS TO VICTIMS AFTER TRAFFICKING

Russia's anti-trafficking response is not victim-centered, nor does it sufficiently recognize human trafficking as a violation of the rights of the individual (Tiurukanova, 2006). The government has not developed or employed a formal system to guide officials in proactive identification of trafficking victims. Identified foreign victims are not always referred to NGOs for assistance but instead held in detention centers and deported. For instance, in January 2010 the government placed four identified victims of sex trafficking from Africa in a temporary detention facility for foreign nationals pending deportation, instead of referring them to NGOs for assistance. It is unknown whether the victims were deported (U.S. Department of State, 2010, 2012). The number of victims referred by the government to obtain assistance appears to be decreasing. In 2008 roughly 56 victims were referred for assistance by authorities compared to "at least" 12 victims in 2009. It is difficult to determine how many victims the government or NGOs have assisted, as there continue to be no official statistics on the matter (U.S. Department of State, 2010, 2012). Few municipalities have referral and identification systems in place. Although 226 trafficking victims were assisted in 2007, most were referred outside Russia by international NGOs or the IOM (U.S. Department of State, 2008).

Government assistance is not adequately targeted to the particular issues faced by trafficking victims. Victims tend to be placed in homeless or domestic-violence shelters, which are not able to address their needs. This situation makes NGOs responsible for victim services by default. However, local anti-trafficking NGOs lack the government funding necessary to supply victims with adequate resources and aid. As a result, even when the police do refer victims to a local anti-trafficking NGO, the NGO simply does not have the means to provide the critical services required by trafficking victims, such as medical aid, legal assistance, shelter, and psychological counseling. For instance, the shelter Oratorium, located in the southern city of Astrakhan, has a staff of only four employees and nine part-time volunteers (former trafficking victims). The shelter aided seven victims between 2010 and 2011 (U.S. Department of State, 2008, 2010; Narizhnaya, 2011).

There are no formal legal alternatives to deportation for foreign victims, though victims who participate in the prosecution of their trafficker are allowed to stay in Russia until the investigation and prosecution are complete. There is a witness protection program, but only two
trafficking victims benefited from the program in 2007, and no victims
of trafficking were assisted by the program in 2008. At least one victim
benefited from the program in 2009 (U.S. Department of State, 2008,
2009, 2010, 2012). Victims who are from other nations or even different regions of Russia (from where they are residing) are often refused
access to state-run social assistance and health care (U.S. Department
of State, 2008). The reality is that most foreign victims are neither deported nor supported as witnesses in a prosecution. Instead, they are
often released (U.S. Department of State, 2012). This leaves victims
without proper services and places them in a position where they are at
risk for potential re-trafficking or retribution.

Of particular concern is the number of shelters and rehabilitation
centers that have closed. For instance, in 2009 alone, nine rehabilitation centers operated by NGOs in Russia were closed (Arutunyan, 2010).
Among them was an IOM-run shelter and rehabilitation center in Moscow (U.S. Department of State, 2010). From the time it opened (with
foreign funding) in March 2006 until its closure in November 2009, the
IOM-run shelter assisted 423 female and male victims of sex and labor
trafficking. The Russian government failed to allocate funding to prevent the closure. The result is even fewer available resources for victims
(U.S. Department of State, 2010, 2012).

WHAT HAPPENS TO TRAFFICKERS

The Russian government does not collect, maintain, or perform statistical analysis on data from trafficking cases, so the exact number of prosecutions, convictions, and sentences of human traffickers in Russia is
not known (U.S. Department of State, 2008). Part of the problem is that
Russia does not have a comprehensive anti-trafficking law. As a result of
international and domestic pressures, Russia created a draft of such a
law. But instead of building upon the draft, a general and skeletal bill,
"On Introducing Changes and Amendments to the Criminal Code of

the Russian Federation," was passed in 2003, adding Articles 127.1 and 127.2 to the Criminal Code. Unlike the draft bill, Article 127 fails to give law enforcement the infrastructure necessary to enforce the laws effectively (McCarthy, 2010). "This makes it more difficult to investigate and prosecute recruiters, and to aid victims," Lyudmila Churkina said (Arutunyan, 2010).

Available statistics on human trafficking in Russia make it clear that Article 127 is not always used. When it is used, it is typically applied only in cases of women trafficked for sexual exploitation within Russia (90 percent of registered cases) and from Russia to other nations (10 percent of registered cases), not in cases of people trafficked from other nations into Russia (Tiurukanova, 2006). The largest number of identified human trafficking cases in 2006 and 2007 were identified under Article 241 (organization of prostitution) and Article 242 (criminalizing the production and distribution of illegal pornographic material). Roughly 3,000 cases were identified under Article 241 and more than 6,000 under Article 242. There were 584 cases identified under Article 240 (forcing to engage in prostitution) in 2006, and 655 in 2007. Fewer cases were identified under the specific offense of trafficking in persons. Under Article 127.1, only 106 cases of trafficking for commercial sexual exploitation were identified in 2006, and 112 in 2007. Even fewer cases of slave labor were identified under Article 127.2—19 in 2006 and 39 in 2007 (UNODC, 2009a). These numbers are significant because it appears that only Article 127.1 and Article 242 are deemed to be grave crimes.[2] Even those charged under 242 tend to face minimal sentencing. According to Tiurukanova, there are negligible consequences for persons who perform acts that fall under 242.1:

> As a rule criminal article 73 is used in sentencing for individuals who commit crimes under article 242.1, resulting in probation sentences or sentences using the lowest sanctions defined under article 242.1. For example, Moscow's Dorogomilovsky district court reviewed a criminal case against [a] citizen, Kuznetsov, for distribution of child pornography, including sexual acts with children, on the internet network. Kuznetsov was sentenced to three years' imprisonment. In a similar case, [another] citizen, Drozdov, was sentenced by Ekaterinburg's Kirovsky district court to three

years' probation, with a probation period of two years. (Tiuru-kanova, 2006: p. 44)

Available conviction and sentencing information on traffickers in Russia is scant. In 2004, 6 people were sentenced under Article 127.1 and 3 under 127.2 (Tiurukanova, 2006). In 2007, 46 persons were convicted of trafficking offenses, and 45 persons were sentenced and imprisoned. In 2008 there were 38 convictions under Article 127, 2 of which were for forced-labor offenses. In 2009 the number of convictions rose significantly: 76 persons were convicted under Article 127, 10 of them for forced-labor offenses (U.S. Department of State, 2008). In 2009 and 2010 the government convicted 76 and 42 traffickers, respectively. Media reports reveal that 24 of the convicted traffickers in 2009 received sentences ranging from 6 months to 13 years' imprisonment. Of the 42 traffickers convicted in 2010, only 31 received sentences, which ranged from several months' to 12 years' imprisonment. The Ministry of Internal Affairs is undergoing a massive reorganization that officials state has adversely affected law enforcement's ability to perform trafficking investigations. That said, convictions have not yet declined. In 2011, 42 persons were convicted of trafficking offenses under Article 127.1 or 127.2; 11 were convicted of forced-labor offenses. Not all sentences are known, but 19 of those convicted of sex-trafficking offenses in 2011 received sentences ranging from 4 to 19 years' imprisonment (U.S. Department of State, 2010, 2011, 2012).

There are reports of continuing collusion among government officials in human trafficking cases. In January 2010 a senior district police commissioner was convicted and sentenced to 8 years' imprisonment for taking passports and travel documents from migrants and forcing them to work as agricultural laborers. Another instance of complicity involves a senior military officer who organized an international human trafficking ring. Dmitry Strykanova, a lieutenant colonel in Russia's foreign military intelligence agency (GRU), and 10 others trafficked 129 women and girls from eastern Europe to western Europe and the Middle East from 1999 to 2007 for the purposes of forced prostitution. Strykanova was sentenced to 12 years' imprisonment on April 25, 2011 (U.S. Department of State, 2010; World News—Russian Opinion, 2011). In February 2010 media sources reported on a forced-labor trafficking ring that was in existence between 2006 and 2008 and allegedly involved a high-level official in the Ministry of Internal Affairs. Experts believe that members of the riot police kidnapped migrant workers and forced them to work in the homes of officials and on police construction projects (U.S. Department of State, 2010).

INTERNAL EFFORTS TO DECREASE TRAFFICKING

Russia ratified the UN Convention Against Transnational Organized Crime and its supplementing Protocol on Trafficking in Persons in 2004. Yet there are no coordinating mechanisms to address human trafficking that would put Russia in full conformity with its international obligations under the ratified conventions (Tiurukanova, 2006). In addition to having defined human trafficking in its criminal code, the nation has taken some internal steps to eliminate trafficking— such as active monitoring of emigration and immigration patterns and an increase in state-controlled media coverage and documentaries on trafficking. But minimal government money is given to local anti-trafficking NGOs, and overall, anti-trafficking initiatives are fragmented and lack coordination (Tiurukanova, 2006; U.S. Department of State, 2008).

Until November 2008, Article 127.1 of Russia's Criminal Code read: "Trafficking in persons, i.e., the buying-selling of a person or other actions committed for the purpose of such person's exploitation in the form of recruitment, transportation, transfer, harboring, or receipt of such person—shall be punishable by a term of imprisonment of up to 5 years." This language was deemed confusing to law enforcement, since the wording created uncertainty as to whether the buying and selling had to relate to the exploitation or whether it could stand alone (McCarthy, 2010). In November 2008 an amendment to Article 127.1 was passed specifying that *any* transaction involving a human being is a crime. The amendment also added two aggravating factors: (1) trafficking of persons known to be helpless or dependent on the accused and (2) trafficking committed against a woman whom the accused knew to be pregnant. The minimum prison sentence for 127.1 rose from "up to 5 years" to "up to 6 years." This step qualified it as a grave crime and thereby grants law enforcement additional investigative tools that they did not have previously (McCarthy, 2010).

Despite the amendment, the existing law-enforcement system presents significant obstacles to the success of anti-trafficking efforts. A strict separation between investigative and prosecutorial functions creates a situation in which there is no ownership of a case from start to finish. There are various points during the investigative and prosecutorial process when a case can have its classification changed. For instance, the criminal investigator can alter the charges after opening a case and during the investigation. Also, the classification of a case can be changed in the oversight process by the head of the investigative agency to which the criminal investigator reports. The state prosecutor can change his or her mind and refuse to support the charges in court, and the judge can reclassify the charges upon hearing the case (McCarthy, 2010).

Another potential problem is that promotion among law-enforcement personnel largely depends on an officer's success rate—the number of case wins compared to losses. This situation makes officials wary of taking on cases—such as human trafficking cases—that are new and/or unfamiliar. Additionally, investigation of trafficking cases is time-consuming and complicated. Criminal investigators are required by law to finish an investigation within a 40-day period. Although they can obtain an extension from a judge, with such pressure to clear cases quickly investigators may choose another route if they think they have enough evidence to go forward with a different charge. Lauren A. McCarthy writes that there is no incentive for any of the key players to investigate cases thoroughly to determine if there is trafficking and properly classify the crime:

If at any point after the sledovatel [criminal investigator] finishes his/her investigation, the classification is changed (by the gosobvintel or the judge), it is a negative for the sledovatel's record. The gosobvinitel [state prosecutor] may not have an incentive to uphold the sledovatel's charge of trafficking if they fear that the judge will return a not-guilty verdict. This is often because judges are unfamiliar with the new laws. An acquittal would negatively affect the gosobvinitel's statistics. If the case is returned for further investigation because of a technical error or if the case is overturned in a court of higher instance, this is a blemish on everyone's record. Concerns over promotion (*prodvizhenie*) were mentioned by a number of my respondents as the reason they did not want to risk using the human trafficking laws. (McCarthy, 2010: p. 17)

The government has adopted some potentially significant anti-trafficking measures. For instance, Prime Minister (then-President) Dmitry Anatolyevich Medvedev signed the Commonwealth of Independent States Program to Combat Human Trafficking for 2011–2013 in Moscow in December 2010. The program of Cooperation in the Prevention of Human Trafficking outlines commitments to form a national anti-trafficking structure and fund NGOs to provide victim protections (Embassy of the Russian Federation Thailand, 2010; U.S. Department of State, 2012). Immediately afterward the Ministry of Health and Social Development formed an interagency committee that includes anti-trafficking NGOs to specifically address human trafficking (U.S. Department of State, 2011, 2012). If properly implemented, these two undertakings could greatly benefit trafficking victims.

It would behoove Russia to adopt a comprehensive anti-trafficking law that clarifies the investigative and prosecutorial process as it relates to human trafficking. Article 127.1 criminalized human trafficking and thereby allows law enforcement to charge offenders with that specific offense, but the law is meaningless if not accompanied by effective prosecutions. At the present time, it appears that law enforcement would prefer to utilize tried-and-true—and often lesser—charges against traffickers. In addition to the challenges this situation presents to the collection of trafficking data, the lack of uniformity creates a systemic inefficiency in the government's efforts against traffickers. Finally, in order to improve the protection and treatment of victims as well as strengthen cases against traffickers, it is essential that identified foreign victims be referred to NGOs for assistance instead of held in detention centers, deported, or released without protection and services.

CHAPTER 24

Brazil

There's lots of girls working around here. I'm not the youngest,
my sister is 12, and there's an 11-year-old. I've been doing it for so long now,
I don't even think about the dangers. Foreign guys just show up here.
I've been with lots of them. They just show up like you.

—PIA, A CHILD PROSTITUTE

Governments and environmentalists worldwide have been desperate to find an alternative renewable energy source that could alleviate dependence on crude oil and create a much-needed break for the environment. At the forefront of the biofuel movement stands Brazil with sugarcane ethanol. Some experts call it clean energy; others argue that it is not sustainable.[1] Some experts assert that it could actually have an adverse impact on the environment—warning of potential deforestation and other ecological impacts of making room for biofuel plantations (Fargione et al., 2008). This debate is certain to continue, but there is one critical issue that is not arguable: owners of sugarcane plantations are the number-one abusers of slave labor in Brazil. In 2009 alone, 45 percent of slave laborers discovered by the Ministry of Labor's Special Mobile Enforcement Unit were found on sugarcane plantations (Gomes, 2010a). The international community has responded harshly to the treatment of workers on sugarcane plantations. In an attempt to diffuse the negative attention on Brazilian sugarcane ethanol, the government launched the National Commitment to Improve Labor Conditions in the Sugarcane Industry in June 2009 (Sugarcaneblog, 2009; Gomes, 2010b).

Brazil has had a National Policy on Trafficking in Persons in place since 2006 and a National Plan of Action from January 2008 to January 2010. The second draft plan is aimed for 2012–2016, although as of April 2012 the plan had not been passed or implemented. Taking their cue from the national plan, some of the federal states and larger municipalities have begun to draft their own plans of action to address human trafficking (UNODC, 2009a). Various Penal Code laws address human trafficking. Sections 231 and 231-A prohibit promoting or facilitating movement to, from, or within the country for the purposes of prostitution or other forms of sexual exploitation. Amendments to the two sections went into effect in August 2009. The amendments strengthen penalties against sex-trafficking offenders. Prescribed penalties range from 3 to 8 years' imprisonment. Sentences may be increased to up to 12 years in cases that involve violence, threats, or fraud or if the victim is a child (U.S. Department of State, 2010).

Article 149 of the Penal Code prohibits worker exposure to conditions akin to those of slavery. Under the code, slave labor is defined as an unyielding work schedule in degrading working and living conditions under the threat or use of violence. The code also prohibits the use of malevolent persuasion to take workers to remote locations in other parts of the country. The code prohibits impairment of the enjoyment of labor rights via violence or fraud. Finally, landowners are prohibited from holding worker documents (Hall, 2004). In addition, the Ministry of Labor and Employment makes public a Dirty List (*Lista Suja*) of companies where slave labor has been discovered by inspectors. The list is updated every six months, and companies remain on the list for two years. During that time the companies may not receive public funds (Biofuel Watch Center, 2009; Anti-Slavery International, 2010).

Even though the law is rapidly changing to protect potential victims and punish those who have committed trafficking offenses, few traffickers are actually convicted, and even fewer have been sentenced.

TRAFFICKING WITHIN BRAZIL

Forced labor of its own citizens is a major problem in Brazil. Experts assert that more than 25,000 Brazilian men are subjected to slave labor, but the number of identified victims has fluctuated. It is unclear how many of these persons are victims of forced labor as opposed to degrading work conditions or exhausting workdays, as all fall under the definition of *trabalho escravo* (slave labor). In 2003 the number of identified slave-labor victims was 5,223 as compared to 2,887 in 2004, 4,348 in

2005, 3,417 in 2006, 5,975 in 2007, 5,016 in 2008, 3,769 in 2009, 2,628 in 2010, and 2,428 in 2011 (UNODC, 2009a; U.S. Department of State, 2010, 2011, 2012). The Ministry of Labor's Mobile Enforcement Unit has rescued over 41,500 workers since the unit's creation in 1995 to 2011 (Anti-Slavery International, 2010; U.S. Department of State, 2010; Lehman, 2012). The primary industries in which slave labor has been discovered are sugarcane plantations and cattle ranches. From 2007 through 2009, half of identified slave-labor victims were found on sugar plantations (Anti-Slavery International, 2010). In 2009 alone, 45 percent of 4,234 persons released from slave labor were rescued from sugar plantations. Sixteen percent (682) of the slave laborers were found on cattle ranches, while 18 percent (773) were discovered on "other crops" farms and plantations (Gomes, 2010a).

Anti-Slavery International estimates that half a million persons work as sugarcane cutters in Brazil. Typically middlemen known as *gatos* (cats) entice workers from poor areas in northeastern Brazil with a wage advance. Upon arrival at the plantations, the workers are commonly forced to work without pay and face threats and abuse. The life expectancy for sugarcane cutters from the time they begin work is 10 years (Anti-Slavery International, 2010). "The dramatic expansion of agribusiness crops in southern and central Brazil lies at the heart of the country's slavery problem. The existence of slavery totally undermines the idea that sugarcane ethanol is a 'clean' biofuel," Brother Xavier Plassat of the Pastoral Land Commission said (Anti-Slavery International, 2010).

As in other forced-labor scenarios across the globe, victims in Brazil are often offered decent-paying jobs that also provide food and lodging. Instead, the victims are charged exorbitant fees for housing, travel, food, and even work equipment. These fees are "deducted" from the victims' wages, and as debts continue to mount the victims are never paid. In many instances, forced-labor victims' movements are restricted not only physically by close monitoring and armed patrols, but also geographically, as many forced-labor settings are in isolated areas. One such case is that of Gomes da Silva, a Brazilian worker who accepted a good job with decent pay, free lodging, and free food, offered by trafficking recruiters. Instead he was taken by bus to a cattle ranch surrounded by armed guards in a desolate area of the jungle. "It was 12 years before

I was finally able to escape and make my way back home," Da Silva told the *New York Times* (Rohter, 2002).

Da Silva was charged for basic necessities such as lodging, travel, and food. His traffickers would not allow him to leave until the rapidly accruing (and inflated) debt was paid. "We were forced to work at 6 a.m. and continued sometimes until 11 p.m., but I was never paid that entire time because they always claimed that I owed them money." Da Silva said that he was sometimes instructed, under suspicious circumstances, to burn the documentation of fellow workers. "Maybe a half-dozen times I was ordered to burn identity cards and work documents of workers whom I had last seen walking down the road, supposedly on their way out," Da Silva told the *New York Times*. "We also found heaps of bones out in the jungle, but none of us ever talked about it" (Rohter, 2002).

Internal sex trafficking of Brazilians is also a problem. It is estimated that 500,000 children are exploited for prostitution (Bischoff, 2006; U.S. Department of State, 2006, 2007b). Race and socioeconomic status appear to make some women more susceptible to targeting. Women and girls who are trafficked for sexual commercial means are predominantly black or of mixed race and ages 15 to 27. Thirty-one percent of these are 16 or 17 years old. Male children and adolescent boys are also trafficked for sexual commercial purposes; some of them work as transvestites (CLADEM, 2004; U.S. Department of State, 2007a). Previously, as recently as 2009, NGOs reported that many cases involving sex-trafficking victims were dismissed on the basis that the victims worked in prostitution. Today, police still often dismiss sex-trafficking cases, and some victims face prejudice from authorities if they engaged in prostitution prior to experiencing coercive conditions (U.S. Department of State, 2010, 2012). These discriminatory practices hinder the identification process, the ability of victims to obtain necessary shelter and services, and the gathering of accurate trafficking statistics.

Despite the government's efforts, child sexual tourism is a serious problem in the cities of Brazil. Many of the persons exploited by sex tourists are underage. One taxi driver who works in Recife and drives young girls and their tricks to motels/hotels (most likely for a cut of the profit) states that underage sex workers are "so much cheaper than the older ones" (BBC News, 2010a). Sarah de Carvalho of Happy Child International says sex tourism is on the rise in Brazil. "The crisis for these children turning to prostitution has increased significantly in the northeast of Brazil over the last few years, fuelled by increasing numbers of foreign tourists who travel to Brazil for sex holidays," Carvalho told the BBC (BBC News, 2010a). One child prostitute, Pia, stated that she turned 10 tricks a night in order to support her mother's crack addiction. At the time she was interviewed, Pia was 13 years old and was not the youngest child prostitute in her group. "There's lots of girls working around here," Pia told the BBC. "I'm not the youngest, my sister is 12, and there's an 11-year-old." Pia had been a prostitute since she was 7 years old. "I've been doing it for so long now, I don't even think about the dangers. Foreign guys just show up here. I've been with lots of them. They just show up like you" (BBC News, 2010a).

Boys are also exploited by sex tourists. Two boys, 14 and 12 years old, said their families knew that they are working in prostitution. "We need to earn money to buy rice and staple foods for our families," the 14-year-old told the BBC. "Our parents don't worry about us too much. We tell them when we are leaving and when we're coming back. And then we give the money to them to buy food. They know how we get the money, we just don't discuss it" (BBC News, 2010a).

TRAFFICKING ABROAD

Brazilian women and children are forced to prostitute in France, French Guiana, Germany, Italy, the Netherlands, Paraguay, Portugal, Spain, Suriname, Switzerland, the United Kingdom, the United States, and Venezuela (U.S. Department of State, 2010). Young men are also subject to forced prostitution abroad. In August 2010 Spanish authorities broke up a syndicate that trafficked young Brazilian men to Spain for commercial sexual exploitation (BBC News, 2010b). The victims, an estimated 60–80 men in their early twenties from northern Brazil, were offered and accepted legitimate employment as models and dancers. Instead, after large travel fees, the men found themselves in debt bondage. Some of the other workers knew that they would be working as prostitutes but did not know the conditions they would face upon arrival in Spain. "If the men complained or caused any kind of problem, the gang leaders would threaten them, even with death," the police statement said (BBC News, 2010b).

NGOs estimate that 75,000 Brazilian women and girls, many of them trafficked, are engaged in prostitution in neighboring South American nations, the United States, and western Europe. Because of the covert nature of both prostitution and trafficking it is difficult to know exact numbers. The United Nations Office in Drugs and Crime states that the main victims of international human trafficking for commercial sexual exploitation in Argentina and Europe are women from Brazil (U.S. Department of State, 2006, 2007a). These women usually have modest educational backgrounds and are between the ages of 18 and 30 (People's Daily Online, 2006). It is unknown whether these estimates have changed since the release of these two reports. What is known is that Brazil is a major source nation for both sex trafficking and forced-labor trafficking. In France, Brazilians account for 24 percent of identified forced-labor victims (UNODC, 2009b).

Victims who manage to escape their trafficking situations are vulnerable to reentry into the informal economy and even re-trafficking when they do not have access to work visas. One such case is that of a 28-year-old Brazilian woman, Elsa, trafficked from Brazil to Madrid, Spain: "In the beginning, I did not work for 15 days for the gang because I could not stop crying and [was] begging them to let me go back to Brazil," Elsa told the BBC. None of the clients wanted to go with me because of that. Then they [the traffickers] threatened to kill me and to kill my whole family. It was so horrible that after that I lost my fear, I lost my dignity, I lost everything" (Infante, 2009).

Elsa was able to escape her trafficking experience and found legitimate work as a manicurist. She returned to prostitution when the money she was earning as a manicurist simply was not enough. But although Elsa knew that she would be working as a prostitute she did not realize that she was returning to a situation of human trafficking. She received death threats from her traffickers if she did not cooperate and was guarded 24 hours a day. She escaped again and received shelter and counseling through the Association for the Prevention, Reintegration and Attention of Prostituted Women in Spain. When the salon where she worked closed she again returned to prostitution. "The beauty parlor closed its doors. Without proper documents, I did not have much chance of finding another job. I did what I could, but without a working visa, I had to go back to prostitution" (Infante, 2009).

WHAT HAPPENS TO VICTIMS AFTER TRAFFICKING

The Ministry of Social Development provides female victims of sex trafficking with shelter, counseling, and medical aid through a network of 187 centers and 72 shelters for victims of sexual abuse and domestic violence. It is unclear how many of the persons helped by the centers and shelters are trafficking victims. NGOs state that many centers are underfunded, have limited services, and are simply not equipped to handle trafficking cases, and long-term shelter is not typically available. Forced-labor victims—who are predominantly domestically trafficked adult men—are not eligible for government-provided shelter assistance, and assistance for transgender sex-trafficking victims is lacking. The only government-funded shelter specifically designated for trafficking victims is in Salvador; it aids female minors (U.S. Department of State, 2010, 2012). There are government-funded regional anti-trafficking offices in 14 states: Acre, Algoas, Amapa, Bahia, Ceara, the Federal District, Goias, Minas Gerais, Para, Parana, Pernambuco, Rio de Janeiro, Rio Grande do Sul, and São Paulo. The offices are designed to coordinate victim assistance, and prevent and combat human trafficking, but experts report that the quality of services vary and that some offices are more focused on public awareness than on victim assistance. In 2011 the São Paulo office aided 179 victims, 114 of whom were transgendered Brazilians. In the same year the Fortaleza office helped 241 victims. NGOs also provide aid to victims, such as helping them file charges against traffickers and obtain police protection, sometimes with limited government funding (U.S. Department of State, 2010, 2012).

Not all victims are treated equally. Internal forced-labor victims of trafficking do not have access to government-provided shelters. However, internal forced-labor victims are allegedly provided with three months' minimum-wage salary, job training, and travel assistance (when available). The Ministry of Labor also awards forced-labor victims a portion of fines charged against offenders. According to the ministry $2.9 million was paid in labor compensation to slave-labor victims in 2011

(U.S. Department of State, 2011, 2012; Lehman, 2012). That said, according to NGOs, many forced-labor victims do not receive services, and only half of complaints of slave labor that are referred to authorities are investigated. The result is that a significant number of rescued slave-labor victims (some of whom are forced-labor victims) are re-trafficked. An NGO in Maranhao stated that none of the 70 forced-labor victims it aided from 2009 to 2011 received government assistance with lodging, education, or job training. Victims of sex trafficking are eligible for short-term protection under a program for witnesses in some states, but the program lacks sufficient resources. In December 2010 the national immigration council issued a decree granting permanent visa status to foreign victims of trafficking, although no victims were reported to have received this status in 2011 (U.S. Department of State, 2011, 2012).

Procedural or referral issues are not the only obstacles. Dalila Figueiredo, the founder of the Brazilian Association for the Defense of Women and Youth, says some marginalized women face multiple instances of trafficking. "Sometimes we pick up the same woman from the airport twice," Figueiredo said. The reason some women return to their life of being trafficked abroad is because "they get paid. It's more money than they [would] make in Brazil and they can even send money home" (Ross, 2005). Figueiredo believes that inequality and poverty are partly to blame for the trafficking situation in Brazil: "While investments in social problems are helping there's still a long way to go to create conditions that would stop Brazilians from taking such risks in the first place" (Ross, 2005).

Although people continue to be marginalized in Brazil, it does appear that the federal initiatives—and an economy that is relatively unaffected by the global financial recession—are helping to improve the trafficking situation within Brazil, particularly when it comes to child labor. "Child labor has been steadily declining (in the early nineties, there were around eight million underage workers in the country)," Regina Scharf, journalist and former Social and Environmental risk analyst for Banco Real, said on her blog *Deep Brazil*. "One of the reasons is that the Brazilian economy and middle class are growing. Many families that had to find their kids a job [can] now afford to keep them in school" (Scharf, 2009).

WHAT HAPPENS TO TRAFFICKERS

Transnational and internal trafficking for commercial sexual exploitation are criminalized under Sections 231 and 231-A of the Brazilian Penal Code. Accused persons face 3 to 8 years in prison. The sentence can be increased to 12 years in cases that involve fraud, violence, or threats, or if the victim is a child (U.S. Department of State, 2010). Article 207 of the Penal Code prohibits fraudulent recruitment of workers, but sentences are minimal and range from 1 to 3 years' imprisonment. Labor trafficking is prohibited under Article 149 of the Penal Code. Under the code slave labor (*trabalho escravo*) is the act of reducing a person to conditions analogous to slavery. This includes forced labor and forcing a person to work or subjecting a worker to degrading work conditions or exhausting workdays. Imprisonment ranges from 2 to 8 years. It is unclear how many individuals identified in slave labor are forced-labor victims, though a 2011 study stated that 60 percent of workers interviewed in rural slave labor experienced primary characteristics of forced labor (U.S. Department of State, 2010, 2012).

The government has significantly increased the number of people assigned to investigations of forced labor. There has also been an increase in the number of civil actions brought against ranch owners and direct traffickers of forced laborers. Moreover, in December 2006 Brazil's Supreme Court ruled that crimes of slave/forced labor fell under federal, not state, jurisdiction. This judgment helped resolve a long-disputed issue of jurisdiction that had previously delayed and hindered prosecution (U.S. Department of State, 2006, 2007a). Another measure taken in 2006 by the government is the Dirty List. The list is public, and state financial institutions may not provide financial services to those on it. The Dirty List includes the names of companies and property owners who employ workers under slave-labor conditions. Violators stay on the list for two years and are removed only if they have stopped the use of slave labor and paid all due wages to workers (U.S. Department of State, 2007b; U.S. Department of Labor, 2009). The list is updated every six months. In January 2010 there were 164 employers on the Dirty List. The number of employers on the list increased to 392 in 2012. According to Alexandre da Cunha Lyra, head of the Labor Ministry's inspection service, the surge is due to increased surveillance by ministry inspectors, not to an increase in the number of workers subjected to slave-labor conditions (U.S. Department of State, 2010; Lehman, 2012; Repórter Brasil, 2012).

Business dealings between companies on the Dirty List and those that have signed Brazil's nonslavery commitment are automatically suspended, so there is a strong incentive for companies to get off the list. Of concern is that some companies are able to do so. For instance, Cosan, Brazil's most powerful ethanol producer, was able to get a temporary injunction to remove it from the Dirty List. A June 2007 inspection resulted in the rescue of 42 people from a Cosan refinery. The company promised good jobs and wages, but instead the workers were not paid or even provided with clean drinking water (Anti-Slavery International, 2010). As a result, Cosan was added to the Dirty List on December 31, 2009 (Gomes, 2010b). The judge who removed Cosan from the list stated that the subcontractor, not Cosan, was responsible and that the situation did not amount to slavery. The statement that subcontractors alone—not the companies that hire them—are solely responsible for slave labor seriously undermines the nation's anti-trafficking agenda. "The fact that workers in this case were not directly employed by Cosan does not absolve the company of the responsibility to ensure that workers producing their goods are employed in decent conditions," said Joanna Ewart-James, Anti-Slavery International's supply chain program coordinator (Anti-Slavery International, 2010).

Despite the various legislative changes, the number of sex and forced-labor convictions remains quite low. There were 14 convictions in 2006, 7 in 2007, 45 in 2008, and 20 in 2009. There were 23 slave-labor traffickers convicted in 2008 and 15 in 2009. In those 2 years sentencing ranged from 14 months to more than 13 years' imprisonment for sex traffickers and 30 months to 10½ years' imprisonment as well as fines for slave-labor traffickers. In 2010, 4 persons were convicted of sex trafficking under Article 231, while 4 other trafficking offenders were convicted under charges of forming a gang. Sentences of those convicted under Article 231 ranged from community service to nearly 9 years' imprisonment, while the sentences of those convicted of forming a gang ranged from fines and community service to 11 years' imprisonment. Eight slave-labor offenders were convicted under Article 149 in 2010, but 7 of the 8 were given fines, and 1 offender was fined and sentenced to 3½ years' imprisonment, which was converted to community service. In 2011, 2 transnational sex traffickers were convicted under Article 231; they were each sentenced to 5 years' imprisonment. It is unclear how many slave-labor traffickers were convicted in 2011, but media reports indicate that 7 labor trafficking offenders were convicted, including a former congressman. Sentences ranged from 4 years to 5 years and 10 months' imprisonment. Three of these sentences were converted to community service. In one case the trafficker's service was fulfilled by the payment of one month's minimum wage salary to a health center. Convicted traffickers—both sex and slave-labor traffickers—are able to appeal their convictions while out on bail, and slave-labor traffickers are able to serve sentences in a halfway home (U.S. Department of State, 2006, 2007b, 2008, 2009, 2010, 2011, 2012).

INTERNAL EFFORTS TO DECREASE TRAFFICKING

The international human rights community has brought attention to the multiple abuses and exploitations of sugarcane plantation workers. In response, the Brazilian government launched the National Commitment to Improve Labor Conditions in the Sugarcane Industry in June 2009. The commitment was signed by 331 Brazilian companies (Sugarcaneblog, 2009; Gomes, 2010b). In signing the commitment, signatories agree to carry out exemplary business practices regarding workers. The commitment also forbids labor intermediation for sugarcane and ethanol production. This step would eliminate the middleman (*gato*) position that recruits workers from rural areas of Brazil and offers workers an advance in order to lure them to the plantation jobs. The agreement also includes a requirement to provide adequate housing facilities, strengthen collective bargaining, and provide workers with proper protective equipment as well as safe transportation (Gomes, 2010b).

Contrary to the intent of the agreement, companies that commonly violate workers' rights were accepted as signatories, and those that violated workers' rights after they signed onto the commitment were allowed to remain as signatories (Gomes, 2010b). One such signatory was Usina Santa Cruz, purchased by the José Pessoa Group in 2002 (EMII, 2002). Hundreds upon hundreds of slave laborers have been discovered at the Usina Santa Cruz plant—150 on May 15, 324 on June 6, and 5 on November 11, 2009. Additionally, 122 slave laborers were found at a property (Lagoa de Cima farm) that was leased by the José Pessoa Group. The José Pessoa Group was also found to have slave laborers at its facilities in November 2007 and June 2008 (Gomes, 2010b). Despite vast human rights offenses and although the José Pessoa Group was excluded in 2008 from the National Pact for the Eradication of Slave Labor, Usina Santa Cruz could still advertise itself as a signatory of the National Commitment to Improve Labor Conditions in the Sugarcane Industry (Gomes, 2010b).

On the Dirty List was another company owned by the José Pessoa Group, Agrisul Agrícola Ltda., which was a signatory to the National Pact for the Eradication of Slave Labor (Instituto ETHOS, 2007; Repórter Brasil, 2010). In 2007, 831 workers were rescued from Agrisul Agrícola's Debrasa facility. Located in Brasilândia, the facility cultivates cane sugar and manufactures alcohol (Camargo & Hashizume, 2007). In 2007, 50 indigenous workers there were discovered living in a small ($15\,m \times 6.8\,m$) prison cell–like cement block of masonry, while smaller blocks ($9.4\,m \times 2.8\,m$) each housed 20 persons. The structures were infested with insects and covered with mold, the mattresses were dirty, and sewage flowed in the open. The José Pessoa Group did not accept responsibility for negligence and simply stated that had the inspection occurred at the beginning of the sugarcane season the outcome would have been different. It also argued—in contradiction to the mobile unit report—that indigenous persons were treated the same as all other workers. "The accommodations are more than 20 years [old] and have gone through checks before . . . and there never was a reaction like this," said Pessoa. "They were dirty because of the use throughout the season." When addressing the inhumane treatment of indigenous workers compared to other workers, a representative said: "The company has only one kitchen. Everyone who works in the industry has their meals in the cafeteria. It's the same food that goes to the field [and is eaten by indigenous workers]. . . . There was never differentiation" (Camargo & Hashizume, 2007). The issue is that until 2012 there was no monitoring system to confirm whether signatory companies were compliant with the National Commitment to Improve Labor Conditions in the

Sugarcane Industry. Violators did not face punishment and could still use the fact that they were a signatory to further their interests (Gomes, 2010b). Verification of compliance with the National Commitment, conducted by independent auditing firms, started in 2012. As of June 2012, 169 companies had obtained a seal signifying that they were compliant with the best working practices established by the agreement, and 86 companies, also signatories of the National Commitment, were being audited to receive the seal (General Secretariat of the Presidency of Brazil, 2012; SugarCane, 2012).

Brazil has added two critical anti-trafficking legal tools to combat slave labor. In 2012 the government passed a constitutional amendment that allows for the expropriation of land used by businesses that employ workers in slave labor. The senate still needs to determine the official criteria for defining slave labor and the process by which land is seized. Experts are concerned that the nation's powerful agricultural lobby will push to make the rules so complex that it will be difficult to implement the amendment. Also, in 2012, Brazil's Penal Code was updated to add the employment of workers in slave labor to a list of heinous crimes, which doubles the possible detention for those charged with labor violations from 30 to 60 days (Looft, 2012).

The government has made great efforts to collaborate with the nations where Brazilians are trafficked in order to interrupt and weaken international trafficking rings. Brazil has teamed with Argentina, Canada, Italy, Mexico, the Netherlands, Portugal, Spain, Sweden, Switzerland, and the United States on cases that involve the trafficking of Brazilian victims. As a result of these investigations there have been at least 56 arrests (U.S. Department of State, 2006, 2010). The federal police investigate international trafficking as well as internal trafficking when it involves more than one state. Within the federal police, the Central Division of Human Rights specializes in investigations of crimes against human rights, including human trafficking. The Federal Road Police Patrol has a unit dedicated to human trafficking cases that occur on the roadways (UNODC, 2009a). Additionally, after three years of testing, an integrated human-trafficking database that collects data from law enforcement, the judicial branch, and anti-trafficking centers around the country was launched in 2011. The data collected is on sex trafficking and slave labor as well as other federal-level crimes. Implementation so far has been uneven (U.S. Department of State, 2010, 2011, 2012).

The dearth of trafficking convictions is a serious problem. The number of convicted sex-trafficking offenders has decreased each year since 2008. Additionally, sentencing for those involved in fraudulent recruiting is not sufficiently stringent. Access to shelters, assistance, and protection for victims is often inconsistent, with the result that victims do not receive the services they need.

The National Commitment to Improve Labor Conditions in the Sugarcane Industry is an extremely positive step in Brazil's anti-trafficking efforts. Still, the fact that companies on the Dirty List and companies who have exploited laborers before or after signing the agreement have remained signatories undermines the effectiveness of the agreement. This situation stands in direct contradiction to the goal and intent of the agreement and allows exploitative companies to reap financial benefits from their alleged commitment to human rights practices. Fortunately, this may change with the recent verification of compliance for all signatories.

Conclusion

In examining the human trafficking scenarios in 24 nations, we discovered that each country has its own environmental, cultural, and geopolitical factors that create a unique set of anti-trafficking issues and obstacles. For instance, in India you cannot address the issue of trafficking without also discussing the caste system, an ancient tradition that places countless people into slavery and indentured servitude at birth. Under what is called the silent apartheid, members of the Scheduled and Backward Castes are born into servitude and forced to work in brick kilns, embroidery factories, and rice mills as well as perform as domestic servants and workers in the agricultural sector. NGOs estimate that at least 2 million human trafficking victims in India are Dalit (formerly the Untouchables, now known as the Scheduled Castes) bonded laborers. Slavery also exists in Niger, where an estimated 8,800 to 43,000 persons are subjected to traditional hereditary slavery. Despite the fact that the Nigerien Penal Code prohibits slavery, slaves are forced to work as shepherds, agricultural workers, domestic servants, and sexual servants. In a landmark case, Hadijatou Mani Koraou, a victim of hereditary slavery, brought suit against the Nigerien government before the Economic Community of West African States Community Court of Justice. The court found that Nigerien courts had failed in their opportunity and obligation to protect Mani when she came before them. Instead, in a previous court proceeding, a judge had held that a marriage between a free man and a slave woman is lawful as long as he cannot afford to marry a free woman and if he fears to fall into fornication. The Nigerien ruling illustrates the power of customary law and tradition over written law.

In South Africa, custom and the role of traditional healers are so powerful that activists must work with members of the healing community to facilitate awareness and change. This has been particularly true of AIDS awareness. Many South Africans once believed that a person could be cleansed of HIV through sex. When NGOs, such as the Jo'burg Child Welfare in Marshalltown, began to collaborate and build relationships with traditional healers, they were much more successful in spreading the word on how to protect oneself and prevent the spread of HIV. This collaboration could be immensely helpful in disseminating information on Muti murders, in which people are abducted and killed, and their body parts and organs removed for the purpose of traditional healing. Some of the female victims are raped before they are killed, and body parts such as ears, tongues, head, heart, kidneys, and genitalia are removed from both female and male victims. Supporters of these traditional practices believe the use of human body parts can bring wealth and fertility, and altering client belief in this practice will be a challenge. Healing groups such as the National Traditional Healers Organization have met with the Department of Women, Children, Youth and People with Disabilities to discuss how to end this form of trafficking and the demand for body parts. Collaborations at the community level between human rights advocates and traditional healers would help healers and community leaders to spread awareness about Muti murders in a direct and meaningful way.

Despite nation-specific differences, the characteristics of human trafficking are remarkably similar the world over. There are common methods used by traffickers, regardless of whether they are trafficking for commercial sexual exploitation or forced labor. Fraudulent recruitment, often through newspaper advertisements or in person, is used to lure trafficking victims. For instance, in India, recruitment advertisements for a U.S. company, Signal International, allegedly promised participating workers permanent residence in the United States and—for additional fees— permanent residence for their spouses and children. Of course, none of it was true. False promises do not come only in paper form but also through fake romantic relationships that are used to manipulate potential victims.

Members of the Carreto family, who ran a Mexican sex-trafficking ring, did just that; the men wooed young girls, one whom was only 14 at the time of her trafficking experience. The traffickers would first court the women, then, when they had the victims' trust, they would rape and physically isolate them. To extend their control the traffickers told the women, many of whom had children with the traffickers, that they would never see their children again if they did not cooperate. Physical isolation, which was essential in the trafficking cases of the convicted Carreto family and the alleged cases of human trafficking by Signal International, is a common tool to limit and control the movement of victims. Another method is the use of armed guards, which is illustrated in a case that involved Thai agricultural workers who had come to the United States on temporary work visas. An armed guard not only controlled their movements but also charged them for food, even though the traffickers refused to pay the victims. The workers, who were taken to Katrina-ravaged buildings in New Orleans to perform demolition, lived in squalid shelters riddled with debris and mold. There was no electricity or running water, so the victims cooked with contaminated water, and because the guard charged the unpaid workers for food, they soon began to go hungry and had to build traps to capture pigeons to eat.

Other methods used to control and limit the movements of victims include physical and mental abuse, withholding victims' visas and other identifying documentation, threats of deportation, and threats of harm to the victims or the families of the victims. Furthermore, debt bondage makes it nearly impossible for victims to escape, as they have no financial means to do so. Charging victims exorbitant initial fees is an efficient and profitable means of manipulating and controlling victims. In order to pay the fees, victims sell land, borrow money from family members, sell family heirlooms with cultural and symbolic value, and take out loans from loan sharks who charge astronomical interest rates. As inflated debts continue to mount, the victims' nominal wages are allegedly perpetually deducted as partial payment. The traffickers obtain free labor, and the victims are placed in debt bondage. This is exactly what happened to Gomes da Silva, a forced-labor victim in Brazil. He accepted a job with decent pay, free lodging, and free food. Instead, traffickers took him to a cattle ranch that was surrounded by armed guards in a desolate area of the jungle and charged high fees for basic necessities such as travel, food, and lodging. His debt, of course, continuously outweighed his pay, and the traffickers told him that he was not allowed to leave until his debt was paid. Not until 12 years later was he able to escape.

One way to destabilize these trafficking methods is to increase transparency in the labor and sex industries. Of course, that is easier said than done. Many nations do have laws in place that, if adequately enforced, would sufficiently monitor the formal labor market. Yet, without enough labor inspectors, as is the case in Poland and South Africa, satisfactory enforcement is next to impossible. Even in countries where there may be a sufficient number of inspectors, such as Germany, they are often not adequately trained to properly identify human trafficking. The same is true for police, prosecutors, judges, and even counseling centers. Since many nations have just recently introduced forced labor as a form of human trafficking to their criminal codes, these groups are regularly unfamiliar with how to recognize and protect potential victims of forced labor, in particular. The result is that victims are often not recognized and face arrest and punishment for offenses they committed as a result of their trafficking experience, such as immigration violations. The commercial sex industry has been identified as a haven for human trafficking for far longer, and most police and other critical players have a better understanding of sex trafficking than labor trafficking. That said, commercial sexual exploitation is often part of the informal labor market and is incredibly difficult to monitor. Potential sex-trafficking victims are often identified during brothel raids. Foreign victims are recognized because of their immigration status, a red flag for police and investigators. But internally trafficked victims who are citizens or residents slip through the cracks and, in nations where prostitution is illegal, frequently face arrest and punishment. In order to increase transparency in the sex industry, some experts recommend legalizing prostitution in nations where it is illegal, arguing that decriminalizing prostitution would help regulate the sex industry and thereby limit potential trafficking. Others hold that most nations simply do not have the infrastructure and resources to adequately regulate the sex industry. While prostitution is legal in many nations, few governments actually regulate it. Whether those countries that regulate prostitution, such as Germany and Mexico, do so successfully and what impact this has on sex trafficking are worthy of further investigation.

Not surprisingly, a consistent factor in the trafficking scenarios of all nations is that persons who are marginalized are often the most vulnerable. In both the trafficking itself and the treatment of victims afterward, race, socioeconomic status, and gender are all significant factors. So is a lack of national status. For instance, persons of the hill tribes in Thailand are often without citizenship, despite having been born and raised in the nation for generations. By law, they are entitled to identification, but the registration process for permanent residence and citizenship requires a DNA test or a witness who can testify on their behalf for persons without a birth certificate—and there are many who lack them. David A. Feingold, director of the Ophidian Research Institute and UNESCO international coordinator for HIV/AIDS and trafficking, claims that citizenship is the single greatest risk factor for a hill tribe person in Thailand to be trafficked or otherwise exploited.[1] Residency is no small matter—it allows access to health care and education, which are the building blocks of social and economic stability and mobility. Without it, people hover on the periphery of society, struggling to survive and taking jobs that are available to them. They commonly have no choice but to accept jobs in the informal economy, where regulation is nonexistent. Their situation makes them ripe for exploitation by traffickers. In China, the nation's Household Registration System (*hukou*) creates a semicaste structure in which people are defined by the place where their parents were born and by urban or rural origin. (They can choose the *hukou* of either parent.) The rules are relaxed for those who can satisfy the strict housing and high income requirements, but others must attain temporary permits that allow them to find work in other cities. According to James Farrer, former director of the Institute of Comparative Culture at Sophia University in Tokyo, these workers experience much of what illegal migrants and temporary visa workers face in other nations, such as long hours and underpayment or nonpayment of wages.[2] They also have few social resources and are left without access to public services such as child education and health care.

The status of "belonging" and its connection to human trafficking exist in every nation, whether the specific determining issue is citizenship, migration, or displacement of persons forced to flee their home, town, or country on account of unrest. In the United States, Japan, and the United Arab Emirates (UAE), temporary foreign workers are particularly vulnerable to human trafficking. In Japan, foreign unskilled laborers are prohibited from employment. Yet, as is the case in most nations, there is demand for low-wage workers. To help satisfy this need the government-run Industrial Training Program and Technical Internship Program, revised in 2010 as the Technical Intern Training Program, has created a means for employers to obtain low-cost migrant workers. In what was designed as a three-year training and technical intern program, enrollees are supposed to spend the first year as trainees and the remaining two as technical interns. The worker's dependence on legal employment is tied to one employer, creating the opportunity for unfair treatment and abuse. Scheming employers take advantage of the system and—after withholding worker passports—force laborers to work excessive hours, restrict their movements, and either do not pay workers or pay them nominal amounts. Workers also face physical and sexual abuse. In the UAE, migrant workers make up more than 90 percent of the UAE's private-sector workforce. The recruitment of foreign workers involves a system of brokers and agents who swindle workers out of large sums of money. Foreign nationals are promised high-paying jobs in the UAE, but upon arrival they often earn less than 50 percent of what they were promised, or are simply not paid. As with the system in Japan, workers are linked to just one employer, their sponsor. If the worker tries to find better employment—except in instances in which the employer has failed to pay the worker for more than two months—the employer is obligated to trigger the worker's deportation. In fact, companies face heavy fines if they fail to ask the UAE government to cancel absconding workers' visas. Ironically, although it is illegal for employers in the UAE to withhold worker passports, the common method for an employer to trigger the deportation of a worker is to turn in the worker's passport to the Ministry of Interior. Under the Victims of Trafficking and Violence Protection Act of 2000, the United States has taken significant measures against human trafficking. At the same time the highly unregulated one-sponsor H-2B guestworker visa program has contradicted the nation's pledge to protect victims of trafficking by creating the opportunity to exploit legal migrant workers. The H-2B visa allows for the hire of temporary nonimmigrant workers to perform nonagricultural labor on a onetime, seasonal, peak-load or intermittent basis. Even with the amended regulations, there are significant flaws in the current H-2B visa program, but it is lack of enforcement of the program that has enabled unscrupulous employers to exploit and traffic workers with little to no consequence. Part of the problem is that no agency took responsibility for the program from 2005 through 2008. It is now monitored under the U.S. Department of Labor.

In Colombia and Iraq, displaced persons, particularly women and children, are the most vulnerable. As of December 2009 there were between 3.3 and 4.9 million internally displaced persons in Colombia. In the first half of 2011, according to the Observatory on Human Rights and Displacement, 89,000 people were displaced. Displaced Colombians have little access to education, health care services, and housing. Consequently, they are more vulnerable to exploitation, including human trafficking and domestic violence. In addition to displacement that results from civil unrest, guerrilla and paramilitary groups have forcibly taken land from the poor, particularly Afro-Colombians. They also recruit disadvantaged children for use as combatants, informants, messengers, sexual partners, transporters, placers of bombs, guarders of hostages, kidnappers, spies, and couriers or dealers in the illegal drug trade. In Iraq, the U.S. invasion resulted in the displacement of an estimated 4.8 million Iraqis between 2003 and 2009, but what exacerbated the problem was the immunity from Iraqi law and the Iraqi legal process granted by the U.S. government to U.S. contractors and U.S. and Iraqi military personnel. In 2004 the United States, through Paul Bremer, then administrator of the Coalition Provisional Authority (CPA), granted the Multi-National Force–Iraq (MNF-I), the CPA, foreign liaison missions, their personnel, property, funds, and assets, and all international consultants immunity from Iraqi law and the Iraqi legal process. The order was not lifted until 2008, when the Iraqi government passed legislation rescinding CPA Order 17, but the legislation does not specifically address how past incidents will be addressed. Also in 2004, coalition troops were barred from investigating any violations committed by Iraqi troops against other Iraqis. The combination of an immensely vulnerable population and the carte blanche enjoyed by U.S. companies, U.S. contractors, and Iraqi military personnel created an ideal scenario for human trafficking.

Marginalization does not necessarily end with a person's escape from a trafficking experience. In most nations throughout the world, criminalization of victims continues, with variations in the severity. Victims are most commonly charged with prostitution and immigration violations. As economic times continue to be tough, governments have increased implementation of immigration policies, often in direct conflict with a nation's pledge to adequately protect trafficking victims. For instance, in the United States there is often a race against the clock as to what will happen first to trafficking victims applying for visas— deportation or protection. This scenario is, of course, in direct conflict with the intent of the nation's federal anti-trafficking law, since it treats the applicant as a criminal instead of a potential victim. Yet this contradiction exists in most nations. Furthermore, many recent immigration agendas have targeted vulnerable populations. For instance, in August 2010 France began a controversial deportation of Roma persons to Romania and Bulgaria. In response, the European Parliament passed a resolution calling on France to suspend the program; after some resistance, the nation did so. Yet, as of August 2012, the nation continues to deport Roma from France. Italy previously had a victim-centered approach, but NGOs believe that there is a recent decrease in the identification of trafficking victims by the government. This is likely because illegal migrants commonly face fines and expedited deportation without a thorough evaluation as to whether they are trafficking victims. On July 2, 2009, Italy's legislature approved a law criminalizing illegal immigration, which is punishable by a fine and an immediate order to leave the country. Shockingly, it also permits the creation of unarmed citizen patrol groups to help police keep order. To prevent the entry of migrants, Italy is part of an agreement with Libya that allows Italy to forcibly return and reroute boat migrants back to Libya. These persons are not screened by Italian authorities to determine whether they are trafficking victims. In Israel, the newly created immigration and border control authority, called the Oz Unit, replaced the Immigration Police. NGOs assert that Oz inspectors do not convey information to police when they encounter a suspected crime against migrant workers. The nation has also announced its intention to cancel the temporary B1 visas—unrestricted work visas—to trafficking victims. In the United Kingdom, the conflict between the nation's immigration and anti-trafficking agenda is exacerbated by the fact that the nation's border agency is the lead anti-trafficking agency. The U.K. Border Agency's objective to monitor immigration clashes with its ability to properly identify, protect, and support victims of human trafficking. This conflict was demonstrated when 49 officially recognized trafficking victims, identified by the Border Agency and police, were not effectively referred and instead were housed in an immigration detention center and a young offenders' institution.

In many nations, cultural norms dictate that sex-trafficking victims not be excused for committing prostitution despite having been forced to commit the offense. Victims are punished and in some cases killed for the crime. For instance, in Iran—where Norma Ramos states there exists a gender apartheid—the unequal footing of women in relation to men has not only created a highly marginalized population vulnerable to trafficking but also led to the criminalization of identified victims. In February 2010, at the Trafficking in Persons Working Group in Vienna, the Iranian delegate stated that Iran would not accept any recommendations calling for the absolution of trafficking victims for their crimes. The delegate stated that while the victim status of a woman in prostitution might be taken into account by the judge, he opposed the idea that such a woman should not be prosecuted. A similar situation exists in Syria and Iraq, where prostitution is illegal and those arrested face detainment. In Iraq almost half the women in the central women's prison of Kadhimiya (Baghdad) have been convicted of prostitution. Some of the women face death. From 2006 through 2008 there were mass killings of women in the cities of Basra and Umara. A number of the women were accused of prostitution, while others were convicted of being unveiled and wearing makeup.

In cases of forced labor—maybe because of gender bias or simply because of lack of awareness among governments and critical players such as law enforcement and other first responders—adult men are often not acknowledged as human trafficking victims. In those nations men are rarely provided with shelter or equal access to services or prosecutorial options. This is the case in Australia, Brazil, Germany, and Japan. This issue has begun to be acknowledged by governments. For instance, the government of Japan, in its 2009 Action Plan to Combat Trafficking in Persons, emphasized that victims of trafficking include non-Japanese men, women, and children. Joy Ngozi Ezeilo, the United Nations special rapporteur on trafficking in persons, has expressed concern that Japan's trafficking response is gendered and focuses solely on women and sexual exploitation. She points out that other forms of trafficking besides sex trafficking affect men and women as well as boys and girls. Ezeilo's concerns about the action plan remained unaddressed as of 2010, when only one male victim (a sex-trafficking victim) received services at an NGO shelter. In 2011 no male victims of either forced labor or forced prostitution were identified.

Globally, forced labor and commercial sexual exploitation are the primary identified forms of human trafficking. There is widespread debate about which is more prevalent. Not surprisingly—as it is most regularly included in anti-trafficking legislation and is more familiar to police, judges, and prosecutors—commercial sexual exploitation is more frequently identified. As awareness and inclusion of forced labor in anti-trafficking legislation increases, so does its identification. Our guess is that forced labor, which affects men, women, boys, and girls, is more prevalent, but the reality is that both forms of trafficking at their core are forced labor and that separating the two categories merely triggers unequal treatment of victims and disparate sentencing for traffickers. This result can be clearly seen in the anti-trafficking law of New York State, which makes sex trafficking a class B felony with a maximum sentence of 25 years' imprisonment and labor trafficking a class D felony with a maximum sentence of 7 years' imprisonment. In other nations, forced labor is simply not acknowledged. This is the case in China, where trafficking is defined as the abduction, kidnapping, buying, fetching, sending, or transfer of a woman or child for the purposes of selling. The law does not include forced labor, involuntary servitude, or debt bondage, nor does it include trafficking of adult males. In Chile, neither forced labor nor internal trafficking was criminalized until March 2011, when Chilean congress passed a comprehensive anti-trafficking law that prohibits all forms of human trafficking. Fortunately, nations are quickly taking the measures to adopt comprehensive anti-trafficking laws, if they did not already have them, or to expand upon existing anti-trafficking legislation to make it more comprehensive. Yet in most nations, the fact remains that although forced labor is acknowledged in law it is less so in practice, resulting in numerous victims that do not have equal access to services, shelters, or the prosecutorial system. These victims, often foreign and without valid visas, are treated as illegal migrants and promptly deported without any sort of adequate screening to determine if they are in fact trafficking victims.

Across the globe, while victims are criminalized and in many instances have little recourse against their traffickers, the traffickers themselves often face minimal or suspended sentencing. For instance, in Germany 92 of the 115 convicted traffickers did not have to face jail time in 2010. Human traffickers are also commonly granted suspended sentences in Poland, Niger, and Japan. Suspended sentences are also granted in Australia. Another source of concern is the occasional granting of 2-for-1 credits to offenders, including human traffickers, whereby one year in pretrial custody is counted as two. This was the case in Canada until October 2009, where a federal cap was placed on time served at 1-to-1. Today, the ratio can be raised to 1.5-to-1 when the circumstances justify doing so.

In trying to obtain data on arrests, investigations, prosecutions, and sentencing, we found that many nations do not adequately collect trafficking data. One reason is that prosecutors habitually turn to tried-and-true lesser charges, such as prostitution and pimping. This practice results in traffickers' commonly receiving less stringent sentencing; it also means that cases are classified under separate offenses. This is the case in Russia, where human trafficking cases are predominantly identified under Article 241, organization of prostitution; Article 242, criminalizing the production and distribution of illegal pornographic material; and Article 240, forcing to engage in prostitution. Significantly fewer cases are identified under the specific offense of trafficking in persons, Article 127. A similar situation exists in Italy, where trafficking cases are categorized under multiple articles of the Penal Code. This information would need to be integrated to yield a more accurate picture of the trafficking situation and the government response. Another impediment to obtaining trafficking data is the failure of some nations to criminalize certain forms of human trafficking, such as forced labor or internal trafficking. Such nations are not likely to collect data on these forms of trafficking, and if they do, the offenses will not be classified as human trafficking. Often it is these unacknowledged forms of trafficking that are the most prevalent, and the lack of their inclusion in a nation's anti-trafficking law poses a significant hindrance both to obtaining an accurate view of the trafficking scenario and to adequately protecting existing and potential victims. To bridge this gap, nations should take steps to ensure that their anti-trafficking laws cover all forms of human trafficking and provide adequate protections to potential and existing victims. Many nations focus most of their anti-trafficking efforts on the prosecution of traffickers. A crucial ingredient in the complicated battle against human trafficking is to ensure that victims do not get revictimized. According to Joy Ngozi Ezeilo, governments must remember the three R's—rehabilitation, reintegration, and redress for victims. These can be implemented only when the post-trafficking experience is a priority and not a sidenote for a nation's government. Of course, while the inclusiveness of the law is essential, how the law is enforced and whether a nation has the infrastructure to enforce it are equally essential.

Many nations make common mistakes in defining or interpreting human trafficking. Some conflate it with human smuggling. While smuggled persons can become trafficking victims, the experience of smuggling alone does not automatically make them victims of human trafficking. What is true is that smuggled persons are often in a position of vulnerability that can put them at risk for a variety of exploitations, including human trafficking. Some nations insist on including movement as a required element of human trafficking. For instance, legislation in the United Kingdom mistakenly makes movement an essential component in proving human trafficking. In order to use the anti-trafficking laws, prosecutors must demonstrate the trafficker's intent to both transport and exploit the victim. The double-intent criterion is particularly unfitting in instances of trafficking within the United Kingdom, both in regard to British citizens who are trafficked internally and in regard to migrant workers who travel voluntarily to the United Kingdom but then experience involuntary servitude. Under the laws, the trafficker must have intent to move the victim, even if just from one part of the country to another. The mistake is that at the heart of human trafficking is its exploitative purpose not movement. The result is that prosecutors often veer away from the stringent criterion and use lesser offenses to prosecute traffickers. This practice not only reduces the severity of the sentence for traffickers but also deprives the victim of access to the same level of protection and support.

To some degree, it is understandable that governments and societies get tangled in the definition of human trafficking. After all, the word *traffic,* though it means to trade or barter—which does not require movement—is often associated with the movement of something: the transportation of goods, whether canned items, drugs, or people. The intent of the term *human trafficking* was clearly originally designed to include the movement of persons from one place to another. Yet as time has passed and this phenomenon has become better understood, it has become clear that the issue of human trafficking turns on its exploitative purpose, and as a result movement itself has become less and less significant. A more inclusive term would be *modern-day slavery.* Many nations have already identified this activity as human trafficking and have simply added to the definition as time has passed. An age-old issue, slavery is not new to our world, but with the ease of global trade the game has changed. What was once village tradition has become a quick and efficient transaction—regardless of whether it occurs across borders or down the street.

Notes

INTRODUCTION

1. Interview with James Farrer on February 9, 2010.

1. UNITED STATES

1. Adult trafficking victims are certified, and child trafficking victims receive eligibility letters. Persons certified or given eligibility letters by HHS are eligible for federal and state benefits and services.

2. Since her rescue, Bennu has become a ward of the Orange County Superior Court. She has decided not to return to Egypt and is living in foster care and going to school. Bennu and Eshe are not the girls' real names.

3. All defendants were associated with California-based labor recruiting company Global Horizons Manpower, Inc., and the recruiters that served the company in Thailand.

4. Interview with Lori J. Johnson on June 25, 2009.

5. This includes the 130 persons allegedly trafficked by Matt Redd of Louisiana Labor, LLC. A suit has not yet been filed against Redd or Louisiana Labor, LLC.

6. The other defendants in this case are Bianca Nikole Vierra (19 years old), Ryan Lia Rasmussen (29 years old), Deairick Dante Newsome (22 years old), and Mark Anthony Grayned (22 years old) (Villa & Collom, 2005a; Park, 2008).

7. Under the TVPA, severe forms of trafficking in persons include sex trafficking and trafficking for labor or services where there was the presence of

force, fraud, or coercion, except when the victim is a child (U.S. Department of State, 2000).

8. Interview with Alia El-Sawi on February 19, 2009.

9. Interview with Kavitha Sreeharsha on March 4, 2009.

10. Personal communication with Thom Mrozek, Public Affairs Officer, U.S. Department of Justice, Central District of California, on November 18, 2009.

11. Interview with Christa M. Stewart on March 18, 2009.

12. Interview with anonymous expert in April 2009.

13. Interview with Suzanne B. Seltzer on April 7, 2009.

14. Interview with Christa M. Stewart on March 18, 2009.

15. Interview with Suzanne B. Seltzer on April 7, 2009.

16. Signal allegedly trafficked 500–550 persons from India to the Gulf region after Hurricane Katrina. Victims each paid roughly $20,000 to traffickers and their agents and thus entered a situation of debt bondage (David et al. v. Signal International, LLC et al., 2008; Cole, 2009).

17. Interview with Barry Nelson on September 25, 2009.

18. Ibid.

19. The Migration Policy Institute report included the arrest date from the inception of the Fugitive Operations Program in 2003 until early 2008 (Gorman, 2009c).

20. Interview with Caitlin Ryland on September 16, 2009, and correspondence on February 25, 2011.

21. Ryland says this may be changing. "Several law enforcement counterparts already involved in statewide anti-trafficking efforts have made great progress training their staff and reaching out to other law enforcement agencies throughout the state with trainings regarding trafficking and recognizing the red flags of trafficking when a victim does not self-identify right away." Ryland notes that many agents have still not received this training.

2. JAPAN

1. Interview with James Farrer on December 21, 2009.

2. Interview with Michiko Yokoyama on December 28, 2009.

3. Interview with James Farrer on December 21, 2009.

4. Interview with Michiko Yokoyama on December 28, 2009.

5. Interview with James Farrer on December 21, 2009.

6. Interview with Michiko Yokoyama on December 28, 2009.

7. Interview with James Farrer on December 21, 2009.

8. The U.S. *Trafficking in Persons Report* comes out annually in June. For ease of reading, the reporting period is labeled as the year from which the majority

of data arose. For example, the TIP report released in June 2010 is labeled 2009.

9. Interview with Michiko Yokoyama on December 28, 2009.

10. Ibid.

11. Ibid.

3. UNITED ARAB EMIRATES

1. All the victims identified in 2005 and 2006 were trafficked for sexual exploitation (UNODC, 2009).

2. There is videotape evidence that appears to show royal family member Sheikh Issa bin Zayed al-Nahyan and the police beating, using electric cattle prods on, and driving over an Afghani man. Sheikh Issa bin Zayed al-Nahyan was acquitted in January 2010 of charges related to the abuse of the man (HRW, 2010a).

4. THAILAND

1. Interview with David A. Feingold on August 10, 2009.

2. This number may also include other persons in need—i.e., nontrafficking victims (UNODC, 2009).

3. To interview and provide legal and outreach services to migrants and Thai workers in the shrimp industry, the Solidarity Center partners with, among others, the Federation of Trade Unions–Burma, the Seafarers' Union of Burma, and the Labour Rights Promotion Network (Solidarity Center, 2008).

4. Interview with Lori J. Johnson on June 25, 2009.

5. Interview with Luigi Acquisto on March 4, 2009.

6. Interview with David A. Feingold on August 10, 2009.

7. Cabinet resolutions from December 18, 2008; May 26, 2009; July 28, 2009; and November 3, 2009.

5. ISRAEL AND THE OCCUPIED PALESTINIAN TERRITORIES

1. The B1 visa is not contingent on cooperation with law-enforcement officials (U.S. Department of State, 2010a).

6. COLOMBIA

1. While historically the FARC and ELN were identified as guerrilla groups, recently the terms *guerrilla* and *paramilitary* have been used interchangeably to describe them.

7. IRAQ

1. KBR separated from Halliburton in April 2007 (KBR, n.d.).

12. IRAN

1. One incorrect statistic repeatedly cited in newspaper articles throughout the past 10 years is that 10–15 percent of the prostitutes in Belgium, Italy, and the Netherlands are Iranian. While cited as the source of the statistic, the report *Research Based on Case Studies of Victims of Trafficking in Human Beings in 3 EU Member States, i.e., Belgium, Italy and the Netherlands* never makes this claim. It does discuss forced prostitution but does not discuss Iran in that context (Commission of the European Communities, 2001).

2. Under Article 90 of the new code, children and juveniles who are under the age of 18 but have reached the age of maturity (8 years and 9 months for girls; 14 years and 7 months for boys) but "do not understand the nature of the committed crime or its prohibition, or if there is a doubt about their mental development and perfection," may be exempt from severe punishment or the death penalty and face correctional measures instead. The court can ask for the opinion of forensic medicine to determine the mental development of the child (Nayyeri, 2012).

3. Whether the Quran actually indicates that the testimony of two women equals that of one man is highly disputed (Roald, 2001).

13. INDIA

1. Interview with Patricia Aliperti on February 22, 2010.
2. Ibid.
3. Interview with Dan Werner on July 13, 2009.
4. Ibid.
5. Ibid.
6. Interview with Patricia Aliperti on February 22, 2010.

14. NIGER

1. Interview with Alia El-Sawi on February 16, 2009.

2. Local attorneys received assistance and support from the International Centre for Legal Protection of Human Rights (INTERIGHTS), Anti-Slavery International, and Timidria.

3. Interview with Helen Duffy on November 28, 2009.

4. Ibid.

15. CHINA

1. Interview with James Farrer on February 9, 2010.

2. Ibid.

3. Ibid.

4. The Action Plan to Crack Down on the Abduction and Trafficking in Women and Children (2008–2012) is part of the National Human Rights Action Plan of China (2009–2010).

5. Interview with James Farrer on February 9, 2010.

16. SOUTH AFRICA

1. Patric Solomons, personal communication, April 22, 2010.

2. Interview with Carol Bews on April 22, 2010.

3. The number of Thai victims trafficked to South Africa may be decreasing. It seems that fewer Thai women are now being trafficked for forced prostitution in South Africa's illegal brothels (U.S. Department of State, 2010).

4. Nde Ndifonka, personal communication, April 22, 2010.

5. Media24 owns the Johannesburg newspaper *City Press*.

6. Nde Ndifonka, personal communication, April 22, 2010.

7. Interview with Carol Bews on April 22, 2010.

8. Nde Ndifonka, personal communication, April 22, 2010.

9. Interview with Carol Bews on April 22, 2010.

10. Ibid.

11. Nde Ndifonka, personal communication, April 22, 2010.

12. Interview with anonymous source in April 2010.

13. Nde Ndifonka, personal communication, April 22, 2010.

14. Ibid.

15. Interview with Carol Bews on April 22, 2010.

16. Ibid.

17. Ibid.

18. Nde Ndifonka, personal communication, April 22, 2010.

19. Interview with Carol Bews on April 22, 2010.

17. AUSTRALIA

1. In 2010 the Parliamentary Joint Committee on the Australian Crime Commission became the Parliamentary Joint Committee on Law Enforcement (Parliament of Australia, 2010b). The Department of Immigration, Multicultural and Indigenous Affairs became the Department of Immigration and Multicultural Affairs in 2006 and then the Department of Immigration and Citizenship in 2007 (Department of Immigration and Citizenship, 2012b).

2. Interview with Luigi Acquisto on March 4, 2009.

3. The debt-bondage offenses are included in Division 271 but are considered to be less serious than the trafficking-in-persons, sexual-servitude, and slavery offenses (Schloenhardt, 2009).

18. UNITED KINGDOM

1. Interview with Klara Skrivankova on February 20, 2009.

2. Ibid.

20. GERMANY

1. Interview with Heike Rabe of the German Institute for Human Rights (DIMR) on July 30, 2010.

2. Ibid.

3. Ibid.

4. Personal communication with Heike Rabe on October 12, 2012.

5. Interview with Heike Rabe on July 30, 2010.

6. Ibid.

22. MEXICO

1. The 2009 ABA report has been supplemented by an interview with Gretchen Kuhner on October 27, 2009.

2. Interview with anonymous source, November 2009.

3. Interview with Gretchen Kuhner on October 27, 2009.

4. Since this interview there have been some convictions of traffickers. But the numbers are minimal, making Kuhner's comment still relevant.

5. Interview with Gretchen Kuhner on October 27, 2009.

6. Ibid.

7. Ibid.

8. Ibid.

23. RUSSIA

1. In addition to Russia, member or participating CIS nations are Azerbaijan, Armenia, Belarus, Kazakhstan, Kyrgyzstan, Moldova, Tajikistan, Turkmenistan, Uzbekistan, and Ukraine (Embassy of the Russian Federation Thailand, 2010; CIS, 2011).

2. Under Article 242, offenders face imprisonment for up to 6 years (Government of Russia, 2003). Under Article 15 of the Criminal Code, medium-gravity offenses are deliberate offenses, for which maximum punishment does not exceed 5 years' imprisonment. Careless crimes have maximum sentences not to exceed 2 years' imprisonment. Grave crimes are defined as intentional acts for which the maximum penalty does not exceed 10 years' imprisonment (Government of Russia, 1996).

24. BRAZIL

1. A study conducted by Illinois University on plantations in several countries—including Brazil—indicates that sugarcane plantations have worsened global warming, while a study conducted by São Paulo University's Center for Nuclear Energy in Agriculture indicates that soils on sugarcane plantations remove carbon dioxide from the atmosphere (Gomes, 2010a).

CONCLUSION

1. Interview with David A. Feingold on August 10, 2009.

2. Interview with James Farrer on December 21, 2009.

References

INTRODUCTION

Belser, P. (2005). *Forced labor and human trafficking: Estimating the profits*. Geneva: ILO.

ILO. (2006). *Forced labor statistics*. Retrieved February 17, 2011, from Cornell University ILR School: http://digitalcommons.ilr.cornell.edu/cgi/viewcontent .cgi?article=1019&context=forcedlabor.

———. (2012). *ILO global estimate of forced labor: Results and methodology*. Geneva: ILO.

OHCHR. (2009). UN expert on trafficking in persons ends visit to Poland. Press release, May 29. Retrieved June 2, 2010, from United Nations Office of the High Commissioner for Human Rights: www2.ohchr.org/english/issues /trafficking/docs/PressReleaseVisitPoland.doc.

UNODC. (2004). United Nations Convention Against Transnational Organized Crime and the protocols thereto. New York: United Nations.

UNTC. (2011). United Nations Convention Against Transnational Organized Crime. Retrieved August 24, 2011, from United Nations Treaty Collection: http://treaties.un.org/Pages/ViewDetails.aspx?src=IND&mtdsg_no=XVIII-12 &chapter=18&lang=en.

1. UNITED STATES

Andert, S. (2007). The new slavery: Human trafficking flies below the radar of most people's consciousness, but it happens—even in New Orleans. *Gambit Weekly*, December 18, pp. 27–31.

Asanok et al. v. Million Express Manpower, Inc. et al. (2007). 5:2007cv00048 (North Carolina Eastern District Court, February 12, 2007).

Bales, K., et al. (2004). *Hidden slaves: Forced labor in the United States*. Berkeley: Free the Slaves and Human Rights Center, University of California.

Bauer, M. (2007). *Close to slavery, guestworker programs in the United States*. Montgomery: The Southern Poverty Law Center.

CBS News. (2004). Porn in the U.S.A. *60 Minutes*, September 5. Retrieved February 17, 2011, from www.cbsnews.com/stories/2003/11/21/60minutes/main585049 .shtml.

Clawson, H. J., et al. (2009). *Human trafficking into and within the United States: A review of the literature*. Washington, D.C.: U.S. Department of Health and Human Services.

Cole, J. (2009). Bill sponsor pushes for human trafficking ban. *The Forum*, January 20, p. C2.

Crary, D. (2005). Human trafficking goes on in U.S., too. *Zwire*, November 1. Retrieved February 18, 2011, from http://web.archive.org/web/20070209072044 /http:/www.zwire.com/site/news.cfm?newsid=15491503&BRD=1817& PAG=461&dept_id=222087&rfi=6.

Daniel Castellanos-Contreras et al. v. Decatur Hotels, LLC et al., 07-30942 (U.S. Court of Appeals, Fifth Circuit, October 11, 2007).

David et al. v. Signal International, LLC et al., 2:2008cv01220 (Louisiana Eastern District Court, March 7, 2008).

Donato, K., & Hakimzadeh, S. (2009). *The changing face of the Gulf Coast: Immigration to Louisiana, Mississippi, and Alabama*. Retrieved February 17, 2011, from Migration Information Source, Migration Policy Institute: www.migrationinformation.org/Feature/display.cfm?ID=368.

Estes, R. J., & Weiner, N. A. (2002). *The commercial sexual exploitation of children in the U.S., Canada and Mexico*. Philadelphia: University of Pennsylvania–School of Social Work, Center for the Study of Youth Policy.

Frundt, T. (2005). *Enslaved in America: Sex trafficking in the United States*. Retrieved February 2011, from Women's Funding Network: www.womensfundingnet work.org/resource/past-articles/enslaved-in-america-sex-trafficking-in-the -united-states.

Gorman, A. (2009a). Victims' U-visa program falters; illegal immigrants who help law enforcement officials are eligible, but few receive them. *Los Angeles Times*, January 26, p. B1.

———. (2009b). California; Between protection, deportation; The U-visa program is designed to safeguard undocumented crime victims. But approval is too late for some. *Los Angeles Times*, July 13, p. A3.

———. (2009c). ICE drops arrest quotas for illegal immigrants. *Chicago Tribune*, August 18, p. 11.

Hess, B. (2007). *Children in the fields: An American problem.* Washington, D.C.: Association of Farmworker Opportunity Programs.

HHS. (2009). *About human trafficking: Overview of human trafficking issue.* Retrieved February 18, 2011, from U.S. Department of Health and Human Services: www.acf.hhs.gov/trafficking/about/index.html.

iAbolish, American Anti-Slavery Group. (2006). *Country report: USA.* Retrieved February 18, 2011, from www.iabolish.org/slavery_today/country_reports/us .html.

Kaiser, E. (2005). To stop a forced sex trade. *Minnesota Daily,* November 1. Retrieved February 17, 2011, p. 1A.

Kerr, K. (2010). Hawaii home to largest human trafficking case in U.S. history. KITV, September 2. Retrieved February 18, 2011, from www.kitv.com/r /24866750/detail.html.

Lin, S. (2012). Feds give up on Global Horizons human trafficking case. *Honolulu Civil Beat.* July 20. Retrieved July 21, 2012, from www.civilbeat.com/ar ticles/2012/07/20/16529-feds-give-up-on-global-horizons-human-traffick ing-case/.

Mairi Nunag-Tañedo et al. v. East Baton Rouge Parish School Board et al., 10-1172-JAK (MLGx) (U.S. District Court for the Central District of California, August 5, 2010).

Mendelson, M. S., Strom, S., & Wishnie, M. (2009). *Collateral damage: An examination of ICE's Fugitive Operations Program.* Retrieved February 18, 2011, from Migration Policy Institute: www.migrationpolicy.org/pubs/NFOP _Feb09.pdf.

NOWCRJ. (2008). *ICE raid targets, snares human trafficking victims.* Retrieved February 18, 2011, from New Orleans Workers' Center for Racial Justice: http://nolaworkerscenter.wordpress.com/2008/11/01/ice-raid-target-snares -victims-of-human-trafficking/.

OAS/PAHO. (2001). *Trafficking of women and children for sexual exploitation in the Americas: Fact sheet.* Retrieved February 17, 2011, from www.paho.org/english /hdp/hdw/traffickingfactsheeteng.pdf.

Park, M. (2008). Man sentenced in kidnapping, gang rape. *Arizona Republic,* March 7. Retrieved February 18, 2011, from www.azcentral.com/news/articles /0307abrk-graysentence0307.html.

Richard, A. O. (2000). *International trafficking in women to the United States: A contemporary manifestation of slavery and organized crime.* Washington, D.C.: Center for the Study of Intelligence.

Rood, L. (2009). Register exclusive: Many ICE arrests are not of criminals, data show. *Des Moines Register,* September 16, p. 1.

Siskin, A., & Wyler, L. S. (2010). CRS Report RL34317, *Trafficking in persons: U.S. policy and issues for Congress,* p. 7.

———. (2012). CRS Report RL34317, *Trafficking in persons: U.S. policy and issues for Congress*, p. 5.

Springer, P. (2008a). Illegal workers bust "largest single case"—Sweep arrests 23 involved in building ethanol plant. *The Forum*, October 29, p. A1.

———. (2008b). Trial date set for men in illegal worker raid. *The Forum*, November 14, p. C1.

———. (2008c). 14 of "Cass 23" plead guilty to charges, supporters including more than 30 pastors begin a daylong fast to pressure authorities. *The Forum*, December 18, p. A1.

Srisavasdi, R. (2006). Irvine pair guilty in child slave case. *Orange County Register*, June 30. Retrieved February 17, 2011, from www.ocregister.com/ocregister /news/homepage/article_1198476.php.

Taxin, A. (2009). Immigration boss says agents no longer have arrest quotas. *San Diego Union-Tribune*, August 17. Retrieved February 18, 2011, from www .utsandiego.com/news/2009/aug/17/us-socal-immigration-enforcement -081709/?print&page=all.

University of Nevada. (2004). *Sex industry and sex workers in Nevada*. Retrieved February 17, 2011, from www.unlv.edu/centers/cdclv/healthnv/sexindustry .html.

U.S. Department of Homeland Security. (2009a). *Improving the process for victims of human trafficking and certain criminal activity: The T and U Visa*. Retrieved February 18, 2011, from U.S. Department of Homeland Security, Office of the Citizenship and Immigration Services Ombudsman: www.dhs.gov/xlibrary /assets/cisomb_tandu_visa_recommendation_2009-01-26.pdf.

———. (2009b). *I-914, application for T nonimmigrant status*. Retrieved February 18, 2011, from U.S. Department of Homeland Security, U.S. Citizenship and Immigration Services: www.uscis.gov/files/form/i-914.pdf.

———. (2009c). *Instructions for Form I-918, Petition for U Nonimmigrant Status*. Retrieved February 18, 2011, from U.S. Department of Homeland Security, U.S. Citizenship and Immigration Services: www.uscis.gov/files/form/i-918instr .pdf.

U.S. Department of Justice. (2006a). *Attorney General's annual report to Congress on U.S. government activities to combat trafficking in persons fiscal year 2005*. Retrieved February 18, 2011, from www.justice.gov/archive/ag/annualreports /tr2005/agreporthumantrafficing2005.pdf.

———. (2006b). *Fact sheet: Protect Act*. Retrieved February 18, 2011, from U.S. Department of Justice: www.usdoj.gov/opa/pr/2003/April/03_ag_266 .htm.

———. (2009). Three American men accused of traveling to Cambodia to have sex with children now en route to United States to face prosecution on federal "sex tourism" charges. Press release. Retrieved February 18, 2011, from Federal Bureau of Investigation (FBI): http://losangeles.fbi.gov/dojpressrel /pressrel09/la083109.htm.

———. (2011a). Two additional defendants charged in human trafficking case involving scheme to hold 400 Thai nationals in forced agricultural labor. Press release, January 14. Retrieved February 18, 2011, from Federal Bureau of Investigation (FBI): http://honolulu.fbi.gov/dojpressrel/pressrel11/hn011411.htm.

———. (2011b). Three defendants plead guilty in Honolulu in connection with human trafficking scheme that exploited 600 Thai workers. Press briefing, June 15. Retrieved September 19, 2011, from www.justice.gov/opa/pr/2011 /June/11-crt-774.html.

U.S. Department of Labor. (1994). *General Administration Letter No. 1–95*. Retrieved July 11, 2010, from Employment and Training Administration, United States Department of Labor: http://wdr.doleta.gov/directives/attach /GAL1-95_attach.pdf.

———. (2008). *ETA final rules, labor certification process and enforcement for temporary employment in occupations other than agriculture or registered nursing (H-2B workers)*. Retrieved June 30, 2010, from webapps.dol.gov/FederalRegister /PdfDisplay.aspx?DocId=21887.

———. (2009a). *The Department of Labor's list of goods produced by child labor or forced labor*. Retrieved February 18, 2011, from www.dol.gov/ilab/programs /ocft/PDF/2009TVPRA.pdf.

———. (2009b). *Fact sheet no. 69: Requirements to participate in the H-2B Program*. Retrieved June 30, 2010, from www.dol.gov/whd/regs/compliance /whdfs69.htm.

———. (2012a). Office of Foreign Labor Certification, H-1B, H-1B1 and E-3 Specialty (Professional) Workers. Retrieved August 24, 2012, from www.foreign laborcert.doleta.gov/h-1b.cfm.

———. (2012b). Office of Foreign Labor Certification, H-2A Temporary Agricultural Program. Retrieved August 24, 2012, from www.foreignlaborcert.doleta .gov/h-2a.cfm.

———. (2012c). Office of Foreign Labor Certification, H-2B Certification for Temporary Non-Agricultural Work. Retrieved August 24, 2012, from www. foreignlaborcert.doleta.gov/h-2b.cfm.

U.S. Department of State. (2000). Victims of Trafficking and Violence Protection Act of 2000 (P.L. 106-386).

———. (2005a). *Inspection of the Office to Monitor and Combat Trafficking in Persons (OIG report ISP I-06-04)*. Retrieved February 18, 2011, from U.S. Department of State and the Broadcasting Board of Governors Office of Inspector General: http://oig.state.gov/documents/organization/57174.pdf.

————. (2005b). *U.S. cooperates with Europe to combat sex trafficking. Fact sheet: Provides overview of U.S. assistance in combating sex trafficking.* Retrieved February 18, 2011, from America.gov: www.america.gov/st/washfile-english/2005/January/20050106133608cjsamoht4.548281e-02.html.

————. (2009a). *Anti–human trafficking programs awarded in fiscal year 2009.* Retrieved February 18, 2011, from www.state.gov/j/tip/rls/other/2009/131167.htm.

————. (2009b). *The President's Interagency Task Force to Monitor and Combat Trafficking in Persons and the Senior Policy Operating Group. Fact sheet.* Retrieved February 18, 2011, from www.state.gov/g/tip/rls/fs/2009/120224.htm.

————. (2009c). *Trafficking in persons report.* Retrieved January 28, 2010, from www.state.gov/documents/organization/123357.pdf.

————. (2010). *Trafficking in persons report.* Retrieved June 20, 2010, from www.state.gov/documents/organization/142979.pdf.

————. (2011). *Trafficking in persons report.* Retrieved September 16, 2011, from www.state.gov/g/tip/rls/tiprpt/2011/.

U.S. House of Representatives. (2007). *Hearing on adequacy of labor law enforcement in New Orleans.* Retrieved February 17, 2011, from U.S. House of Representatives, Committee on Oversight and Government Reform: http://frwebgate.access.gpo.gov/cgi-bin/getdoc.cgi?dbname=110_house_hearings&docid=f:51702.pdf.

————. (2008). *U.S. House of Representatives Subcommittee on Immigration, Citizenship, Refugees, Border Security and International Law. Testimony of Mary Bauer, Director, Immigrant Justice Project, Southern Poverty Law Center, before the House.* Retrieved February 18, 2011, from Southern Poverty Law Center: www.splcenter.org/get-informed/news/h-2b-guestworkers-facing-rampant-abuse.

————. (2010a). *18 USC Chapter 63—Mail fraud and other fraud offenses.* Retrieved February 23, 2011, from http://uscode.house.gov/download/pls/18C63.txt.

————. (2010b). *18 USC Chapter 77—Peonage, slavery, and trafficking in persons.* Retrieved February 23, 2011, from http://uscode.house.gov/download/pls/18C77.txt.

Villa, J., & Collom, L. (2005a). Runaway raped, held as sex slave. *Arizona Republic,* November 9, p. A1.

————. (2005b). Kidnap suspect was child prostitute. *Arizona Republic,* November 10, p. B1.

World Vision. (2009). *Child sex tourism FAQs.* Retrieved February 18, 2011, from www.worldvision.org/content.nsf/learn/globalissues-stp.

2. JAPAN

Adelstein, J. (2009). *Tokyo vice: An American reporter on the police beat in Japan.* New York: Pantheon Books.

Arudou, D. (2009). "Golden parachutes" mark failure of race-based policy. *Japan Times*, April 7. Retrieved December 18, 2009, from http://search.japantimes.co.jp/cgi-bin/fl20090407ad.html.

Bangkok Post. (2009). "How I was tricked into becoming a sex slave in Japan." After months of frustrating and seemingly hopeless investigations, a 53-year-old teacher has been implicated in a human trafficking racket. *Bangkok Post*, October 26. Retrieved December 6, 2009, from www.bangkokpost.com/news/local/26267/how-i-was-tricked-into-becoming-a-sex-slave-in-japan.

Convention on the Rights of the Child. (2010). *Optional Protocol to the Convention on the Rights of the Child on the sale of children, child prostitution and child pornography: Replies to the list of issues to the consideration of the initial report of Japan.* Retrieved January 2, 2011, from UN Office of the High Commissioner for Human Rights: www2.ohchr.org/english/bodies/crc/docs/CRC.C.OPSC.JPN.Q.1.Add.1.doc.

DAW/DESA. (2005). Amendment to the Penal Code (2005). Retrieved December 16, 2009, from UN Secretary-General's database on violence against women, the United Nations Entity for Gender Equality and the Empowerment of Women: http://sgdatabase.unwomen.org/searchDetail.action?measureId=5290&baseHREF=country&baseHREFId=689.

———. (2009). *Women's consulting offices.* Retrieved December 16, 2009, from UN Secretary-General's database on violence against women, the United Nations Entity for Gender Equality and the Empowerment of Women: http://sgdatabase.unwomen.org/searchDetail.action?measureId=5401&baseHREF=country&baseHREFId=689.

Government of Japan. (2006). Penal Code (Act No. 45 of 1907). Retrieved January 3, 2011, from Cabinet Secretariat: www.cas.go.jp/jp/seisaku/hourei/data/PC.pdf. This English translation of the Penal Code has been prepared up to the revisions of Act No. 36 of 2006 (Effective May 28, 2006).

Hongo, J. (2006). New round of entertainer visa changes—help or hindrance? *Japan Times*, June 2. Retrieved December 10, 2009, from http://search.japantimes.co.jp/cgi-bin/nn20060602f2.html.

Hughes, D. M., Sporcic, L. J., Mendelsohn, N. Z., & Chirgwin, V. (1999). *The factbook on global sexual exploitation.* Retrieved December 7, 2009, from University of Rhode Island: www.uri.edu/artsci/wms/hughes/factbook.htm.

ILO. (2005). Efforts Mount in Japan to counter human trafficking. Press release, January 5. Retrieved December 4, 2009, from International Labour

Organization: www.ilo.org/global/about-the-ilo/press-and-media-centre/news /WCMS_075528/lang--en/index.htm.

Inter-Ministerial Liaison Committee. (2009). *Japan's 2009 Action Plan to Combat Trafficking in Persons*. Retrieved January 2, 2011, from Cabinet Secretariat: www.cas.go.jp/jp/seisaku/jinsin/kettei/2009gaiyou_en.pdf.

Ishiwata, C. (2011). Sexual health education for school children in Japan: The timing and contents. *Japan Medical Association Journal (JMAJ)* 54, no.3, May– June 2011, pp. 155–160.

JITCO. (2010). *Technical Intern Training Program: Operative manual for sending organizations*. Retrieved September 20, 2011, from Japan International Training Cooperation Organization: www.jitco.or.jp/download/data/okuridashi _English.pdf.

Johnston, E. (2009). Child porn hard to define. Laws limited in huge market where possession, animated sex know no bounds. *Japan Times,* March 31. Retrieved December 22, 2009, from http://search.japantimes.co.jp/cgi-bin/ nn2009033li1.html.

Kakuchi, S. (2004). Experts put new spin on sex education. May 27. Retrieved December 2, 2011, from Inter Press Service: http://ipsnews.net/news.asp? idnews=23923.

Kuhn, A. (2009). Japan's treatment of foreign workers criticized. National Public Radio, *All Things Considered,* May 12. Retrieved December 17, 2009, from www.npr.org/templates/story/story.php?storyId=104065603.

Labor Standards Act (Act No. 49 of April 7, 1947). (2005). Retrieved August 27, 2012, from the International Labour Organization: www.ilo.org/dyn/travail /docs/2021/Labor%20Standards%20Act%20-%20www.cas.go.jp%20version .pdf. This English translation of the Labor Standards Act has been prepared up to the revisions of ActNo. 147 of 2004 (Effective April 1, 2005).

Matsumoto, S. (1995). Sex education and sexual behaviour of adolescents in Japan. *Annals of the Academy of Medicine Singapore*, vol. 24, no.5, pp. 696–699.

McCabe, K., S. Yi-Ying Lin, & H. Tanaka. (2009). Pay to go: Countries offer cash to immigrants willing to pack their bags. Retrieved December 18, 2009, from *Migration Information Source*: www.migrationinformation.org/Feature /display.cfm?ID=749.

McCurry, J. (2009). Japan's yakuza gangsters swot up on the law. *The Guardian*, September 7, p. 26.

McNeill, D. (2004). Japan: Pink heaven for traffickers. *Japan Times,* February 1. Retrieved January 2, 2011, from http://search.japantimes.co.jp/cgi-bin/ fl20040201a2.html.

MOFA. (1999). Fourth periodic report on implementation of Convention on the Elimination of All Forms of Discrimination Against Women. Retrieved De-

cember 2, 2011, from Ministry of Foreign Affairs of Japan: www.mofa.go.jp/
policy/human/women_rep4/index.html.

———. (2000). Recommendations of Overseas Emigration Council future policy
regarding cooperation with overseas communities of Nikkei. Retrieved December 18, 2009, from Ministry of Foreign Affairs of Japan: www.mofa.go.jp
/policy/emigration/nikkei.html.

———. (2008a). Statement by Mr. Masatoshi Shimbo, Deputy Director-General,
Foreign Policy Bureau, Ministry of Foreign Affairs of Japan, at the Vienna
Forum to Fight Human Trafficking. Retrieved December 9, 2009, from Ministry of Foreign Affairs of Japan: www.mofa.go.jp/policy/i_crime/people
/state0802.html.

———. (2008b). The recent actions Japan has taken to combat TIP (trafficking in
persons). Retrieved December 5, 2009, from Ministry of Foreign Affairs of
Japan: www.mofa.go.jp/POLICY/i_crime/people/action0508.html.

———. (2012). A guide to Japanese visas—exemption of visas. Retrieved August
27, 2012, from Ministry of Foreign Affairs of Japan: www.mofa.go.jp/j_info
/visit/visa/short/novisa.html.

Nambu Foreign Workers Caucus. (2008). Foreign workers need social security.
Retrieved December 17, 2009, from http://nambufwc.org.

NPA. (2009). The situation of child protection in Japan: Overview of Japanese
police. Retrieved December 16, 2009, from National Police Agency: www.npa
.go.jp/english/syonen2/The_situation_of_child_protection_in_Japan.pdf.

OAS. (2005). *Rapid assessment report: Trafficking in persons from Latin America and
Caribbean (LAC) region to Japan.* Retrieved November 26, 2009, from Organization of American States: www.oas.org/atip/PDFs/Rapid%20Assessment
%20(English).pdf.

OHCHR. (2009a). UN expert on trafficking in persons ends visit to Japan. Press
statement, July 17. Retrieved January 3, 2011, from Office of the United
Nations High Commissioner for Human Rights: www2.ohchr.org/ . . . /
trafficking/docs/PressStatementJapan170709.doc.

———. (2009b). Japan: "Human trafficking affects every country," warns UN
expert. Press release, July 17. Retrieved November 25, 2009, from United Nations Office at Geneva: www.ohchr.org/en/NewsEvents/Pages/DisplayNews
.aspx?NewsID=8466&LangID=E.

PBS. (2009). Dying to leave. The business of human trafficking: Criminal
groups. *Wide Angle,* September 25. Retrieved December 4, 2009, from Public
Broadcasting Service: www.pbs.org/wnet/wideangle/episodes/dying-to-leave
/business-of-human-trafficking/criminal-groups/1423/.

Reynolds, I. (2009). Author gets too close for comfort with Tokyo's yakuza
gangs. October 13. Retrieved December 4, 2009, from Reuters: www.reuters
.com/article/idUSTRE59C0NX20091013.

SMC. (2009). (Draft) Asian migration atlas: Japan. Retrieved December 9, 2009, from Scalabrini Migration Center: www.smc.org.ph.

Sour strawberries: Japan's hidden guest workers. Directed by König, T., & D. Kremers. 2008. Germany: Cinemabstruso Leipzig, 2008. DVD.

UN News Center. (2009). UN expert calls on Japan to boost action in combating human trafficking. Press release, July 17. Retrieved November 25, 2009, from United Nations News Center: www.un.org/apps/news/story.asp?NewsID=31500&Cr=&Cr1.

U.S. Department of State. (2008). *Trafficking in persons report.* Retrieved July 20, 2008, from www.state.gov/documents/organization/105501.pdf.

———. (2009). *Trafficking in persons report.* Retrieved January 28, 2010, from www.state.gov/documents/organization/123357.pdf.

———. (2010). *Trafficking in persons report.* Retrieved June 20, 2010, from www.state.gov/documents/organization/142979.pdf.

———. (2011). *Trafficking in persons report.* Retrieved September 16, 2011, from www.state.gov/g/tip/rls/tiprpt/2011/.

———. (2012). *Trafficking in persons report.* Retrieved August 30, 2012, from www.state.gov/j/tip/rls/tiprpt/2012/.

Vital Voices. (2004). *Memorandum: Summary of Japanese laws.* Retrieved December 4, 2009, from www.vitalvoices.org/. Copy in author's possession.

3. UNITED ARAB EMIRATES

Caplin, J. (2009). Mirage in the desert oasis: Forced labor in Dubai and the United Arab Emirates. *Harvard International Review*, March 21. Retrieved February 9, 2011, from http://hir.harvard.edu/rethinking-finance/mirage-in-the-desert-oasis.

Emarat Al Youm. (2010). Dubai to set up special human trafficking court. *Emarat Al Youm*, October 25. Retrieved September 18, 2011, from U.S. Library of Congress: www.loc.gov/lawweb/servlet/lloc_news?disp3_1205402339_text.

Gulf News. (2010). New UAE shelters to help combat human trafficking. *Gulf News*, June 6. Retrieved February 8, 2011, from http://gulfnews.com/news/gulf/uae/government/new-uae-shelters-to-help-combat-human-trafficking-1.637288.

HRW. (2009). "The Island of Happiness": Exploitation of migrant workers on Saadiyat Island, Abu Dhabi. Human Rights Watch, May 19. Retrieved February 7, 2011, from www.hrw.org/en/reports/2009/05/18/island-happiness.

———. (2010a). UAE: Sheikh's trial insufficient to stop torture. News release, Human Rights Watch, January 10. Retrieved February 10, 2011, from www.hrw.org/en/news/2010/01/10/uae-sheikh-s-trial-insufficient-stop-torture.

———. (2010b). India/UAE: Use visit to raise migrant worker issue. News release, Human Rights Watch, November 22. Retrieved February 7, 2011, from www .hrw.org/en/news/2010/11/22/indiauae-use-visit-raise-migrant-worker-issue.

———. (2012). UAE: Proposed law to benefit domestic workers important opportunity to ensure legislation meets international standards. Human Rights Watch, May 11. Retrieved August 29, 2012, from http://www.hrw.org/news /2012/05/11/uae-proposed-law-benefit-domestic-workers.

IRIN. (2006). Iraq-Syria: Sex traffickers target women in war-torn Iraq. October 26. Retrieved October 19, 2008, from Integrated Regional Information Networks, the humanitarian news and analysis service of the UN Office for the Coordination of Humanitarian Affairs: www.irinnews.org/Report.aspx ?ReportId=61903.

———. (2007). UAE-PAKISTAN: Gov't steps up efforts to help former child jockeys. Press release, April 30. Retrieved October 21, 2008, from Integrated Regional Information Networks, the humanitarian news and analysis service of the UN Office for the Coordination of Humanitarian Affairs: www .irinnews.org/Report.aspx?ReportId=71860.

NCCHT. (2010). *Combating human trafficking in the UAE: Annual report, 2009–2010*. Retrieved September 18, 2011, from United Arab Emirates National Committee to Combat Human Trafficking: www.nccht.gov.ae/en/Publica tions/PDF/81020111102143972500.pdf.

Noueihed, L. (2008). Trafficking tough to tame in rich Gulf states. February 24. Retrieved October 22, 2008, from Reuters Africa: http://africa.reuters .com/world/news/usnL20906164.html.

Peachey, P. (2010). UAE defies ban on child camel jockeys. *The Independent*, March 3. Retrieved February 11, 2011, from www.independent.co.uk/news /world/middle-east/uae-defies-ban-on-child-camel-jockeys-1914915.html.

Sambidge, A. (2010). UAE says committed to human trafficking fight. *Arabian Business*, June 16. Retrieved February 9, 2011, from www.arabianbusiness. com/uae-says-committed-human-trafficking-fight-291713.html.

Sunderland, J. (2006). Swept under the rug: Abuses against domestic workers around the world. *Human Rights Watch*, July, vol. 18, no. 7 (C).

UAE Interact. (2008). Mohammed Bin Zayed's contribution to anti human trafficking lauded. *UAE Interact*, February 15. Retrieved October 19, 2008, from www.uaeinteract.com/docs/Mohammed_bin_Zayeds_contribution_to_anti _human_trafficking_lauded/28647.htm.

UNODC. (2009). *Global report on trafficking in persons*. Retrieved June 6, 2010, from United Nations Office on Drugs and Crime: www.unodc.org/documents /Global_Report_on_TIP.pdf.

———. (2011). *Ongoing projects in eastern Africa*. Retrieved February 10, 2011, from United Nations Office on Drugs and Crime: www.unodc.org/eastern

africa/en/ongoing-projects/global-initiative-to-fight-human-trafficking.
html.

U.S. Department of State. (2008). *Trafficking in persons report*. Retrieved July 20, 2008, from http://www.state.gov/documents/organization/105501.pdf.

———. (2010). *Trafficking in persons report*. Retrieved June 20, 2010, from www.state.gov/documents/organization/142979.pdf.

———. (2011). *Trafficking in persons report*. Retrieved September 16, 2011, from www.state.gov/g/tip/rls/tiprpt/2011/.

———. (2012). *Trafficking in persons report*. Retrieved August 30, 2012, from http://www.state.gov/j/tip/rls/tiprpt/2012/.

4. THAILAND

Andert, S. (2007). The new slavery: Human trafficking flies below the radar of most people's consciousness, but it happens—even in New Orleans. *Gambit Weekly*, December 18. Retrieved June 3, 2009, from www.bestofneworleans.com/gambit/the-new-slavery/Content?oid=1248877.

Asanok et al. v. Million Express Manpower, Inc. et al. (2007). 5:2007cv00048 (North Carolina Eastern District Court, February 12, 2007).

AVERT. (2011). *HIV & AIDS in Thailand*. Retrieved December 14, 2011, from www.avert.org/thailand-aids-hiv.htm#contentTable1.

Bales, K. (1999). *Disposable people: New slavery in the global economy*. Berkeley: University of California Press.

Bangkok Post. (2010). Fisheries "face sanctions." *Bangkok Post*, May 6. Retrieved February 5, 2011, from www.bangkokpost.com/news/local/38225/fisheries-face-sanctions.

Batstone, D. (2010). *Not for sale: The return of the global slave trade—and how we can fight*. New York: HarperOne.

BBC News. (2011). Burma transfer of power complete. *BBC News*, March 30. Retrieved December 4, 2011, from www.bbc.co.uk/news/world-asia-pacific-12903507.

Branigan, T. (2011). Thailand elections yield surprise gains for former brothel tycoon. *The Guardian*, July 5. Retrieved December 14, 2011, from www.guardian.co.uk/world/2011/jul/05/thailand-elections-chuwit-kamolvisit-seats.

Civil Registration Act No. 2. (2008). *Civil Registration Act No. 2, B.E. 2551*. February 15. Retrieved August 11, 2009, from United Nations High Commission on Refugees: www.unhcr.org/refworld/docid/4a5464942.html.

The Code. (2011). Code of Conduct for the Protection of Children from Sexual Exploitation in Travel and Tourism: An industry driven responsible tourism initiative co-funded by the Swiss Government (SECO) and by the tourism private sector and supported by the ECPAT International network. Advisory partners: UNICEF and UNWTO. Retrieved December 24, 2011, from www .thecode.org/.

Cropley, E. (2007). In Thai shrimp industry, child labor and rights abuses persist. *New York Times,* April 25. Retrieved August 6, 2009, from www.nytimes .com/2007/04/25/business/worldbusiness/25iht-baht.4.5438244.html?_r=3.

Duthel, H. (2011). *Wordwide prostitution: Facts and details of global prostitution.* Charleston: CreateSpace Independent Publishing Platform.

Eckert, P. (2008). Shrimp industry blasted for "modern-day slavery." *International Herald Tribune,* April 23. Retrieved February 12, 2009, from www.iht .com/articles/reuters/2008/04/23/europe/OUKWD-UK-ASIA-SHRIMP-USA .php.

Extension. (2010). *Extension of the time period for nationality verification and granting an amnesty.* January 19. Retrieved February 4, 2011, from Burma/Myanmar Library: www.burmalibrary.org/docs08/Nationality-verification%28en %29.pdf.

Freedom House. (2009). *Freedom in the world 2009—Thailand.* July 16. Retrieved August 8, 2009, from Office of the United Nations High Commissioner for Human Rights: www.unhcr.org/refworld/docid/4a64527bc.html.

Friends-International, Inc. (2011). *Thailand.* Retrieved December 24, 2011, from www.friends-international.org/wherewework/thailand.asp?main menu=wherewework&page=thailand.

Head, J. (2008). New trafficking law for Thailand. *BBC News,* June 5. Retrieved July 23, 2009, from http://news.bbc.co.uk/2/hi/asia-pacific/7437016.stm.

Hongthong, P. (2007). New law on trafficking, protection for male victims, but corruption behind "slave trade" still the main concern. *The Nation,* October 1. Retrieved July 29, 2009, from www.nationmultimedia.com/2007/10/01 /national/national_30050827.php.

IMF. (2011). *Regional economic outlook: Asia and Pacific.* October. Retrieved December 13, 2011, from International Monetary Fund: www.imf.org/external /pubs/ft/reo/2011/apd/eng/areo1011.pdf.

IRIN. (2009). Thailand: Burmese migrant children missing out on education. June 15. Retrieved August 21, 2009, from Integrated Regional Information Networks, the humanitarian news and analysis service of the UN Office for the Coordination of Humanitarian Affairs: www.irinnews.org/Report.aspx ?ReportId=84844.

———. (2010). Myanmar: Smuggled abroad and shunned at home. September 14. Retrieved February 4, 2011, from Integrated Regional Information Networks, the humanitarian news and analysis service of the UN Office for the

Coordination of Humanitarian Affairs: www.irinnews.org/Report.aspx?ReportId=90467.

———. (2011). Myanmar-Thailand: Undocumented workers exploited post-floods. November 8. Retrieved December 24, 2011, from Integrated Regional Information Networks, the humanitarian news and analysis service of the UN Office for the Coordination of Humanitarian Affairs: www.irinnews.org/report.aspx?reportid=94162.

Karen Women's Organization. (2004). *Shattering silences: Karen women speak out about the Burmese military regime's use of rape as a strategy of war in Karen State.* Retrieved August 30, 2012, from The Women's League of Burma: www.womenofburma.org/Report/Shattering_Silences.doc.

Kerr, K. (2010). Hawaii home to largest human trafficking case in U.S. history. KITV, September 2. Retrieved September 19, 2011, from www.kitv.com/r/24866750/detail.html.

Leiter, K., et al. (2004). No status: Migration, trafficking and exploitation of women in Thailand. A report by Physicians for Human Rights, June. Retrieved December 4, 2011, from http://s3.amazonaws.com/PHR_Reports/thailand-women-trafficking-2004.pdf.

Leithead, A. (2011). Burmese "slavery" fishermen are trafficked and abused. *BBC News,* April 25. Retrieved December 26, 2011, from www.bbc.co.uk/news/world-asia-pacific-12881982.

Lertcharoenchok, Y. (2001). Searching for identity. Retrieved July 21, 2009, from UNESCO Bangkok, Asia and Pacific Regional Bureau for Education: www.unescobkk.org/fileadmin/user_upload/culture/Trafficking/citizenship/YINDEE_SearchingforIdentity_article_1_.pdf.

Lin, S. (2012). Feds give up on Global Horizons human trafficking case. *Honolulu Civil Beat.* July 20. Retrieved July 21, 2012, from www.civilbeat.com/articles/2012/07/20/16529-feds-give-up-on-global-horizons-human-trafficking-case/.

Myint-U, T. (2012). The 100 most influential people in the world, U Thein Sein. *Time,* April 18. Retrieved August 31, 2012 from www.time.com/time/specials/packages/article/0,28804,2111975_2111976_2112089,00.html.

Naing, S. Y. (2012). The start of a second wave of reform, or a sign of trouble? *The Irrawaddy,* August 29. Retrieved August 29, 2012 from www.irrawaddy.org/archives/12815.

National AIDS Prevention and Alleviation Committee. (2010). *UNGASS Country Progress Report.* Retrieved December 27, 2011, from Joint United Nations Program on HIV/AIDS: www.unaids.org/en/dataanalysis/monitoringcountry-progress/2010progressreportssubmittedbycountries/thailand_2010_country_progress_report_en.pdf.

Nationality Act No.4. (2008). *Nationality Act (No.4), B.E. 2551.* Retrieved August 8, 2009, from United Nations High Commission on Refugees: www.unhcr .org/refworld/docid/4a54695f2.html.

National Statistical Office Thailand. (2004). *Core economic indicators of Thailand.* Retrieved December 13, 2011, from United Nations Public Administration Network: http://unpan1.un.org/intradoc/groups/public/documents/apcity/ unpan015286.pdf.

NOAA Fisheries Service. (2011). *FishWatch,* September 13. Retrieved December 26, 2011, from National Oceanic and Atmospheric Administration, U.S. Department of Commerce: www.nmfs.noaa.gov/fishwatch/trade_and_aqua culture.htm.

OHCHR. (2011). Human trafficking: Thailand must show clear leadership against it in the region and beyond, urges UN expert. Press release, August 22. Retrieved September 19, 2011, from United Nations Human Rights Office of the High Commissioner for Human Rights: www.ohchr.org/EN/News Events/Pages/DisplayNews.aspx?NewsID=11323&LangID=E.

PATA. (2012). International arrivals increase in April but growth rate slows. Press Release, July 31. Retrieved August 30, 2012, from Pacific Asia Travel Association: www.pata.org/press/pata-international-arrivals-increase-in-april-but -growth-rate-slows.

Pimonsaengsuriya, K. (2008). *Understanding the linkages between child sex tourism and other forms of commercial sexual exploitation of children in East Asia and the Pacific.* Retrieved December 24, 2011, from End Child Prostitution, Child Pornography and Trafficking in Children for Sexual Purposes, ECPAT International: www.ecpat.net/worldcongressIII/PDF/Journals/Understanding_ linkages.pdf.

Prospect Magazine. (2005). Learning the Thai sex trade. *Prospect Magazine,* May 21. Retrieved December 24, 2011, from www.prospectmagazine.co.uk/2005 /05/learningthethaisextrade/.

Royal Thai Government. (2008). Anti-Trafficking in Persons Act B.E. 2551. Retrieved July 29, 2009, from United Nations High Commission on Refugees: www.unhcr.org/refworld/pdfid/4a546ab42.pdf.

Shan Women's Action Network. (2002). *Licence to rape.* Retrieved December 4, 2011, from www.shanwomen.org/pdf/Licence%20to%20Rape%20B .pdf.

Solidarity Center. (2008). *The true cost of shrimp—how shrimp industry workers in Bangladesh and Thailand pay the price for affordable shrimp.* Degradation of Work series. Retrieved August 6, 2009, from American Center for International Labor Solidarity: www.solidaritycenter.org/files/pubs_True_Cost_of _Shrimp.pdf.

Thawdar, The Irrawaddy. (2009a). Bleak future for Burmese stateless children. *The Irrawaddy,* July 11. Retrieved August 21, 2009, from www2.irrawaddy.org /article.php?art_id=16310.

———. (2009b). No country to call their own. *The Irrawaddy,* August, vol. 17, no. 5. Retrieved August 21, 2009, from www2.irrawaddy.org/article.php?art _id=16438.

UNESCO Bangkok. (2008). Press release regarding the June 2008 FCCT/ UNESCO Panel on the Impact of Legal Status on Hill Tribes, Asia and Pacific Regional Bureau for Education, Press release, June 9. Retrieved July 21, 2009, from United Nations Educational, Scientific and Cultural Organization Bangkok: www.unescobkk.org/fileadmin/user_upload/culture/Trafficking/ citizenship/Press_Release_16_June_08.pdf.

United Nations Radio. (2011). IOM report reveals widespread human trafficking in Thai fishing industry. United Nations Radio, May 6. Retrieved December 26, 2011, from www.unmultimedia.org/radio/english/2011/05/iom-report -reveals-widespread-human-trafficking-in-thai-fishing-industry/.

UNODC. (2009). *Global report on trafficking in persons.* Retrieved June 6, 2010, from United Nations Office on Drugs and Crime: www.unodc.org/documents /Global_Report_on_TIP.pdf.

UNWTO. (2011). *Arrivals of non resident tourists/visitors, departures and tourism expenditure in the country and in other countries.* Retrieved December 13, 2011, from United Nations Statistics Division, United Nations World Tourism Organization: http://data.un.org/DocumentData.aspx?id=292.

U.S. Department of Justice. (2011a). Two additional defendants charged in human trafficking case involving scheme to hold 400 Thai nationals in forced agricultural labor. Press release, January 14. Retrieved February 18, 2011, from Federal Bureau of Investigation (FBI): www.fbi.gov/honolulu/press -releases/2011/hn011411.htm.

———. (2011b). Three defendants plead guilty in Honolulu in connection with human trafficking scheme that exploited 600 Thai Workers. Press release, June 15. Retrieved September 19, 2011, from United States Department of Justice: www.justice.gov/opa/pr/2011/June/11-crt-774.html.

U.S. Department of Labor. (2008). *Testimony of Thea Mei Lee, policy director of the American Federation of Labor and Congress of Industrial Organizations (AFL-CIO).* Retrieved August 6, 2009, from www.dol.gov/ilab/programs/ocft/pdf /20080423e.pdf.

———. (2009). *2008 findings on the worst forms of child labor.* Retrieved December 2, 2010, from www.dol.gov/ilab/programs/ocft/PDF/2008OCFTreport.pdf.

———. (2010). *2009 findings on the worst forms of child labor.* Retrieved December 2, 2010, from www.dol.gov/ilab/media/reports/tda/tda2009/Thailand.pdf.

U.S. Department of State. (2009). *Trafficking in persons report*. Retrieved January 28, 2010, from www.state.gov/documents/organization/123357.pdf.

———. (2010). *Trafficking in persons report*. Retrieved June 20, 2010, from www .state.gov/documents/organization/142979.pdf.

———. (2011). *Trafficking in persons report*. Retrieved September 16, 2011, from www.state.gov/g/tip/rls/tiprpt/2011/.

———. (2012). *Trafficking in persons report*. Retrieved August 31, 2012, from www.state.gov/g/tip/rls/tiprpt/2012/.

WLB. (2004). *System of impunity: Nationwide patterns of sexual violence by the military regime's army and authorities in Burma*. Retrieved December 4, 2011, from The Women's League of Burma: www.womenofburma.org/Report /SYSTEM_OF_IMPUNITY.pdf.

5. ISRAEL AND THE OCCUPIED PALESTINIAN TERRITORIES

BBC News. (2010). Police smash Israeli organ-trafficking ring. *BBC News*, April 7. Retrieved May 28, 2010, from http://news.bbc.co.uk/2/hi/middle_east /8608053.stm.

Cohen, G., & Mozgovaya, N. (2011). State Dept.: Israel not doing its part to stop human trafficking. *Haaretz*, June 29. Retrieved September 18, 2011, from www .haaretz.com/print-edition/news/state-dept-israel-not-doing-its-part-to-stop -human-trafficking-1.370143.

Dickman, O. (2011). Employing of asylum seekers in Israel—Regulations and problems. Retrieved September 3, 2012 from The Hotline for Migrant Workers: www.hotline.org.il/english/pdf/Employment_and_CR_Visas_Eng.pdf.

Goren, Y. (2009). Police arrest 12 in raid on Israel's largest human-trafficking ring. *Haaretz*, March 9. Retrieved April 21, 2010, from www.haaretz.com/ hasen/spages/1069609.html.

Hass, A. (2010a). Israel withholding NGO employees' work permits. *Haaretz*, January 20. Retrieved May 21, 2010, from www.haaretz.com/print-edition/ news/israel-withholding-ngo-employees-work-permits-1.265728.

———. (2010b). Israel to resume issue of visas for foreign NGO workers in West Bank. *Haaretz*, March 9. Retrieved May 21, 2010, from www.haaretz.com /print-edition/news/israel-to-resume-issue-of-visas-for-foreign-ngo-workers -in-west-bank-1.264362.

IRIN. (2009). Israel: People-trafficking gang uncovered. Press release, March 12. Retrieved April 21, 2010, from Integrated Regional Information Networks, the humanitarian news and analysis service of the UN Office for the Coordination of Humanitarian Affairs: www.irinnews.org/report.aspx?ReportId=83436.

Jerusalem Post. (2009). Eight men charged in human trafficking. *Jerusalem Post*, March 29. Retrieved April 24, 2010, from www.jpost.com/Home/Article.aspx ?id=137483.

Khoury, J., & Ashkenazi, E. (2010). Israel police uncover organ trafficking ring in north. *Haaretz*, April 9. Retrieved April 21, 2010, from www.haaretz.com /news/israel-police-uncovers-organ-trafficking-ring-in-north-1.905.

Kliger, R. (2009). 77% of women in Gaza Strip are exposed to violence. December 20. Retrieved May 24, 2010, from Palestinian Women's Information and Media Center: www.pwic.org.

The Knesset. (2011a). *National programme to meet the problem of infiltrators and asylum seekers entering Israel across the Egyptian border.* January 25. Retrieved September 18, 2011, from www.knesset.gov.il/mmm/eng/doc_eng.asp?doc =me02765&type=pdf.

———. (2011b). *Israel: Increased penalties for prostitution advertising.* March 28. Retrieved September 18, 2011, from U.S. Library of Congress: www.loc.gov /lawweb/servlet/lloc_news?disp3_l205402669_text.

———. (2011c). *Israel: Regulation of employment visas of providers of elder care.* June 6. Retrieved September 18, 2011, from U.S. Library of Congress: www .loc.gov/lawweb/servlet/lloc_news?disp3_l205402699_text.

Ma'an News Agency. (2010). Report: 6 detained for organ trafficking in Israel. April 7. Retrieved April 21, 2010, from Ma'an News Agency: Ma'an News Agency, www.maannews.net/eng/ViewDetails.aspx?ID=274771.

Menkedick, S. (2010). Palestinian women victim to increasing violence and discrimination. March 24. Retrieved May 24, 2010, from Change.org: news. change.org.

Ministry of Justice and the Ministry of Foreign Affairs. (2009). The implementation of the International Convention on the Elimination of All Forms of Discrimination Against Women (CEDAW). Retrieved April 26, 2010, from www.justice.gov.il/NR/rdonlyres/2EE793D7-E486-48E4-9000-8D1E7CC747F7 /15366/CEDAW2009.pdf.

———. (2010). *Israel replies to CEDAW.* Retrieved February 10, 2012, from www .justice.gov.il/NR/rdonlyres/898A7D08-2738-4A3D-8E2C-BE75689D7EF2 /28810/IsraelsrepliestoCEDAWLOI61211.pdf.

National Economic Council. (2007). *Socio-economic agenda, Israel 2008–2010.* Retrieved February 10, 2012, from the Prime Minister's Office: www.pmo. gov.il/English/PrimeMinistersOffice/DivisionsAndAuthorities/TheNation alEconomicCouncil/Pages/Socio-EconomicAgenda,Israel2008-2010.aspx.

OCHA. (2007). *OCHA closure update, occupied Palestinian territory.* Retrieved May 24, 2010, from United Nations Office for the Coordination of Humanitarian Affairs: www.ochaopt.org/documents/ClosureUpdateOctober2007.pdf.

Roffe-Ofir, S. (2010). Organ-trafficking suspects indicted. *Yedioth News*, April 22. Retrieved May 28, 2010, from www.ynet.co.il/english/articles/0,7340,L-3879327,00.html.

SAWA/UNIFEM. (2008). *Trafficking and forced prostitution of Palestinian women and girls: Forms of modern day slavery*. A Briefing Paper. Retrieved May 22, 2010, from www.unifem.org/attachments/products/forms_of_modern_day_slavery_opt_en.pdf.

UNODC. (2009). *Human trafficking country profiles, Middle East and North Africa*. Retrieved April 26, 2010, from United Nations Office on Drugs and Crime: www.unodc.org/documents/Global_Report_on_TIP.pdf.

U.S. Department of State. (2009). *Trafficking in persons report*. Retrieved January 28, 2010, from www.state.gov/documents/organization/123357.pdf.

———. (2010a). *Trafficking in persons report, 2010*. Retrieved June 20, 2010, from www.state.gov/documents/organization/142979.pdf.

———. (2010b). *2009 human rights reports: Israel and the occupied territories*. Retrieved May 25, 2010, from www.state.gov/g/drl/rls/hrrpt/2009/nea/136070.htm.

———. (2011). *Trafficking in persons report*. Retrieved September 16, 2011, from www.state.gov/g/tip/rls/tiprpt/2011/.

———. (2012). *Trafficking in persons report*. Retrieved August 30, 2012, from www.state.gov/j/tip/rls/tiprpt/2012/.

WCLAC & DCAF. (2012). Palestinian Women and Penal Law. Policy Brief. Retrieved September 3, 2012, from the Geneva Centre for the Democratic Control of Armed Forces: www.dcaf.ch/content/download/.../Policy_Brief_Penal_EN_Final.pdf.

Zebede, M. (2009). Traffickers target Israeli girls to replace foreign sex slaves. *Haaretz*, August 16. Retrieved May 22, 2010, from www.haaretz.com/news/traffickers-target-israeli-girls-to-replace-foreign-sex-slaves-1.282091.

6. COLOMBIA

ABColombia. (2012). *Colombia the current panorama: Victims and Land Restitution Law 1448*. August 3. Retrieved September 4, 2012, from ReliefWeb: http://reliefweb.int/sites/reliefweb.int/files/resources/ABColombia_land_report_-_Colombia_the_Current_Panorama.pdf.

Act 4786 of 2008. (2008). *Comprehensive national strategy against trafficking in persons*. December 12. Retrieved October 2, 2010, from Alcaldia Bogota: www.alcaldiabogota.gov.co/sisjur/normas/Norma1.jsp?i=34645.

Alsema, A. (2010). FARC commander "Mono Jojoy" killed. September 23. Retrieved September 4, 2012, from *Colombia Reports*: http://colombiareports

.com/colombia-news/news/12002-mono-jojoy-killed-colombian-media
.html.

Arrington, V. (2004). Sexual exploitation of minors taints Colombia's Caribbean tourist city. *Times Argus*, November 7. Retrieved March 20, 2007, from www.timesargus.com/apps/pbcs.dll/article?AID=/20041107/NEWS/411070325/1014.

Asahi Shimbun. (2005). Colombia, Japan to tackle trafficking. January 19. Retrieved January 19, 2005, from *Asahi Shimbun*: www.asahi.com/english/nation/TKY200501190138.html.

Begg, K. (2010). Ecuador: FARC launched Putumayo attack from Colombia. September 13. Retrieved October 6, 2010, from *Colombia Reports*: http://colombiareports.com/colombia-news/news/11802-ecuador-putumayo-farc-attack-launched-in-colombia.html.

El Colombiano. (2009). Growing concern for Colombians trapped in Trinidad. December 7. Retrieved October 7, 2010, from *El Colombiano*: www.ecbloguer.com/globalnewsroom/?p=6733.

El Universal. (2009). ELN members seek refuge in Venezuela, says Colombia. December 14. Retrieved October 6, 2010, from *El Universal*: http://english.eluniversal.com/2009/12/14/en_pol_esp_eln-members-seek-ref_14A3190691.shtml.

Gill, L. (2009). *Durable disorder: Parapolitics in Barrancabermeja; NACLA report on the Americas*. July/August. Retrieved October 5, 2010, from North American Congress on Latin America: https://nacla.org/files/A04204022_1.pdf.

Hanson, S. (2009). *FARC, ELN: Colombia's left-wing guerrillas*. August 19. Retrieved October 7, 2010, from Council on Foreign Relations: www.cfr.org/publication/9272/farc_eln.html#p4.

HRI. (2006). *Intra-Caribbean migration and the conflict nexus*. August 31. Retrieved March 20, 2007, from the UN High Commissioner for Refugees: www.unhcr.org/4bfb92099.pdf.

IDMC. (2009). *Colombia: New displacement continues, response still ineffective*. July 3. Retrieved October 3, 2010, from Internal Displacement Monitoring Centre: www.internal-displacement.org/8025708F004BE3B1/(httpInfoFiles)/5BCA28006BFAA8ADC12575E8005CBF23/$file/Colombia%20-%20July%202009.pdf.

———. (2011). *Colombia: Improved government response yet to have impact for IDPs*. December 29. Retrieved January 10, 2012, Internal Displacement Monitoring Centre: from www.internal-displacement.org/8025708F004BE3B1/%28httpInfoFiles%29/4C851081FBE3FB10C1257975005E685E/$file/colombia-overview-Dect2011.pdf.

IOM. (2009). *Mission in Colombia*. Retrieved October 2, 2010, from International Organization for Migration: www.iom.int.

———. (2011). Key regional figures. Retrieved September 4, 2012, from International Organization for Migration: www.iom.int/jahia/Jahia/about-migration/facts-and-figures/americas-facts-and-figures.

Martínez, H. (2009). Trafficking victims' ordeal never over. June 10. Retrieved October 7, 2010, from Inter Press Service: http://ipsnews.net/news.asp?idnews=47163.

MOFA. (2008). *The recent actions Japan has taken to combat TIP (trafficking in persons)*. Retrieved December 5, 2009, from Ministry of Foreign Affairs of Japan: www.mofa.go.jp/POLICY/i_crime/people/action0508.html.

OAS. (2010). OAS calls for dialogue and cooperation in bilateral relations between Colombia and Venezuela. Press release. July 22. Retrieved October 6, 2010, from Organization of American States: www.oas.org/OASpage/press_releases/press_release.asp?sCodigo=E-276/10.

Pachico, E. (2010). Intelligence shows extent of FARC-Venezuela links. May 20. Retrieved October 6, 2010, from *Colombia Reports*: www.colombiareports.com/colombia-news/news/9798-intelligence-shows-extent-of-farc-venezuela-links.html.

Palmer, L. (2010). General confirms: We know location of "Ivan Marquez." July 7. Retrieved October 6, 2010, from *Colombia Reports*: http://colombiareports.com/colombia-news/news/10678-general-backs-uribe-we-know-location-of-farcs-ivan-marquez.html.

Pearson, E. (2002). *Human traffic, human rights: Redefining victim protection*. Retrieved April 8, 2007, from Anti-Slavery International: www.antislavery.org/includes/documents/cm_docs/2009/h/hum_traff_hum_rights_redef_vic_protec_final_full.pdf.

UNCRC. (2000). *Concluding observations of the United Nations Committee on the Rights of the Child, Colombia*. Retrieved March 20, 2007, from the University of Minnesota: www1.umn.edu/humanrts/crc/colombia2000.html.

UNHCR. (2004). *UN Commission on Human Rights, Racism, Racial Discrimination, Xenophobia and All Forms of Discrimination, Report submitted by Mr. Doudou Diène, special rapporteur on contemporary forms of racism, racial discrimination, xenophobia and related intolerance*. February 24. Retrieved August 24, 2009, from UN Commission on Human Rights: www.unhchr.ch/huridocda/huridoca.nsf/0/9f78a478fb97d407c1256e60003e77cc/$FILE/G0411140.doc.

UNODC. (2009a). *Global report on trafficking in persons*. Retrieved June 6, 2010, from United Nations Office on Drugs and Crime: www.unodc.org/documents/Global_Report_on_TIP.pdf.

———. (2009b). *Trafficking in persons; analysis on Europe*. Retrieved June 6, 2010, from United Nations Office on Drugs and Crime: www.ungift.org/docs/ungift/pdf/humantrafficking/Trafficking_in_Persons_in_Europe-Final_09.pdf.

U.S. Department of Labor. (2004). *Colombia, incidence and nature of child labor.* Retrieved March 20, 2007, from www.dol.gov/ilab/media/reports/iclp/tda2004 /colombia.htm.

———. (2009). *List of goods produced by child labor or forced labor.* September 10. Retrieved August 28, 2010, from www.dol.gov/ilab/programs/ocft/PDF /2009TVPRA.pdf.

U.S. Department of State. (2006). *Trafficking in persons report.* Retrieved May 10, 2007, from www.state.gov/documents/organization/66086.pdf.

———. (2007). *Trafficking in persons report.* Retrieved October 14, 2007, from www.state.gov/documents/organization/82902.pdf.

———. (2008). *Trafficking in persons report.* Retrieved July 20, 2008, from www .state.gov/documents/organization/105501.pdf.

———. (2009). *Trafficking in persons report.* Retrieved January 28, 2010, from www.state.gov/documents/organization/123357.pdf.

———. (2010a). *Trafficking in persons report.* Retrieved June 20, 2010, from www .state.gov/documents/organization/142979.pdf.

———. (2010b). *2009 Human rights report: Colombia.* Retrieved October 7, 2010, from www.state.gov/g/drl/rls/hrrpt/2009/wha/136106.htm.

———. (2011). *Trafficking in persons report.* Retrieved September 16, 2011, from www.state.gov/g/tip/rls/tiprpt/2011/.

———. (2012). *Trafficking in persons report.* Retrieved August 30, 2012, from www.state.gov/j/tip/rls/tiprpt/2012/.

USOC. (2004). *The impact of war on women: Colombian women's struggle.* Understanding Colombia Series. Retrieved March 20, 2007, from U.S. Office on Colombia: www.usofficeoncolombia.org/Women%20and%20Children/.

Vanovac, N. (2009). 54 Colombian women victims of human trafficking. September 1. Retrieved October 7, 2010, from *Colombia Reports*: http://colombi areports.com/colombia-news/news/5689-54-colombian-women-victims-of -human-trafficking.html.

Vieira, C. (2010). Paramilitaries don't want to take the blame alone. July 11. Retrieved October 5, 2010, from Inter Press Service: http://ipsnews.net/news .asp?idnews=52115.

War Child International. (2007). *Child soldiers: The shadow of their existence.* Retrieved October 3, 2010, from ReliefWeb: http://reliefweb.int/sites/reliefweb .int/files/resources/2AE1161A29A21AF28525735D006ABB9E-war%20child -child%20soldiers-2007.pdf.

7. IRAQ

Bennett, B. (2006). Stolen away. *Time,* April 23. Retrieved October 7, 2008, from www.time.com/time/magazine/article/0,9171,1186558,00.html.

Business Wire. (2012). Federal court upholds right to sue Jordanian defense contractor in U.S.; Judge rejects argument that U.S. court lacks jurisdiction in Nepali human trafficking case. March 5. Retrieved September 5, 2012, from Bloomberg: http://origin-www.bloomberg.com/apps/news?pid=cone-wsstory&tkr=KBR:US&sid=apcOTh5CLN5o.

Coalition to Stop the Use of Child Soldiers. (2008). *Child soldier, global reports.* Retrieved December 18, 2010, from www.childsoldiersglobalreport.org/files /country_pdfs/FINAL_2008_Global_Report.pdf.

Commission on Wartime Contracting. (2010). Subcontracting risks in combat zones to be probed at July 26 Wartime Contracting hearing on Capitol Hill. Press release, July 20. Retrieved December 20, 2010, from www.wartimecon-tracting.gov/index.php/pressroom/pressreleases/154-cwc-nr-29.

CPA. (2004). *Coalition Provisional Authority order number 17 (revised): Status of the Coalition Provisional Authority, MNF—IRAQ.* Retrieved December 20, 2010, from UN High Commissioner for Refugees: www.unhcr.org/refworld/pdfid /49997ada3.pdf.

Democracy Now. (2010). WikiLeaks Iraq War logs expose U.S.-backed Iraqi tor-ture, 15,000 more civilian deaths, and contractors run amok. *Democracy Now,* October 25. Retrieved December 20, 2010, from www.democracynow .org/2010/10/25/wikileaks_iraq_war_logs_expose_us.

Global Policy Forum. (2005). Iraq: Focus on boys trapped. Press release, August 8. Retrieved October 6, 2008, from www.globalpolicy.org/security/issues /iraq/attack/consequences/2005/0808trapped.htm.

Handley M., & M. McOwen. (2009). Combating human trafficking in Iraq: Ad-hikari v. Daoud. *International Law News,* 38, no. 1. Retrieved October 7, 2008, from Cohen Milstein Sellers & Toll, PLLC: www.cohenmilstein.com /media/pnc/2/media.682.pdf.

Hedgpeth, D. (2008). KBR, partner in Iraq contract, sued in human trafficking case. *Washington Post,* August 28. Retrieved October 7, 2008, from www .washingtonpost.com/wp-dyn/content/article/2008/08/27/AR2008082703237 .html?nav=rss_world/mideast/iraq.

Hirsh, M. (2007). The age of irresponsibility: How Bush has created a moral vacuum in Iraq in which Americans can kill for free. *Newsweek,* September 20. Retrieved December 23, 2010, from http://web.archive.org/web /20071001161845/http://www.msnbc.msn.com/id/20892483/site/news week/.

HRW. (2008). Iraq: Pass new law ending immunity for contractors. News release, Human Rights Watch, January 9. Retrieved December 24, 2010, from www. hrw.org/news/2008/01/08/iraq-pass-new-law-ending-immunity-contractors.

IILHR. (2010). *Women and the law in Iraq.* Retrieved February 10, 2012, from Institute for International Law and Human Rights: http://iilhr.org/documents/womenandlawiniraqEN.pdf.

IRIN. (2008). Iraq: Move to prevent children being exploited by militants. Press release, July 29. Retrieved December 18, 2010, from Integrated Regional Information Networks, the humanitarian news and analysis service of the UN Office for the Coordination of Humanitarian Affairs: www.irinnews.org /Report.aspx?ReportId=79498.

KBR. (n.d.). History. Retrieved October 7, 2008, from Kellogg Brown & Root, Inc.: www.kbr.com/About/History/.

Kubota, S. (2010). Human trafficking alleged in Iraq contracting. Federal News Radio, July 27. Retrieved December 20, 2010, from www.federalnewsradio. com/?nid=15&sid=2012421.

Lavender, L. (2012). Human trafficking in Iraq: 2003 and beyond. Retrieved September 5, 2012, from Civil-Military Fusion Centre: https://www.cimic web.org/cmo/medbasin/Holder/Documents/r015%20CFC%20Monthly %20Thematic%20Report%20(14-May-12).pdf.

Mason, R. C. (2009). U.S.-Iraq Withdrawal/Status of Forces Agreement: Issues for Congressional oversight. July 13. Retrieved on September 5, 2012, from Federation of American Scientists: www.fas.org/sgp/crs/natsec/R40011.pdf.

OWFI. (2010). Prostitution and trafficking of women and girls in Iraq. March 5. Retrieved December 27, 2010, from Organization of Women's Freedom in Iraq: www.equalityiniraq.com/images/stories/pdf/prostitutionandtrafficking -OWFIreport.pdf.

Pincus, W. (2008). U.S. has detained 2,500 juveniles as enemy combatants. *Washington Post,* May 25. Retrieved December 24, 2010, from www.washing tonpost.com/wp-dyn/content/story/2008/05/14/ST2008051404032.html.

Presidency Council. (2012). Law of 2012, Trafficking in Persons. Retrieved September 6, 2012, from Civil-Military Fusion Centre: https://www.cimicweb. org/cmo/ComplexCoverage/Documents/Iraq/TIP%20Law%202012_FINAL %20TEXT.pdf

Ramchandra Adhikari et. al v. Daoud & Partners et. al., filed April 24, 2009. Case no.: 4:2009cv01237 (U.S. District Court, Southern District of Texas).

Republic of Iraq. (2010). Penal Code No. 111 of 1969 updated to include all amendments made up to 14 March 2010. March 14. Retrieved December 2, 2010, from Global Justice Project: Iraq: gjpi.org/wp-content/uploads/gjpi -pc-1969-v1-eng.doc.

Risen, J. (2008). End of immunity worries U.S. contractors in Iraq. *New York Times*, November 30. Retrieved December 24, 2010, from www.nytimes.com /2008/12/01/world/middleeast/01contractors.html.

Sarhan, A. (2009). Iraqi babies for sale: People trafficking crisis grows as gangs exploit poor families and corrupt system. *The Guardian*, April 6. Retrieved December 2, 2010, from www.guardian.co.uk/world/2009/apr/06/child -trafficking-iraq.

Schwellenbach, N., & Leonnig, C. (2010). U.S. policy a paper tiger against sex trade in war zones. *Washington Post,* July 18. Retrieved December 20, 2010, from www.washingtonpost.com/wp-dyn/content/article/2010/07/17 /AR2010071701401.html.

Simpson, C. (2006). Iraq War contractors ordered to end abuses. *Chicago Tribune,* April 23. Retrieved October 7, 2008, from http://articles.chicagotribune.com/2006–04–24/news/0604240221_1_orders-promise-harsh-actions -iraq-from-impoverished-countries-return-passports.

Switzky, B. R. (2008). D.C. attorneys win human trafficking case in Iraq. *Washington Business Journal,* July 11. Retrieved October 7, 2008, from http:// washington.bizjournals.com/washington/stories/2008/07/14/story3.html.

United Nations Security Council. (2007). *Children and armed conflict: Report of the secretary-general.* Retrieved December 18, 2010, from www.ceipaz.org /images/contenido/Children%20and%20armed%20conflict_ENG.pdf.

U.S. Department of Labor. (2009). *2008 findings on the worst forms of child labor.* Retrieved December 2, 2010, from www.dol.gov/ilab/media/reports/iclp/.

U.S. Department of State. (2003). *Trafficking in persons report.* Retrieved November 18, 2010, from www.state.gov/documents/organization/21555.pdf.

———. (2009). *Trafficking in persons report.* Retrieved January 28, 2010, from www.state.gov/documents/organization/123357.pdf.

———. (2010). *Trafficking in persons report.* Retrieved June 20, 2010, from www .state.gov/documents/organization/142979.pdf.

8. SYRIA

ABS-CBN. (2011). Many OFWs victims of human trafficking in Syria. ABS-CBN, August 18. Retrieved September 15, 2011, from www.abs-cbnnews.com/ global-filipino/08/17/11/many-ofws-victims-human-trafficking-syria.

AFP (American Free Press). (2010). Syria nabs 11 alleged organ traffickers. *Sydney Morning Herald,* October 5. Retrieved January 26, 2011, from http://news .smh.com.au/breaking-news-world/syria-nabs-11-alleged-organ-traffickers -20101005-164lz.html.

Al-Masry Al-Youm. (2010). Eleven arrested for alleged Damascus-to-Cairo organ trafficking. *Al-Masry Al-Youm,* October 4. Retrieved January 25, 2011, from www.almasryalyoum.com/en/news/eleven-arrested-alleged-organ-trafficking-damascus-cairo.

Associated Press. (2011). UN: Death toll In Syria unrest at least 2,600. National Public Radio, September 12. Retrieved September 15, 2011, from www.npr.org/templates/story/story.php?storyId=140395286.

Bulos, N. (2012). Jordan feels the strain of Syria refugee influx. *Los Angeles Times,* September 6. Retrieved September 6, 2012, from www.latimes.com/news/nationworld/world/la-fg-syria-jordan-refugees-20120903,0,853146.story.

Doha Debates. (2012). Arabs want Syria's President Assad to go—opinion poll. *Doha Debates,* January 2. Retrieved January 17, 2012, from www.thedohadebates.com/news/item/index.asp?n=14312.

GAO. (2009). *Iraqi refugee assistance, improvements needed in measuring progress, assessing needs, tracking funds, and developing an international strategic plan.* Retrieved January 25, 2011, from the U.S. Government Accountability Office: www.gao.gov/new.items/d09120.pdf.

Hassan, N. (2007). "50,000 Iraqi refugees" forced into prostitution. *The Independent,* June 24. Retrieved January 26, 2011, from www.independent.co.uk/news/world/middle-east/50000-iraqi-refugees-forced-into-prostitution-454424.html.

HRW. (2011). *World report 2011: Syria.* Human Rights Watch. Retrieved February 11, 2012, from www.hrw.org/world-report-2011/syria.

IOM. (2010a). Initiative helps vulnerable Iraqi female-headed households and victims of trafficking in Syria. Press briefing, October 22. Retrieved January 26, 2011, from International Organization for Migration: www.iom.int/jahia/Jahia/media/press-briefing-notes/pbnAF/cache/offonce/lang/en?entryId=28537.

———. (2010b). Syria, facts and figures. Retrieved January 25, 2011, from International Organization for Migration: www.iom.int/jahia/Jahia/pid/427.

IRIN. (2005). Syria: Authorities tackle issue of human trafficking. September 13. Retrieved October 16, 2008, from Integrated Regional Information Networks, the humanitarian news and analysis service of the UN Office for the Coordination of Humanitarian Affairs: www.irinnews.org/Report.aspx?ReportId=25472.

———. (2006). Iraq-Syria: Sex traffickers target women in war-torn Iraq. October 16. Retrieved October 12, 2008, from Integrated Regional Information Networks, the humanitarian news and analysis service of the UN Office for the Coordination of Humanitarian Affairs: www.irinnews.org/Report.aspx?ReportId=61903.

———. (2008). Syria: New draft law targets sex traffickers. March 17. Retrieved January 25, 2011, from Integrated Regional Information Networks, the humanitarian news and analysis service of the UN Office for the Coordination of Humanitarian Affairs: www.irinnews.org/Report.aspx?ReportId=77311.

———. (2010). Syria: Number of Iraqi refugees revised downwards. June 20. Retrieved January 25, 2011, from Integrated Regional Information Networks, the humanitarian news and analysis service of the UN Office for the Coordination of Humanitarian Affairs: ww.irinnews.org/Report.aspx?ReportId=89549.

———. (2012). Analysis: Syria's forgotten refugees. April 23. Retrieved from Integrated Regional Information Networks, the humanitarian news and analysis service of the UN Office for the Coordination of Humanitarian Affairs: www.irinnews.org/Report/95336/Analysis-Syria-s-forgotten-refugees.

Moschella, G. (2010). Syria steps up anti-trafficking measures. *Eurosapiens*, September 27. Retrieved January 26, 2011, from www.eurosapiens.it/?p=1954.

New York Times. (2011). Events in Syria: A chronology. *New York Times*. Retrieved September 15, 2011, from www.nytimes.com/ref/timestopics/syriatimeline.html.

Peel, M. (2012). Diplomats seek UN Syria consensus. *Financial Times,* January 17. Retrieved January 17, 2012, from www.ft.com/cms/s/0/bd2d7756–40f1–11e1-b521–00144feab49a.html#axzz1jkpIVMnE.

Rashwan, H. (2010). Organ trafficking active between Egypt and Syria, says report. *Al-Masry Al-Youm,* November 30. Retrieved January 26, 2011, from www.almasryalyoum.com/en/news/organ-trafficking-active-between-egypt-and-syria-says-report.

Sawah, W. (2010). "Trafficking in persons in Syria." January 12. *Syrian Glow* (blog). Retrieved January 26, 2011, from http://syrianglow.blogspot.com/2010/01/trafficking-in-persons-in-syria.html.

Syrian Arab Republic. (2004). *Legislative Decree 59.* Retrieved January 26, 2011, from Commercial Bank of Syria: www.cbs-bank.sy/files/en_699.pdf.

UNCRC. (2012). *Consideration of reports submitted by states parties under article 44 of the Convention, concluding observations: Syrian Arab Republic.* February 9. Retrieved September 6, 2012, from Bayefsky: www.bayefsky.com/pdf/syria_t4_crc_58.pdf.

UN International Convention on the Protection of the Rights of All Migrant Workers and Members of Their Families. (2008). May 2. Retrieved September 6, 2012, from the Office of the United Nations High Commissioner for Human Rights: www2.ohchr.org/english/bodies/cmw/docs/CMW.C.SYR.CO.1_final.doc

UN News Centre. (2011). As Syrian death toll tops 5,000, UN human rights chief warns about key city. December 12. Retrieved January 17, 2012, from www.un.org/apps/news/story.asp?NewsID=40708&Cr=syria.

———. (2012). Syria: UNICEF scales up health and nutrition response for children affected by crisis. September 6. Retrieved September 6, 2012, from www.un .org/apps/news/story.asp?NewsID=42817&Cr=Syria&Cr1=#.UElvw0JgPFI.

U.S. Department of State. (2008). *Trafficking in persons report.* Retrieved June 9, 2008, from www.state.gov/documents/organization/105501.pdf.

———. (2009). *Trafficking in persons report.* Retrieved January 28, 2010, from www.state.gov/documents/organization/123357.pdf.

———. (2010). *Trafficking in persons report.* Retrieved June 20, 2010, from www .state.gov/documents/organization/142979.pdf.

———. (2011). *Trafficking in persons report.* Retrieved September 2011, from www.state.gov/g/tip/rls/tiprpt/2011/.

———. (2012). *Trafficking in persons report.* Retrieved August 30, 2012, from www.state.gov/j/tip/rls/tiprpt/2012/.

9. CANADA

Akin, D. (2010). Tories promise new law on human trafficking. *Toronto Sun,* September 5. Retrieved September 7, 2010, from www.torontosun.com/news /canada/2010/09/05/15255101.html.

Barnett, L. (2006). Bill C-49: An Act to Amend the Criminal Code (Trafficking in Persons). January 12. Retrieved January 13, 2012, from Parliament of Canada: www.parl.gc.ca/About/Parliament/LegislativeSummaries/bills_ls .asp?ls=C49&Parl=38&Ses=1.

Bell, S. (2012a). Sri Lankan smuggled into Canada on MV Ocean Lady accepted as refugee due to possible danger. *National Post,* August 13. Retrieved September 8, 2012, from http://news.nationalpost.com/2012/08/13/sri-lankan -smuggled-into-canada-on-mv-ocean-lady-granted-refugee-status-due-to -possible-danger/.

———. (2012b). Two more refugee claimants from MV Sun Sea ordered de-ported to Sri Lanka. *National Post,* May 1. Retrieved September 7, 2012, from http://news.nationalpost.com/2012/05/01/two-more-refugee-claimants -from-mv-sun-sea-ordered-deported-to-sri-lanka/.

Bolan, K. (2010). Province to investigate complaints of abuse, filthy conditions at bush camp. *Vancouver Sun,* August 11. Retrieved September 8, 2010, from 199.71.40.195/vancouversun/news/story.html?id=f89b8d74-7d5d-47cc-a65b -c03549d86a0a&p=2.

Canadian Immigration Information Centre. (2011). Report suggests human trafficking in Tamil migration to Canada. February 13. Retrieved September

7, 2012, from www.canadianimmigrationinformation.com/2011/02/report-suggests-human-trafficking-in-tamil-migration-to-canada.html.

CBC News. (2009). New law ends 2-for-1 credit on jail sentences. *CBC News*, October 23. Retrieved September 10, 2010, from www.cbc.ca/canada/story/2009/10/23/prison-sentencing-credit-limited.html.

———. (2010). Prostitution laws struck down by Ont. court. *CBC News*, September 28. Retrieved from www.cbc.ca/news/canada/story/2010/09/28/prostitution-law028.html.

CCR. (2012). Anti-smuggling or anti-refugee? Press release, June 16. Retrieved January 12, 2012, from Canadian Council for Refugees: http://ccrweb.ca/en/c4.

Chan, L. (2007). Reforming Canada's record on human trafficking. *UBC (University of British Columbia) Reports*, September 6, vol. 53, no. 9. Retrieved November 2, 2007, from www.publicaffairs.ubc.ca/ubcreports/2007/07sep06/reform.html.

Cherry, T. (2010). Human trafficking bill passes Senate. *Toronto Sun*, June 17. Retrieved September 7, 2010, from www.torontosun.com/news/torontoandgta/2010/06/17/14428941.html.

CIC. (2007). Strengthening protection and assistance for victims of human trafficking. June 19. Retrieved November 2, 2007, from Citizenship and Immigration Canada: www.cic.gc.ca/English/information/applications/trp.asp.

———. (2012). Legislation to protect Canada's immigration system receives royal assent. News Release, June 29. Retrieved from Citizenship and Immigration Canada: http://www.cic.gc.ca/english/department/media/releases/2012/2012-06-29.asp.

CISC. (2008). *Organized crime and domestic trafficking in persons in Canada*. Retrieved September 8, 2010, from Criminal Intelligence Service Canada: www.cisc.gc.ca/products_services/domestic_trafficking_persons/document/sib_web_en.pdf.

CityNews. (2006). Local sex crime conference focuses on human trafficking. *CityNews*, November 20. Retrieved October 29, 2007, from http://www.citytv.com/toronto/citynews/news/local/article/24605.

Dalley, M. (2010). *Hidden abuse, hidden crime: The domestic trafficking of children and youth in Canada; the relationship to sexual exploitation, running away and children at risk of harm*. Retrieved February 13, 2012, from http://cpc.phippsinc.com/cpclib/pdf/74192.pdf.

Department of Justice, Canada. (2001). Immigration and Refugee Protection Act, S.C. 2001, c. 27. Retrieved September 8, 2012, from http://laws-lois.justice.gc.ca/PDF/I-2.5.pdf.

———. (2012). *Funding*. Retrieved September 6, 2012, from http://canada.justice.gc.ca/eng/pi/pcvi-cpcv/fun-fin2.html.

Dhillon, S. (2011). "Perversion of the law" forces migrants to pay smugglers, lawyer argues. *Globe and Mail*, March 30. Retrieved April 2, 2011, from www .theglobeandmail.com/news/national/british-columbia/perversion-of-the -law-forces-migrants-to-pay-smugglers-lawyer-argues/article1964235/.

Fitzpatrick, M. (2006). MP calls for action to combat human trafficking. *Vancouver Sun*, December 8. Retrieved October 29, 2007, from www.canada.com/ vancouversun/news/story.html?id=827e2ece-6b58-49d3-9733-a1a 77451366d&k=7165.

Legislative Assembly of Ontario. (2009). *An Act to protect foreign nationals employed as live-in caregivers and in other prescribed employment and to amend the Employment Standards Act, 2000.* December 15. Retrieved September 8, 2010, from Service Ontario e-laws: www.e-laws.gov.on.ca/html/source/statutes /english/2009/elaws_src_s09032_e.htm.

Mayes, A. (2010). Awareness campaign takes aim at human trafficking. *Winnipeg Free Press*, September 8. Retrieved September 9, 2010, from www.winni-pegfreepress.com/local/awareness-campaign-takes-aim-at-human-traffick ing-102436379.html.

NUPGE. (2009). President's commentary: Canada's shameful refusal to ratify the ILO convention on forced labour. Press release, June 18. Retrieved September 8, 2010, from National Union of Public and General Employees: www.nupge.ca/node/2372.

———. (2010). Canada ratifies ILO Convention on Maritime Labour. Press release, July 27. Retrieved September 8, 2010, from National Union of Public and General Employees: www.nupge.ca/content/3426/canada-ratifies-ilo -convention-maritime-labour.

Parliament of Canada. (2010a). Bill C-25: Truth in Sentencing Act. January 25. Retrieved September 10, 2010, from Parliament of Canada: www2.parl.gc.ca/ Sites/LOP/LegislativeSummaries/Bills_ls.asp?lang=E&ls=c25&source=library _prb&Parl=40&Ses=2.

———. (2010b). Bill C-268: An Act to amend the Criminal Code (minimum sentence for offences involving trafficking of persons under the age of eighteen years). March 3. Retrieved September 7, 2010, from Parliament of Canada: www2.parl.gc.ca/HousePublications/Publication.aspx?Docid=4330350&file=4.

———. (2010c). *Proceedings of the Standing Senate Committee on Social Affairs, Science and Technology.* June 2. Retrieved September 8, 2010, from Parliament of Canada: www.parl.gc.ca/40/3/parlbus/commbus/senate/Com-e/soci-e/08eva -e.htm?Language=E&Parl=40&Ses=3&comm_id=47.

Payton, L. (2009). Ottawa woman gets seven years in teen-luring case. *Vancouver Sun*, April 9. Retrieved September 9, 2010, from www.vancouversun.com /news/Ottawa+woman+gets+seven+years+teen+luring+case/1483290/story .html.

Perrin, B. (2009a). Bill C-268: Minimum sentences for child trafficking needed. *Alberta Law Review Online Supplement,* March 12. Retrieved September 8, 2010, from http://ualbertalaw.typepad.com/alr_supplement/2009/03/bill-c-268-minimum-sentences-for-child-trafficking-needed.html.

———. (2009b). Confronting human trafficking in Canada. LexisNexis Canada, February 6. Retrieved January 13, 2012, from www.lawyersweekly.ca/index.php?section=article&articleid=849.

———. (2011). Migrant smuggling, Canada's response to a global criminal enterprise. October 2. Retrieved September 7, 2012, from the Macdonald-Laurier Institute: http://www.macdonaldlaurier.ca/files/pdf/Migrant-Smuggling-Canadas-Response-to-a-Global-Criminal-Enterprise-October-2011.pdf.

Rabson, M. (2009). Legislation targets traffickers of children. *Winnipeg Free Press,* January 30. Retrieved September 7, 2010, from www.winnipegfreepress.com/canada/legislation_targets_traffickers_of_children38687727.html.

RCMP. (2010). *Human trafficking in Canada.* Retrieved January 13, 2012, from Royal Canadian Mounted Police: http://publications.gc.ca/collections/collection_2011/grc-rcmp/PS64-78-2010-eng.pdf.

UNODC. (2009). *Global report on trafficking in persons: A threat assessment.* Retrieved June 6, 2010, from United Nations Office on Drugs and Crime: www.unodc.org/documents/Global_Report_on_TIP.pdf.

U.S. Department of State. (2007a). *Country report on human rights practices, 2006, Canada, released by the Bureau of Democracy, Human Rights, and Labor.* Retrieved October 29, 2007, www.state.gov/g/drl/rls/hrrpt/2006/78883.htm.

———. (2007b). *Trafficking in persons report.* Retrieved August 31, 2010, from www.state.gov/documents/organization/82902.pdf.

———. (2010). *Trafficking in persons report.* Retrieved June 20, 2010, from www.state.gov/documents/organization/142979.pdf.

———. (2011). *Trafficking in persons report.* Retrieved September 16, 2011, from www.state.gov/g/tip/rls/tiprpt/2011/.

———. (2012). *Trafficking in persons report.* Retrieved August 30, 2012, from www.state.gov/j/tip/rls/tiprpt/2012/.

Whittington, L. (2010). Police investigating refugee boat to see if human smuggling laws violated: Vic Toews. *The Star,* August 13. Retrieved September 7, 2010, from www.thestar.com/news/canada/article/847883—police-investigating-refugee-boat-to-see-if-human-smuggling-laws-violated-toews.

10. ITALY

AFP. (2010). Romanian and Italian police dismantle human trafficking gang. *Vancouver Sun,* June 21. Retrieved August 13, 2010, from www.vancouversun

.com/news/Romanian+Italian+police+dismantle+human+trafficking+gang
/3171273/story.html#ixzz0wWIMKK6K.

Aminu, M. (2010). Nigeria: Naptip moves against human traffickers. AllAfrica,
February 23. Retrieved August 13, 2010, from http://allafrica.com/stories
/201002240816.html.

Carling, J. (2005). Trafficking in women from Nigeria to Europe. Retrieved August 13, 2010, from Migration Information Source: www.migrationinforma
tion.org/feature/display.cfm?ID=318.

———. (2006). *Migration, human smuggling and trafficking from Nigeria to Europe.*
Retrieved August 13, 2010, from Peace Reseach Institute Oslo: www.prio.no
/sptrans/1326102309/file48438_carling_2006_migration_human_smug
gling_and_trafficking_from_nigeria_to_europe.pdf.

Chamber of Deputies and Senate. (2003). Law n. 228. Measures against trafficking in persons. August 11. Retrieved January 1, 2011, from www.e-notes
-observatory.org/legislation/italy-measures-trafficking-persons/.

Council of Europe. (n.d.). *Action against trafficking in human beings.* Retrieved
December 29, 2010, from www.coe.int/t/dghl/monitoring/trafficking/default
_en.asp.

Day, M. (2010). Immigrant riots rock southern Italian town as tensions ex-
plode. *The Independent,* January 9. Retrieved August 16, 2010, from www
.independent.co.uk/news/world/europe/immigrant-riots-rock-southern-ital
ian-town-as-tensions-explode-1862413.html.

Donadio, R. (2010). Race riots grip Italian town, and Mafia is suspected. *New York
Times,* January 10. Retrieved August 21, 2010, from www.nytimes.com/2010
/01/11/world/europe/11italy.html?_r=1.

European Parliament. (2010). Compatibility of Italy's "second security package" with EC law. Press release, November 26. Retrieved September 17, 2011,
from www.europarl.europa.eu/sides/getDoc.do?pubRef=-//EP//TEXT+WQ+E
-2010–9731+0+DOC+XML+V0//EN.

Fruehauf, U. (2011). EU-Libya agreements on refugees and asylum seekers: The
need for a reassessment. Retrieved January 16, 2012, from Heinrich Böll Stif-
tung: www.boell.de/downloads/perspectives_02-37_urs_fruehauf.pdf.

Germano, G. (2001). "Human trafficking as a transnational problem: The responses of destination countries." *Proceedings of the First Pan-African Conference
on Human Trafficking, Abuja, Nigeria,* February 19-23, 2001, pp.117–127.

HRW. (2010). Libya: End live fire against suspected boat migrants; Italy should
halt joint patrols after Libyans fire on Italian fishing vessel. News release,
September 16. Retrieved January 16, 2012, from Human Rights Watch: www
.hrw.org/news/2010/09/16/libya-end-live-fire-against-suspected-boat-mi
grants.

IOM. (2006). Human trafficking from Nigeria to Europe. Press briefing, September 26. Retrieved August 13, 2010, from International Organization for Migration: www.iom.int/jahia/Jahia/media/press-briefing-notes/pbnEU/cache/of fonce/lang/en?entryId=11038.

Owen, R. (2008). Woman, 19, forced to swim with piranhas at circus. *The Times*, March 26. Retrieved August 2, 2010, from www.timesonline.co.uk/tol /news/world/europe/article3624431.ece.

Povoledo, E. (2007). With scars that will never heal, one woman fights human trafficking. *New York Times*, September 21. Retrieved August 2, 2010, from www.nytimes.com/2007/09/21/world/europe/21iht-traffic.4.7597912.html? _r=2.

Tripoli Post. (2011). Libya, Italy Reactivate Friendship Treaty. December 16. Retrieved September 10, 2012, from www.tripolipost.com/articledetail.asp?c=1 &i=7503.

Truscott, C. (2008). Circus sisters rescued from snake and piranha acts. *The Guardian*, March 26. Retrieved December 30, 2010, from www.guardian.co .uk/world/2008/mar/26/italy.

UNODC. (2009a). *Global report on trafficking in persons.* Retrieved June 6, 2010, from United Nations Office on Drugs and Crime: http://www.unodc.org/docu ments/Global_Report_on_TIP.pdf.

———. (2009b). *Trafficking in persons: Analysis on Europe.* Retrieved June 6, 2010, from United Nations Office on Drugs and Crime: www.ungift.org/docs/un gift/pdf/humantrafficking/Trafficking_in_Persons_in_Europe-Final_09 .pdf.

U.S. Department of State. (2010a). *Trafficking in persons report.* Retrieved June 20, 2010, from www.state.gov/documents/organization/142979.pdf.

———. (2010b). *2009 human rights report: Italy.* Retrieved December 30, 2010, from www.state.gov/g/drl/rls/hrrpt/2009/eur/136038.htm.

———. (2011a). *Trafficking in persons report.* Retrieved September 16, 2011, from www.state.gov/g/tip/rls/tiprpt/2011/.

———. (2011b). *2010 human rights report: Italy.* Retrieved September 10, 2012, from www.state.gov/j/drl/rls/hrrpt/2010/eur/154431.htm.

———. (2012a). *Trafficking in persons report.* Retrieved August 30, 2012, from www.state.gov/j/tip/rls/tiprpt/2012/.

———. (2012b). *2011 human rights report: Italy.* Retrieved September 10, 2012, from www.state.gov/j/drl/rls/hrrpt/2011/eur/186366.htm.

Watkins, T. (2011). Italy suspends friendship treaty with Libya. February 28. CNN. Retrieved September 10, 2012, from http://articles.cnn.com/2011-02 -28/world/libya.italy_1_moammar-gadhafi-friendship-treaty-italian-ministry ?_s=PM:WORLD.

Zaccaro, S. (2009). Trafficking from Nigeria rises sharply. Inter Press Service, September 11. Retrieved August 13, 2010, from http://ipsnews.net/news.asp?idnews=48405.

11. FRANCE

Amnesty International Canada. (2006). France: Women trafficked and forced to work in the sex trade. June 7. Retrieved November 2, 2008, from www.amnesty.ca.

Audi, N., & Brothers, C. (2009). French police dismantle migrant camp. *New York Times*, September 22. Retrieved 22 2010, October, from www.nytimes.com/2009/09/23/world/europe/23france.html.

BBC News. (2010a). Euro MPs tell France to stop deporting Roma. *BBC News*, September 9. Retrieved October 20, 2010, from www.bbc.co.uk/news/world-europe-11243923.

———. (2010b). Q&A: France Roma expulsions. *BBC News*, October 19. Retrieved September 12, 2012, from www.bbc.co.uk/news/world-europe-11027288.

Coatnet. (2004). National law—France. Retrieved October 25, 2010, from http://www.coatnet.org/en/21211.asp.

COE. (2006). Roma and Travellers glossary. December 11. Retrieved September 10, 2012, from the Council of Europe: www.coe.int/t/dg3/romatravellers/default_en.asp.

CRC. (2009). *Committee on the Rights of the Child.* Retrieved October 22, 2010, from United Nations Convention on the Rights of the Child: www2.ohchr.org/english/bodies/crc/docs/CRC.C.FRA.Q.4.Add.1.pdf.

Davies, L. (2010). Bring back the brothel, says female French MP. *The Guardian*, March 18. Retrieved October 25, 2010, from www.guardian.co.uk/world/2010/mar/18/france-brothel-prostitution-female-mp.

ECHR. (2010). Case of Rantsev v. Cyprus and Russia. January 7. Retrieved October 22, 2010, from European Court of Human Rights: http://hudoc.echr.coe.int/sites/eng/pages/search.aspx?i=001-96549.

Embassy of the United States in Paris, France. (2010). France: Input for the 2010 trafficking in persons report (part 1 of 3). Retrieved September 10, 2012, from WikiLeaks: http://wikileaks.org/cable/2010/02/10PARIS196.html.

European Parliament. (2010). European Parliament resolution of 9 September 2010 on the situation of Roma and on freedom of movement in the European Union. September 9. Retrieved October 20, 2010, from www.europarl.europa.eu/sides/getDoc.do?pubRef=-//EP//TEXT+TA+P7-TA-2010-0312+0+DOC+XML+V0//EN.

French Republic. (2005). Penal Code. July 4. Retrieved October 25, 2010, from Legifrance: www.legifrance.gouv.fr/content/download/1957/13715/version/4/file/Code_33.pdf.

HRW. (2009). Lost in transit. Human Rights Watch, October 29. Retrieved October 22, 2010, from www.hrw.org/en/node/86208/section/7.

———. (2012). France: Renewed crackdown on Roma. August 10. Retrieved September 10, 2012, from www.hrw.org/news/2012/08/10/france-renewed-crackdown-roma.

IOL. (2007). Shocking human trafficking case. *Independent Online*, April 20. Retrieved November 13, 2008, from www.int.iol.co.za/index.php?set_id=1&click_id=3&art_id=nw20070420172522805C534913

Lichfield, J. (2005). French police turn attention to "the pimp on the corner." *The Independent*, March 21. Retrieved October 25, 2010, from www.independent.co.uk/news/world/europe/french-police-turn-attention-to-the-pimp-on-the-corner-529320.html.

Novinite. (2010). Bulgarians busted for human trafficking to Germany, France. *Novinite*, October 21. Retrieved October 22, 2010, from www.novinite.com/view_news.php?id=121351.

People's Daily. (2008). France pledges co-op to end human trafficking in Africa. *People's Daily*, May 30. Retrieved October 30, 2008, from http://english.peopledaily.com.cn/90001/90777/6421971.html.

Phillips L., & A. Chrisafis. (2011). Roma campaigners dismiss Brussels' claim on evictions and expulsions; France and Italy among member states still breaking up camps and deporting EU citizens contrary to announcement, NGOs say. *The Guardian*, August 25. Retrieved January 16, 2012, from www.guardian.co.uk/world/2011/aug/25/roma-campaigners-dismiss-brussels-deportations-claim.

Rossi, A. (2010). Thousands of Roma Gypsies deported from France will head for Britain, Germany or Spain, according to members of their community. September 10. Retrieved January 16, 2012, from Sky News: http://news.sky.com/story/808159/roma-migrants-heading-for-western-europe.

Sofia Echo. (2010). Police take action in Varna against human trafficking. *Sofia Echo*, April 26. Retrieved October 20, 2010, from http://sofiaecho.com/2010/04/26/892591_police-take-action-in-varna-against-human-trafficking.

Telegraph. (2010). France debates the return of bordellos. *The Telegraph*, March 18. Retrieved October 25, 2010, from www.telegraph.co.uk/news/worldnews/europe/france/7473343/France-debates-the-return-of-bordellos.html.

UNODC. (2009a). *Global report on trafficking in persons.* Retrieved June 6, 2010, from United Nations Office on Drugs and Crime: www.unodc.org/documents/Global_Report_on_TIP.pdf.

———. (2009b). *Trafficking in persons; Analysis on Europe.* Retrieved June 6, 2010, from United Nations Office on Drugs and Crime: www.ungift.org/docs/ungift /pdf/humantrafficking/Trafficking_in_Persons_in_Europe-Final_09.pdf.

UPI. (2010). France skirts Roma expulsion punishment. United Press International, October 20. Retrieved October 21, 2010, from www.upi.com/Top_ News/World-News/2010/10/20/France-skirts-Roma-expulsion-punishment/ UPI-50851287583356/.

U.S. Department of State. (2008). *Trafficking in persons report.* Retrieved October 24, 2008, from www.state.gov/documents/organization/105501.pdf.

———. (2009). *Trafficking in persons report.* Retrieved June 5, 2010, from www .state.gov/documents/organization/123357.pdf.

———. (2010). *Trafficking in persons report.* Retrieved June 20, 2010, from www .state.gov/documents/organization/142979.pdf.

———. (2011). *Trafficking in persons report.* Retrieved September 16, 2011, from www.state.gov/g/tip/rls/tiprpt/2011/.

———. (2012). *Trafficking in persons report.* Retrieved August 30, 2012, from www.state.gov/j/tip/rls/tiprpt/2012/.

12. IRAN

Biklou, L. M. (2012). The influence of age on criminal responsibility in Iran and Azerbaijan law. *Journal of Basic and Applied Scientific Research*, vol. 2. no. 1., pp. 322–326. Retrieved January 18, 2012, from TextRoad Publication: www .textroad.com/pdf/JBASR/J.%20Basic.%20Appl.%20Sci.%20Res.,%202(1)322 -326,%202012.pdf.

Commission of the European Communities. (2001). *Research based on case studies of victims of trafficking in human beings in 3 EU member states, i.e., Belgium, Italy and the Netherlands.* Retrieved November 22, 2010, from Commission of the European Communities, DG Justice & Home Affairs: http://ec.europa.eu /justice_home/daphnetoolkit/files/projects/2001_010/int_trafficking_case _studies_be_it_nl_hippokrates.pdf.

Fehresti, Z. (2010). Legislative approaches towards human trafficking in pre- versus post-Islamic Revolution Iran. *Iran and the Caucasus*, vol. 14, no. 2, pp. 431–447. Copy in author's possession.

Harrison, F. (2007). Iran talks up temporary marriages. *BBC News*, June 2. Retrieved November 28, 2010, from http://news.bbc.co.uk/2/hi/6714885.stm.

Hepburn, S., & Simon, R. J. (2007). *Women's roles and statuses the world over.* Lanham, Md.: Lexington Books.

Hosseini-Divkolaye, N. S. (2009). Iran: Migrant smuggling and trafficking in persons. Retrieved November 26, 2010, from Forced Migration Review

(FMR), published by the Refugee Studies Centre of the Oxford Department of International Development, University of Oxford: www.fmreview.org /FMRpdfs/FMR32/66–67.pdf.

Hughes, D. M. (2004). Sex slave jihad. *Front Page Magazine*, January 27. Retrieved October 1, 2008, from http://archive.frontpagemag.com/readArticle.aspx ?ARTID=14542.

———. (2006). *Report on human trafficking in Iran, trafficking: Modern day slavery.* February 7. McLean: Women's Freedom Forum. Copy in author's possession.

IANS (Indo-Asian News Service). (2010). Pakistan orders probe into human trafficking to Iran. *Deccan Herald*, November 19. Retrieved November 22, 2010, from www.deccanherald.com/content/114200/pakistan-orders-probe-human -trafficking.html.

IOM. (2009). Migration initiatives appeal, Islamic Republic of Iran. Retrieved November 26, 2010, from International Organization for Migration: www .iom.ch/jahia/webdav/shared/shared/mainsite/activities/countries/mi/iran. pdf.

IRIN. (2009). Afghanistan-Iran: Sharp rise in deportations from Iran. July 21. Retrieved November 26, 2010, from Integrated Regional Information Networks, the humanitarian news and analysis service of the UN Office for the Coordination of Humanitarian Affairs: www.irinnews.org/Report.aspx ?ReportId=85355.

———. (2010). Iran-Pakistan: Focus on human smuggling. Retrieved November 22, 2010, from Integrated Regional Information Networks, the humanitarian news and analysis service of the UN Office for the Coordination of Humanitarian Affairs: ww.irinnews.org/Report.aspx?ReportID=33957.

Islamic Republic of Iran. (1979). Constitution of Islamic Republic of Iran. Retrieved November 28, 2010, from Iran Online: www.iranonline.com/iran /iran-info/government/constitution.html.

———. (1991). Islamic Penal Code of Iran. Retrieved December 1, 2010, from from the UN High Commissioner for Refugees: www.unhcr.org/refworld /pdfid/4d384ae32.pdf.

Kahn, M. (2008). Human trafficking victims return from Iran. *Dawn*, March 9. Retrieved September 19, 2008, from Pakistan Herald Publication: http:// archives.dawn.com/2008/03/09/top15.htm.

Khan, S. (2010). FIA fails to stop human trafficking. *Daily Times*, April 11. Retrieved November 26, 2010, from http://dailytimes.com.pk/default.asp ?page=2010%5C04%5C11%5Cstory_11-4-2010_pg7_12.

Nayyeri, M. H. (2012). *Research paper series: New Islamic Penal Code of the Islamic Republic of Iran; An overview.* March 31. Retrieved September 14, 2012, from the Iran Human Rights Documentation Center: www.iranhrdc.org/english/ human-rights-documents/ngo-reports/university-of-essex-university-of

-essex-iran-unit/1000000159-new-islamic-penal-code-of-the-islamic-repub
lic-of-iran-an-overview.html.

ODVV. (2009). *The European Parliament*. Retrieved November 22, 2010, from
Report submitted to the Human Rights Council by the Organization for
Defending Victims of Violence: www.europarl.europa.eu/meetdocs/2009
_2014/documents/droi/dv/droi_20100426_67odvv_/droi_20100426_67odvv
_en.pdf.

Prostitution behind the veil. Directed by Nahid Persson Sarvestani. 2004. Denmark: Jakob Kirstein Høgel for Cosmo Film A/S, 2004. DVD.

Rafsanjani, A. H. (1997). "Sigheh" or "temporary marriage" & "the bomb." *60
Minutes*, March 8. Retrieved November 22, 2010, from World News: http://
wn.com/rafsanjani_on_sigheh,_or_temporary_marriage_the_bomb,
_with_mike_wallac,_march_8,_1997.

Reporters Uncensored. (2010). Iran sex slaves and child prostitution. Reporters
Uncensored, Episode 106, March 23. Retrieved November 28, 2010, from
www.livestream.com/reportersuncensored/video?clipId=pla_0f15f5d4-e2f2
-452c-be6f-05b57a8f5445.

Roald, A. S. (2001). *Women in Islam: The western experience*. London & New York:
Routledge.

UNODC. (2006). *Report of the special rapporteur on violence against women, its
causes and consequences, Yakin Ertürk, Mission to the Islamic Republic of Iran*.
Retrieved November 28, 2010, from United Nations on Drugs and Crime:
www2.ohchr.org/english/issues/women/rapporteur/annual.htm.

———. (2007). *Drug and crime situation in Iran, crime prevention*. Retrieved November 26, 2010, from United Nations Office on Drugs and Crime: www.unodc.org.

———. (2008). *Signatories to the CTOC Trafficking Protocol*. Retrieved November
28, 2010, from United Nations Office on Drugs and Crime: www.unodc.org
/unodc/en/treaties/CTOC/countrylist-traffickingprotocol.html#EndDec.

U.S. Department of State. (2003). *Trafficking in persons report*. Retrieved November 18, 2010, from www.state.gov/documents/organization/21555.pdf.

———. (2004). *Trafficking in persons report*. Retrieved November 18, 2010, from
www.state.gov/documents/organization/34158.pdf.

———. (2005). *Trafficking in persons report*. Retrieved September 30, 2008, from
www.state.gov/documents/organization/47255.pdf.

———. (2006). *Trafficking in persons report*. Retrieved May 10, 2007, from www
.state.gov/documents/organization/66086.pdf.

———. (2007). *Trafficking in persons report*. Retrieved August 31, 2010, from
www.state.gov/documents/organization/82902.pdf.

———. (2008a). *Country report on human rights practices, 2007, Iran, released by
the Bureau of Democracy, Human Rights, and Labor*. Retrieved September 19,
2008, from www.state.gov/g/drl/rls/hrrpt/2007/100595.htm.

———. (2008b). *Trafficking in persons report*. Retrieved October 24, 2008, from www.state.gov/documents/organization/105501.pdf.

———. (2010). *Trafficking in persons report*. Retrieved June 20, 2010, from www .state.gov/documents/organization/142979.pdf.

———. (2011). *Trafficking in persons report*. Retrieved September 16, 2011, from www.state.gov/g/tip/rls/tiprpt/2011/.

Vaidya, S. K. (2008). Iran battles human trafficking to Gulf. *Gulf News*, February 8. Retrieved September 19, 2008, from http://gulfnews.com/news/gulf/oman /iran-battles-human-trafficking-to-gulf-1.83623.

Wahab, A. (2009). Journey to nowhere. *Newsline*, May 5. Retrieved November 22, 2010, from www.newslinemagazine.com/2009/05/journey-to-nowhere/.

13. INDIA

Aliperti, P. (2009). *The role of education to prevent the trafficking in children for forced and bonded labor in India*. Thesis, Division of Public Administration, International Christian University (ICU) Graduate School. Copy in author's possession.

Anti-Slavery International. (2009). Bonded labor. Retrieved March 16, 2010, from www.antislavery.org/includes/documents/cm_docs/2009/b/1_bonded _labour.pdf.

Asian Development Bank. (2002). *Combating trafficking of women and children in South Asia: Country paper, India*. Retrieved February 23, 2010, from www .childtrafficking.com/Docs/adb_2002__trafficking_india.pdf.

Bamforth, S. S., Poulton, L., Tait, M., & Timberlake, J. (2009). India's invisible poor: Child trafficking. Child's eye series. *The Guardian*, May 16. Retrieved February 18, 2010, from www.guardian.co.uk/world/video/2009/may/16/ india-child-trafficking.

BBA. (2010). What we do. Retrieved March 16, 2010, from Bachpan Bachao An-dolan: www.bba.org.in/whatwedo/index.php.

Dastidar, S. (2007). Never too young to be sold. *The Telegraph*, October 16. Re-trieved February 19, 2010, from www.telegraphindia.com/1071016/asp /opinion/story_8436850.asp.

David et al. v. Signal International LLC et al., 2:2008cv01220 (Louisiana East-ern District Court, March 7, 2008).

David et al. v. Signal International LLC, complaint. (2008). Retrieved May 28, 2009, from Southern Poverty Law Center: http://www.splcenter.org/pdf/dy namic/legal/Signal_Complaint_080321.pdf.

D'souza, D. J. (2006). *Modern-day slavery's biggest challenge: Setting the agenda for Dalit emancipation within the twenty-first century*. Retrieved February 20, 2010, from Dalit Freedom Network: www.dalitnetwork.org/go?/dfn/who_are_the _dalit/C102/.

Government of India, Ministry of Human Resource Development. (2010). *Department of Women and Child Development*. Retrieved March 1, 2010, from http://wcdhry.gov.in/swadhar_f.htm.

Government of India, Ministry of Women and Child Development. (2007). *UJ-JAWALA, a comprehensive scheme for prevention of trafficking and rescue, rehabilitation and re-integration of victims of trafficking for commercial sexual exploitation*. Retrieved March 3, 2010, from http://wcd.nic.in/schemes/ujjawala .pdf.

Heitzman, J., & Worden, R. L. (1995). *India: A country study*. Retrieved February 20, 2010, from Library of Congress: http://countrystudies.us/india/89.htm.

Hindustan Times. (2010). India becoming hub of child sex abuse: SC [Supreme Court]. *Hindustan Times*, January 29. Retrieved February 20, 2010, from www.hindustantimes.com/India-news/NewDelhi/India-becoming-hub-of -child-sex-abuse-SC/Article1-503122.aspx.

Human Trafficking Project. (2010). Human trafficking in India, Part II: Interview with Dr. Joseph D'souza. Press release, February 11. Retrieved February 22, 2010, from http://traffickingproject.blogspot.com/2010/02/human-traf-ficking-in-india-part-ii_05.html.

ILO. (2012). India propose [*sic*] a ban on the employment of children younger than 14. August 29. Retrieved September 15, 2012, from International Labour Organization: www.ilo.org/ipec/WCMS_189552/lang--en/index.htm.

Kumar, N. (2011). Share of child labour in India's growth story. Retrieved September 14, 2012, from Childline India Foundation: www.childlineindia.org .in/pdf/Share-of-Child-Labour-in-India.pdf.

Magnier, M. (2009). The world; changing climate, changing lives; droughts worsen, crops fail, feeding a cycle of debt. *Los Angeles Times*, December 1, A18.

Ministry of Overseas Indian Affairs. (2009). Emigration (Amendment) Rules 2009. Retrieved September 14, 2012, from: http://moia.gov.in/writereaddata /pdf/gazettenotification_eng.pdf.

NACDOR. (2001). Who are the Dalit? Retrieved February 20, 2010, from National Conference of Dalit Organizations: www.nacdor.org/TEXT%20FILES /Dalit.htm.

Negi, S. (2006). Reply to SC daunting task for government. *The Tribune*, June 11. Retrieved March 17, 2010, from www.tribuneindia.com/2006/20060611 /main2.htm.

Shahin, S. (2001). Indian census could produce "the most complicated lies." *Asia Times Online*, February 21. Retrieved February 20, 2010, from www .atimes.com/ind-pak/CB21Df01.html.

Singh, H. S. (2010). India's "untouchables" declare own religion. CNN, February 3. Retrieved February 27, 2010, from www.cnn.com/2010/WORLD/asiapcf /02/03/india.new.religion/index.html.

Thaindian News. (2009). Emigration Act to be amended to protect workers overseas. *Thaindian News*, October 23. Retrieved March 3, 2010, from www .thaindian.com/newsportal/uncategorized/emigration-act-to-be-amended -to-protect-workers-overseas_100264807.html.

U.S. Department of State. (2009). *Trafficking in persons report*. Retrieved 16 November, 2009, from www.state.gov/documents/organization/123357.pdf.

———. (2010). *Trafficking in persons report*. Retrieved June 20, 2010, from www .state.gov/documents/organization/142979.pdf.

———. (2011). *Trafficking in persons report*. Retrieved September 16, 2011, from www.state.gov/g/tip/rls/tiprpt/2011/.

———. (2012). *Trafficking in persons report*. Retrieved August 30, 2012, from www.state.gov/j/tip/rls/tiprpt/2012/.

14. NIGER

Anti-Slavery International. (2008a). Anti-Slavery—reporter in brief—news. Press release, October 27. Retrieved November 23, 2009, from http://old .antislavery.org/archive/reporter/reporter_autumn_2008_news.htm.

———. (2008b). *Briefing paper: Hadijatou Mani Koraou v. Niger at the ECOWAS Court of Justice*. Retrieved November 4, 2009, from www.antislavery.org /includes/documents/cm_docs/2008/n/niger_case_at_ecowas.pdf.

———. (2008c). Historic slavery case launched against Niger. Press release, April 3. Retrieved November 4, 2009, from www.antislavery.org/.

———. (2008d). *Information on Niger compliance with ILO Convention No. 29 on Forced Labour* (ratified in 1961). Retrieved November 23, 2009, from www .antislavery.org/includes/documents/cm_docs/2009/2/2008_niger.pdf.

———. (2008e). Niger slavery: Background. *The Guardian*, October 27. Retrieved November 3, 2009, from : http://www.guardian.co.uk/world/2008/oct/27 /humanrights1.

BBC News. (2004). Testimony: Former slave. *BBC News*, November 3. Retrieved November 23, 2009, from http://news.bbc.co.uk/2/hi/africa/3972669.stm.

———. (2008). West Africa slavery still widespread. *BBC News*, October 27. Retrieved November 9, 2009, from http://news.bbc.co.uk/2/hi/africa/7693397.stm.

———. (2010). Niger coup leaders name transitional government. *BBC News*, March 2. Retrieved March 13, 2010, from http://news.bbc.co.uk/2/hi/africa /8544647.stm.

Callimachi, R. (2012). Poverty forcing girls into marriage. *San Francisco Chronicle*, September 15. Retrieved September 15, 2012, from www.sfgate.com/news/article/Poverty-forcing-girls-into-marriage-3868308.php#page-3.

ECOWAS. (2008). *ECOWAS Community Court of Justice, Hadijatou Mani Koraou v. The Republic of Niger: Unofficial transcript of ECOWAS judgment in English*. Retrieved November 6, 2009, from the United Nations High Commissioner for Refugees: www.unhcr.org/refworld/pdfid/496b41fa2.pdf.

IFES. (2010). *Election guide*. Retrieved January 10, 2011, from International Foundation for Electoral Systems: www.electionguide.org/country.php?ID=157.

ILO. (1996). *General legislative prohibitions of forced or compulsory labour*. Retrieved November 22, 2009, from International Labour Organization: www.ilo.org/public/english/dialogue/ifpdial/llg/ch6/ex1.htm.

The Independent. (2004). Freedom fighter. *The Independent*, November 18. Retrieved November 23, 2009, from www.independent.co.uk/news/world/africa/freedom-fighter-533599.html.

INTERIGHTS. (2009a). *Hadijatou Mani v. Niger*. Retrieved November 9, 2009, from the International Centre for the Legal Protection of Human Rights: www.interights.org/niger-slavery.

———. (2009b). *Hadijatou Mani v Niger, update*. Retrieved November 4, 2009, from the International Centre for the Legal Protection of Human Rights: www.interights.org/niger-slavery#UpdateJuly2009.

IRIN. (2008). Niger-Nigeria: Porous border aids human trafficking. Press release, May 21. Retrieved November 2, 2009, from Integrated Regional Information Networks, the humanitarian news and analysis service of the UN Office for the Coordination of Humanitarian Affairs: www.unhcr.org/refworld/docid/483692991c.html.

———. (2009a). Niger: Early marriage—from rural custom to urban business. Press release, January 16. Retrieved November 2, 2009, from Integrated Regional Information Networks, the humanitarian news and analysis service of the UN Office for the Coordination of Humanitarian Affairs: www.irinnews.org/report.aspx?reportid=82419.

———. (2009b). Niger: When religious teachers traffic their students. Press release, August 26. Retrieved January 11, 2011, from Integrated Regional Information Networks, the humanitarian news and analysis service of the UN Office for the Coordination of Humanitarian Affairs: www.irinnews.org/Report.aspx?ReportID=85857.

Kaye, M. (2008). *Arrested development: Discrimination and slavery in the 21st century*. Retrieved November 9, 2009, from Anti-Slavery International: www.antislavery.org/includes/documents/cm_docs/2009/a/arresteddevelopment.pdf.

Kumolu, C. (2012). Almajiri education: Modern gang up against ancient tradition? *Vanguard*, April 26. Retrieved September 16, 2012, from www.van guardngr.com/2012/04/almajiri-education-modern-gang-up-against-an cient-tradition/.

Mebrahtu, S. (2012). UNICEF supports efforts to eradicate child marriage in Niger. Retrieved September 16, 2012, from UNICEF: www.unicef.org/infoby-country/niger_65336.html.

Pflanz, M. (2008). Former slave wins historic case against Niger government. *The Telegraph*, October 27. Retrieved November 3, 2009, from www.telegraph.co.uk/news/worldnews/africaandindianocean/niger/3268371/Former-slave-wins-historic-case-against-Niger-government.html.

Raghavan, S. (2012). In Niger, hunger crisis raises fears of more child marriages. *Washington Post*, July 9. Retrieved September 16, 2012, from www.washing-tonpost.com/world/africa/in-niger-hunger-crisis-raises-fears-of-more-child-marriages/2012/07/09/gJQA8xD9YW_story.html.

UNODC. (2009). *Global report on trafficking in persons.* Retrieved June 6, 2010, from United Nations Office on Drugs and Crime: www.unodc.org/documents/Global_Report_on_TIP.pdf.

U.S. Department of Labor. (2009a). *List of goods produced by child labor or forced labor.* Retrieved August 28, 2010, from www.dol.gov/ilab/programs/ocft/PDF/2009TVPRA.pdf.

———. (2009b). *2008 findings on the worst forms of child labor.* Retrieved December 2, 2010, from www.dol.gov/ilab/media/reports/iclp/.

U.S. Department of State. (2009). *Trafficking in persons report.* Retrieved January 28, 2010, from www.state.gov/documents/organization/123357.pdf.

———. (2010). *Trafficking in persons report.* Retrieved June 20, 2010, from www.state.gov/documents/organization/142979.pdf.

———. (2011). *Trafficking in persons report.* Retrieved September 16, 2011, from www.state.gov/g/tip/rls/tiprpt/2011/.

———. (2012). *Trafficking in persons report.* Retrieved August 30, 2012, from www.state.gov/j/tip/rls/tiprpt/2012/.

VOANews. (2011a). Niger postpones elections. *VOANews,* January 7. Retrieved January 10, 2011, from Voice of America: www.voanews.com/english/news/africa/west/Niger-Postpones-Local-Elections-113072029.html.

———. (2011b). Provisional results have Issoufou winning Niger presidency. *VOANews,* March 13. Retrieved September 18, 2011, from Voice of America: www.voanews.com/content/niger-opposition-candidate-wins-presidential-run-off----117928819/136464.html.

15. CHINA

ADB. (2006). *Gender, law, and policy in ADB Operations: A tool kit, II. Gender, law, and policy in country partnership strategies.* Retrieved January 20, 2011, from Asian Development Bank: http://beta.adb.org/documents/gender-law-and -policy-adb-operations-tool-kit.

BBC News. (2010). China faces growing gender imbalance. *BBC News,* January 11. Retrieved January 26, 2010, from http://news.bbc.co.uk/2/hi/asia-pacific /8451289.stm.

Beijing Review. (2009). National Human Rights Action Plan of China (2009–2010). *Beijing Review,* December 2. Retrieved January 27, 2010, from www .bjreview.com.cn/special/Human_Rights_Action_Plan_2009–2010/2009– 12/02/content_232193_21.htm.

Branigan, T. (2010). Chinese newspapers in joint call to end curb on migrant workers. *The Guardian,* March 1. Retrieved September 25, 2010, from www .guardian.co.uk/world/2010/mar/01/chinese-newspapers-migrant-workers -rights.

CECC. (2006). China's household registration system: Sustained reform needed to protect China's rural migrants. Congressional-Executive Commission on China, March 29. Retrieved February 10, 2010, from www.cecc.gov/pages/ news/hukou.php.

China Daily. (2003). Uprooting poppy fields forever: Villagers in Golden Triangle struggle to reap a dollar from new cash crops. *China Daily,* March 5. Retrieved September 16, 2012, from www.asiantribune.com/news/2003/03/06/uproot ing-poppy-fields-forever-villagers-golden-triangle-struggle-reap-dollar-new.

———. (2004). Checking imbalance in gender ratio. *China Daily,* May 26. Retrieved January 26, 2010, from www.chinadaily.com.cn/english/doc/2004 -05/26/content_333725.htm.

Chou, J. (2006). Who's in China's prisons? *Weekly Standard,* April 24. Retrieved February 8, 2010, from www.weeklystandard.com/Content/Public/Articles /000/000/012/107hobbw.asp.

CIA. (2011). *China.* Retrieved September 16, 2012, from Central Intelligence Agency: www.cia.gov/library/publications/the-world-factbook/geos/ch.html.

French, H. W. (2007). Reports of forced labor unsettle China. *New York Times,* June 16. Retrieved January 20, 2010, from www.nytimes.com/2007/06/16/ world/asia/16china.html?_r=1.

GhanaWeb. (2009). Three Chinese jailed for human trafficking. GhanaWeb, June 23. Retrieved January 30, 2010, from www.ghanaweb.com/Ghana-HomePage/NewsArchive/artikel.php?ID=164179.

Guihua, M. (2009). China joins Mekong countries in fighting cross-border human trafficking. Xinhua News Agency, November 29. Retrieved January

24, 2010, from http://news.xinhuanet.com/english/2009-11/29/content
_12558880.htm.

Haixing, J. (2012). Guangdong urged to prevent gender imbalance. *China Daily*,
September 5. Retrieved September 16, 2012, from http://usa.chinadaily.com
.cn/china/2012-09/05/content_15736175.htm.

Human Rights Watch. (2010). *"Where darkness knows no limits": Incarcerating, ill-
treatment and forced labor as drug rehabilitation in China.* Retrieved January 21,
2010, from www.hrw.org/sites/default/files/reports/china0110webwcover.pdf.

Jia, C. (2010). China joins UN fight against human trafficking. *China Daily*, December 23. Retrieved January 24, 2010, from www.chinadaily.com.cn/china
/2009–12/23/content_9216980.htm.

Juma, M. (2009). Child labor alleged at factory. Radio Free Asia, May 12. Re-
trievied September 16, 2012, from www.rfa.org/english/news/uyghur/under
ageworkers-05112009162537.html.

Lam, W. (2010). Powerful interests stifle China reforms. *Asia Times*, March 20.
Retrieved September 25, 201, from www.atimes.com/atimes/China/LC20Ad01
.html.

Ministry of Justice. (2010). *Supreme People's Procuratorate, the Ministry of Justice
issued "on the trafficking of women and children to punish the views of" notice.*
March 15. Retrieved September 2011, from Chinalawinfo: http://www.law
infochina.com.

People's Daily. (2008). Human trafficking ring head sentenced to death in
southwest China. *People's Daily*, December 17. Retrieved February 9, 2010,
from http://english.peopledaily.com.cn/90001/90776/90882/6556421.html.

RFA. (2010). China vows action on trafficking. *Radio Free Asia*, May 21. Retrieved February 1, 2010, from www.rfa.org/english/news/china/chinatraf
ficking-05212009114049.html.

Spencer, R. (2005). The refugees forced to be sex slaves in China. *The Telegraph*,
October 1. Retrieved January 28, 2010, from www.telegraph.co.uk/news
/worldnews/asia/northkorea/1499675/The-refugees-forced-to-be-sex-slaves
-in-China.html.

Taipei Times. (2007). Chinese police detain Shanxi kiln foreman. *Taipei Times*,
June 18. Retrieved January 20, 2010, from www.taipeitimes.com/News
/world/archives/2007/06/18/2003365767/wiki.

The Telegraph. (2010). Chinese gender imbalance will leave millions of men
without wives. *The Telegraph*, January 11. Retrieved January 26, 2010, from
www.telegraph.co.uk/news/worldnews/asia/china/6966037/Chinese-gender
-imbalance-will-leave-millions-of-men-without-wives.html.

UNIAP. (2008). *The trafficking situation in China.* Retrieved January 31, 2010,
from United Nations Inter-Agency Project on Human Trafficking: www.no
-trafficking.org/china.html.

U.S. Department of State. (2009). *Trafficking in persons report*. Retrieved September 24, 2010, from www.state.gov/documents/organization/123357.pdf.

———. (2010). *Trafficking in persons report*. Retrieved June 20, 2010, from www.state.gov/documents/organization/142979.pdf.

———. (2011). *Trafficking in persons report*. Retrieved September 16, 2011, from www.state.gov/g/tip/rls/tiprpt/2011/.

———. (2012). *Trafficking in persons report*. Retrieved August 30, 2012, from www.state.gov/j/tip/rls/tiprpt/2012/.

Windrow, H., & Guha, A. (2005). The hukou system, migrant workers, & state power in the People's Republic of China. April 8. *Northwestern University Journal of International Human Rights*. Retrieved January 20, 2012, from Northwestern University School of Law: www.law.northwestern.edu/journals/JIHR/v3/3.

Wong, T. C., & J. Rigg. (2011). *Asian cities, migrant labour and contested spaces*. New York: Routledge.

Xiaohuo, C. (2010). Students without hukou struggle to get in classrooms. *China Daily*, April 16. Retrieved January 20, 2011, from www.chinadaily.com.cn/cndy/2010–04/16/content_9737770.htm.

Xin, C. (2012). Equality urged for migrant workers. *China Daily*, September 13. Retrieved September 16, 2012, from http://usa.chinadaily.com.cn/business/2012-09/13/content_15754560.htm.

Xinhua News Agency. (2006). Human trafficking in the Greater Mekong Subregion (series). Xinhua News Agency, December 31. Retrieved January 31, 2010, from www.yn.xinhuanet.com/newscenter/2006-12/31/content_8943255.htm.

———. (2010a). China to maintain low birth rate: Vice premier. Xinhua News Agency, January 20. Retrieved January 26, 2010, from http://news.xinhuanet.com/english2010/china/2010-01/20/c_13143071.htm.

———. (2010b). Five sentenced over child trafficking in south China. Xinhua News Agency, January 9. Retrieved February 8, 2010, from http://news.xinhuanet.com/english/2010–01/09/content_12782617.htm.

Yanzhao Metropolis Daily. (2007). The story of Chen Chenggong. *Yanzhao Metropolis Daily*, June 18. Retrieved January 21, 2010, from www.zonaeuropa.com/20070701_2.htm.

16. SOUTH AFRICA

AllAfrica. (2010). Mozambique: Network of human traffickers exposed. *All Africa.com*, March 26. Retrieved March 31, 2010, from http://allafrica.com/stories/201003260975.html.

Attwood, V. (2009). Crime and courts: Human traffickers aim to exploit 2010. *Independent Online*, February 19. Retrieved April 1, 2010, from www.iol.co

.za/news/south-africa/human-traffickers-aim-to-exploit-2010-1.435090#.
UFgGgEJgPFJ.

BBC News. (2012). Jackie Selebi: South Africa's ex-police chief to be freed. *BBC News*, July 20. Retrieved September 17, 2012, from www.bbc.co.uk/news /world-africa-18924772.

Carte Blanche. (2007). Caught in traffic. *Carte Blanche*, January 28. Retrieved March 31, 2010, from http://beta.mnet.co.za/carteblanche/Article.aspx ?Id=3239.

Club of Mozambique. (2008). "Diana" denies all charges of human trafficking. Press release, October 22. Retrieved January 23, 2011, from www.clubof mozambique.com/solutions1/sectionnews.php?secao=international& id=13225&tipo=one.

Cole, B. (2008). South Africa: Human trafficking expands in KZN. *Independent Online*, September 15. Retrieved April 1 , 2010, from www.iol.co.za/index.php ?set_id=1&click_id=13&art_id=vn20080915105033971C236617&singlep age=1.

Donne, R. D. (2007). Alleged child trafficker walks free. *Independent Online*, December 1. Retrieved April 3, 2010, from www.iol.co.za/news/south-africa /alleged-child-trafficker-walks-free-1.380989#.UFfefEJgNlJ.

Dynes, M. (2003). "Magic medicine" murders bedevil South Africa: Rogue traditional traders are still using human body parts to increase their potions' power. *The Times*, October 4. Retrieved January 20, 2011, from www.scribd .com/doc/23729171/03–10–04-Times-Live-Magic-Medicine-Murders-Be devil-South-Africa-Pg1.

Fellows, S. (2008). *Trafficking body parts in Mozambique and South Africa*. Human Rights League, Mozambique. Mozambique: Human Rights League in Mozambique. Copy in author's possession.

Hosken, G.. (2010). Little Masego found dead. *Independent Online*, January 11. Retrieved May 18, 2010, from www.iol.co.za/index.php?art_id=vn201001110 71835984C960700&page_number=1.

Independent Online. (2007). Judges asked to clamp down on trafficking. *Independent Online*, October 19. Retrieved April 3, 2010, from www.int.iol .co.za/index.php?set_id=1&click_id=13&art_id=vn20071019043927178C 735488.

———. (2010). Further delay in human trafficking case. *Independent Online*, November 24. Retrieved March 30, 2010, from www.iol.co.za/news /south-africa/kwazulu-natal/further-delay-in-human-trafficking-case-1 .876361.

Khumalo, G. (2008). South Africa: Bill to allow for prosecution of all forms of human trafficking. *AllAfrica*, August 14. Retrieved March 30, 2010, from http://allafrica.com/stories/200808150106.html.

Kwong, M. (2010). SA cabbies quit over "false promises." *The National*, February 28. Retrieved September 17, 2012: www.thenational.ae/news/uae-news/sa -cabbies-quit-over-false-promises.

Labuschagne, G.. (2004). Features and investigative implications of muti murder in South Africa. *Journal of Investigative Psychology and Offender Profiling*, 191–206.

Mail & Guardian. (2007). Human trafficking "as evil as slave trade of the past." *Mail & Guardian*, October 19. Retrieved May 16, 2010, from www.mg.co.za /article/2007-10-19-human-trafficking-as-evil-slave-trade-of-the-past.

Mbanjwa, X. (2007). Legalise prostitution for 2010. *Independent Online*, December 7. Retrieved April 2 , 2010, from http://www.iol.co.za/news/south -africa/legalise-prostitution-for-2010-1.381832#.UFgMX0JgNFI.

Molo Songololo. (2000). *The trafficking of children for purposes of sexual exploitation—South Africa*. Cape Town: Molo Songololo. Copy in author's possession.

Ndawonde, P. (2009). Illegal crossings a major security concern. Press release, November 17. Retrieved March 31, 2010, from South African Government News Agency: www.buanews.gov.za/rss/09/09111716451003.

NPA (National Prosecuting Authority) / HSRC (Human Sciences Research Council). (2010). *Tsireledzani: Understanding the dimensions of human trafficking in Southern Africa: Research report*. Retrieved March 26, 2010, from www. hsrc.ac.za/Document-3562.phtml.

NPR. (2007). South Africa considers legalizing prostitution. National Public Radio, October 11. Retrieved April 2, 2010, from www.npr.org/templates /story/story.php?storyId=15180189.

Regchand, S. (2012). Brothel duo may go free. *The Mercury*, June 1. Retrieved September 17, 2012, from *Independent Online*: www.iol.co.za/mercury/brothel -duo-may-go-free-1.1309663#.UFgCnUJgPFJ.

SANews. (2010a). Dept, healers declare war on muthi killings. Press release, February 18. Retrieved March 30, 2010, from South African Government News Agency: www.buanews.gov.za/news/10/10021814251001.

———. (2010b). Human trafficking is modern-day slavery—Gigaba. Press release, February 22. Retrieved March 30, 2010, from www.buanews.gov.za/ news/10/10022213551003.

SAPA (South African Press Association). (2009). Thai woman in court for trafficking. December 30. Retrieved March 30, 2010, from *Independent Online*: www.iol.co.za/news/south-africa/thai-woman-in-court-for-trafficking-1 .469072#.UFfZqEJgNlI

———. (2011). Killer grins at muti murder sentence. November 28. Retrieved January 20, 2011, from *Independent Online*: www.iol.co.za/news/crime-courts /killer-grins-at-muti-murder-sentence-1.1187916.

South Africa: The Good News. (2010). SA convicts first sex trafficker. *South Africa—The Good News*, March 24. Retrieved March 30, 2010, from www .sagoodnews.co.za/crime/sa_convicts_first_sex_traffickers_2.html.

South Africa Department of Social Development. (n.d.). *Grant for caring for a young child (child support grant).* Retrieved January 23, 2011, from Western Cape government: http://www.westerncape.gov.za/eng/directories/services /11586/47468.

Statistics South Africa. (2010). Quarterly labour force survey: Quarter 1 (January to March), 2010. Press statement, May 4. Retrieved May 11, 2010, from www.statssa.gov.za/keyindicators/QLFS/Press/Q1_2010_Press_Statement.pdf.

Stuurman, L. (2008). SA must enact laws to nail perpetrators. *Sowetan*, March 12. Retrieved April 1, 2010, from www.sowetan.co.za/News/Article.aspx?id= 724885.

UNESCO. (2007). *Human trafficking in South Africa: Root causes and recommendations.* Retrieved March 30, 2010, from United Nations Educational, Scientific and Cultural Organization: http://unesdoc.unesco.org/images/0015/001528 /152823E.pdf.

UNODC. (2009). *Global report on trafficking in persons.* Retrieved June 6, 2010, from United Nations Office on Drugs and Crime: www.unodc.org/docu ments/Global_Report_on_TIP.pdf.

U.S. Department of Labor. (2009). *2008 findings on the worst forms of child labor.* Retrieved December 2, 2010, from www.dol.gov/ilab/media/reports/iclp/.

U.S. Department of State. (2009). *Trafficking in persons report.* Retrieved January 28, 2010, from www.state.gov/documents/organization/123357.pdf.

———. (2010). *Trafficking in persons report.* Retrieved June 20, 2010, from www .state.gov/documents/organization/142979.pdf.

———. (2011). *Trafficking in persons report.* Retrieved September 16, 2011, from www.state.gov/g/tip/rls/tiprpt/2011/.

———. (2012). *Trafficking in persons report.* Retrieved August 30, 2012, from www.state.gov/j/tip/rls/tiprpt/2012/.

Williams, M. J. (2007). The social and economic impacts of South Africa's child support grant. May 7. Unpublished BA thesis, Williams College, Williamstown, Massachusetts. Retrieved September 18, 2012, from Williams College: http://web.williams.edu/Economics/Honors/2007/Williams _thesis.pdf.

World Bank. (2012). World Development Indicators 2012—South Africa. Retrieved September 17, 2012, from http://data.worldbank.org/country/south -africa.

17. AUSTRALIA

ABC News. (2008). Farm denies abusing Indian workers. *ABC News,* January 15. Retrieved June 10, 2008, from www.abc.net.au/news/stories/2008/01/15 /2138675.htm.

Amnesty International. (2001). Australia: Asylum seekers—where to now? Press release, December 5. Retrieved December 17, 2008, from www.amnesty.org /en/library/asset/ASA12/010/2001/en/81b01933-fb06-11dd-9fca -0d1f97c98a21/asa120102001en.pdf.

———. (2007). The Pacific solution—welcome first steps. Press release, December 11. Retrieved December 17, 2008, from www.amnesty.org.au/news/comments/7099/.

An Phoblacht. (2012). Sinn Féin TD Pearse Doherty visits Australia. September 2. Retrieved September 20, 2012, from www.anphoblacht.com/contents /22181.

ARTIP. (2011). On 25 August 2011 the Asia Regional Trafficking in Persons Project (ARTIP) ended its five year contribution to the prevention of trafficking in persons in the Asia region. Retrieved September 19, 2012, from www .artipproject.org.

Australian Government. (2005). Criminal Code Amendment (Trafficking in Persons Offences) Act 2005. July 6. Retrieved September 23, 2012, from www.comlaw.gov.au/Details/C2005A00096.

———. (2012). Criminal Code Act 1995, taking into account amendments up to Act No. 44 of 2012. July 11. Retrieved September 23, 2012, from www.comlaw.gov.au/Details/C2012C00547/Download.

BBC News. (2002). Q&A: Australia's "Pacific Solution." *BBC News,* February 5. Retrieved December 17, 2008, from http://news.bbc.co.uk/2/hi/asia-pacific /1802364.stm.

———. (2007). Australia's Pacific solution. *BBC News,* September 26. Retrieved December 17, 2008, from http://news.bbc.co.uk/2/hi/programmes/corre spondent/2279330.stm.

Craig, N. (2007). Sex slave victim wins abuse claim. *The Age,* May 29. Retrieved June 8, 2008, from www.theage.com.au/articles/2007/05/28/1180205160434 .html.

David, F. (2010). *Labour trafficking.* Retrieved September 21, 2011, from Australian Institute of Criminology: www.aic.gov.au/documents/A/9/0/%7BA90867A2– 1558–4B01-A233–34B3381D2F6D%7Drpp108.pdf.

Deegan, B. (2008). *Visa Subclass 457 integrity review report, final.* Retrieved December 3, 2009, from www.minister.immi.gov.au/media/media-releases /2008/457-integrity-review-report.pdf.

Department of Immigration and Citizenship. (2009). Act amendments to strengthen the integrity of the temporary skilled visa program. September 14. Retrieved August 24, 2010, from www.immi.gov.au/legislation/amend ments/2009/090914/lc14092009-01.htm.

———. (2012a). Simplifying sponsorship for permanent skilled migrants. Press release, March 9. Retrieved September 20, 2012, from www.minister.immi .gov.au/media/cb/2012/cb183639.htm.

———. (2012b). What's in a name? Retrieved September 19, 2012, from www .immi.gov.au/about/anniversary/whats-in-a-name.htm.

Duff, E. (2008a). Sent to squalor in a small country town. *Sydney Morning Herald*, January 13. Retrieved December 2, 2009, from www.smh.com.au/articles/2008/01/12/1199988650397.html.

———. (2008b). "Worst" illegal migration racket busted. *Sydney Morning Herald*, May 11. Retrieved December 2, 2009, from www.smh.com.au/news/national /worst-illegal-migration-racket-busted/2008/05/10/1210131327011.html.

———. (2009). Agency sacks Prassad. *Sydney Morning Herald*, July 6. Retrieved December 3, 2009, from www.smh.com.au/news/national/agency-sacks -prassad/2008/07/05/1214951110502.html.

FaHCSIA. (2009). *Anti–people trafficking strategy.* Retrieved December 4, 2009, from Department of Families, Housing, Community Services and Indigenous Affairs, Australian Anti-People Trafficking Strategy: www.fahcsia.gov .au/sa/women/progserv/violence/Pages/AntiPeopleTraffickingStrategy.aspx.

Fergus, L. (2005). *Trafficking in women for sexual exploitation.* Retrieved June 4, 2008, from Australian Institute of Family Studies: www.aifs.gov.au/acssa/ pubs/briefing/acssa_briefing5.pdf.

Ford, M. (2001). *Sex slaves and legal loopholes: Exploring the legal framework and federal responses to the trafficking of Thai "contract girls" for sex exploitation to Melbourne, Australia.* Retrieved June 5, 2008, from Australian Insititute of Family Studies: www.projectrespect.org.au/files/sexslaves.pdf.

Gillis Delaney Lawyers. (2008). *GD News,* March. Retrieved December 3, 2009, from www.gdlaw.com.au/Services/March08.pdf.

Khalik, A. (2007). Australia gives aid to slave trade fight. *Jakarta Post,* August 28. Retrieved February 5, 2009, from www.thejakartapost.com/news/2007/08/28 /australia-gives-aid-to-slave-trade-fight.html.

McGlade, H. (2006). Aboriginal women, girls and sexual assault. *ACSSA Newsletter,* September. Retrieved December 2, 2009, from Australian Institute of Family Studies: www.aifs.gov.au/acssa/pubs/newsletter/n12.html#aboriginal.

Mercer, P. (2007). Thai woman wins landmark compensation in Australian sex trafficking case. *Voice of America News,* June 1. Retrieved February 10, 2008, from www.voanews.com/content/a-13-2007-06-01-voa8-66777222/564824.html.

Parliamentary Joint Committee on the Australian Crime Commission. (2004). *To examine Australian Crime Commission's response to trafficking in women for sexual servitude: Inquiry into the trafficking of women for sexual servitude.* Retrieved December 1, 2009, from Parliament of Australia: www.aph.gov.au /binaries/senate/committee/acc_ctte/completed_inquiries/2002-04/sexual _servitude/report/report.pdf.

Parliament of Australia. (2010a). Crimes Legislation Amendment (Sexual Offences Against Children) Act 2010. April 14. Retrieved March 18, 2011, from ComLaw, Australian Government: www.comlaw.gov.au/Details/C2010A00042.

——. (2010b). Parliamentary Joint Committee on Law Enforcement Act 2010. November 24. Retrieved September 19, 2012, from Commonwealth of Australia: www.comlaw.gov.au/Details/C2010A00128.

——. (2012). Crimes Legislation Amendment (Slavery, Slavery-Like Conditions and People Trafficking) Bill 2012. August 24. Retrieved September 19, 2012 from www.aph.gov.au/Parliamentary_Business/Bills_Legislation/bd/bd1213a /13bd014.

Raymond, J. G. (2001). *Guide to the new UN trafficking protocol.* Retrieved January 25, 2005, from Coalition Against Trafficking in Women: http://action.web. ca/home/catw/attach/Guideun_protocolENG.pdf.

Schloenhardt, A. (2009). *Human Trafficking Working Group.* Retrieved September 21, 2011, from University of Queensland, T. C. Beirne School of Law: www .law.uq.edu.au/documents/humantraffic/legislation/Criminal-Code-Cth -Div-271-trafficking-in-persons-offences.pdf.

University of Queensland. (2009a). Case report: R. v. Yogalingham Rasalingam. Retrieved January 27, 2012, from University of Queensland, T. C. Beirne School of Law: www.law.uq.edu.au/documents/humantraffic/case-reports /trafficking-offences/rasalingham.pdf.

——. (2009b). Labour trafficking in Australia. Retrieved December 1, 2009, from University of Queensland, T. C. Beirne School of Law: www.law.uq.edu .au/labour-trafficking-in-australia.

——. (2009c). Slavery, sexual servitude, and deceptive recruiting offenses Division 270 Criminal Code. October 10. Retrieved September 20, 2012, from University of Queensland, T. C. Beirne School of Law: www.law.uq.edu.au /documents/humantraffic/legislation/Criminal-Code-Cth-Div-270-sexual -slavery-offences.pdf.

——. (2009d). Trafficking in persons and debt bondage offenses Division 271 Criminal Code. April 21. Retrieved September 20, 2012, from University of Queensland, T. C. Beirne School of Law: www.law.uq.edu.au/documents/hu mantraffic/legislation/Criminal-Code-Cth-Div-271-trafficking-in-persons -offences.pdf.

———. (2010). Slavery, sexual servitude and debt bondage. Retrieved January 27, 2012, from University of Queensland, T. C. Beirne School of Law: www.law.uq.edu.au/case-report-slavery-sexual-servitude-debt-bondage.

———. (2011a). Case report: R. v. Divje Trivedi. Retrieved January 26, 2012, from University of Queensland, T. C. Beirne School of Law: www.law.uq.edu.au/documents/humantraffic/case-reports/trafficking-offences/Trivedi.pdf.

———. (2011b). Cases of labour trafficking in Australia. Retrieved January 26, 2012, from University of Queensland, T. C. Beirne School of Law: www.law.uq.edu.au/cases-of-labour-trafficking-in-australia.

———. (2011c). Trafficking offences. Retrieved January 27, 2012, from University of Queensland, T. C. Beirne School of Law: www.law.uq.edu.au/case-report-trafficking-offences.

———. (2012). Law relating to trafficking in persons. Retrieved September 19, 2012 from www.law.uq.edu.au/ht-legislation.

UNODC. (2012). *Signatories to the CTOC Trafficking Protocol.* August 15. Retrieved August 19, 2012, from the United Nations Office on Drugs and Crime: http://treaties.un.org/Pages/ViewDetails.aspx?src=TREATY&mtdsg_no=XVIII-12-a&chapter=18&lang=en.

U.S. Department of State. (2007a). *Country report on human rights practices, 2006, Australia.* Retrieved February 12, 2007, from www.state.gov/j/drl/rls/hrrpt/2006/78766.htm.

———. (2007b). *Trafficking in persons report.* Retrieved November 11, 2007, from www.state.gov/g/tip/rls/tiprpt/2007/82805.htm.

———. (2008). *Trafficking in persons report.* Retrieved June 9, 2008, from www.state.gov/documents/organization/105501.pdf.

———. (2009). *Trafficking in persons report.* Retrieved November 16, 2009, from www.state.gov/documents/organization/123357.pdf.

———. (2010). *Trafficking in persons report.* Retrieved June 20, 2010, from www.state.gov/documents/organization/142979.pdf.

———. (2011). *Trafficking in persons report.* Retrieved September 16, 2011, from www.state.gov/g/tip/rls/tiprpt/2011/.

———. (2012). *Trafficking in persons report.* Retrieved August 30, 2012, from www.state.gov/j/tip/rls/tiprpt/2012/.

18. UNITED KINGDOM

ACPO. (2011). *ACPO strategy and supporting operational guidance for policing prostitution and sexual exploitation.* Retrieved September 20, 2012, from the

Association of Chief Police Officers: www.acpo.police.uk/documents/ crime/2011/20111102%20CBA%20Policing%20Prostitution%20and %20%20Sexual%20Exploitation%20Strategy_Website_October%202011 .pdf.

Asylum Aid. (2012). *Women's Asylum News*. Issue 112, May/ August 2012. Retrieved September 20, 2012, from United Nations High Commissioner for Refugees: www.unhcr.org/refworld/pdfid/5021497a2.pdf.

Cambridgeshire Constabulary. (2009). Freedom of Information Request No. 0439/2009. Retrieved March 11, 2011, from www.cambs.police.uk/about/foi /disclosure/PUB0439-2009.pdf.

Channel 4 News. (2011). Trafficking victims claim human rights breach. *Channel 4 News*, February 14. Retrieved March 2, 2011, from www.channel4.com /news/trafficking-victims-claim-human-rights-breach.

Cutler, S. (2007). *Refusal factory: Women's experience of the Detained Fast Track Asylum Process at Yarl's Wood Immigration Removal Centre*. Retrieved December 3, 2007, from Bail for Immigration Detainees: www.statewatch.org/news /2007/sep/bid-refusal-factory-07.pdf.

Daily Mail. (2011). Father and son who ran family business trafficking women for sex are jailed. *Daily Mail,* January 26. Retrieved February 16, 2011, from www.dailymail.co.uk/news/article-1350790/Bogdan-Nejloveanu-51-Marius -Nejloveanu-23-jailed-sex-trafficking.html.

David, F. (2010). *Labour trafficking*. Retrieved September 21, 2011, from Australian Institute of Criminology: www.aic.gov.au/documents/A/9/0/%7BA 90867A2-1558-4B01-A233-34B3381D2F6D%7Drpp108.pdf.

Department of Justice, Equality and Law Reform (Ireland) (2007). Human trafficking bill published. October 11. Retrieved November 23, 2007, from www .justice.ie/en/JELR/Pages/Human_Trafficking_Bill_Published.

ECRE. (2009). Complementary protection in Europe. Retrieved September 20, 2012, from European Council on Refugees and Exiles: www.unhcr.org/ref-world/pdfid/4a72c9a72.pdf.

Equality and Human Rights Commission. (2011). EU trafficking directive. Retrieved September 17, 2011, from www.equalityhumanrights.com/legal-and -policy/european-policy/eu-trafficking-directive/.

EU. (2011). Directive 2011/36/EU of the European Parliament and of the Council of 5 April 2011. *Official Journal of the European Union,* April 15. Retrieved September 17, 2011, from http://eur-lex.europa.eu/LexUriServ/LexUriServ .do?uri=OJ:L:2011:101:0001:0011:EN:PDF.

Government of the United Kingdom (2003). Sexual Offences Act 2003. November 20. Retrieved March 11, 2011, from Legislation.gov.uk, National Archives: www.legislation.gov.uk/ukpga/2003/42/section/58.

————. (2004). Asylum and Immigration (Treatment of Claimants, etc.) Act 2004. July 22. Retrieved March 11, 2011, from Legislation.gov.uk, National Archives: www.legislation.gov.uk/ukpga/2004/19/section/4.

————. (2009). The Coroners and Justice Act 2009. November 12. Retrieved March 1, 2011, from Legislation.gov.uk, the National Archives: www.legislation.gov.uk/ukpga/2009/25/contents.

Hill, A. (2011). Poppy Project funding redirected to Salvation Army. *The Guardian*, May 9. Retrieved September 20, 2012, from www.guardian.co.uk/law/2011/may/09/poppy-project-funding-salvation-army.

HRW. (2010a). *Fast-tracked unfairness, detention and denial of women asylum seekers in the U.K.* Human Rights Watch, February 23. Retrieved March 1, 2011, from www.hrw.org/sites/default/files/reports/uk0210webwcover.pdf.

————. (2010b). UK: "Fast track" asylum system fails women. Press release, Human Rights Watch, February 23. Retrieved March 1, 2011, from www.hrw.org/en/news/2010/02/19/uk-fast-track-asylum-system-fails-women.

Lewis, P. (2006). Nightmare world of suburban sex slaves. *The Guardian,* May 8. Retrieved November 22, 2007, from www.guardian.co.uk/crime/article/0,,1769962,00.html.

Lipscombe, S. (2012). Human trafficking: UK responses. March 16. Retrieved September 20, 2012, from Parliament: www.parliament.uk/briefing-papers/SN04324.pdf.

Mantouvalou, V. (2012). Human rights for precarious workers: The legislative precariousness of domestic labour. Retrieved September 20, 2012, from University College London: www.ucl.ac.uk/laws/lri/papers/VM%20precarious%20workers.pdf.

Office for National Statistics. (2007). Asylum seekers, control of immigration. August 21. Retrieved December 2, 2007, from www.statistics.gov.uk.

Police Oracle. (2007). ACPO On Op Pentameter 2. October 2007. Retrieved on September 20, 2012, from www.policeoracle.com/news/ACPO-On-Op-Pentameter-2_14562.html.

Politics.co.uk. (2010). Immigration removal/detention centres. Retrieved March 11, 2011, from www.politics.co.uk/briefings-guides/issue-briefs/policing-and-crime/immigration-removal-detention-centres-$366686.htm.

Puffett, N. (2010). Concerns raised over low number of convictions for child trafficking. Press release, September 7. Retrieved March 11, 2011, from Children & Young People Now, National Children's Bureau and National Youth Agency: www.cypnow.co.uk/cyp/news/1046533/concerns-raised-low-convictions-child-trafficking.

Queen v. Matyas Pis, Icos no. 11/10962 (Belfast Crown Court, April 23). (2012). Copy in author's possession.

Scottish Government. (2012). Trafficking in Human Beings: Investigation, enforcement and prosecution. Retrieved September 21, 2012, from www.scotland.gov.uk/Topics/Justice/crimes/humantraffick/enforcement1.

Skrivankova, K. (2010). *Between decent work and forced labour: Examining the continuum of exploitation.* Retrieved March 2, 2011, from the Joseph Rowntree Foundation: www.jrf.org.uk/sites/files/jrf/forced-labour-exploitation-full.pdf.

SOCA. (2012). Introduction to UKHTC. Retrieved January 23, 2009, from Serious Organized Crime Agency: www.soca.gov.uk/about-soca/about-the-ukhtc.

Townsend, M. (2011). Target brothels or sex trafficking in UK will rise. *The Guardian*, February 5. Retrieved September 17, 2011, from www.guardian.co.uk/law/2011/feb/06/sex-slave-trafficking-brothel-crackdown.

UKHTC. (2008). About the UKHTC. Retrieved January 23, 2009, from United Kingdom Human Trafficking Centre: www.ukhtc.org.

U.S. Department of State. (2007a). *Country report on human rights practices, 2006: United Kingdom.* Retrieved November 11, 2007, from www.state.gov/g/drl/rls/hrrpt/2006/78847.htm.

———. (2007b). *Trafficking in persons report.* Retrieved August 31, 2010, from www.state.gov/documents/organization/82902.pdf.

———. (2010). *Trafficking in persons report.* Retrieved June 20, 2010, from www.state.gov/documents/organization/142979.pdf.

———. (2011). *Trafficking in persons report.* Retrieved September 16, 2011, from www.state.gov/g/tip/rls/tiprpt/2011/.

———. (2012). *Trafficking in persons report.* Retrieved August 30, 2012, from www.state.gov/j/tip/rls/tiprpt/2012/.

19. CHILE

ADOC. (2009a). UNICEF and Vicaria warn that child labor is worsening in Chile. Press release, June 23. Retrieved September 19, 2010, APEC Digital Opportunity Center: from www.apecdoc.org/post/7/4350.

———. (2009b). UN manual aims to stop child labor in Chile. Press release, June 30. Retrieved September 19, 2010, APEC Digital Opportunity Center: from www.apecdoc.org/post/7/4349.

Banco Central de Chile. (2012). Indicators. Retrieved September 22, 2012 from www.bcentral.cl/eng/index.asp.

Bernasoni, C. (2008). Spiniak's sentence increased to 12 years. *Santiago Times*, August 10. Retrieved September 20, 2010, from www.santiagotimes.cl/index.php?option=com_content&view=article&id=14396:SPINIAK%E2%80%99S-SENTENCE-INCREASED-TO-12-YEARS&catid=19:other&Itemid=142.

El Colombiano. (2011). Chile tipificó el delito de trata de personas. *El Colombiano*, March 8. Retrieved September 15, 2011, from www.elcolombiano.com/ BancoConocimiento/C/chile_tipifico_el_delito_de_trata_de_personas/chile _tipifico_el_delito_de_trata_de_personas.asp.

D'Alessandro, A., & H. Tobar. (2004). Chilean sex scandal strains political ties: Lawmaker is ostracized after she implicates colleagues in alleged orgies and pedophilia. *Los Angeles Times*, January 3, p. A3.

IOM. (2009). Research sheds new light on human trafficking in Chile. Press release, July 31. Retrieved September 12, 2010, from International Organization for Migration: www.iom.int/jahia/Jahia/media/press-briefing-notes /pbnAM/cache/offonce?entryId=25844.

Mazars Communication Group. (2011). *Chile taxation guide 2011*. Retrieved September 22, 2012, from www.mazars.cl.

El Mercurio. (2011). Francisco Javier Errázuriz recibe multa de más de $100 millones por paraguayos ilegales. *El Mercurio*, May 27. Retrieved September 15, 2011, from: http://blogs.elmercurio.com/cronica/2011/05/27/caso-errazuriz -menor-paraguayo.asp.

New York Times. (2009). Sichuan earthquake. *New York Times*, May 6. Retrieved September 12, 2010, from http://topics.nytimes.com/topics/news/science /topics/earthquakes/sichuan_province_china/index.html.

Quillier, M. (2011). Caso paraguayos: Demandas en contra del empresario Francisco Javier Errázuriz. *El Ciudadano*, June 7. Retrieved September 15, 2011, from www.elciudadano.cl/2011/06/07/caso-paraguayos-demandas-en-contra -del-empresario-francisco-javier-errazuriz/.

Radio Universidad de Chile. (2012). Justicia chilena dicta primera sentencia por trata de personas. September 1. Retrieved September 22, 2012, from http:// radio.uchile.cl/noticias/169778/.

Republic of Chile. (2011). Tipifica los delitos de tráfico ilícito de migrantes y trata de personas, y establece normas para su prevención y más efectiva persecución criminal. *La Biblioteca del Congreso Nacional de Chile*. March 17. Retrieved September 15, 2011, from www.leychile.cl/Navegar?idNorma= 1024319&buscar=Ley+20507.

Rivera, E. (2011). Chile: Former presidential candidate accused of "enslaving" employees. *Global Voices*, July 9. Retrieved September 15, 2011, from http:// globalvoicesonline.org/2011/07/09/chile-former-presidential-candidate- accused-of-enslaving-employees/.

Ross, J. (2003). Chile awakens to child prostitution after scandal—one organization finds 65,000 online pedophile networks. *San Francisco Chronicle*, November 24. Retrieved October 25, 2007, from www.sfgate.com/ news/article/Chile-awakens-to-child-prostitution-after-scandal-2526032 .php.

———. (2004). Chile tackles child-sex trade; a new law protecting children went into effect last week in the wake of a major scandal. *Christian Science Monitor,* January 13. Retrieved September 12, 2010, from www.csmonitor.com/2004 /0113/p06s01-woam.html.

Tauran, E. (2011). Investigan presunta trata de personas en fundo de Francisco Javier Errázuriz. *Radio Bio-Bio,* May 22. Retrieved September 15, 2011, from www.biobiochile.cl/2011/05/22/investigan-presunta-trata-de-personas-en -fundo-de-francisco-javier-errazuriz.shtml.

Le Tercera. (2011). Corte de Rancagua ratifica multas a empresa agrícola de Francisco Javier Errázuriz. November 22. Retrieved September 22, 2012, from www.latercera.com/noticia/nacional/2011/11/680-406874-9-corte-de -rancagua-ratifica-multas-a-empresa-de-francisco-javier-errazuriz.shtml.

UNESCO. (2004). *Struggles against slavery: International year to commemorate the struggle against slavery and its abolition.* Retrieved October 25, 2007, from United Nations Educational, Scientific and Cultural Organization: unesdoc. unesco.org/images/0013/001337/133738e.pdf.

UNODC. (2009). *Global report on trafficking in persons.* Retrieved June 6, 2010, from United Nations Office on Drugs and Crime: http://www.unodc.org /documents/Global_Report_on_TIP.pdf.

U.S. Department of Labor. (2004). *Incidence and nature of child labor, Bureau of International Labor Affairs (ILAB).* Retrieved October 22, 2007, from www.dol .gov/ilab/media/reports/iclp/tda2004/chile.htm.

———. (2007). *The Department of Labor's 2006 findings on the worst forms of child labor.* Retrieved October 25, 2007, from www.dol.gov/ILAB/media/reports /iclp/main.htm.

U.S. Department of State. (2006). *Trafficking in persons report.* Retrieved October 20, 2007, from www.state.gov/documents/organization/66086.pdf.

———. (2007a). *Country report on human rights practices, 2006, Chile, released by the Bureau of Democracy, Human Rights, and Labor.* Retrieved October 21, 2007, from www.state.gov/g/drl/rls/hrrpt/2006/78884.htm.

———. (2007b). *Trafficking in persons report.* Retrieved August 31, 2010, from www.state.gov/documents/organization/82902.pdf.

———. (2009). *Trafficking in persons report.* Retrieved September 24, 2010, from www.state.gov/g/tip/rls/tiprpt/2009/.

———. (2010). *Trafficking in persons report.* Retrieved June 20, 2010, from www .state.gov/documents/organization/142979.pdf.

———. (2011). *Trafficking in persons report.* Retrieved September 15, 2011, from www.state.gov/g/tip/rls/tiprpt/2011/.

———. (2012). *Trafficking in persons report.* Retrieved August 30, 2012, from www.state.gov/j/tip/rls/tiprpt/2012/.

van de Glind, H. (2010). Migration and child labour: Exploring child migrant vulnerabilities and those of children left behind. Retrieved September 22, 2012, from the International Labour Organization: www.ilo.org/ipecinfo /product/viewProduct.do?productId=14313.

20. GERMANY

BNO News. (2011). HIV-infected German sentenced to nine years for child sex tourism in Thailand. *Lincoln Tribune*, March 3. Retrieved September 16, 2011, from WireUpdate: http://wireupdate.com/wires/15573/hiv-infected-german -sentenced-to-nine-years-for-child-sex-tourism-in-thailand/.

Bundeskriminalamt. (2009). *Human trafficking: National situation report 2008.* Retrieved June 24, 2010, from www.bka.de/nn_194550/EN/SubjectsAZ/Traf-fickingInHumanBeings/traffickingInHumanBeings_node.html?_nnn=true.

———. (2010). *Trafficking in human beings: 2009 national situation report.* Retrieved June 24, 2010, from www.bka.de. Copy in author's possession.

———. (2011). *Trafficking in human beings: 2010 national situation report.* Retrieved September 23, 2012, from www.bka.de. Copy in author's possession.

———. (2012). *Trafficking in Human Beings: 2011 national situation report.* Retrieved October 17, 2012, from www.bka.de/nn_193360/DE/Publikationen /JahresberichteUndLagebilder/Menschenhandel/menschenhandel_node .html?_nnn=true. Copy in author's possession.

Council of Europe. (2012). Council of Europe Convention on Action Against Trafficking in Human Beings. Retrieved September 23, 2012, from www. conventions.coe.int/Treaty/Commun/ChercheSig.asp?NT=197&CM=1&DF =&CL=ENG.

ECPAT. (2009). *Offenders beware: Child sex tourism case studies.* Retrieved September 23, 2012, from Fair Trade in Tourism South Africa: www.fairtourismsa.org .za/thecode/resources/training/ECPAT_ReportChildSexTourismCases.pdf.

Follmar-Otto, P., & H. Rabe. (2009). *Human trafficking in Germany: Strengthening victims' human rights.* Retrieved July 16, from German Institute for Human Rights: www.institut-fuer-menschenrechte.de/uploads/tx_commerce/study_ human_trafficking_in_germany.pdf.

IOM. (2012). REAG/GARP Program 2012—Information sheet. Retrieved September 23, 2012, from www.iom.int/germany/de/downloads/REAG/REAG -GARP%202012%20-%20Infoblatt%20Englisch%20%20(Stand%20Juni %202012).pdf.

OHCHR. (2009). Victims must be at the centre of anti-trafficking action. Press release, May 14. Retrieved August 1, 2010, Office of the United Nations High

Commissioner for Human Rights: from www.ohchr.org/EN/NEWSEVENTS /Pages/Victimsofanti-traffickingaction.aspx.

Press TV. (2010). Human trafficking climbs in Germany. Press TV, May 24. Retrieved June 24, 2010, from www.presstv.ir/detail.aspx?id=127565&sectio nid=351020604.

Saas, Claire. (2012). Exceptional law in Europe with emphasis on "enemies." Draft. Conference presentation in Preventive Detention and Criminal Justice, Ravenna, May 11–12, 2012. Retrieved September 23, 2012, from the University of North Carolina School of Law: www.law.unc.edu/documents /faculty/adversaryconference/exceptionallawsineuropewithemphasisonene-miesapril2012.pdf.

UNODC. (2009). *Global report on trafficking in persons.* Retrieved June 6, 2010, from United Nations Office on Drugs and Crime: www.unodc.org/documents/Global_Report_on_TIP.pdf.

U.S. Department of State. (2010). *Trafficking in persons report.* Retrieved June 20, 2010, from www.state.gov/documents/organization/142979.pdf.

———. (2011). *Trafficking in persons report.* Retrieved June 7, 2010, from www .state.gov/g/tip/rls/tiprpt/2011/.

———. (2012). *Trafficking in persons report.* Retrieved August 30, 2012, from www .state.gov/j/tip/rls/tiprpt/2012/.

Zündorf-Hinte, N. (2010). Cooperation and coordination are the keys to counter trafficking. June 10. Retrieved June 24, 2010, from Council of the Baltic Sea States: www.cbss.org/component/option,com_attachments/id,775/lang ,en/task,download/+Cooperation+and+coordination+are+the+keys+to+cou nter+trafficking.

21. POLAND

Bielawska, A. (2008). On the right track. Polish Radio External Service, February 11. Retrieved June 10, 2010, from www.thenews.pl/News/?id=75616.

Buchowska, S. (2007). *Social aspects of human trafficking.* Retrieved December 29, 2011, from the Peer Review and Assessment in Social Inclusion Program, European Commission DG Employment, Social Affairs and Inclusion: www .peer-review-social-inclusion.eu/peer-reviews/2007/social-aspects-of-human -trafficking/poland-dk07.

———. (2011). *The challenges of implementing anti-trafficking policies in Poland.* Retrieved December 28, 2011, from Vienna Institute for International Dialogue and Cooperation: www.vidc.org/index.php?id=1568#c3942.

Bunnag, S. (2010). Poland "exploiting Thai farm workers." *Bangkok Post,* March 20. Retrieved June 11, 2010, from www.bangkokpost.com.

Campbell, F., & Thorne, B. (2007). Another export. Radio Netherlands World-wide, December 21. Retrieved June 11, 2010, from www.rnw.nl.

Charoensuthipan, P., & Tansubhapol, T. (2010). Thais in Polish "job swindle" want help. *Bangkok Post*, March 6. Retrieved June 12, 2010, from www.bang kokpost.com.

CRIN. (2011). *Status of the Optional Protocol to the Convention on the Rights of the Child on the sale of children, child prostitution and child pornography in national law—Poland*. Retrieved December 29, 2011, from Child Abuse and Neglect in Eastern Europe: www.canee.net/files/CRIN%20OPSC%20Report%20Poland.pdf.

European Union. (2009). The Schengen area and cooperation. March 3. Retrieved June 2, 2010, from http://europa.eu/legislation_summaries/justice_freedom_security/free_movement_of_persons_asylum_immigration/l33020_en.htm.

———. (2012). Together against trafficking in human beings: Poland. November 6. Retrieved October 12, 2012, from http://ec.europa.eu/anti-trafficking/showNIPsection.action;jsessionid=tZmTPbGGqSvs4VtCqjvB9mSXP3yjgfM2FPJ0qPVCT7kskrL7FNDT!-637572467?country=Poland.

Garnier, J. (2009). *Prostitution in Polish legal system*. Retrieved June 21, 2010, from De Rode Draad: http://rodedraad.nl/index.php?id=1130.

General Headquarters of Police. (2010). *Combating trafficking in human beings in Poland*. Retrieved June 2, 2010, from Council of the Baltic Sea States: www.cbss.org/Civil-Security-and-the-Human-Dimension/diplomatic-training.

Human Trafficking Foundation. (2012). EU agency fears human trafficking during Euro 2012. Press release, June 5. Retrieved October 12, 2012, from www.humantraffickingfoundation.org/06/eu-agency-fears-human-trafficking-during-euro-2012/.

Interpol. (2009). Polish Penal Code—Chapter XXV offences against sexual liberty and decency. Retrieved June 21, 2010, from www.interpol.int/Public/Children/SexualAbuse/NationalLaws/CsaPoland.pdf.

IOM. (2010). New report on labour migration trends in the western Balkans. International Organization for Migration, Regional Office in Budapest. Newsletter issue no. 10. Retrieved June 5, 2010, from www.iom.pl/Shared%20Documents/LINK%2010-%20January%202010.pdf.

Ministry of Interior and Administration. (2008). *Trafficking in human beings in Poland*. Retrieved December 28, 2011, from ProCon.org: http://prostitution.procon.org/sourcefiles/PolandTraffickingInHumanBeingsReport2008.pdf.

———. (2010). Statistics. Retrieved December 30, 2011, from www.msw.gov.pl/portal/pl/684/8974/Statistics.html.

———. (2011). *National action plan against trafficking in human beings for 2011–2012*. Retrieved December 29, 2011, from www.msw.gov.pl/download.php?s=1&id=13928.

OHCHR. (2009a). *Report of the special rapporteur on trafficking in persons*. United Nations Office of the High Commissioner for Human Rights, August 12. Retrieved June 2, 2010, from www.ohchr.org.

———. (2009b). UN expert on trafficking in persons ends visit to Poland. Press release, May 29. Retrieved June 2, 2010, from United Nations Office of the High Commissioner for Human Rights: www2.ohchr.org/english/issues/trafficking/docs/PressReleaseVisitPoland.doc.

Plant, R. (2009). Trafficking for labour exploitation: Challenges for criminal law enforcement. In *The Cambridge International Symposium on Economic Crime, Cambridge, United Kingdom*. Retrieved October 11, 2012, from the International Labour Organization: www.ilo.org/sapfl/Informationresources/Speeches/WCM_041995/lang--en/index.htm.

Polish Radio External Service. (2009a). Ugandan woman victim of trafficking to Poland. Polish Radio External Service, January 12. Retrieved June 9, 2010, from www.thenews.pl.

———. (2009b). Women traffickers prey on jobless in Poland. Polish Radio External Service, November 6. Retrieved June 9, 2010, from www.thenews.pl.

———. (2010a). One in five Poles worked abroad. Polish Radio External Service, March 31. Retrieved June 5, 2010, from www.thenews.pl.

———. (2010b). Polish nannies exploited by Swede. Polish Radio External Service, February 1. Retrieved June 5, 2010, from www.thenews.pl.

Seattle Times. (2012). Poland to reinstate border checks during Euro 2012. *Seattle Times*, April 23. Retrieved October 12, 2012, from www.seattletimes.com/html/nationworld/2018051441_apeupolandeuro2012checks.html.

Simpson, P. V. (2010). Stockholm mum charged over Polish "slaves." *The Local*, February 1. Retrieved June 5, 2010, from www.thelocal.se/24718/20100201/.

Sykiotou, A. P. (2007). *Trafficking in human beings: Internet recruitment*. Retrieved June 21, 2010, from Council of Europe: www.coe.int/t/dg2/trafficking/campaign/Source/THB_Internetstudy_en.pdf.

UNHCR. (2011). *Submission by the United Nations High Commissioner for Refugees for the Office of the High Commissioner for Human Rights' Compilation Report—universal periodic review: Poland*. Retrieved October 12, 2012, from http://lib.ohchr.org/HRBodies/UPR/Documents/session13/PL/UNHCR_UPR_POL_S13_2012_UNHCR_E.pdf.

UNODC. (2009a). *Global report on trafficking in persons*. Retrieved June 6, 2010, from United Nations Office on Drugs and Crime: www.unodc.org/documents/Global_Report_on_TIP.pdf.

———. (2009b). *Trafficking in persons; analysis on Europe.* Retrieved June 6, 2010, from United Nations Office on Drugs and Crime: www.ungift.org/docs/ungift /pdf/humantrafficking/Trafficking_in_Persons_in_Europe-Final_09.pdf.

U.S. Department of State. (2009). *Trafficking in persons report.* Retrieved June 5, 2010, from www.state.gov/documents/organization/123357.pdf.

———. (2010). *Trafficking in persons report.* Retrieved June 20, 2010, from www .state.gov/documents/organization/142979.pdf.

———. (2011). *Trafficking in persons report.* Retrieved September 16, 2011, from www.state.gov/g/tip/rls/tiprpt/2011/.

———.(2012). *Trafficking in persons report.* Retrieved August 30, 2012, from http:// www.state.gov/j/tip/rls/tiprpt/2012/.

Wiśniewski, M. (2010). The phenomenon of trafficking in human beings: The case of Poland. In G. Wylie & P. McRedmond (eds.), *Human trafficking in Europe: Character, causes and consequences.* Houndmills, U.K.: Palgrave Macmillan.

Wroblewski, W. (2009). Results of CI EQUAL and their mainstreaming—examples from Poland. EQUAL seminar. Bratislava, Slovakia. May 28. Retrieved December 29, 2011, from www.esf.gov.sk/new/index.php?id=2151.

22. MEXICO

ABA. (2009). *Human trafficking assessment tool report for Mexico.* Retrieved October 8, 2009, from American Bar Association: www.abanet.org/rol/publications/mexico_2009_htat_en.pdf.

Alcocer, G. (2011). Mexican businessman convicted of child pornography. *El Paso Times.* March 31. Retrieved October 17, 2012, from www.elpasotimes .com/ci_17739671?source=most_viewed.

Antonio-Morales et al. v. Bimbo's Best Produce, Inc. et al., Case no. 2:2008cv05105 (Eastern District of Louisiana, April 20, 2009).

Bauer, M. (2007). *Close to slavery: Guestworker programs in the United States.* Retrieved January 3, 2010, from Southern Poverty Law Center: www.splcenter .org/pdf/static/SPLCguestworker.pdf.

Brundage, R. (2012). Movement for Peace with Justice calls Calderon's proposed "Victims Law" opportunistic. March 24. Retrieved October 17, 2012, http:// mexicovoices.blogspot.com/2012/03/moverment-for-peace-with-justice -calls.html.

CNN. (2011a). Mexican police arrest more than 1,000 in human trafficking raids. July 25. Retrieved October 16, 2012, from http://articles.cnn.com/2011 -07-25/world/mexico.human.trafficking_1_human-trafficking-mexican -police-arrest-trafficking-and-sexual-exploitation?_s=PM:WORLD.

————. (2011b). Mexico changes constitution to combat human trafficking. July 14. Retrieved October 16, 2012, from http://thecnnfreedomproject.blogs.cnn.com/2011/07/14/mexico-changes-constitution-to-combat-human-trafficking/.

————. (2012a). Felipe Calderón firma una ley contra la trata de personas y feminicidios, La nueva legislación establece una pena de 40 a 60 años de prisión a quien prive de la vida a una mujer por razones de género. June 13. Retrieved October 31, 2012, from http://mexico.cnn.com/nacional/2012/06/13/felipe-calderon-firma-una-ley-contra-la-trata-de-personas-y-feminicidios.

————. (2012b). The PGR creates a coordination to prosecute trafficking offenses. September 12. Retrieved October 18, 2012, from http://mexico.cnn.com/nacional/2012/09/12/la-pgr-crea-una-coordinacion-para-perseguir-delitos-de-trata-de-personas.

DeWeese, J. (2004). Feds arrest six in Corona human trafficking ring. Times-Ledger Newspapers, November 26. Retrieved October 5, 2009, from www.safehorizon.org.

EFE. (2012). El presidente Calderón promulga ley que castiga hasta con 60 años la trata de personas. June 14. Retrieved October 17, 2012, from http://efe.vistasemanal.com/189_mexico/1625924_el-presidente-calderon-promulga-ley-que-castiga-hasta-con-60-anos-la-trata-de-personas.html.

Government of Mexico. (2012a). The General Law to Prevent, Punish and Eradicate Crimes Related to People Trafficking. June 14. Retrieved October 17, 2012, from www.diputados.gob.mx/LeyesBiblio/pdf/LGPSEDMTP.pdf.

————. (2012b). Marisela Morales Ibáñez, attorney general of the Republic during the signing of the Decree Against Trafficking Act and reform to combat crimes against women. June 13. Retrieved October 18, 2012, from www.presidencia.gob.mx/2012/06/marisela-morales-ibanez-procuradora-general-de-la-republica-durante-la-firma-del-decreto-de-ley-contra-trata-de-personas-y-reformas-para-combatir-delitos-contra-la-mujer.

Gutierrez, N. (2011). Mexico: Constitutional reforms to fight human trafficking. July 25. Retrieved October 16, 2012, from the United States Library of Congress: www.loc.gov/lawweb/servlet/lloc_news?disp3_1205402754_text.

Hernández, S. A. (2008). El juez de control en México. Milenio, December 9. Retrieved November 9, 2009, from www.milenio.com.

HRW. (2012). World report 2012: Mexico. Retrieved February 3, 2012, from Human Rights Watch: www.hrw.org/world-report-2012/mexico.

ICE. (2007). Gabriel Garcia, chief, Human Smuggling and Trafficking, U.S. Immigration and Customs Enforcement Department of Homeland Security regarding a hearing on "crossing the border: Immigrants in detention and victims of trafficking, part II." U.S. Immigration and Customs Enforcement,

March 20. Retrieved October 6, 2009, from www.ice.gov/doclib/news/library /speeches/070320garcia.pdf.

———. (2008). Mexican woman pleads guilty to sex trafficking, admits role in family organization that forced young women into sexual slavery in New York. Press release, July 22. Retrieved September 22, 2009, from U.S. Immigration and Customs Enforcement: www.ice.gov/news/releases/0807/080722 brooklyn.htm.

iEmpathize. (2012). Empower survivors. Retrieved October 16, 2012, from http:// iempathize.org/empower/empower-survivors.

Justice in Mexico Project. (2009). *October 2009 news report.* Retrieved November 9, 2009, from www.justiceinmexico.org.

McAdams, M. (2010). Modern day slavery in Mexico and the United States. Retrieved January 5, 2011, from Council on Hemispheric Affairs: www.coha .org/modern-day-slavery-in-mexico-and-the-united-states/.

Mexico Institute. (2012). Mexico's congress approves bill to combat human trafficking. April 28. Retrieved October 17, 2012, from http://mexicoinstitute.wordpress.com/2012/04/28/mexicos-congress-approves-bill-to-combat -human-trafficking-read-more-httplatino-foxnews-comlatinonews 20120428mexico-congress-approves-bill-to-combat-human-traffickingixzz 1txxtolbx/.

Mosso, R. (2011). Dan más de 112 años de cárcel a Succar Kuri por delitos sexuales. *Milenio,* August 31. Retrieved September 16, 2011, from www.milenio .com/cdb/doc/noticias2011/6eab88d5b6b4e276fa728948bd5c3253.

Semple, K. (2008). Woman in family-run prostitution ring pleads guilty. *New York Times,* July 23. Retrieved October 5, 2009, from www.nytimes.com /2008/07/23/nyregion/23madam.html.

Shirk, D. A. (2010). *Judicial reform in Mexico: Change & challenges in the justice sector.* Retrieved February 3, 2012, from Trans-Border Institute, University of San Diego: http://catcher.sandiego.edu/items/peacestudies/Shirk-Justice%20 Reform%20in%20Mexico.pdf.

United States v. Carreto et al., Case no. 1:04-cr-00140-FB (United States District Court, Eastern District of New York, November 17, 2009).

UNODC. (2009). *Global report on trafficking in persons.* Retrieved June 6, 2010, from United Nations Office on Drugs and Crime: www.unodc.org/docu ments/Global_Report_on_TIP.pdf.

USAID. (2009). Mexico TIP shelter project. *Quarterly report no. 11, October 1–December 31, 2008.* January 29. Retrieved November 9, 2009, from US Agency for International Development: http://pdf.usaid.gov/pdf_docs/PDACO422.pdf.

U.S. Department of Justice. (2005). *Anti-trafficking news bulletin.* Retrieved October 7, 2009, from Department of Justice, Civil Rights Division: www.usdoj. gov/crt/crim/trafficking_newsletter/antitraffnews_apr05.pdf.

———. (2006). *Anti-trafficking news bulletin.* Retrieved October 7, 2009, from U.S. Department of Justice, Civil Rights Division: www.usdoj.gov/crt/crim/traf ficking_newsletter/antitraffnews_aug06.pdf.

———. (2007a). Mexican citizen charged with forcing young Mexican women into sexual slavery in New York extradited to U.S. Press release, March 2. Retrieved October 5, 2009, from U.S. Department of Justice, United States Attorney's Office, Eastern District of New York: www.usdoj.gov/usao/nye/pr /2007/2007Mar02.html.

———. (2007b). Statement of Grace Chung Becker, Deputy Assistant Attorney General, Civil Rights, Division, before the Subcommittee on Human Rights and the Law Committee on the Judiciary, United States Senate, concerning "legal options to stop human trafficking." March 26. Retrieved October 7, 2009, from Department of Justice, Civil Rights Division: www.usdoj.gov/crt /speeches/chung-becker_trafficking.pdf.

———. (2008). *Report on activities to combat human trafficking.* October 21. Retrieved October 7, 2009, from Department of Justice, Civil Rights Division: www.usdoj.gov/crt/crim/appendices.pdf.

———. (2009). *Criminal selection: Selected case summaries.* Retrieved October 7, 2009, from U.S. Department of Justice, Civil Rights Division: www.usdoj.gov /crt/crim/selcases.php.

U.S. Department of Labor. (2008). *ETA final rules, labor certification process and enforcement for temporary employment in occupations other than agriculture or registered nursing (H-2B workers).* Retrieved June 30, 2010, from webapps.dol. gov/FederalRegister/PdfDisplay.aspx?DocId=21887.

———. (2009a). *Fact sheet no. 69: Requirements to participate in the H-2B program.* Retrieved June 30, 2010, from U.S. Department of Labor, Wage and Hour Division: www.dol.gov/whd/regs/compliance/whdfs69.htm.

———. (2009b). *List of goods produced by child labor or forced labor.* Retrieved August 28, 2010, from www.dol.gov/ilab/programs/ocft/PDF/2009TVPRA.pdf.

U.S. Department of State. (2008). *Trafficking in persons report.* Retrieved June 9, 2008, from www.state.gov/documents/organization/105501.pdf.

———. (2009). *Trafficking in persons report.* Retrieved January 28, 2010, from www .state.gov/documents/organization/123357.pdf.

———. (2010). *Trafficking in persons report.* Retrieved June 20, 2010, from www .state.gov/documents/organization/142979.pdf.

———. (2011). *Trafficking in persons report.* Retrieved September 16, 2011, from www.state.gov/g/tip/rls/tiprpt/2011/.

———. (2012). *Trafficking in persons report.* Retrieved August 30, 2012, from www .state.gov/j/tip/rls/tiprpt/2012/.

U.S. Embassy in Mexico. (2007). Ambassador Garza expresses his condolences to the family of José Nemesio Lugo Félix. News release, May 14. Retrieved October 28, 2009, from www.usembassy-mexico.gov/eng/releases/ep070514 Lugo.html.

U.S. House of Representatives. (2008). *U.S. House of Representatives Subcommittee on Immigration, Citizenship, Refugees, Border Security and International Law. Testimony of Mary Bauer, director, Immigrant Justice Project, Southern Poverty Law Center, before the House.* Retrieved February 18, 2011, from Southern Poverty Law Center: www.splcenter.org/get-informed/news/h-2b-guestworkers-facing-rampant-abuse.

23. RUSSIA

Alexandrova, L. (2011). Average wage in Russia barely enough to survive. ITAR-TASS, November 8. Retrieved December 31, 2011, from www.itar-tass.com /en/c39/266542.html.

Arutunyan, A. (2010). Russian father wins sex trafficking case. *Moscow News,* January 2. Retrieved January 15, 2011, from http://themoscownews.com /news/20100201/55407511.html?referfrommn.

Burkov, A. (2010). *Russia and the Council of Europe Convention on Action Against Trafficking in Human Beings.* Retrieved January 19, 2011, from EU-Russia Centre: www.eu-russiacentre.org/our-publications/column/russia-council-europe -convention-action-trafficking-human-beings.html.

Chance, M. (2008). Russia's sex slave industry thrives, rights groups say. CNN, July 18. Retrieved December 23, 2008, from www.cnn.com/2008/WORLD /europe/07/18/russia.prostitution/index.html.

CIS. (2011). States-participants of CIS. Retrieved September 17, 2011, from Commonwealth of Independent States (CIS): http://e-cis.info/index.php?id=2.

ECHR. (2010). Judgement, case of Rantsev v. Cyprus and Russia. European Court of Human Rights, January 7. Retrieved January 21, 2011, from the European Union: http://ec.europa.eu/anti-trafficking/download.action?nodeId= b97ffd56-003f-485c-a2b3-7361bac43c35&fileName=Rantsev+vs+Russia+Cy prus_en.pdf&fileType=pdf.

Economy Watch. (2010). Russia economy, April 8. Retrieved January 19, 2011, from www.economywatch.com/world_economy/russia/.

Embassy of the Russian Federation Thailand. (2010). Domestic news. Press release, December 10. Retrieved September 17, 2011, from www.thailand.mid .ru/Win_work/Bulletin_2010/WIB171210.htm.

Goldman Sachs. (2011). Introducing "growth markets": A perspective from Goldman Sachs Asset Management. Retrieved December 30, 2011, from www2 .goldmansachs.com/our-thinking/global-economic-outlook/intro-growth -markets/index.html.

Government of Russia. (1996). The Criminal Code of the Russian Federation. Article 15. Categories of crimes. Retrieved January 19, 2011, from http://www .russian-criminal-code.com/PartI/SectionII/Chapter3.html.

———. (2003). Excerpts from Federal Law No. 162-FZ "On Introducing Changes and Amendments to the Criminal Code of the Russian Federation." Retrieved January 18, 2011, from the Harvard School of Public Health: www .hsph.harvard.edu/population/trafficking/russianfed.traf.03.htm.

HRW. (2009). "Are you happy to cheat us?": Exploitation of migrant construction workers in Russia. Human Rights Watch, February 10. Retrieved January 5, 2012, from www.hrw.org/sites/default/files/reports/russia0209web_0.pdf.

ILO. (2009). *Forced labour: Facts and figures, the cost of coercion: Regional perspectives.* Retrieved December 30, 2011, from International Labour Organization: www.ilo.org/wcmsp5/groups/public/@dgreports/@dcomm/documents /publication/wcms_106245.pdf.

Inman, P. (2011). Brazil overtakes UK as sixth-largest economy. *The Guardian,* December 25. Retrieved February 7, 2012, from www.guardian.co.uk/busi ness/2011/dec/26/brazil-overtakes-uk-economy.

International Business Times. (2011). Russian economy to grow 5.4 pct this year, says Nordea Bank. *International Business Times,* January 19. Retrieved January 19, 2011, from www.ibtimes.com/articles/102597/20110119/russian -economy-to-grow-5–4-pct-this-year-says-nordea-bank.htm.

ITAR-TASS. (2011a). About 70 pct people trafficking victims—women in sexual slavery. ITAR-TASS, December 22. Retrieved December 30, 2011, from www .itar-tass.com/c154/303597_print.html.

———. (2011b). Members of intl human trafficking group detained in Vladivostok. ITAR-TASS, August 12. Retrieved December 30, 2011, from www.itar -tass.com/en/c32/202851.html.

———. (2011c). Number of human trafficking cases decreases by two times from 2010. ITAR-TASS, December 20. Retrieved December 30, 2011, from www .itar-tass.com/en/c154/302054.html.

Malarek, V. (2004). *The Natashas: Inside the new global sex trade.* New York: Arcade Publishing.

McCarthy, L. A. (2010). *Beyond corruption: An assessment of Russian law enforcement's fight against human trafficking.* Retrieved January 18, 2011, from Demokratizatsiya, The World Affairs Institute: www.demokratizatsiya.org.

Narizhnaya, K. (2011). Human trafficking increasing at home. *Moscow Times,* November 9. Retrieved October 20, 2012, from www.themoscowtimes.com /news/article/human-trafficking-increasing-at-home/447405.html.

Polina, C. (2011). BRICS' prospects look bright. *Voice of Russia,* December 30. Retrieved December 30, 2011, from http://english.ruvr.ru/2011/12/30 /63187311.html.

Reuters. (2011). Brazil joins fellow-BRIC China in world's top 5. Reuters, March 7. Retrieved December 30, 2011, from http://blogs.reuters.com/macroscope /2011/03/07/brazil-joins-fellow-bric-china-in-worlds-top-5/.

Rosenberg, S. (2003). Guilty secrets of Russia's sex slaves. BBC News, February 17. Retrieved December 20, 2008, from http://news.bbc.co.uk/2/hi/europe /2770617.stm.

Russia Today. (2008). Russian Girls trapped in sex-slave nightmare. Russia Today, January 27. Retrieved December 17, 2008, from http://rt.com/news/ russian-girls-trapped-in-sex-slave-nightmare/.

Saidazimova, G. (2008). Central Asian migrant laborers trapped in modern-day slavery. Radio Free Europe/Radio Liberty, July 7. Retrieved August 28, 2009, from www.rferl.org/content/Central_Asian_Migrant_Laborers_Trapped_ Modern_Slavery/1182191.html.

Shelley, L. (2010). Human trafficking: A global perspective. Cambridge: Cambridge University Press.

Stoecker, S. W., & Shelley, L. (2005). Human traffic and transnational crime: Eurasian and American perspectives. Lanham, Md.: Rowman & Littlefield.

Tiurukanova, E. V., & the Institute for Urban Economics for the UN/IOM Working Group on Trafficking in Human Beings. (2006). Human trafficking in the Russian Federation: Inventory and analysis of the current situation and responses. Retrieved December 30, 2011, from La Strada International: http://lastradain ternational.org/lsidocs/118%20Human%20Trafficking%20in%20Russian %20%28UNICEF,%20ILO,%20CIDA%29.pdf.

Trading Economics. (2011). Russia GDP annual growth rate. Retrieved December 30, 2011, from www.tradingeconomics.com/russia/gdp-growth-annual.

UNODC. (2009a). Global report on trafficking in persons. Retrieved June 6, 2010, from United Nations Office on Drugs and Crime: www.unodc.org/docu ments/Global_Report_on_TIP.pdf.

——. (2009b). Trafficking in persons; analysis on Europe. Retrieved June 6, 2010, from United Nations Office on Drugs and Crime: www.ungift.org/docs/un gift/pdf/humantrafficking/Trafficking_in_Persons_in_Europe-Final_09 .pdf.

U.S. Department of Labor. (2009). List of goods produced by child labor or forced labor. Retrieved August 28, 2010, from www.dol.gov/ilab/programs/ocft/PDF /2009TVPRA.pdf.

——. (2010). 2009 findings on the worst forms of child labor. Retrieved December 2, 2010, from http://www.dol.gov/ilab/media/reports/tda/tda2009/Russia.pdf.

U.S. Department of State. (2008). Trafficking in persons report. Retrieved October 24, 2008, from http://www.state.gov/documents/organization/105501.pdf.

——. (2009). Trafficking in persons report. Retrieved January 28, 2010, from www .state.gov/documents/organization/123357.pdf.

———. (2010). *Trafficking in persons report.* Retrieved June 20, 2010, from www .state.gov/documents/organization/142979.pdf.

———. (2011). *Trafficking in persons report.* Retrieved September 16, 2011, from www.state.gov/g/tip/rls/tiprpt/2011/.

———. (2012). *Trafficking in persons report.* Retrieved August 30, 2012, from www .state.gov/j/tip/rls/tiprpt/2012/.

WageIndicator Foundation. (2011). The average salary in Russia by a first quarter 2011. Retrieved December 31, 2011, from www.mojazarplata.ru/main/ srednemesjachnaja-nominalnaja-nachislennaja-zarabotnaja-plata/srednjaja -zarplata-v-rossii-po-oblastjam-v-1-om-kvartale-2011-goda.

World Bank in Russia. (2012). Russian economic report: Reinvigorating the economy. October 8. Retrieved October 20, 2012, from www-wds.worldbank .org/external/default/WDSContentServer/WDSP/IB/2012/10/10/000333038 _20121010010923/Rendered/PDF/731210NWP0Russ0sed0100901200ENG LISH.pdf.

World News—Russian Opinion. (2011). GRU officers have given 12 years for trafficking in women. *World News—Russian Opinion,* April 25. Retrieved September 17, 2011, from http://mysouth.su/2011/04/gru-officers-have-given -12-years-for-trafficking-in-women/.

24. BRAZIL

Anti-Slavery International. (2010). Shell makes deal with Cosan in Brazil despite slave labour claims. Press release, February 3. Retrieved August 28, 2010, from www.antislavery.org/english/press_and_news/news_and_press_releases_2009 /030210_shell_makes_deal_with_cosan_despite_slave_labour_claims.aspx.

———. (2010a). Brazil's sex tourism boom. *BBC News,* July 30. Retrieved August 28, 2010, from www.bbc.co.uk/news/world-10764371.

———. (2010b). Spain breaks up male-sex trafficking ring. *BBC News,* August 31. Retrieved September 2, 2010, from www.bbc.co.uk/news/world-europe -11142264.

Biofuel Watch Center. (2009). Gameleira, a company at the power center. *Repórter Brasil,* November 2. Retrieved August 30, 2010, from www.report erbrasil.org.br/biofuel/exibe.php?id=79.

Bischoff, J. L. (2006). Forced labour in Brazil: International criminal law as the *ultima ratio* modality of human rights protection. *Leiden Journal of International Law.* March. Retrieved October 20, 2007, from Leiden Journal of International Law: www.oit.org.br/sites/all/forced_labour/brasil/documentos /bischoff_brazilian_forced_labour_ljil_mar_2006.pdf.

Camargo, B., & Hashizume, M. (2007). Fiscal rescue 831 indigenous plant cane sugar in MS [Brasilândia]. *Repórter Brasil*, November 21. Retrieved August 30, 2010, from www.reporterbrasil.org.br/exibe.php?id=1233.

CLADEM. (2004). *Alternative report to the Convention on the Rights of the Child —contribution from a gender perspective*. Retrieved October 17, 2007, from Childs Rights Information Network (CRIN): www.crin.org/docs/Brazil_ alternative_report_full.doc.

EMII. (2002). Grupo Jose Pessoa buys Brazilian Usina Santa Cruz sugar and alcohol mill. *Euromoney Institutional Investor*, May 6. Retrieved September 3, 2010, from www.emii.com/article.aspx?ArticleID=1037533.

Fargione, J., Hill, J., Tilman. D., Polasky, S., and Hawthorne, P. (2008). Land clearing and the biofuel carbon debt. *Science*, February 29. Retrieved August 31, 2010, from www.sciencemag.org/cgi/content/abstract/319/5867/1235 ?hits=10&RESULTFORMAT=&FIRSTINDEX=0&maxtoshow=&HITS=10&ful ltext=land+clearing+and+the+Carbon+Biofuel+Debt+&searchid=1 &resourcetype=HWCIT.

General Secretariat of the Presidency of Brazil. (2012). Empresas agraciadas com o selo "empresa compromissada." June 12. Retrieved October 27, 2012, from www.secretariageral.gov.br/noticias/ultimas_noticias/empresas-agraviadas -13dejunho.

Gomes, M. (2010a). Clean development mechanism "endorses" expansion of sugarcane. *Repórter Brasil*, May 19. Retrieved August 29, 2010, from www .reporterbrasil.org.br/biofuel/exibe.php?id=129.

———. (2010b). Cosan damaged the public image of the companies in 2009, but was not the only. *Repórter Brasil*, March 18. Retrieved August 28, 2010, from www.reporterbrasil.org.br/biofuel/exibe.php?id=121.

Hall, K. G. (2004). Slavery exists out of sight in Brazil. Knight Ridder, September 5. Retrieved May 20, 2007, from www.mongabay.com/external/slavery_ in_brazil.htm.

Infante, A. (2009). Recession moves migration patterns. *BBC News*, September 8. Retrieved September 2, 2010, from http://news.bbc.co.uk/2/hi/business /8244474.stm.

Instituto ETHOS. (2007). Pacto nacional pela erradicação do trabalho escravo. November 6. Retrieved September 3, 2010, from www.ethos.org.br/_Rain- bow/Documents/Microsoft%20Word%20-%20Pacto_Signat%C3%A1rios _06112007.pdf.

Lehman, S. (2012). Brazil employers accused of slave-like conditions, Brazil says nearly 300 employers submitted workers to slave-like conditions. January 3. Retrieved October 24, 2012, from http://finance.yahoo.com/news/Brazil -employers-accused-apf-3044240482.html.

Looft, C. (2012). After decade of struggle, Brazil Anti-Slave Labor Law moves forward. June 19. Retrieved October 24, 2012, from InSightCrime–Organized Crime in the Americas: www.insightcrime.org/news-analysis/after-decade -of-struggle-brazil-anti-slave-labor-law-moves-forward.

People's Daily Online. (2006). Brazil to launch campaign against human trafficking. *People's Daily Online*, June 29. Retrieved May 10, 2007, from http:// english.people.com.cn/200606/29/eng20060629_278431.html.

Repórter Brasil. (2010). Lista suja do trabalho escravo. *Repórter Brasil*. Retrieved August 28, 2010, from www.reporterbrasil.com.br/listasuja/.

———. (2012). Lista suja do trabalho escravo. *Repórter Brasil*. Retrieved October 27, 2012, from www.reporterbrasil.com.br/listasuja/resultado.php.

Rohter, L. (2002). Brazil's prized exports rely on slaves and scorched land. *The New York Times*, March 25. Retrieved May 22, 2007, from www.nytimes.com /2002/03/25/world/brazil-s-prized-exports-rely-on-slaves-and-scorched-land .html.

Ross, J. (2005). Brazil tries to stem tide of sex slavery. *Women's E News*, June 19. Retrieved October 16, 2007, from www.womensenews.org/article.cfm/dyn/ aid/2342/context/cover/.

Scharf, R. (2009). 5 million workers under age. *Deep Brazil,* November 17. Retrieved August 28, 2010, from http://deepbrazil.com/2009/11/17/5-million -workers-under-age/.

SugarCane. (2012). Responsible labor conditions. Retrieved October 27, 2012, from http://sugarcane.org/sustainability/responsible-labor-conditions.

Sugarcaneblog. (2009). Brazil's lula and sugarcane industry launch new national labor commitment. *Sugarcaneblog*, June 26. Retrieved August 30, 2010, from http://sugarcaneblog.com/2009/06/26/brazil%E2%80%99s-lula-and-sugar-cane-industry-launch-new-national-labor-commitment/.

UNODC. (2009a). *Global report on trafficking in persons.* Retrieved June 6, 2010, from United Nations Office on Drugs and Crime: www.unodc.org/docu-ments/Global_Report_on_TIP.pdf.

———. (2009b). *Trafficking in persons; analysis on Europe.* Retrieved June 6, 2010, from United Nations Office on Drugs and Crime: www.ungift.org/docs/un-gift/pdf/humantrafficking/Trafficking_in_Persons_in_Europe-Final_09.pdf.

U.S. Department of Labor. (2009). *List of goods produced by child labor or forced labor.* Retrieved August 28, 2010, from www.dol.gov/ilab/programs/ocft/PDF /2009TVPRA.pdf.

U.S. Department of State. (2006). *Trafficking in persons report.* Retrieved May 10, 2007, from www.state.gov/g/tip/rls/tiprpt/2006/.

———. (2007a). *Country report on human rights practices, 2006: Brazil.* Retrieved October 14, 2007, from www.state.gov/g/drl/rls/hrrpt/2006/78882.htm.

———. (2007b). *Trafficking in persons report*. Retrieved October 14, 2007, from www.state.gov/documents/organization/82902.pdf.

———. (2008). *Trafficking in persons report*. Retrieved July 20, 2008, from http://www.state.gov/documents/organization/105501.pdf.

———. (2009). *Trafficking in persons report*. Retrieved September 24, 2010, from www.state.gov/documents/organization/123357.pdf.

———. (2010). *Trafficking in persons report*. Retrieved June 20, 2010, from www.state.gov/documents/organization/142979.pdf.

———. (2011). *Trafficking in persons report*. Retrieved September 16, 2011, from www.state.gov/g/tip/rls/tiprpt/2011/.

———. (2012). *Trafficking in persons report*. Retrieved August 30, 2012, from www.state.gov/j/tip/rls/tiprpt/2012/.

Index

Page references followed by *t* and n indicate tables and notes, respectively.

Aye Than (migrant worker), 80
Azerbaijan, 66–67, 201, 356. *See also* Commonwealth of Independent States (CIS)

Bachpan Bachao Andolan (BBA), 220–21, 223–24
Badea, Marinela, 326
Bahrain, 85–86
Bal Ashram, 221, 223–26
Bali Process on People Smuggling, Trafficking in Persons, and Related Transnational Crime, 313
Balika Ashram, 221, 226
Bangladesh: child trafficking, 71; human trafficking, 71, 178–79, 229–30, 234, 356, 357; labor trafficking, 63, 137
Barker, Christine, 166
battered-child syndrome, 26
BBA. *See* Bachpan Bachao Andolan
begging, 241–42, 276, 357, 360–61, 393, 400, 401
Belarus: human trafficking, 96, 97, 148, 356; migrant workers, 397–98; sex trafficking, 66–67. *See also* Commonwealth of Independent States (CIS)
Belfiore, Gaetano, 180
Belgium, 360, 444n1
Belize, 390
Benin, 238–39, 243–44
Bennu (victim), 15, 441n2
Berlusconi, Silvio, 184–85
Bews, Carol, 291–92
Bielefeldt, Heiner, 346
Bimbo's Best Produce, 22*t*, 375
biofuel, 394, 413
body-parts trafficking, 289–90; *muti* (or *muthi*) killings for, 2, 269–70, 278, 280–81, 282, 286, 293. *See also* organ trafficking
Boere (trafficker), 276–77
Bolivia: anti-trafficking efforts, 127; human trafficking, 21*t*, 46, 49; labor trafficking, 17; sex trafficking, 331
bonded labor, 231–32, 233–34, 312–13
border checks, 353–54, 368, 390, 400
borders, transparent, 351–52
Botswana, 284
Bowen, Chris, 313

Boyajian, Ronald Gerard, 27
boys, 134, 136; child prostitutes, 417; commercial sexual exploitation of, 222; education of, 223–24, 224–25; forced labor, 276; koranic students (*almajiris*), 241–42; trafficking of, 241, 261–62. *See also* children; men and boys; women and children
Brazil: anti-trafficking centers, 425–26; anti-trafficking cooperation, 425–26; anti-trafficking initiatives, 420; anti-trafficking law, 413–14, 425; anti-trafficking offices, 419; Central Division of Human Rights, 425; child labor, 393–94, 420; child prostitution, 413; child sex tourism, 416–17; economic growth, 393–94, 395–96, 420; efforts to decrease trafficking, 423–26; Federal Road Police Patrol, 425; forced labor, 9, 17, 394, 414–15, 421–22, 429–30; human trafficking, 22*t*, 46, 49, 176, 186–87, 195, 413–26; labor trafficking, 9; Ministry of Labor, 414, 415, 419–20; Ministry of Social Development, 419; National Commitment to Improve Labor Conditions in the Sugarcane Industry, 423–26; National Pact for the Eradication of Slave Labor, 424; National Plan of Action, 413; National Policy on Trafficking in Persons, 413; natural resources, 393, 394, 413; and Palermo Protocol, 3–4; Penal Code, 414, 421, 425; permanent visa status to foreign victims of trafficking, 420; poverty, 393–94, 420; sex tourism, 181; sex trafficking, 416; shelters, 419–20; slave labor (*trabalho escravo*), 413, 414–15, 421, 423–24; sugarcane industry, 394, 413, 414, 421–22, 423–24, 447n1; trafficking abroad, 417–19; trafficking within, 414–17; what happens to traffickers, 421–23; what happens to victims, 419–20, 435–36
Bremer, Paul, 131–32, 433
BRICs (Brazil, Russia, India, and China), 395